A Critical Introduction to Sport Psychology

Third edition

**Aidan Moran
and John Toner**

Routledge
Taylor & Francis Group

LONDON AND NEW YORK

Third edition published 2017
by Routledge
2 Park Square, Milton Park, Abingdon, Oxon OX14 4RN

and by Routledge
711 Third Avenue, New York, NY 10017

Routledge is an imprint of the Taylor & Francis Group, an informa business

First edition published 2004 by Routledge

Second edition published 2012 by Routledge

British Library Cataloguing in Publication Data
A catalogue record for this book is available from the British Library

Library of Congress Cataloging in Publication Data
Names: Moran, Aidan P., author.
Title: A critical introduction to sport psychology / Aidan Moran &
John Toner.
Description: Third edition. | New York : Routledge, 2017.
Identifiers: LCCN 2016042622| ISBN 9781138999961 (hbk :
alk. paper) | ISBN 9781138999978 (pbk : alk. paper) | ISBN
9781315657974 (ebook)
Subjects: LCSH: Sports--Psychological aspects.
Classification: LCC GV706.4 .M64 2017 | DDC 796.01/9--dc23
LC record available at https://lccn.loc.gov/2016042622

ISBN: 978-1-138-99996-1 (hbk)
ISBN: 978-1-138-99997-8 (pbk)
ISBN: 978-1-315-65797-4 (ebk)

Typeset in Bembo
by HWA Text and Data Management, London

A Critical Introduction to Sport Psychology

Third edition

WITHDRAWN

The new third edition of *A Critical Introduction to Sport Psychology* is the only textbook in the field that provides a detailed overview of key theories, concepts and findings within the discipline of sport psychology, as well as a critical perspective that examines and challenges these core foundations.

Fully revised and updated, the new edition covers key research findings affecting both participation and performance in sport, including topics such as motivation, anxiety, emotional coping, concentration, mental imagery, expertise and team cohesion. In addition, the book includes a range of helpful features that bring the science to life, including critical thinking exercises, suggestions for student projects and new "In the spotlight" boxes that highlight key advances in theory or practice. A comprehensive glossary is also included, whilst a final chapter examines some new horizons in sport psychology, including embodied cognition and socio-cultural perspectives.

Sport is played with the body but often won in the mind; that is the theory. *A Critical Introduction to Sport Psychology* is the definitive textbook for anyone wishing to engage critically with this fascinating idea.

Aidan Moran is Professor of Cognitive Psychology and Director of the Psychology Research Laboratory in University College Dublin, Ireland. A Fulbright Scholar, he has written sixteen books and many scientific papers on cognitive processes such as mental imagery and attention (including eye-tracking) in athletes. He is the Founding Editor-in-Chief of the *International Review of Sport and Exercise Psychology*, has advised many of Ireland's leading professional athletes and teams and is a former psychologist to the Irish Olympic Squad.

John Toner is a lecturer in sports coaching and performance in the Department of Sport, Health, and Exercise Science at the University of Hull, UK. His research and teaching interests include skill acquisition, expertise in sports performance and pedagogy in sports coaching.

Contents

Preface to the third edition: what's new?

Sport psychology is flourishing both as an academic discipline and as a profession. For example, since 2007, at least five new scholarly journals have been published, and many new graduate training courses developed, in this field. To keep you abreast of such exciting developments, we have made a lot of changes to the third edition of *A Critical Introduction to Sport Psychology*. These changes can be summarized as follows. First, and perhaps most obviously, we have narrowed the focus of the book to increase the depth of our coverage of sport psychology – removing two chapters on exercise psychology and replacing them with new chapters on "Emotions and coping" (Chapter 4) and "New horizons" in sport psychology (Chapter 9). Second, we have included over 500 new references (many of which have been published between 2012 and 2017), thereby updating greatly the topical coverage (especially in the neuroscientific and embodied foundations of athletic performance) provided by the book. Third, as a consequence of the inclusion of this new material, we have extensively rewritten the text and lengthened it from about 157,000 words to over 180,000 words. Similarly, we have revised and extended the glossary.

Turning to specific chapters, among the new topics that we have included are the development of critical thinking skills (Chapter 1), how action planning can facilitate goal-directed behaviour (Chapter 2), simulation training to prevent "choking" in sport (Chapter 3), hemispheric-specific priming (Chapter 3), emotional contagion (Chapter 4), the use of music to manipulate emotional states (Chapter 4), pupillometry (Chapter 5), the "quiet-eye" phenomenon (Chapter 5), the neural substrates of motor imagery (Chapter 6), the mental chronometry approach to imagery measurement (Chapter 6), the phenomenon of "continuous improvement" in elite performers (Chapter 7), the hazards of pursuing elite-level sport (Chapter 7), a critical re-appraisal of Triplett's classic research on social facilitation (Chapter 8), embodiment theory in sport psychology (Chapter 9) and cultural sport psychology (Chapter 9). Next, building on some of the unique features of the second edition, we have devised additional critical thinking exercises (increased from 25 to 31) and have also revised, updated and increased (from 41 to 44) our suggestions for independent research projects throughout the book. Finally, we have tried to enrich the text and bridge the gap between theory and practice by including a wealth of vivid contemporary examples and compelling insights from the world's leading athletes (e.g., Rory McIlroy, Serena Williams) and coaches (e.g., Arsène Wenger, José Mourinho) as well as by including many new photographs of sport stars to accompany the text.

The book is divided into three parts. In Chapter 1, we introduce the field of sport psychology as both an academic discipline and as a profession. In this chapter, we've added a new section on developing critical thinking skills, revised and updated the coverage of mental toughness, sport psychology as an academic discipline, research methods in sport psychology, and new journals in the field. In Part 1, we investigate the various psychological processes that affect individual athletes in their pursuit of excellence. Included here are chapters on motivation, anxiety, emotions and coping, concentration, mental imagery and expertise. In Chapter 2, we've updated the coverage of achievement goal theory, attribution theory and goal-setting (and have developed a new critical thinking box on this topic) and we've also included some new suggestions for research projects on motivation in athletes. In Chapter 3, we've updated coverage of the topics of anxiety in athletes and the conscious processing hypothesis. We've added new material on simulation training and on choking behaviour in athletes. We've also developed some new suggestions for research projects on anxiety in athletes. In Chapter 4, we critically evaluate the role that emotions and coping play in determining an athlete's potential success in competitive sport. We introduce three prominent theories that have sought to explain the emotion–performance relationship in sport and we discuss a variety of the regulatory processes that athletes use to deal with emotions and stressors. We've included critical thinking boxes on emotional contagion in sport and the use of music to manipulate emotional states. In Chapter 5, we've updated the material on concentration training exercises and techniques. We've developed a new critical thinking box on attentional training and offered some new suggestions for research on concentration processes in athletes. Chapter 6 features several new topics such as the latest research findings on the neural substrates of motor imagery as well as on the relationship between self-report and mental chronometry measures of imagery. We have also expanded our coverage of theories of mental practice and included several new ideas for research projects on imagery processes in athletes. In Chapter 7, we've updated material on the nature and determinants of expertise in sport and on the research methods used in the study of expertise. In addition, we've updated research findings on expert–novice differences in athletes as well as on Ericsson's theory of deliberate practice. We've also included new boxes on "continuous improvement" in elite performers and on whether or not high performance sport is a healthy pursuit and also some new suggestions for research on expertise in athletes. In Part 2, we address the role of team cohesion in athletic performance. Specifically, in Chapter 8, we've updated our coverage of research on groups, teams and team dynamics in sport. We've also included some new suggestions for research on team cohesion in athletes. In Part 3, we explore potentially fruitful new directions in sport psychology – a topic that is rarely addressed by other textbooks in this field. In particular, Chapter 9 evaluates the importance of the embodiment approach (which argues that cognitive processes are rooted in sensorimotor experience) and cultural sport psychology (which emphasizes the importance of contextualized studies of marginalized topics in sport psychology). To conclude, we hope that this book manages to convey the scope and excitement of contemporary sport psychology in an accurate, comprehensive and accessible manner.

Acknowledgements

This book would not have been possible without the help that we received from a large number of our friends and colleagues and also from our families. To begin with, we would like to acknowledge the wonderful editorial support, encouragement and guidance that we received from Russell George, Elizabeth Rankin, Katie Hemmings and Libby Volke of Routledge and Psychology Press. Also, we are very grateful for the rigorous assistance provided by Ciara Smith, John Hodgson and the team at HWA Text and Data Management. Next, we wish to acknowledge the help that we received from Georgina Dwyer (University College Dublin Sport), Stephen Heaney (Inpho Photography), Seán O'Dómhnaill (University College Dublin Audio Visual Services), Mark McDermott (Irish Rugby Football Union), and Colin Burke and Andrew Flood (both of University College Dublin, School of Psychology) with regard to the photographs and other illustrations that we used in the book. Furthermore, we wish to express our gratitude to our colleagues and friends in the School of Psychology, University College Dublin, and in the School of Life Sciences, University of Hull. On a personal level, I (Aidan) would like to thank Mark Campbell, John Kremer, Kate Kirby, David Lavallee, Tadhg MacIntyre, and James Matthews for their friendship, insights and support over many years. Finally, we wish to acknowledge the love, support and understanding that we have received from our families. Thanks to you all.

Introduction

Overview

Many prominent athletes and coaches believe that although sport is played with the body, it is won in the mind. If so, sport offers psychologists an exciting opportunity to develop academic theories (e.g. about how expert athletes differ from novices in a variety of mental skills) and practical strategies (e.g. teaching athletes how to cope with pressure situations) about mental aspects of skilled performance. Chapter 1 of this book introduces **sport psychology** as both an academic discipline and as a profession.

1

Introducing sport psychology
Discipline and profession

Introduction

Many prominent athletes and coaches believe that although sport is played with the body, it is won in the mind (see Figure 1.1). This idea applies both to individual and to team sports. For example, tennis star Novak Djokovic claimed that "the difference between the top players is the mental ability to cope with the pressure and hit the right shots at the right time and stay calm" (cited in Harman, 2009, p. 5). Likewise, consider what Tiger Woods, one of the greatest golfers in the history of the game, said about the importance of the mental side of the game:

> You have to keep pushing yourself from within. It's not about what other people think and what other people say. It's about what you want to accomplish and do you want to go out there and be prepared to beat everyone you play or face?
>
> (cited in Gola, 2008, p. 5)

Similarly, the celebrated footballer Xavi Hernández (a World Cup winner with Spain in 2010) revealed that when he joined Barcelona, "the first thing they teach is: Think, think, think" (cited in Lowe, 2011, pp. 6–7). If mental processes are crucial for athletic success, psychologists should be able to help sports competitors to enhance their athletic performance by providing them with practical advice on how to do their best when it matters most. Influenced by this possibility, increasing numbers of athletes, coaches and **teams** have turned to sport psychologists in an effort to gain a winning edge over their rivals. For example, when Tiger Woods was only 6 years old, his late father, Earl Woods, gave him an audiocassette containing inspirational affirmation phrases (e.g. "I focus and give it my all") which he would dutifully write out and pin to his bedroom wall (Shannon, 2008). Although such an early exposure to mental aspects of sport

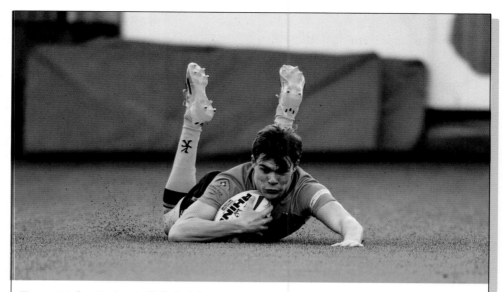

Figure 1.1 Sport is played with the body but won in the mind (*source:* courtesy of University College Dublin, Sport)

is unusual, the quest to increase psychological strength is apparent in virtually all competitive games, it is especially evident in mentally demanding individual sports such as golf. Not surprisingly, therefore, major championship winning golfers such as Justin Rose (Brown, 2013) and Pádraig Harrington (P. Dixon, 2008) have acknowledged the contribution of sport psychologists to their success in recent years. Interestingly, Phil Mickelson, one of the best players in the world, has a degree in psychology. Also, according to D. Davies (2003), Davis Love III, whose twenty wins on the PGA tour have earned him a lifetime exemption from pre-qualification, has consulted up to *three* sport psychologists on a regular basis! It would be wrong, however, to assume that athlete–psychologist consultations are always about performance enhancement. Thus Keefe (2003, p. 73) suggested that one reason why so many professional golfers hire psychologists is simply that they "need to tell their story to someone" who has little direct involvement in their lives. Until recently, this idea that athletes have a story to tell in order to make sense of their existence has attracted little research attention. However, with the emergence of a new research method called **narrative inquiry** in sport psychology (see C. Douglas and Carless, 2014; B. Smith and Sparkes, 2009; see also Chapter 9), a tool is now available by which to elicit and analyse the "stories" of athletes' lives.

Regardless of whether its origins are pragmatic or therapeutic, athletes' interest in consulting psychologists is particularly noticeable at the elite grade of sport performance where minimal differences exist between competitors in technical ability and/or **physical fitness** (G. Jones et al., 2002). This observation is endorsed by Novak Djokovic who remarked after beating Andy Murray in the final of the 2015 Australian Open that "In these particular matches and circumstances mental strength probably plays the most important role" (cited in Cohn, 2015). Perhaps more importantly, mental resilience can be developed through appropriate practice and training. Thus Pádraig Harrington, a three times major championship winner, said: "I know I can't swing it well every day but there's no reason why I can't think well every day" (cited in K. Morris, 2006, p. 24). Although anecdotal, these insights into the importance of psychological factors in sport are supported by scientific evidence. For example, research on the "peak performance" experiences of athletes (S. Jackson et al., 2008; see also Chapter 5) as well as in-depth interviews with Olympic champions (Gould et al., 2002a) indicate that **mental toughness** (to be considered later in the chapter) and the ability to concentrate effectively are among the factors which distinguish top athletes from less successful counterparts. But apart from having some vague awareness of its importance to athletic success, what do we really know about the "mental side" of sport? More generally, how did the discipline of sport psychology originate? What type of work do sport psychologists engage in with their clients and do their interventions actually work? How can one qualify as a professional in this field? The purpose of this chapter is to provide some answers to these and other relevant questions, thereby introducing you to sport psychology both as a scientific discipline and as a profession.

This chapter is organized as follows. First, in this section, we introduce the field of sport psychology. In the second section, we critically explore the mental side of sport – paying special critical attention to two related terms that are widely associated with athletic success: **confidence** and mental toughness. Interestingly, some researchers (e.g. Vealey, 2009) believe that the key to mental toughness is a level of self-belief "that is robust and resilient in the face of obstacles and setbacks" (p. 43). This section also provides some practical tips on developing your critical thinking skills and contains a brief discussion of the factors that influence the mental demands of a given sport. In the third section, we briefly review the nature and history of, and research methods used in, the academic discipline of sport psychology. The fourth section of the chapter focuses on professional aspects of this field. Included here will be a discussion of four key questions: What type of work do sport psychologists actually do? What is the best way to deliver sport psychology services to athletes and coaches? How can I qualify professionally as a sport psychologist? Where can I learn more about sport psychology? In the fifth section, we provide a brief evaluation of the current status of sport psychology. This section considers not only the scientific standing of this discipline but also people's views of it. Finally, we suggest an idea for a possible research project on the mental side of sport.

At the outset, some words of caution are necessary. From the initial paragraphs, you may have assumed that sport psychology has a single objective (namely, performance enhancement), a coherent identity (i.e. as an accepted sub-discipline of psychology), clearly agreed academic pathways to professional qualifications, and an established role within the sporting community. Unfortunately, each of these four assumptions is questionable. First, as we indicated earlier, performance enhancement is not the only goal of sport psychology. Since the late 1990s, this discipline has been concerned increasingly with the promotion of health and exercise among people of all ages – whether they are athletic or not. Also, sport psychologists have begun to apply their theories and techniques to business (Ievleva and Terry, 2008) and to everyday work settings (Gordon, 2008) as part of the burgeoning field of coaching psychology. Second, the assumption that sport psychology is an applied field within the discipline of psychology is only partly true – simply because not all *sport* psychologists are professional psychologists. To explain, consider the case of sport psychologists in the United States and United Kingdom. Although some of them belong to Division 47 (Exercise and Sport Psychology) of the American Psychological Association (APA) and/or to the Division of Sport and Exercise Psychology (DSEP) of the British Psychological Society (BPS), others have an academic background in sport science and are members of interdisciplinary organizations such as the North American Society for Psychology of Sport and Physical Activity (NASPSPA) and/or the British Association of Sport and Exercise Sciences (BASES) (these organizations are listed later in the chapter in Box 1.3). Third, in view of this "twin-track" identity of sport psychologists, there are several ways of qualifying professionally in this field (see details of professional training routes in Cotterill, 2010; Cremades and Tashman, 2014; Eubank et al., 2009). For students of psychology, there are four steps to becoming a chartered sport and exercise psychologist. First, one has to obtain a BPS-accredited undergraduate qualification in psychology (i.e. by having a recognized undergraduate degree or a recognized graduate conversion course in this subject). Second, one has to obtain a BPS-accredited master's degree in **sport and exercise psychology** (or pass the BPS's Stage 1 qualification). Third, one must obtain either the BPS's own Stage 2 Qualification in Sport and Exercise Psychology or a BPS-accredited Stage 2 Qualification in Sport and Exercise Psychology. Fourth, one can apply for registration as a chartered sport and exercise psychologist. Finally, and perhaps most controversially, it is important to point out that sport psychology has not always been welcomed or appreciated by athletes. In this regard, a number of examples spring to mind from a variety of team and individual sports. For instance, Pelé, arguably the greatest footballer of all time, was almost excluded from the Brazilian soccer team that won the 1958 World Cup on the advice of the team psychologist, Dr Joao Carvalho. Apparently, Carvalho considered Pelé to be "infantile" and lacking in the fighting spirit that was required for the team's success. Fortunately, Vicente Feola, the manager of the team, ignored this advice and stated that "If Pelé's knee is ready, he plays" (Pelé, 2006, p. 8). More recently, Magnus Hedman, the former Celtic goalkeeper, related a story about his first encounter with a sport psychologist during his playing career.

> The first thing he asked me was what I would do if I found an intruder trying to break into my apartment – I told him that I would attack the guy and kick him down the stairs. So he says to me "I want you to I imagine the penalty area is your apartment and you have to kick out like that to protect your goal". I knew then that he had never thought about referees and me getting

sent off in every game I played for violent conduct. So, I decided to handle my own problems after that.

(cited in Hannigan, 2003)

Also consider what Gary Player the golfer had to say about sport psychology:

When you need to put a two iron on the back of the green to win the Open, how is a psychologist going to help you? If he hasn't got the experience, what can he tell you? I'm not totally against psychologists but you have to do a certain amount yourself.

(cited in Buckley, 2005, p. 12)

Similar views were expressed by Butch Harmon, the golf coach who worked with Tiger Woods for over a decade, who remarked of sport psychologists:

They may not be doing any harm but I fail to see what good they are doing. When a player is facing a crucial shot and the red dot (camera) is trained on him, alone ... where is the mental coach then?

(cited in Browne, 2008, p. 182)

Another pot-shot at sport psychology was taken by Andy Murray, one of the world's best tennis players, who said that a sport psychologist had approached him during Wimbledon in 2006 and offered to help him with a book that the psychologist had written on the mental side of tennis. His response was somewhat jaundiced: "I had the last laugh – I chucked it in the bin!" (cited in Harman, 2006, p. 67). Murray seems to have changed his mind on this issue, however, as he acknowledged working with a sport psychologist in 2015 (Flatman and Gadher, 2015). But another sceptical view of sport psychology was offered by Ronnie "The Rocket" O'Sullivan, a five-time world champion in **snooker**, and arguably the most gifted ball-potter in the game (e.g. he holds the record for the fastest maximum score in snooker – 147 – achieved in five minutes and twenty seconds). Specifically, he said "I tried a sports [*sic*] psychologist once and I never really got much out of it ... if you're on, you're on; if you're off, you're off and there's not a lot you can do about it" (cited in White, 2002c, p. 10). Unfortunately, this fatalistic view of his sporting performance appears to reflect a deeper struggle that O'Sullivan has experienced throughout his remarkable career – a volatility spawned by recurrent bouts of depression (Everton, 2011). Thus he has revealed paradoxically that "I love the game but I don't really care whether I play or not" (cited in Everton, 2009, p. 12). We hope that this book will convince you that O'Sullivan is wrong to believe that there is nothing one can do to increase one's chance of success in sport. Nevertheless, the preceding quotations suggest that some athletes are indifferent to, if not openly sceptical of, sport psychology. But how typical are these attitudes? One way of answering this question is to examine what sport performers think of this field. In this regard, Lavallee et al. (2005) investigated the attitudes of a large sample of elite Irish athletes (n=240) to seeking a consultation with a sport psychologist. Using the Sport Psychology Attitudes – Revised (SPA-R) questionnaire (S. Martin et al., 2002), these authors discovered a generally positive attitude to sport psychology among the athletes in the sample. In addition, contrary to previous studies (e.g. Leffingwell et al., 2001) indicating that some US athletes perceived a stigma associated with consulting a sport psychologist, Irish athletes showed an openness to this form of help. Interestingly, some years ago, Hoberman (1992) compared the discipline of sport psychology to the "human potential" movement of the 1960s because it appeared to propagate "romantic theories of untapped energy and mind-body unity [that] recall the naïve **psychophysiology** of the *fin de siècle* and its speculations about human limits". Overall, his critique led him to conclude that sport psychology was not an established discipline but merely "an eclectic group of theories and therapies in search of scientific respectability" (Hoberman, 1992, pp. 187–188). Although this latter criticism is now outdated because sport psychology *is* now regarded as an established field of psychology (see Box 1.3 later in the chapter), Hoberman's criticism challenges us to adopt an evidence-based approach in evaluating any claims made about this discipline. For this reason, Hoberman's (1992) critique should be welcomed not dismissed. We shall return to this issue of scepticism towards sport psychology in the fourth section of this chapter. To summarize, having examined four mistaken assumptions about sport and exercise psychology, let us return from our preamble to explore the first topic in the chapter – namely, an analysis of the mental side of sport.

The mental side of sport

Sport scientists typically distinguish between four hypothetical aspects of athletic performance: physical, technical, tactical and psychological (see Figure 1.2). First, within this quadrant, physical aspects of sport performance refer to phenomena such as **fitness**, strength and stamina which can be measured objectively. Second, technical aspects of performance refer mainly to the proficiency with which athletes can execute fundamental skills required by their specialist sport. For example, a competitive swimmer in freestyle events must be able to perform a turn. This skill involves approaching the wall, dropping one's leading arm, lowering one's chin to one's chest, tucking in one's knees and then flipping over one's feet when they hit the wall. Third, the tactical part of the quadrant in Figure 1.2 concerns strategic aspects of athletic performance. Included here are such skills as planning and decision making. For example, a shrewd tactical performer can devise and adhere to a specific game plan in competitive situations. Fourth, we come to the familiar yet mysterious domain called the psychological (or mental) side of performance in sport. At this stage, you should note the paradox of psychology in sport. How can something be familiar yet mysterious? To explain, this domain is *familiar* because, almost every week, we hear about or see athletes who make uncharacteristic mistakes (e.g. missing a penalty kick in football or a short putt in golf) due to the temporary influence of psychological factors like **anxiety** (see also Chapter 3). In a sense, therefore, lapses in performance allow us to catch a glimpse of the psychological side of athletes' minds. Unfortunately, despite their ubiquity, mental influences on athletic performance are not well understood in mainstream

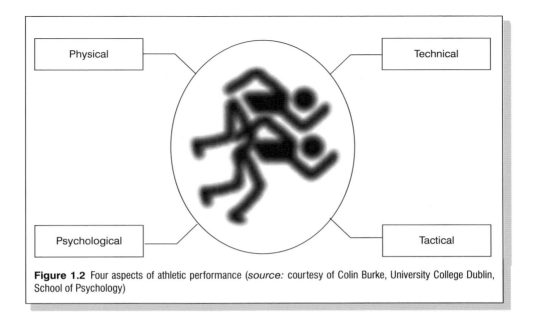

Figure 1.2 Four aspects of athletic performance (*source:* courtesy of Colin Burke, University College Dublin, School of Psychology)

psychology. This regrettable situation owes its origins to a historical reluctance by psychologists to regard sport as a suitable domain in which to explore how the mind works (Moran, 1996). Given such reluctance to investigate the sporting mind, how do we go about exploring the mental side of athletes' competitive experiences?

Perhaps the most obvious way to investigate the mental side of sport is to ask athletes what they have learned from their personal experience about the mental factors that seem to affect their performance. Using this strategy, we can gain useful insights into the psychological challenges of team and individual sports. For example, Nick Faldo, who won six major tournaments, highlighted the importance of maintaining momentum and **concentration** when he observed that "golf is unusual in that you have to pick up where you left off the day before. Four days of mental intensity take it out of you" (cited in Nicholas, 2002). Unfortunately, despite its superficial plausibility, the practice of asking athletes about mental aspects of sport performance has at least two major limitations as a research strategy. First, it is hard to be unbiased when editing or analysing interview data. After all, most people (including scientists) tend to see what they *believe* – rather than believe what they see! However, researchers can address this issue by using phenomenological approaches which encourage the use of "bracketing" (i.e. identifying potential biases and heightening consciousness of one's presuppositions about the topic of interest). Second, as athletes' insights are invariably sport-specific, they are rather limited in their generality of application. For example, the world of sailing is full of unknown variables (e.g. variability of wind speed and direction) whereas that of snooker is very predictable. Given these environmental constraints, it would be naive to expect identical mental preparation strategies to be as effective among competitive sailors as among snooker players.

In seeking to overcome the preceding difficulties, researchers often use systematic and objective research strategies to explore mental aspects of athletic performance. An obvious technique in this regard is the research questionnaire. Using a specially designed survey instrument, Scully and Hume (1995) elicited the views of a sample of elite athletes and coaches about mental aspects of sport. In particular, they asked these participants what the term "sport psychology" meant to them and also inquired about the psychological attributes that they believed to be most influential in determining athletic success. Results revealed that sport psychology was defined mainly in terms of mental preparation for competition (a point to which we shall return later in the chapter). In addition, these researchers found that mental toughness was perceived to be the most important determinant of success in sport. Interestingly, this latter **construct** was also identified by the golfer Nick Faldo (Nicholas, 2002) and by a sample of Olympic gold medallists as a crucial prerequisite of athletic success (Gould et al., 2002a). Before we analyse this term, however, let us consider briefly a key characteristic of mentally tough athletes – self-confidence.

What is confidence?

Confidence, or "the belief that one has the internal resources, particularly abilities, to achieve success" (Vealey, 2009, p. 43), is usually correlated positively with peak athletic performance (Beaumont et al., 2015; Zinsser et al., 2010). Not surprisingly, many elite athletes regard self-belief as the cornerstone of mental toughness (Connaughton et al., 2008; Gucciardi et al., 2009a). Conversely, at a practical level, an apparent *lack* of confidence is one of the problems most commonly reported by athletes to sport psychologists (Kremer and Moran, 2013). At first glance, the fragility of confidence, even in successful athletes, may seem surprising. But when we discover from Bandura's (1997) theory of **self-efficacy** that confidence is essentially a belief, then we can understand why it may vary significantly from one context to another. According to Bandura (1997, p. 3), self-efficacy is the belief that one has the capacity to "execute the courses of action required to produce given attainments" – or, put simply, to achieve a specific **goal**. This "I can do it" belief, however, is not all pervasive but actually situation-specific. Thus, a golfer may be more confident in driving the ball from the teebox than in chipping it from the rough. Similarly, a tennis player may be more confident in playing groundstrokes from the baseline than in volleying at the net. And because confidence is largely belief-based rather than fact-based, it requires constant replenishment. For example, Mia Hamm, the former US soccer player who has scored more international goals than any other player in history, revealed that confidence "takes constant nurturing. It's not something you go in and turn on the light switch and say 'I'm confident' and it stays on until the light bulb burns out" (cited in Vealey and Chase, 2008, p. 66). In summary, self-confidence is a vital yet fragile ingredient of athletic success.

Although a considerable amount of research has been conducted on the origins of self-confidence in sport (e.g. see Vealey et al., 1998) and on ways of building confidence in athletes (e.g. see Beaumont et al., 2015; Vealey and Vernau, 2010; Zinsser et al., 2010), few investigators have attempted to measure the "robustness" of self-confidence or the capacity to maintain one's belief in one's ability in the face of adversity. Filling this gap in the research literature, Beattie et al. (2011) developed the Trait Robustness of Self-Confidence Inventory (TROSCI) to measure "the ability to maintain confidence beliefs in the face of adversity" (Beattie et al., 2011, p. 184). This eight-item inventory contains items such as "A bad result in competition has a very negative effect on my self-confidence" (item 1) and "My self-confidence is stable; it does not vary much at all" (item 5). Initial psychometric analysis suggests that this scale shows satisfactory internal consistency, good test–retest reliability and reasonable predictive **validity**. Beaumont et al. (2015) recently sought to identify the strategies advocated by sport psychology consultants as effective in developing and maintaining robust sport-confidence in athletes. Ten highly experienced sport psychology consultants took part in interviews which probed their understanding of how confidence is developed and how they advocated maintaining confidence over time. Psychologists identified six key strategies to develop robust sport-confidence (i.e. logging evidence, developing understanding and awareness, manipulating the coaching environment, tailoring interventions for the individual, using psychological skills, and developing an athlete's signature strengths) and four strategies to maintain it (i.e. a continuation of the development process, influence the athlete's environment, stable beliefs, and reinforcing abilities).

What is mental toughness? Meaning and measurement

"Mental toughness" is one of the most widely used terms in everyday sporting discourse. Garside (2008, p. 15) claimed that "a common trait in all the champions … including Prost, Senna, Michael Schumacher and Mika Hakkinen has been an immense mental toughness … the difference between winning and losing". Typically, the term mental toughness is used as a synonym for determination, resilience and/or an exceptional immunity to pressure situations. Ronald Smith (2006) described it as a characteristic that enables athletes to react well to adversity and to persist in the face of setbacks. Despite its popularity, the term mental toughness is a relatively recent addition to the vernacular of academic psychology. Nevertheless, mental toughness has attracted a great deal of attention from sport psychologists in recent years (for an account of research in this field, see Anthony et al., in press; Sheard, 2010). Not surprisingly, there is now a profusion of definitions of this term and theories about how to develop it. Unfortunately, as Connaughton and Hanton (2009) pointed out in their valuable critique of research on this topic, most of the definitions of mental toughness are atheoretical in nature, owing more to *anecdotal* plausibility than to empirical research. Therefore, considerable caution is required when attempting to draw conclusions about the nature, characteristics, determinants and development of mental toughness in sport.

Since 2001, a number of researchers (e.g. Anthony et al. in press; Chang et al., 2012; Clough et al., 2002; Connaughton et al., 2008; Crust, 2008; Gucciardi et al., 2016; G. Jones et al., 2002) have explored theoretical and practical aspects of this construct in detail (for a popular book on this topic, see also Hemmings et al., 2007). Two key themes emerge from empirical studies of this construct. First, mental toughness is widely regarded as the key to sporting success. Second, little agreement exists about what the construct itself actually means – or about what theoretical mechanisms underlie it. Before we consider these themes, however, let us examine some athletes' views on mental toughness.

Athletes' views on mental toughness can be gauged from anecdotal sources and also from formal interviews with top performers. With regard to the former, according to Josh Lewsey, England's full back on their 2003 rugby World Cup winning team,

> England won the World Cup because we were mentally tougher than any other side. That sort of mental toughness is born out of experience, both of winning competitions and of losing. It was by losing Grand Slam games, by losing every now and then at the final hurdle despite the fact that people are calling you the best team in the world, and going through those lows together that England built up that experience. When you get to that stage again you know what you have to do not to slip up.
>
> (cited in Thatcher et al., 2011, p. 261)

Similar sentiments were echoed by the Australian cricketer Glenn McGrath (the fourth leading wicket taker of all-time in test cricket) who argued that when gauging what factors contribute to sporting success "ability is a 10 to 20 per cent requirement, you need 80 to 90 per cent mental strength" (cited in Barker and Slater, 2015, p. 552). In an effort to complement such anecdotal insights, Connaughton et al. (2008) interviewed a sample (n=7) of elite international athletes about the development and maintenance of mental toughness. Results indicated that these athletes believed that mental toughness develops as a long-term outcome of a complex range of interacting factors. Among these factors was a **motivational climate** (see also Chapter 2 for further discussion of this term) surrounding the athlete's training that was challenging yet enjoyable.

Historically, one of the earliest references to mental toughness is found in Loehr's (1982) popular self-help book on athletic excellence. Loehr (1982) proposed that mental toughness involved the possession of a positive attitude to stressful and/or challenging situations in sport. Unfortunately, Loehr's intuitive but atheoretical approach appears somewhat simplistic and is hampered by a lack of empirical evidence. Since the early 1990s, however, the construct of mental toughness has attracted interest from a number of research groups in the United Kingdom and Australia. The studies that have emerged in these countries have developed in three main waves: first, intuitive accounts of mental toughness (Loehr, 1982), second, descriptive studies of mental toughness in samples of elite athletes (e.g. Clough et al., 2002; G. Jones et al., 2002), and third, theoretical syntheses of the field (Crust, 2008; Sheard, 2010). What is clear from these publications is that mental toughness is a complex multidimensional construct. Let us now review some key studies in this field.

Clough et al. (2002), influenced by Kobasa's (1979) research on **hardiness**, used a specially devised questionnaire to measure mental toughness. By way of background, Kobasa (1979) proposed that hardiness is a constellation of personality characteristics that enables people to mitigate the adverse effects of stressful situations. Building on this idea, Clough et al. (2002) postulated four key components of mental toughness in their 4Cs model of this construct. The first of these four components is *control* or the capacity to feel and act as if one could exert an influence in the situation in question. The second component of the construct is *challenge*, which refers to the habit of perceiving potentially stressful situations as positive opportunities rather than as threats. For example, a challenge-oriented golfer may see a par-five hole as an opportunity to make a birdie than as a potential bogey situation (Earle et al., 2008). The third component of mental toughness is *commitment* or stickability (Earle et al., 2008). Fourth, and differentiating this model from the hardiness approach, *confidence* was defined as a component of mental toughness that designates a strong belief in one's ability to complete a task successfully. Combining these four elements, Clough et al. (2002) defined mentally tough athletes as people who have "a high sense of self-belief and an unshakeable faith that they can control their own destiny" and who can "remain relatively unaffected by competition or adversity" (Clough et al., 2002, p. 38). In addition, these researchers devised an eighteen-item measure called the Mental Toughness Questionnaire, which requires respondents to use a five-point **Likert scale** to indicate their level of agreement with such items as "Even when under considerable pressure, I usually remain calm" (item 1) or "I generally feel in control" (item 10) or "I usually find it difficult to make a mental effort when I am tired" (item 17). These authors reported a **reliability coefficient** for this scale of $r=0.90$ and **construct validity** data based on predicted relationships with such constructs as self-efficacy or a belief in one's ability to achieve certain outcomes regardless of the situation ($r=0.56, p<0.05$). Although such **psychometric data** are encouraging, a great deal of additional validation evidence is required before this scale can be accepted as a worthwhile tool for the measurement of the rather nebulous construct of mental toughness (Gucciardi et al., 2012).

Another study of mental toughness was carried out by G. Jones et al. (2002) using **qualitative research** methodology (described later in the chapter in Box 1.4; for a practical guide, see also Sparkes and Smith, 2014). G. Jones et al. (2002, p. 209) postulated that it involves having a psychological edge that enables an athlete to cope better than opponents with the demands of competitive sport – thereby remaining focused and in control under pressure. G. Jones et al. (2002) believed that mental toughness denoted a range of psychological processes such as the ability to cope with pressure, the ability to rebound from failure, a determination to persist in the face of adversity, and mental resilience. They adopted the theoretical framework of personal construct psychology (G. Kelly, 1955) – an approach that emphasizes the unique ways in which people perceive and strive to make sense of their experience. Using a combination of a **focus group** (i.e. a data collection technique based on group discussion that is led by a trained facilitator) and individual interviews with a sample (n=10) of international sport performers, G. Jones et al. (2002) tried to elicit the meaning of mental toughness as well as the characteristics associated with it. Results showed that mental toughness was perceived to comprise both general and specific components. The general component of this construct was a perception of having a "natural or developed psychological edge" that enables an athlete to cope better than his or her opponents with competitive lifestyle and training demands. The specific components of mental toughness were perceived to be the capacity to remain more determined, focused, confident and in control than one's athletic rivals. Although superficially compelling, the theory of mental toughness (G. Jones et al., 2002) has several weaknesses (Gucciardi et al., 2009a, 2012). For example, little detail is provided on the precise components of the psychological edge that mentally tough athletes are assumed to possess. Similarly, the idea that mental toughness is apparent only when one surpasses an opponent's performance seems short-sighted as it neglects the possibility that true mental toughness requires the ability to achieve one's goals – irrespective of the performance of one's opponent. Nevertheless, G. Jones et al. (2002) provided some valuable data on twelve perceived characteristics of mental toughness. These characteristics included having an unshakeable belief in one's ability, having an unshakeable belief in one's unique qualities, having an insatiable desire to succeed, having the ability to bounce back from setbacks, being able to thrive on the pressure of competition, being able to cope with competition and performance anxiety, being able to ignore others' performance, being able to switch focus when required, the ability to remain focused on the task at hand, the ability to push oneself through physical and emotional pain, and the ability to regain control after unexpected events. The authors classified these twelve attributes into such categories as **motivation**, **focus** (or concentration), the ability to deal with pressure and anxiety, and the ability to cope with physical and emotional pain. Unfortunately, the results of this study must be interpreted cautiously due to the small sample size (e.g. the focus group comprised only three participants) and the restricted range of sports represented by the participants. In a later study, G. Jones et al. (2007) interviewed a sample of eight Olympic or world champion athletes, three top coaches and four sport psychologists. From these interviews, a number of features of mental toughness were identified and organized along four key dimensions: the attitudes and beliefs of the performer (mindset) and the three major contexts of athletic performance – namely, training (e.g. using long-term goals as a source of motivation and pushing oneself to the limit), competition (e.g. ability to handle pressure) and post-competition (e.g. ability to handle failure and setbacks). In addition to these generic studies of mental toughness, several sport-specific investigations have been conducted on this construct. Cook et al. (2014) recently interviewed eight key staff responsible for a range of roles in the development of young soccer players at English Premier League academies about their perceptions regarding mental toughness and its development. In seeking to enhance mental toughness in young players, coaches emphasized the importance of developing two characteristics: independence and resourcefulness (e.g. through increasing self-awareness and encouraging reflection). Thelwell et al. (2005) interviewed forty-three professional soccer players and asked them to rank the perceived attributes of mental toughness. Results showed that self-belief, wanting the ball at all times (even when playing badly) and having the ability to remain calm under pressure were among the key characteristics of mental toughness in soccer.

One of the more recent theoretically driven accounts of mental toughness was provided by Gucciardi et al. (2009a). Adopting the perspective of personal construct psychology (G. Kelly, 1955), as G. Jones et al. (2002) had done previously, these researchers postulated that this construct can be understood best by probing how athletes perceive and respond to a range of challenging situations in sport. Gucciardi et al. (2009a) suggested that questions such as "What did you predict would happen?" or "What did you learn from this experience?" could be helpful in eliciting athletes' perceptions of mental toughness. Interestingly, Gucciardi et al. (2009c) developed and evaluated a mental toughness training programme for Australian Rules football players. Connaughton et al. (2010) interviewed a sample of world-class performers (including athletes and coaches) about the development and maintenance of mental toughness. Among the factors perceived to influence mental toughness development were skill-mastery, competitiveness and the use of psychological skills. However, it is notable that these authors concluded their study by highlighting "the overriding need to develop ... a conceptually accurate and psychometrically valid and reliable measure of mental toughness" (Connaughton et al., 2010, p. 192).

Anthony et al. (in press) conducted a meta-study (i.e. a systematic collection and analysis of qualitative research findings) on mental toughness development. The main aims of this study were to establish a detailed conceptualization of mental toughness (i.e. what it is and what it is not) and to identify the key features evident in mentally tough athletes. The meta-data analysis revealed four key categories: (1) personal characteristics (e.g. malleable personal skills such as heightened awareness); (2) interactions within the environment (e.g. receiving encouragement from significant others); (3) progressive development (training in an environment that fosters independence but also provides necessary support); and (4) breadth of experience (e.g. significant events/diverse experiences such as overcoming hardship that, over time, facilitate adaptive and positive growth). On the basis of these findings, Anthony et al. proposed that the development of mental toughness requires an approach that addresses the interaction between an individual's personal capacity (i.e. person) and varying degrees of situational demands (i.e. context). The authors suggested that Bronfenbrenner and Morris' (2006) bioecological model of human development – which encompasses four components of process–person–context–time that align with the themes identified in the **meta-analysis** – can be used as a heuristic to guide future research in this area. The model may help to identify interrelated areas that can be targeted to foster mental toughness (e.g. a coach increasing his/her expectations in order to increase an athlete's competitiveness). In summary, we have learned in this section that athletes and researchers regard mental toughness as a key characteristic of successful athletes. But are you really convinced about the validity of this construct? As Box 1.1 shows, there are several unresolved conceptual and ethical issues arising from research on mental toughness, and the term mental toughness is far from clear.

Developing your critical thinking skills

Although we think all the time, few of us are skilled at *critical* thinking – or the ability and willingness to evaluate claims (whether in science or in everyday life) in an open-minded and careful manner (Bensley, 2010; Lilienfeld et al., 2009). In the following section we discuss how you might develop and improve your critical thinking skills. Our goal here is to introduce a systematic approach that you can apply not only in this book but also, more generally, to your reading and analysis of other academic books and papers.

Let us start by considering the nature, components and importance of critical thinking. Based on a review of relevant critical thinking literature, Moran et al. (2006) defined this process as a "form of intelligent criticism which helps people to reach independent and justifiable conclusions about their experiences" (p. 38). These authors argued that critical thinking comprises a *motivational* component (i.e. a disposition to engage in analytical thinking) and a *cognitive* component (i.e. a set of questioning and reasoning skills). The motivation to engage in critical thinking is characterized by the adoption of open-mindedness, inquisitiveness and scepticism. However, these characteristics must be supplemented by a "toolbox" of cognitive skills such as analysis, evaluation, inference, deductive reasoning and inductive reasoning (see Facione et al., 1997 for a detailed explanation of each of these skills).

Critical thinking is important for both theoretical and practical reasons. From a theoretical perspective, an important aim in higher education teaching is "to improve students' ability to think critically, to reason, and to evaluate and weigh evidence judiciously in making decisions and choices among alternative courses of action" (Pascarella, 1999, p. 562). The need to think critically assumes practical importance when we consider the extraordinary volume of information which people receive in their everyday lives. For example, consider peoples' use of the internet to collect information to answer queries and to solve problems. The web is an unregulated resource and so people with little or no **expertise** in a subject area can post anything at anytime. As a result, many sources on the web have proven to be inaccurate and unreliable (Harmon and Jones, 1999). In fact, an over-reliance on the web when completing course work could have a detrimental impact on a student's grades. Thus, there is a need for students to learn how to critically sift through the profusion of information available to them and recognize what is meaningful and trustworthy.

To do so will require students to *read* material in a critical manner. Let us briefly address what we mean by "critical reading". University lecturers and tutors will expect you to consult a wide range of sources (including books and journal articles) when completing assignments or preparing for exams. However, obtaining high marks will require students to develop and showcase a critical understanding of relevant material. Your first step in achieving this aim is to ensure that you avoid uncritically accepting everything that you read. Indeed, you should be aware that although authors rarely attempt to deliberately mislead readers their work can be based on a misinterpretation of existent evidence or on certain biases they may hold. Also, authors might occasionally overemphasize the importance of "weak" results. For example, correlational research might indicate that there is a significant correlation between two or more variables but this does *not* mean that one of those variables *caused* the other(s). Although an important element of critical reading is the identification of any weaknesses in an author's argument you should also seek to identify positions that are well grounded and difficult to argue against. In the following section we draw on Moran et al.'s (2006) guidelines to outline a number of practical steps that might be taken by a student who wishes to develop their critical thinking skills (each of these steps also applies to the process of critical reading).

The *first* step in critical thinking is to ask "what exactly is the claim/idea/conclusion that I am being asked to believe and who or what is the source of that claim?" Your goal here is to *interpret* or establish the credibility of a source of information. For example, is the author an acknowledged expert in his/her field? You must also be careful not to be overly reliant on "second hand" information. If possible, you should consult primary sources (i.e. the original book or article by an author) in order to validate claims encountered in "secondary" books.

Second, you can *analyse* a source by asking "what type of evidence is used to support the main argument or central claims(s)?" Arguments might be based on "hunches" (e.g. one's impressions of an experience or phenomena) or on more objective data (e.g. information derived from a series of controlled laboratory experiments). According to Forshaw (2012), an author's argument generally falls into one of three camps; it is based on fact, theory or faith. Critical reading requires you to ascertain which camp an argument belongs to as your conclusions will need to be grounded in this analysis. Arguments based on faith are least useful when attempting to critically understand an issue. You should ensure that an author has not presented an argument based on faith which he/she has disguised as being based on theory. Also, authors may claim that their arguments are based on fact when they are actually based on theoretical ideas (which may yet to have been subjected to rigorous empirical testing).

Having identified the evidence used by an author to reach his/her conclusions, you need to *evaluate* this information by asking "how valid is the evidence cited? What type of evidence would go against/reject the claim/idea being proposed?" In this case, you need to establish the validity and reliability of the information used to support a claim. For example, an author's explanation can be undermined if it is based solely on their own personal observations or if they are reliant on a single episode of a specific phenomenon or incident as these interpretations can be distorted by their attitudes and expectations.

Next, you can use *inference* to establish whether there are alternative explanations for the evidence provided. If this is the case, you'll also need to determine the plausibility of these rival theories. In doing so, your goal is to establish an interpretation of the evidence which is at least as plausible as that offered by the theorist. The fifth step in the critical thinking process is *explanation* which requires you to determine the most likely conclusion based on available evidence. The final step for students wishing to show a capacity to think for themselves is demonstrating the skill of *self-regulation*. This process requires students to consolidate what they know by establishing links between what they have learnt and other fields of knowledge/relevant material.

Our goal in the preceding section was to introduce the notion of critical thinking and to outline a series of steps that you can take in seeking to develop this key academic skill. Of course, we recognize that learning to think critically is a challenging process and, like any other skill, one that takes dedication and hard work to excel at. With this in mind, one of the key aims of the forthcoming chapters is to introduce academic material and provide you with a series of questions (listed in each box) which will encourage you to engage with it in a critical manner. As you work your way through each chapter we also recommend that you use the steps outlined above in order to critically evaluate each of the ideas we present.

Box 1.1 Thinking critically about ... mental toughness in sport

In an effort to help you to think more critically about key topics and issues in sport psychology (e.g. in this case, mental toughness) here are some questions to consider (see also the conceptual critiques offered by Connaughton and Hanton (2009) and Sheard (2010) and a good discussion by Gucciardi and Mallett (2010) of some practical implications of mental toughness for applied sport psychology).

Critical thinking questions

First, do you think that it is valid to define mental toughness without reference to any aspect of behaviour *other* than the end-state of winning? Put differently, has mental toughness become the "default explanation" (Barnes, 2009) for athletic success? Recall that the athletes interviewed by G. Jones et al. (2002) claimed that this construct gives performers a "psychological edge" over their rivals. But how is this edge evident? Is it present only if an athlete defeats someone else? Could mental toughness not also influence athletes to perform better than they have done previously – regardless of the presence of others? Can you think of a way of defining mental toughness in a more objective manner? Is there a danger of circularity defining this construct because of the lack of an independent index of mental toughness? Second, is there a danger that in presenting mental toughness as a complex, multifaceted construct which is difficult to define (e.g. Gucciardi and Mallett, 2010), its explanatory efficiency and scientific utility are diminished? Third, if we adopt the perspective of personal construct psychology (G. Kelly, 1955), one way of exploring people's understanding of a term is to ask them to identify the opposite of it. But what exactly is the *opposite* of mental toughness? If you are not "tough" then surely this means that you are "soft" or "weak" and these are not labels that are highly sought after by elite athletes (Gilbourne and Andersen, 2011). Are advocates of "toughness" in danger of perpetuating a macho notion that athletes should showcase their physical strength and commitment by playing through pain and injury? Is it ethically responsible for psychologists to promote "toughness" (given its current conceptualization) in sport? Is mental toughness the sole preserve of elite athletes or can "everyday" exercisers also be tough? Fourth, do you think that mental toughness is learned or innate? Which view do you favour and why?

In summary, having explored the mental side of sport in general, and having examined the specific construct of mental toughness in athletes, there is one more question to address in this section of the chapter. Specifically, what factors influence the mental demands of a given sport?

What factors influence the mental demands of a given sport?

Although a considerable amount of research has been conducted on mental factors in athletic performance, surprisingly little analysis has been undertaken on the different mental challenges posed by different athletic activities. What follows is a brief analysis of this important issue.

At the outset, it is widely agreed that sports differ significantly in the *physical* demands that they make of performers. For example, sprinting requires a short burst of explosive power whereas marathon running demands not only great stamina but also the ability to maintain a steady pace throughout a race. Interestingly, research on marathon runners indicates that they can lose up to 8 per cent of their body mass during the race (Cooper, 2003) and face the risk of dehydration, muscular damage and possible sudden death. Perhaps not surprisingly, the psychological requirements of different sports also appear to vary widely. To illustrate, whereas some sports like weightlifting require short periods of intense concentration for a limited duration, other athletic activities like cycling demand sustained alertness for longer periods of time. But what causes such differences in the mental demands of these activities?

Among the most important determinants of the psychological demands of any sport are its nature and structure. For example, consider some differences between a field game like soccer and an indoor game such as snooker. Whereas the former is a timed, physical contact, team game, the latter is an untimed, non-contact, individual sport. These differences are likely to affect the mental challenges posed by these activities. For example, whereas motivation, communication skills, and an ability to anticipate opponents' moves would seem to be vital for soccer players, snooker performers appear to depend more on cognitive skills like concentration, decision making and the ability to recover mentally from errors. Put simply, a footballer can try to win the ball back off an opponent by chasing and tackling him or her, but a snooker player can only sit and watch while his or her opponent is potting balls on the table. In short, the structure of a sport can affect its psychological requirements. To emphasize this point, consider the phenomenon of sitting passively "in the chair" in snooker. Briefly, in this game, the player who is not scoring (or building breaks) at the snooker table has to sit and wait for his or her opponent to miss before returning to the table. Clearly, the challenge of sitting in the chair is to retain one's focus rather than becoming annoyed at oneself for previous mistakes. But what goes through snooker players' minds as they wait for their opponents? Stephen Hendry (seven times world champion snooker star) referred to "hoping you don't have to play a certain shot, dreading that you might" (cited in White, 2001, p. 18) when forced to watch and wait. But not all snooker players feel as helpless as does Hendry in this situation. For example, Peter Ebdon, who won the world championship in 2002, claimed that although the chair is the toughest place in sport ... Well it is and it isn't. *It depends on what you do with your time there.* There's certain routines that you can be going through mentally which help you for when you get your chance.

(cited in White, 2003, p. 20, italics ours)

One of the most popular "chair routines" used by former world snooker champions such as Steve Davis or Ken Doherty (cited in BBC, 2003) is to imagine oneself playing the shots that one's opponent is confronted with (see also Chapter 6) so that one will be ready to recommence at the table when the opportunity arises. Another psychological technique that helps players to maintain their concentration is to scrutinize the layout of the balls facing one's opponent – hoping that one can anticipate precisely when the opponent might miss a shot or lose position on the table. To summarize, most top snooker players use psychological strategies to prevent lapses in concentration in situations where passivity is likely (see also Chapter 5 on concentration).

Let us now consider the mental demands of a popular sport – golf. This sport is interesting because, as mentioned earlier, many of its leading players are enthusiastic advocates of sport psychology. What is so special about golf from a psychological point of view?

Golf is a psychologically demanding game for at least three reasons. First, it is an untimed sport so players have to be prepared to play for as long as it takes (often, up to five hours) to complete a round or match. Sadly, many club-level and leisure players allow themselves to become upset at the apparently slow play of those ahead of them. Naturally, this self-generated annoyance usually hampers their performance. Second, golf is a tough sport mentally because players have to take full responsibility for their own performance on the course. They cannot be substituted if they are playing poorly. Unfortunately, many players try to evade this responsibility by making excuses: blaming course conditions, their clubs, the weather and/or the balls that they are using. In this regard, an old adage in sport psychology is relevant: "Winners are workers – only *losers* make excuses" (but see Box 1.2). Third, the "stop-start" nature of golf means that players spend more time *thinking* about playing than actually hitting the ball. Indeed, some golf analysts believe that less than 20 per cent of the time on a course is devoted to hitting the ball. Usually, the remainder of the time is spent walking, talking, looking for balls, regretting mistakes, losing concentration and, of course, making excuses! Unfortunately, it is during this fallow time that players lose concentration either by thinking too far ahead or by regretting mistakes and/or lost opportunities in the past. Overall, this disjunction in golf between playing time and thinking time may explain why Sam Snead, a former player, once remarked that *thinking* was the biggest problem in the game (Moran, 2000a). In summary, golf is demanding mentally because it is an untimed, individual and discontinuous sport. In the light of these unique features, the mental challenge for golfers is to learn to concentrate on playing one shot at a time (see also Chapter 5). One way in which this challenge can be accomplished is for golfers to learn to *restructure* the game in their minds. For example, instead of perceiving golf as an eighteen-hole competition against others, people can be trained to see it as a *single-shot* contest between themselves and the target at which they are aiming. Using this technique of **mindfulness** (see also Chapter 5), they can learn to adopt a moment-to-moment non-judgemental awareness that can help them to focus on the here-and-now. Before we conclude this section, let us return briefly to the ubiquitous phenomenon of excuse-making in sport. The worst sporting excuses have been documented by Hodgkinson (2002) and *The Observer Magazine* (*The Observer*, 2004) (see Box 1.2).

One interesting point about excuses is that some athletes love to hear competitors using them. Jack Nicklaus, who won eighteen professional major golf tournaments in his career, loved to hear rival players making excuses before a competition: "The rough is too high. The greens are too fast. Check him off. You just check guys off as they complain themselves right out of this

---

Box 1.2 In the spotlight Some classic excuses in sport: can they be serious?

Athletes and coaches often make excuses to avoid taking personal responsibility for errors, mistakes, misdemeanours or missed opportunities in sport. Sometimes, however, these excuses are presented in an ironic fashion. Consider what Brian Little, the former Wrexham Football Club manager, said after his team was defeated by Wycombe Wanderers in March 2008: "I'm not looking for excuses but another 24 hours would have been nice to have prepared for the game. But that's about the only excuse if I'm looking for an excuse, which I'm not but it was a factor" (cited in BBC Sport, 2008). Among the most famous excuses in sport are such gems as:

- The suggestion that the grey colour of Manchester United's shirts prevented teammates from seeing and passing to each other properly (Alex Ferguson, manager of Manchester United, after his team's 3–1 defeat by Southampton in 1996).

- The claim that "the balls were too bouncy" (Kenny Dalglish, then manager of Newcastle, after his team's 1–1 draw with Stevenage in an FA Cup match in 1998).

- The explanation that England's defeat by South Africa in 1999 in a cricket test match held in Johannesburg was due to "low cloud" conditions.

- The claim by the Sri Lankan cricket team that their loss to Pakistan in the 2001 International Cricket Council (ICC) Champions Trophy was due to the intolerably tight sports clothes that they had been required to wear during the match (*The Observer*, 2004).

- Having bitten Italian defender Giorgio Chiellini's shoulder during a world cup 2014 soccer match, Luis Suarez (Uruguay's mercurial striker) claimed to a FIFA investigatory panel that "I lost my balance, making my body unstable and falling on top of my opponent … at that moment I hit my face against the player leaving a small bruise on my cheek and a strong pain in my teeth" (cited in *The Observer*, 2014). The panel would appear to have had little sympathy for Suarez's apparent "misfortune" as he was subsequently banned from football for four months!

championship" (cited in Gilleece, 1999a, p. 2). A similar view was expressed by Michael Campbell, the New Zealand golfer and US Open winner in 2005, when he remarked that when players make excuses, "they've added a two-shot penalty before they even tee off" (cited in McGinty, 2006).

Sport psychology as an academic discipline

Having scratched the surface of the mental dimension of sport, let us now introduce the discipline of sport psychology. Sport psychology can be defined as the application of psychological theory and methods to understand the performance, mental processes and well-being of people who are involved in sport. As the history of this discipline has been well documented (e.g. see Kornspan, 2011; Kremer et al., 2012), it is sufficient to note here that empirical research on mental aspects of athletic performance is at least as old as psychology itself. In the nineteenth century, Triplett (1898) found that racing cyclists tended to perform at least 25 per cent faster when competing against other cyclists (or pacemakers) than when performing alone against the clock. This discovery that individual athletic activity is facilitated by the presence of others became known as **social facilitation** and was attributed to the capacity of rival performers to "liberate latent energy not ordinarily available" (Triplett, 1898, p. 532). Triplett's research led to a robust empirical principle in social psychology. Specifically, the presence of other people tends to enhance the performance of well-learned skills but to impair the performance of poorly learned skills (Cashmore, 2008).

Despite having a research tradition spanning more than a century (for brief historical accounts, see Kornspan, 2007; Kremer and Moran, 2008) the field of sport psychology is difficult to define precisely. This is due, in part, to the twin-track identity of the discipline. To explain, as we indicated in the previous section, not only is sport psychology regarded as a subfield of mainstream psychology but also it is seen as one of the sport sciences. Indeed, in 2000, Diane Gill (2000, p. 7) classified sport and exercise psychology as a "branch of exercise and sport science" rather than of psychology.

Despite this semantic difficulty of defining the discipline precisely, three characteristics of sport psychology are noteworthy. First, it is generally regarded as a science. As such, it is committed to the principle that its claims should be falsifiable or capable of being tested through objective and systematic methods of empirical inquiry (see Box 1.4 later in the chapter). Second, sport psychology is not just about sport – it involves the study of *exercise* as well as of competitive athletic behaviour. Thus **physical activity** undertaken for health and leisure is just as important to sport and exercise psychologists as is competitive sport. In formal recognition of the increasing importance of physical activity to sport science researchers, the title of the *Journal of Sport Psychology* was changed to the *Journal of Sport and Exercise Psychology* in 1988. Third, sport psychology is a *profession* as well as a science. Therefore, there are *applied* as well as theoretical dimensions to this discipline. So whereas some sport psychologists are engaged in basic research designed to establish how the mind works in a variety of athletic and exercise settings, others provide practical advice and training on performance enhancement and/or on healthy living. Recognizing this distinction, in 1986, the Association for Applied Sport Psychology (AASP) was established in order to cater for the growing interests of applied sport psychologists (see also Box 1.3 later in the chapter). Two of these three key features of sport psychology – the commitment to scientific procedures and the existence of an applied dimension to the discipline – will be emphasized throughout this book. However, the study of exercise psychology lies outside the scope of our coverage. In passing, it should be noted that the relationship between theorists and applied professionals in sport psychology has not always been harmonious. Kontos and Feltz (2008) observed that some basic researchers in the field believe that professional services should not be provided to athletes and coaches until a solid body of knowledge has been established using empirical methods. However, many applied researchers argue that there is an urgent demand for psychological services within the sporting community and that such work should drive the theory and practice of sport psychology.

In spite of this debate between theorists and practitioners, applied sport psychology has grown rapidly in recent years. To illustrate, this subfield has its own professional organizations (e.g. the AASP), a number of international journals (see Box 1.8 later in the chapter) and over one hundred postgraduate training programmes in the United States, Canada, Australia, Finland, Singapore and the United Kingdom (see K. Burke et al., 2008). However, the vast majority of these programmes are located in exercise science departments rather than in departments of psychology, a fact which suggests that applied sport and exercise psychology has not yet been fully integrated into mainstream psychology. We shall deal with this issue of professional qualification and training in more detail in the next section of the chapter. At this point, however, let us outline briefly some key events in the history of the discipline.

A brief history of sport and exercise psychology

In the two decades which followed Triplett's (1898) research, investigators such as Swift (1910) and Lashley (1915) explored the determinants of sport skills such as ball-tossing and archery. Interestingly, such research was complemented by applied work in actual sport settings. In the 1920s, the Chicago Cubs baseball team employed the services of a sport psychologist at the University of Illinois named Coleman Griffith. This researcher and practitioner is widely regarded as the progenitor of this discipline (see Green, 2003). Indeed, it was Griffith who had established the first sport psychology research facility, called the Athletic Research Laboratory, in the United States in 1925 (at the University of Illinois). Unfortunately, this laboratory closed in 1932 and despite Griffith's pioneering fusion of theory and practice in this field, research in sport psychology encountered a barren era between the 1920s and 1960s. It was during the 1960s, however, that sport psychology emerged as an independent discipline. Specifically, in 1965 the International Society of Sport Psychology was established by an Italian named Ferruccio Antonelli (LeUnes, 2008). This development heralded the arrival of sport psychology as a distinct subfield of sport science. Unfortunately, within mainstream academic psychology, formal recognition of the burgeoning subfield of sport psychology was slow to arrive: it was not until 1986 that Division 47 (Exercise and Sport Psychology) was established by the American Psychological Association. A similar pattern of late recognition of sport psychology was apparent in Australia and Britain. For example, it was 1991 before the Board of Sport Psychologists was established within the Australian Psychological Society and 1993 before a sport and **exercise psychology** section was formed by the BPS. For a short summary of some key dates in the evolution of this discipline, see Box 1.3.

Box 1.3 In the spotlight Key dates in the history of sport and exercise psychology

	Significant event
1897–1898	Triplett's experimental research on psychological factors in cycling
1925	Coleman Roberts Griffith established the Athletic Research Laboratory in the University of Illinois
1965	Establishment of International Society of Sport Psychology (ISSP) / First International Congress of Sport Psychology held in Rome
1967	Establishment of North American Society for the Psychology of Sport and Physical Activity (NASPSPA)
1969	Establishment of Fédération Européenne de Psychologie des Sports et des Activités Corporelles (FEPSAC)
1970	Publication of first issue of *International Journal of Sport Psychology*
1979	Publication of first issue of the *Journal of Sport Psychology* (changed to the *Journal of Sport and Exercise Psychology* in 1988)
1984	Foundation of the British Association of Sport and Exercise Sciences (BASES)
1986	Formation of Association for the Advancement of Applied Sport Psychology (AAASP) – later renamed Association for Applied Sport Psychology (AASP)
1986	Publication of first issue of *The Sport Psychologist*
1986	Establishment of Division 47 of American Psychological Association on Exercise and Sport Psychology
1989	Publication of first issue of *Journal of Applied Sport Psychology*
1991	Formation of Board of Sport Psychologists within the Australian Psychological Society
1993	Establishment of Sport and Exercise Psychology Section of the British Psychological Society (later became Division of Sport and Exercise Psychology)
2000	Publication of first issue of *Psychology of Sport and Exercise*

2003	Renaming *International Journal of Sport Psychology* as *International Journal of Sport and Exercise Psychology*
2004	Establishment of Division of Sport and Exercise Psychology (DSEP) within the British Psychological Society
2008	Publication of first issue of *International Review of Sport and Exercise Psychology*
2009	Publication of first issue of *Qualitative Research in Sport and Exercise*
2010	Publication of first issue of *Journal of Sport Psychology in Action* (official journal of Association for Applied Sport Psychology)
2012	Publication of first issue of *Sport, Exercise and Performance Psychology* (official publication of APA Division 47, Exercise and Sport Psychology)

As you can see from Box 1.3, the discipline of sport and **exercise** psychology has had many landmarks since Norman Triplett conducted his cycling studies in the 1890s. Since the mid-1960s, however, many important developments have occurred in this field, but space restrictions in this chapter prevent a detailed analysis of these developments. For accounts of the history of sport and exercise psychology, see Green and Benjamin (2009), Kremer and Moran (2008) and Schinke, McGannon and Smith (2016).

Research methods in sport psychology

In the previous section, we indicated that sport psychology is commonly regarded as an applied science. If so, what research techniques does it use? As you might expect, there is a large toolbox of research methods available to sport psychologists. One way of classifying these techniques is to distinguish between traditional quantitative or numbers-based methods (i.e. where measurement is used to assess the "amount" of something and where statistical analysis is then applied to make sense of the resulting data; see Conroy et al., 2008) and more recently developed qualitative approaches that are concerned more with understanding the meaning of events, situations and actions for people involved in a given study (see Brustad, 2008; Culver et al., 2003). An example of a qualitative study in sport comes from Bishop et al. (2007), who investigated young tennis players' use of music to manipulate their moods and emotional states using an approach called **grounded theory** (whereby a researcher attempts to develop a theory of a phenomenon from the analysis of a set of qualitative data derived from people's experience of that phenomenon). Not surprisingly, in light of their potential richness, qualitative techniques have become increasingly popular in sport and exercise psychology since 2000 and have led to the development of a journal dedicated to this field – *Qualitative Research in Sport, Exercise and Health* (first published in 2009 – see Gilbourne and Smith, 2009). Another way to classify research methods in sport and exercise psychology is to distinguish between descriptive, correlational and experimental techniques (Passer et al., 2009). Let us now consider each of these three categories briefly.

First, the aim of **descriptive research** is to record and analyse certain aspects of behaviour, especially in natural settings. Included in this category are such methods as **case study** (which is an intensive or in-depth analysis of individuals, **groups** or events), **naturalistic observation** (where researchers observe behaviour as it occurs in its own natural environment), **survey research** (where information is collected about the behaviour, experiences or attitudes of many people using a series of questions about the topic of interest) and **psychometric testing** (where differences between people on some psychological construct are assessed using specially designed, standardized instruments). Second, the purpose of **correlational research** is to measure the relationship or degree of association between two or more variables. For example, what is the relationship between athletes' anxiety levels and their performance in athletic competition? (see Chapter 3.) Third, the objective of **experimental research** is to determine cause-and-effect relationships between two or more variables. Using this method, a researcher tries to manipulate an independent variable under controlled conditions in order to study its effects on a dependent variable. For example, what is the relative efficacy of mental versus physical practice in the learning and performance of a motor skill (see Chapter 6)?

Before we conclude this section, it is important to mention a research design that is attracting increasing attention in sport and exercise psychology – namely, the single-case design. **Single-case research designs** are a group of quasi-experimental methods that grew out of attempts in the applied behaviour analysis tradition to understand an individual's behaviour – especially his or her response to an intervention programme (Kratochwill and Levin, 2010). They can be used to study the effect, time course, or variability of an independent variable (e.g. an intervention programme or psychological process) on some designated dependent (outcome) variables. Single-case research is typically used both for theoretical reasons (e.g. to test conceptually derived hypotheses) and for practical reasons (e.g. to validate the efficacy of a specific intervention programme in order to establish evidence-based practice). Barker et al. (2011) provided a comprehensive review of the nature and applications of single-case research designs in sport and exercise psychology.

As you have probably encountered these various categories of research methods already in other academic courses (e.g. in your laboratory practicals and methodology courses), we shall provide only a brief outline of their strengths and weaknesses here. Therefore, in Box 1.4, we have summarized the main research methods used in sport and exercise psychology along with appropriate sample studies drawn from different areas of the field.

Sport psychology as a profession

In the previous section, sport psychology as an academic discipline was discussed. This section examines its status as a profession. In this regard, three important questions need to be addressed. First, what exactly do sport psychologists do? Second, what is the best model for the provision of sport psychology services to clients such as athletes and coaches? Third, how can one qualify as a sport psychologist? Let us now consider each of these questions in turn (for a discussion of these issues, see also Lavallee et al., 2012).

What type of work do sport psychologists actually do?

For a quick overview of what sport psychologists do, it is worth reading books by Keegan (2016) and Cremades and Tashman (2014) and also visiting the web pages of the Division of Sport and Exercise Psychology of the British Psychological Society (see www.bps.org.uk/spex/) and also of the Division of Exercise and Sport Psychology (Division 47) of the American Psychological Association (see http://apa47.org/). Typically, the professional activities of sport psychologists fall into three main categories: applied consultancy work (including advice on performance enhancement as well as the provision of counselling and clinical psychology services); education; and research. Before we explore these functions, however, two cautions should be noted. First, there is considerable overlap between these three categories in practice (a point to which we shall return later in this section). Second, the majority of sport psychologists work only part-time in this field. Usually, the professional work from which they derive most of their income (i.e. their "day job") lies in some other area of psychology or sport science such as lecturing and research.

Applied consultancy work

This category of sport psychology services may be subdivided into two types of work: advice on performance enhancement and the provision of counselling/clinical psychology services. Interestingly, demand for the latter services has increased with the public admission by some top athletes that they have suffered from psychological problems such as depression. Mark Allen (one of the world's top snooker players) and Michael Trescothick (the former England cricket star) have revealed their susceptibility to this latter problem (Goulding, 2011; Hopps, 2011). Not surprisingly, there has been an upsurge of research on mental health issues in athletes (e.g. Gulliver et al., 2015; Sebbens et al., 2016; Uphill et al., 2016). At the same time, a debate has arisen amongst sport psychologists concerning what they should focus upon when working with elite level athletes (see Brady and Maynard, 2010). In this debate, Brady argued that if the sport psychologist believes that their sole focus is to enhance performance then this would potentially contravene professional codes of conduct (such as those endorsed by AASP) which state that recognition and support of the athlete's health and welfare is paramount. Maynard responded to this argument by claiming that a focus on performance enhancement is essential for psychologists working in ultra-competitive, high performance settings and that a focus solely on health and welfare would mean that they would seldom see athletes back for another session. This debate has raised a number of interesting ethical issues that psychologists face working in high-performance environments, but let us now get back to the main reasons why athletes consult sport psychologists in the first place.

Box 1.4 In the spotlight Research methods in sport psychology

Method	Goal	Data obtained	Advantages	Limitations	Example
Experiments	To study cause–effect relationships by manipulation of certain variables and control of others	Quantitative – usually interval level of measurement	• Random assignment of participants • Precise control of independent variables • Causal inference possible	• May be somewhat artificial – not always possible to generalize results beyond lab setting • Vulnerable to certain biases	Abdollahipour et al. (2015) examined the effects of different foci of attention (internal movement of the hands; or external – tape marker attached to the chest) on gymnastic performance
Surveys, questionnaires and psychological tests	To measure people's attitudes, beliefs and/or skills and abilities	Quantitative or qualitative	• Easy to administer, score and analyse • Can be tailored to specific populations	• Limited to conscious experiences and processes • Vulnerable to certain biases	Gucciardi et al. (2009b) developed a scale to measure mental toughness in Australian Rules football
Interviews and focus groups (see also "narrative inquiry", a form of qualitative research focusing on people's stories as they unfold over time; see B. Smith, 2010)	To explore people's knowledge and experiences of a topic "in-depth"	Qualitative (main themes) and quantitative (e.g. frequency analysis of key words)	• Richness of data collected • Flexible • Can lead to "grounded theory"	• Very laborious and time-consuming to analyse • Interviewer may contaminate findings	Swann et al. (2015c) interviewed a sample of elite golfers about their "flow" experiences

Case studies	To provide an intensive analysis of a single case or example	Qualitative	Can yield detailed information of a phenomenon over time	Difficult to generalize from findings	Carson et al. (2014) designed an intervention to help an elite weight lifter regain technical proficiency following an injury
Naturalistic observation	To observe and analyse naturally occurring behaviour in real-life settings	Qualitative	Can help to understand the nature and context of certain behaviour	No experimental control over variables Presence of observer may influence findings	Lang (2010) explored how swimming coaches used "surveillance" to ensure that athletes complied with intensive training protocols.

The most obvious reason for such consultation is to gain practical advice on ways of improving their mental preparation and/or competitive performance. Such requests may come directly as self-referrals or indirectly through coaches, general practitioners, governing bodies of sports and/or national "carding schemes" whereby elite athletes may be given funded access to medical and sport science advisers. Typically, these consultations are motivated by a desire to realize some unfulfilled athletic potential and/or to gain a competitive edge over rival performers. Indeed, research suggests that a desire to perform better is the reason most frequently cited by athletes for their decision to consult sport psychologists. As well as providing practical strategies to enhance athletic performance, sport psychologists are often asked to help athletes to resolve a heterogeneous array of alleged "psychological problems" (e.g. poor concentration, performance anxiety, low self-confidence) which tend to be self-diagnosed and vaguely expressed. Indeed, Clough et al. (2002, p. 32) captured the frustration engendered by this unreliable referral system when they remarked that "being asked to solve a problem that is ill-conceived, ill-defined and ill-considered is the lifeblood of sport psychology. Coaches and athletes are more prone than most to using clichés, abbreviations, or shorthand phrases." Interestingly, the demand for sport psychology services at the Olympics continues to increase. For example, whereas only one official sport psychologist was part of the US team prior to the 2000 Games in Sydney, the 2008 Games in Beijing was attended by five full-time official psychologists in the US team as well as a number of colleagues hired privately by national governing bodies (J. Bauman, 2008).

Does sport psychology work? A number of meta-analyses (meta-analysis is a statistical technique that involves summarizing and reviewing previous quantitative studies) have been conducted in order to evaluate the efficacy of psychological skills training (PST) interventions in sport. First, Greenspan and Feltz (1989) reviewed nineteen studies that assessed the effects of PST in competitive sport situations. The results revealed that such interventions were generally effective in over 80 per cent of these studies. Second, Vealey (1994) reported a figure of over 75 per cent effectiveness of PST following a similar review. Third, Weinberg and Comar (1994) showed that psychological skills training is effective for athletes in competitive settings. Finally, Brown and Fletcher (2017) conducted a meta-analysis of research studies that have evaluated psychological and psychosocial interventions with sport performers on a variety of variables relating to athletic performance. The analysis revealed that the interventions had a moderate positive effect on performance and that this effect lasted for at least a month following the intervention.

Let us now consider the second type of applied professional services that sport psychologists tend to provide for their clients – namely, consultations in the fields of counselling and clinical psychology. Since 2000, there has been a growth of research interest in the personal problems (e.g. eating disorders, alcohol abuse, stress and **burnout**) that may afflict those involved in sport and exercise. Torstveit et al. (2008) found that clinical eating disorders were significantly more prevalent in elite female athletes in "leanness" sports (i.e. those in which a specific body shape and weight are important – such as gymnastics, diving, bodybuilding) than in "non-leanness" sports (such as most ball-sport team games). On a different note, a survey of professional soccer players in Britain for the BBC current affairs programme *Real Story* found that 46 per cent of them were aware of colleagues who used illegal recreational and/or performance-enhancing drugs on a regular basis (Jacob, 2003). Not surprisingly, such shocking findings have led to a call for the provision of medical and psychological services for athletes who suffer from drug and/or alcohol dependence problems. In a related vein, Samulski (2008) edited a special issue of the *International Journal of Sport and Exercise Psychology* on counselling Olympic athletes. This special issue examined theoretical and practical aspects of the counselling interventions provided for athletes from different countries at the Olympic Games.

Not surprisingly, appropriate formal postgraduate qualifications and a great deal of sensitivity are required by sport psychologists who offer counselling and/or clinical services because many athletes are afraid or embarrassed to seek professional help for personal problems. Typically, such performers fear the possibility of ridicule from their peers for seeking a consultation with a "shrink". Unfortunately, media coverage of sport psychology may serve only to exaggerate this problem due to the way in which this discipline is portrayed. For example, *The Times* (2002) reported that Graham Taylor (former manager of Aston Villa) called in "the shrinks" to offer psychological services to the players. In view of this caricature of the discipline, it is interesting to note that a scale has been developed by researchers to assess athletes' attitudes to seeking help from sport psychologists (see S. Martin et al., 2002).

Education

Many sport psychologists are involved in educational aspects of the discipline. This professional role usually involves teaching students, athletes, coaches and perhaps business people about the principles, methods and findings of sport psychology. Such educational services are extremely important. For example, in the absence of accurate and up-to-date information conveyed by sport psychology professionals, myths and false assumptions about the discipline can arise. At a more practical level, coaches and managers are usually eager to obtain advice from psychologists about practical strategies for forging **team spirit** in their players (see also Chapter 8). Finally, there is an increasing demand for the services of sport and exercise psychologists in translating certain mental skills displayed by top athletes (e.g. **goal-setting**, coping with pressure) into practical life skills for business people.

Research

Research in sport psychology is extremely important because it can provide evidence-based answers to a number of practical questions. For example, is there a link between the way in which athletes prepare mentally for a competition and how they perform in it subsequently? What are the greatest mental challenges of a particular sport? Do relaxation CDs really work for athletes? What is the most effective way of promoting the benefits of physical activity among a sample of sedentary young people?

So far, we have seen that the work of sport psychologists falls into three main categories. Nevertheless, as we explained earlier, these categories overlap considerably in practice. To illustrate, consider the types of professional services which sport psychologists provide at the Olympic Games (see Box 1.5).

Box 1.5 In the spotlight What do sport psychologists do at the Olympics? Insights from the front line

For most athletes, coaches and applied sport psychologists, the opportunity to participate in the Olympic Games is a highly cherished ambition. However, due to its global importance and unique competitive environment, the Olympics can overwhelm even the most experienced international athletes. In an effort to help people to prepare optimally for such a pressure cauldron, several applied researchers (e.g. Hodge, 2010; Samulski, 2008) have analysed the type of services that sport psychologists are typically required to deliver at the Games. To begin with, Hodge (2010) explained that the most common athletic challenges that he addressed concerned stress management (e.g. arising from athletes living together in close proximity under cramped conditions in the Olympic Village), pre-event mental preparation (e.g. to maintain a focus on one's performance rather than on the possibility of winning a medal), "Games wobbles" (i.e. the tendency to radically change one's routine in response to the perceived pressure of the event), interpersonal conflict (e.g. with teammates, coaches, managers and other officials), psychological aspects of injury and illness, "second-week blues" (i.e. a tendency to become homesick after the first week of the competition), and unintentional distractions posed by family and friends. In dealing with these problems, the most important practical advice offered by Hodge (2010) was "be available, but don't get in the way!" Birrer et al. (2012) analysed the sport psychology consultancy of the Swiss team at three consecutive Olympic Games (two winter games, 2006 Turin and 2010 Vancouver; and one summer games, 2008 Beijing). Results revealed that between 11 per cent and 25 per cent of the Swiss delegation consulted a psychologist across the three games. The sport psychologist conducted between 2.1 and 4.6 interventions per day and the most commonly addressed issues were performance related (e.g. pre-event preparation).

Another fascinating account of psychology at the Olympic Games is available from a special issue of the *International Journal of Sport and Exercise Psychology* on the provision of sport psychology services at this event (Samulski, 2008). In this issue, McCann (2008) reflected on his experience of providing sport psychology services to US athletes at *seven* Olympic Games as part of the US Olympic Committee (USOC) Sport Psychology Department. The scale of this service provision is remarkable because the United States typically sends over 200 athletes to the Winter Olympics and over 500 to the Summer Olympics. Not surprisingly, given the significance of these Games, US Olympic athletes have sought help from McCann and his colleagues for a wide spectrum of difficulties. These problems include clinical issues (e.g. depression arising from a family bereavement), adjustment problems (e.g. financial difficulties, homesickness), interpersonal conflicts (e.g. with coaches, fellow athletes), countless distractions (e.g. dealing with the media) and various types of performance pressure (e.g. those arising from national expectations of success). In such circumstances, McCann (2008, p. 269) claims that "every issue, whether it is difficulty focusing in the starting gate, a conflict between coaches, or mourning a grandmother who died the day before, is a performance issue". Clearly, the ability to deal effectively with these problems involves a mixture of performance-enhancement and educational activities. In 2008, five sport psychologists from the USOC attended the 2008 Olympic Games in Beijing. Apart from this official group, a number of other US psychologists worked privately with teams from sports such as diving, taekwondo and rowing. A flavour of the philosophy underlying the work of these sport psychologists can be gleaned from the following quotations (Schwartz, 2008):

- Dr James Bauman (who worked with US athletes in swimming and track and field): "People now understand we're there to help them with their strengths."

- Dr Chris Carr (who worked with the US diving team): "My role is to help the divers focus on what they can control ... their thoughts, their emotions and their preparation to dive at their best each time."

- Dr Colleen Hacker (who worked with the US field hockey team): "I try to empower athletes to have the skills necessary to produce optimal performance at elite levels, to be at their best more often and to play at their best when it counts most."

- Dr Sean McCann (who worked with the US shooting and weightlifting teams): "It's my job to help them deal with what they can control."

- Dr Margaret Ottley (who worked with the US track and field team): "I support athletes' self-determination and drive to achieve their personal goals."

- Dr Marshall Mintz (who worked with the US men's and women's rowing teams): "My goal is to try to help the athletes to stay intensely focused and committed to the task at hand."

From these quotations, a common theme emerges – namely, the importance of helping athletes to focus only on what they can control. We'll return to this principle later, in Chapter 5.

In summary, this section shows that sport psychologists have multifaceted professional roles. Unfortunately, these roles cannot be performed adequately until an important question has been explored. Specifically, what model facilitates the optimal delivery of sport psychology services to athletes and coaches?

What is the best way to deliver sport psychology services to athletes and coaches?

Although discussion of the theoretical basis of service delivery may seem somewhat removed from the practical concerns of applied sport psychology, it has profound practical importance for the field. To explain, if sport psychologists work according to a traditional medical model, they will be expected to provide "quick fixes" and instant "cures" for athletes with problems in much the same way as physicians are expected to treat their patients through the prescription of suitable medication. What is wrong with this traditional medical model of service delivery and is there any alternative to it?

Unfortunately, there are at least three problems associated with a medical model of applied sport psychology (Kremer and Moran, 2013; Kremer and Scully, 1998). First, it places the burden of responsibility on the "expert" psychologist to "cure" whatever problems are presented by the athlete or coach. This situation may encourage clients to depend excessively on their sport psychologist, thereby impeding their growth towards self-reliance. Interestingly, in a discussion of his service delivery philosophies, Gordin (2003) advocated the importance of empowering athletes when he remarked that

> it is my intent to put myself out of a job with a client. That is, a goal of mine is to make the client self-sufficient and independent. Once these athletes have achieved independence, then the relationship is appropriately terminated or altered.
>
> (Gordin, 2003, pp. 64–65)

A second problem with the medical model of intervention is that "expert" sport psychologists are often on shaky ground theoretically because many of the intervention techniques which they recommend have not been validated adequately. Third, the distinction between "expert" and "client" ignores the fact that sportspeople, including athletes and coaches, are naive psychologists in the sense that they have already developed informal theoretical intuitive psychological theories to account for the behaviour of players. In these cases, such intuitive theories need to be deconstructed through discussion with sport psychologists before a client can be helped. Taken together, these three problems highlight the weaknesses of the traditional role of the medically oriented sport psychologist.

Fortunately, an alternative model has been proposed for the delivery of sport psychology services to athletes and coaches (see Kremer and Scully, 1998). This model identifies the *coach* rather than the athlete as the primary target for psychological education. Accordingly, the role of the sport psychologist changes from that of a medical expert to that of a management consultant – somebody who works as part of a team with the coach or manager and his or her support staff. Of course, this new model does not eliminate the need for individual consultation. There will always be situations which warrant "one-to-one" consultations between athletes and sport psychologists. However, the adoption of Kremer and Scully's (1998) model does change one feature of the client–psychologist relationship. Specifically, it challenges the myth that sport psychologists are "shrinks" or "mind benders" who can provide instant solutions for athletes whose problems have baffled their coaches. Evaluating the model that underlies one's services is not the only self-appraisal task faced by sport and exercise psychologists. Increasingly, in this era of accountability and evidence-based practice, there is a need for psychologists to *demonstrate* the efficacy of the professional services that they provide. How can a sport psychologist tackle this question? This issue is examined in Box 1.6.

Box 1.6 Thinking critically about ... evaluating the efficacy of sport psychology consultations

How can sport psychologists assess the efficacy of their professional work? At first glance, the answer to this question is simple. All they have to do is to evaluate their interventions and services empirically from time to time and publish the results accordingly. Unfortunately, for at least three reasons, this strategy has not proved popular in sport and exercise psychology. First, many practitioners are too busy to engage in evaluative activities. Second, until recently, few assessment tools were available for this purpose. Third, given certain inherent biases of the publication system, there is a danger that the only outcomes which sport psychologists might be willing to publish are *successful* ones. To illustrate, how often do you come across an article by a sport psychologist in which he or she revealed the complete *failure* of an intervention? Have you ever read a paper by a sport psychologist in which he or she referred to clients' failure to follow up on his or her advice? Given these problems, how can a sport psychologist evaluate his or her consultancy services? Anderson (2002) developed an instrument called the Assessment of Consultant Effectiveness (ACE) to help practitioners to assess the quality of their professional services. Briefly, this instrument asks clients to evaluate statements concerning "customer service" using a rating scale. Typical items include "The sport psychologist was a good listener" (item 5) or "The sport psychologist presented information in a clear and easy to understand way" (item 22).

Critical thinking questions

Is there any danger that clients may not tell the truth when answering this questionnaire? How can this problem be overcome? How could this instrument be validated? Can you think of any other ways of evaluating the efficacy of a sport psychologist's professional services?

In this section of the chapter, we have explored the type of work that sport psychologists do as well as issues concerning the optimal delivery of psychological services to athletes and coaches. Now it is time to examine the question of how one can qualify as a sport psychologist.

How can I qualify professionally as a sport psychologist?

Earlier in this chapter, we introduced sport psychology as a hybrid discipline with roots in both psychology and sport science. Given this dual-track disciplinary background, perhaps it is not surprising that there is no simple or universally agreed academic pathway to professional qualification in sport psychology at present. And so, the crucial question of who is certified to call themselves sport psychologists has been debated vigorously in such countries as Australia, Canada, the United Kingdom and the United States. In most of these countries, there has been a disjunction between psychology associations and sport science organizations with regard to the issue of labelling and/or accrediting people as sport psychologists. For example, in the United States, anyone who receives a recognized doctoral degree in psychology qualifies for licensure (or statutory registration) as a "psychologist". Unfortunately, the APA does not yet accredit programmes in *sport* psychology. Therefore, this organization accepts that a psychologist's decision to claim a professional specialization in sport psychology is a personal one which should be taken only in the light of full awareness of relevant APA ethical guidelines. For example, one of these guidelines stipulates that psychologists should work only within the boundaries of their competence. Working apart from the APA, sport science organizations have made important advances in accrediting sport psychology practitioners. For example, in the United States, the AASP developed a certification procedure for sport psychology in 1989. People who satisfy the criteria stipulated by AASP are entitled to call themselves "Certified Consultant, AASP" but not "Certified Sport Psychologist". This latter title is precluded because, as explained above, the term psychologist is protected by state licence in the United States. For the Certified Consultant, AASP requirements, professionals must have knowledge in a number of areas: professional ethics and standards; biomechanical or physiological bases of physical activity; historical, philosophical, social, or motor bases of physical activity; psychopathology and its assessment; counselling skills; research design; statistics, or psychological assessment; biological bases of behaviour; cognitive-affective bases of behaviour; and individual behaviour. The majority of these courses must be taken at the graduate level and individuals are expected to have completed a masters or a doctoral programme. Certification also requires individuals to undertake mentored structured experiences within the field and certified consultants must demonstrate engagement in continued professional development.

Similar certification processes have been established in Britain where the BASES has a psychology section. So, how can one qualify as a sport psychologist in Britain?

In Britain, at the time of writing, there are two main routes to professional practice as a chartered psychologist practising in sport psychology. The first route is through the BPS. Here, one must have a primary degree in psychology from a degree or conversion course that is approved by the BPS (i.e. a course that confers eligibility for "Graduate Basis for Chartered Membership", or GBC, previously known as "Graduate Basis for Registration" or GBR). Having obtained GBC, one needs to have achieved either a BPS accredited masters in sport and exercise psychology or Stage 1 of the BPS's qualification in sport and exercise psychology and then Stage 2 of this qualification (two years of relevant supervised practice). In order to use the title "sport and exercise psychologist", however, one will need to register with the Health Professionals Council (HPC). The second route to professional training in Britain is for people who do not have qualifications leading to GBC in psychology but who have either completed, or are in the process of completing, the accreditation procedure established by the BASES. At the time of writing, to qualify as an accredited sport and exercise psychologist with the BASES, one needs to have a primary degree in sport and exercise science (which includes subjects such as physiology and biomechanics), a master's degree in sport and exercise science/psychology and at least three years' supervision by a BASES accredited sport and exercise psychology practitioner. What is the difference between these routes? As we have indicated, the main difference between Chartered (BPS) and Accredited (BASES) sport psychologists concerns the nature of the undergraduate training received. Whereas psychology degrees provide undergraduates with a rich coverage of psychological fields and topics, they do not normally provide information on coaching techniques or on disciplines such as biomechanics. By contrast, whereas sport and exercise science degrees provide core modules in physiology and biomechanics, they do not normally cover a wide a variety of psychology modules. In the late 1990s, a European Master's Programme in Sport and Exercise Psychology was established as an interdisciplinary mobility course run by a consortium of twelve European universities. This programme is organized by the FEPSAC, takes place over a minimum of one year of study and aims to educate highly qualified researchers and practitioners in the field of sport and exercise psychology (see FEPSAC website in Box 1.7 for further details). In summary, the issue of titles and certification in sport psychology is quite complex. But this complexity is not surprising, however, in view of the interdisciplinary foundations of sport and exercise psychology.

Where can I learn more about sport psychology?

If you would like to find out more about sport psychology using the internet, there are at least two options. First, you could subscribe to an electronic bulletin board devoted to sport and exercise psychology. At present, there are two such bulletin boards in the field: Division 47 of the APA and "SportPsy". Division 47 of the APA has an email list for members (remember that to join APA Division 47, you must be a member or affiliate of the APA and also request affiliation to Division 47). The purpose of this list is to post issues, questions and findings concerning research in sport and exercise psychology as well as related professional practice issues in this field. In order to join this list, you should send an email message to: listserv@lists.apa.org

Leave the subject field blank and type <subscribe div47 your name> in the body of the text. When your application is approved, you may send messages to the list by using the following address: div47@lists.apa.org

The SportPsy list has well over 1,000 members and is maintained at Temple University. To join it, go to http://listserv.temple.edu/archives/sportpsy/html and select "Join or leave the list" which will take you to a secure page, or send a message to listserv@listserv.temple.edu with nothing in the subject heading and only the following in the text: SUB SPORTPSY [your name].

The second option is to consult the websites of some of the professional organizations listed in Box 1.7.

Box 1.7 In the spotlight Learning more about sport psychology: locating websites of professional organizations in the field

- **American Psychological Association – Division 47 (Exercise and Sport Psychology)**
  - www.psyc.unt.edu/apadiv47/
  - Provides articles, information on the division, newsletter updates, membership news, book reviews and a conference calendar

- **Association for Applied Sport Psychology (AASP)**
  - www.aaasponline.org/index2.html
  - Aims to promote the development of psychological theory, research and intervention strategies in sport and exercise psychology

- **British Association of Sport and Exercise Sciences (BASES)**
  - www.bases.org.uk
  - Aims to develop and spread knowledge about the application of science to sport and exercise

- **British Psychological Society (Division of Sport and Exercise Psychology)**
  - www.bps.org.uk/sub-syst/SPEX/about.cfm
  - Section aims to promote the development of psychology in sport and exercise through academic study and research

- **Fédération Européenne de Psychologie des Sports et des Activités Corporelles** (FEPSAC; European Federation of Sport Psychology)
  - www.itplu.se/fepsac/
  - Aims to promote scientific, educational and professional work in sport psychology

- **International Society of Sport Psychology (ISSP)** www.phyed.duth.gr/sportpsy/international.html
  - Devoted to promoting research and development in the discipline of sport and exercise psychology

- **North American Society for Psychology of Sport and Physical Activity (NASPSPA)**
  - www.naspspa.org/info/
  - An interdisciplinary association which aims to develop and advance the scientific study of human behaviour when individuals are engaged in sport and physical activity.

To conclude this section, Martindale and Collins (2011) provide some good practical advice on how to get help in your search for a sport psychologist.

Current status of sport psychology: respect or scepticism?

Now that we have explored the scientific foundations and professional applications of sport and exercise psychology, let us consider its status as a discipline. At first glance, the field of sport psychology appears to be an intellectually challenging, vibrant and highly valued interdisciplinary enterprise. This conclusion is based on four strands of evidence.

First, since the 1970s, sport psychology has expanded its topical coverage as well as the range of populations at which its interventions have been aimed. To explain, whereas this discipline used to be concerned mainly with performance enhancement in sport performers, its scope has now enlarged to accommodate aspects of exercise and health in people of all ages – regardless of their athletic status. Second, the extent and quality of research in sport and exercise are indicated by the number of international peer-reviewed journals in this field: since 2007, five new international journals have been published in sport psychology. A selection of scholarly journals which contain the words "sport" in their titles is presented in Box 1.8.

Box 1.8 In the spotlight Alphabetical list of selected journals in the field of sport psychology

- *International Journal of Sport and Exercise Psychology* (the official publication of the International Society of Sport Psychology and published by Fitness Information Technology; first published in 1970 and renamed in 2003)

- *International Journal of Sport Psychology* (published by Edizioni Luigi Pozzi, Italy; first published in 1970 and renamed in 2003)

- *International Review of Sport and Exercise Psychology* (published by Routledge/ Taylor & Francis; first published in 2008)

- *Journal of Applied Sport Psychology* (published by the Association for Applied Sport Psychology; first published in 1989)

- *Journal of Clinical Sport Psychology* (published by Human Kinetics; first published in 2007)

- *Journal of Sport and Exercise Psychology* (published by the North American Society for the Psychology of Sport and Physical Activity; first published in 1979)

- *Journal of Sport Behaviour* (published by the United States Sports Academy; first published in 1978)

- *Journal of Sport Psychology in Action* (published by Taylor & Francis; first published in 2010)

- *Journal of Sports Sciences* (published by Taylor & Francis; first published in 1982)

- *Psychology of Sport and Exercise* (published by Elsevier; first published in 2000)

- *Qualitative Research in Sport, Exercise and Health* (published by Routledge; first published in 2009)

- *Research Quarterly for Exercise and Sport* (published by American Alliance for Health, Physical Education, Recreation and Dance; first published in 1930)

- *Sport, Exercise, and Performance Psychology* (published by the American Psychological Association; first published in 2012)

- *The Sport Psychologist* (published by the International Society of Sport Psychology; first published in 1987)

The third reason for attributing a healthy status to the field of sport psychology comes from the formal recognition of this discipline by mainstream psychology. In particular, as indicated earlier in Box 1.3, professional psychological associations in the United States (in 1986), Australia (in 1991) and Britain (in 2004) have established special divisions or sections to cater for the needs of members who are interested in the application of psychology to sport and exercise settings. Fourth, the practical value of sport psychology is evident from the increasing number of performers and coaches around the world who are using its services mainly for performance enhancement. For example, among the top athletes who have publicly acknowledged the help of sport psychologists are major golf championship winners such as Pádraig Harrington and Trevor Immelman. But it is not just individual athletes who have emerged as enthusiastic advocates of sport psychology. Many countries competing at the Olympic Games employ sport psychologists as advisers (see Box 1.5 above) as do teams in soccer (e.g. Arsenal: King and Ridley, 2006), baseball (Seppa, 1996), cricket (e.g. the Australian squad: see Wilde, 1998) and rugby (e.g. the Irish national team: see Thornley, 1997). In addition, sport psychologist Ken Way appears to have played an important role in Leicester City's extraordinary and entirely unexpected march to the 2016 English Premier League Football title (they were 5,000–1 odds on to win the title at the start of the season with many bookmakers; see Kay, 2016). In summary, the preceding strands of evidence suggest that sport psychology is now firmly established as a scientifically respectable and useful discipline. Unfortunately, this conclusion has been challenged by critics both from within and outside the discipline. Let us now consider briefly the nature and validity of their counter-arguments.

Within the discipline, Dishman (1983) argued that sport psychology is deeply flawed due to a combination of shaky theoretical foundations and unreliable intervention strategies. These sentiments were echoed by Morgan (1997) who bemoaned the absence of scientific evidence to support many of the intervention techniques promulgated by practitioners in this field. A similar point was made by Moran (1996) who noted that few concentration skills training programmes in applied sport psychology have been subjected to either conceptual or empirical evaluation. Augmenting these criticisms of theory and research in sport psychology are accounts of practitioners' disenchantment with the professional side of this discipline. For example, consider Meyers' (1997) candid account of his experiences as an "on site" sport psychologist at the US Olympic Festival. Working in this situation, he noted that although there was a clear demand for sport psychological services, "there exists little respect for what we do" (Meyers, 1997, p. 466).

As indicated earlier in our analysis of the work of Hoberman (1992), criticisms have also been levelled at sport psychology from sceptical athletes and journalists. For example, Goran Ivanisevic, the former Wimbledon champion, dismissed the value of sport psychologists by saying that "You lie on a couch, they take your money, and you walk out more bananas than when you walk in" (cited in LeUnes and Nation, 2002, p. 18; see also Figure 1.3). Likewise, Sergio Garcia, the Spanish golfer who has been ranked consistently among the top ten players in the world, claimed that, with reference to sport psychology, "I've never been a big believer in it and you can't try to do something if you don't believe in it" (cited in Corrigan, 2007). For some journalists, golf psychologists are especially irksome. Thus Paul Mahoney (2007) proclaimed that they are "the latest gurus to milk millions of pounds by teaching mantras of the bleeding [*sic*] obvious to golfers short on confidence and the ability to think for themselves". Similar scepticism of the value of sport psychology is evident in professional football in England. For example, in 1997, a survey of forty-four football clubs was conducted by the BBC Radio 5 Live documentary team On the Line. Results showed that three quarters of the clubs questioned either had never used, or would not ever consider using, a sport psychologist (see Bent et al., 2000). These clubs justified this decision by claiming that their own coaching staff, who are usually former professional players, knew best how to deal with the psychological needs of their footballers. Fortunately for psychology, Sven-Göran Eriksson, the former England team manager, did not share this view and emphasized the importance of recruiting sport psychologists to deal with the mental side of football. Thus he suggested that "if we go into the heads of players we need a specialist to do it, but I believe that this is the future of the game" (cited in Every, 2002, p. 1). For a fascinating account of the work of sport psychologists in professional football, see Nesti (2010).

What is the origin of this scepticism of sport psychology among athletes, coaches and journalists? One possibility is that it stems from a popular myth – the misidentification of psychology with psychiatry. Unfortunately, headlines that refer to managers who consult "shrinks" promulgate two potentially damaging ideas about sport psychology. First, by using the word "shrinks" (which is a

Figure 1.3 It is a myth that sport psychologists are "shrinks"

popular slang abbreviation of the term "head shrinkers"), the headline suggests that sport psychologists are psychiatrists. Second, it implies that they are consulted or called in only when there is a problem to be solved. It is worth noting that this view of sport psychology as a branch of psychiatry is based on the medical model that we explored in the previous section of this chapter. Perhaps it is this myth that players are "patients" who need to be "shrunk" by medical specialists that lies at the heart of certain athletes', coaches' and journalists' scepticism of sport psychology (see also an article on this issue by Gee, 2010). Unfortunately, as Box 1.9 shows, this discipline has also been associated in the popular mind with spoon bending and faith healing. In the light of this caricature of sport psychology as portrayed by some media, is it any wonder that Graham Taylor was pilloried in certain quarters for using a psychologist with the England team in the European Championships in 1992 (G. Taylor, 2002)?

Fortunately, in spite of the myths surrounding the discipline and the negative publicity engendered by the events described in Box 1.9, sport psychology has begun to make inroads into the world of professional football in Britain since the late 1990s. This upsurge of interest in psychology has been caused by three key changes in the sport.

Box 1.9 Thinking critically about ... sport psychology, plasticine and faith healing

Advice on sport psychology has not always received a universal welcome from the athletic community – especially in British soccer. To illustrate, Dickinson (2007) and Simon Hartley (7 January 2011, personal communication) described what happened when Howard Wilkinson, who was manager of Sunderland in the 2002–2003 season of the Premier League, hired a management consultancy firm to provide some **team building** strategies to improve the club's fortunes. In one of the management consultants' first sessions with the squad, they allegedly gave the players some plasticine with which to make a shape that reflected their perceived role in the team. When the "shrink" (Dickinson's term) examined what the players had produced, he found "five pairs of breasts, 14 phalluses and one group who had clubbed together to build a substitutes' bench!" Sadly, but not too surprisingly, Sunderland were relegated that year. A few years earlier, Glenn Hoddle, who was then manager of the England national soccer team, appointed a faith-healer named Eileen Drewery to his backroom staff. One of the reasons which Hoddle gave in justification for this decision was that Drewery "is a bit of a psychologist because she puts your mind at ease when she talks to you" (cited in Thorp, 1998).

Critical thinking questions

Do you think that the public image of sport psychology is affected by incidents such as the ones described above? What are the similarities and differences between faith healing and applied sport psychology? If putting "your mind at ease" is all that footballers require in order to play well, does it matter whether or not a technique that achieves this purpose is accepted as "scientific"? How can sport psychologists change the popular image of their profession? List two or three practical strategies to address this issue.

First, improvements in the standard of coach education programmes have led to increased acceptance of the role that sport science (including psychology) plays in professional football. Put simply, if clubs are willing to accept the principle that regular physiological testing is a good way of maintaining physical fitness among players, then they should also accept the notion that footballers' mental fitness can be facilitated by advice from sport psychologists. Second, there has been an influx of foreign coaches and players into British football since 1990, when Dr Jozef Vengloš was appointed manager of a top-flight club, Aston Villa. These people have introduced indigenous players to the benefits of such sport scientific practices as "warming down" after games, adhering to a balanced diet, and preparing mentally for matches (L. Dixon, 2002). Third, and perhaps most importantly, the fact that successful coaches such as Sven-Göran Eriksson and Alex Ferguson have employed sport psychologists (H. Winter, 2002) has influenced other coaches to copy them. Mindful of these three developments, the Football Association in England launched a campaign to encourage football clubs in Britain to recruit more sport psychologists (H. Winter, 2002). In summary, available evidence suggests that sport psychology in football is expanding not "shrinking" (Moran, 2002b).

To summarize this section, in spite of its struggle against certain persistent criticisms and misconceptions, sport psychology is making encouraging progress in establishing itself as a respected discipline. Of course, this conclusion must be tempered by awareness of at least two unresolved issues in the field. First, it is essential for the long-term viability of sport psychology that professional psychological organizations such as the APA and the BPS should develop accreditation criteria for postgraduate training courses in this field. Second, in an effort to safeguard the public against the possibility of malpractice, professional issues concerning titles and certification need to be addressed urgently. For a more extensive discussion of ethical issues in applied sport and exercise psychology, see Kremer et al. (2012), Oliver (2010) and Stapleton et al. (2010).

An idea for a research project on sport psychology

Here is an idea for a possible research project on the psychological aspects of sport. Its objectives are:

1. to find out what athletes mean by "mental preparation"
2. to establish how important it is to them
3. to estimate what proportion of their training time they devote to it on average.

To conduct this project, you will need a digital voice recorder and some volunteer athletes. Find three people who play different types of sports (e.g. a team game, an individual game) who have been actively involved in competitive performance for at least five years. Request their permission to record your interview with them on the voice recorder. Then, ask them the following questions:

■ What does the term "mental preparation" mean to you?

- On a scale of 0 (meaning "not at all important") to 5 (meaning "extremely important"), how important do you think that proper mental preparation is for successful performance in your sport?
- What sort of things do you do as physical training for your sport?
- What sort of things, if any, do you do as mental preparation for your sport?
- About what percentage of your training time do you devote to physical preparation? Give a rough percentage figure.
- And to mental preparation? Give an approximate percentage figure, please.

Compare and contrast the athletes' answers to your questions. You will probably discover that although these people think that mental preparation is important for optimal performance, they devote relatively little time to it. If this finding emerges, how do you interpret it? If not, what did the athletes say? Did the type of sport make a difference to the athletes' views?

Summary

- Sport psychology is both a science and a profession in which the principles and methods of psychology are applied in sport and exercise settings.

- The second section investigated the nature and determinants of the mental side of sport as well as the related constructs of confidence and mental toughness in athletes. It also provided some practical tips on how to develop your critical thinking skills.

- The third section outlined the nature, history and research methods of the discipline of sport psychology.

- The fourth section explored professional aspects of this field. Included here was a discussion of four key questions:

  1. What type of work do sport psychologists actually do?
  2. What is the best way to deliver sport psychology services to athletes and coaches?
  3. How can I qualify professionally as a sport psychologist?
  4. Where can I learn more about sport psychology?

- The fifth section provided a brief evaluation of the current status of sport psychology. This section addressed this question by assessing both the scientific standing of this discipline as well as people's perception of it.

- Finally, the chapter provided a practical suggestion for a research project on the mental side of sport.

Exploring athletic performance
Key constructs

Overview

Chapter 1 of the book examined the nature of the discipline and profession of sport psychology. Part 1 investigates the various psychological processes that affect individual athletes in their pursuit of excellence. Whereas Chapter 2 explores the psychology of motivation, Chapter 3 examines anxiety in athletes. Chapter 4 addresses coping and emotion. After that, Chapter 5 explores concentration and Chapter 6 tackles imagery processes in athletes. Finally, Chapter 7 investigates the question of what determines expertise in sport performers.

2

Motivation and
goal-setting in sport

Introduction

According to Arsène Wenger (current manager of Arsenal football club), "the biggest difficulty you have in this job is not to motivate the players but to get them relaxed enough to express their talent" (cited in Fanning, 2004a, p. 5). More generally, motivation plays a crucial if somewhat misunderstood role in sport. To illustrate the first of these claims, the term "motivation" is commonly invoked by athletes, coaches and psychologists to account for the "energizing", regulation and persistence of behaviour in athletic situations (e.g. when training for endurance events such as marathons). As Standage (2012) explained, the "energy required for an athlete to persist in high-quality training sessions, both across long gruelling seasons and in the face of competitive failure, reveals why motivation is considered a foundation" (p. 233) in sport psychology. Indeed, at the elite level of sport, the role of motivation is *crucial* in the sense that athletic success depends significantly on the willingness of athletes to exert *mental* as well as physical effort in pursuit of excellence (see detailed discussion in Chapter 7). In this regard, José Mourinho, one of the most successful coaches in world football (e.g. his teams have won titles in four different countries), claimed that "motivation is the most important thing. Some of them can and they don't want [to], some of them want and they can't. We want players who can do it and at the same time *want* to do it" (cited in Honigsbaum, 2004, p. 18; italics ours). Delving deeper into this idea, Alex Ferguson (the former Manchester United manager), another extraordinarily successful coach, revealed that athletes' motivation can be manipulated by shrewd managers by understanding how players differ from each other with regard to the factors that drive their behaviour. Specifically, he said:

> footballers are all different human beings. Some are self-motivators, they need to be left alone ... For some, you need causes, your country, them and us, your religion. And those causes can be created by the manager ... at Manchester United, we have to be better than everyone else.
>
> (cited in White, 1999)

Despite these valuable insights from successful coaches, the contribution of motivation to optimal performance in sport is widely misunderstood. For example, as Glyn Roberts (2001) pointed out, motivation is often confused with being "psyched up" (see also Chapter 3) – a view that Arsène Wenger has challenged (see Figure 2.1).

Contrary to popular wisdom, however, there is little research evidence that "psyching up" athletes by emphasizing the disastrous consequences of failure can ever prove to be an effective motivational ploy. Indeed, if anything, such a strategy may prove *counterproductive* because high levels of **arousal** (see Chapter 3) are known to impair both athletes' technical performance (Gee, 2010) and concentration skills (see Chapter 5). To illustrate, Webster (1984) reported that due to the effects of excessive anxiety, *not one* member of an Australian Rules football team could recall any of the coach's instructions in a vital game just *five minutes* after his rousing pre-match address! Interestingly, as the quote at the beginning of the chapter shows, Arsène Wenger, who is the most successful manager in the history of Arsenal football club, observed that his role was not to motivate players – but to help them to relax on the pitch. Similar sentiments were expressed by José Mourinho. Specifically, he said that "… sometimes you may have to shout at them in the face, but fear is not a good emotion" (Campbell, 2015, p. 2). And this brings us to the question of motivation through fear. This issue was highlighted sharply by reports that, in the early 1990s, Iraqi footballers were regularly beaten and tortured for losing matches under the brutal regime of Uday Hussein, son of the notorious Saddam Hussein (Goldenberg, 2003) – a cruel practice which did nothing to enhance team morale or performance.

Figure 2.1 Arsène Wenger believes that footballers perform best when they are relaxed (*source*: courtesy of Inpho photography)

Nevertheless, anecdotal reports suggest that some athletes have used fear to motivate themselves in certain situations. For example, Pádraig Harrington, a three-time golf major winner, admitted that

> fear has always been a motivating factor in my golf ... This is my 12th year on Tour and certainly for eight or nine years, every time I took my winter break, I was very anxious I would come out and it would still be there ... Yes, fear is a big part of me.
>
> (Pádraig Harrington, cited in *The Irish Times*, 2008)

By contrast, Arsène Wenger claims that the fear is incompatible with peak performance. Specifically, he said that "fear is the best way *not* to achieve what you want to achieve" (cited in J. Jackson, 2010; italics ours). In general, empirical research supports Wenger's rather than Harrington's position because a strong fear of failure is associated with psychological problems such as excessive anxiety, depression and even withdrawal from sport, especially among young athletes (Travers et al., 2013).

Given this background of confusion and inconsistency about the role of motivational factors in sport psychology, the present chapter attempts to answer the following questions. What exactly does the term "motivation" mean? What types of motivation have been identified? What theoretical approaches have been used to explore this construct? How can athletes increase their motivation? Finally, what factors motivate people to participate in dangerous sports? In order to address these issues, the chapter is organized as follows.

To begin with, we consider the nature and types of motivation that are evident among athletes. Next, we present a brief overview of theoretical approaches to motivation in sport psychology. Special consideration will be given here to three influential cognitive models of motivational processes in athletes: **achievement goal theory** (AGT; Ames, 1992; J. Nicholls, 1984), **attribution theory** (AT; e.g. Heider, 1958; Kelley, 1967) and **self-determination theory** (see Deci and Ryan, 1985, 2000, 2008). The third section explores the theory and practice of increasing motivation in athletes through goal-setting techniques. The fourth section examines a motivational question that has attracted popular debate: why do some people take part in risky or dangerous sports activities? In the final section of the chapter, we provide some practical suggestions for possible research projects on the psychology of motivation in athletes.

Nature and types of motivation

The term motivation refers to "the direction and intensity of one's effort" (Weinberg, 2009, p. 7). It is derived from the Latin word *movere* (meaning "to move": Onions, 1996) and is concerned with those factors that "move" (or energize), direct and regulate achievement behaviour. More precisely, within sport psychology, motivational processes are implicated whenever "a person undertakes a task at which he or she is evaluated or enters into competition with others, or attempts to attain some standard of excellence" (G. Roberts, 2001, p. 6).

Box 2.1 Thinking critically about ... popular understanding of "motivation"

According to Roberts and Kristiansen (2010), motivation is widely misunderstood. In particular, three myths about it need to be debunked. First, motivation is not the same as arousal. Research suggests that athletes cannot be motivated effectively simply by "psyching" them up into a frenzy of adrenaline. For optimal motivation and performance to occur, arousal needs to be *channelled* in a specific direction (see also Chapter 3). The second myth about motivation is that it can be enhanced purely through positive thinking. For example, it may be assumed that if athletes can be encouraged to imagine themselves holding up the winner's trophy, their motivation will be strengthened. Unfortunately, research on goal-setting (see later in this chapter) shows that people's objectives have to be controllable and realistic in order to be effective. The third myth is the assumption that motivation is a genetically inherited characteristic – something that one either has or does not have. Again, this view is contradicted by research evidence which shows that motivation can be changed through appropriate instruction (see later in chapter). Given these popular misconceptions, is it any wonder that sport psychologists have to be careful when using the term motivation? As Glyn Roberts warned in 2001, "it is defined so broadly by some that it incorporates the whole field of psychology, so narrowly by others that it is almost useless as an organising construct" (G. Roberts, 2001, p. 3).

Critical thinking questions

Do you agree with Roberts and Kristiansen (2010) that motivation is widely misunderstood in sport? Why do you think that many people mistake a heightened state of arousal for motivation? Are there any distinctive behavioural signs or expressions of motivation? How would you design a study to explore athletes' understanding of motivation? From reading the popular press, do you think that the myth of motivation extend to everyday understanding of the work that sport psychologists do with their clients? If so, why do you think so many people believe that sport psychology is concerned only with motivating athletes to perform well?

Unfortunately, as we have suggested already, the term motivation is plagued by a great deal of conceptual confusion. Box 2.1 presents some persistent myths surrounding this construct.

In the light of the confusion surrounding motivational processes in sport, how should we approach this construct scientifically? Traditionally, sport psychologists have distinguished between two different types of motivation – intrinsic and extrinsic (see review by Vallerand and Rousseau, 2001). **Intrinsic motivation** refers to people's impetus to perform an activity for its own sake – "for itself and the pleasure and satisfaction derived from participation" (Vallerand and Rousseau, 2001, p. 390). For example, many people love walking or running simply because it gives them a feeling of fun and freedom and enhances their sense of well-being (see also Chapter 5 for an analysis of what runners actually think about when running). Anecdotally, it is precisely this sense of intrinsic joy or satisfaction which seems to characterize the motivation of top athletes in sports like swimming, golf and cricket. Thus, consider the importance which Kieren Perkins, the Australian former swimmer and four-time Olympic medallist, attached to intrinsic motivational influences in his sport when he said: "I always *race against myself to improve my own performances*. The fact that I sometimes set world records in the process is a bonus. My personal best performance is the goal, not necessarily the world record" (Clews and Gross, 1995, pp. 98–99; italics ours). A similar emphasis on intrinsic satisfaction is evident in the approach of Phil Taylor, sixteen times world champion darts player. He said: "I love everything about my job – getting up every morning, practising and dedicating myself; I always try to better myself ... There's always that 1 per cent that I can improve" (cited in P. Newman, 2010, p. 12). Finally, the former cricket star Sachin Tendulkar, who inspired India to victory in the 2011 World Cup and who is widely regarded as one of the greatest batsmen of all time, claimed that "I don't set myself any targets. I just concentrate on trying to bat well ... When I was a kid, I played cricket because I loved it and I still love it now" (*Funday Times*, 2002). Interestingly, an in-depth study of the motivational processes of elite track-and-field athletes (those who had finished in the top ten at either the Olympic Games or the world championships) supports these anecdotal insights. Specifically, Mallett and Hanrahan (2003) interviewed such expert performers in an effort to identify the factors which sustained their motivation to compete at the highest level. Results showed that these athletes were driven mainly by personal goals and achievements rather than by financial incentives. Not surprisingly (according to M. Martens and Webber, 2002), intrinsic motivation is associated with increased enjoyment of physical activities and a reduced likelihood of dropping out of sport.

As the name implies, **extrinsic motivation** applies whenever a person is involved in a task largely as a result of external factors or constraints. More precisely this term refers to "engaging in an activity as a means to an end and not for its own sake" (Vallerand and Rousseau, 2001, p. 391). Typical extrinsic factors held to motivate athletes include money, trophies, praise and/or other forms of social approval from others. For example, golfers would be regarded as extrinsically motivated if they joined a golf club because they wanted to make new business contacts – not because they actually enjoyed the game of golf. In summary, extrinsic motivators are factors which influence a person to do something either because they provide a reward for such behaviour or because they provide some punishment or sanction for *not* doing it. In general, research shows that extrinsic motivation is associated with increased anxiety in, and increased likelihood of dropping out from, sporting activities (see M. Martens and Webber, 2002). More recently, researchers have explored children's reasons either for taking part in or for dropping out from organized sport. For example, C. Foster et al. (2007) discovered that extrinsic factors such as gender and cultural stereotyping of certain sports, the costs of participation in organized activities and increasing emphasis on technical and performance issues rather than on having fun were cited as facilitating variables for children under 8 years old. By contrast, the "turn ons" for these children were enjoyment of the activities and parental and peer support. Perhaps not surprisingly, feelings of burnout (i.e. a syndrome characterized by withdrawal from one's sport and overriding sense of physical and psychological exhaustion; see Chunxiao et al., 2013; Goodger et al., 2010;

Gustafsson et al., 2011) in elite athletes are often associated with an extrinsic motivational orientation (Lemyre et al., 2006).

Theoretically, intrinsic and extrinsic motivation can be differentiated on at least three criteria (Vallerand and Fortier, 1998). First, consider the purpose of the activity. As indicated earlier, whereas intrinsically motivated activities are undertaken for their own sake, extrinsically motivated tasks are typically conducted for some perceived instrumental benefit. Second, although people who are intrinsically motivated tend to seek experiential rewards, those who are extrinsically motivated tend to be influenced more by social and/or objective rewards (e.g. money). Third, Vallerand and Fortier (1998) proposed that intrinsically motivated performers tend to experience less pressure than extrinsically motivated counterparts when competing because the former people are largely concerned with the experience of participation itself.

Despite these theoretical distinctions, intrinsic and extrinsic motivation often overlap in real life. Indeed, as Box 2.2 shows, extrinsic rewards can affect intrinsic motivation under certain circumstances.

Box 2.2 Thinking critically about ... how rewards can change people's motivation

The National Coaching Foundation (1996) presented an apocryphal tale that nicely captures the idea that the withdrawal of rewards can sometimes change people's motivation in surprising ways. By the way, this tale has a long history in psychology (e.g. see another version of this story in Myers et al., 2010, p. 172).

An old man was plagued by teenagers playing football and making noise on the street outside his house. No matter what he said to them, they ignored him. In fact, the more he pleaded with them to stop, the more they persisted and the more obnoxiously they behaved. He was at his wits' end. Then one day, following a chat with a psychologist friend, he decided to try a new approach to the problem. Briefly, instead of scolding the boys, he decided to give them a *reward* (two euros each) for playing noisily outside his house. Of course, the boys were delighted with this decision. Imagine getting paid for doing something which they really enjoyed – making the old man's life miserable! When the boys returned the following evening, they received the same reward again – another two euros each. This practice puzzled the boys but they continued to wreak havoc on the old man. After a week, however, the man told them that he could not afford to pay each of them the two euros that they had been given previously. In fact, all he could manage was fifty cents each. This disappointed the boys a little but they continued to torment the man. Another week elapsed and this time, the old man reduced the reward to twenty cents each. Again, this was very frustrating to the boys who had grown used to receiving a larger reward. Eventually, the old man reduced the reward to two cents each – at which time, the leader of the boys grew very angry. Shouting at the old man, he said, "We've had enough of your meanness. If you think that we're going to play football for your entertainment outside your house for two cents, then you've got another thing coming! We're off!" Clearly, the moral of this tale is that when the old man removed extrinsic motivation for the football, the boys lost interest in doing what they had done previously for nothing.

Critical thinking questions

Do you think that this story has any relevance for understanding why highly paid sports performers sometimes lose their motivation? From your knowledge of other areas of psychology (e.g. behaviour modification), can you think of any other explanation of the boys' loss of motivation? Can cognitive evaluation theory (see text for description) offer any insights into what happened in this story?

As you can see from Box 2.2, if people who are performing an activity for the sheer fun of it are given external rewards, their level of intrinsic motivation may decrease (Deci, 1971). Interestingly, there is evidence that athletes who engage in sporting activity to receive a trophy tend to show a subsequent decrease in intrinsic motivation as measured by self-report scales (Vallerand and Rousseau, 2001). In an effort to explain this somewhat surprising finding, **cognitive evaluation theory** (Deci and Ryan, 1991) suggested that the way in which rewards are perceived must be considered. Briefly, this theory assumes that rewards can fulfil one of two functions: *controlling* (i.e. those which influence behaviour) or *informational* (i.e. those which provide feedback about the performer's level of performance on a given task). Depending on how athletes perceive rewards, their intrinsic motivation may be either enhanced or reduced. For example, if they believe that their sporting behaviour is controlled by external rewards, their level of intrinsic motivation may decline. However, if rewards are perceived as merely providing feedback, intrinsic motivation will probably increase. According to cognitive evaluation theory, controlling rewards tend to impair intrinsic motivation whereas informational rewards may strengthen it. Before we conclude this section, it is important to consider the relationship between praise (which we can define as communicating a positive evaluation of another person's performance or attributes to him or her) and motivation. It has long been assumed that praise enhances children's motivation. But is this really true? In a critique of this claim, Henderlong and Lepper (2002) argued that when praise is perceived as being sincere, it is beneficial to motivation as long as it conveys attainable standards and expectations and encourages people to make **attributions** (i.e. to seek possible causes of behaviour; see later in chapter) to controllable factors. Interestingly, praise may inadvertently undermine children's motivation – perhaps because it encourages invidious social comparison processes.

In an effort to understand the subtleties of motivational processes in athletes, Vallerand and his colleagues postulated a hierarchical model of intrinsic/extrinsic motivation (HMIEM; see Lalande and Vallerand, 2014). Briefly, the HMIEM proposes that three types of motivation (intrinsic motivation; extrinsic motivation; and "amotivation" – or the absence of motivation) may be identified at three different levels of generality (i.e. global, contextual and situational). Furthermore, it speculates that the type of motivation one has at a given level will influence one's motivation at the other levels. For example, if a person displays a relatively high level of global intrinsic motivation, then she or he is likely to also demonstrate a high level of intrinsic motivation at the contextual level (e.g. in sport).

Theories of motivation: from personality to cognition

Having considered the nature and main types of motivation, let us now review key theoretical approaches to this construct in sport psychology. Historically, at least four major theoretical approaches have dominated research on motivational processes in sport and exercise since the 1960s – the personality model (epitomized by research on individual differences in people's need for achievement) and three social-cognitive models (including the goal-orientation approach, attribution theory and self-determination theory). Perhaps the most important difference between these two categories of models is that whereas personality theorists view people as being driven by deep-seated psychological needs (see review by Allen et al., 2013), social-cognitive researchers are more concerned with understanding how people's thoughts and perceptions guide their behaviour. Another difference between these approaches is that whereas personality theorists are concerned mainly with the origins of people's achievement strivings (i.e. the past determinants of their needs), cognitive motivational researchers are more interested in people's choice of future actions (G. Roberts, 2001). The theoretical rationale of each of these approaches is reviewed in more detail below.

The personality approach

Initially, sport psychologists tried to account for athletes' motivational processes by referring to two types of variables – innate instincts and learned drives. Superficially, such theories seem plausible. For example, aggressive behaviour on the football field is commonly attributed to the possession of an aggressive nature. But on closer inspection, this approach is flawed by the "circularity" of the reasoning involved (i.e. the fact that the argument assumes what it is trying to prove). The difficulty here is that any scientific explanation for a phenomenon must be independent of the phenomenon itself. Otherwise, one unknown variable is used to "explain" another. This problem of proposing circular explanations for people's behaviour has a long history and was satirized by Molière in *La Malade Imaginaire* when he made fun of doctors who had suggested that what gives opium its soporific quality is its *virtus dormitiva* – or soporific quality! In a similar vein, aggressive actions cannot be explained adequately by appealing to hypothetical aggressive instincts, because the existence of these instincts depends on evidence of aggressive behaviour. On logical grounds, therefore, instinct theories of motivation have been discredited significantly in psychology.

Following the demise of instinct theory, sport psychologists turned to *personality traits* in an effort to account for motivational phenomena. One trait of particular interest was a construct called "need for achievement" (see McClelland et al., 1953; also Conroy, 2014). Briefly, this trait was believed to be elicited by situations involving approach-avoidance conflicts. In such situations, people face a dilemma in which their natural desire to achieve success (i.e. their "need to achieve") is challenged by their fear of failure. Theoretically, athletes were said to have a relatively high level of **achievement motivation** if their need to achieve was greater than their fear of failure. Conversely, they were alleged to have a relatively low level of achievement motivation when their fear of failure exceeded their desire to succeed. According to McClelland et al. (1953), people with high achievement needs are impelled to seek challenging but realistic objectives for their performance in competitive settings. Applied to sport, this principle suggests that athletes who have a high need to achieve should prefer to compete against opponents of a similar, or slightly higher, level of ability. By contrast, athletes with low achievement motivation tend to avoid challenging situations and should prefer to compete against opponents of lower ability levels. Despite its intuitive appeal, this theory has made little progress in accounting for the motivational behaviour of sport performers. This situation is attributable to two main problems. First, there is a dearth of valid objective instruments available for the measurement of achievement motivation in athletes (Conroy, 2014). Second, researchers have criticized the assumption in traditional achievement motivation theory that success and failure may be defined objectively. For example, Maehr and Nicholls (1980) argued that these variables are largely subjective because they are usually defined in relation to people's *perception* of goal achievement. So, whereas some athletes may regard "success" as being defined by defeating an opponent or winning a competition, others may perceive it in relation to achieving a "personal best" performance or impressing their coach or parents (we shall return to this point in the next section).

Recognition of this subjective influence on people's achievement strivings influenced researchers to switch from a personality-based to a social-cognitive approach in the study of motivation in athletes (see Doerksen and Elavsky, 2014). This change in emphasis had important theoretical implications for sport psychology. As Kremer et al. (2003, p. 188) observed, it "switched attention from the 'what' or content of motivation to the 'why' or process whereby we are or are not motivated". Within the social-cognitive **paradigm** (see also Chapter 9 for a discussion of this term) of motivation research, two conceptual models deserve special mention: achievement goal theory and attribution theory. Let us now examine each of these approaches briefly.

The social-cognitive approach: achievement goal theory

Achievement goals concern the aim or purpose of a person's achievement behaviour which can be defined as "behaviour directed at developing or demonstrating high rather than low competence" (J. Nicholls, 1984, p. 328). Therefore, "achievement goal theory" (see J. Nicholls, 1984; also Conroy and Hyde, 2014) seeks to understand people's adaptive and maladaptive responses to achievement challenges. Two main types of goals were identified: **task** or **mastery goals** (which focus mainly on acquiring competence in a given skill) and **ego** or performance goals (which emphasize instead the importance of demonstrating one's competence by performing better than others). For an excellent critique of the evolution of this theory, see Senko et al. (2011).

Applied to sport psychology, AGT is also known as **"goal orientation theory"** (see reviews by Harwood et al., 2008; G. Roberts et al. 2007) and is concerned mainly with how people perceive and define *successful* achievement. The cornerstone of this theoretical approach to motivation in sport is the assumption that athletes' behaviour in competitive situations is a consequence of their perception of "success". More precisely, this approach suggests that in order to understand athletes' motivation, we need to explore what success *means* to them. Put differently, whether athletes consider a given outcome as a success or failure depends on how they define "success" and "failure" initially (Weinberg, 2009). Arising from this fundamental assumption, Maehr and Nicholls (1980, p. 228) proposed that success and failure "are not concrete events. They are psychological states consequent on perception of reaching or not reaching goals."

Achievement goal theory postulates a dichotomous model whereby two main types of motivation (or goal orientations) may be identified in athletes – depending on how they interpret the goal of their achievements (or success). These two type of motivation are task motivation (also known as mastery motivation) and ego motivation (also known as competitive orientation). Overall, AGT proposes that the way in which athletes define competence and success (i.e. their goal orientation) and the way in which they interpret their psychological environment (i.e. their perceived motivational climate) will influence their behaviour. For athletes, this term "motivational climate" refers to the psychological environment created by the coach and involves the athlete's perception of the "situational cues and structures that are evident within an achievement setting" (Roberts et al., 2015, p. 536). Theoretically, with a task goal orientation and in a mastery motivational climate, competence and success are typically defined in self-referenced terms such as personal improvement and development. In contrast, an **ego orientation** and a performance motivational climate define competence and success in reference to others (normative) such as outperforming others and winning. Consistently, research on motivational climates has shown that mastery climates (i.e. those that emphasize rewarding of task mastery and of effort more than ability) lead to more desirable outcomes than do ego-involving performance climates (i.e. those that emphasize the importance of minimizing mistakes and performing better than others). To illustrate, compared to performance climates, mastery motivational climates have been shown to be associated with enhanced effort, enjoyment and persistence in the face of adversity and lowered levels of anxiety (e.g. O'Rourke et al., 2014).

According to AGT, task-motivated athletes are interested mainly in subjective indices of success such as skill-learning, tactical development, mastery of challenges and technical self-improvement. For example, task-oriented athletes may perceive themselves to be successful if they can perform a specific sport skill (e.g. serving a tennis ball) better today than they did three weeks ago. By contrast, ego-motivated athletes tend to view "success" normatively, through comparison with the attainments of other people. For example, ego-oriented athletes regard themselves as successful only if they perform better than others, regardless of any personal improvements in performance that they may have achieved. By defeating others, they believe, they have demonstrated superior ability to rival athletes. Therefore, winning and beating others are the main preoccupations of ego-oriented athletes. Originally, these two goal orientations were assumed to be "orthogonal" or independent (J. Nicholls, 1989). In other words, a person may achieve a high or a low score on either goal orientation or on both at the same time. Subsequently, however, this assumption was challenged. In particular, Harwood et al. (2008) proposed that athletes cannot be task-oriented and ego-oriented at the same time. However, as Kremer et al. (2012) noted, there is evidence that many elite athletes regard an ego-orientation as complementary, rather than inimical, to a **task orientation**. To complicate matters further, Elliott and Conroy (2005) proposed a trichotomous model of AGT. Specifically they argued that as well as investigating the distinction between task-orientation and ego-orientation, we need to explore whether athletes are influenced by *approach* motives (striving to be competent) or *avoidance* motives (fear of being seen to be incompetent). More precisely, they postulated that achievement targets that are motivated by a desire to meet a specific challenge (approach goals) are likely to encourage persistence whereas targets that are motivated by a desire not to fail (avoidance goals) are unlikely to sustain commitment. Based on Elliott and Conroy's (2005) theory, we can distinguish between four different achievement goals:

- *mastery approach* (i.e. striving to learn or improve skills: "I want to learn as much as possible from this group coaching session")
- *mastery avoidance* (i.e. striving to avoid learning failures or a decline in skills: e.g. "I'm concerned that I may not learn what I need to learn in this session")
- *performance approach* (i.e. striving to perform better than others: e.g. "It's important for me to do better than the other students in this session")
- *performance avoidance* (i.e. striving to avoid doing worse than others e.g. "My priority in this session is to avoid performing poorly").

Returning to the original distinction between task-motivation and ego-motivation, what does research reveal about the correlates of these two motives? According to Lemyre et al. (2002), task-oriented athletes perceive achievement in sport in self-referenced terms involving skill improvement/mastery and technical development. As a consequence, they tend to be intrinsically interested in the task, willing to expend effort in persisting with it and, above all, guided by personal standards of achievement rather than by prevailing social norms. Conversely, ego-oriented athletes strive to "demonstrate superior normative ability, or avoid the demonstration of incompetence at the task at hand" (Lemyre et al., 2002, p. 122). In other words, they judge their own success by the degree to which they can perform better than others. Thus winning and defeating others is their primary concern in athletic situations. This description of ego-oriented performers brings to mind a quotation attributed to the writer Gore Vidal: "it's not enough to succeed – others must fail!" (cited in *The Guardian*, 2012). Another correlate of task and ego orientation is sportspersonship, Thus Kavussanu (2007) reported that an ego goal orientation is associated with relatively low levels of moral functioning – as indicated by expressing unsportspersonlike attitudes, engaging in unsportspersonlike behaviours, and employing relatively immature moral reasoning. By contrast, a task orientation tends to be associated with sportspersonship. More generally, in a recent meta-analysis of research in the field, Van Yperen et al. (2014) concluded that across the domains of sport, work and education, mastery-*approach* goals (i.e. those that emphasize doing better than one has done before) and performance-*approach* goals (i.e. those with a focus on doing better than others) were generally related positively to performance achievement. By contrast, performance-*avoidance* goals (i.e. those with a focus on not doing worse than others) and mastery-*avoidance* goals (i.e. those with a focus on not doing worse than one has done before) were, in general, related negatively to performance attainment.

Having outlined briefly what these two goal orientations involve, let us now consider how they can be measured psychologically before sketching some general findings in this field.

Measuring achievement goal orientations

Task and ego goal orientations may be assessed using questionnaires such as the Task and Ego Orientation in Sport Questionnaire (TEOSQ: Duda and Nicholls, 1992) and/or the Perceptions of Success Questionnaire (POSQ: G. Roberts et al., 1998). The TEOSQ consists of thirteen items – seven of which measure a task orientation and six of which assess an ego orientation. Participants are required to respond to the generic stem "I feel most successful in my sport when ..." using a five-point Likert scale. Responses range from 1 (strongly disagree) to 5 (strongly agree). Typical items in the task orientation scale are "I learn a new skill by trying hard" or "I do my very best". Similarly, typical items on the ego orientation scale include "The others can't do as well as me" or "I'm the best". Early psychometric research indicates that these scales possess adequate reliability (Duda and Whitehead, 1998). More recently, Hanrahan and Cerin (2009) reported that the internal consistency of the task orientation scale was 0.80 and that for the ego orientation scale was 0.83. The POSQ is a twelve-item test of task and ego orientation with six items in each subscale. In this test, the stem item is "When playing my sport, I feel most successful when ...". Typical items in the task orientation subscale include: "I work hard" (item 1) or "I master something I couldn't do before". Meanwhile, the ego orientation subscale comprises items such as "I am the best" or "I accomplish something others can't do". As with the TEOSQ, there is evidence of acceptable validity and reliability for the POSQ (Harwood, 2002).

Some research findings on achievement goal theory

At least four predictions from achievement goal theory have been tested by researchers. First, children who hold task-oriented goals (e.g. wanting to learn new skills) should show persistence in sport situations whereas more ego-motivated counterparts may drop out of sport at an earlier stage. Some support for this prediction has been found (see review by Weiss and Ferrer-Caja, 2002). Second, achievement goal theory predicts that athletes with different goal orientations will have different beliefs about the causes of their success. As in the previous case, this hypothesis has received some empirical support. Thus task-oriented athletes tend to regard athletic success as being determined significantly by the expenditure of effort. By contrast, athletes with an ego orientation typically believe that success is achieved mainly by having high ability (G. Roberts, 2001). Interestingly, the belief that effort rather than ability leads to success may help to explain why task-oriented athletes tend to persist longer in sport than do ego-oriented counterparts. A third trend in research findings in this field is that athletes' goal orientations are related to the way in which they cope with anxiety. For example, Ntoumanis et al. (1999) discovered that when exposed to stressful situations, task-oriented student athletes tended to use problem-solving strategies (e.g. exerting more effort, seeking social support) whereas those with a predominant ego orientation tended to rely on emotion-focused coping strategies (e.g. venting their emotions). Furthermore, a task orientation was found to be negatively associated with thoughts about wanting to escape from a losing situation in sport whereas an ego orientation was positively associated with such thoughts (Hatzigeorgiadis, 2002). Fourth, the relationship between goal orientation and sportspersonship has been investigated with some interesting results. In general, greater levels of ego orientation are associated with lower levels of moral reasoning and a greater likelihood of approval of unsportspersonlike behaviour. By contrast, higher levels of task orientation are associated with good sportspersonship and less tolerance for aggression and cheating (Weiss et al., 2008).

So far, we have examined the predictions of achievement goal theory in sport as if no moderating variables were involved. Unfortunately, the impact of situational factors in this field needs to be considered carefully. Not surprisingly, therefore, researchers in this field have postulated that an intervening variable called "motivational climate" regulates the relationship between goal orientation and athletic performance. According to Ames (1992), motivational climate refers to the perceived structure of the achievement environment as mediated by the coach's attitudes and behaviour. In general, two types of climate may be identified. A "mastery" climate is perceived when the coach places the emphasis on personal effort and skill development. In such an environment, mistakes are regarded as sources of feedback and learning. By contrast, an "ego-oriented" motivational climate is said to prevail when athletes are compared with, and pitted against, each other and when their mistakes are criticized and punished (Duda and Pensgaard, 2002). A scale has been developed by Walling et al. (1993) to measure the Perceived Motivational Climate in Sport.

Several trends are evident from research findings on motivational climates in sport. To begin with, an ego-oriented climate is typically correlated negatively with similar motivational indices (approximate $r=0.3$) (Harwood and Biddle, 2002). One possible reason for the perceived advantage of the task-oriented climate over the ego-oriented one is that in the former, the athlete is encouraged to focus on factors within his or her control whereas in the latter, athletes tend to use social comparison processes when assessing their own competence (Duda and Hall, 2001). Generally, most achievement goal theorists (e.g. Ames, 1992; J. Nicholls, 1992) advocate the importance of cultivating a task-oriented climate in which athletes are taught to value effort, skill-mastery and intrinsic motivation rather than an ego-oriented climate in which the goal of defeating others is paramount. Theoretically, task-oriented motivational climates can be cultivated by the provision of coaching feedback that focuses on athletes' performance relative to self-referenced criteria of achievement and improvement. The value of an ego-oriented climate should not be dismissed completely, however. Thus L. Hardy et al. (1996) argued that some degree of ego involvement is a necessary prerequisite of success for any elite athlete. Recently, Harwood et al. (2015) explored the intrapersonal correlates of motivational climate perceptions in sport and physical activity. They found that perceived task/mastery motivational climates were associated positively with a range of adaptive outcomes such as perceived competence, feelings of autonomy, intrinsic forms of motivation, positive affect and dispositional flow. By contrast, perceived ego/performance motivational climates were associated with negative affect and negative thoughts/worries.

Having sketched the nature, measurement and predictions of achievement goal theory, it is time to evaluate its contribution to motivational research in sport. Box 2.3 presents a brief critical appraisal of this theory.

Box 2.3 Thinking critically about ... achievement goal theory in sport

In 2001, Duda and Hall (2001, p. 417) hailed achievement goal theory as "a major theoretical paradigm in sport psychology". Is this claim still valid? Unfortunately, this theory has been plagued by a number of troublesome issues (for reviews of achievement goal theory, see also Harwood et al., 2008; Senko et al., 2011). First, as Duda and Hall (2001) acknowledged, achievement goal theorists are rather vague about the ways in which athletes' goal orientations interact with situational factors such as perceived motivational climate in order to determine motivational behaviour. Second, a preoccupation with task-oriented and ego-oriented goal orientations has led to the neglect of *other* possible goal perspectives in sport such as affiliative needs. A third problem with achievement goal theory was noted by Kremer and Busby (1998) in relation to understanding participant motivation – the question of why some people persist with physical activity whereas other people drop out of it. In particular, these authors pointed out that it is somewhat naive to expect that task and ego orientations do not overlap considerably in real life. For example, whereas some people may initially involve themselves in physical activity for task-oriented reasons (such as losing weight), they may learn to love such activity for its own sake over time. In other words, people's motivational orientation is neither fixed nor static. A fourth problem with achievement goal theory in sport psychology is that although there have been many studies on athletes' goal orientations, there have been fewer studies on athletes' "goal states" – or the type of achievement goals that athletes pursue in specific sport situations (Harwood and Biddle, 2002). Finally, as Harwood (2002) pointed out, **nomothetic** measures of goal orientation (i.e. ones that seek to establish general laws of human behaviour from data mainly obtained through group comparisons) such as the TEOSQ (Duda and Nicholls, 1992) are often used inappropriately for the purposes of quantitative **idiographic** assessment of individual athletes (i.e. evaluation of the intensive study of individuals over time) even though such tests are poor at identifying the differences between high, moderate and low task-orientation scores. Furthermore, there is some evidence (Harwood, 2002) that athletes' goal orientations may be more context-specific than had previously been realized. For example, an athlete's goal orientation in training may differ significantly from that which the athlete displays in competitive settings. Also, as Glyn Roberts (2001) acknowledged, athletes may shift their goal orientation within a game. To illustrate, a tennis player may begin a match with the ego-related aim of defeating an opponent but may soon realize that this will probably prove impossible. So, gradually, this player may choose instead to disregard the score and use the game as an opportunity to practise some new technical skills that he or she has acquired.

In summary, achievement goal theory has historically been plagued by a variety of conceptual and methodological issues.

Critical thinking questions

Does a typology like task-oriented versus ego-oriented motivation really explain anything – or is it merely a convenient way of classifying behaviour? What specific predictions does goal achievement theory make about the relationship between goal orientation and athletic performance? As there are many anecdotal examples of elite athletes with prominent ego orientations (e.g. Muhammad Ali), is this type of goal perspective necessarily a bad thing for athletes?

Social-cognitive approach: attribution theory

Having reviewed research on achievement goal theory, let us now turn to the second of the social-cognitive approaches to motivation in sport psychology – namely, attribution theory (AT) or the study of how people construct explanations for everyday events, including the successes and failures which they experience. AT was recently identified as the first major theoretical wave in the scientific study of how people make causal/explanatory inferences about behaviour (see review by Alicke et al., 2015).

The cornerstone of AT is the "intuitive scientist" metaphor – the idea that we all act like intuitive scientists in our everyday lives by trying to decide whether or not a behaviour that we experience reflects something unique about the person who performed it or was instead due to certain features of the situation in which it occurred. As a theory in social psychology, AT explores people's explanations for the causes of events that occur in their lives as well as of their own and other people's behaviour. Such explanations are especially likely in the face of negative, novel or unexpected events (Coffee, 2014). In sport psychology, attribution theory was a "hot topic" in the 1980s (see reviews by Biddle and Hanrahan, 1998; Biddle et al., 2001; McAuley and Blissmer, 2002) but declined considerably in popularity since 2000 (although see Rees et al., 2005). Before analysing the relevance of this theory for understanding motivational processes in sport, some background information is required.

To begin with, the term *attribution* (which is associated with Heider (1958), one of the progenitors of this field) refers to the cause or reason which people propose when they try to explain why something happened to them. For example, a tennis player may attribute her victory over an opponent in a long match to her own "never say die" attitude on court. Conversely, a manager of a football team may ascribe a defeat to some misfortune over which he had no control (e.g. a series of unfair refereeing decisions during the match). There is an important difference between these two examples of attribution, however. In the first case, the tennis player's attribution is made to a *personal* quality – namely, her high motivation – whereas in the second case, the football manager's attribution is made to an external cause (the referee). This distinction highlights the difference between internal or **dispositional attributions** (i.e. explanations that invoke stable individual personality characteristics of the person in question) and external or **situational attributions** (i.e. explanations that refer to environmental causes of a given outcome or event). Attributions may also vary in dimensions other than this one of internal versus external locus of causality. Thus some attribution theorists postulate that people's explanations for events vary in stability (i.e. whether the perceived cause is consistent or variable over time) as well as **controllability** (i.e. the degree to which the person involved – the "actor" – could exert personal influence over the outcome in question). In summary, based on Heider's (1958) ideas, Weiner (1985) proposed that people's attributions may be classified along three causal dimensions as follows: *locus of control* (internal or external), *stability* (stable or unstable) and *personal control* (personally controllable or uncontrollable). A great deal of attribution theory research in sport psychology has been inspired by Weiner's (1985) model.

Some research findings on attribution theory in sport

In sport psychology, one of the earliest attributional questions addressed was whether or not winners differ from losers in the type of explanation which they provide for their sporting behaviour. As one might expect, research findings have generally supported this hypothesis (see Biddle and Hanrahan, 1998). Specifically, in contrast to their less successful counterparts, winners in sport tend to favour attributions to *internal* and *personally controllable* factors such as degree of preparation or amount of practice conducted. This general finding applies to winners in individual sports (e.g. table tennis: McAuley, 1985) as well as to successful counterparts in team sports (e.g. soccer: Robinson and Howe, 1987). Such attributions for success are important because of their practical implications. To illustrate, they may be predictive of *future* athletic achievement. Thus if a young sprinter attributes a sequence of poor performances to a lack of ability (a relatively stable internal factor) rather than to the high quality of his or her opponents (a variable external factor), then the sprinter may become demoralized and lose motivation. In this way, attribution theory, or the study of how people construct explanations for their successes and failures, has a number of practical implications for everyday life. To illustrate, consider the common finding that people tend to accept personal responsibility for successful outcomes but blame others for significant failures (the so-called "credit for success, blame for failure" tendency). For example, a student who passes an exam is likely to attribute this result to internal factors like hard work or high intelligence but a student who fails an exam may explain it with reference to bad luck or being asked the "wrong" questions. In a similar vein, managers of losing teams tend to make excuses for poor results (see Figure 2.2). Of course, players are not immune from excuse-making either. For example, in the wake of England's poor performance at the 2010 World Cup in South Africa, the players had a rebellious team meeting and blamed their manager, Fabio Capello. Specifically, they claimed that he had picked the wrong team, played the wrong formation and introduced the wrong substitutes (Northcroft and Walsh, 2010)! Commenting on this display of player power, a former England international, and current England manager, Gareth Southgate (2010), remarked that "we are breeding players that look for excuses, that don't want to take responsibility".

Why do managers tend to make excuses for poor results or performances by their teams? One obvious explanation is that managers may use excuses in order to preserve their sense of self-esteem in the fickle world of sporting success. Another possible explanation is that excuses help people to present a favourable image to others. In order to explore further this tendency for people to *internalize* their successes and to *externalize* their failures, try the research exercise in Box 2.4.

Figure 2.2 Managers of losing teams tend to make excuses

Box 2.4 In the spotlight Exploring the self-serving bias by analysing sports reports in newspapers (based on McIlveen, 1992)

The **self-serving attributional bias** is a tendency for people to make internal attributions for success and external (usually situational) attributions for failures. For example, after Chelsea's 2-1 defeat by Leicester City in December 2015, the club's manager, José Mourinho accused his team of "betraying" his meticulous preparation and tactical planning (Barlow, 2015). Such excuses are offered mainly to protect coaches' self-esteem. This interpretation is strengthened by the fact that in the days leading up to his departure from Chelsea in December 2015, Mourinho had stopped referring to "my players" and had started to use the phrase "the players" instead (Campbell, 2015). So far, the self-serving attributional tendency

continued …

Box 2.4 continued

has been tested mainly using laboratory paradigms in which the participants have little personal interest in the outcomes under consideration. Accordingly, it is difficult to generalize such research to everyday life settings. This problem can be overcome, however, by taking advantage of a naturally occurring situation in which people are asked to give explanations for events which occurred in their lives and which affect them in significant ways (Lau and Russell, 1980). A good example of such a situation is the post match interview with football managers. In this situation, self-serving biases are likely to occur as managers try to explain the apparent causes of match outcomes (see McIlveen, 1992).

Hypotheses

That victories in football matches will be attributed more frequently to internal than to external factors whereas defeats will be attributed more frequently to external than to internal factors.

Instructions

The first step in this exercise is to locate possible attributional content in online newspaper coverage of football matches. In particular, you should try to find twenty attributions for team success or failure in matches involving the Premier League and/or Championship in England. Both tabloid and broadsheet daily newspapers should be consulted in this regard. Look out especially for quotations from players or managers that contain a possible explanation for the outcome of the match. The match result could be coded crudely as a success if the attributor's team won the match and a failure if the team lost the match. The perceived cause of the attribution should be deemed internal if the player or manager referred to something personal about the team (e.g. its character or ability) in the explanation provided. Conversely, the locus of causality may be deemed external if the player or manager attributed the result to something *outside* the team or its players (e.g. bad weather).

Analysis

A 2 × 2 contingency table should be constructed in which outcome (success or failure) and perceived cause (internal or external) are the row and column variables, respectively. Next, enter the number of attributions that fall into each of the four categories in this table. Then, using a chi-square test (check your statistics book or notes to find out how to use this test), work out the statistical relationship between match outcome and type of attribution. If the self-serving bias is present, we would expect a significantly higher proportion of internal than external attributions for successful results and a significantly higher proportion of external than internal attributions for failure outcomes.

Issues for discussion

Are success and failure objective events? How would achievement goal theorists answer this question? In any case, can we be sure that people's attributions expressed in public situations reflect what they really believe? How do you think that the emotional state of the person may affect the self-serving bias? Note that Mezulis et al. (2004) found that depressed people are much less likely than non-depressed peers to display a self-serving bias. Indeed, depressed people tend to take too little credit for success and too much credit for their failures.

A more recent line of inquiry in attribution research in sport psychology concerns the relationship between athletes' attributions and their emotional responses to poor performances in competition. Investigating this topic, M. Allen et al. (2011a) asked a large sample (86) of golfers to report their emotional states before a competition and then asked them to complete measures of attribution and **emotion** after this competition. Results showed that these golfers' emotions were linked to the attributions that they provided for poor performances. For example, high levels of anger were apparent when poor performances were attributed to internal factors – and this emotion intensified when the causes of their performance were perceived as being relatively stable over time.

According to Rees et al. (2005), attribution research in sport psychology could benefit from a move away from testing main effects of attributions to an approach which investigates instead the interactive effects of controllability and generalizability attributions on sport performance. As Coffee (2014) pointed out, attributing less successful performances to uncontrollable causes may induce negative effects only when causes are also perceived as stable (i.e. unlikely to change over time), global (i.e. likely to affect a wide array of situations) and personal (i.e. unique to the person concerned). Thus, if an athlete attributed a poor performance to a cause (e.g. poor concentration) that was perceived as uncontrollable ("there was nothing I could do about it"), stable ("it is unlikely to change"), global ("it affects many situations in my sport") and personal ("it only happens to me"), then his or her athletic performance will probably suffer. Theoretically, however, more successful performance should follow if the athlete were able to combine his or her uncontrollable attribution with an unstable ("but this can change"), specific ("this affects only a few situations in my sport") and universal attribution ("this affects lots of people – not just me"). Later in this section of the chapter, we explore further the idea of helping athletes to change their preferred way of explaining things – a phenomenon known as "attributional retraining".

Weaknesses of attribution theory

So far, we have presented classic attribution theory's intuitive scientist approach as a powerful way of analysing people's attempt to make sense of their world. But when viewed critically, this theory suffers from several limitations (e.g. Alicke et al., 2015). For example, it is ill-suited to the task of explaining events that have multiple causes or that include actors occupying different roles with unique responsibilities. Applied to sport psychology, at least four weaknesses have been identified in AT (Biddle et al., 2001; Rees et al., 2005). First, it seems clear that athletic success and failure are neither objective events nor synonymous with winning and losing, respectively. To illustrate, imagine interviewing an athlete who had won a competitive race – but by a very close margin. Superficially, this performer embodies a winning mentality. But what if this person's opponents were of a low athletic standard? In this case, the athlete may not regard barely winning a race against a poor field as being a successful performance at all. Therefore, Biddle et al. (2001) argued that a win is not always perceived as being a success and a loss is not always seen as an index of failure. The practical implication of this principle is that attribution researchers in sport psychology now tend to use *subjective* indices of success and failure whenever possible. A second problem for attribution theory in sport is that researchers cannot always be sure about what participants mean when they use certain words or phrases. For example, if a golfer says that his or her opponent "played better" than he or she did in a match-play event, does this signal a stable attribution ("My opponent is likely to defeat me again because they are simply a better player") or an unstable attribution ("My opponent defeated me on the day – but I believe that I can defeat them the next time we play")? Clearly, researchers in this field should adopt a painstaking approach when investigating what participants mean in using certain phrases (Biddle et al., 2001). Third, another complication for attribution research in sport is that individual differences in explanatory tendencies may affect the attributions that athletes make. Indeed, research suggests that there is a link between the way in which athletes tend to explain events (their **attributional style**) and their motivation to compete. Put simply, optimism and pessimism have motivational consequences. For example, when sport performers habitually explain negative outcomes (such as losing a match) by references to personal factors (i.e. to perceived causes which are internal, stable and global, such as "It's down to me; I can't change it and it seems to affect my whole life"), they are said to display a *pessimistic* explanatory style. In this frame of mind, people may behave as if they are powerless to change their situation. Not surprisingly, this despondency often leads to a loss in motivation. By contrast, when athletes attribute negative outcomes to external, unstable and specific causes (e.g. "My defeat was just a freak occurrence and it doesn't affect the most important things in my life"), they are displaying an *optimistic* explanatory style – which helps them to learn from their defeat and to work harder in the future. Clearly, certain athletes can achieve a healthy resilience by thinking optimistically in the face of adversity. Why does optimism make athletes more resilient? One possible explanation (Seligman, 1998) is that an optimistic outlook allows athletes to keep their confidence levels high – encouraging them to believe that they have the ability to overcome any temporary setbacks. Put simply, therefore, athletes with low motivation tend to interpret setbacks as being permanent. Optimists tend to believe that positive outcomes (e.g. winning a football match) are not caused by luck but have causes that are relatively permanent in nature (such as ability). Fourth, attributional researchers in sport have not always acknowledged the role of timing in the explanations offered by athletes and coaches. For example, Schoenemann and Curry (1990) suggested that although the self-serving bias (see Box 2.4) is often evident immediately after an event, it may change over time. Specifically, these authors argued that with the benefit of hindsight, people tend to take personal responsibility for their failures as well as their successes. Clearly, this theory indicates that immediate attributions for a sporting outcome may differ from delayed attributions for the same event.

Attributional style and athletic performance

Earlier, we examined the theory of achievement goal orientation which analyses how people perceive and define "success". Now, we turn to a related idea – the notion of attributional or explanatory style, defined as how people typically seek to explain success and failure in their lives. In general, the terms attributional style or explanatory style refer to people's tendency to offer similar kinds of explanations for different events in their lives. More precisely, they reflect "how people habitually explain the causes of events" (Peterson et al., 1995, p. 19). Attributional style can be measured using a general self-report instrument called the Attributional Style Questionnaire (ASQ: Peterson et al., 1982), which requires people to identify causes for twelve hypothetical situations (involving six "good" outcomes and six "bad" outcomes) and to rate these causes along three bipolar dimensions: locus of causality, stability and globality. As explained earlier, the first of these dimensions refers to whether the alleged causal event is internal (due to the person involved) or external (due to someone else). The second dimension relates to whether the cause in question is stable (or likely to last for the foreseeable future) or unstable (i.e. short-lived). The third dimension refers to whether it is global (i.e. likely to affect every aspect of one's life) or specific (i.e. highly circumscribed in its effects). Although the ASQ is psychometrically adequate, it is not designed specifically for athletic populations. Therefore, an alternative test called the Sport Attributional Style Scale (SASS; Hanrahan et al., 1989) was devised for use in sport and exercise settings. This sixteen-item scale is also available in a shortened (ten-item) format (Hanrahan and Grove, 1990). In general, psychometric evidence in support of the SASS has been encouraging (Biddle and Hanrahan, 1998). For example, most of its subscales appear to be correlated significantly with those of the criterion instrument, the ASQ.

Research on the relationship between explanatory style and athletic performance has generated some interesting findings. For example, first, Carron et al. (2014) explored whether or not explanatory style (i.e. a tendency to seek optimistic rather than pessimistic attributions for sporting outcomes) differentiates between more and less successful sport teams. Team success was measured in terms of winning percentages. In order to assess explanatory style, athletes (n=442) from a variety of sport teams estimated the controllability, universality, stability and globality of a number of hypothetical negative events. Results revealed that more successful teams (i.e. those with a winning percentage of 0.501 or above) were significantly ($p<0.05$) more optimistic than were less successful teams (winning percentage of 0.500 or below) on the attributional dimensions of controllability (e.g. "we can fix this") and universality (e.g. "every team has this happen"). Second, Seligman et al. (1990) discovered that university swimmers with a pessimistic explanatory style (ES) were more likely to perform below the level of coaches' expectations during the season than were swimmers with a more optimistic outlook. In fact, the pessimists on the ASQ had about twice as many unexpectedly poor swims as did their optimistic colleagues. Third, pessimistic swimmers were less likely to "bounce back" from simulated defeats than were optimistic counterparts. Fourth, the explanatory style scores of the swimmers were significantly predictive of swimming performance even after coaches' judgements of ability to overcome a setback had been controlled for in the data analysis. Interestingly, these findings show that explanatory style is quite separate from athletic ability. Thus pessimistic ES profiles were as prevalent among high-level as among low-level performers. One implication of this finding is that a successful performance by itself will not engender confidence in an athlete. In other words, a sports performer has to *learn* to attribute successful events constructively in order to benefit optimally from them.

Overall, available evidence suggests that explanatory style can predict certain aspects of team performance in sport – even when athletic ability levels are taken into consideration. As mentioned earlier, a practical implication of these findings concerns **attributional retraining**. Specifically, Rettew and Reivich (1995, p. 185) suggest that the most helpful ES in terms of future athletic success is one "that motivates the individual to continue doing whatever he or she does when things are going well but galvanises the player when things are not going well".

Hanrahan and Cerin (2009) investigated the relationship between type of sport and attributional style. They found that athletes competing in individual sports (e.g. diving, track-and-field and golf) made more internal, stable and global, and less externally controllable attributions, for positive events, and more internal attributions for negative events, than did team sport (e.g. field hockey) athletes. Hanrahan and Cerin (2009) suggested that it is logical for athletes competing in individual sports to make more internal attributions than those in team sports because the former do not have teammates to whom they can assign credit or blame.

So far, our discussion of attributional styles has been largely theoretical. But for a practical insight into this topic, try the exercise in Box 2.5.

Box 2.5 In the spotlight What is your typical explanatory style?

When something unpleasant or negative happens to you (e.g. failing an examination), ask yourself the following questions. First, what do you think was the main cause of the event? More precisely, are you responsible for it or is it due to some external circumstances? This question relates to the internal–external attributional dimension. Second, do you think that the cause will persist in the future? This question concerns the permanence of the attribution. Third, there is the pervasiveness issue. How much will this event affect other areas of your life? By the way, if you cannot see the difference between "permanence" and "pervasiveness", try thinking of the former as relating to time and the latter to space.

Overall, if you attributed the event to yourself (Q 1) and to things which will not change in the future (Q 2) and if you believe that it affects all of your life (Q 3), then you probably have a *pessimistic* explanatory style. If so, then you have a tendency to explain misfortune by saying "it's my fault" (personalization), "it will never change" (permanence) and "it's going to ruin my whole life" (pervasiveness). *Optimists* tend to interpret setbacks as being caused by temporary circumstances which may change in the future.

Implications of research on explanatory styles

Before concluding this section of the chapter, we would like to explore the coaching implications of research on explanatory styles. According to Seligman (1998), research on attributional style has several practical implications for sport performance. First, an optimistic explanatory style is not something that is immediately apparent to coaches. As this author put it, the ASQ "measures something you can't. It predicts success beyond experienced coaches' judgements and handicappers' expertise" (Seligman, 1998, p. 166). Second, athletes' or players' levels of optimism have implications for when to use them in team events. Thus, in general, pessimistic players should be used only after they have done well – not when they are in a run of poor form. Third, in talent search programmes, optimists may be better bets than pessimists as they will probably perform better in the long run. Fourth, pessimistic athletes can be trained to become more optimistic. As Seligman put it, "unlike IQ or your waistline, pessimism is one of those characteristics that is entirely changeable" (cited in DeAngelis, 1996, p. 33).

Having learned about the nature of athletes' attributional tendencies, can these thinking patterns be changed through professional intervention? On the basis that this practice has produced some encouraging results in clinical psychology (see Fosterling, 1988), attributional retraining may be worth trying in sport settings. For example, if a coach could change a lazy athlete's tendency to make attributions to unstable/internal dimensions, such a performer may discover that the expenditure of additional effort is helpful. Conversely, performers who are prone to "depressogenic" attributions (e.g. by ascribing unwanted outcomes to stable/internal factors) may be helped by encouraging them to externalize their explanations. In general, coaches can help athletes to become more self-reliant by helping them to decrease their tendency to use external attributions after poor performances and instead to use internal attributions. For example, a golfer may confide in her coach that she had been lucky to get away with a bunker shot that barely skimmed the rim of the bunker before landing on the green. This attribution to an external unstable factor (e.g. luck) may erode a player's confidence over time. But if the golfer could be trained to rephrase this attribution to an internal source (e.g. "If I concentrate on getting more elevation on my sand shots, I will become a much better bunker player"), she will probably be more motivated to practise her bunker play more assiduously. In a study of this topic, Orbach et al. (1999) investigated the effects of an attributional training programme on the manner in which thirty-five tennis players explained failure on a tennis skills test. Performers were assigned to one of three treatment groups: those involving controllable and unstable attributions (CU group), those involving uncontrollable and stable attributions (US group) and those in a non-attributional control condition. Results showed that not only is it possible to alter people's attributions for their performance, but also such modified attributions remained stable for at least three weeks afterwards. Interestingly, attributional retraining has also been applied successfully to young athletes. Sinnott and Biddle (1998) tested twelve children aged between 11 and 12 years. Half of these children rated their performance on a ball-dribbling task as being poor while the other half rated themselves as performing this skill successfully. Following attributional retraining, the former group showed significant increases not only in their self-ratings but also in their level of intrinsic motivation (see earlier discussion of this topic). More recently, Parkes and Mallett (2011) sought to develop "mental toughness" (see Chapter 1) by evaluating the utility of an optimism intervention for rugby union athletes. This intervention involved systematic exposure to various cognitive-behavioural techniques (e.g. identifying automatic thoughts) in a bid to retrain the rugby players' attributional style. The effectiveness of this intervention programme was assessed in part using self-reports based on the Sport Attributional Style Scale (Hanrahan et al., 1989). Qualitative data were also collected via a focus group and some semi-structured interviews. Results revealed that participants' attributions became more external for negative events. In addition, the qualitative data suggested that participants developed greater resilience in the face of adversity, were more confident in their sport, and also developed a more optimistic explanatory style for negative events.

Although the potential value of attributional retraining is impressive, a great deal of additional research is required to evaluate the nature and scope of this phenomenon in sport psychology.

Social-cognitive approach: self-determination theory

Self-determination theory (SDT), which was developed by Deci and Ryan (e.g. see Deci and Ryan, 1985, 2000, 2008), is a meta-theory of the study of human motivation – especially of the autonomous control of behaviour and volitional engagement (see brief overview by Standage et al., 2014). It is a "dialectical framework" (Weiss and Amorose, 2008, p. 129) because it argues that motivation emerges from constant interaction between human nature and social contextual factors. According to Hagger and Chatzisarantis (2008, p. 80), self-determination theory attempts "to explain human motivation and behaviour based on individual differences in motivational orientations, contextual influences on motivation, and interpersonal perceptions".

SDT begins with the assumption that people are inherently growth-oriented and actively seek optimal challenges. This growth orientation is apparent in SDT's construct of intrinsic motivation (discussed earlier in the chapter) or the tendency to partake in activities "for the enjoyment and interest that is inherent within the activity itself" (Standage et al., 2014, p. 630). Furthermore, SDT postulates that optimal performance and maximal subjective well-being tend to occur when people's innate needs for *relatedness* (i.e. feeling connected with, and close to, others in one's community), *competence* (i.e. feeling proficient in producing desired outcomes) and *autonomy* (i.e. feeling that one has a sense of agency in, or control over, one's actions – which provides a sense of self-determination) are satisfied (P. Wilson and Rodgers, 2007). Put simply, having meaningful personal relationships, being able to perform proficiently in different situations, and feeling in control of one's actions tend to promote health and happiness. Next, Ryan and Deci (2000) proposed that social-contextual factors (or "autonomy supportive" environments) that satisfy these three basic needs are more likely to increase people's effort, persistence and sense of well-being than are environments that inhibit these needs. This hypothesis has been supported by empirical research in sport and exercise psychology (see reviews by Hagger and Chatzisarantis, 2007, 2008; Ryan and Deci, 2007). For example, Vallerand (2007) reported that self-determined (or autonomously regulated) behaviour such as intrinsic motivation is associated with positive outcomes such as increased effort and persistence and enhanced well-being when compared with more "controlling" environments (e.g. where behaviour is motivated by consequences that are extrinsic to, or separate from, the activity in question). It is also associated with increased prosocial behaviour towards teammates and opponents (Hodge and Gucciardi, 2015; Sheehy and Hodge, 2015). Similarly, Amorose and Anderson-Butcher (2015) discovered that for a large (over 300) sample of athletes, positive motivational responses increased as perceptions of autonomy support increased – especially when the athletes also perceived a relatively lower level of controlling behaviours in the coaching environment. Overall, therefore, SDT's distinction between autonomous (or self-determined) motivation and non-self-determined (or controlling) motivation is important both theoretically and practically.

Since the mid-1990s, SDT has shifted its emphasis away from the old distinction between intrinsic and extrinsic motivation and towards one between *autonomous* and *controlled* motivation (Deci and Ryan, 2008). In this regard, evidence has accumulated to suggest that the benefits of "self-control" training can generalize from one domain to another. For example, Oaten and Cheng (2006) found that students who had learned self-control skills through a regime of daily exercise and regular study habits became more adept at self-regulation in other environments (e.g. when sitting examinations).

Self-determination theory currently comprises five interrelated mini-theories – cognitive evaluation theory (CET), organismic integration theory (OIT), causality orientations theory (COT), basic psychological needs theory (BPNT) and goal contents theory (GCT). Although a detailed treatment of these five mini-theories is beyond the scope of this chapter (but see Hagger and Chatzisarantis, 2008, for a more detailed treatment), here is a brief summary of their relevance to sport behaviour (adapted from Standage et al., 2014).

To begin with, CET was postulated to account for the effects of various social-contextual factors (e.g. rewards, provision of choice, feedback and deadlines) on people's intrinsic motivation (defined as behaviour based on the inherent satisfaction associated with the activity itself). Specifically, it proposes that if people believe that a given task (e.g. performing a sprint in training) lies within their capacity, they will be intrinsically motivated to perform it (Cashmore, 2008). However, if an extrinsic reward is offered for successful performance of the behaviour in question, their intrinsic motivation will probably decrease. This "undermining effect" of rewards is well known in psychology. For example, Lepper and Greene (1975) showed that providing rewards to individuals for activities that they *already* find interesting and challenging tends to lead to a *decrease* in their reported intrinsic motivation. This phenomenon has been termed the "over-justification effect" and refers to a "tendency to devalue those activities that we perform in order to get something else" (Gilovich et al., 2011, p. 222). You may recall that we encountered this phenomenon earlier in this chapter (see Box 2.2). The second mini-theory of the SDT framework is OIT, which attempts to explain the process by which people assimilate behaviour that is initially *externally* regulated into their own repertoire. Consider the motivational processes at work when a young athlete is told by her coach that she needs to increase her weight training regime in the gym before going to college (an example borrowed from Weiss and Amorose, 2008). In this case, she might comply with this request not only because she was *advised* to do so (external regulation) but also because she feels that she would *not like to let her coach down* (introjected regulation). In this way, OIT examines the psychological processes by which social-contextual factors may be internalized by people. The third mini-theory in SDT is COT which analyses the way in which people not only orient themselves towards environments but also regulate their behaviour. Specifically, COT postulates that people differ from each other in three orientations: *autonomy orientation* (an orientation towards intrinsic motivation), *controlled orientation* (an orientation towards being motivated by reward contingencies) and *interpersonal orientation* (a tendency to act without intentionality). The fourth mini-theory in SDT is entitled basic psychological needs theory (BPNT). It postulates that the origin of self-determined motivation lies in satisfaction of three universal psychological needs or "nutriments to wellness" (Standage et al., 2014, p. 631) described earlier, namely, relatedness, competence and autonomy. Specifically, SDT proposes that people's development, growth and general well-being depend on the extent to which the preceding three needs are supported by their social environment. In short, the construct of basic psychological needs (BPN) is the main predictor of human motivation. However, as Martinent et al. (2015) pointed out, the precise causal ordering between BPN and motivation is still largely unresolved. Thus, although classical SDT held that BPN is an antecedent of motivation, some recent studies (e.g. Gunnell et al., 2014) indicate that BPN may be a *consequence* of motivation. Overall, a considerable amount of research has tested BNT propositions in the sporting domain. For example, the hypothesized relationship between need satisfaction and subjective well-being has been tested with gymnasts and dancers. Thus, Gagné et al. (2003) found that gymnasts' sense of well-being from pre-practice to post-practice sessions changed in accordance with satisfaction of the needs that they experienced during practice. Similarly, Quested and Duda (2010) discovered that need satisfaction according to SDT predicted **positive emotions** among dancers. The final mini-theory in SDT is goal contents theory which seeks to understand the relationship between people's goals and their motivation and well-being. GCT pays special attention to intrinsic and extrinsic goals (discussed earlier in this chapter). As the former type of goals are typically concerned with personal growth, GCT assumes that they are directly related to people's basic psychological need satisfaction. By contrast, extrinsic goals are postulated to be less supportive of – and perhaps even inimical to – such basic need satisfaction.

Although Hagger and Chatzisarantis (2008) acknowledged that SDT has contributed significantly to increased theoretical understanding of factors that predict sport and exercise behaviour, they highlighted certain unresolved issues that need to be addressed by proponents of this approach. For example, not enough experimental or intervention studies have been conducted on SDT in sport and exercise behaviour. Also, further research is required on the role of implicit processes in self-determined motivation. As Hyde et al. (2010) pointed out, an exclusive focus on *conscious* motivational factors neglects the role of unconscious, automatic processes in sport and exercise behaviour. Overall, however, Standage et al. (2014) concluded that SDT has much to offer sport psychology in its quest to understand such phenomena as the study of "vitality (i.e. a marker of mental and physical energy"; p. 632) and the role of mindfulness in autonomous behaviour in sport settings.

Increasing motivation in athletes: goal-setting in sport

Now that we have explored the nature of motivation and the main theoretical perspectives on it, let us turn to the question of how it can be *increased* in athletes. Effective motivation requires a sense of *direction* as well as drive or energy. To understand this idea, consider the following analogy. Imagine a car being driven around in circles in a carpark. Although its engine is in perfect working order, the vehicle is not actually going anywhere. Clearly, what is needed is a signpost that can direct the driver out of the carpark and towards his or her destination. By analogy, athletes require a map or signpost which will channel their motivational energy effectively. One way of providing this signpost is through goal-setting – the process by which people set "goals" or targets (i.e. **mental representations** of desired outcomes: Harkin et al., 2016; see also Kingston, 2014; Weinberg, 2014). As we shall see, goal-setting can enhance athletic performance significantly, which explains why this technique is perhaps the most frequently used psychological intervention among US Olympic athletes and coaches (Weinberg, 2009; K. Williams, 2013) and "arguably the most effective performance enhancement technique on the behavioural sciences" (Burton and Weiss, 2008, p. 344). Reviews of research on goal-setting have been published by Burton and Weiss (2008), Gould (2010), Kingston and Wilson (2009), Locke and Latham (2013) and Williams (2013). Before we summarize the findings of these reviews, however, some clarification of terminology is necessary.

What is goal-setting?

A goal is a target or objective which people strive to attain – "what an individual is trying to accomplish; it is the object or aim of an action" (Locke et al., 1981, p. 126). Technically, it involves "attaining a specific standard of proficiency on a task, usually within a specific time frame" (Locke et al., 1981, p. 145) Typical goals in sport include winning a match, playing better than one has done before, being selected for a club team or national squad, or becoming fitter than one is at present. Arising from this explanation of terms, goal-setting may be defined simply as the deliberate process by which people establish, and evaluate progress towards, desirable aims or objectives for their actions. It should be noted, however, that goals are not always held consciously (Locke and Latham, 1990). For example, focusing on a goal such as winning a tennis match (a conscious goal) may interfere with a player's performance of habitual skills such as serving or volleying (Burton and Weiss, 2008). Within sport psychology, research on goal-setting has been influenced by two distinct theoretical traditions: cognitive learning theory and organizational psychology (where it was studied originally under the heading of "management by objectives": Burton and Weiss, 2008). To illustrate the former source of influence, cognitive researchers such as Tolman (1932) proclaimed that human actions are understood best as the outcome of internally represented conscious goals rather than as the product of environmental forces. The organizational roots of research in this field are more prominent, however, and may be traced back to theorists like F. W. Taylor (1967) and Locke and Latham (1985) who extolled the merits of goal-setting for enhanced productivity in the workplace. In an early review of this topic within organizational psychology, Locke et al. (1981, p. 145) concluded that "the beneficial effect of goal-setting on task performance is one of the most replicable findings in the psychological literature. Ninety per cent of the studies showed positive or partially positive effects." Later Locke and Latham (1990) claimed that of 201 studies on goal-setting, positive effects on performance were shown for 183 of them – resulting in an estimate of 91 per cent success rate for goal-setting. More generally, from over 500 studies on goal-setting (Burton and Weiss, 2008), two key findings have emerged (Kingston and Wilson, 2009). First, "difficult" goals tend to elicit higher levels of performance than do "easy" goals. Second, goals that are phrased more specifically tend to be more effective than vague "do your best" goals or no goals at all. But how well do these findings transfer to the domain of sport? Similar, but more modest, claims about the efficacy of goal-setting have emerged from studies in sport settings. To illustrate, Burton et al. (2001) reported that forty-four out of fifty-six published studies (almost 79 per cent) yielded moderate to strong effects of goal-setting on athletic performance. From a cursory inspection of these figures, it appears that the effects of goal-setting in sport are not quite as impressive as they are in organizational settings. We shall return to this issue later. At this stage, however, we need to explore what psychological research reveals about goal-setting in athletes.

Types of goals

Three main types of goals have been identified in sport psychology research (Hardy and Nelson, 1988). First, **outcome goals** or **result goals** are based on the outcome of a specific event and usually require some kind of interpersonal comparison. They represent the *why* of motivational processes (Kremer et al., 2012) and are objective targets such as winning a competition, defeating an opponent or achieving a desired finishing position (e.g. "making the cut" in a golf tournament). What is not often appreciated about such goals, however, is the extent to which their achievement depends on the ability and performance of one's *opponents*. For example, a tennis player could play the best game of his or her life but still lose a match because the opposing player has played better on the day. So, outcome goals usually involve performing better than one's opponents and are largely uncontrollable. The second type of objective encountered in sport is the **performance goal**. This type of goal, which represents the *what* of sporting motivation (Kremer et al., 2012), is usually self-referenced (i.e. it relates only to one's own performance) and involves a numeric value of some kind (e.g. trying to reduce the total number of putts one takes in a round of golf). Performance goals usually refer to the attainment of a designated personal standard of competence with regard to technique (e.g. learning to hit a top-spin backhand in tennis), effort (e.g. "giving 100 per cent effort at all times in a match"), time (running a marathon in less than four hours) distance and/or height (in certain athletic events) or form (e.g. adopting a certain gymnastics position). Unlike outcome goals, performance goals are largely under the control of the person who sets them. For example, a golfer could set as her performance goal the task of putting to within 30cm of the hole every time she is on the green. Nobody can stop the player from achieving this level of accuracy because putting is a self-paced skill. The third type of goal studied in sport psychology is the **process goal** – a behavioural strategy by which an athlete executes a particular skill or tries to attain a specific performance outcome. For example, in golf, a process goal in putting might be to keep one's head steady while taking a slow backswing. Similarly, for the free throw in basketball, a process goal might involve focusing on a high follow-through after releasing the ball. In general, process goals reflect the *how* of motivation in sport (Kremer et al., 2012).

As they can be controlled directly, performance and process goals are usually regarded as being more motivational for athletes than are result goals. Weinberg (2002, p. 38) exhorted people "to set goals that are based on their own levels of performance rather than on the outcome of winning and losing". Likewise, Orlick (1986) proclaimed that

> day-to-day goals for training and for competition should focus on the means by which you can draw out your own potential. Daily goals should be aimed at the improvement of personal control over your performance, yourself, and the obstacles you face.
>
> (Orlick 1986, p. 10)

In a similar vein, Gould (1998, p. 187) proposed that athletes should "set process and performance goals as opposed to outcome goals" and Hodge and McKenzie (1999, p. 31) advised athletes to "set performance goals rather than outcome goals". Unfortunately, this emphasis on performance goals is not completely supported by research findings. A quantitative literature review by Kyllo and Landers (1995) found that performance goals were no more effective than result goals in enhancing skills. But why exactly do goals motivate athletes and improve their performance?

Why do goals enhance performance?

From available research, it seems that goal-setting affects athletic performance for at least five reasons (Locke and Latham, 2002; Weinberg, 2009, 2014). First, goals serve to focus and direct **attention** towards relevant actions. For example, if an athlete is told that unless she becomes fitter she will be dropped from a basketball team, she may not know what action to take. But if she is advised to improve her performance on a specific index of fitness such as the "bleep test" by a certain date, she is clearer about what is expected of her. Likewise, a tennis player who tries to achieve at least 70 per cent accuracy on his first serve should be less distractible on court than a player who has no objective for the match. Second, goals help to elicit effort and commitment from athletes. Presumably, that is why coaches give "pep talks" at half-time in football matches (see Chapter 3): to remind players what they are striving for collectively. Third, goals provide incentives that may foster persistence in athletes, especially if they can measure their progress towards the targets in question. For example, a weekly fitness or speed chart could be maintained for all members of a sports squad in order to encourage them to adhere to prescribed training regimes. According to Burton et al. (2001), the preceding theoretical mechanisms may explain why goals tend to have impressive short-term influences on athletic performance. But how do they enhance the development of new strategies over a longer period of time? This leads us to the fourth putative mechanism of goal-setting effects. Specifically, goals may work simply because they help athletes to break large problems into smaller components and then develop action plans (or jobs that are within one's control) for dealing with these sub-goals. For example, golfers who want to achieve greater accuracy off the tee may go to the driving range to hit buckets of balls at a designated target – not finishing until they hit that target a certain number of times. In so doing, they have begun to practise using a problem-solving approach to the game. Fifth, goals may influence athletic performance indirectly by boosting athletes' self-confidence (e.g. "I'm delighted to have achieved that goal – it restores my faith in my own ability") as well as their sense of satisfaction ("That win felt really great"). This latter possibility that goals may influence performance through the mediation of cognitive factors reminds us of the achievement goal theory that we mentioned earlier in this chapter. As you may recall, this theory proposes that athletes' motivational behaviour is influenced by their goal orientation (whether task-related or ego-related) as well as by their perception of their own athletic ability.

Research on goal-setting in sport psychology: key principles, findings and issues

Goal-setting is not only one of the most widely used performance-enhancement techniques in sport psychology but also one of the most extensively researched. The typical paradigm for such research involves a comparison between the performance of people who have been instructed to set goals according to certain criteria (e.g. specific goals) with that of counterparts who have been told simply to "do your best". Often, a third sample of participants is used: a control group of people who are given no advice on goal-setting. Unfortunately, a difficulty that can afflict control groups in goal-setting research is that participants in such groups may spontaneously set goals for themselves – whether consciously or unconsciously. Clearly, this is a potentially serious methodological concern as it threatens the validity of comparisons between experimental and control groups in this field. Nevertheless, using this experimental paradigm, researchers have sought to explore the characteristics of goals that make them most effective in sport settings. This topic is known as "goal attribute" research (Burton and Naylor, 2002).

Based originally on organizational psychology (see Locke and Latham, 1985, 2013) but subsequently on sport research (Weinberg, 2014), at least nine theoretical principles have emerged from research on goal-setting in sport. First, the more specific and measurable the goal (e.g. trying to achieve a target of 70 per cent accuracy in one's first serve in tennis), the more likely it is to be effective. Second, goals are alleged to work best when they are realistic but challenging. For example, experienced 10 kilometre distance runners may set themselves a target of reducing their best time (e.g. forty minutes) by three minutes over three months of carefully designed training. Third, goals should be set for both practice and competition. Often, athletes neglect the former type of goal-setting because they focus excessively on competitive results. Useful practice goals include arriving punctually at the training site, displaying a high level (self-rated) of intensity in every training session and achieving certain designated standards for every drill undertaken. Fourth, goals should be written down (note the old coaching maxim, "ink it, don't think it") to ensure maximum compliance and concentration. Fifth, separate goals should be established for practice and competition. Sixth, in order to increase the likelihood of goal attainment, goal **action plans** (i.e. specific behavioural acts that serve as stepping stones to goal attainment) should be specified as clearly and explicitly as possible. For example, Weinberg (2014) cites the case of Michael Johnson (Olympic gold-medal winning sprinter over both 200m and 400m in Atlanta in 1996): "I'd crafted a decade of dreams into ambitions, refined ambitions into goals, and finally hammered goals into plans" (p. 44). Interestingly, goal action plans have been postulated as important intervening variables in filling the well-known gap between people's intentions and their actions (see Box 2.6).

Seventh, athletes should always endeavour to set outcome, performance and process goals (described earlier). Interestingly, as Weinberg (2014) pointed out, when athletes achieve their specific performance and process goals, their outcome goals tend to occur as a consequence. For example, if a soccer team achieves its targets in relation to effort expended, tackles won, passes completed successfully, and shots on target (i.e. at the goal), then its chances of winning a particular match will improve significantly. Eighth, both individual and team goals should be designated in advance of training and competition. Finally, progress towards goal achievement should be monitored regularly for optimal benefits to occur. Empirical support for this principle was provided recently by Harkin et al. (2016) who conducted a meta-analytic review of 138 interventions designed to promote goal progress monitoring. Briefly, from this review, they concluded that "progress monitoring has a robust effect on goal attainment and constitutes a key component of effective self-regulation" (p. 219).

Box 2.6 In the spotlight Can action plans bridge the gap between people's goal intentions and their subsequent behaviour?

It has long been known in psychology that there is a major gap between what people intend to do (e.g. their stated goals) and what they *actually* do (i.e. their behaviour). This disjunction, which has been called the "(goal) intention-action gap" (Sheeran, 2002), is caused mainly by the fact that due to the fragility of their **working memories** (see Chapter 5), people tend to forget their intentions whenever they encounter either internal or external distractions. Not surprisingly, the intention-behaviour gap has spawned a plethora of studies in social psychology on the factors that influence consistency between people's intentions and their subsequent behaviour (see review by Harkin et al., 2016). Two of the most important of these factors are the amount of actual control wielded by people over their behaviour and the extent to which people engage in "**action planning**" – a deliberate, prospective self-regulation strategy in which people forge mental links between concrete behavioural responses and specific triggering cues/situations (Sheeran and Orbell, 1999). To illustrate such attempted executive control over behaviour, an athlete who intends to improve her race times may formulate an action plan such that "on Mondays, Wednesdays and Fridays, I will go for a 5k road run before dinner". The rationale here is that on these specified evenings, little or no conscious decision making is required by the athlete and her intended behaviour will be triggered automatically by the temporal cues designated in her action plan. Presumably, forging links between actions and environmental cues increases the likelihood of automatic processing and circumvents possible reliance on conscious executive control processes (Allan, 2008). Considerable research evidence has accumulated to indicate that action planning helps people to achieve their goals. For example, regular generation of action plans helps to increase people's engagement in exercise behaviour (Lippke et al., 2010). Overall, action implementation (*if ... then*) plans appear to provide a promising research avenue for studies attempting to bridge the gap between goals and behaviour. Indeed, based on a recent **systematic review** in the field of rehabilitation psychology, Kersten et al. (2015) concluded that people who form '*if-then*' action plans achieved better outcomes in adhering to medication for stroke and epilepsy than did control participants.

How well have these principles been supported in other studies? Overall, the following general findings have emerged (see comprehensive reviews by Burton et al., 2001; Burton and Naylor, 2002; Weinberg, 2014). First, although goal-setting is one of the most widely used interventions in applied sport psychology, most athletes rate goals as being "only moderately effective" (Burton et al., 2001, p. 497) facilitators of performance. This is largely because sport performers are not entirely clear about how best to maximize the effectiveness of their goals. In the next section, we consider some practical ways of setting effective goals. Second, there is general agreement among researchers that specific goals are more effective than general goals, vague goals or no goals at all (H. Hall and Kerr, 2001). This finding, which is called the "goal specificity" effect, may be attributable to the greater precision of specific goals than general goals. However, an important caveat must be noted here. To explain, research on goal-setting in sport shows that it may not provide any incremental benefits to athletes who are *already* motivated to do their best (a phenomenon called the "ceiling effect"; see also Box 2.7 later in the chapter). This point is illustrated by the fact that not all top athletes set goals for their performance. For example, as we learned earlier in this chapter, the Indian former batsman Sachin Tendulkar claimed that he did not set any targets before matches. Another complicating factor here is that the complexity of the skill in question may serve as a mediating variable. Burton (1989) investigated the effects of specific versus general goals on basketball skills of varying degrees of complexity. Results showed that although specific goals *did* enhance performance relative to general goals as predicted, this benefit was mediated by the level of complexity of the task – a fact which had not been predicted. As a third general finding in goal-setting research, Burton et al. (2001) claimed that performance goals are more effective than result goals in improving athletic performance – presumably because the former type of goals facilitate improved concentration processes in athletes (for a discussion of goal-setting as a concentration technique, see Chapter 5). It should be noted, however, that goal-setting practice studies show that athletes tend to set both types of goals – performance and result – equally often (Burton et al., 2001). A fourth general finding in the goal-setting research literature is that athletes and coaches are not systematic in writing down their goals (Weinberg, 2002). Fifth, research has accumulated on the "goal proximity" prediction – namely, the suggestion that short-term goals should be more effective motivationally than long-term goals. Surprisingly, this hypothesis has received only modest support in sport psychology (H. Hall and Kerr, 2001). Sixth, a number of practical barriers appear to hamper goal-setting practices among athletes. These barriers include such factors as a lack of time and distractions arising from social relationships (Weinberg, 2002). Seventh, the relationship between goals and performance is mediated by a host of intervening variables. For example, the level of ability of the performer, the extent to which he or she is committed to the goal, and the quantity and quality of feedback provided are all important factors in moderating the influence of goals on performance (H. Hall and Kerr, 2001). Finally, research evidence is accumulating to suggest that goal-setting skills can be taught to athletes. Thus Swain and Jones (1995) used a single-subject, multiple-baseline research design to examine the effects of a goal-setting intervention programme on the selected basketball skills (e.g. getting rebounds) of four elite university performers over a series of sixteen matches in a competitive season. Results showed that the intervention yielded significant positive effects on the targeted basketball skills for three out of four of the participants in the study.

In addition to the preceding findings, research in sport psychology has yielded three recurrent themes: "first, goals work well in sport, but not as well as in business; second, goal-setting is a paradox because this simple technique is somewhat more complicated than it looks" (Burton et al., 2001, p. 497). Interestingly, it seems that although goal-setting affects performance, many of its principles derived from organizational contexts do not generalize well to athletic domains. For example, setting specific goals is not always more effective in sport than is the practice of exhorting people to do their best. The third recurrent theme is that in sport, "an individual's primary focus should be on personal task-focused objectives rather than social comparison" (Kingston, 2014, p. 315). Having summarized the main principles and findings in this field, let us conclude this section by evaluating some unresolved issues in goal-setting research.

One of the most contentious issues in this field is the fact that goal-setting seems to be more effective in business settings than in sport. In an effort to explain this anomaly, Locke (1991) suggested that methodological factors may be involved. Specifically, he claimed that perhaps participants in the "no goal" and the "do your best" goal conditions actually set goals for themselves spontaneously. Also, there are many important conceptual differences between the fields of work and sport. For example, consider the issue of choice. To explain, H. Hall and Kerr (2001) noted that whereas most athletes have chosen to invest time and effort in pursuit of their sporting goals, the decision about whether or not to work is far less influenced by personal factors. In short, people *choose* to play sport – but they *have* to work, for economic reasons. This is why Weinberg and Weigand (1996) suggested that as they have chosen to participate in their chosen activities, sports performers are usually more motivated than average workers. Another problem with goal-setting studies in sport is that they are rather atheoretical. To explain, few researchers in this field have attempted to find out *why* people set the goals that they do. As H. Hall and Kerr (2001, p. 186) observed, few investigators have studied "the causes underlying the particular goals an individual might adopt".

Practical application: motivational properties of goals

Having outlined relevant theory and research on goal-setting in sport, we should now consider some practical applications. As indicated earlier, goal-attribute research suggests that certain properties of goals should elicit increased effort from or energize the behaviour of athletes. In particular, four characteristics of goals have been deemed to be especially motivational for athletes of all levels. These properties concern goal difficulty, goal specificity, goal proximity and goal focus (Kingston and Wilson, 2009).

Goal difficulty
According to Locke and Latham (1990), the more challenging or difficult a goal is, the more motivation it should elicit. More precisely, these authors suggested that there is a positive linear relationship between goal difficulty and task performance and that difficult goals encourage greater effort and persistence than do simple goals. In general, this prediction has been supported in the general goal-setting research literature (with mean **effect sizes** ranging between 0.52 and 0.82) but it has not been supported consistently in research on goal-setting in sport psychology. Furthermore, surveys of goal-setting practices in athletes (reviewed in Burton and Naylor, 2002) indicated that sports performers are motivated best by *moderately* challenging goals.

Goal specificity
Available evidence suggests that **goal specificity** – or the extent to which goals are stated in clear, specific and attainable terms – tends to elicit more effort and

better performance than does goal generality (i.e. where goals which are stated in more vague terms). For example, a golfer who is told to "drive the ball straight down the fairway – but don't worry about the distance you achieve" should try harder than someone who is told simply to "do your best". In this regard, Weinberg et al. (1994) found that college lacrosse players who had been given specific tasks to achieve during a season performed significantly better than did counterparts assigned to "do your best" goals.

Goal proximity
The issue of how far into the future goals are projected tends to affect people's motivation. Interestingly, Bandura (1997) claimed that whereas proximal or short-term goals mobilize effort and persistence effectively, "distal goals alone are too far removed in time to provide effective incentives and guides for present action" (Bandura, 1997, p. 134).

Goal focus
The term "**goal focus**" refers to whether a designated goal is an outcome (e.g. finishing first in a race), a performance (e.g. self-referenced targets such as the number of putts taken in a round of golf) or a process (e.g. keeping one's head steady as one putts). Research suggests that there is a pattern to the type of goal that is selected by athletes in different situations. For example, Munroe-Chandler et al. (2004) found that athletes tended to use performance and process goals in training but are focused more on outcome goals in competition.

In addition to these features, goals should be stated positively as much as possible. For example, in soccer, it is better for a striker to set a positive goal, such as "I am going to practise timing my runs into the box", than a negative goal, such as "I must try not to get caught off-side so often". The reason for this advice is that a goal which is stated positively tells the person what to do, whereas a negatively stated goal does not provide such explicit guidance.

Does goal-setting really work?

A classic meta-analytic review on the effects of goal-setting was conducted by Kyllo and Landers (1995) using data from thirty-six studies in this field. To explain this type of review, meta-analysis is a quantitative statistical technique which combines the results of a large number of studies in order to determine the overall size of a statistical effect. According to Kyllo and Landers (1995), goal-setting was effective in enhancing performance in sport over baseline measures by about one third of a standard deviation (mean effect size of 0.34). This effect was increased when goals of a moderate level of difficulty were used. Also, as mentioned earlier, these researchers found that the greatest effects were obtained when the goals were result based (which contradicts the received wisdom that performance goals work best), moderately difficult and agreed by the athletes themselves (i.e. self-set) rather than imposed from outside. Burton and Weiss (2008) reported that of eighty-eight published goal-setting studies in sport and physical activity settings, seventy demonstrated moderate to strong goal-setting effects. Nevertheless, sceptical voices have been raised about unequivocal support for the efficacy of goal-setting. For example, King and Burton (2003) argued that such efficacy depends on a variety of complex factors such as the amount of success attained by the goal-setter, the structural properties of the goal itself, and, of course, its content.

Earlier, we learned that most studies on goal-setting have been based on the theories of Locke and Latham (1985, 2002, 2013) in organizational psychology. These authors predicted that relative to either "no goal" or vague "do your best" instructions, athletes' performance should be enhanced when they use goals that are specific, short term and difficult yet realistic. Unfortunately, research designed to test Locke and Latham's predictions in sport has produced equivocal findings. Several studies have failed to establish the allegedly beneficial effects of specific and realistic goals on people's performance of motor tasks. Weinberg et al. (1990) found that the performance of hand strength and "sit-up" tasks was related neither to goal difficulty nor to goal specificity. In an effort to explain this anomaly, a variety of conceptual and methodological issues in research on goal-setting in sport may be identified (Weinberg, 2002). These issues are discussed in Box 2.7.

Box 2.7 Thinking critically about ... research on goal-setting in sport

Sport psychology is replete with claims about the value of goal-setting as a performance-enhancement strategy in sport. Thus H. Hall and Kerr (2001, p. 183) asserted that "not only is the efficacy of goal setting assumed; it is also claimed that the technique is a fundamental psychological skill that all athletes must develop if they are to maximize athletic potential". But are these claims warranted by available evidence? Although Locke (1991) claimed that goal-setting effects in sport are similar to those in business, Weinberg et al. (1985) argued that there are significant differences between these two spheres. Kremer and Scully (1994, p. 145) observed that the extrinsic rewards arising from the world of work "stand in contrast to the intrinsic motivators which have been identified as being so crucial to maintaining an interest in amateur sport". Other problems in this field come from the following methodological flaws in research on goal-setting (see Burton et al., 2001; Burton and Naylor, 2002; Burton and Weiss, 2008).

- *Possible ceiling effects:* There is evidence that the goal effectiveness curve flattens out or reaches a ceiling as people approach the limits of their ability. In other words, ability factors restrict the amount of improvement that can be made through goal-setting.

- *Complexity of task or skill:* Goal-setting effects may not be noticeable when the tasks used to assess them require complex skills. In fact, research indicates that as tasks become more complex, athletes must learn to adopt strategic plans to extract maximum benefit from goal-setting practices (H. Hall and Kerr, 2001).

- *Individual differences:* The relationship between goal-setting and performance may be moderated by strategic factors. Burton et al. (2001) claimed that such factors as self-efficacy can affect the impact of goal-setting practices on skilled performance.

■ *Spontaneous goal-setting in control group:* As mentioned earlier in the chapter, in the typical experimental paradigm used to study goal-setting effects (see earlier in chapter), it is difficult to ensure that participants in control groups do not set goals spontaneously for themselves. Indeed, there is evidence (Weinberg et al., 1985) that over 80 per cent of participants in a "no goal" control group admitted later that they had set goals for themselves.

Critical thinking questions

What are the similarities and differences between goal-setting processes in business and sport? What factors could account for the tendency for goal-setting to be less effective in sport than in business contexts? In sport, is it possible to eliminate the possibility of spontaneous goal-setting among people in control groups? Why do you think so few studies on goal-setting have used athletes studied in field settings?

Future directions in research on goal-setting

In general, at least six new directions can be sketched for research on goal-setting in athletes. First, more research is required to establish the optimal level of goal difficulty for athletes in specific types of sports. Second, despite persuasive evidence supporting the importance of goal-monitoring for intention fulfilment (see Harkin et al., 2016), relatively little is known about the relationship between the frequency with which people monitor their goal-setting behaviour and the efficacy of their goals. Third, additional research needs to be conducted on the role that "action plans" play in goal-setting effectiveness. Fourth, goal-setting researchers need to move on from studying atheoretical questions such as "what types of goals are most effective?" to investigating the psychological mechanisms underlying the motivational effects of goals on specific sport skills. Fifth, more longitudinal field studies are required to establish the actual goal-setting practices of athletes and coaches over the course of a competitive season. Finally, in an effort to counteract an over-reliance on individual attributional processes, additional studies are required to investigate team-based goal-setting (see Box 2.8). A promising new psychometric instrument in this regard is The "Team-Referent Attributions Measure in Sport" (TRAMS; Coffee et al., 2015).

Practical goal-setting: the SMART approach

To be effective as a motivational technique, goal-setting should be conducted according to sound psychological principles. These principles have been encapsulated in various acronyms in applied sport psychology. For example, Weinberg (2009) refers to INSPIRED where I stands for "internalized", N for "nurturing", S for "specific", P for "planned", I for "in your control", R for "reviewed regularly", E for "energizing" and D for "documented". Another well-known acronym is the SMART approach to goal-setting (Bull et al., 1996). This approach is illustrated in Box 2.9 with regard to the task of motivating oneself to exercise more regularly.

Box 2.8 Thinking critically about ... goal-setting in a team environment

Although a lot of research has been conducted on goal-setting in individual athletes, relatively few studies have investigated **team goal-setting** – or the process by which teams plan "the future state of affairs desired by enough members of a group to work towards its achievement" (D. Johnson and F. Johnson, 1987, p. 132). Team goal-setting is believed to enhance team performance by increasing **team cohesion** (U. Schmidt et al., 2005) and/or by improving collective efficacy (Greenlees et al., 2000).

In the early days of goal-setting research, Locke and Latham (1985, p. 212) suggested that the process of setting goals in team sports is similar to that in individual sports because "each individual has a specific job to do that requires particular skills". Over time, however, it became clear that this position is somewhat simplistic. For example, O'Leary-Kelly et al. (1994) suggested that team goal-setting is more complex than individual goal-setting for at least two reasons. First, team planning requires more coordination than individual goal-setting. Second, team goal-setting may take place at several levels (e.g. individual, unit, team) whereas individual goal-setting largely takes place at only one level. The different levels of team goal-setting may not always be mutually compatible. In Formula One motor racing, the Ferrari team was fined $100,000 by the FIA World Motor Sport Council in July 2010 for bringing the sport into disrepute in a controversial "team orders" (whereby a racing team decides which of its team members it wishes to win a race) incident in which one of its drivers, the Brazilian Felipe Massa, was apparently ordered to stand aside and let a teammate, the Spanish Fernando Alonso, win the German Grand Prix (Cary, 2010). A similar incident occurred in the 2002 Austrian Grand Prix when the Brazilian Rubens Barrichello was ordered by Ferrari to pull over on the finishing straight to allow his German teammate Michael Schumacher to win the race (Owen, 2010). In one case study, Thelwell (2009) described how he had developed and evaluated a psychological intervention programme in an effort to improve team goal-setting for a professional soccer team playing in the Championship (second tier of the Football League in England). Following some initial focus group meetings with the coaching staff to plan aspects of the intervention, a *performance profiling* exercise was conducted with the squad. Using this technique (based on Butler, 1996; see review by Weston et al., 2013), athletes are typically requested to indicate on a diagram (resembling a dartboard) "where I am now" and "where I would like to be" on a list of attributes deemed essential for success in their field (see example of use in Kremer and Moran, 2013). As an illustration of its applicability in sport psychology, Thelwell (2009) used performance profiling to elicit from the players and staff the team characteristics that would be required to secure the team's promotion to the Premier League. Evaluation of the intervention showed an improvement in perceived team qualities such as "being able to keep winning" and "positive responses to going behind/conceding late".

Critical thinking questions

Is there really such a thing as "team" goal-setting? In other words, is goal-setting not always an *individual* process? Can you think of any psychological theories that may help to explain why an individual athlete's goals could be different from those of a team? Do you think that a coach's communication style could influence how athletes in a team game interpret the goals that they strive to achieve during a competitive season? Give reasons for your answer. Based on Thelwell's (2009) research, what methods could you use – apart from performance profiling – to elicit team goals? What are the strengths and weaknesses of these methods?

Box 2.9 In the spotlight The SMART approach to goal-setting (based on Bull et al., 1996)

How can you motivate yourself to take physical exercise more regularly? One way of achieving this goal is to use the SMART approach to goal-setting. This approach is based on the idea that goal-setting works best when it follows certain principles that are captured by the acronym SMART. The SMART approach can be applied to your exercise behaviour as follows.

S = specific

The clearer and more specific your goal is, the more likely you are to achieve it. For example, "I want to visit the gym three times a week for the next three months" is better than saying "I would like to become fitter in the future".

M = measurable

If you cannot measure your progress towards your goal, you will quickly lose interest in it, so it is important to keep a record of your progress towards your fitness objective. For example, you could measure the length of time it takes you to run three kilometres and then try to improve on it every three weeks.

A = action-related

Unless you identify a number of stepping stones (i.e. tasks which take you a step nearer to your goal and which involve specific actions that are under your control) for your goals, you may feel confused about what to do next. One action step is to join a gym and a second is to get a weekly assessment of your progress from a qualified fitness instructor.

R = realistic

Your goals should be realistic for your present level of health and fitness. Therefore, it is important that you get a full health check-up before you begin an exercise programme so that your fitness level and exercise aspirations can be assessed. Otherwise, your fitness goals may be unrealistic.

T = timetabled

In order to motivate yourself to exercise regularly, you must build some daily physical activity into your timetable. Planned exercise is the key to better fitness levels.

So far in this chapter, we have explored the nature and types of motivation, various theoretical approaches to the study of this construct and a strategy (goal-setting) that attempts to increase motivation in athletes. The final section will address a rather puzzling question in this field. Specifically, what motivates people to participate in dangerous or high-risk sports – ones "where you have to reckon with the possibility of serious injury or death as an inherent part of the activity" (Breivik, 1999, p. 10)? This question is perplexing because people's involvement in risky sports is psychologically counter-intuitive. To explain, dangerous sports elicit fear – and fear is supposed to *dissuade* people from danger, not attract them to it. So, why do people engage in sporting behaviour that does not seem to make any psychological sense?

What motivates people to take part in high-risk sports?

On 8 August 2010, a Russian man named Vladimir Ladyzhenskiy collapsed and died with severe burns while competing in the Sauna World Championships in Heinola, Finland. Contestants in this extreme endurance event had to sit in a sweltering room and withstand temperatures as high as 230 degrees Fahrenheit (110 degrees Celsius) while water was tossed onto a searing stove. Why did he push his body to its final physiological limit? Similarly, what motivates someone to skydive from very tall urban buildings, bridges, cranes and cliffs? This latter activity is known as BASE (Buildings, Aerials, Spans and Earth) jumping and it has a fatality rate of about one in six participants (Wollaston, 2010). According to Dan Witchalls, one of the world's most famous BASE jumpers who has leaped off Wembley Stadium, Nelson's Column and the Millennium Dome, it's a matter of intrinsic thrill-seeking: "I like doing it because it's fun ... only get one chance. You can't make mistakes up there" (cited in Ronay, 2010, p. 8).

A sport is usually defined as being risky or dangerous if the consequences of something going wrong in it are life-threatening for the participants involved (Woodman et al., 2010). Based on this definition, sports such as mountain-climbing, ballooning, free-diving (a form of underwater diving in which participants hold their breath until they resurface rather than use breathing equipment; see Skolnick, 2016), hang-gliding, parachute-jumping, white-water kayaking, skydiving and motorcycle racing are highly risky. So, what motivates people to engage in such dangerous activities? At least four psychological theories have been proposed to answer this question.

First, at a general level, some theorists believe that dangerous activities offer people an escape from a world that the poet and novelist Al Alvarez described as increasingly "constricted by comfort" (cited in Delingpole, 2001, p. 8). According to this theory, many people feel excessively cosseted by the materialistic comforts of our contemporary society and hence seek dangerous experiences in an effort to fill a gap in their lives. Furthermore, as western city life "is now tame and increasingly controlled" (Vidal, 2001, p. 2), some people may look increasingly for danger in outdoor experiences. Therefore, risk-taking behaviour may represent a conscious backlash against the bland and sterile security of everyday life. Although this theory is rather speculative, it has a ring of plausibility about it because it seems likely that alienated people may experience a heightened state of awareness when they are faced with the prospect of injury or death. Indeed, Schrader and Wann (1999, p. 427) suggested that one way to achieve the illusion of control over one's mortality is by "cheating death" through involvement in high-risk activities.

A second theory of risk-taking behaviour is the proposition that it stems from a personality trait called **sensation seeking**. According to Zuckerman (1979, 2007), this trait involves the propensity to seek "novel and complex sensations and experiences and the willingness to take physical and social risks for the sake of such experiences" (Zuckerman 1979, p. 10). Originally, Zuckerman speculated that people who participated in risky sports were high sensation seekers who displayed a tendency to underestimate the dangers posed by these sports. Subsequently, however, he revised this view by suggesting instead that sensation seekers are actually accurate in their risk assessment – even though they apparently believe that the rewards of arousal outweigh the degree of risk involved by the activity in question (Zuckerman, 1994). This trait of sensation seeking can be measured using the Sensation Seeking Scale (Zuckerman, 1984) which assesses such dimensions of the construct as "thrill and adventure seeking" (the desire to engage in adventurous activities), "experience seeking" (the tendency to seek arousal through mental and sensory means), "disinhibition" (seeking a release through such activities as drinking and gambling) and "boredom susceptibility" (an aversion to monotony). For a critical perspective on this test, see Box 2.10.

Box 2.10 Thinking critically about ... sensation seeking in sport

What factors are associated with people's involvement in risky sporting activities? Schrader and Wann (1999) investigated the role of variables such as gender, "death anxiety" (i.e. the degree to which one feels that one can cheat death by participating in high-risk activities) and sensation seeking (Zuckerman, 1979, 2007) in people's involvement in dangerous sports. Results showed that only two variables accounted for significant amounts of variance in thrill-seeking behaviour. These variables were gender and sensation seeking. Schrader and Wann (1999) found that a much higher proportion of males (about 62 per cent) than females (approximately 37 per cent) participated in high-risk recreation activities. In addition, sensation seeking, as measured by the Sensation Seeking Scale V (SSSV: Zuckerman 1979, 1994), was significantly associated with involvement in high-risk activities.

Critical thinking questions

Are you satisfied with the defintion above for "risky" sports? Is it too simplistic? Note that Woodman et al. (2010) pointed out that although proportionately more people are injured playing soccer than bungee-jumping, soccer is not regarded as a dangerous sport. In any case, do you think that correlations between risk-taking behaviour and personality variables really explain anything? After all, to say that someone chooses dangerous sports because they enjoy the thrill of danger seems rather circular. Furthermore, how can we be sure that participants regard their chosen athletic behaviour as "risky" unless we assess their perceptions of the actual danger involved in it? What other implicit assumptions do researchers in this field make? Why do you think that proportionately more males than females tend to participate in risky sporting activities? If thrill-seeking behaviour is as addictive as is often claimed (Vidal, 2001), why do people tend to choose *only one* outlet for their risky behaviour? For example, why do rock-climbers rarely become interested in other dangerous sports like motor-racing or bungee-jumping?

A third theoretical approach to risky behaviour in sports comes from the cognitive tradition. To illustrate, consider the idiosyncratic ways in which people estimate the risks associated with certain activities. John Kerr (1997) noted that athletes who participate in dangerous sports often confess to a fear of participating in *other* sports which are equally dangerous. Carl Llewellyn, a British National Hunt jockey who has suffered a catalogue of serious injuries in his sport, confessed to being petrified of activities like bungee-jumping. Presumably, familiarity with the risks of one's sport blinds one to the dangers which they pose. In an effort to explain this phenomenon, Kerr (1997) speculated that athletes who take part in dangerous sports tend to construct subjective "protective frames" which give them a feeling of invincibility, although such frames do not appear to extend to less familiar sports.

The fourth theoretical account of risk-taking behaviour comes from research on the phenomenon of "alexithymia" or the apparent inability by some people to experience, describe and/or to verbalize their emotions adequately (Chen et al., 2011; Taylor et al., 1999). According to Barlow et al. (2015), alexithymic athletes may be attracted to high-risk sports because these activities offer such individuals the opportunity "to move from experiencing nonspecific, ambiguous and internal emotions (e.g. anxiety) to experiencing specific and intense emotions (e.g. fear), which are attached to an objective danger" (p. 84). Interestingly, there is evidence that alexithymic people can compensate, to some extent, for their emotional regulation difficulties by taking part in high-risk sports (Woodman et al., 2008). In a recent study, Barlow et al. (2015) argued that alexithymia exerts a causal influence on risk-taking behaviour. Another perspective on risk-taking was offered by Gamble and Walker (2016) in a rather counter-intuitive study. Briefly, these researchers discovered that people's risk-taking propensity *increased* when they were not explicitly aware that they had been wearing protective equipment (a helmet rather than a baseball cap). They attributed this finding to "social priming" (a phenomenon whereby thinking about or interacting with a particular object can affect subsequent behaviour concerning that object). Clearly, this finding deserves attempted replication.

Before we conclude this section, however, it is notable that there may be a neurochemical basis to risk-taking behaviour. For example, Zorpette (1999) claimed that such behaviour is addictive physiologically because dopamine is released by the brain as a chemical reward for experiencing dangerous situations. As yet, however, there have been few systematic attempts to explore the brains of thrill-seekers using **neuroscientific imaging** technology.

Ideas for research projects on motivation in athletes

Here are six ideas for possible research projects on motivation in athletes.

1. Is there a relationship between the motivation of athletes and the type of sport which they play? To answer this question, you could compare and contrast the motivation of performers from individual and team sports using a questionnaire such as the Sport Motivation Scale (M. Martens and Webber, 2002).

2. Can goal-setting help to increase the performance of endurance athletes – those engaged in "whole-body, dynamic exercise that involves continuous effort and lasts for 75 s or longer" (McCormick et al., 2015, p. 998)? Typical endurance sports include (but are not limited to) running, cycling and swimming events (e.g. marathons, triathlons, ultra-marathons), rowing, canoeing, cross-country skiing and speed skating. Interestingly, a recent systematic review by McCormick et al. (2015) found that mental imagery, self-talk and goal-setting were among the most useful of a variety of psychological strategies designed to improve the performance of such endurance athletes. So far, only a few studies have been conducted on goal-setting in endurance athletes (e.g. see Tenenbaum et al., 1999). Therefore, it would be interesting to fill this gap in the research literature by investigating the efficacy of a goal-setting intervention programme on endurance athletes.

3. Can goal-setting help to increase the activity levels of older adults? In a recent study of such a population (with a mean age of about 65 year), Floegel et al. (2015) found that the more physically active members of their sample had cited more specific goals and specific actions to achieve these goals than did less physically active participants. It would be interesting to extend this study by investigating whether or not a custom-designed goal-setting intervention programme could increase physical activity levels in an older adult population.

4. Relatively little is known about the actual goal-setting practices of athletes who have been tested in field settings (but see Mellalieu et al., 2006b). Historically, most goal-setting studies have been conducted in laboratory settings on non-athlete samples. In view of this oversight in the research literature, you may wish to investigate the goal-setting practices of athletes in a specific sport over the course of a season. For example, Mellalieu et al. (2006b) explored goal-setting in five collegiate rugby players over a competitive season. This study may give you some ideas on how to proceed with your own research.

5. What factors motivate prolonged engagement in high-risk sports? It would be interesting to extend the studies by Woodman et al. (2010) or Barlow et al. (2015) which addressed this question.

6. It would be interesting to investigate how team-attributions change over time using a test such as the Team-Referent Attributions Measure in Sport (Coffee et al., 2015).

Summary

■ Motivation plays a vital but often misunderstood role in sport psychology. The role is *critical* because athletic success depends significantly on people's willingness to exert mental as well as physical effort in pursuit of excellence. Unfortunately, the role of motivation in sport is also potentially *confusing* because of certain myths that have surrounded this term (e.g. the idea that being "psyched up" is synonymous with being appropriately motivated for competitive action). Therefore, the goal of this chapter was to outline and evaluate selected theories and research on motivational processes in athletes.

- We began by considering the nature and types of motivation (e.g. intrinsic and extrinsic) that are evident among athletes.

- Next, we presented a brief review of four theoretical approaches to motivation in sport psychology – namely, the personality perspective and three social-cognitive models (i.e. the goal-orientation, attribution and self-determination theories).

- The third section explored the theory and practice of increasing motivation in athletes through the use of goal-setting techniques.

- The fourth section examined a motivational question that has attracted much popular debate – why do some people take part in risky or dangerous sports activities?

- In the final section of the chapter, we provided six practical suggestions for possible research projects on the psychology of motivation in athletes.

3

"Psyching up" and calming down
Anxiety in sport

Introduction

After his uncharacteristically poor final round at the 2011 US Masters championship in August, golfer Rory McIlroy admitted that

> I was still one shot ahead going into the 10th and then things went all pear-shaped after that ... I can't really put my finger on what went wrong ... I just hit a poor tee shot on 10 and sort of unravelled from there.
>
> (cited in Garrod, 2011, p. 64)

Clearly, competitive sport can make even the world's most successful athletes feel nervous. For example, consider the anxiety experienced by seasoned performers such as England Rugby World Cup winner Jonny Wilkinson and golf major tournament winner Justin Rose. Interestingly, Wilkinson admitted that "I am always nervous before a rugby match. I always have been ... the condition wasn't physical fear ... it was the thought of losing and letting myself down at something which meant so much to me" (Wilkinson, 2006, pp. 49–50). Surprisingly, Rose suggested that athletes' ability to cope with anxiety may not improve with experience. For example, although he has represented Europe in four Ryder Cup teams since 2008, he still feels nervous on the first tee of this competition. As he pointed out:

> the Ryder cup ... you never get accustomed to it. You don't do it often enough to get comfortable. No matter how much it means to you personally, you know what it means to everyone around you. You feel it more. The tension is more palpable.
>
> (cited in Harig, 2014) (see Figure 3.1)

Extrapolating from these experiences, we can conclude that most athletes have discovered that if they wish to perform consistently well in competition, they must learn to acknowledge and control their arousal levels effectively. And the first step in this process is for athletes to admit that they get anxious from time to time. So, the current world number 1 tennis player Novak Djokovic claimed that under pressure

Figure 3.1 According to Justin Rose, playing in the Ryder Cup can be a nerve-racking experience (*source*: courtesy of Inpho photography)

the body sometimes has "reactions and movements that you're not in control of … sometimes these things happen and it's important to re-group, bounce back and focus on the next one" (cited in ontennis.com, 2015). With this realization comes empowerment. Andy Murray, a Wimbledon and US Open champion, proclaimed: "I'm happy with nerves. For a sportsperson to go into matches being nervous is good. Having that adrenaline gets your mind focused on the match" (cited in Mitchell, 2010). Clearly, athletes have to be able either to "psych themselves up" (see Chapter 2) or to calm themselves down as required by the situation. As an example of the latter, Jessica Hill-Ennis (the gold medal winning heptathlete in the 2012 Olympic games) revealed that she liked watching other athletes get themselves psyched up but that if she experienced similar levels of physiological arousal then she would "tense up, so I would quietly slip into my blocks instead. People would tell me I wasn't trying, but I always was" (cited in Ennis, 2012, p. 56) (see Figure 3.2). Similarly, José Mourinho (current manager of Manchester United and twice a coach of Champions' League winning teams) observed that in his experience, "without emotional control, you cannot play … you cannot react. You have to know what you have to do … You have to be cool (cited in *The Guardian*, 2005) (see Figure 3.3). Nevertheless, some sports challenge the performer to *alternate* regularly between psyching up and calming down within the same competition. For example, gymnasts must be able to energize themselves before attempting a vault exercise but must then switch to relaxation mode when preparing to perform a routine on the beam. Otherwise, they may slip – literally, as happened to Gabby Douglas, the 2012

Figure 3.2 Jessica Ennis-Hill believes that she performs the best when she is calm (*source*: courtesy of Inpho photography)

all-round Olympic gymnastics champion, who fell off the balance beam during the individual routine ruining her chances of a gold medal in that event. Interestingly, the importance of arousal control in sport was highlighted by Mike Atherton, a former captain of England's cricket team, who observed:

> there are two sorts of player: those who are quite placid people ... who need an adrenaline flow to get them up for it, and so find nerves a real help. And then there are those who are naturally hyper for whom that additional flow may not be such a good thing. When I look at players now I can see who fits into which category and then *their ability to cope depends on whether they can either bring themselves up or take themselves down.*

(cited in Selvey, 1998; italics ours)

Similar sentiments were expressed by Sam Torrance, the captain of the victorious European golf team before the 2002 Ryder Cup, when he urged his players to use their nervous energy effectively (see O'Sullivan, 2002a, p. 19), and by Mo Farah, the British 2012 Olympic champion 10,000 metres athlete, who admitted to drinking two shots of espresso so that he would be "pumped up" before the final. Given the importance of anxiety control in sport, how can athletes manage to calm themselves down or psych themselves up before or during a competition? More generally, what does "anxiety" mean to athletes and does it help or hinder their performance? What causes it and how can it be measured in sport settings? The purpose of this chapter is to provide answers to these and other questions raised by the study of arousal and anxiety in sport.

Figure 3.3 José Mourinho believes that emotional control is essential for success in sport (*source*: courtesy of Inpho photography)

The chapter is organized as follows. To begin with, we explore the nature, causes and types of anxiety in sport performers as well as what anxiety means to athletes themselves. In the next section, various ways of measuring anxiety in athletes are evaluated briefly. The following section reviews research findings on the relationship between anxiety and athletic performance. This section also features a discussion of the nature and causes of "choking" under pressure in sport. In the following section, the topic of anxiety *control* is addressed. The next section highlights some unresolved issues and new directions in research on anxiety in athletes, and we present some practical suggestions for research projects in this field.

Anxiety in athletes

According to Onions (1996), the term anxiety is derived from the Latin word *angere*, meaning "to choke". This Latin origin is interesting because it shows that anxiety is at the root of "choking" under pressure – a phenomenon in which athletes perform worse than expected in pressure situations that have a degree of perceived importance (Jordet, 2009). We discuss this topic of choking in more detail later in this chapter. For the present, however, anxiety in sport psychology refers to an unpleasant emotion which is characterized by vague but persistent feelings of apprehension and dread (Cashmore, 2008). A similar view of this construct was provided by Buckworth and Dishman (2002, p. 116) who defined anxiety as a state of "worry, apprehension, or tension that often occurs in the absence of real or obvious danger". Typically, the tension felt by anxious people is accompanied by a heightened state of physiological arousal mediated by the **autonomic nervous system** (ANS) which regulates certain bodily processes such as blood pressure and our rate of breathing. It works automatically (autonomously) – without conscious effort.

In order to understand anxiety properly, we need to explore its psychological components and also to distinguish it from similar constructs such as *fear*, a brief emotional reaction to a stimulus that is perceived as threatening, and *arousal*, a diffuse state of bodily alertness or "readiness" (Cashmore, 2008). The latter distinctions are very important because anxiety research in sport has been plagued by conceptual confusion (Fletcher et al., 2006; Gould et al., 2002b; Mellalieu et al., 2006a). For example, the terms anxiety, fear and arousal are sometimes used interchangeably even though these constructs have quite different meanings – as we shall explain shortly.

Components of anxiety: cognitive, somatic and behavioural

Most psychologists regard anxiety as a multidimensional construct with at least three dimensions or components: cognitive (i.e. mental), somatic (i.e. physical) and behavioural (Gould et al., 2002b). Let us now examine each of these components in turn.

First, **cognitive anxiety** involves worrying or having negative expectations about some impending situation or performance and engaging in task-irrelevant thinking as a consequence (see also Chapter 5 on concentration in athletes). More precisely, it refers to "negative expectations and cognitive concerns about oneself, the situation at hand and potential consequences" (L. Morris et al., 1981, p. 541). But what do athletes worry about in sport? Although relatively little research has been conducted on this issue, John Dunn (1999) and Dunn and Syrotuik (2003) discovered four main themes in their analysis of cognitive anxiety in intercollegiate ice-hockey players. These themes were a fear of performance failure, apprehension about negative evaluation by others, concerns about physical injury or danger, and an unspecified fear of the unknown. On average, the players in this study were more concerned about performance failure and negative evaluation by others than about the other two worry domains. A similar concern about poor performance (specifically, the fear of failure and being negatively evaluated by one's coach or spectators) was evident among a group of elite golfers interviewed by Hill et al. (2010b). In general, cognitive anxiety has a debilitating effect on athletic performance (Cashmore, 2008). We return to this issue in the fourth section of the chapter when we explore why some athletes "choke" under pressure. By the way, cognitive anxiety about future performance is also widespread among performers other than athletes. For example, performance anxiety or stage fright has blighted the careers of such talented people as the singer Barbra Streisand, who forgot the words of one of her songs during a concert in Central Park, New York, in front of 135,000 people – an event which prompted her to avoid singing "live" for another twenty-seven years (Sutcliffe, 1997).

The second component of the construct of anxiety involves somatic or bodily processes. **Somatic anxiety** refers to the *physical* (including psychophysiological) manifestation of anxiety and may be defined as "one's perception of the physiological-affective elements of the anxiety experience, that is, indications of autonomic arousal and unpleasant feeling states such as nervousness and tension" (L. Morris et al., 1981, p. 541). In sport, this component of anxiety is apparent when an athlete is afflicted by such physical markers as neuroendocrine responses (e.g. secretion of cortisol – the "stress hormone"), increased perspiration, a pounding heart, rapid shallow breathing, clammy hands and a feeling of butterflies in the stomach. Whereas cognitive anxiety is characterized by negative thoughts and worries, somatic anxiety is associated with signs of autonomic arousal such as the release of hormones such as cortisol. It should be noted, however, that some researchers (e.g. J. Kerr, 1997) have suggested that increases in physiological arousal may accompany emotions other than anxiety. In particular, excitement and anger appear to have physiological substrates similar to those of anxiety.

The third component of the construct of anxiety is **behavioural anxiety**. In this domain, indices of anxiety include tense facial expressions, changes in communication patterns (e.g. unusually rapid speech delivery) and agitation and restlessness (Gould et al., 2002b). Surprisingly, relatively little research has been conducted on the behavioural manifestations of anxiety in athletes – mainly because of the dearth of objective measures and suitable checklists for the assessment of such phenomena. Nevertheless, it is widely believed that anxiety produces jerky and inefficient muscular movements in athletes which can be assessed using kinematic measures. In this regard, a good example of how these three dimensions of anxiety interact comes from a study by Cooke et al. (2010). Briefly, these researchers conducted an experiment designed to compare the effects of a pressure manipulation on novice golfers' putting performance. They manipulated the level of anxiety among the participants through the use of monetary rewards (a stack of £1 coins were placed in clear view during the experiment) and punishments (the loss of £1 every time they failed to achieve an agreed upon standard of performance). Results revealed that, as predicted, the effects of anxiety were evident psychologically at three different levels. First, at the experiential level, the novice golfers reported feeling more anxiety and an increase in perceived pressure when performing under the pressure manipulation. Second, at the physiological level, performing under pressure resulted in greater heart rates and heart rate variability. Third, anxiety affected the participants' bodily movements which was apparent in indices such as an increase in muscle activity and lateral clubhead acceleration. Before concluding this section, two important theoretical issues need to be addressed concerning the tri-dimensional nature of anxiety.

In the first theoretical issue, given the inextricable links between mind and body in sport, is it valid to postulate that cognitive and somatic anxiety are truly separate dimensions of this construct? There are at least two sources of evidence to support this distinction (Burton, 1998). First, factor analyses of self-report state anxiety scales tend to reveal a multidimensional rather than a unidimensional structure. Second, there are grounds for believing that cognitive and somatic anxiety emanate from different types of pre-competitive patterns. For example, research suggests that whereas cognitive anxiety remains relatively high and stable prior to competition for most athletes, somatic anxiety tends to remain low until one or two days before the event – at which point it increases steadily before peaking at the start of a competition. After that, it tends to dissipate rapidly. With regard to this issue, Fenz and Epstein (1967) explored the temporal pattern of physiological arousal responses among expert and novice skydivers prior to performance. Results showed that in the expert performers, peak arousal levels were reached significantly in advance of the jump. By contrast, the physiological arousal of the novice parachutists started at a relatively low level but increased progressively in the time leading up to the jump. More recently, Strahler et al. (2010) examined the anticipatory anxiety – as manifested in psychological and neuroendocrine stress responses – of athletes one week before an important competition. They were especially interested in the cortisol awakening response (CAR), which is a marker of hypothalamic-pituitary-adrenal activity. Typically obtained from saliva samples, CAR may provide insight into how people react psychophysiologically over time to the anticipated demands of an impending challenge. Strahler et al. (2010) were surprised to discover that whereas the athletes in their study reported experiencing a significant rise in somatic anxiety as the day of a competition loomed, there was no significant increase in CAR activity. The authors interpreted this finding as indicating that experienced athletes appear to habituate certain hormonal activity in response to repeated exposure to stressful situations. However, contradictory findings have emerged from a study by Cunniffe et al. (2015) who explored the influence of game venue (home versus away) and starting status on precompetitive psychophysiology measures in elite rugby union. Saliva samples revealed higher pregame cortisol levels than on a baseline control day and similar findings were observed for measures of cognitive and somatic anxiety. Given these findings, one might also ask whether self-report and neuroendocrine responses to anxiety are capable of offering accurate predictors of performance. In one of the few studies to address this issue, Lautenbach et al. (2014) found that cortisol levels could better predict variance in tennis serve performance than a subjective anxiety measure (i.e. Competitive State Anxiety Inventory-2). In a more recent study, Lautenbach et al. (2015b), using a single-case design (see Chapter 1), found that cortisol levels were higher on a competition day than a rest day in two competitive tennis players. The researchers also found that cortisol levels were higher before, during, and after, a match-*losing* performance compared to a match-*winning* one. Cortisol concentration was negatively correlated with certain performance measures such as the percentage of points won after making the first serve and return performance. In summary, evidence from psychometric studies of self-report scales and that from studies of changes in the pattern of athletes' affect over time suggest that cognitive and somatic anxiety are in fact independent dimensions of anxiety.

The second theoretical issue that arises from the tri-dimensional model of anxiety concerns the distinction between *intensity* and *directionality* of this construct. To explain, until the early 1990s, most anxiety researchers tended to focus only on the intensity or level (or amount) of symptoms experienced by performers when assessing their cognitive and somatic anxiety (Thomas et al., 2009). However, with the discovery that the experience of anxiety was *not* always detrimental to performance (see subsection below on "Athletes' interpretation of anxiety symptoms"), researchers began to investigate the *directional* interpretation of anxiety. In other words, is it perceived by the performer as being facilitative or debilitative of performance? As we shall see later in the chapter, this emphasis on the importance of perception as a mediating factor in athletes' experience of anxiety has led to useful **coping** strategies such as "**cognitive restructuring**" (illustrated in Box 3.7 later in the chapter).

Anxiety, fear and arousal

So far, we have been using the terms anxiety, arousal and fear quite loosely. Let us now distinguish between them more precisely. Anxiety is believed to differ from fear in lasting longer (Buckworth and Dishman, 2002) and in tending to be more undifferentiated than fear – because people can be anxious about something that is not physically present or immediately perceptible. Despite these differences, however, anxiety is similar to a fear in some ways. To explain, anxiety is elicited whenever people interpret a particular person, event or situation as posing a *threat* to them in some way. This perception of threat may be based on realistic or imaginary fears – although the distinction between these two factors is often blurred in everyday life. For example, if you are a tennis player and serving at match point in your local club championship, you will probably feel a little anxious – even though your feelings in this case are completely disproportionate to the physical danger involved in the situation (unless, of course, your opponent has a reputation for being physically violent on court if he or she loses!). But if you are a novice parachutist facing your first jump with no instructor around, you may have every reason to feel nervous because of the potential danger to your life. Let us turn now to the distinction between anxiety and arousal.

In psychology, the term "arousal" refers to a type of bodily energy which primes or prepares us for emergency action. For example, when we are threatened physically, our body's sympathetic nervous system prepares us either to confront the source of danger or to run away from it. This fight or flight response triggers such bodily reactions as a faster heartbeat, release of glucose into the bloodstream and heightened levels of arousal. But what does arousal involve? According to Gould et al. (2002b, p. 227), it is a "general physiological and psychological activation of the organism which varies on a continuum from deep sleep to intense excitement". In other words, arousal is an undifferentiated somatic state which prepares people to respond to anticipated demands for action (Whelan et al., 1990). Physiologically, feelings of arousal are mediated by the sympathetic nervous system. Thus when we become aroused, our brain's reticular activating system triggers the release of biochemical substances like **epinephrine** and **norepinephrine** into the bloodstream so that our body is energized appropriately for action. Therefore, anxiety can be distinguished from arousal as follows. Although arousal involves undifferentiated bodily energy, anxiety is an emotional label for a *particular type* of arousal experience (L. Hardy et al., 1996). This view is endorsed in a model of arousal developed by Gould et al. (2002b). In this model, cognitive anxiety is believed to emerge from the interpretation or appraisal of arousal. Therefore, anxiety can be regarded as *negatively interpreted* arousal. This proposition raises the question of individual differences in arousal interpretation.

It has long been known that athletes differ from each other in the labels that they attach to their arousal states. Thus certain bodily symptoms (e.g. rapid heartbeat, shortness of breath) may be perceived as "pleasant excitement" by one athlete but regarded as unpleasant anxiety by another performer. To illustrate a *positive* interpretation of an arousal state, note what Sam Torrance, captain of the victorious 2002 European Ryder Cup golf team, said to his players before the competition started:

> If you're not nervous then there is something wrong with you. Nerves create adrenaline and I told them to use that, use it in your own advantageous way, to make you feel better, get pumped up; just get psyched up.
>
> (cited in O'Sullivan, 2002a, p. 19)

A similarly positive attitude to nervousness was shown by the tennis star Roger Federer, who described how he felt about playing on Centre Court in Wimbledon: "I mean, it's nerves. It's exciting. But after all, it's a privilege to be there" (cited in Wimbledon.com, 2015). Notice that Federer labelled his nervousness as excitement. In a similar vein, Tiger Woods revealed that "the challenge is hitting good golf shots when you have to ... to do it when the nerves are fluttering, the heart pounding, the palms sweating ... that's the *thrill*" (cited in D. Davies, 2001; italics ours).

These comments by Federer and Woods highlight the role that perception plays in the emotional experiences of elite athletes. For example, a low level of arousal may be experienced either as a relaxed state of readiness or as an undesirable "flat", lethargic or sluggish feeling. This idea that athletes' arousal levels may be *interpreted* in either positive or negative terms raises the issue of what anxiety means to sport performers.

Athletes' interpretation of anxiety symptoms: help or hindrance?

Traditionally, arousal and anxiety have been regarded as factors to be controlled in case they hampered athletic performance. However, this assumption was challenged by research which showed that, in many athletic situations, it is not the *amount* of arousal that affects performance but the way in which such arousal is interpreted. For example, M. Mahoney and Avener (1977) found that successful gymnasts (i.e. those who qualified for the 1976 US Olympic squad) tended to perceive pre-competitive arousal as a form of anticipatory excitement – a view which apparently facilitated their subsequent performance. Conversely, less successful counterparts (i.e. athletes who failed to qualify for the US team) tended to treat their arousal levels negatively, interpreting them as unwelcome signs of impending failure. Influenced by this finding, Jones and his colleagues in the early 1990s began to investigate the directional interpretation of anxiety (i.e.

the extent to which athletes perceived anxiety as a help or a hindrance to their performance). Thus G. Jones and Swain (1992, 1995) and Hanton and Jones (1999) showed that somatic symptoms of anxiety can have either a *facilitative* effect or a *debilitative* effect on sport performance depending on how the athlete perceives them. To illustrate, a performer who interprets sweaty palms as a sign of uncertainty is experiencing debilitative anxiety whereas someone who regards similar symptoms as a sign of readiness to do well is experiencing facilitative anxiety (as in the cases of Roger Federer and Tiger Woods above).

Since the early 1990s, a substantial volume of studies has been conducted on the benefits of perceiving anxiety symptoms as facilitative of performance. Thomas et al. (2009) highlighted research showing that athletes with this latter view tend to perform better, have higher levels of self-confidence, use more effective coping strategies and display more resilience than do counterparts who perceive anxiety symptoms as debilitative of performance. Clearly, it is beneficial to see anxiety as a help rather than a hindrance. But although this directional perception theory of anxiety in sport seems plausible, it is marred by conceptual and methodological difficulties. The former stem mainly from the terminology involved. G. Jones and Hanton (2001) acknowledged that the term "facilitative anxiety" seems like an oxymoron. To explain, as the term "anxiety" has negative connotations, and as it is difficult to distinguish between somatic anxiety and other emotions (J. Kerr, 1997), then perhaps athletes who label "anxiety" symptoms as facilitative may not be experiencing anxiety at all, but rather a sense of excitement or challenge (see the preceding quote from Tiger Woods). Burton and Naylor (1997) argued that anxiety is by definition a negatively toned and unpleasant emotion. These researchers believe that anxiety does not facilitate performance proficiency and that anxiety researchers have mistakenly labelled other positive emotions such as challenge and self-confidence as facilitative anxiety.

To shed light on this issue, Nicholls et al. (2012) administered a series of pre-competitive measures of stress and emotion and post-competitive measures of coping and subjective performance to a large sample of athletes and found a strong correlation between anxiety and *excitement*. Because excitement was positively correlated with subjective performance the authors argued that its presence may account for the "fallacy" that anxiety can facilitate performance. Despite these concerns, Cheng et al. (2011) proposed that anxiety may have a regulatory function. In their three-dimensional framework, including cognitive, physiological and regulatory dimensions, the latter dimension represents the potentially adaptive capacity of anxiety. The authors argue that this adaptive capacity is consistent with the evolutionary root of anxiety as a defence mechanism which allows individuals to mobilize resources for vigorous reaction to perceived threat when performing a task under pressure. Compounding this semantic issue is a formidable methodological challenge (Uphill, 2008). Specifically, how can researchers distinguish empirically between athletes' anxiety state, their perception of that state, their perception of the impact of that state on their performance, and the actual impact of that state on their performance? Additional research is required to resolve these conceptual and methodological issues. Despite such problems, it is clear that the way in which athletes *label* their arousal levels (if not their anxiety) seems to play a significant role in whether they feel challenged or overwhelmed by pressure situations.

This idea that a given level of arousal is amenable to different interpretative labels has significant theoretical and practical implications. On the theoretical side, it suggests that attempts to measure anxiety should include indices of *direction* or interpretation as well as of intensity. With regard to practical implications, directionality effects highlight the importance of teaching athletes to reframe their physiological symptoms constructively. Hanton and Jones (1999) reported that elite swimmers benefited from learning to interpret pre-race anxiety symptoms in a positive manner. As these authors put it so memorably, the elite swimmers in their study had learned to make their butterflies "fly in formation"! Moore et al. (2015) claimed that athletes can be trained to interpret heightened physiological arousal as a tool that can help to maximize performance resulting in more adaptive cardiovascular responses. We consider this possibility in greater detail later in the chapter. In an effort to explore the meaning of anxiety to athletes, try the exercise in Box 3.1.

Box 3.1 In the spotlight Exploring the meaning of anxiety to athletes

The purpose of this exercise is to explore what performance anxiety means to athletes and to investigate how they cope with it. In order to complete this exercise, you will need to interview three competitive athletes – preferably from different sports. Before you begin, however, please ensure that these participants have been informed about the purpose of the study and have consented to have their views recorded and analysed. Then, using an electronic voice-recorder, ask them the following questions:

1. What does the word "anxiety" mean to you? Do you think that it is helpful or harmful to your performance?

2. On a scale of 0 (meaning "not at all important") to 5 (meaning "extremely important"), how important do you think that the ability to control anxiety is for successful performance in your sport?

3. Do you prefer to be psyched up or calm before a competitive event in your sport? Why? Please explain.

4. What things make you anxious *before* a competition? How do these factors affect your performance? Explain.

5. What things make you anxious *during* a competition? How do these factors affect your performance? Explain.

6. What techniques do you use, if any, to cope with anxiety in your sport? Where did you learn these techniques?

Analysis

Do the athletes differ in their understanding of anxiety? If so, are these differences related to the sports that they play? From the athletes' experiences, what factors make them anxious before and/or during competition? Do the athletes use any specific techniques to cope with anxiety? If so, where did they learn these techniques?

In summary, we have learned so far that anxiety is a multidimensional construct with cognitive, somatic and behavioural components. We have also discovered that this construct can be distinguished from fear and arousal experiences. In addition, we saw how athletes differed in the way in which they interpret their arousal levels as being either facilitative or debilitative of their sport performance. At this stage, however, we need to tackle the question of whether or not different *types* of anxiety can be identified.

Types of anxiety: state and trait

Since the seminal research of Spielberger (1966), a distinction has been drawn by psychologists between anxiety as a mood state (state anxiety) and anxiety as a personality characteristic (trait anxiety). Whereas the former term (also known as "A-state") describes transient, situation-specific feelings of fear, worry and physiological arousal, the latter one (also called "A-trait") refers to a relatively stable personality trait (or chronic predisposition) which is characterized by a tendency to perceive certain situations as anxiety-provoking. Thus as Spielberger (1966, p. 17) explained, **state anxiety** may be defined as "subjective, consciously perceived feelings of tension and apprehension", whereas **trait anxiety** refers to a general disposition among people to feel anxious in certain environmental situations (e.g. when playing an important match). Applied to sport, the concept of state anxiety may be used to describe situations in which an athlete's feelings of tension may change during a match. A footballer may feel nervous in the dressing-room before an important match but may become calmer once the competitive action begins. However, a player who scores highly on trait anxiety may feel pessimistic most of the time. Another way of explaining this distinction is to say that trait anxiety is a predisposition to experience state anxiety under certain circumstances. According to this view, athletes who display a high degree of trait anxiety are more likely to interpret sport situations as threatening than are less anxious counterparts.

What causes anxiety in athletes?

Although it is easy to identify typical *antecedents* of anxiety in athletes, it is very difficult to establish the precise causal nature of these factors because of ethical issues. To explain, researchers are often precluded from manipulating any variable that may induce anxiety among the participants in their studies. Accordingly, most research on anxiety in sport is correlational rather than experimental in nature. Overall, the personal and situational antecedents of anxiety may be summarized as follows (see also Uphill, 2008).

Perceived importance of the competition

In general, the more importance that is attached to a forthcoming competition by athletes, the more anxiety they are likely to experience in it (Dowthwaite and Armstrong, 1984).

Predispositions: trait anxiety

Many sport psychologists (e.g. Anshel, 1995) believe that athletes' levels of trait anxiety are important determinants of the amount of state anxiety which they are likely to experience in a given situation. But, as we indicated in Chapter 2, it is not valid to use a personality trait as an "explanation" for a mental state. After all, one cannot explain aggressive behaviour by saying that a person has an "aggressive" personality. Clearly, we must be careful to avoid circular reasoning when seeking to explain why athletes become anxious in certain situations.

Attribution/expectations

As we explained in Chapter 2, a tendency to attribute successful outcomes to external and unstable factors (e.g. luck) and to attribute unsuccessful outcomes to internal and stable factors (e.g. low levels of skill) is likely to induce anxiety in athletes. Perceptions of audience expectations are also important determinants of performance anxiety. For example, the soprano June Anderson said:

> in the beginning of your career ... nobody knows who you are, and they don't have any expectations. There's less to lose. Later on, when you're known, people are coming to see you, and they have certain expectations. You have a lot to lose.
> (cited in Blau, 1998, p. 17)

Perfectionism

Research on the question of how **perfectionism** (or the striving for flawlessness and the setting of excessively high standards for one's performance: Stoeber and Stoeber, 2009) is related to anxiety and athletic performance is equivocal. Whereas some investigators (e.g. Gould et al., 2002b) regard perfectionism as a stepping-stone to Olympic excellence, others (e.g. Flett and Hewitt, 2005) view it as an impediment to sport success. To illustrate the latter opinion, Flett and Hewitt (2005, p. 14) argued that perfectionism is "primarily a negative factor that contributes to maladaptive outcomes among athletes and exercisers". One reason for this apparent disagreement is that perfectionism is a *multidimensional* construct with at least two components (Slaney et al., 2002) – adaptive perfectionism (e.g. striving to achieve high standards) and maladaptive perfectionism (e.g. displaying excessive concern about mistakes). In relation to making mistakes, research suggests that athletes who set impossibly high standards for their performances may feel anxious when things go wrong for them. Frost and Henderson (1991) discovered that athletes who displayed a significant concern for their mistakes (a key dimension of perfectionism) tended to experience more anxiety than did less perfectionistic colleagues. A similar problem is apparent in the performing arts. For example, the pianist Louis Lortie attributed stage fright and other forms of anxiety to the fact that "we were brought up with the idea that there shouldn't be mistakes" (cited in Blau, 1998, p. 17). Gotwals and Dunn (2009) developed a test of perfectionism in sport called the Sport Multidimensional Perfectionism Scale-2 (Sport-MPS-2). Support for the validity of this scale was provided by Gotwals et al. (2010).

Fear of failure

Many athletes are indoctrinated to adopt a "win at all costs" attitude, which ultimately makes them vulnerable to performance anxiety. If they believe that their self-esteem is tied inextricably to what they achieve, they are especially likely to become nervous at the prospect of defeat as it constitutes a threat to their self-worth. Although fear of failure may invoke performance anxiety some athletes appear to use this state as a motivational tool. For example, Dame Kelly Holmes, who won the 800m and 1500m races at the 2004 Olympic games in Athens, revealed that "the fear of failure drove me on as I hated the thought that I could come off the track feeling I hadn't done absolutely everything I could have to win" (cited in Crutchley, 2014). However, Holmes revealed that she felt the pressure to win was so great in the lead-up to the Olympics that she had suicidal thoughts and engaged in self-harm. Although some performers might claim that fear of failure acts as a source of motivation there seems little doubt that this is a highly undesirable state – one that is associated with a host of negative psychological and physical effects including shame and depression (see Conroy, 2001 for a review).

Lack of confidence

Some sport psychologists have speculated that athletes who have little confidence in their own abilities are likely to experience high levels of anxiety in competitive situations. This hypothesis is supported by research (e.g. J. Martin and Gill, 1991) which shows that runners who scored highly in self-confidence reported experiencing little cognitive anxiety. Koehn (2013) found positive correlations between confidence (intensity and direction) and anxiety symptoms (only directional perceptions) with flow state amongst a sample of junior tennis players. The results indicated that confidence may serve a protective function against debilitating anxiety interpretations.

Time to competition

Research suggests that different types of anxiety follow different temporal patterns before competition (Uphill, 2008). Specifically, whereas cognitive anxiety tends to remain high and stable in the days preceding an important competitive event, somatic anxiety remains relatively low until one or two days before this encounter. At this point, it tends to increase until the competition begins.

In summary, at least four conclusions have emerged from studying anxiety in athletes. First, even the world's best athletes get nervous before competition. Second, many athletes and coaches (e.g. José Mourinho, who is widely regarded as one of the top managers in world football) believe that competitive performance is determined significantly by the ability to control and channel one's nervous energy effectively. Third, we have learned that anxiety tends to affect people at different levels – via their thinking, feeling and behaviour. In short, anxiety causes athletes to think pessimistically about the future and to feel tense and agitated. Fourth, we have identified a number of antecedents of anxiety in athletes.

Measuring anxiety in athletes

In the previous section, we learned that the construct of anxiety has three different dimensions: cognitive, somatic and behavioural. Within sport psychology, attempts to measure anxiety have focused largely on the first and second of these dimensions, with fewer studies available on the behavioural aspect of this construct (but see Pijpers et al. (2003), who measured climbers' rigid posture and jerky muscular movement characteristics as behavioural indices of anxiety). Of the measures developed, the most popular tools for anxiety assessment have been self-report scales – probably as a result of the availability and convenience of these instruments – but psychophysiological measures are becoming increasingly popular.

Physiological measures

As anxiety is analogous to a fear reaction, it has a strong physiological basis. Thus Spielberger (1966, p. 17) proposed that anxiety states are "accompanied by or associated with activation of the autonomic nervous system". This activation results in such typical symptoms of anxiety as elevated heart rate, increased blood pressure, fast and shallow breathing, sweaty palms and tense musculature. If such indices could be measured conveniently, they would facilitate research in this area as they are relatively unaffected by **response sets** such as people's tendency to guess the purposes of questionnaire items so that they can present themselves in a maximally desirable light (a tendency called **social desirability**). Unfortunately, until the 1990s, physiological measures of anxiety were relatively rare in sport psychology for at least five reasons. First, there is no single, universally agreed physiological index of anxiety. Second, as athletes differ in the way in which they *interpret* autonomic arousal (i.e. as facilitative or debilitative of their performance), physiological measures of anxiety are of limited value. Third, most physiological measures assess *arousal* not anxiety. Fourth, physiological indices of arousal are not highly intercorrelated, a fact which suggests that they are not all measuring the same construct. Fifth, physiological assessment of athletes is time-consuming and inconvenient. For these reasons, researchers in sport psychology have tended to use self-report rather than physiological instruments to measure anxiety states in athletes. Since 2000, however, there has been a surge of interest among psychology researchers in the use of neuroendocrine responses (e.g. the release of hormones such as cortisol) to measure anxiety (recall the study by Strahler et al. 2010, discussed earlier in the section on components of anxiety). Additional research is required to establish the validity and utility of cortisol-based measures of anxiety in athletes.

Self-report instruments

Given their simplicity, brevity and convenience, paper-and-pencil tests of anxiety have proliferated in sport psychology research. Unfortunately, as we shall see, almost all of these instruments have psychometric limitations which threaten their validity. These limitations led Uphill (2008, p. 41) to conclude that we need a "healthy dose of skepticism when interpreting the results" of anxiety tests. With this caveat in mind, let us now briefly consider three of the most popular self-report instruments in this field – namely, the "Sport Competition Anxiety Test" (SCAT; R. Martens, 1977), the "Sport Anxiety Scale" (SAS; R. Smith et al., 1990; see also the SAS-2; R. Smith et al., 2006) and the "Competitive State Anxiety Inventory-2" (CSAI-2; R. Martens et al., 1990). (By the way, the "Mental Readiness Form" (MRF; Krane, 1994) was devised as a short version of the CSAI-2.) In general, these scales have focused largely on the measurement of anxiety intensity in athletes rather than on how anxiety is interpreted by them.

Sport Competition Anxiety Test

The SCAT (R. Martens, 1977) is a ten-item unidimensional inventory which purports to measure trait anxiety in sport performers. Parallel versions of this test are available for children (aged 10–14 years) and for adults (of 15 years and above). Typical items include "When I compete I worry about making mistakes" and "Before I compete I get a queasy feeling in my stomach". Respondents are required to indicate their agreement with each item by selecting their preferred answer from the three categories of "hardly ever", "sometimes" and "often". Reverse scoring is used on certain items (e.g. "Before I compete I feel calm") and overall test scores can range from 10 to 30. **Internal consistency coefficients** range from 0.8 to 0.9 and test–retest reliability values cluster around 0.77 (R. Smith et al., 1998). Validation studies suggest that the SCAT is mainly a measure of somatic anxiety (R. Smith et al., 1998). Evidence of convergent validity comes from studies which show that the test is correlated moderately with various general anxiety inventories. Unfortunately, as the SCAT does not distinguish between or measure adequately individual differences in cognitive and somatic anxiety, its utility is limited (R. Smith et al., 2006). A revised version of this instrument entitled the Competitive State Anxiety Inventory-2 (CSAI-2) was published by R. Martens et al. (1990).

Sport Anxiety Scale-2

The SAS-2 (R. Smith et al., 2006), which is a revised version of the SAS (R. Smith et al., 1990), is a multidimensional instrument that purports to measure individual differences in somatic anxiety, worry and concentration disruption in children (from the age of 9) and adults. It contains fifteen items that load onto three subscales, each comprising five items: somatic anxiety (e.g. "My body feels tense"), worry (e.g. "I worry that I will not play well") and concentration disruption (e.g. "It is hard to concentrate on the game"). According to R. Smith et al. (2006), the SAS-2 not only correlates highly ($r=0.90$) with its predecessor, the SAS – a sign of convergent validity – but also has strong reliability. For example, subscale reliabilities were estimated at 0.84 (for somatic anxiety), 0.89 (for worry) and 0.84 (for concentration disruption). In summary, the SAS-2 appears to be a reliable and valid measure of multidimensional anxiety in children and adults. The original version of the SAS contains twenty-one items which are divided into three subscales: somatic anxiety (nine items such as "I feel nervous"), worry (seven items such as "I have self-doubts") and a "concentration disruption" (five items such as "My mind wanders during sport competition") subscale. Reliability data for this scale are encouraging, with internal consistency estimated at between 0.88 (somatic anxiety), 0.87 (worry) and 0.69 (concentration-disruption) (J. Dunn et al., 2000) and test–retest figures at 0.77 for an inter-test interval of eighteen days (R. Smith et al., 1990). Evidence of convergent validity for this scale was reported by R. Smith et al. (1990), who calculated significant correlations (ranging between 0.47 and 0.81) between its subscales and the Sport Competition Anxiety Test (R. Martens, 1977). Discriminant validity for the SAS is supported by evidence of low correlations between it and general mental health measures (see R. Smith et al., 1998). Factor analyses have also confirmed that the SAS assesses three separate dimensions: somatic anxiety, cognitive anxiety/worry, and concentration-disruption (J. Dunn et al., 2000). Unfortunately, the SAS was not suitable for children – a fact that prompted the SAS-2.

Competitive State Anxiety Inventory-2

The CSAI-2 (R. Martens et al., 1990) is a popular test of cognitive and somatic anxiety. It comprises twenty-seven items which are divided into three subscales (with each containing nine items): cognitive anxiety, somatic anxiety and self-confidence. Typical items in the somatic anxiety subscale include "I feel nervous" and "My body feels tense". A sample item in the cognitive anxiety subscale is "I am concerned about losing". The "self-confidence" subscale is included in the test because a lack of confidence is believed to be a sign of cognitive anxiety (R. Martens et al., 1990). On a four-point scale (with 1 = "not at all" and 4 = "very much so"), respondents are required to rate the intensity of their anxiety experiences prior to competition. Following a review of forty-nine studies using the CSAI-2, Burton (1998) reported that internal consistency estimates for these three subscales ranged from 0.76 to 0.91. Doubts about the factorial validity of the CSAI-2 were raised by Lane et al. (1999). For example, these authors suggested that only one of the items on the cognitive anxiety subscale ("I have self-doubts") validly measures this type of anxiety. In response to some of the early criticisms of this scale (summarized in Uphill, 2008), a revised version of this test, called the Revised Competitive State Anxiety Inventory (CSAI-2R), was developed by Cox et al. (2003). This seventeen-item scale purports to measure the intensity components of cognitive anxiety (five items), somatic anxiety (seven items) and self-confidence (five items).

The previous section of the chapter indicated the importance of athletes' interpretations of their arousal symptoms. In this regard, the CSAI-2 is hampered by a significant methodological deficiency – namely, its neglect of the issue of "direction" or personal meaning of anxiety symptoms for athletes (G. Jones, 1995). To rectify this problem, some researchers advocate the addition of a *directional* measure to all "intensity" indices of anxiety (G. Jones and Swain, 1992). In this case, respondents may be required first to complete the CSAI-2 in order to elicit the intensity with which they experience the twenty-seven symptoms listed in this test. Then, they may be asked to rate the degree to which the experienced intensity of each symptom is facilitative or debilitative of their subsequent athletic performance. A seven-item Likert response scale is used, with values ranging from –3 (indicating "very negative") to +3 (indicating "very positive"). To illustrate, an athlete might respond with a maximum "4" to the statement "I am concerned about losing" but might then rate this concern with a +3 on the interpretation scale. Through these scores, the performer is indicating that he or she feels that this concern about losing is likely to have a facilitative effect on his or her forthcoming performance. With this modification, CSAI-2 **direction of anxiety** scores can vary between –27 and +27. Internal consistency reliability estimates for this facilitative/debilitative measure range from 0.72 (for the somatic anxiety subscale) to 0.83 (for the cognitive anxiety subscale) (Swain and Jones, 1996). When this directional modification scale has been used in conjunction with the CSAI-2, the resulting instrument is called the DM-CSAI-2 (Burton, 1998) or the CSAI-2(d) (M. Jones and Uphill, 2004). But how valid is this procedure? See Box 3.2.

Box 3.2 Thinking critically about ... research on direction of anxiety

In sport psychology, the term "direction of anxiety" refers to whether an athlete sees anxiety as facilitative or debilitative of athletic performance. To indicate the value of this variable, G. Jones and Swain (1992) added a Likert scale of directionality to each item of the Competitive State Anxiety Inventory-2 to explore the degree to which athletes viewed anxiety as facilitative of their performance. They also administered a test of competitiveness to each athlete. Results showed that highly competitive athletes believed more significantly in the facilitative effects of anxiety than did less successful counterparts. Another study by G. Jones et al. (1994) found that successful swimmers viewed their anxiety as being more facilitative of performance than did less successful swimmers – even though the groups did not differ significantly on anxiety intensity. Based on such evidence, G. Jones (1995) recommended a "directional modification" of the Competitive State Anxiety Inventory-2. Since the late 1990s, however, at least three conceptual and methodological criticisms of direction of anxiety have been raised, as well as an alternative model of the relationship between arousal and performance.

First, Burton (1998) has queried the rationale underlying G. Jones' approach. In particular, he wondered whether or not anxiety can ever be regarded as "facilitative". Is it possible that researchers have been confusing somatic anxiety with more positive emotional states such as excitement or challenge (see also J. Kerr, 1997)? Burton (1998) argued that **cognitive**

appraisal processes determine whether people experience a positive emotion, such as excitement/challenge, or a negative emotion, such as anxiety, when they are aroused in athletic competition. Clearly, more research is required to distinguish between the different emotional experiences of athletes. The second weakness of G. Jones' approach is that measurement of direction of anxiety relies on self-report data. As indicated in Chapter 1, however, people are not always reliable judges of their own behaviour. Therefore, we should not assume that athletes are always correct when they tell us that anxiety had a *facilitative* effect on their performance. Third, **reversal theory** (a conceptual model of motivation and emotion which suggests that people switch back and forth between different frames of mind: see J. Kerr, 1997) also highlights the importance of individual differences in the interpretation of arousal symptoms. For example, when athletes are in a **telic dominance** state (i.e. highly task oriented), high arousal may be interpreted as unpleasant anxiety whereas low anxiety may be interpreted as pleasant relaxation. By contrast, athletes who are in a **paratelic dominance** state (characterized by a fun-loving, present-centred focus) may regard high arousal as pleasantly exciting whereas they may perceive low arousal as unpleasant boredom. In summary, despite its intuitive plausibility, the concept of direction of anxiety has not been validated adequately in sport psychology.

Critical thinking questions

Can you think of a way of assessing whether anxiety facilitates or hampers athletic performance without using a **quantitative research** design or self-report scales? In particular, would qualitative research methodology (see Chapter 1) offer a viable alternative to the self-report approach? How could you validate athletes' insights into their own emotional experiences? Can reversal theory help to explain why athletes may switch from perceiving anxiety as facilitative to perceiving it as debilitative of their performance (see Hudson and Walker, 2002)?

Despite the issues raised in Box 3.2, several studies have supported the validity of the DM-CSAI-2. For example, G. Jones et al. (1994) discovered that elite swimmers reported that they had interpreted cognitive and somatic anxiety as being more facilitative of their performance than did their less successful counterparts. Not surprisingly, a significant proportion of the non-elite swimmers reported anxiety as being debilitative to their performance. Before we conclude this section, it should be noted that concern has been expressed about the psychometric adequacy of the CSAI-2. Briefly, Craft et al. (2003) conducted a meta-analysis of the association between this test and athletic performance. Unfortunately, relationships between the three subscales (cognitive anxiety, somatic anxiety and self-confidence) and sport performance were generally weak – thereby raising doubts about the construct validity of the CSAI-2.

Three-Factor Anxiety Inventory

The Three-Factor Anxiety Inventory is a twenty-five-item measure of performance anxiety. The inventory, developed by Cheng et al. (2009), comprises three subscales including cognitive anxiety (including worry and self-focus), physiological anxiety (autonomic hyperactivity and somatic tension) and the regulatory dimension of anxiety (perceived control). The scale is based on the first theoretical model in sport psychology that emphasizes the potentially adaptive nature of anxiety by highlighting its regulatory function. The authors argued that the scale addresses the failure of the CSAI-2 to consider the coping capacity involved in anxiety. The validation of this model came from a prospective study using a small group of elite athletes from one sport (see Cheng et al. 2009). Cheng and Hardy (2016) strengthened the generalizability of the construct validity of the model by administering the inventory to a sample of 1280 performers from a wide range of sports and found convergent evidence consistent with their hypothesis (e.g. the regulatory dimension of anxiety was strongly positively related with adaptive dimensions of perfectionism). Despite these promising results the authors acknowledge that the model would benefit from further validation.

Let us now consider in more detail the issue of how anxiety affects athletic performance.

Arousal, anxiety and athletic performance

At the beginning of this chapter, we suggested that the ability to regulate one's arousal level is a vital determinant of success in sport. Endorsing this principle, many athletes and coaches have developed informal methods of either energizing themselves or lowering their arousal levels before important competitions. For example, athletes who are involved in sports which require strength and power (e.g. wrestling and weightlifting) and/or physical contact (e.g. soccer, rugby) tend to favour "psych up" strategies such as listening to inspirational music in the hours or minutes before the competition begins (for a list of popular music tracks that are used for psych up purposes, see Karageorghis, 2008; see also Box 4.3 in Chapter 4 for a summary of some recent research on the effects of music on endurance performance). Of course, music is not the only psych up strategy used in sport: some coaches believe that if players are taunted or made *angry* before they compete, their performance will be improved. Laurent Seigne, the French rugby coach, is reported to have punched members of his team, Brive, before a match in order to psych them up appropriately (S. Jones, 1997). As yet, however, this theory has not been tested empirically in sport psychology – and ethical prohibitions make this possibility unlikely if not impossible! Arousal regulation strategies are also used in precision sports such as golf, snooker and archery where performers need to calm down in order to play well. For example, the American archer Darrell Pace, twice an Olympic gold medal winner, extolled the benefits of a controlled breathing technique as a preparation strategy before competitions. In this breathing technique, Pace synchronized the pattern of his inhalations and exhalations with covert repetition of the word "relax" (Vealey and Walter, 1994). Another way of dealing with anxiety in ball-sports is to exhale as one strikes the ball. This idea brings us to the controversial issue of "grunting" in tennis (see Box 3.3).

Box 3.3 Thinking critically about ... grunting in tennis: what a racket!

Since 2000, at almost all the leading international tennis tournaments, the distinctive "thwack" of the ball being hit by a racket has been drowned out by a rather more grating sound – the extraordinary grunt, moan, shriek or piercing wail that increasingly accompanies many tennis players' serves and groundstrokes. Although this problem may seem recent, grunting in tennis has been practised since the 1970s, with Jimmy Connors being one of its famous early exponents. Indeed, according to the journalist Clive James, Connors' grunt was faster than the ball he was hitting and his opponent had no option but to return the grunt *before* the ball (Fraser, 2009)!

The controversy raised by grunting in tennis may be presented as an argument between two factions. On one side of the fence, grunting has been complained about by players (who claim that it is a form of intimidation or gamesmanship), spectators (who regard it as an aural abomination that is incompatible with the genteel spirit of the game of tennis) and tennis officials (who have noted that a player's grunt can extend into the hitting preparation time of his or her opponent). Among these objectors is Martina Navratilova, the former world number 1 player, who proclaimed, "I call it cheating and it has to stop" (Navratilova, 2009). On the other side of the fence, the practice of grunting has been defended on the grounds that it is simply a habit resulting from a natural and harmless exhalation of air. In other words, it is simply a way of releasing tension by players. Indeed, Jo Durie, the former British champion, claimed that grunting can benefit a player's timing if it is performed quietly like a gentle exhale (Geoghegan, 2009). Interestingly, O'Connell et al. (2014) found that velocity, force and peak muscle activity (as measured using **electromyographic** data) during tennis serves and forehand strokes were enhanced significantly in a condition in which tennis players were allowed to grunt compared to a non-grunting condition. Similarly, the veteran tennis coach Nick Bollettieri believes that grunting *relaxes* players by helping them to release tension on court (Geoghegan, 2009). Although these rival arguments have been debated widely, what is not in dispute is the actual decibel level achieved by top tennis grunters. To illustrate, Maria Sharapova's grunts have been recorded at 101 decibels – about 9 decibels below the sound of a lion's roar (Flatman, 2009)! The Williams sisters are also inveterate grunters, with 2009 Wimbledon champion Serena reaching 93.2 decibels and Venus hitting 85 decibels (Morrissey, 2009). Debate about this issue came to a head in the 2009 French Open when a French player, Aravane Rezai, complained that the shrieks of her teenage opponent, the Portuguese player Michelle Larcher de Brito, were distracting her. No action was taken against the "grunter" on this occasion, however.

Moving from speculation to science, does grunting *actually* give tennis players an advantage over their rivals? The first study to address this question empirically was published by Sinnett and Kingstone (2010). Briefly, these researchers created a number of video clips of a professional tennis player hitting the ball either to the left or right of a video camera. These clips were edited to include an accompanying grunt or not. Then, a sample of recreational tennis players was required to indicate, as quickly and as accurately as possible, the direction of the shot in each clip. Results showed that

continued ...

Box 3.3 continued

participants' response times and accuracy were significantly adversely affected by the presence of grunting sounds. What are the precise mechanisms underlying this effect? Farhead and Punt (2015) sought to shed light on this issue and found that grunting had a disruptive effect on participants' serve-speed perception. Accordingly, grunting may act as a form of auditory masking (the possibility that grunting prevents opponents from hearing the sound of the ball being struck by the racket) which hinders their ability to plan their own shots. Further research is required to corroborate this interesting finding. In conclusion, despite the preceding findings, there are no explicit *rules* against grunting in tennis. An umpire *can* penalize a player for "noise hindrance", but it is up to the official to decide whether such noise is intentional or not.

Critical thinking questions

The professional tennis community is divided on the issue of grunting. What do you make of Michelle Larcher de Brito's claim that "nobody can tell me to stop grunting. Tennis is an individual sport and I'm an individual player" (cited in Fraser, 2009, p. 77). How does this view compare with Martina Navratilova's opinion that grunting is a diversionary tactic that prevents opposing players from using auditory cues to anticipate the type of shot that is being played by the grunter. Can you think of a way of extending Sinnett and Kingstone's (2010) research to arbitrate between "masking" and "attentional" explanations of the adverse effects of grunting?

Theories of arousal–performance and anxiety–performance relationships

Although the preceding discussion has highlighted the importance of arousal control to athletes, it does not really illuminate the relationship between anxiety and performance. Fortunately, there is a considerable empirical research literature on this topic (e.g. see reviews by Gould et al., 2002b; M. Wilson, 2008; Woodman and Hardy, 2003). Let us now evaluate briefly the main theories and findings emerging from this research literature. Since the early 1990s, a considerable amount of psychological research has been conducted on the relationship between people's arousal levels and their subsequent performance on skilled tasks. In general, this research has been influenced by at least five main theories: **drive theory** (based on Hull, 1943), the **inverted-U hypothesis** (based on Yerkes and Dodson, 1908), **catastrophe theory** (e.g. L. Hardy, 1990, 1996; L. Hardy and Parfitt, 1991; L. Hardy et al., 2007), the **conscious processing hypothesis** or **reinvestment hypothesis** (R. Masters, 1992; R. Masters and Maxwell, 2008) and **attentional control theory** (Eysenck et al., 2007). Although the earlier theories (e.g. drive theory, the inverted-U hypothesis) applied mainly to arousal–performance relationships, the more recent ones (e.g. catastrophe theory, conscious processing hypothesis and attentional control theory) deal more with anxiety–performance relationships. Other theoretical approaches such as the **individual zone of optimal functioning** hypothesis (Hagtvet and Hanin, 2007; Hanin, 1997) and reversal theory (J. Kerr, 1997) have also been postulated.

Drive theory

In learning theory, a "drive" is regarded as a psychological state of arousal that is created by an imbalance in the homeostatic mechanisms of the body and that impels the organism to take ameliorative action. In general, two types of drives have been identified (Cashmore, 2008). Primary drives arise from the pursuit of basic biological needs such as eating, drinking and restoring homeostasis (or the internal equilibrium of the body). Secondary drives are stimuli (e.g. earning money, winning titles) that acquire the motivational characteristics of primary drives as a result of conditioning or other forms of learning. Applied to sport, drive theory postulates a positive and linear relationship between arousal level and performance. In other words, the more aroused an athlete is, the better his or her performance should be. Initially, support for this theory was claimed by researchers like Oxendine (1984), who argued that in power and/or speed sports such as weightlifting or sprinting, a high level of arousal tends to enhance athletic performance. Although superficially plausible, this theory does not stand up to scientific scrutiny. Consider the problem of false starts in sprinting. Here, athletes may become so aroused physiologically that they anticipate wrongly and end up "jumping the gun". This very problem occurred in the 1996 Olympic Games when the British sprinter Linford Christie made *two* false starts in the 100 metres race and was subsequently disqualified. Since 2010, athletes who make even *one* false start are disqualified from races. In the 100 metres final at the 2011 World Athletics Championships, the world record holder Usain Bolt (see also Chapter 5) was disqualified because he had made a single false start. In an effort to counteract this problem of over-anticipation, official starters in sprint competitions tend to use variable foreperiods before firing their pistols. Similar problems stemming from over-arousal can occur in weightlifting when athletes fail to "chalk up" before lifting the barbell. In team sports, over-arousal may be prompted by rousing pep talks delivered by a coach to his or her players before a game. Such talks may capture the attention of the players, especially if they refer to alleged insults by opponents. Thus Jeremy Guscott, the former England and Lions rugby player, remarked that "nothing is a better motivator than being bad-mouthed by the opposition" (Guscott, 1997, p. 44). In one of the few studies to explore how pep talks might channel players' arousal Gonzalez et al. (2011) found that a simulated pep talk (involving a movie clip of a coach giving an inspirational speech) resulted in greater emotional dominance amongst collegiate football players but had no effect on their arousal. Recall from Chapter 2 that motivation requires *direction* as well as intensity. Clearly, the problem with rousing pep talks is that they usually lack this important directional component (Anshel, 1995).

The inverted-U hypothesis

According to the inverted-U hypothesis (Oxendine, 1984), the relationship between arousal and performance is curvilinear rather than linear. In other words, increased arousal is postulated to improve skilled performance up to a certain point, beyond which further increases in arousal may impair it. To illustrate this theory, imagine being required to sit an examination just after you wake up (low arousal) or after you have run a marathon (high arousal). At both of these extreme ends of the arousal continuum, your academic performance would probably be poor, whereas if you had a good night's sleep and felt properly prepared for the exam, you should perform at your best. This proposition that arousal has diminishing returns on task performance is derived from the Yerkes–Dodson law (Yerkes and Dodson, 1908). Briefly, this law proposed that there is an optimal level of arousal for performance on any task. Specifically, performance tends to be poor at low or high levels of arousal but is best at intermediate levels of arousal. A summary of the Yerkes–Dodson law is presented in Box 3.4.

Box 3.4 In the spotlight Of mice and men (and women) ... the Yerkes–Dodson law

Although the Yerkes–Dodson law is widely cited in sport psychology, its origins lie in research on animal learning in the early 1900s. Specifically, in 1908, Robert Yerkes and John Dodson reported experiments on the relationship between arousal level and task difficulty. Briefly, they devised a paradigm in which mice could avoid electrical shocks by entering the brighter of two compartments. Arousal level was varied by changing the intensity of the electrical shocks administered to the mice. Task difficulty was manipulated by varying the contrast in brightness between the two compartments. Results showed that the amount of practice required by the mice to learn the discrimination task increased as the difference in brightness between the compartments decreased. In other words, when the task was easy (i.e. when the brighter compartment was easy to identify), the mice performed best at high levels of arousal (i.e. larger electric shocks). However, when the task was difficult (i.e. when there was little difference between the brightness of the two compartments), the mice performed best at low levels of arousal (i.e. small electrical shocks). These findings led Yerkes and Dodson (1908, pp. 481–482) to conclude that "an easily acquired habit, that is, one which does not demand difficult sense discrimination or complex associations, may readily be formed under strong stimulation, whereas a difficult habit may be acquired readily only under relatively weak stimulation". Thus the Yerkes–Dodson law consists of two parts.

Part one suggests that people's performance on skilled tasks is best when their level of arousal is intermediate and that it deteriorates as their arousal either increases or decreases from that optimal level. In other words, the relationship between arousal and performance looks like an inverted "U". For example, when you are either drowsy (under-aroused) or very excited (over-aroused), it is difficult to do an exam to the best of your ability. Part two of the Yerkes–Dodson law suggests that as the complexity of a skill increases, the amount of arousal required for optimal performance of it *decreases*. In other words, the performance of difficult tasks decreases as arousal increases whereas the performance of easy tasks increases as arousal increases. In summary, the Yerkes–Dodson law suggests that optimal performance occurs when people's arousal levels are intermediate in strength. Further details of this law may be found in Teigen (1994).

If the Yerkes–Dodson theory is correct, athletic performance that occurs under conditions of either high or low arousal should be inferior to that displayed at intermediate levels. This hypothesis has received some empirical support. For example, Klavora (1978) found that within a sample of high-school basketball players, the highest levels of performance were displayed by people who had reported moderate levels of somatic anxiety. Unfortunately, despite its plausibility, the Yerkes–Dodson principle is marred by at least four conceptual and methodological weaknesses. First, as Landers and Arent (2010) pointed out, the inverted-U hypothesis does not provide a satisfactory explanation of arousal–performance relationships because it does not address the putative internal mechanisms underlying it. Second, as we learned earlier, it is not easy to devise or agree on a satisfactory independent measure of the construct of arousal. As a result, researchers find it difficult to decide whether a given arousal level is too low or too high for a performer. Third, there is an inherent flaw at the heart of this law. In particular, as researchers cannot predict in advance the point of diminishing returns for the effects of arousal on skilled performance, the inverted-U hypothesis is "immune to falsification" (Neiss, 1988, p. 353). Fourth, researchers disagree about the best way in which to induce different levels of arousal in participants. For ethical reasons, contemporary investigators cannot use electric shocks or other forms of aversive stimuli for this purpose – unlike their predecessors Yerkes and Dodson (1908). In summary, the inverted-U theory has several flaws as a possible explanation of the link between arousal and performance. Perhaps most significantly, it does not elucidate putative theoretical mechanisms which might account for the link between arousal and performance. Thus the inverted-U is "a general prediction, not a theory that explains how, why, or precisely when arousal affects performance" (Gould et al., 2002b, p. 214). Unfortunately, despite these limitations, this hypothesis has been promulgated as an established fact by some applied sport psychologists. To illustrate, G. Winter and Martin (1991, p. 17) used it to justify their advice to tennis players on "controlling 'psych' levels".

Catastrophe theory

The cusp catastrophe theory of anxiety (e.g. L. Hardy, 1990, 1996; L. Hardy and Parfitt, 1991; L. Hardy et al., 2007) is based on the assumption that anxiety is a multidimensional construct comprising a cognitive component and a physiological arousal component. This theory is different from the two previous arousal–performance models in proposing that physiological arousal *interacts* with certain aspects of anxiety (in this case, cognitive state anxiety or worry) to influence athletic performance. More precisely, this theory postulates that arousal is associated with athletic performance in a manner described by the inverted-U curve – but only when athletes have low cognitive state anxiety (i.e. when they are not worried). When cognitive anxiety is high, however, increases in arousal tend to improve performance up to a certain point beyond which further increases may produce a swift, dramatic and discontinuous (hence the term "catastrophic") decline in performance rather than a slow or gradual deterioration. Therefore, the cornerstone of catastrophe theory is the assumption that arousal may have different effects on athletic performance depending on the prevailing level of cognitive anxiety in the performer.

Based on this assumption, at least two predictions are possible (Gould et al., 2002b). First, the interaction of physiological arousal and cognitive state anxiety will determine athletic performance more than will the absolute value of either variable alone. Thus high cognitive anxiety should enhance performance at low levels of physiological arousal but should hinder performance at relatively higher levels of arousal. This prediction is interesting because it suggests that, contrary to popular opinion, cognitive anxiety does not always hamper performance (L. Hardy, 1997). The second prediction is that when an athlete experiences high cognitive anxiety, the arousal–performance curve should follow a different path under conditions of increasing versus decreasing physiological arousal (a phenomenon known as "hysteresis"). This hypothesis was supported, in part, by Vickers and Williams (2007), who discovered that a high level of cognitive anxiety combined with a high level of physiological arousal sometimes led to "choking" (see later in chapter) among biathlon performers – but not when these athletes were able to pay attention to task-relevant information. Put differently, these authors showed that visual attentional processes mediate the relationship between anxiety and performance. Although the cusp catastrophe theory has received some empirical support in sport psychology (e.g. see Edwards et al., 2002), it has also been challenged. A. Cohen et al. (2003) found no support for the hysteresis hypothesis in a dart-throwing task. The complexity of catastrophe theory (stemming from its three-dimensional nature) renders it difficult to test. Nevertheless, this approach remains an intriguing model which deserves additional empirical scrutiny.

Conscious processing (or reinvestment) hypothesis

The conscious processing (or reinvestment) hypothesis (CPH; R. Masters, 1992; R. Masters and Maxwell, 2008) attempts to investigate what happens when people become conscious of the task-related movements that they are performing. It has generated a considerable amount of research in sport and exercise psychology (see review by R. Masters and Maxwell, 2008) – especially with regard to the relationship between conscious (motor) processing and skilled performance under anxiety-provoking conditions. It was spawned, in part, by an attempt to explain the well-known "paralysis-by-analysis" phenomenon whereby skilled performance tends to deteriorate whenever people try to exert conscious control over movements that had previously been under automatic control (see Figure 3.4). Note that once a skill has become automatic, its execution is implemented implicitly and does not require the resources of working memory (a cognitive system that regulates the storage and manipulation of currently relevant information).

According to R. Masters (1992), the performance impairment suffered by skilled but highly anxious athletes is caused mainly by the disruption of automatic control processes. To explain in more detail, when athletes experience increases in their anxiety levels, they attempt to ensure task success by reverting

Figure 3.4 Over-analysis can unravel people's sport skills

to a mode of conscious control that is associated mainly with an *early* stage of motor learning (i.e. one that relies on explicit rules and that typically results in slow and effortful movements). This temporary regression is held to involve a "reinvestment" of **cognitive processes** in perceptual-motor control. So, the conscious processing hypothesis postulates that performance breakdown occurs when performers "reinvest" their verbal knowledge of task components in an effort to consciously control their movements. This reinvestment is most likely to happen, according to R. Masters and Maxwell (2008), in pressure situations. In other words, anxiety is postulated to exert its debilitating influence upon performance by *increasing a participant's self-consciousness* of their movements. This heightened self-consciousness may result in the performer manipulating "conscious, explicit, rule based knowledge, by working memory, to control the mechanics of one's movements during motor output" (R. Masters and Maxwell, 2004, p. 208). If this conscious processing theory is correct, anxiety should have *differential* effects on skilled performance – depending on how the skill had been acquired originally (i.e. whether it had been learned explicitly or implicitly).

In an effort to test this prediction using the skill of golf putting, R. Masters (1992) devised an intriguing experimental paradigm in which participants who acquired the skill of golf putting using explicit knowledge subsequently experienced impaired performance when tested under conditions of high anxiety. To explain this experiment in more detail, participants were initially required to perform putting skills in both training and testing phases. Two conditions were crucial to the experiment. In the explicit condition, participants were instructed to read coaching manuals on golf putting. Conversely, in the implicit condition, participants were given no instructions but had to putt golf balls while performing a secondary task which had been designed to prevent them from thinking about the instructions on putting. There were four training sessions in which participants had to try to hole one hundred golf balls. The number of putts holed was measured in each case. After the fourth training session, a source of stress was introduced. This stress was induced by a combination of evaluation apprehension (e.g. requesting an alleged golfing expert to judge their putting performance) and financial inducement. Results suggested that the implicit learning group showed no deterioration in performance under stress in contrast to the golfers in the explicit learning condition. R. Masters (1992) interpreted this to mean that the skills of athletes with a small pool of explicit knowledge were less likely to fail than were those of performers with relatively larger amounts of explicit knowledge. In other words, the prediction of the conscious processing theory was corroborated. Anxiety appears to have *different* effects on performance depending on how the skill was acquired in the first place (i.e. through *explicit* or *implicit* learning). Subsequently, R. Masters et al. (1993) developed a measure of individual differences in dispositional reinvestment – or people's tendency to attempt to gain conscious control over an automatic skill in pressure situations – called the Reinvestment Scale. This twenty-item scale purports to measure the extent of people's self-consciousness in everyday situations.

However, Masters recognized that the Reinvestment Scale suffered from a number of limitations (e.g. it did not directly specify movement) and decided to develop a movement specific version of the original scale which was subsequently termed the Movement Specific Reinvestment Scale (MSRS). The scale yielded two movement related factors referred to as *movement self-consciousness* and *conscious motor processing*. Predictive validity for the scale has been found in sport where "high reinvesters" display greater susceptibility to skill failure under pressure compared to "low reinvesters", and in rehabilitation settings where "high reinvesting" stroke patients report greater difficulty in regaining functional independence than their low reinvesting counterparts. Although these results point to the potential dangers associated with "reinvesting" conscious attention in proceduralized skills, it is important to note that some confusion exists concerning the relative influence of different "types" of reinvestment. To explain, Malhotra et al. (2015) argued that *conscious motor processing* may represent an individual's propensity to control movement mechanics while *movement self-consciousness* reflects a tendency to hold concerns about one's "style" of movement (i.e. how it might appear to onlookers). Interestingly, the authors argue that while conscious motor processing (i.e. deliberately controlling an aspect of one's movement) may prove deleterious to the performance of well-learned movements, high levels of movement self-consciousness (which involves "conscious monitoring", that is, attending to one's movement as skill execution unfolds) might allow performers to utilize exteroceptive (visual, auditory) and kinesthetic (tactile) feedback to assess the discrepancy between actual and desired movement patterns. This intriguing possibility warrants experimental investigation. Kinrade et al. (2010) modified the original reinvestment scale to create a decision-specific version of the scale. Decision-Specific Reinvestment Scale scores of fifty-nine skilled team sport players were found to be highly correlated with coaches' ratings of players' tendency to choke under pressure ($r=0.74$). High scores on this scale are indicative of greater susceptibility to poorer decision making under pressure. This scale has been validated in a number of recent studies (e.g. Laborde et al., 2014).

To summarize, the conscious processing hypothesis predicts that athletes whose cognitive anxiety increases will tend to revert to conscious control of normally automatic skills. This theory has received considerable empirical support in sport and exercise psychology (R. Masters and Maxwell, 2008). For example, many experimental studies have shown that people's performance deteriorates when pressure manipulations require them to consciously attend to their movements (e.g. see Pijpers et al., 2003; M. Wilson et al., 2007b).

Attentional control theory

Attentional control theory (ACT: Derakshan and Eysenck, 2009; Eysenck et al., 2007), which is a successor to **processing efficiency theory** (PET: Eysenck and Calvo, 1992), was postulated to investigate theoretical relationships between anxiety, working memory (our mental system for storing and manipulating currently relevant information for a brief period of time) and skilled performance. ACT and PET make three key assumptions. First, they assume that we can distinguish between performance *effectiveness* (i.e. the quality of task performance) and performance *efficiency* (i.e. the relationship between performance effectiveness and use of processing resources). Second, they assume that anxiety impairs processing efficiency more than performance effectiveness. Third, both theories assume that cognitive anxiety (or worrying) impairs the efficiency of the central executive component of the working memory system and diverts the performer's attention from task-relevant to *task-irrelevant* information. ACT, however, goes beyond PET in addressing the putative theoretical mechanisms by which anxiety impairs cognitive performance.

To explain, a central prediction of ACT is that anxiety hampers performance via "attentional control" – which is a key function of the central executive. According to Corbetta and Shulman (2002), there are two attentional systems – one influenced by a person's current goals and expectations (a top-down, goal-driven system) and the other, a bottom-up, stimulus driven system which is triggered by salient environmental events. According to ACT, anxiety affects attentional control. Specifically, it "disrupts the balance between these two systems by enhancing the influence of the stimulus driven, bottom-up processes over the efficient top-down goal-driven processes" (Derakshan and Eysenck, 2009, p. 170). Furthermore, ACT predicts that anxiety "increases attention to task irrelevant stimuli (especially threat-related)" and "reduces attentional focus on concurrent task demands" (Derakshan and Eysenck, 2009, p. 170). More precisely, ACT predicts that anxiety disrupts performance not only by impairing *attentional inhibition* (the process by which, under normal circumstances, people can restrain themselves from directing their attention at task-irrelevant factors) but also by impairing *attentional shifting* (the process by which people can normally switch their attention in response to changing task requirements).

Research provides some empirical support for the predictions of ACT. M. Wilson et al. (2009) used **eye-tracking technology** (see also Chapters 5 and 7) to analyse the visual search behaviour of soccer players as they prepared to take penalties in five-a-side matches (where there is a smaller distance between the goal posts than in eleven-a-side matches) under various conditions of anxiety. Results supported a prediction of ACT by indicating that when anxious, the penalty takers displayed an attentional bias towards a salient and threatening stimulus (the goalkeeper) rather than to the ideal target for their kick (just inside the goal post). Extending this research, G. Wood and Wilson (2010) investigated the performance of experienced footballers who took penalties while wearing eye-tracking equipment under counterbalanced conditions of threat (low versus high) and goalkeeper movement (stationary versus arm-waving). Results revealed that under high-threat conditions, the kickers found it difficult to disengage their attention from the moving/distracting goalkeepers – which again corroborates the predictions of ACT. Eysenck and Wilson (2016) recently presented an extension of the ACT (namely the Attentional Control Theory: Sport; ACTS). The ACTS focuses more than ACT on the factors which jointly determine an individual's anxiety level in competition. One of the ACTS main predictions is that pressure will prove deleterious to performance if it promotes anxiety via attentional and interpretative biases for threat-related information. Athletes who lack these biases are likely to outperform those who possess them because they are less likely to believe that losing in high-pressured environments will have high costs. Further research is required in sport psychology to test the predictions of this emerging theory of the relationship between anxiety and performance.

Conclusions about arousal–performance and anxiety–performance relationship

At least three general conclusions have emerged from the preceding theories and research (see also Weinberg and Gould, 2007). First, anxiety and arousal are multidimensional constructs which do not have simple linear relationships with athletic performance. Second, increases in physiological arousal and cognitive state anxiety do not inevitably lead to a deterioration in athletic performance. Recall that the effects of both of these variables depend crucially on how the performer *interprets* the perceived changes in arousal. For example, increased arousal may be perceived as energizing rather than overwhelming and hence facilitative of performance. Third, the interaction between arousal and cognitive anxiety seems to be more important in determining performance than is the absolute value of either variable on its own. With these general conclusions in mind, let us now consider what happens when anxiety hampers athletic performance.

Performance anxiety in sport: "choking" under pressure

Earlier in the chapter, we learned that the term anxiety is derived from the Latin word *angere*, which means "to choke". Not surprisingly, the phenomenon of **choking under pressure**, whereby athletic performance is suddenly impaired by intense anxiety, has attracted both popular interest (e.g. Beilock, 2010a; Dobson, 1998) and scientific scrutiny (e.g. Gucciardi and Dimmock, 2008; Hill and Hemmings, 2015; Otten, 2009). As we shall see in Box 3.5, however, researchers disagree not only about how to define this term but also about the psychological mechanisms that explain its impact on behaviour. Nevertheless, choking is such a ubiquitous experience among competitive athletes that it has a variety of sport-specific synonyms, such as "icing" (in basketball), "dartitis" (in darts) and the "yips" (in golf). Although it affects athletes of all levels of ability and/or experience, choking is especially prevalent among performers of individual precision sports such as golf, tennis, snooker, darts and cricket. To illustrate, successful golfers like Greg Norman, Stewart Cink, Scott Hoch, Jean van de Velde (who led by three strokes at the final hole of 1999 Open Championship at Carnoustie but who triple-bogied it before losing to Paul Lawrie in a play-off: P. Dixon and Kidd, 2006) and more recently, the Irish prodigy Rory McIlroy, who squandered a four-shot lead in the final round of the 2011 US Masters championship in Augusta and ended up shooting an 8 over par score of 80 and finishing ten shots behind the winner, Charl Schwartzel. Despite this setback, McIlroy displayed remarkable mental strength to win the next major championship that he played after the US Masters – namely, the 2011 US Open (see Figure 3.5). Of course, choking also happens in team sports. For example, in 2004, the New York Yankees became the first team in baseball history to lose a best-of-seven series, having held a 3–0 lead against the Boston Red Sox (Viner, 2011). Choking is widespread in soccer. For example, consider how some of the world's best footballers appear to crumble under the pressure of penalty-taking (see Box 3.5).

Unfortunately, choking not only is debilitating but also can affect athletes over a long period of time. For example, the Welsh golfer Ian Woosnam admitted that he had suffered from the "yips" for three years. More precisely, he said:

> it got to the stage where the right hand would suddenly jerk into action and you'd putt to the left ... Then, as it goes on, you don't know where the right path is and you get even more tense. I was suffering so much when I got onto the green I was feeling physically sick.

> (cited in White, 2002b, p. 22)

Fortunately, this problem disappeared when he made a technical adjustment to his stroke by switching to a "broom handle" putter. Similarly, Eric Bristow, who won the world darts championship five times, choked so badly at times that he could not release the dart from his fingers. It took him years to overcome this problem (Middleton, 1996). Other athletes have not been so lucky. The former snooker star Patsy Fagan had to abandon the sport because of his failure to overcome anxiety problems which affected his cueing action (Dobson, 1998).

Figure 3.5 Rory McIlroy displayed remarkable mental strength to win the 2011 US Open golf championship (*source:* courtesy of Inpho photography)

Box 3.5 In the spotlight   Choking under pressure in soccer: why do top players miss penalty kicks?

Ever since the penalty shootout was introduced by the Fédération Internationale de Football Association (FIFA) in 1970 to resolve elimination matches when two teams are tied after extra time, it has attracted praise and controversy in equal measure. But is it really a test of players' nerve and skill or merely a contest based entirely on chance? At first glance, the penalty kick presents a straightforward technical challenge. It is a self-paced task in which the kicker tries to beat the goalkeeper from a distance of approximately 11 metres. Furthermore, the kicker is allowed to place the static ball on the penalty spot and no interference to his or her "run-up" or kick is allowed from other players. But closer examination of the psychological factors involved in penalty taking raises an obvious question. Specifically, if penalty kicks are so easy to take, why do so many top professional players miss them in important matches (e.g. recall the misses of Italy's Roberto Baggio against Brazil in the 1994 World Cup final and of England's Gareth Southgate against Germany in the European Championship semi-final in 1996)?

Some possible answers to this question have emerged from empirical studies on the anxiety mechanisms underlying poor penalty taking in soccer. For example, consider the research of Jordet and his colleagues (e.g. Jordet, 2009; Jordet and Hartman, 2008; Jordet et al., 2006, 2007) on choking in penalty takers in major international soccer tournaments. Jordet et al. (2006) investigated the relationship between players' *perception of control* and penalty outcome. He discovered that players who felt that a penalty shootout was a lottery were more likely to miss their shots than those who believed that they were in control of the outcome of the kick. Furthermore, Jordet and Hartman (2008) found that a key factor associated with penalty misses was the *immediate importance* of the shot. To illustrate, consider the success rate of penalty kicks in situations either where a kicker's shot can ensure that his or her team wins, or alternatively, where *missing* the kick can mean instant defeat for his or her team. Jordet and Hartman (2008) discovered that in the latter situations (i.e. in cases of shots where a miss instantly produces a team loss), players typically respond anxiously (e.g. by speeding up their preparation for the kick) and perform considerably worse than in situations where a successful kick can ensure an immediate team win. This might represent a form of escapist behaviour where the player tries to get the situation "over and done with" as quickly as possible. Unfortunately, this action might contribute to the goalkeeper forming a negative impression of the penalty taker and may actually increase their confidence in saving the penalty kick (Furley et al., 2012). According to Keh (2010), whereas the success rate for kickers whose penalties can mean an immediate win for their teams is about 92 per cent, it drops to about 60 per cent for players whose missed penalties would lead to instant defeat for their teams. Jordet (2009) discovered from analysis of video footage taken at major international tournaments that publicly esteemed "superstar" players (i.e. those who had received prestigious awards for their skills) tended to perform worse than less renowned players in penalty shootouts – presumably because of the perceived pressure they experienced.

Interestingly, recent evidence (see Misirlisoy and Haggard, 2014) suggests that goalkeepers may be prone to what is known as the "gambler's fallacy" (e.g. when we flip a coin a number of times and there is a run of "heads" and subsequently believe that there is now an increased chance that the next flip will be "tails"). This example represents a fallacy as there is actually a fifty–fifty chance of "heads" or "tails" on every toss – irrespective of the length of a preceding sequence of tosses. Misirlisoy and Haggard (2014) found that after a series of penalty kicks taken in the same direction (e.g. to the left hand side of the goal) that goalkeepers were more likely to dive in the opposite direction (i.e. to the right) at the next kick. The authors argued that if penalty takers paid close attention to the sequence of the preceding kicks they will be better able to predict where the goalkeeper will dive next. By contrast, goalkeepers may be best advised to vary the direction in which they dive as they are more likely to be exploited by the penalty taker if they produce a specific pattern of dives.

Less dramatically, anxiety has prompted remarkable collapses in the performance of such athletes as Jana Novotna and Greg Norman. To illustrate, consider what happened in the 1993 Wimbledon Ladies' Singles final between Jana Novotna (Czech Republic) and Steffi Graf (Germany). Serving at 4–1 in the third set, with a point for 5–1, Novotna began to lose control. She produced a double fault and some wild shots to lose that game. Later, she served *three* consecutive double faults in her anxiety to increase her 4–3 lead over Graf (Thornley, 1993, p. 6). Interestingly, Novotna played in a similar fashion in the third round of the 1995 French Open championship in Paris when she lost a match to the American player Chanda Rubin despite having nine match points when leading 5–0, 40–0 in the third set. The golfer Jean Van De Velde surrendered a three-shot lead on the final hole of the 1999 British Open Championship in Carnoustie and subsequently lost out in a play-off to Paul Lawrie. Likewise, the American golfer John Daly admitted that "when the heat was on, I choked" (*The Title*, 1998) in the 1998 golf World Cup in New Zealand. Interestingly, in the case of Daly, a curious moderating factor was at work – namely, the effects of alcohol. Daly believed that the effects of anxiety on his golf performance had been intensified by the fact that he had given up drinking before the tournament. Ironically, Daly's sobriety had caused him to feel more nervous than he would have been in the past:

> Usually, when I have that situation I don't feel the pressure, I usually just knock them in. But now it's totally different. I guess I used to be so drunk I didn't care. Now it's tough, I feel all the nerves and the pressure more than ever.
>
> (*The Title*, 1998)

In summary, the preceding examples show clearly that choking is a potentially significant problem for many athletes. But what do we really know about the nature and causes of this problem?

What exactly is choking?

The term choking is used by sport psychologists to refer to a phenomenon in which athletic performance is impaired suddenly by anxiety. Baumeister (1984) offered an early and seminal definition of this term when he claimed that it referred to "the occurrence of suboptimal performance under pressure conditions" (Baumeister and Showers, 1986, p. 362). But there are at least three problems with this definition. First, as Hill et al. (2010a) pointed out, for any suboptimal performance to be regarded as a choke in sport, and hence distinguished from a random lapse, we must be sure that the athlete in question was *capable* of performing better, was *motivated* sufficiently to succeed, and perceived the sport situation as *important*. Second, Gucciardi and Dimmock (2008) argued that the deterioration in performance that characterizes choking should be *significant* – not trivial. Third, as Hill et al. (2010a) noted, in order to qualify as a choke, the performance impairment should be *acute* rather than gradual. Mesagno and Hill (2013) recently sought to bring clarity to this issue by arguing that there appears to be a number of factors that distinguish a choke from an *underperformance* including: (1) the magnitude of the performance decrement, (2) negative cognitive appraisal of anxiety, (3) a lack of perceived control, and (4) self-presentational concerns. They also argued that choking arises when the performer has a strong desire to succeed rather than when performance is compromised by physiological factors such as injury and fatigue. Furthermore, they point to their own work (see Hill et al., 2011) which has shown that recovering performance proficiency after a choking episode is hampered by the continued presence of negative affect. Regardless of these semantic issues, choking is an intriguing mental state because it stems from a motivational paradox. To explain, in the pressure situations that prompt choking, the more effort the athlete puts into his or her performance, the *worse* it becomes. Put simply, choking occurs paradoxically because people try *too* hard to perform well.

The symptoms of choking are similar to those of any arousal state (see earlier in chapter). They include tense muscles, shaky limbs, rapid heart and pulse rates, shortness of breath, butterflies in the stomach, racing thoughts and feelings of panic. In addition, choking may involve the sensation that one cannot complete the stroke or movement that one intends. In this way, choking is similar to another form of performance failure called the yips (a type of focal dystonia). Golfers who suffer from this condition often feel themselves getting tense over the ball and struggle to complete a putting stroke without interference from sudden involuntary movements. Likewise, bowlers in cricket who suffer from anxiety attacks suddenly feel as if they cannot release the ball. Phil Edmonds, the former Middlesex and England bowler, was so badly afflicted with anxiety that he ended up standing in the crease and lobbing the ball at the batter's end (Middleton, 1996). Choking reactions may also be characterized by a tiny muscular spasm that occurs just as the stroke is about to be executed even in practice situations. Eric Bristow, a world champion in darts for three consecutive years, revealed: "I had it so bad I was even getting it when I was practising ... It took me six or seven years to sort it out" (cited in Dobson, 1998, p. 16). Unfortunately, although Bristow claimed that he had rid himself of this problem he never enjoyed the same success that he had experienced earlier in his career.

Before concluding this section, it should be noted that choking seems to occur more frequently in untimed individual sports (e.g. golf, tennis) than in timed team games (e.g. football, rugby). As yet, however, the precise reasons for this phenomenon remain unknown. Happily, some progress has been made in understanding the aetiology of the "yips" in golf (see Clarke et al., 2015, for a recent review). Briefly, A. Smith et al. (2003) distinguished between two types of yips phenomena on the basis of whether they were caused by neurological or psychological factors. "Type 1" yips was postulated to reflect a neurological condition called dystonia, in which a deterioration occurs in the motor pathways involving the basal ganglia. "Type 2" yips probably results from severe performance anxiety or choking. These authors speculated that golfers who suffer from the neurologically mediated type 1 yips may have to learn a new stance or else switch to a longer putter as the prognosis for this condition is poor. Research suggests that neurologically based yips conditions appear to be exacerbated by stress (Clark et al., 2005). Despite these advances, researchers have yet to identify a standardized method (involving the use of appropriate psychometric and behavioural measurements) for the diagnosis of this condition or an agreement concerning the best strategies to alleviate the yips.

What causes choking in sport? Attentional theories

In contemporary sport psychology, choking is regarded as an anxiety-based attentional difficulty (see also Chapter 5) rather than as a personality problem. This distinction is important because it suggests that the propensity to choke is not some sort of character flaw but, instead, a cognitive problem arising from an interaction between anxiety and attention. If this *attentional* perspective is correct, then any athletes, regardless of their personality, can choke if they concentrate on the "wrong" target – anything which is outside their control or which is irrelevant to the task at hand. But what psychological mechanisms could underlie this choking effect?

According to Gucciardi and Dimmock (2008) and Hill et al. (2010a), two types of attentional theories of choking may be identified – *distraction* theories, such as processing efficiency theory (Eysenck and Calvo, 1992) and *self-focus* theories (e.g. Baumeister, 1984; Beilock and Carr, 2001; R. Masters, 1992). In general, distraction theories postulate that pressure (as perceived by the performer) induces anxiety which consumes working memory resources and causes inefficient processing of task-relevant information – thereby shifting attention away from task execution. By contrast, self-focus models of choking propose that anxiety increases athletes' levels of self-consciousness and causes them to focus their attention inwards (see also Chapter 5). This shift to self-focused attention encourages athletes to attempt to consciously monitor and/ or control their skill execution which may induce choking through a form of "paralysis by analysis" (see above). In general, PET explains choking by suggesting that anxious athletes may try to maintain their level of performance by investing extra effort in it. Although this increased effort investment may appear to generate immediate benefits, it soon reaches a point of diminishing returns. At this stage, athletes may conclude that too much effort is required and so they give up. For example, an elite golfer in Hill et al.'s (2010b) study revealed that instead of adopting a task-relevant focus during a choking episode he thought about "what they [the spectators] are thinking. What are they going to say if I hit a bad shot . . . so I rush the shot, in order to get away from them" (p. 226). At that point, the athlete's performance deteriorated rapidly. Unfortunately, this theory is hampered by the difficulty of measuring mental effort objectively. Turning to self-focus theories of choking, two models are especially prominent – the conscious processing (or reinvestment) hypothesis (R. Masters, 1992, explained on p. 105) and the "explicit monitoring" hypothesis (EMH; Beilock and Carr, 2001). Although these two approaches share many similarities (see R. Masters and Maxwell, 2004), they differ in at least one important issue (Hill et al., 2010a). Whereas the EMH suggests that athletic performance is disrupted by performers *monitoring* their step-by-step execution of the skill, CPH postulates that the disruption is caused by athletes consciously *controlling* (e.g. altering or changing) the skill involved.

Applying the self-focus model to sport, when people experience a great deal of pressure to perform well they tend to think more about themselves and the importance of the event in which they are competing than they would normally. This excessive self-consciousness causes people to attempt to gain conscious control over previously automatic skills – just as a novice would do. As a result of this attempt to invest automatic processes with conscious control, skilled performance tends to unravel. According to some athletes, this unravelling of skill, which is caused by thinking too much about automatic movements, may happen more frequently as one gets older. For example, consider Ian Woosnam's experience of trying to correct his putting stroke in golf. In particular, he said:

> putting shouldn't be hard ... but that's where the mind comes in. So much is running through your mind – hold it this way, keep the blade square whereas when you're young, you just get hold of it and hit it. When you get old too much *goes* through your mind.
>
> (cited in White, 2002b, p. 22)

This self-consciousness approach is similar to the conscious processing hypothesis (R. Masters, 1992) discussed in the previous section. Indeed, this latter hypothesis suggests that under pressure, "the individual begins thinking about how he or she is executing the skill, and endeavours to operate it with his or her explicit knowledge of its mechanics" (R. Masters, 1992, p. 345).

Overall, according to Gucciardi and Dimmock (2008), empirical support for distraction models of choking is strongest for tasks (e.g. mathematical computation) that load heavily on working memory resources. By contrast, self-focus models of choking appear to be supported best by studies involving tasks that make few demands on working memory (e.g. golf putting). Interestingly, Nieuwenhuys and Oudejans (2012) proposed that both distraction and self-focus models can be explained with the same distraction principles. To explain, when anxious, performers' attention is biased towards threat-related stimuli and this leaves fewer attentional resources to adjust and calibrate movements on the basis of task-relevant information. On certain occasions (e.g. when under monitoring pressure) this might mean that the performer engages in self-focused attention which is not a task-relevant focus for expert performers and will likely prove debilitative to performance. For a brief account of conceptual issues in psychological explanations of choking, see Box 3.6.

Box 3.6 Thinking critically about ... explanations of choking behaviour in athletes

At first glance, the phenomenon of choking in sport is simple to define and easy to explain. Is it not just a case of an athlete performing poorly due to nervousness? When we delve a little deeper into this lay "explanation" of this phenomenon, however, we discover a hornet's nest of conceptual problems. As we explained in the subsection on "What exactly is choking?", there is no universal agreement among researchers as to the precise meaning of the term choking. In addition, the idea that we can attribute choking behaviour to nervousness is fraught with difficulty. To explain, as we learned in Chapter 2, trait explanations of behaviour are rather dubious. Logically, traits are inferences from, rather than causes of, behaviour. Therefore, there is always a danger of circularity when "explaining" behaviour using traits (e.g. "she acted nervously because she is an anxious person"). Instead of explaining choking in terms of anxiety-proneness, modern sport psychology researchers tend to consider it as an attentional problem. Some researchers have suggested that it seems to be caused by focusing on oneself when one should be concentrating on the task at hand. More recently, however, researchers have argued that distraction (i.e. having one's focus of attention diverted to task-irrelevant thoughts such as fear of negative evaluation by one's coach) is the primary cause of choking. Let us consider evidence for the former argument by outlining the research of Roy Baumeister in this field (see Azar, 1996). Baumeister (1984) began by distinguishing between sports that are dominated primarily by skill (e.g. golf, gymnastics) and those which require sustained effort (e.g. running, weightlifting). According to him, the pressure of a competition can facilitate performance of an "effortful" skill but can impede the performance of a precision skill. This theory was tested using simulated pressure situations in laboratory conditions. Baumeister (1984) devised an effortful task by timing the speed and accuracy with which college students could arrange a deck of cards in numerical order. However, he introduced a pressure component into this task by telling the respondents that if they did better than their previous score, he would pay them $5. In general, results showed an improvement in sport performance in the pressure group. But when Baumeister used a skilful task (e.g. playing a videogame), different findings emerged. Thus Baumeister suggested that although pressure from competition or from public scrutiny makes people try harder on effortful tasks, it does not make them perform better on skill-based tasks. This happens because pressure tends to make people pay attention to automatic (i.e. highly practised) aspects of a given task. But here the picture becomes more complex. To explain, Baumeister (1984) proposes that athletes who are used to focusing on themselves choke less frequently than do counterparts who engage in less self-focused observation. But participants in Baumeister's studies were novices and hence may have maintained their performance level under pressure conditions not because they were trained under high levels of self-consciousness but instead, because skill-focused attention is required for effective performance at their level of ability (J. Wang et al., 2004). In other words, pressure may not alter the chronic self-focus achieved by some people – but it *does* seem to affect the behaviour of people who do not normally concentrate on their own actions.

Although Baumeister proposed that choking is most likely to arise when automatic processes are disrupted via conscious reinvestment, a series of recent qualitative studies (see Gucciardi et al., 2010; Hill et al., 2010b, 2011) has revealed distraction as the primary mechanism responsible for this phenomenon. For example, Hill et al. (2010b) discovered that choking episodes amongst a group of elite golfers were characterized by a focus on thoughts such as fear of failure and negative evaluation. Interestingly, the perceived choking episodes were only alleviated once performers adopted an internal rather than an external focus of attention. Although this runs contradictory to the advice of a number of researchers (e.g. Wulf; see Chapter 5) Hill et al. (2010b) argued that the internal thoughts were functional and task-related in nature (e.g. holistic swing thoughts such as getting their weight through the ball) and that this may have enhanced the participants' confidence and perceived control. Of course, we must acknowledge that these studies are reliant on the retrospective recall of complex and potentially dynamic attentional mechanisms but they do suggest that distraction has an important role to play in the choking process. In fact, this explanation has been corroborated in a recent experimental study by Englert and Oudejans (2014). In this study, semi-professional tennis players were assigned to an anxiety or neutral group. Anxiety led to a significant reduction in serve accuracy and this relationship was mediated by self-reported distraction rather than self-focus.

Critical thinking questions

Can you think of any alternative explanation of Baumeister's (1984) results? What do you make of Baumeister's claims given recent research findings which suggest that distraction is the primary cause of choking? Why do you think choking is more prevalent in untimed individual sports rather than timed group sports?

In summary, we have learned that choking under pressure is a pervasive problem in sport. Unfortunately, no consensus has been reached as yet about the theoretical mechanisms that cause it. Nevertheless, most theories of this phenomenon agree that anxiety impairs performance by inducing the athlete to think too much, thereby regressing to an earlier stage of skill acquisition. By the way, some helpful practical tips on how to counteract choking are provided by Beilock (2010a). This leads us to the next section of the chapter, which explains how athletes can learn to control anxiety and cope with pressure situations in sport.

Controlling anxiety in sport: how do athletes and coaches cope with pressure situations?

Given the ubiquity of performance anxiety in sport, it is not surprising that psychologists have devised a variety of strategies in an effort to reduce athletes' anxiety levels. In this section, we describe the most popular of these coping strategies and outline some recent research on the coping techniques used by elite athletes and coaches. Before we address these two objectives, however, some important background information is required. First, we must distinguish between pressure *situations* and pressure *reactions* in sport. This distinction is extremely important in applied sport psychology because athletes need to be trained to understand that they do not automatically have to experience "pressure" (i.e. an anxiety response) in pressure situations.

With these two ideas in mind – that pressure lies in the mind of the beholder and that different strategies are available to facilitate active coping – here is a summary of some of the most popular techniques used by athletes to counteract the effects of unwanted anxiety in sport.

Understanding the experience of pressure

According to psychologists, we experience pressure and concomitant anxiety symptoms whenever we believe that a current or impending situation threatens us in some way. For example, a soccer player might be apprehensive about making a mistake in an important match in front of the home supporters. A swimmer may feel tense at the prospect of competing under the watchful eye of a feared coach. More generally, whenever there is a discrepancy between what we *think* we can do (i.e. our assessment of our own abilities) and what we believe we are *expected* to do (i.e. the perceived demands of the situation), we put *ourselves* under pressure. Psychologically, therefore, pressure is a subjective interpretation of certain objective circumstances (the "pressure situation"). Another point to note is that although we cannot change a pressure situation, we *can* change our reaction to it. Specifically, by restructuring the situation in our minds, we can learn to interpret it as a challenge to our abilities rather than as a threat to our well-being.

Unfortunately, this skill of perceiving pressure situations as *challenges* does not normally develop spontaneously in athletes. It can be cultivated through specialist advice and training, however. For example, consider a recent study by Moore et al. (2015). In this research, participants received either **arousal reappraisal** instructions (e.g. "the increase in arousal you may feel during stressful situations is not harmful. In fact, recent research has shown that this response to stress can be beneficial and aid performance in stressful situations …") or control instructions before performing a pressurized, single-trial, motor task. Although both groups initially displayed cardiovascular responses that were consistent with a *threat* state, the reappraisal group displayed a cardiovascular response more reflective of a *challenge* state (i.e. by showing relatively higher cardiac output) after the reappraisal manipulation. Even more significantly, despite performing similarly at baseline, the reappraisal group performed better than the control group on the pressurized task. These results show that encouraging athletes to interpret heightened physiological arousal as a potential *facilitator* of performance can result in enhanced adaptive cardiovascular responses and motor performance under pressure.

To learn the rudiments of cognitive restructuring in practical terms, try the exercise in Box 3.7.

Becoming more aware of anxiety: interpreting arousal signals constructively

Having learned how athletes can restructure pressures as challenges, our next step is to examine some practical techniques for reducing anxiety in pressure situations. Despite their talent and experience, many athletes have a poor understanding of

Box 3.7 In the spotlight Cognitive restructuring in action: turning a pressure situation into a challenge

The purpose of this exercise is to show you how to use a technique called cognitive restructuring to turn a feared pressure situation into a manageable challenge (based on Moran, 1998). To begin, think of a situation in your sport or daily life that usually makes you feel anxious. Now, describe this situation by finishing the following sentence:

"I hate the pressure of ..."

Fill in the missing words with reference to the pressure situation you have experienced. For example, you might write down "I hate the pressure of serving for the match when playing tennis". Alternatively, it could be "I hate the pressure of facing exams when I have not studied for them".

Now, think of this pressure situation again. This time, however, I would like you to *restructure* it in your head so that you think about it differently:

"I love the challenge of ..."

Please note that you are not allowed to simply repeat what you wrote before. For example, you cannot say "I love the challenge of serving for the match when playing tennis". Instead, you have to pick something else to focus on in that pressure situation besides the fear of making mistakes. As we shall see in Chapter 5, the secret of maintaining your focus under pressure is to concentrate on something that is specific, relevant and under your own control. Usually, that means concentrating on some aspect of your *preparation* for the feared situation. For example, you could write "I love the challenge of preparing in the same way for every serve – no matter what the score is in the match". Notice how restructuring a situation can make you feel differently about it. You no longer see it as something to fear but as something which challenges your skills. If athletes perceive competition as a challenge rather than a threat they are likely to have less cause to regulate their responses. Jones and Lavallee (2010) proposed that performers will experience a challenge state when they possess high self-confidence in their ability to meet task demands; a perception of control and a focus on approach goals. In the next section we consider how performers may be encouraged to reinterpret their physiological arousal and thereby promote a challenge state.

what their body is telling them when they are anxious. In particular, they need to be educated to realize that anxiety is not necessarily a bad thing but merely a sign that they *care* about the results of what they are doing. Without such education, athletes tend to make the mistake of misinterpreting physical signs of *readiness* (e.g. a rapid heartbeat, a surge of adrenaline) as harbingers of impending disaster. Therefore, sport performers must learn to perceive somatic arousal as an essential prerequisite of a good performance. Some players realize this intuitively when they concede that they cannot play well unless they feel appropriately "juiced" or pumped up for a contest. Interestingly, Thomas et al. (2007) investigated the effects of a psychological skills training programme on elite hockey players' anxiety symptoms. Results showed that the intervention was successful in helping these players to interpret their symptoms more constructively. More recently, Moore et al. (2013) explored whether arousal reappraisal could be used to help individuals overcome a threat state. This approach encourages performers to perceive pressure-induced changes in physiological arousal (e.g. increased heartbeat) as a tool that can aid performance. Participants in the latter study received either arousal reappraisal or control instructions before performing a golf putting task under baseline and pressurized conditions. A reappraisal manipulation, which encouraged participants to perceive increases in arousal as being beneficial to performance, resulted in a cardiovascular response more indicative of a challenge state (relatively higher cardiac output and/or lower total peripheral resistance) and led to superior performance during the pressurized task (when compared to a control condition). This result suggests that performers may be able to learn to interpret their physiological arousal as being facilitative to performance rather than representing an unwanted negative experience. In a similar vein, the use of **rational emotive behaviour therapy** (REBT; Ellis, 1957) could be effective for players who have a predisposition for threat appraisals (see Turner et al., 2014). The goal of REBT is to replace irrational thoughts with rational ones in order to reduce dysfunctional emotions such as anxiety. In summary, the first step in helping athletes to cope with anxiety is to educate them as to what it means and how to detect it. The psychological principle here is that awareness precedes control of psychological states.

Using physical relaxation techniques: lowering shoulders, slowing down and breathing deeply

Earlier in the chapter, we explained that anxiety causes certain behavioural characteristics. For example, anxious athletes tend to speed up their behaviour. The obvious solution to this problem is to encourage them to breathe deeply, slow down and relax whenever tension strikes. For example, after his defeat of Jay Haas (USA) on the eighteenth hole in the 1995 Ryder Cup at the Oak Hill Club, Pittsford, New York, Europe golfer Philip Walton revealed how he had used a diaphragmatic breathing technique to counteract his anxiety. "What saved me ... was something I learned ... about how to breathe properly in a stressful situation. You do it from your belly not high up in your chest" (cited in L. Kelly, 1998). A recent study by Wells et al. (2012) found that trained musicians who engaged in a slow breathing intervention showed significantly greater improvements in high frequency (HF) and low frequency (LF)/HF ratio measures of heart rate variability (HRV) relative to a control group. Intriguingly, a group of American athletes (including Olympic skiers) have advocated prolonged breath holding as a relaxation technique (see Futterman, 2014). This process involves learning to hold one's breath for a period of up to five minutes while doing a deep sea dive. By practicing this activity, the athletes hope to learn how to control their breathing and stay relaxed under extremely challenging and uncomfortable conditions. The aim is to take what they learn from this experience and apply it to stress-inducing moments they might encounter in the heat of competition –

for example, a skier staring down an icy mountain slope or a snowboarder faced with new aerial tricks that involve numerous spins and flips above a hard and icy surface. Holding one's breath for such a prolonged period is a highly dangerous activity and one which recreational athletes should avoid engaging in.

Of course, any advice on relaxation must be tailored to the demands of the particular sport in question. Indeed, the feasibility of using physical relaxation techniques such as progressive muscular relaxation (see practical tips offered by J. Williams, 2010) depends heavily on the amount of "break time" offered by the sport in question. For example, in stop–start, untimed sports like golf or tennis, there are moments where it may be possible to lower one's shoulders, flap out the tension from one's arms and engage in deep-breathing exercises. Interestingly, some professional tennis players use a relaxation strategy whereby they visualize an imaginary area (e.g. behind the baseline of a tennis court) which serves as a relaxation zone where they can switch off mentally during breaks in play (for a discussion of mental **imagery** in sport, see also Chapter 5). However, this procedure may be impossible to use in athletic activities where play is fast and continuous (e.g. hockey). Also, another caution is necessary when teaching relaxation skills to athletes. In our experience, downloading relaxation exercise programmes does not work effectively with many sport performers as these exercises are invariably perceived as being too passive and generic for their needs. However, Karageorghis and Terry (2010) advocated what they refer to as the "relaxing place technique" which involves the use of **visualization** exercises designed to transport you from a stressful situation to a place you associate with peace and quiet. As noted above, such an approach might prove fruitful in self-paced tasks (where the performer has time to "regroup") but is unlikely to be used by performers in dynamic and fast-paced tasks. A comprehensive account of relaxation techniques in sport may be found in J. Williams (2010).

Giving oneself specific instructions

Anxiety is unhelpful because it makes people focus on what might go *wrong* (i.e. possible negative consequences) rather than on what exactly they have to do (the immediate challenge of the situation). Therefore, a useful way to counteract pressure in a competition is to ask oneself: "What exactly do I have to do right now?" By focusing on what they have to do, athletes can learn to avoid the trap of confusing the *facts* of the situation (e.g. "We're 1–0 down with ten minutes to go") with an anxious *interpretation* of those facts ("It's no use, we're going to lose"). Therefore, when athletes experience pressure, they should give themselves specific commands which help them to focus on actions that can be performed immediately.

Adhering to pre-performance routines

Most athletes use **pre-performance routines** (PPRs), or systematic sequences of preparatory thoughts and actions, in an effort to concentrate optimally before they execute important skills (e.g. golf putts, penalty kicks; see also Chapter 5). Briefly, these routines serve as a cocoon against the adverse effects of anxiety. In particular, by concentrating on each step of the routine, athletes learn to focus on only what they can control – a vital principle of anxiety management. In fact, Hazell et al. (2014) found that the introduction of a new pre-performance routine led to a significant reduction in somatic anxiety (as measured by the CSAI-2) amongst semi-professional football players during a penalty taking task. Mesagno and Mullane-Grant (2010) investigated the efficacy of different PPRs in attempting to alleviate choking behaviour in a sample of Australian Rules football players as they performed free kicks under low- and high-pressure conditions. Results showed that choking was *least* likely when the footballers' attention was taken up by task-relevant thoughts. Based on this finding, Mesagno and Mullane-Grant (2010, p. 358) recommended that choking can be reduced if athletes use a non-automated PPR that "occupies attention prior to execution and decreases involuntary shifts to pressure-related threat". Lautenbach et al. (2015a) subsequently explored the effect of a non-automated pre-performance routine on tennis serve performance in a high-pressure situation. Practicing with the non-automated routine for four weeks led to a reduction in subjective, but not objective (i.e. cortisol), levels of stress in a high-pressure test condition and helped these participants to maintain performance proficiency.

Developing "quiet eye"

In eye-tracking research in sport (see Chapter 5), the phenomenon of "**quiet eye**" (QE; Vickers, 1992, 2007) refers to the time that elapses between a skilled performer's last visual fixation on a specific target and the subsequent initiation of a relevant motor response. Briefly, research suggests that expert athletes tend to display significantly longer durations of final fixation on targets than do "near-expert" counterparts. Furthermore, within a given target sport, successful aiming is often associated with longer QE periods than is unsuccessful aiming (e.g. Rienhoff et al., 2015). Interestingly, QE appears to be trainable (i.e. its duration can be lengthened) both for experts (Causer et al., 2011) and for novices (Vine and Wilson, 2011). Based on these findings, QE training could offer a potential method of combating the debilitating effects of anxiety. Encouragingly, recent evidence suggests that quiet eye can be quite easily incorporated within a performer's existing pre-performance routine. Wilson et al. (2015) described a series of steps that are involved in this process. First, trainees need to perform a specific task while wearing mobile eye tracking equipment. Data collected is then compared with the quiet eye characteristics (e.g. the specific location of visual gaze or an early onset prior to a critical movement) of experts who have performed the same task. The trainees are then taught how to mirror the quiet eye focus through the use of video modelling, feedback and questioning. This combination of pedagogical approaches should help them to learn the task through the eyes of an expert. Trainees are then shown their own quiet eye data and this is compared to the quiet eye characteristics of the expert. Finally, the trainee then selects one of the QE characteristics to adopt and practices this over a number of trials or until it can be effortlessly incorporated within their normal routine. Given our earlier discussion on how anxiety may lead to choking in penalty shootouts, it is worth briefly considering how the development of the quiet eye might help prevent performance breakdown in this situation. In a penalty taking task, Wood and Wilson (2012) taught players to focus on what is considered to be the optimal target areas of the goal (i.e. top corner) for a period of time considered necessary to process aiming information needed for accurate shooting. The quiet eye trained participants demonstrated superior performance during a "live" penalty shootout compared to a control group (who practiced without instructions). Additional testing revealed that those who had undergone quiet eye training reduced their perceptions of outcome uncertainty and increased their perceptions of shooting ability and perceived control (e.g. ability to cope with the pressure). Furthermore, and perhaps most importantly, those participants with high perceptions of control were more likely to aim optimally (i.e. further from the goalkeeper). On the basis of these results, Wood et al. (2015) recommended that PPRs should contain a gaze-control element to optimize aiming behaviour and prevent anxiety-induced disruptions to attentional control. This should involve focusing on where they are aiming for a significant period of time before their run-up in order to process target-related information. Although some players may worry that this practice would concede a certain amount of predictive information to the goalkeeper, they should be reassured that goalkeepers have a tendency to focus on the kicker's lower-leg kinematics rather than the kicker's gaze direction.

Constructive thinking: encouraging oneself

When sports performers are anxious, their **self-talk** (i.e. what they say to themselves inside their heads; see also Chapter 5) tends to become hostile and sarcastic. Although such frustration is understandable, it is *never* helpful to the person involved and may even make the situation worse. So, athletes need to talk to themselves with two objectives: to encourage themselves for their efforts (positive reinforcement) and to instruct themselves on what to do next (guidance). For example, an anxious tennis player might say, "Come on, this point now: go cross-court on my next return". Cheng and Hardy (2016) found that motivational self-talk was the best predictor of the adaptive (i.e. regulatory) dimension of anxiety. When faced with a pressurized situation, engaging in motivational self-talk may allow performers to maintain performance proficiency by mobilizing appropriate cognitive and emotional resources (e.g. increasing effort). The performance of complex motor skills in fast-paced and dynamic environments may also benefit from self-talk. Miles and Neil (2013) discovered that elite cricketers used self-talk to redirect their thoughts to performance-related cues and that this strategy reduced their competitive anxiety. This approach was found to be particularly effective during periods of declining performance.

Simulation training

If anxiety in athletes is associated with a fear of the unknown, then one way of counteracting it is by reducing uncertainty through the use of **simulation training** (i.e. practising under conditions that replicate key aspects of an impending challenge; see also Chapter 5). This idea is supported by both anecdotal and descriptive evidence. To illustrate the former, many coaches of elite athletes try to inoculate their performers against the unwanted effects of anticipated anxiety. In preparation for the Beijing Olympics – where American shooters were competing against a Chinese shooter who was favourite to win a gold medal – the American team psychologist, Sean McCann, prepared the athletes to face the boisterous and partisan home support by encouraging them to listen to iPod files of crowd noises during workouts. The renowned swimming coach Bob Bowman admitted deliberately breaking the goggles of Michael Phelps (who has won more Olympic gold medals than any other athlete) during practice so that he could learn to swim calmly without them if necessary in a competition. Remarkably, this situation actually arose in the 2008 Olympics when Phelps won the 200 metres butterfly event even though his goggles had been broken for the last 100 metres of the race (Whitworth, 2008). Jordan Spieth, the winner of two major golf championships in 2015, would appear to have become accustomed to practicing under pressure from a very early age. Indeed, his coach Cameron McCormick, has argued that it is "really hard to expect a player who practises in a state of little stress that it's going to be like that on the course … You want to simulate as much pressure as you can" (cited in Hoggard, 2015). To achieve this, McCormick taught Spieth that there should be "consequences" when he practises such as the possibility of losing a nominal amount or money or "symbolic gestures" (such as buying a nice dinner for his girlfriend should he fail a particular task). Descriptive evidence on the value of simulation training comes from Uphill and Jones (2004) who reported that athletes used "what if?" scenarios in an effort to minimize the likely anxiety that would be prompted by imminent pressure situations. Although these sources of evidence are interesting, they are not compelling. But an experiment by Oudejans and Pijpers (2010) may fill this gap in the relevant research literature. The question addressed by these researchers was as follows. Can simulating mild levels of anxiety in practice conditions help to prevent athletes from choking in a subsequent competitive situation? See Box 3.8.

Hemispheric-specific priming

Recent evidence (Beckmann et al., 2013) suggests that some athletes may improve their performance under pressure simply by squeezing a ball or clenching their left hand before competition. Specifically, in a series of experiments with experienced soccer players, badminton players and tae kwon do athletes, participants performed a ball-squeezing task prior to task execution – during practice and then in stressful competitions before a large crowd or video camera. The ball-squeezing task was used because unilateral muscle contractions in the upper limb are believed to activate contralateral hemispheres and the functions associated with them. Participants who squeezed the ball in their *left* hand (thereby, presumably priming right-hemispheric

Sometimes, players and coaches claim that it is difficult to prepare for the anxiety experienced by athletes in real-life competition because the pressure situations in question are too intense and/or too sport-specific to be replicable in practice. Until 2010, this proposition was untested empirically in psychology. But using an experimental paradigm, Oudejans and Pijpers (2010) investigated whether or not simulation training helps to counteract choking behaviour in athletes. In this study, a sample of novices was assigned to one of two groups. In the experimental group, participants practised darts throwing under experimentally induced levels of mild anxiety – achieved by requiring participants to hang high rather than low on an indoor climbing wall. In the control group, participants practised without any additional anxiety. Manipulation checks using heart rate (an index of arousal/anxiety) were conducted to ensure that the anxiety manipulation had been effective. State anxiety was measured before and after the training programme using a visual-analogue anxiety scale called the "anxiety thermometer" (Oudejans and Pijpers, 2010). After training, participants were tested under conditions of low, mild and high anxiety. Results showed that despite systematic increases in anxiety, heart rate and effort from low to mid to high anxiety, the experimental group (i.e. the one that had trained under mild anxiety) performed *equally well* on all three tests whereas the performance of the control group *deteriorated* in the high anxiety condition. Oudejans and Pijpers (2010) interpreted their results to indicate that training with mild anxiety helps to prevent choking under conditions of high anxiety. They acknowledged, however, that this apparently beneficial simulation effect is short term, and that additional research is required to explore its efficacy over longer periods of time.

Recently, Lawrence et al. (2014) examined whether Oudejans and Pijpers' results could be explained through a "specificity of practice" (i.e. learning will be most effective when training conditions replicate the environmental demands encountered in "real-life" competitive performance) perspective. In this study the authors explored whether the benefits of practicing with anxiety is influenced by the *amount* of exposure, and the *timing* of exposure, in relation to what point in the learning process that exposure occurs. In two experiments, the authors found that learning a golf putting and a rock climbing task under anxiety provoking conditions eliminated choking. However, perhaps the most interesting finding was that performers who experienced anxiety from the start of learning were less effective in subsequent low anxiety conditions compared to those who were introduced to anxiety-provoking practice conditions later in the learning process. Performance at anxiety transfer was significantly greater in anxiety control (participants who performed the first half of practice under anxiety before changing to non-anxiety conditions) and control-anxiety groups (those who performed under non-anxiety conditions before moving to an anxiety-provoking condition) compared to those who practiced in an anxiety condition alone. The authors argued that a mixture of anxiety and control conditions may be the most efficacious approach to immunizing performers against performance anxiety. Having practiced under anxiety, performance in a transfer test may have served to activate the emotions associated with this mood state and prompted the recall of the muscular patterns that were required during transfer of both motor skills.

continued ...

Box 3.8 continued

Critical thinking questions

Do you think that Oudejans and Pijpers' (2010) conclusions are warranted by the experimental method that they used? Specifically, are you satisfied that heart rate (an index of arousal) was used as one of the anxiety manipulation measures? Do you think that the ecological validity of this study is questionable in view of the rather contrived nature of experimental task – namely, throwing darts while *hanging* from a climbing wall? Can you think of any alternative explanations as to why practice under pressurized conditions might immunize performers against the debilitating effects of anxiety?

activity) outperformed participants who performed the same task with their *right* hand. From these studies, Beckman and colleagues concluded that "**hemispheric-specific priming**" (i.e. imposing concurrent activity that selectively activates one hemisphere and, hence, creates an advantage for the performance of an activity that relies on the functions of that hemisphere) could prevent choking. There may be two possible explanations for this finding. On the one hand, priming right-hemispheric activity may have promoted automated behaviour and, on the other, it may have suppressed conscious control in the left hemisphere. The authors acknowledged that the precise mechanisms underlying the effect of priming remain unknown but argue that the procedure could be implemented as part of the pre-performance routine. In fact, **anecdotal evidence** from the participants indicated that they found the task helpful rather than disruptive and that they could quite easily incorporate the approach in their current routines.

In summary, this section of the chapter suggests that athletes can learn to cope with pressure situations by using at least four psychological strategies. First, they must be trained to believe that pressure lies in the eye of the beholder. Therefore, they must be taught to cognitively restructure competitive events so that they can be perceived as opportunities to display their talents (the challenge response) rather than as potential sources of failure (the fear response). Second, athletes must learn for themselves that systematic preparation tends to reduce pressure. One way of doing this is to use simulation training and mental rehearsal (or "**mental practice**"; see also Chapter 6) to inure themselves against anticipated difficulties. Third, anxious athletes can benefit from using self-talk techniques to guide themselves through pressure situations. Fourth, when anxiety strikes, athletes must be prepared to deepen their routines and to use physical relaxation procedures in accordance with the temporal demands of the sport that they are performing.

Unresolved issues and new directions in research on anxiety in athletes

Despite a long tradition of research on anxiety in athletes, many issues remain unresolved in this field. Identification of these issues can help us to outline six areas for further research on anxiety in sport performers. First, the fact that researchers tend to use terms such as arousal, fear, anxiety and stress interchangeably in sport psychology suggests that greater conceptual rigour is required throughout this field. Fortunately, some progress in this regard is evident with the development of a model designed to clarify the relationship between arousal-related constructs (see Gould et al., 2002b; Thomas et al., 2009). Second, idiographic research designs (i.e. ones which reflect the uniqueness or individuality of the phenomena of interest; Cashmore, 2008) are required to augment the traditional nomothetic approach (i.e. the search for general principles of psychology based on large samples of participants) to anxiety in sport. A good example of the idiographic approach comes from the work of Hill and colleagues on the catastrophic experiences of elite athletes when choking competitively. Single-case research designs (see Barker et al., 2011) and qualitative methodology such as focus groups (see Chapter 1) could be especially useful in exploring the meaning of anxiety to athletes. Third, some researchers (e.g. Wilson et al., 2007a) have questioned the validity of the **dual-task paradigm** used in many studies of anxiety on the grounds that the difficulty of secondary tasks is hard to evaluate independently. Land and Tenenbaum (2012) and Toner and Moran's (2011) use of "relevant" tasks offer some promise in this regard, but more work needs to be done to identify ecological valid measurements of attentional focus during online skill execution. Fourth, researchers know very little about how performers may be immunized against the debilitating effects of anxiety. The use of simulation training has been found to increase athletes' robustness to competitive anxiety but further research is required to establish how training conditions can be best manipulated to ensure that they replicate the challenges and demands athletes face in "real-world" competitive situations. In a similar vein, some confusion also remains about the specific mechanisms (i.e. distraction versus self-focus) responsible for choking amongst skilled performers. Further research is required in order to shed light on this issue. Fifth, little research has been conducted to date on the interaction between anxiety and attentional control. For example, we know very little about how athletes inhibit information (i.e. prevent irrelevant stimuli and responses influencing performance) or shift their attentional focus within and between tasks when performing under pressure. Both functions are believed to become less efficient when athletes are anxious. Eysenck and Wilson's (2016) ACTS may represent a useful framework for researchers wishing to address this issue. Finally, relatively little research has been conducted on the anxiety experienced by athletes close to and during competitive performance (but see Hanton et al., 2004). Field studies in this area are particularly welcome.

Ideas for research projects on anxiety in athletes

Here are six ideas for research projects on anxiety in athletes.

1. Based on the research of Hanton et al. (2004), you could investigate possible changes in the intensity and direction of athletes' experiences of cognitive and somatic anxiety in the days preceding a competitive match. Neuroendocrine responses such as cortisol levels could also be collected (see Lautenbach et al., 2015b). Interviews with athletes might provide another means of understanding how they interpret changes in emotional and bodily responses before competition. Of course, in such a study,

you would have to be extremely careful to be as unobtrusive as possible in your data collection to prevent possible interference with the athletes' preparation.

2. Findings from a pioneering study using trained musicians (see Wells et al., 2012) suggest that slow breathing techniques can help to control physiological arousal in anticipation of psychosocial stress. Researchers interested in helping athletes to control their anxiety could use this latter approach alongside the use of heart rate variability **biofeedback** and explore their respective influence on anxiety and sympathetic nervous system arousal.

3. Few studies have evaluated theoretically based interventions designed to alleviate choking behaviour in athletes. In order to address this gap in the research literature, you could explore whether methods such as selectively priming hemispheric specific activity (e.g. see our discussion above of Beckmann et al., 2013) can be incorporated into athletes' pre-performance routines and how this approach influences both movement (as determined by kinematic measures) and performance proficiency. Also, further experimental studies are required to tease out the respective effects of distraction and self-focus on the performance of self-paced tasks under pressurized conditions.

4. You could evaluate the psychometric adequacy of one of the self-report anxiety scales described in this chapter (e.g. the Revised Competitive State Anxiety Inventory-2: Cox et al., 2003). Surprisingly little data on these tests have been gathered from elite athletes.

5. In a recent study, Gardner et al. (2015) investigated the relationship between soccer players' implicit beliefs, attribution style and competitive anxiety levels. Briefly, these researchers found that higher "entity" beliefs (i.e. those involving uncontrollable, external, specific and unstable attributions for positive events and uncontrollable, global and stable attributions for negative events) were associated with higher levels of competitive anxiety. By contrast, "incremental" beliefs (i.e. those involving controllable, internal, global and stable attributions for positive events and controllable and specific attributions for negative events) were associated with lower levels of competitive anxiety. Following the suggestions of Gardner et al. (2015), it would be interesting to replicate and extend this study using a more recent test of competitive anxiety (e.g. the Sport Anxiety Scale-2; Smith et al., 2006) and a sample of athletes other than soccer players.

6. If you have access to eye-tracking technology in your academic department's research laboratory, it would be intriguing to explore the eye movement patterns of participants who experience either ironic processes or implicit overcompensation when provided with negative self-instructions. Does quiet eye training reduce the likelihood of these undesirable outcomes?

Summary

- It is widely agreed that athletic success depends significantly on the ability to regulate one's arousal levels effectively. Put simply, sport performers need to know how and when to either psych themselves up or to calm themselves down in competitive situations.

- The second section examined the nature, causes and types of anxiety experienced by athletes. It also distinguished between anxiety and related constructs such as fear and arousal and explored the question of whether anxiety facilitates or impairs performance in sport.

- The third section reviewed the most popular instruments available for the measurement of anxiety in athletes.

- Theories and research on the relationship between arousal, anxiety and performance were examined in the fourth section, which also contained a brief discussion of the nature and causes of choking under pressure in sports.

- The fifth section addressed the practical issue of how to control anxiety and cope effectively with pressure situations in sport.

- Finally, some unresolved issues on anxiety in athletes were identified along with several potentially fruitful new directions for future research in this field.

4

Emotions and coping

Introduction

Competitive athletes devote an extraordinary amount of time and effort in seeking to attain elite status in their sport. Given the personal significance they are likely to attach to performance, the financial rewards that may be at stake, and the fact that they are required to perform extremely complex movements with great precision in front of large audiences, it is little wonder that they have been found to experience a wide range of both negative and positive emotions in competitive environments. As Roger Federer (a seventeen-times Grand Slam tennis champion) admitted recently, "I need to find a balance. I can't just be ice, it becomes horribly boring. I need the fire, the excitement, the passion, the whole rollercoaster. But I need it at a level where I can handle it" (cited in Hattenstone, 2016, pp. 22–23). More generally, competitive athletes experience such emotions as excitement, joy, relief, anger, dejection, happiness and anxiety (e.g. Hanin, 2000; M. Jones et al., 2005).

Perhaps not surprisingly, there is widespread debate amongst commentators, spectators and the media about whether sportspeople should contain or display their emotions during competitive performance. While some believe that the venting of emotions (e.g. displaying anger or frustration with one's performance) may allow the performer to "let off steam" others propose that such overt displays disrupt performance proficiency by distracting the athlete from the task at hand. Media coverage surrounding the behaviour of three-time Grand Slam winning tennis player Andy Murray serves as a useful illustration of this latter point. Murray has often been chastised by commentators and the media for his outbursts of anger on the tennis court. In fact, the media has suggested that it is his inability to control his emotions that have held him back from winning further Grand Slam titles. His approach has been described as "negative" on British television while the famous American tennis player Chris Evert has argued that Murray should not get so heated or emotional on court but should just "chill". However, Murray has argued that expressing his emotions is an important feature of performance: "It wouldn't make me feel good, bottling up my emotions – saying nothing and standing there makes me feel flat" (Hodgkinson, 2013). For Murray, and other athletes like him, venting his frustration appears to serve a motivational function by encouraging him to redouble effort and to divert even greater energy and mental resources to the task at hand (see Figure 4.1).

Figure 4.1 Andy Murray likes to express his emotions overtly (*source*: courtesy of Inpho Photography)

Interestingly, a number of prominent coaches have expressed a reluctance to rein in or curb their players' emotions in case it lowers their drive on the field of play. For example, after the England soccer star Wayne Rooney had been sent off for stamping on Richard Carvalho in the 2006 World Cup quarter final match against Portugal, Sven-Göran Eriksson (England's manager at the time) revealed that, "Of course, he has a temperament [*sic*] but you have to live with that. You can't take that away from him because he would never be the same player" (cited in Kremer and Moran, 2013, p. 112). However, there is anecdotal evidence which suggests that performance improves when athletes learn to curb their temper. For example, Björn Borg, the winner of eleven Grand Slam titles over the course of his tennis career, earned the nickname "ice man" for the cool and unflappable demeanour he displayed on court. It may come as a surprise that Borg had been extremely angry and volatile in his early years: "When I was twelve, I behaved badly on court, swearing, cheating, throwing rackets – so my club suspended me for six months. When I came back ... I felt that I played my best tennis being focused" (cited in Kremer and Moran, 2013, p. 113). Indeed, other elite athletes have acknowledged the importance of controlling their emotions if they are to perform at their best. Rory McIlroy, the winner of four major golf championships, revealed that there are times when "I need to stay in control of my emotions ... If I am a little tired or a little fatigued mentally I'll start to be hard on myself and start to get down on myself" (Austin, 2015).

The preceding anecdotal evidence complements a large volume of empirical research which has shown that emotions have an important bearing on the process and outcome of athletic performance. This body of research has raised some interesting questions regarding the role that "negative" and "positive" emotions may play in athletic performance. To explain, one might assume that certain negative emotions will automatically prove deleterious to athletic performance but there may be occasions when they can actually improve performance proficiency. For example, experiencing anger or fear might result in athletes recruiting more resources in order to combat these feelings or to deal with the cause of these emotions (Eysenck and Calvo, 1992; Fredrickson, 2001; Lazarus, 2000). On the other hand, the same emotion can also prove dysfunctional such as when a show of anger or petulance towards a referee might result in a sending off or sin-binning. Researchers (e.g. Moore et al. 2015) have found that athletes will appraise situations differently (e.g. as a challenge or a threat) and, as a result, may display very different emotional responses (i.e. either negative or positive) to the same sporting situation. This emphasizes the complexity of the emotion–performance relationship in sport and may explain why this topic has become of increasing interest to researchers and practitioners working in this field.

Of course, emotions also play an important role outside the competitive arena by influencing athletes' motivation to train, their adherence to injury rehabilitation programmes, and the way in which they deal with retirement from sport. Given the wide range of stressors that athletes encounter in training and competitive environments (e.g. injury, deselection) it would be foolhardy to think that they could go through their entire career without ever experiencing debilitating emotions. Accordingly, it is important that they are aware of a variety of strategies that can be used for emotional control. One might argue that sport psychologists' principal aim should be to help athletes to prevent certain emotions from occurring rather than seeking to react to the emotion when it arises. The former approach appears to be a more effective strategy as attempts to reappraise a stimulus (i.e. the cognitive evaluation a person makes regarding the significance of an event) may stop the emotion from occurring and are less cognitively demanding than strategies that suppress an emotion once it arises. As a result, many sport psychologists seek to help athletes to reappraise stressors but they may also develop strategies that allow performers to cope with and/or regulate these emotions. The ultimate aim is to help athletes attain and maintain the appropriate/functional emotional state during competition.

The purpose of this chapter is to review the findings from a body of literature which has investigated the emotion–performance relationship in sport. To achieve this objective, the chapter is organised as follows. First, we explore the nature of emotions. The next section outlines a number of prominent theories that have sought to explain the emotion–performance relationship. After that, we consider how a number of specific negative and positive emotions might influence performance proficiency, whilst the fourth section examines a variety of instruments and methodological approaches that have been used to measure emotions in athletes. The fifth section reveals some of the regulatory processes that athletes may use in seeking to deal with the stressors and emotions they encounter in competitive environments. The sixth section considers an emerging body of empirical evidence on the coping strategies used by athletes. The chapter concludes by highlighting some unresolved issues and a discussion of some potentially fruitful areas for future research.

What are emotions?

A precise definition of the term "emotion" is likely to remain elusive given the sheer range and complexity of affective states it seeks to describe (M. Jones, 2012). However, researchers generally conceptualize emotions as subjective feelings experienced in response to one's environment (e.g. playing a match in front of a raucous and aggressive home support) or in one's mind such as concern about performance in an upcoming event. More precisely, Fredrickson (2001) defined emotion as a cognitively appraised reaction to an event that "triggers a cascade of response tendencies manifest across loosely coupled component systems, such as subjective experience, facial expression, cognitive processing and physiological changes" (p. 218). It may be useful at this point to clarify the difference between *emotions* and *mood*. Whereas emotions represent a response to a stimulus or event (e.g. delight at scoring a goal), mood is believed to represent a more enduring state whereby the individual may be unaware of the causes of the feelings experienced. Despite this distinction, Jones (2012) argued that the experience of mood and emotion may be very similar to a person who is unable to tease apart feelings that have been triggered by a specific stimulus from those that are already present as part of an underlying mood state. Whilst reading the literature in this area, one should also be aware that the terms emotion and mood are used to describe specific feeling states while *affect* is used as a broad term to capture all valenced responses including preferences, emotions and moods.

Emotions generally elicit three types of response: *physiological* such as increased heart rate; *motivational* such as devoting extra physical and mental resources towards a task; and *cognitive* such as alterations in attention and other information processing capacities. Let us briefly consider the relationship between emotion and each of these types of responses. The effect of physiological arousal on performance is believed to vary across emotions. For example, imagery-induced anger has been found to enhance muscular strength on an isometric extension of the right leg, when compared to imagery-induced happiness (Woodman et al., 2009). Physiological arousal has also been found to positively affect height jumped on the Segeant jump performance (Parfitt et al., 1995) and performance on a standard hand strength task (Perkins et al., 2001). Increased arousal might be positive for performance tasks requiring power but there are few sporting tasks where power or strength is the sole requirement. In fact, increased arousal can prove deleterious to performance on tasks that require coordination or fine motor control (Collins et al., 2001; Pijpers et al., 2005). In addition, experiencing certain emotions may have a motivational effect on performance – such as when a soccer player seeks to overcome feelings of shame for having made an error by attempting to gain possession of the ball as much as possible in order to create a goal-scoring opportunity. However, other emotions, such as anxiety, may lead performers to "hide" on the pitch and to *avoid* calling for the ball for fear that they may make the same mistake again. Emotions also have an important influence on an athlete's cognitive functioning. For example, positive emotions are believed to broaden an athlete's attentional focus whereas negative emotions narrow attention. Positive emotions, such as amusement and contentment, may increase creativity in sport by facilitating the cognitive flexibility that is required by performers attempting to think of a novel game play or approach to break down the defensive resolve of a well organised opponent (M. Jones, 2012). By contrast, certain emotions like anxiety may direct the performer's attention towards potential threats in the environment rather than task-relevant cues.

Theories of emotion

A number of theories have been proposed to explain how emotions arise in sport settings and how they may influence athletic performance. In the following section, we discuss three of the most influential theoretical frameworks in this field (i.e. Lazarus', 2001, cognitive-motivational-relational theory; Hanin's, 2000, Individual Zones of Optimal Functioning Hypothesis; Jones et al.'s, 2009, theory of challenge and threat states in athletes). Let us start by discussing Lazarus' cognitive-motivational-relational theory (CMRT; 1991). The CMRT proposes that individuals are continually evaluating events in their lives with respect to the significance for their well-being. According to this theory, there are two processes involved in the generation and regulation of emotions: *cognitive appraisal* and *coping*. We will address each of these processes in turn.

The CMRT proposes that when performing in stressful environments it is how one appraises the situation, rather than the situation itself, that influences the emotional response. For example, consider how Jack Nicklaus (who has won more major golf championships than any other player) changed the way he labelled the anxiety he felt before competitions:

> Sure you're nervous, but that's the difference between being able to win and not being able to win. And that's the fun of it, to put yourself in the position of being nervous, being excited. I never look on it as pressure. *I look on it as fun and excitement.*
>
> (cited in Gilleece, 1996, italics ours; see also Figure 4.2)

Figure 4.2 Jack Nicklaus labelled the anxiety he felt before competition as fun and excitement

According to the CMRT, an event/situation may be *appraised* in number of ways. To explain, it may be seen as representing a source of *harm* if a loss has already occurred, *threat* if there is the potential of a loss, *challenge* if we are faced with a difficult-to-attain yet anticipated gain, and *benefit* if a gain has already occurred (Lazarus, 2000). According to Lazarus (1991, 2000), emotions arise from what he termed a **"core relational theme"**, which comprises a summary of six separate appraisal judgments, classified as either primary (goal relevance, goal congruence, type of ego involvement) and/or secondary (blame or credit, coping potential, future expectations) appraisals. For example the core relational theme for happiness is "making reasonable progress towards the realization of a goal" (Lazarus, 2000, p. 234). Appraisals of any given situation will be accompanied by a "relational meaning" as the individual takes into account personal factors, environmental demands, constraints and opportunities. This latter concept helps to explain how two different individuals can experience similar emotional reactions when encounters vary and yet different reactions when encounters are the same.

The *coping* process also plays a critical role in Lazarus' approach. Rather than treating coping as a separate process (which occurs independently of the emotional experience), Lazarus proposed that coping starts as soon as an emotion is elicited. If, for example, an athlete fears retaliation from a physically imposing counterpart, they may be more likely to express anger or they may reappraise the conditions for it. This, in turn, will change the relational meaning that led to anger and may result in the athlete experiencing a different emotion such as anxiety or guilt. Lazarus argued that coping mediates the reaction to the emotion-provoking relationship and the subsequent emotion. So, what an individual thinks and does to cope will influence the emotion that emerges from the emotion-provoking encounter. The CMRT represents a nomothetic approach – that is, the core relational theme of each emotion does not change on a person-by-person basis. For example, people will vary greatly in terms of what angers them and they will also express anger in different ways but anger will always correspond to a situation appraised as a "demeaning offense against me and mine" (Lazarus, 2000, p. 234).

How does the CMRT propose that emotions will influence performance? Lazarus believed that emotions may trigger the use of self-statements or ruminative thoughts that disrupt the focused attention required to perform at one's best. The core relational theme of each emotion is also likely to have a significant influence on a performer's level of motivation. Ultimately, emotion will influence performance depending on the match between the action tendencies (impulse to act when we experience a specific emotion) derived from the core relational theme and the task demands. For example, an action tendency that is associated with *anger* is the impulse to counter-attack in order to gain revenge for a perceived affront. A number of studies have found that anger has a positive influence on performance on a maximal force task (Davis et al., 2010; Woodman et al., 2009) – perhaps because the task requirements were similar to anger's associated action tendency (i.e. to lash out).

Neil et al. (2011) interviewed twelve athletes in order to examine their appraisals, emotional reactions, further appraisals and behavioural responses to performance and organizational stressors that they encountered in a competitive environment. Overall, the findings supported Lazarus' contention that emotions are underpinned by unique appraisals. The results also provided some interesting insights into the mechanisms underpinning the performers' interpretations of their felt emotions. To explain, a number of participants positively interpreted what are traditionally considered to be negative emotions (e.g. anxiety) in order to motivate themselves to do well. This interpretation led to an increase in effort and concentration and provides further evidence that anxiety symptoms can be interpreted as beneficial to performance (see Chapter 3 for a detailed discussion). These findings also demonstrate that further appraisals occur once emotions are experienced by the performer. This cognitive process does not involve a reappraisal of the situation itself but an interpretation of the emotion in relation to its anticipated influence on performance. For example, one participant reported feeling anxious (caused by concerns over making mistakes in front of a crowd) as a result of encountering various performance and environmental stressors but interpreted these emotions as facilitative towards the upcoming performance. The performer interpreted these emotions as being positive and used thoughts of making mistakes to motivate him to do better. This reinterpretation led to a reported improvement in his level of concentration during task execution.

While considerable support exists for the CMRT, some studies have failed to find conclusive evidence for the existence of core relational themes. For example, Martinent and Ferrand (2015) used **self-confrontation interviews** with eleven national table-tennis players to explore the cognitive appraisals associated with discrete emotions experienced during competition. This study found no support for the core relational theme for anger. In addition, the athletes in Martinent and Ferrand's study associated hope with "believing the improvement from a difficult situation is possible" rather than Lazarus' (2000) conceptualization which associates hope with "fearing the worst but yearning for better and believing the improvement is possible". Martinent and Ferrand (2015) argued that perceiving that it is possible to overcome a difficult situation may elicit hope while fearing the worst but yearning for better may intensify this emotion. Similarly, Uphill and Jones (2007) interviewed twelve elite athletes about the emotions they experienced during competition and the findings on core relational themes were mixed. Support was found for the core relational themes of guilt, relief and shame but not for the core relational themes of anger and pride.

The CMRT has found considerable support in the sporting literature but Jones (2012) argued that it is an incomplete explanation of emotions. For example, it is possible that Lazarus' notion of core relational themes may account for some emotions better than others (Bennett et al., 2003; Uphill and Jones, 2007). Therefore, further research is required to gain a better understanding of the relationship between action tendency predictions and performance. The model has also been challenged by the "Conservation of Resources Theory" (COR; Hobfoll, 2001) which proposes that stress experience derives from the threat to the loss of resources, and not from the appraisal process itself. Notwithstanding these critiques, one of the main contributions made by the CMRT is the emphasis that it places on cognition in the emotion process. This emphasis has encouraged researchers to consider how changes to an athlete's cognition will influence their emotional response (see later in this chapter for a discussion on how emotions can be regulated). In this regard, Ntoumanis et al. (2009) explored the conceptual links between the Cognitive-Motivational-Relational Theory of coping (Lazarus, 1991) and Self-Determination Theory of Motivation (Deci and Ryan, 1985) and suggested that researchers should also consider how motivational factors are implicated in the coping process. These authors argue that when individuals feel autonomous and competent during a stressful encounter they are more likely to appraise demands or constraints on goals as challenges that need to be overcome rather than threats or losses.

Individual zone of optimal functioning

As we mentioned in Chapter 3, Hanin's (2000) individual zone of optimal functioning theory (IZOF) predicts how a performer's precompetitive emotional state will influence performance during competition. Hanin (2000) proposed that successful performances are characterized by distinct emotional patterns which can be distinguished from those of less successful performances. The theory adopts a multidimensional approach by describing emotional experiences in terms of their form (e.g. cognitive, somatic), intensity, content, time (e.g. duration), and context. Emotions can be categorized on the basis of hedonic tone (pleasant or unpleasant) and on functional impact on performance (optimal or dysfunctional). Proponents of this theory argue that how one perceives emotion is likely to differ on an individual-by-individual basis. For example, anger and joy might be perceived as pleasant or unpleasant depending on their impact upon performance. The athlete who experiences anger during a winning performance is likely to find this hedonically pleasing as this emotion may have enhanced performance. According to Hanin (2000) emotions possess an energizing and organizing function that will result in energy mobilization/demobilization and energy utilization (including misuse). Athletes who possess functional-pleasant and functional-unpleasant emotions are believed to be more capable of mobilizing and utilizing energy in a productive manner (Robazza et al., 2004, 2008). Dysfunctional-pleasant and dysfunctional-unpleasant emotions may result in lethargy and distraction (Hanin and Stambulova, 2002).

Proponents of the theory typically seek to establish individualized performance profiles for each player based on a retrospective analysis of the emotions that accompanied good and bad performances. Performers may also be observed for a period of time – whereby the performer's emotional intensities and performance quality is observed. This data is collected as the IZOF proposes that athletes possess an individually optimal and dysfunctional pre-performance bandwidth or zone of emotional intensity. The IZOF is determined by adding or subtracting 0.25 or 0.50 standard deviations to or from the mean emotional intensity (based on observations and analysis of past performance; Kamata et al., 2002). Optimal performance is most likely to occur when the athlete's emotional level falls within the optimal zone and outside the dysfunctional zone. Poor performance is likely to occur when the athlete's emotional level falls outside the optimal zone and within the dysfunctional zone (Robazza et al., 2008). How does the IZOF propose that emotions will influence performance? The interaction between emotional content (e.g. anger) and the intensity of that emotion (high, moderate, or low) is believed to either facilitate or disrupt performance proficiency. Ultimately, athletes will evaluate if they possess the necessary resources to meet the demands of the task (Hanin, 2007). Optimizing emotions are believed to be linked with increased concentration and confidence, positive sensations and adaptive behaviours.

Kamata et al. (2002) pointed to a number of problems associated with the original IZOF methodology (e.g. emotional intensities associated with optimal performance are also experienced when performance is less than optimal). These authors sought to overcome these limitations by introducing a "probabilistic approach" in order to improve the predictive validity of the model. This methodology helps identify probability-based zones of intensity (including affective and physiological states) within which each athlete is predicted to perform at a certain level (e.g. optimal, moderate, poor). Probability-based zones of intensity have been identified in a variety of sports including golf (Cohen et al., 2006) and archery (Johnson et al., 2007). Edmonds et al. (2006) used perceived affectivity (i.e. arousal and pleasantness) and physiological measures (i.e. heart rate and skin conductance) to define individual zones of functioning for three performers competing in a simulated car racing task. Each performer maintained unique individual affect-related performance zones for each of these latter measures. Overall, findings indicated that athletes are unlikely to share the same level or range of arousal.

In another IZOF inspired study, Robazza et al. (2008) explored the impact of emotions on the performance of sixty-five high-level Italian track and field athletes. Performers were asked to complete an eleven-item post-performance self-evaluation scale with 1 = "very, very poor", 6 = "intermediate" and 11 = "excellent". Self-ratings were taken across one to three competitions and used as independent variables in the analysis of intensity, intra-individual, and direction scores of anxiety, self-confidence, idiosyncratic emotions and bodily symptoms. Performance levels (i.e. poor, average or good) were established based on the athlete's self-ratings and characterized as near to or distant from optimal/dysfunctional zones and used as independent variables to analyse the direction scores of anxiety. Results provided support for the IZOF's predictions as emotional levels that approximated an individual's optimal zone were perceived as facilitative-pleasant and emotional levels approximating an individual's dysfunctional zone were perceived as debilitative-unpleasant.

Bortoli et al. (2012) sought to build on the preceding body of work by exploring the value of the probabilistic approach as a means of studying the time course of physiological indicators of arousal/activation (measured by skin conductance) and vigilance (measured by heart rate) in the moments preceding the onset of skill execution (e.g. just before a pistol shooter pulls the trigger). The researchers found significant differences in affect intensity, hedonic tone, skin conductance level and heart rate, as a function of performance. These findings lend weight to the claim that athletes need to reach and maintain idiosyncratic optimal performance profiles in order to perform at their best.

The IZOF has undoubtedly made an important contribution to our understanding of the emotion–performance relationship in sport. However, a number of researchers have expressed concern at the model's inability to predict how emotion will influence performance proficiency amongst less skilled performers. For example, doubt has been expressed about less skilled performers' capacity to recognize the emotional states that might accompany poor or good performance. That is, inexperienced athletes, who do not have an extensive performance history, may experience difficulties in identifying valid zones (Hanin and Syrjä, 1995) although Woodcock et al. (2012) found that a relatively inexperienced runner was capable of identifying these zones. Hanin (2000) recommended the profiling process to be used predominantly with experienced athletes who are assumed to have a necessary level of awareness for zone identification. Another criticism that may be levelled at the model is that it struggles to explain why some athletes suffer performance decrements whilst experiencing certain emotions whilst others retain performance proficiency. Future research using the IZOF could test its predictions while measuring physiological variables. Indeed, it may be easier to predict optimal performance when emotions are considered in conjunction with physiological measures of vigilance.

The theory of challenge and threat states in athletes

The theory of challenge and threat states (TCTSA; Jones et al., 2009) has recently been put forward as another conceptual perspective seeking to explain the emotion–performance relationship in sport. This theory presents a dichotomy in terms of the way athletes respond to competition. That is, Jones et al. (2009)

propose that athletes can be classified into those who respond positively (i.e. they see competition as a challenge) and those who respond negatively (i.e. they see competition as a threat). The TCSTA seeks to explain *why* athletes may perceive an upcoming competition as either a challenge or a threat, *how* they respond emotionally and physiologically when they do, and *how* challenge and threat states can influence movement and performance proficiency. Let us address each of these questions in turn.

First, the TCTSA argues that a challenge state is experienced when an athlete perceives that they possess sufficient resources to meet the demands of a situation while a threat state is experienced when one believes that they have insufficient resources. Appraisal is an important component of the model and comprises *demand* and *resource* appraisals (Blascovich and Mendes, 2000). *Demand* appraisals may arise when one perceives danger or uncertainty in a competitive situation (see Figure 4.3). For example, a *demand* appraisal may be made by a defender in soccer who is aware that she is marking an opponent who has great speed and dribbling skills (danger of humiliation), is uncertain how she will perform and recognizes that it will take a great deal of mental effort and tactical awareness to gain the upper hand (effort). *Resource* appraisals are related to a person's ability to cope with the demands of a situation and include skills, knowledge and a variety of dispositional factors (e.g. self-esteem) and the external support available to the athlete. As such, a challenge state may be experienced if an athlete has been performing well (skills) and is pitted against an opponent who he/she has beaten on the last few occasions they have met in competition (knowledge).

Figure 4.3 Demand appraisals are made by defenders in team sports

The TCTSA proposes that resource appraisals comprise three interrelated constructs (self-efficacy, perceptions of control and goal orientation). Ultimately, it is the manner in which these three constructs interact which will determine whether a challenge or threat state is experienced. For example, if an individual aims to perform better than an opponent, believes that they have the skills to do so (self-efficacy) and has sufficient perceived control over the situation then the adoption of performance approach goals (i.e. striving for competence) should be associated with a challenge state.

How do athletes respond physiologically when they experience either a challenge or threat state? A challenge response is characterized by an increase in sympathetic-adreno-medullary (SAM) 13 activity and accompanying increases in epinephrine and cardiac activity along with a decrease in peripheral vascular resistance (Jones et al., 2009). A threat response is characterized by an increase in SAM and pituitary-adreno-cortical (PAC) activity, accompanying increases in cortisol, smaller increases in cardiac activity and either no change or an increase in peripheral vascular resistance. When athletes perceive a situation as challenging, the SAM activation enables an organism to mobilize energy for a fight or flight response whereas a threat state resulting from PAC and SAM activation is a distress system associated with perceptions of actual or physical harm.

Researchers have sought to identify whether the **valence** of athletes' emotional states during challenge and threat states are perceived as helpful or unhelpful for performance (see Box 4.1). The TCTSA predicts that positive emotions will typically be associated with a challenge state and negative emotions with a threat response. Of course, there are situations in which negative emotions, such as anger and anxiety, can occur in a challenge state. How might this arise? Challenge and threat represent motivational states and thus are orthogonal to the valence of the emotion experienced (Mendes et al., 2008). Adopting this perspective, one might be able to understand how an athlete experiencing high intensity emotions of a negative valence (like anxiety or anger) can serve as a motivational function that would be consistent with a challenge state. So, it is possible that both cognitive and somatic anxiety could be experienced in a challenge state as many athletes feel anxious as they enter a competition but believe those symptoms will actually help performance (see Chapter 3). Here, emotions of a negative valence might lead the performer to increase their motivation or to reorient their focus of attention. Importantly, high levels of anxiety (or any emotions of a negative valence) will be perceived as being facilitative to performance if the athlete has a high perception of control and high self-efficacy.

Blascovich et al. (2004) required baseball and softball players to provide a two minute speech about a specific baseball/softball playing situation while cardiovascular indices of threat and challenge were recorded. These indices were able to significantly predict athletic performance during the subsequent season and revealed that players who experienced challenge in the laboratory performed better relative to those who experienced threat. In a more recent study, Turner et al. (2013) tested whether cardiovascular reactivity patterns indexing challenge and threat states could predict performance in elite cricket players.

Box 4.1 Thinking critically about … how the manipulation of challenge and threat states influences athletic movement and performance proficiency

In a novel study, Moore et al. (2012) manipulated challenge and threat states in a sample of novice golfers prior to a putting task and explored how these manipulations influenced their movement and performance proficiency. The threat instructions focused on the task's high degree of difficulty and emphasized that previous participants had struggled to perform well on the task. The challenge instructions encouraged participants to perceive the task as a challenge to be met and overcome, and to think of themselves as capable of meeting the challenge and they were reminded that previous participants had performed well on the task. Results revealed that the challenge group performed better on the putting task than the threat group. What mechanisms were responsible for these findings? The challenge group reported lower levels of cognitive anxiety, were found to possess a smoother and more efficient movement pattern, and had longer quiet eye durations (see Chapter 3) and lower activation of task-relevant muscles when compared to the threat group. In another study, Moore et al. (2013) employed a similar procedure with a group of "experienced" golfers (mean handicap = 9). Again, challenge and threat states were successfully manipulated. The challenge group outperformed the threat group in the golf putting task (they held a higher percentage of putts) and demonstrated a cardiovascular response consisting of relatively higher cardiac output and lower total peripheral resistance compared with the threat group. The challenge group also reported lower cognitive and somatic anxiety scores than the threat group and felt that this was facilitative for performance – although subsequent mediation analyses revealed that none of the emotional variables could account for the effect of the experimental manipulation on the performance measures.

Critical thinking questions

The participants in the Moore et al. (2012, 2013) studies were novices and "experienced" participants – do you think researchers would find similar results if the same procedure was used with highly skilled or elite participants? What difficulties do you think you might encounter if you were to attempt to induce a threat state in elite participants? Moore et al.'s (2013) study explored the effects of challenge and threat states over a very short number of trials (in order to prevent participants re-evaluating the task). However, the authors acknowledge that an athlete's demand and resource evaluations are likely to fluctuate quite considerably during competition and that this re-evaluation is likely to impact performance. Are there alternative methodological approaches that you might use to capture these fluctuations during performance?

Batting performance was tested under pressure and cardiovascular reactivity was recorded after participants had been given ego-threatening instructions. Cardiovascular reactivity predicted superior performance in the batting test, compared with threat cardiovascular activity. Although these latter findings are in line with the TCTSA's predictions we should note that other studies have reported inconsistencies in cardiovascular and psychological responses and that the psychology of cardiovascular responses remains unclear (for a review see Hilmert and Kvasnicka, 2010). For example, Meijen et al. (2014) asked collegiate athletes to talk about an upcoming competition whilst cardiovascular and self-report measures were completed. These authors found that perceived control, self-reported measures of challenge and threat, anxiety and happiness, and perception of emotional state did not relate to cardiovascular responses. Meijen et al. noted that only studies that have actually manipulated self-efficacy or threat and challenge states have found an effect on cardiovascular responses.

Perhaps the TCTSA's biggest contribution to this field of study is the emphasis it has placed on understanding an athlete's state response to a competitive situation. This focus seems particularly pertinent given the wide range of evidence which indicates that athletes' responses to stressors are dynamic and that their appraisals of demands and resources fluctuate (Jones et al., 2009). The use of cardiovascular responses also provides a non-invasive means of identifying athletes who are approaching competition in either a challenge or a threat state. However, as the TCTSA is a relatively new theory in this field, further research is required to support some of the predictions outlined above. Further research may wish to establish the neuroendocrine changes that accompany challenge and threat states while additional research could explore the proposal that athletes can experience high levels of negatively valenced emotions in a challenge state and yet still perceive these as being facilitative to performance.

Specific emotions in competitive performance

Negative emotions

Researchers have found that athletes experience a host of negatively toned emotions during performance. These emotions include anger, anxiety, disappointment, guilt, embarrassment, shame, sadness and regret. Inspection of the relevant literature reveals that anxiety is the most heavily researched of these negative emotions but in the following section we discuss findings from a body of research which has sought to understand the anger–performance relationship in sport (perhaps the next most researched negative emotion).

One might assume that experiencing anger will inevitably prove deleterious to sporting performance. Take, for example, the Portuguese football player Pepe's reaction having been struck in the face by the German player Thomas Muller in a match during the 2014 World Cup. Pepe responded by "headbutting" Muller and subsequently earned a red card which virtually ensured that his team would lose the match (they were 2–0 down when the incident occurred).

Although anger typically hampers performance there are occasions when athletes somehow manage to use it as a tool to motivate themselves and to overcome disappointment. For example, consider the controversy that surrounded the 2015 Solheim Cup match (the biennial event between the top twelve ranked American and European female golfers). In a remarkable incident, America's Alison Lee and Brittany Linicome picked up their ball on the seventeeth hole of their match against Europe's Charley Hull and Suzanne Pettersen having mistakenly believed that the putt had been conceded (i.e. that they were not required to hole the putt). The European pair claimed that the putt had not been given to the Americans and therefore the hole was awarded to the European team leading to heated exchanges amongst the players and managers at the conclusion of the match. The Europeans went on to win this particular game and took a formidable four point lead in to the final day's play. Pettersen justified her actions by arguing that the conceded putt was three foot in length (it was in actual fact considerably shorter) but the American team believed that the Europeans had demonstrated extremely poor sportspersonship. So, the Americans harnessed their anger and sense of injustice as a motivational tool for the team. Commenting on this issue, Stacey Lewis observed "if that's how they want to play it, let's use this to motivate us". The American team staged a remarkable comeback to win eight and a half points (out of a possible twelve) in the final day's single matches and win the overall match.

According to Lazarus' CMRT model, the action tendency appraisal for anger is a "powerful impulse to counterattack in order to gain revenge for an affront or to repair wounded self-esteem" (Lazarus, 2000, p. 243). Woodman et al. (2009) explored the effects of anger and happiness on the performance of physical and cognitive tasks. Findings partially supported the authors' hypothesis as participants' performance on the physical task (i.e. gross muscular peak force task requiring isometric extensions of the right leg) was significantly greater when angry compared with the happiness and emotion-neutral condition. In this study, anger may have facilitated performance as the task requirements were similar to anger's associated action tendency (i.e. to lash out). In a second experiment, these authors explored the influence of hope and anger on cognitive performance (using a computer task to measure soccer-related reaction times) amongst a group of semi-professional football players. In line with the authors' hypothesis, effort and performance was greater in the hope condition (imagery scripts were used to elicit this emotion) than in the emotion-neutral condition. By contrast, although participant effort rose in the anger condition, performance was not significantly better than in the emotion-neutral condition. This may have been the case because the action tendency for anger (e.g. lashing out) is less obviously aligned with the cognitive task.

Woodman et al.'s (2009) third study sought to identify individual differences that might moderate the anger–performance relationship. The authors chose extraversion as an individual difference variable that might represent a potential moderator given that extraverts are more sociable and therefore more willing to express themselves in front of others. Similar to the results from experiment 1, anger resulted in superior performance on a gross muscular peak force task and the extraverts' performance gains were better than introverts.

How might anger be measured in competitive athletes? Maxwell and Moores (2007) developed a twelve-item scale (Competitive Aggressiveness and Anger Scale, CAAS) in order to measure trait anger and aggressiveness in competitive athletes (given the widely acknowledged relationship between anger and aggression). Maxwell et al. (2009) administered the CAAS, the Sport Behaviour Inventory (SBI) and the Chinese version of the state/trait anger expression inventory (STAXI-C; Maxwell et al., 2009) to a large sample of Chinese male competitive athletes and found that players of team sports (e.g. basketball, rugby) perceived aggression as more legitimate than did players of squash while players of contact sports scored higher on the CAAS aggressiveness and anger subscales than did players of non-contact sports (see Figure 4.4). In interpreting their findings the authors raised an intriguing question by asking whether contact and collision sports tend to attract players who are more angry/aggressive or whether the nature of these sports socializes them to express these emotions/engage in these behaviours. Further analysis revealed that for these rugby players advanced status was associated with increased aggressiveness and anger – a finding which might suggest that such behaviours are adaptive for success.

Grange and Kerr (2010) interviewed eight of the most aggressive Australian football players (most had been suspended or fined during their careers for aggressive on-field acts) about their use of sanctioned and unsanctioned aggression. Findings revealed that some of these athletes angrily retaliated to an act of aggression by an opponent and, in some cases, the use of aggression as a form of intimidation

Figure 4.4 Aggression may facilitate performance in certain sports

was openly advocated by coaches. Certain players showed examples of "anger aggression" which represents a sudden and immediate response to an opponent's transgression. In a qualitative study with elite athletes, Uphill and Jones (2007) explored athletes' appraisals and their experienced emotions. Anger was the most frequently reported negative emotion experienced by these athletes. It was found to influence athletes' attention by redirecting thoughts to task-irrelevant stimuli. To illustrate, an archer revealed that when angry "your thoughts aren't channelled to the goal of shooting correctly". Anger also appeared to negatively influence athletes' decision making while competing. One badminton player described the impact of anger on shot selection as follows: "You lose control and you don't think. You've got to build rallies up ...but more errors come into the game [through] selecting the wrong shots" (Uphill and Jones, 2011, p. 222). By contrast, anger was reported paradoxically as having either a beneficial or detrimental impact on athletes' motivation. To illustrate, a golfer indicated that anger can prove beneficial by helping him to "get nasty with myself ... swear a lot .... Sometimes you've got no fight, if you start having a go, it just gets you going" but that it can also prove problematic because "sometimes you can go the other way and not give a t★★★" (p. 222). This quote suggests that there may be intra-individual differences in the impact of emotions on motivational states and that strategies employed by athletes to manage their emotions will have an important impact on performance.

Allen et al. (2009) explored how attributions made immediately after a competitive event influence the temporal patterning of emotions experienced in response to competition. Sixty adult female golfers completed measures of performance satisfaction, casual attribution and emotion (using the Sport Emotion Questionnaire; SEQ) immediately after competition, five hours after competition, and two days after competition. Findings revealed that attributions remained consistent over time. Feelings of anger were reduced over the post-competition period only when athletes attributed poor performance to unstable causes (i.e. the cause may not be present again). Feelings of anger did not subside when athletes attributed poor performance to stable causes. The findings from this study indicate that emotional duration should be explored relative to emotional intensity.

Positive emotions

Although mainstream psychology research has devoted greater attention to the exploration of negative emotions (e.g. anxiety) rather than positive emotions (e.g. happiness) sport psychology researchers have started to devote attention to an exploration of the latter (see Figgins et al., 2016; McCarthy, 2011). For example, Figgins et al. (2016) explored the concept of inspiration in sport. Interestingly, McCarthy (2011) argued that positive emotions are likely to have an important influence on certain subcomponents of sport performance including perception, attention and decision making. Positive emotions may be associated with the broadening of one's attentional focus and may increase performers' cognitive flexibility – that is, their ability to sustain and guide their focus of attention. It may be worth noting at this point that we must be careful not to assume that the terms positive and negative emotions imply that the affective content of the emotion is pleasant/unpleasant but also that there are positive/negative effects associated with it. Recent research indicates that the relationship between positive emotions and performance is somewhat complex. For example, Woodman et al.'s (2009) study (see above) found that happiness did not produce any significant differences in cognitive performance in physically active students (as measured by a grammatical reasoning task which required participants to identify whether a sentence describes a letter pair correctly). The authors sought to explain this result by suggesting that happiness may actually result in no change in the cognitive resources one commits to a task. They claimed that the core relational theme of happiness suggests a satiated state, that is, if one feels happy then they may feel no immediate desire to change their mood. In another study exploring the relationship between happiness and performance, Totterdell (2000) required players from two professional cricket teams to use pocket computers to provide ratings of their moods and performances three times a day for 4 days in the lead up to a match between the two sides. Statistical analysis revealed a significant association between the average measure of teammates' happy moods and the players own moods and subjective performances. The results also revealed a relationship between an individual's own mood and the mood of their teammates but only when the individual was happier than usual.

Sport enjoyment is another positive emotion which has been explored by sport psychology researchers. This emotion has been defined as "a positive affective response to the sport experience that reflects generalized feelings such as pleasure, liking and fun" (Scanlan and Simons, 1992, p. 202). Sport enjoyment is seen as playing a crucial role in influencing motivation and commitment to sport across all stages of participation (from novice through to Olympic athlete; see Figure 4.5).

Figure 4.5 Enjoyment strengthens athletes' commitment to their sport

The importance of enjoying participation was emphasized by Caroline Wozniacki, currently ranked number 34 in the world tennis rankings, who revealed that "When you have fun, you play better. You want to spend time on the practice court – it all goes together. When I enjoy life, I do better at tennis" (Dunn, 2015). Scanlan et al. (1993) sought to identify the sources of enjoyment in sport, and their motivational consequences, in a large youth sample. The most significant sources of enjoyment for these participants were greater effort and mastery, positive team interactions and support, and positive coach support and satisfaction with the players' seasonal performance. Participants indicated that these sources of enjoyment played an important role in their commitment to sport. Scanlan et al. (1989) explored the sources of enjoyment amongst former elite figure skaters and found that these athletes derived enjoyment from diverse sources including social and life opportunities, perceived competence, social recognition of competence and the act of skating. Interestingly, these findings demonstrated that enjoyment was not only derived from the achievement aspects of sport (e.g. perceived competence) but also from the social and movement dimensions as well. In the next section we consider how positive emotions may lead to "emotional contagion" in sport (see Box 4.2).

Box 4.2 Thinking critically about … emotional contagion in sport

Behaviour is often contagious. For example, if you see someone yawn, you'll probably find yourself doing likewise. But does this type of "emotional contagion" apply on the sports pitch as well as in everyday life? More precisely, does celebrating your individual success enhance the likelihood of achieving team success? In an interesting study, Moll et al. (2010) explored the association between individually displayed post-shot behaviours and the final result of soccer penalty shootouts held in World Cups and European Championships. These researchers retrospectively rated penalty kicks in terms of distinct and recognizable behaviours associated with positive emotions. Findings revealed that 66 per cent of the players displayed celebratory behaviour and that most of these behaviours were linked with pride. Players who displayed certain celebratory behaviours were more likely to be in the team that ultimately won the shootout. These behaviours included extending both arms either below or above head height, expanding the chest, and making hands into fists. Moll et al. proposed that displaying pride had a positive impact on teammates by inducing what is known as "emotional contagion" (the mimicking of facial expressions, vocalizations, postures and movements to converge emotionally with others). Evidence to support the beneficial influence of this phenomenon has been found in a laboratory study in which the contagion of positive emotions lead to improved cooperation, decreased conflict and increased perceptions of task performance (Barsade, 2002). Moll et al. (2010) argued that displaying pride after a successful penalty kick indicated that the participants were experiencing increased self-esteem and dominance and that these emotions were perceived by their teammates. These convergent emotions may have lead teammates to feel more confident in taking their own penalty kick, helped to increase expectancy levels of winning the penalty shootout and/or resulted in a more positive approach to the shootout.

The authors also argued that their findings were in line with Fredrickson's (1998, 2001) "**broaden-and-build theory**". This theory proposes that certain positive emotions – including joy and contentment – can broaden people's momentary thought–action repertoires and build enduring resources (e.g. physical and psychological). From an evolutionary perspective, these emotions may increase our desire to play and explore thereby enhancing our personal resources and guaranteeing our continued existence. Whereas negative emotions may play an important role in influencing how we respond to a particular situation (e.g. fear leading us to withdraw), positive emotions are designed to encourage us to explore our environment for resources and opportunities (Cohn and Fredrickson, 2006). Positive emotions promote certain urges (joy urges us to be creative), and, over time, are believed to help us achieve psychological growth and improved well-being. Although this theory has only recently been applied by sport psychologists it seems to offer considerable promise as a theoretical framework to explain how positive emotions may influence sporting performance. Findings from the Moll et al. study show how positive emotions may induce emotional contagion thereby leading to superior performance under pressurized conditions. It is possible that positive emotions might lead athletes to adopt a broader attentional focus (i.e. to pursue a wide range of thoughts and actions) rather than attentional narrowing (focusing on task-irrelevant thoughts such as worrying about how they will be judged should they miss). Positive emotions may also prevent players from engaging in escapist behaviours which have been found to be linked with poor performance in penalty shootouts (rushing the kick so as to "get it over with"; Jordet and Hartman, 2008).

Critical thinking questions

O'Neil (2008) argued that emotional contagion mechanisms may be responsible for poorer performance among alpine skiers after they had witnessed a teammate sustain a severe injury. Can you think how or why emotional contagion might exert a negative influence in this scenario? Given that individuals can become quite adept at hiding their true emotions (i.e. engaging in "emotional labour"; see Morris and Feldman, 1996), what are the interpersonal (e.g. **cohesion**) and intrapersonal costs (e.g. fatigue) for team performers?

Measurement of emotions in athletes

Prior to the development of sport-specific scales, researchers of emotions in sport were heavily reliant upon the use of The Profile of Mood States (POMS; McNair et al., 1992) and the Positive and Negative Affect Schedule (PANS; Watson et al., 1988). These instruments assessed a broad range of affective states but were designed for use within the general population. The Brunel Mood Scale (BRUMS; Terry et al., 2003) is a derivative of the POMS scale and was designed as a sport-specific measurement. Criterion and factorial validity have been found for this twenty-four-item scale (Lane et al., 2012a). A limitation of the BRUMS is that vigour is the only positive construct assessed. To provide a more balanced assessment of negative and positive emotion, researchers have extended validation of the scale to include calmness and happiness factors (e.g. Lane and Devonport, 2009; Thelwell et al., 2007). Lane and Devonport (2009) asked 222 male athletes to complete the modified BRUMS in order to examine the interaction between pleasant and unpleasant affect in relation to optimal performance. Results revealed that low scores for tension and anger correlated positively with happiness when athletes did not concurrently experience depression, confusion and fatigue. When athletes reported feeling unpleasant emotions (anxious, tense) they were more likely to experience confusion, depression and fatigue. These findings suggest that when athletes experience tension alongside other unpleasant emotions they are less likely to experience positive emotions. On the basis of these results, the authors recommend that it may be more useful to investigate an athlete's overall emotional profile rather than focus on one emotion.

The lack of a sport-specific questionnaire to explore emotions in sport led Jones et al. (2005) to develop the Sport Emotion Questionnaire (SEQ). This twenty-two-item scale contains five dimensions (i.e. anxiety, dejection, excitement, anger and happiness) and is used in pre-competition settings. Support for the factorial validity and internal validity for the scale was found by Jones et al. (2005). The relationship between SEQ scores and the emotional control in competition subscale from the Test of Performance Strategies (TOPS: Thomas et al., 1999) offered support for the construct validity of the SEQ. Athletes who had high scores on psychological skills used to control emotions during competition had low scores of anger and dejection and high scores of excitement and happiness. The SEQ seems to hold a number of advantages over other measures in this field. First, the five-factor structure of the SEQ allows athletes to report on a broader range of emotional states than the PANS (which measures positive and negative affect only) or the POMS (which primarily measures negative moods). It also has a greater focus on positive emotions than the PANS, POMS or BRUMS. Second, the BRUMS factor structure was based on the POMS (a scale developed specifically for use with clinical populations) and therefore contained a number of subscales such as confusion – emotions which may not be commonly experienced by athletes. Finally, the SEQ was specifically designed to measure emotion rather than mood or affect. Lane (2007) argued that researchers should choose a scale that is best suited to the specific research question and that both BRUMS and SEQ provide valid measures of emotions for use in sport.

A number of studies over the past decade have used the SEQ to measure emotions in athletes. For example, Vast et al. (2010) administered the SEQ to sixty-nine athletes following a national softball competition. Athletes were asked to retrospectively report how their emotions had influenced a number of cognitive processes such as attention and concentration. Positive emotions such as excitement and happiness were perceived as more likely to lead to a performance-related focus and automated physical movements than negative emotions such as anxiety, dejection and anger. In another study, Allen et al. (2009) explored the effect of team-referent attributions on emotions and collective efficacy in a sample of 265 athletes. Following victory, attributions of team control were associated with higher levels of post-competition happiness. These findings provide initial support for the utility of the SEQ for investigating the relationship between emotional changes and various cognitive factors in a sporting context. In addition, Arnold and Fletcher (2015) recently found support for the reliability and validity of the SEQ as a measure of emotions experienced by performers in organizational environments during the past month. In this study, over 1,000 sports performers completed the SEQ and the Organizational Stressor Indicator for Sport Performers (OSI-SP; Arnold et al., 2013 – which measures the frequency, intensity and duration of organizational stressors experienced over the last month).

What are the strengths and weaknesses of using self-report instruments when seeking to explore emotions in athletes? (See also Chapter 1.) There are a number of advantages associated with the use of self-rating measures. For example, they are relatively easy to use (i.e. they can be completed in a variety of settings including a classroom or changing room), cost-effective and capture the subjective nature of emotional experience. However, individuals who score high on measures of social desirability may be less willing or capable of reporting negative emotional states. Some researchers have argued that self-rating measures could be used alongside physiological tests in an attempt to "make emotions organismic" (Lazarus, 2000). The fact that questionnaires require participants to retrospectively rate their emotions is also problematic. Emotions are recognized as dynamic processes that "unfold, linger and then dissipate over time" (Larsen and Fredrickson, 1999, p. 42). According to McCarthy (2011) emotions "also prompt different response systems (heart rate, sweat glands, hormones) with particular onset times and duration" so if they are recorded retrospectively rather than in real time "bodily changes associated with physiological systems become less obvious or redundant, obfuscating the gradation in subjective experience" (p. 53).

How might researchers overcome the preceding limitations? The use of manipulation checks (research strategies designed to ascertain whether the participant has experienced the desired emotion) in research on emotions may represent one means of doing so. In Davis et al.'s (2010) study, elite athletes viewed video footage of a successful or unsuccessful performance (evaluated as such by the athletes themselves) and provided online ratings of their sadness or happiness while undergoing **functional magnetic resonance imaging** (fMRI) scans. Athletes who viewed successful scenes were, perhaps unsurprisingly, significantly happier but also showed greater activation in the right premotor cortex and left sensorimotor cortex. The combination of a manipulation check and neuroscientific measurements may provide a more objective understanding of the emotions experienced by athletes. Of course, the use of neuroscientific measures during many dynamic sporting tasks is deeply impractical as movement is likely to present a number of "confounds" (i.e. variables that were not controlled or eliminated in the study and which could affect the results) (see also Chapter 5).

There are a number of additional methods that researchers use in seeking to explore the relationship between configurations of appraisals and the ensuing discrete emotions. First, they can use vignettes or scenarios that have been manipulated with respect to appraisal dimensions and ask participants to outline the emotions they might experience in these situations (Roseman, 1991). Second, researchers may ask participants to recall specific discrete emotions experienced during competition and then question them about the appraisal dimensions that caused these emotions (see Uphill and Jones, 2007). A potential drawback of the latter approach is the reliance on participants' long-term memory to recall events that may have happened some time before. Third, researchers can record competitive events in order to capture naturally occurring emotional experiences so as to better understand the appraisal process. Take, for example, the methodology used by Martinent and Ferrand (2015) to understand the appraisals associated with discrete emotions experienced by athletes during competition. These authors adopted a naturalistic, video-assisted approach which involved the use of self-confrontation interviews with national-level table tennis players. Here, participants were shown video footage of their performance and invited to describe events and emotions experienced. Analysis revealed that athletes experienced nine discrete emotions (self-, other-, and environmental-oriented anger, anxiety, disgust, joy, relief, hope and pride).

Methods used to elicit positive and negative emotions

The majority of laboratory experiments have sought to elicit negative emotions such as anxiety (e.g. Baumeister's exploration of choking under pressure; Baumeister, 1984; see Chapter 3). However, Woodman et al. (2009) elicited three discrete emotions, two positively (i.e. happiness, hope) and one negatively toned (i.e. anger) by using imagery scripts. The scripts were standardized by recording them onto a compact disc. Davis et al. (2010) used a similar procedure in their study which explored how differences in anger regulation might moderate the anger–performance relationship. These researchers elicited physiological, cognitive and somatic activation consistent with the appropriate emotional state by using imagery scripts which contained detail regarding stimuli, response and meaning propositions. Cover stories are also used by researchers to ensure that participants are unaware that their emotional states are being manipulated. For example, Moore et al. (2012) used a cover story to create challenge/threat state in a group of novice golfers.

Autonomic measures of emotion

Although self-report measures may provide an indication of the subjective experience of emotion, the use of various autonomic measures may also prove helpful in identifying the mechanisms underpinning emotional states. The autonomic nervous system (ANS) is a general-purpose physiological system responsible for modulating peripheral functions (Öhman et al., 2000). The most commonly assessed indices of ANS activation are based on electrodermal (i.e. sweat gland) or cardiovascular (i.e. blood circulatory system) responses. Although rarely used in sport (as movement activity would present a potential confounding variable) some sport psychologists have sought to capture electrodermal activity by measuring skin conductance response (SCR). For example, Appaneal et al. (2007) used measurements of SCR in a study which sought to explore psychophysiological stress reactivity to orthopaedic trauma among male athletes who sustained a severe sport injury. Injured and non-injured athletes completed self-report measures of psychological distress and were then shown video footage of athletes sustaining injuries while measures of heart rate and skin conductance were recorded. Athletes with injuries demonstrated significantly greater skin conductance reactivity and subjective distress compared to controls.

Commonly used cardiovascular measures of emotion include heart rate (HR) and cardiac output (CO). HR is often used as a means of measuring emotional valence and intensity in sporting performance. Unfortunately, this approach is of limited use when measuring individuals as they perform dynamic tasks (a characteristic of many sports) as there are a number of interacting variables in the cardiovascular system (e.g. respiratory anomalies) which can make it difficult to isolate the effect of affective valence. However, in controlled environments involving the performance of a relatively passive task (e.g. golf putting) the use of HR measurements can contribute to the researchers' understanding of an athlete's emotional state. For example, Cooke et al. (2014) found that expert golfers displayed greater HR deceleration in the final seconds preceding movement than their novice counterparts. Combining a number of the preceding approaches, Fenz and Epstein (1967) examined patterns of HR, respiration rate and skin conductance as experienced and inexperienced parachutists performed a jump sequence. HR levels were found to be lower amongst experienced jumpers but novices who performed well had similar physiological reactions as experienced jumpers.

Brain states as a measure of emotion

Mainstream emotion researchers have proposed that the physiological correlates of discrete emotions are likely to be found in the brain rather than in peripheral physiological responses (Mauss and Robinson, 2009). Researchers exploring emotions in athletes have started to take up this challenge by using electroencephalogram (EEG) and neuroimaging methods. For example, Davis et al. (2008) used fMRI to identify changes in regional cerebral activity associated with negative affect which was induced in elite athletes by exposing them to a self-referent video of personal competitive failure. Future research may use neuroimaging to better understand the neural systems invoked with the expression or regulation of affect and emotions.

Emotion regulation

Elite athletes often emphasize the importance of emotional regulation. Consider what the former Indian cricketer Yuvraj Singh had to say about being on the receiving end of "sledging" (being insulted or intimidated by an opposing player):

> … if someone says something, you want to reply, but you realise he is trying to get importance out of picking a fight with you. So then I think, I look and I move. Normally we react emotionally, so I try to keep my emotions

in check. I can't do it every time. This is something I have changed about myself, because in the past I would always react. Then I figured that not saying anything can sometimes be more powerful than talking.

(cited in Barker and Slater, 2015, p. 555)

Researchers have argued that learning to regulate the wide range of emotions experienced in competitive environments will have an important bearing on athletic success and development. **Emotion regulation** has been defined as "the automatic or deliberate use of strategies to initiate, maintain, modify or display emotions" (Lane et al., 2012b, p. 1190). The regulation of emotions appears to be part of a self-regulatory process used by athletes to keep track of the emotions they experience and to develop strategies to maintain or alter these emotions. Research suggests that there are a huge number of possible strategies people may use to regulate their emotions. Many athletes may even use certain psychological skills (such as imagery or self-talk) – without having received formal training in these skills – which will serve as emotion regulation strategies. What emotion-regulation strategies are most commonly used by athletes? Researchers have distinguished between *antecedent-focused* and *response-focused* strategies (Gross, 1998; Lane et al., 2012b). The former strategy involves redirecting one's attention in order to prevent an emotional response while the latter strategy involves the use of certain skills (e.g. self-talk) to regulate the emotion directly. According to Gross' (1998) model of emotion regulation, antecedent-focused strategies may be more efficient, as response-focused approaches take place after the emotion has occurred and are therefore likely to require greater resources to monitor and regulate behaviours.

Antecedent-focused emotion regulation strategies involve the following elements: situation selection and modification; attention deployment; and cognitive change. *Situation selection* involves deciding whether or not to place oneself in a particular situation whereas *situation modification* involves deliberate attempts to change aspects of a situation (Jones, 2012). One might see parallels between these approaches and problem-focused coping techniques which we outline later on. An example of situation selection might involve a soccer player who chooses not to take part in a penalty shootout as they fear how they might be judged should they miss the kick while a teammate might engage in situation modification by choosing to take the first penalty so as to avoid having to dwell on the upcoming task (Jones, 2012). *Attention deployment* involves directing attention away from emotion-inducing stimuli, so a golfer faced with a putt to win his or her first major championship may engage in a pre-shot routine rather than think about the potentially life-changing consequences of victory. *Cognitive change* requires the athlete to alter the meaning or significance of an event or situation and involves the psychological skills of imagery, goal-setting and self-talk (all discussed in detail in Chapter 5).

Response-focused emotional regulation involves the use of response modulation. Regulation of the autonomic arousal that accompanies emotions is a response strategy often used in performance settings. For example, progressive muscular relaxation and music may be used to regulate physiological arousal and emotions (see Figure 4.6). Researchers have devoted considerable attention to

Figure 4.6 Many athletes use music to regulate their emotions

the use of one response-focused strategy in particular: suppression. This body of research has pointed to the cognitively effortful nature of suppression as suppressing emotions or thoughts may leave individuals with fewer cognitive resources to process task-related stimuli or may exacerbate the very thoughts they are trying to suppress (i.e. increase "ironic processes"; see Chapter 3). In a recent study, Wagstaff (2014) found that participants who suppressed emotional reactions to an upsetting video prior to completing a 10k time cycle trial completed the task more slowly, generated lower power outputs, and reached a lower maximum heart rate when compared to a condition in which they were given no self-regulation instructions during the video.

How might athletes enhance their ability to successfully regulate their emotions? As discussed in the preceding section, evidence indicates that athletes should seek to reappraise a situation rather than attempt to suppress an emotion. In line with recommendations by proponents of the IZOF approach, practitioners can help performers to identify emotional states that accompany best and worst performances (see Box 4.3). Practitioners need to identify what strategies are being used by their athletes and the efficacy of these regulatory processes. For example, if athletes are using music to regulate emotions then they need to identify the musical pieces that are most likely to elicit a preferred emotional state.

Recently, researchers have sought to gain a better understanding of the emotion regulation strategies used by athletes. In one such study, Stanley et al. (2012) used an online survey to explore the strategies used by over 500 runners in the hour prior to training and competition. Analysis revealed five general dimensions of strategies used by these runners (task preparation, avoidance, positive thinking, negative thinking, self in relation to others). Task preparation involved goal-setting (e.g. inducing positive emotions by thinking about whether they could set a personal best), listening to music and visualization (e.g. picturing themselves finishing the

Box 4.3 Thinking critically about … the use of music to manipulate emotional states

A number of elite athletes appear to use music in order to manipulate their emotional state. For example, Jessica Ennis, the Olympic gold-winning heptathlete, always has her iPod with her because "it enables you to switch off between events and gets the adrenaline pumping" (John, 2010). Bishop et al. (2007) conducted a qualitative analysis of young tennis players' use of music to manipulate their emotional states. These participants kept diary entries (including a summary of daily activities carried out while listening to music and details of a memorable music listening episode) over a two week period and in a subsequent interview were asked to list emotional states that they deemed crucial for success in tennis. Participants also specified music tracks (taken from the researchers' personal music collection or brought by the participant to the interview) that either made them feel or think about each emotional state. Results from interviews and diary data revealed that participants listened to music for an average of two hours per day. The players listened to music when they were travelling, preparing for tennis, in their bedrooms or when in the gym. The findings revealed that participants consciously selected music to elicit various emotional states including an appropriate mental focus, confidence, positive emotions and to help them "psych-up" or to relax. Music selection by the participants were highly idiosyncratic (i.e. characterized by a broad range of genres and artists). The participants' present emotional state was often quite negative so music was chosen which could lead to improved mood. The authors argued that by increasing the tempo and/ or intensity of a musical excerpt, players may be able to increase the magnitude of an affective response. More recent studies have found that the asynchronous (music that is not synchronized to a concurrent activity) use of music is associated with arousal regulation and the reduction in rated perceived effort. For example, Karageorghis et al. (2013) required six swimmers to perform in two experimental trials (involving motivational and oudeterous music at 130 beats per minute) and a no-music control, during which they engaged in a 200m freestyle swimming time trial. Results revealed that participants swam faster in the two experimental conditions relative to the control condition. The authors suggested that the benefits observed in these conditions may be attributable to "rhythmic entrainment" whereby the music had a metronomic effect and slightly increased the participants' stroke rate. Qualitative findings would appear to support this suggestion as a number of the swimmers revealed that music was used as a rhythmical stimulus. While asynchronous music was used in the latter study, Lim et al. (2014) explored whether synchronizing movement to a musical beat could reduce the metabolic cost of exercise. The authors found that limb discomfort was lower when participants completed a cycle ergometer task when listening to synchronous music when compared to a control condition.

Critical thinking questions

Might music have a blanket effect on the intensity of emotions experienced by athletes (Jones, 2012)? That is, is it possible to use music to target the regulation of certain emotions without influencing others? How might the inclusion of kinematic measurements improve our understanding of how music might influence athletic performance? Why is it important that athletes/exercise participants choose the type of music they listen to during training?

race). Avoidance strategies included distraction (e.g. trying not to think about the run) and downplaying outcomes (e.g. minimizing the importance of the event). Overall, the findings indicated that the emotional regulation strategies focused largely on performance-related factors and were predominantly cognitive – thereby enabling the athletes to concentrate on achievement, appraisal and re-evaluation of performance goals. Surprisingly, behavioural emotional regulation strategies were less frequently reported. The authors speculated that the preference for cognitive strategies may have been because the performers had to deal with these emotions in the immediate run-up to performance so they served a dual purpose of emotional regulation and performance management. Interestingly, Stanley et al. (2012) reported that some participants deliberately sought to increase unpleasant emotions. That is, some dwelt on negative past experiences as a means of spurring themselves on in the present situation. Others focused on negative emotions to make them more competitive or to listen to music to up-regulate anger. These findings point to the situational variability of emotional regulation in sport.

In a more recent study, Lane and colleagues (2016) examined how an emotion regulation intervention influenced 1600m track running performance. One intervention was designed to increase the intensity of unpleasant emotions experienced by one group (e.g. feel more angry) while another motivated participants to reduce the intensity of unpleasant emotions (e.g. feel less angry). Interestingly, the latter intervention was associated with significantly slower times for the first 400m while the former resulted in higher anxiety and lower calmness scores but had no significant effect on running time. Further analysis revealed that there was no significant difference in the intensity of the emotions reported by those who were exposed to the intervention seeking to reduce the intensity of unpleasant emotions and those who took part in a no-treatment condition. The authors argued that in the no-treatment condition, participants may have used non-conscious emotional regulation strategies to achieve the desired emotional state. Participants in this study had no access to their running time and nor could they gauge their pace by following other runners (i.e. following a pacing strategy) – an experience which may increase unpleasant emotions. The authors argued that this lack of feedback may have acted as a stressor and contributed to the lack of significant findings across conditions.

Although these findings provide some insight into how individuals perceive and regulate their emotions, less attention has been devoted to an exploration of athletes' emotional regulation within teams. Tamminen and Crocker (2013) sought to address this issue by conducting a longitudinal case study (including multiple semi-structured interviews and naturalistic observations) of emotional regulation within a high-performance curling team. The results revealed that the athletes' emotional regulation had a significant impact on their teammates over the course of a season. Emotional self-regulatory strategies used by the athletes included body language and self-censorship while interpersonal emotional regulation included humour (e.g. telling funny stories during the team's car ride to the rink before the game) and providing positive feedback. There were also a number of factors that were found to influence emotional regulation including the length of time the athletes had spent together and social norms/team roles. With respect to the latter of these factors, the team's skipper acknowledged that her role as leader influenced her emotional self-regulation and that she regulated her own emotions to avoid upsetting her teammates. These findings highlight some of the challenges or consequences associated with self-regulation within teams. That is, the skipper was concerned that she was "out of her comfort zone" when regulating her teammates' emotions and that this process would make her anxious. The team's "lead" also explained that considerable mental energy was required to combine her own emotional self-regulation with the regulatory demands of her teammates. Such regulation requires self-control which can ultimately lead to a depletion of self-regulatory resources. Future research may wish to explore how emotional self-regulation influences the resources required for interpersonal emotion regulation.

How can practitioners enhance athletes' emotion regulation skills? Woodcock et al. (2012) explored this question using a single case study design with a female cross-country runner. The researchers drew on the IZOF to inform the development of the athlete's emotion regulation skills. The athlete was introduced to imagery techniques and encouraged to refine her goal-setting and self-talk. The process of zone identification enhanced the athlete's awareness and acceptance of desired emotional states. Practicing imagery helped the athlete to re-experience optimal-zone characteristics in her mind and helped to remind her of feelings associated with optimal performance. A post-intervention interview with the athlete suggested that she was able to perform more consistently during the intervention. This interview also revealed that she experienced enhanced perceptions of control and that she adopted a more appropriate focus of attention during performance (e.g. focusing on certain cue words).

Measuring self-regulation in athletes

What instruments might researchers use to measure athletes' emotion regulation use? Uphill et al. (2012) examined the applicability of the emotion regulation questionnaire (ERQ) for use with a sport population. Construct and criterion validity of the instrument provided some support for its applicability but the test–retest results indicate that it lacks stability. Given that one of the main aims of the instrument is to assess stable patterns of emotion regulation, the authors recommended that future research seeks to identify the factors that might be responsible for this effect.

Research on coping strategies of elite athletes and coaches

Crocker et al. (2015) argued that a critical process in self-regulation is coping which involves "volitional thoughts and actions to manage physically and psychologically demanding situations" (p. 28). How do emotion self-regulation and coping differ? Jones (2012) argued that emotional regulation involves attempts to maintain or augment positive emotions whereas the primary aim of coping is to decrease negative emotional experience.

Recent years have seen an upsurge of research interest in the coping strategies used by elite athletes and coaches (e.g. see A. Nicholls and Polman, 2007). This is perhaps unsurprising given that the manner in which performers deal with the various stressors that are a ubiquitous feature of performance environments (e.g. injuries, performance slumps, playing in front of large audiences) often have a hugely important bearing on their development and success. In this section we explore the relationship between emotion and coping in sport. To illustrate the importance of this relationship consider the comment made by Steffi Graf, a former world number 1 tennis player, who revealed the emotional impact of an enforced absence from the game due to injury: "I couldn't do anything. No work-outs, nothing, I was angry, moody, frustrated" (cited in Miller, 1997, p. 124). Based on Lazarus and Folkman's (1984) work, we conceive of coping as a process and review recent empirical research which has sought to identify the strategies used by athletes when experiencing stress. Next, we consider various approaches to train coping and to assess **coping effectiveness**.

Coping involves changes in thoughts or behaviours that are made to manage the perceived demands of a situation (Lazarus and Folkman, 1984). Traditionally, researchers have studied coping using two approaches which can be described as coping *style* and coping *process* approaches (Richards, 2012). Coping style is believed to involve the preferred use of strategies that remain fixed across time and situations (Carver et al., 1989). Researchers adopting this trait approach typically employ methodological approaches which involve questioning participants about how they usually handle a situation. In contrast, the coping process or transactional approach is more fluid in nature and involves the dynamic alteration of cognitive and behavioural efforts to manage specific "external and/or internal demands or conflicts appraised as taxing or exceeding one's resources" (Lazarus and Folkman, 1984, p. 141). Coping is generally believed to involve deliberate and effortful responses (e.g. a conscious process involving thoughts and actions) although some researchers (e.g. Gould et al., 1993) have argued that these responses may be automatic (i.e. they require little mental effort). Exploring the prevalence of automatic responses might require the use of methods that are quite different from the self-report approach that has dominated sport coping research. Therefore, in this section we adopt a definition of coping that excludes automatic and involuntary responses.

Lazarus and Folkman (1984) and Folkman (1991) placed an important emphasis on the role of cognitive appraisal (i.e. the transaction that occurs between person and environment) in the coping process. Appraisal involves two components: **primary appraisal** and **secondary appraisal**. Primary appraisal involves a consideration of whether situational events are relevant to goal commitment, values, beliefs about self, and situational intentions (Nicholls and Polman, 2007). Goal commitment is seen as a particularly crucial factor as without it "'there is nothing of adaptational importance at stake in an encounter to arouse a stress reaction'" (Lazarus, 1999, p. 76). Having identified a situation as relevant the individual will appraise whether it presents *harm* (consists of damage that has already occurred), *threat* (potential damage in the future), *challenge* (when people feel invigorated/excited about an upcoming event) and *benefit* (what one might gain from a stressful situation). Secondary appraisal is a cognitive-evaluative process and might arise when a discrepancy between the demands of the situation and one's resources to deal with the event is perceived. It is important to note that both forms of appraisal occur at roughly the same time and that the resultant emotion is part of this instantaneous process.

Researchers have sought to identify the various categories and dimensions of coping. The most commonly used coping dimensions are problem- and emotion-focused coping (see Box 4.4). Problem-focused coping strategies are used to alter a stressful situation while emotion-focused strategies seek to deal with the distress that arises from a situation. The use of avoidance coping (e.g. behavioural strategies such as removing oneself from the situation and psychological approaches such as distancing oneself from the situation) and approach coping (e.g. confronting the source of stress by increasing effort) have also been identified by researchers.

Box 4.4 Thinking critically about … elite athletes' strategies for coping with emotions experienced during sport

Even elite athletes may find it difficult to cope with some of the emotions they experience during competitive events. For example, Kjetil Andre Aamodt, the four-time alpine skiing Olympic champion revealed that "If I am also the favourite, it can become difficult to cope with the expectations. Pressure increases both tension and fear of failure" (cited in Jordet, 2010, p. 239). Uphill and Jones (2007) employed a qualitative methodology in order to identify the strategies used by elite athletes to cope with emotions during competitive events. Findings revealed that these strategies could be categorized as either problem focused or emotion focused. Problem-focused coping accounted for 24 per cent and emotion-focused 76 per cent of all reported strategies. Problem-focused strategies used by these athletes included attempts to modify the situation (12 per cent of all strategies) and increased task-related effort (12 per cent). Emotion-focused strategies included attentional control (19 per cent), expression (17 per cent), suppression (12 per cent), reappraisal (21 per cent), imagery (3.5 per cent) and breathing techniques (3.5 per cent). The authors acknowledged that athletes may have been more likely to report the use of emotion-focused strategies (which are often used when an athlete perceives the situation to be uncontrollable) because of the transient nature of many of the stressors experienced during sport (e.g. contentious decision by a referee/umpire) and because the athletes may have perceived the stressors to lie outside their control when the incident occurred. These findings seem to run counter to much of the coping literature which has generally found that athletes use more problem-focused strategies than emotion-focused or avoidance coping strategies. Let us consider each of the most frequently cited strategies in turn. First, attempting to modify the situation or one's place within it often involved players reacting to an event in such a way as to ensure that it would not happen again. A rugby player revealed that he lashed out at an opponent having being illegally held back and that this reaction served an instrumental purpose by ensuring that it would not happen again: "I want to prevent it [being held back] from happening again, to make the point that he can't do that to me and expect to get away with it" (Uphill and Jones, 2007, p. 86). A badminton player sought to modify his situation within a performance environment in order to channel pre-competitive anxiety. This athlete remarked

You are walking up and down, and you think that it's not going to do me any good because I'm going to be tired by the time of the race ... I force myself to sit down, and keep all that nervous energy inside me.

(Uphill and Jones, 2011, p. 227)

Players who sought to increase task-related effort as a coping strategy generally did so in order to confront negatively valenced emotions. For example, one rugby player reported feeling guilty for making an error and that he "wanted to make up for the mistake, to make amends ... repair the damage you feel you have done and try harder" (Uphill and Jones, 2011, p. 227). Attentional control emerged as the most commonly used emotion-focused coping strategy. Here, athletes aimed to devote greater attention to task-related cues during competition. Uphill and Jones (2011) acknowledged that the mechanisms underpinning such attentional flexibility (i.e. redirecting one's attention from task-irrelevant towards more task-relevant cues) remains poorly understood. The use of expression and suppression was also frequently used by elite athletes to cope with stressors in their environment. Uphill and Jones (2007) found that athletes often expressed anger (e.g. at a bad line call by an umpire) and speculated that they may have done so as a form of catharsis, or emotional release. Athletes also reported having suppressed emotions in order to remain as calm as possible. Unfortunately, this strategy may prove costly as it will have no impact on how the individual is actually feeling and is likely to use up important cognitive resources. Reappraisal was the coping strategy most frequently reported by athletes in this study. Reappraisal involves reinterpreting a stimulus and is used by athletes to reduce or increase the intensity or quality of an emotion (Uphill et al., 2009). Having made a mistake one golfer recalled how he "wasn't very happy about bogeying the hole, but I thought the best thing to do was to play the next hole well" (Uphill and Jones, 2007, p. 86). Here the golfer reappraised the situation by reminding himself that there was nothing he could do about a shot he had just hit and that he could only control the next shot. Interestingly, social support also played an important role in helping the athletes to either manage the situation or to regulate the emotional response experienced. We discuss this aspect of coping in more detail later.

Critical thinking questions

Can you think of any approaches that might improve an athlete's attentional flexibility thereby improving their ability to devote greater attention to task-relevant cues? According to Lazarus' CMRT why might reappraisal prove more beneficial than either suppression or expression?

In the following section we consider a number of factors which are believed to moderate the coping-outcome relationship in sport.

Coping in sport: does gender make a difference?

Some evidence suggests that men and women use different coping strategies in response to the same stressors. For example, Goyen and Anshel (1998) found that male athletes preferred to use problem-focused coping strategies in response to stressors such as pain and injury while female athletes prefer to use emotion-focused strategies. Conversely, Nicholls et al. (2007) found that female athletes used a variety of problem-solving strategies (e.g. planning, communication) more frequently than male athletes. In studies that have found similarities between the male and female appraisals of stressful situations, females use more social support and are more expressive of their emotions while males used suppression of competing activities to cope with the same stressor (Hammermeister and Burton, 2004). Kaiseler et al. (2012) sought to identify gender differences in stress, appraisal and coping by investigating performance under pressurized conditions on a golf putting task. Stress responses for males and females were similar but gender differences were found in relation to the frequency of stressors cited and the coping strategies used for these stressors. However, these results must be interpreted with some caution as no moderator analysis was conducted to determine if gender interacted with appraisal to predict coping. Moderator analysis may be a useful way of exploring the interactions that are likely to exist between coping and other key variables when participants experience stress and emotion.

Coping in sport: is age important?

Few studies have explored whether there are age differences in the coping responses used by athletes. However, there is some evidence to suggest that older athletes are better at coping with stress than their younger counterparts. Bebetsos and Antoniou (2003) reported that older badminton players were better able to cope with psychological distress and possessed superior emotional self-control. Goyen and Anshel (1998) found that older athletes were more reliant on techniques such as increasing their concentration and focusing on the next task attempt in comparison to adolescents. The authors proposed that these techniques allowed the older athletes to better control their negative emotions following a stressful event.

Coping effectiveness

Coping effectiveness in sport refers to an athlete's success in using certain strategies to alleviate the negative emotions caused by stress. Conceptualizations of coping effectiveness include the goodness-of-fit approach; the choice hypothesis (which suggests that effective coping depends on the choice of particular coping strategies in a given context; Nicholls et al., 2005); or the automaticity perspective (see section above) which postulates that athletes will automatically deploy strategies that have proved effective in similar contexts in the past (Gould et al., 1993). What factors might influence coping effectiveness? Problem-focused approaches such as increasing task-related effort are believed to be more effective when they are used in situations that are controllable (e.g. those arising from one's own behaviour) while emotion-focused approaches such as attentional control are believed to be more effective in situations where the athlete has little control (e.g. those arising from an opponent's performance). This is known as the goodness-of-fit model (Folkman, 1991, 1992). This hypothesis was corroborated by Anshel (1996), who reported that high perceived controllability was linked to problem-focused coping strategies whereas low perceived controllability was associated with emotion-focused coping strategies in competitive athletes. Athletes who report having coped effectively with challenging situations generally report that they focused on elements that they could control.

Similarly, Kim and Duda (2003) discovered that when stressors were perceived to be controllable, intercollegiate athletes tended to use problem-based coping strategies. Weston et al. (2009) used in-depth interviews to explore the stressors faced, and coping strategies employed, by five single-handed, round-the-world sailors. Among the stressors experienced by these sailors were environmental hazards (e.g. isolation and sleep deprivation), competitive stressors (e.g. yacht-related difficulties) and personal issues (e.g. family problems). In response to these stressors, the sailors reported using a combination of problem-focused coping strategies (e.g. making detailed plans for what to do in various hypothetical scenarios) and emotion-focused coping strategies (e.g. relying on social support from family and supporters to counteract the isolation of single-handed sailing). Interestingly, Weston et al. (2009) acknowledged that their research did not establish specific causal or temporal links between the stressors experienced by these sailors and the resulting coping strategies adopted. However, they suggested that future research in this field could benefit from equipping participants with electronic diaries to log the time-course of their stressor-coping strategy interactions. Qualitative methodology was also used by Olusoga et al. (2010) to explore the responses to stress of, and coping techniques used by, a sample of world-class UK coaches from a range of sports (e.g. swimming, field hockey). Thematic analysis showed that the most frequently reported coping strategy was "structuring and planning" – a problem-focused approach that involved using past experience to anticipate and circumvent likely stressors. Attending coaching courses and seeking continuous professional development were also widely cited as preferred coping strategies.

Despite such findings, little progress has been made in understanding the theoretical mechanisms underlying the apparent efficacy of problem-focused and emotion-focused coping strategies. Clearly, additional studies are required in which theoretically derived hypotheses concerning coping strategies are tested using longitudinal research designs. Moreover, much of the research in this area is plagued by a reliance on participants' retrospective accounts of how they coped with stressors. Future research could use diary approaches, ecological momentary assessment or **think aloud protocols** to overcome the limitations associated with retrospective recall. Ideally, researchers would draw on a combination of these approaches and conduct multiple assessments of athletes' coping responses across a number of stressful events that differ in their intensity and controllability (see Box 4.5).

What other factors might influence coping effectiveness? Nicholls et al. (2015) predicted that emotional maturity (the ability to facilitate and guide emotional tendencies to reach intended goals) would have a direct effect on coping effectiveness. Measures of emotional maturity, dispositional coping and coping effectiveness were completed by 790 adolescent athletes. Analysis revealed a significant path (i.e. the dependencies among a group of variables)

Box 4.5 Thinking critically about ... stressors, emotions and the coping experiences of elite athletes as they prepare for, and compete in, a major international championship

Many elite athletes often spend considerable periods of time away from home as they prepare for, and compete in, major international matches or championships. While some might view the opportunity to travel the world whilst earning a living to be a privilege, there is anecdotal evidence to suggest that spending prolonged periods away from one's family and friends can prove to be an extremely stressful experience. In fact, the English cricketer, Marcus Trescothick revealed that "touring" can lead to

> four-wall fever that can strike you when you are stuck inside a hotel bedroom complete with en-suite bathroom for days on end prior to moving on to the next one ... it creates extraordinary strains for the players not to mention their wives and families.
>
> (cited in Forzoni, 2015)

Nicholls and Levy (2016) conducted a longitudinal exploration of the stressors, emotions and coping experiences of four elite gymnasts as they prepared for, and competed in, the world championships. Data was collected over a 28-day competitive period during which participation in the world championships acted as a qualifying competition for the London 2012 Olympic Games. Participants were given a diary pack which included instructions and definitions of the psychological constructs. Participants were also provided with diary sheets which required them to detail the stressors they had experienced that day, how these stressors had made them feel, what they did to cope with these stressors, how they felt after attempting to cope with these stressors, and, finally, which of the coping strategies they used was most effective and why. The researchers used an Interpretive Phenomenological Approach (IPA; a qualitative approach which seeks to gain a detailed understanding of a participant's experience of specific phenomena) to analyse the diary data. Findings revealed that coping (when perceived as being effective) alleviated unpleasant emotions such as anger and that it also generated positive emotions. Interestingly, findings revealed that elite participants experienced pleasant and unpleasant emotions concurrently (e.g. anxiety and excitement). One of the participants felt the weight of expectations leading up to the event and revealed that he felt "anxious and worried, because I don't want to let everybody down, but also makes me excited that it is quite soon". Teammates were found to have an important influence on one another's experiences of stressors, emotions and coping strategies. For example, one participant experienced anxiety when teammates were either ill or injured. This caused "slight panic and worry for him that he gets better, as we can't afford to lose a team member". However, athletes appeared to use different coping strategies to cope with the same stressful event – thereby providing support for Lazarus' (1999) contention that coping is an individualistic process.

Critical thinking questions

Why do incidences of successful coping generate positively toned emotions? This study did not assess the athletes' appraisals of the stressors they had experienced. Given that appraisals are considered to be an important construct within the stress process (Lazarus, 1999), how might an evaluation of appraisals contribute to a better understanding of how stress and emotions influence elite performance? Should we rely on diary entries as the sole method of data collection? How would this research have benefited from the use of semi-structured interviews?

between emotional maturity and task-oriented coping. The authors argued that the emotionally mature participants might have learnt that there are various adaptive outcomes associated with this form of coping. Task-oriented coping has been found to be associated with superior performance in golf (Gaudreau et al., 2010) and collegiate volleyball players achieving their goals (Schellenberg et al., 2013).

Nicholls et al. (2013) sought to explore the relationship between cognitive social maturity, coping effectiveness and dispositional coping. Measures of these constructs were completed by 245 adolescent athletes. Findings revealed that coping is associated with the maturation that occurs across adolescence. Conscientiousness was the most important dimension of maturity in relation to coping and was positively associated with task-oriented coping strategies such as increasing effort and planning. In another study, Nieuwenhuys et al. (2011) explored the role of meta-experiences (i.e. knowledge or beliefs about the impact of experiences and strategies upon performance) in determining the effectiveness of coping strategies amongst a group of ten elite athletes. Athletes were interviewed about their experiences (thoughts, emotions, actions) during good and bad performances over recent weeks/months. The success ratio of coping strategies was higher in good competitions than bad competitions. Results revealed that in good performances a significantly higher percentage of coping strategies were based on meta-experiences. The authors argued that during poor performances athlete's working memory may become increasingly occupied with task-irrelevant thoughts (e.g. worry) thereby causing meta-experiences to be less accessible and/or making it increasingly difficult to select and implement effective coping strategies. The authors argued that mental training programmes could help athletes to become more aware of these meta-experiences and to identify the specific coping processes that arise during poor and good performances. An individual's tendency to reinvest conscious attention (see Chapter 3) also appears to influence coping effectiveness. In a recent study, Laborde et al. (2014) classified one hundred handball players as either low or high reinvesters (on the basis of their scores on the Decision Specific Reinvestment Scale; DSRS) and then measured their stress appraisal and coping effectiveness. Low reinvesters were found to score higher on perceived controllability of stressors and coping effectiveness than their higher reinvesting counterparts. The authors speculated that although high reinvesters appraised the same stress intensity as low reinvesting players they coped less efficiently with the stress, perhaps because reinvestment overloads working memory thereby reducing the attention they can devote to selecting appropriate coping responses. Given the important role that coping effectiveness seems to play in athletic performance one may wonder whether or not this is a skill that can be trained. We consider this issue in Box 4.6

Coaches and parents are also in a position to teach adolescents how to cope with stressful experiences. Tamminen and Holt (2012) interviewed athletes, parents and coaches about the ways adolescent athletes learn about coping in sport. A number of parents sought to create a supportive context for learning by listening and remaining aware of their own reactions as they discussed stressors with their children.

Box 4.6 In the spotlight Can coping effectiveness be trained?

Coping effectiveness training (CET; Chesney et al., 1996) is informed by Lazarus' transactional-theoretical perspective of stress and coping and the goodness-of-fit model. CET aims to reduce the athlete's stress, enhance emotional well-being and improve performance proficiency. CET is typically delivered as a group-based intervention but Reeves et al. (2011) recently delivered an adapted version of this training (referred to as the CETASP; Coping Effectiveness Training for Adolescent Soccer Players) to academy soccer players on an individual basis. Five male soccer players from an English Premier League Soccer Academy participated in the study. Participants took part in 45–60 minute training sessions for 6 consecutive weeks which involved receiving advice regarding cognitively based coping strategies (e.g. reviewing previous coping attempts by considering the specific stressors appraised and the coping responses employed during the previous week) and behaviourally based coping strategies. Results showed that all of the participants' coping self-efficacy scores improved in response to the CETASP and partial support was found for the hypothesis that the intervention would improve coping effectiveness. The researchers acknowledged that the study design was unable to determine whether the improvement in scores was due to an extension of coping repertoires, providing opportunities for coping practice, and/or giving athletes' time to develop their coping self-efficacy. Ideally, future research would compare the efficacy of these training programmes when an intervention group is compared with a comparison group under controlled conditions (i.e. a control group exposed to placebos).

Family environments that are cohesive, supportive and expressive were associated with adaptive coping amongst adolescents. Of course, it is also important to recognize that social networks may have a negative influence on some athlete's stressor appraisals. For example, athletes may be afraid that failure would make their coaches unhappy and have an adverse influence on their relationship (Sagar et al., 2007).

Coping through social support

Social support includes social integration (i.e. the number of different types of relationships in which recipients participate), perceived support (i.e. one's subjective judgement that friends, family etc. would provide support if needed) and enacted support (i.e. actual help received from one's support network during a specific time frame). Of these constructs, an athlete's perception of the social support available to them appears to have the greatest influence on their mental health and emotional well-being (Rees and Freeman, 2012). If athletes believe that they have a great deal of support then they are more likely to conclude that they have the resources to cope with difficult situations and, as a result, are less likely to appraise those situations as stressful. For example, Freeman and Rees (2009) administered questionnaires to a sample of skilled golfers and found that high levels of perceived support were associated with the tendency to appraise competition as less of a threat. By contrast, it is less clear how effective enacted or received support may prove to athletes. Indeed, there is a considerable body of evidence which indicates that pressure from significant others (including parents) is associated with burnout and other undesirable outcomes (Gould et al., 1996). Consider the case of American Olympic gymnast Dumitru Moceanu who, at the age of 17, sued her parents for exploiting her. Moceanu revealed that she "never had a childhood … it was always about the gym. I would think: 'Don't you guys know anything besides gymnastics? Can't we go for ice-cream? Can't you be my mom and dad?'" (cited in Hersh, 1998). Some authors have argued that received support will be most effective if it is based on "optimal matching" – that is, the support is matched to the needs arising from the stressful event. For example, Cutrona and Russell (1990) argued that the controllability or uncontrollability of the stressor may also influence the type of support sought by the athlete. To explain, when faced with uncontrollable events the athlete is likely to require social support that fosters emotion-focused forms of coping (e.g. esteem forms of support such as reassurance) while controllable events may lead to a need for support that promotes problem-focused coping (tangible forms of support). Unfortunately, the optimal matching model has received little empirical support. Supportive behaviours can serve multiple functions and different behaviours can achieve similar objectives. For example, there is considered to be a high degree of overlap between types of support in real-life settings so attempts by a coach to bolster an athlete's sense of competence (esteem support) may also be interpreted as a sign of caring (emotional support).

Researchers have also proposed that the effectiveness of perceived support may partly depend on the context in which it is provided, with participants accruing greater benefit when there is a match between the type of received support and the context. Emotional and esteem forms of support (i.e. instructions provided in a script which sought to bolster the person's sense of competence or self-esteem) have been found to improve performance on a golf putting task (Rees and Freeman, 2010) and when used in a one-to-one intervention with high-level golfers (Freeman et al., 2009). Rees and Freeman (2012) argued that these forms of support may be considered more nurturing, less controlling and less "likely to undermine important mediating mechanisms such as self-efficacy than informational (such as direct advice) and tangible (concrete instructional assistance) forms of support" (p. 108). Unfortunately, the latter two forms of support may undermine an athlete's belief in their skills if provided in the absence of emotional and esteem support. Although the preceding results point to the important role that social support may play in shaping athlete development, further research is required to examine the mechanisms through which this form of support operates. Cognitive appraisal and self-efficacy (Rees and Freeman, 2009) are believed to play an important role in this regard but it is likely that other cognitive, emotional and behavioural mechanisms are influential. Such a line of inquiry will enhance both theoretical understanding and help develop more effective interventions.

Communal coping

The vast majority of the literature on coping in sport has focused on athletes' attempts to deal with stressors individually but there is considerable evidence to suggest that an individual's stressors, emotions and attempts to cope are social in nature. Building on this latter idea, Crocker et al. (2015) argued that researchers might wish to explore the role "communal coping" (i.e. stressors are appraised and acted upon in the context of close relationships) plays in helping individuals cope with stressors collectively as a group. Although researchers have yet to use a communal coping perspective to explore how athletes' cope collectively, Crocker et al. argued that there is some research which is connected to this concept. They point to Son et al.'s (2011) work which investigated the effect of group-focused self-talk (e.g. we are confident performers) on a dart-throwing task. This form of self-talk resulted in superior performance when compared to a neutral self-talk condition (e.g. I am a student). Such performance improvements may have been due to an enhanced perception of the group's ability to perform and this may have reduced individual performer's anxiety.

Measurement of coping

Researchers have used a variety of measurements to capture the coping strategies used by athletes. Carver et al.'s (1989) COPE, and its subscales, have been used extensively in sports coping research, and it has been found to have acceptable reliability and validity (e.g. Eubank and Collins, 2000). Instruments used to differ in terms of their breadth and specificity. The MCOPE (a modified version of the scale) measures specific strategies actually used while the Coping Style Inventory for Athletes (CSIA; Anshel and Kassidis, 1997) explores how an athlete would behave in a hypothetical situation. Unfortunately, there are a number of limitations associated with the use of these instruments, and with others that are commonly used, as researchers failed to take into account factors such as gender, ethnicity or age when developing them. As a result, researchers remain unsure whether the instruments will demonstrate reliability and validity when used with more diverse samples. MCOPE is a hybrid questionnaire and so does not possess a solid theoretical or conceptual foundation (Crocker et al. 2015). An additional concern is that most of the research in this area has explored athletes' voluntary behavioural, emotional or cognitive responses to stressful situations. However, athletes are often reliant on involuntary responses (e.g. controlling physiological arousal) in order to deal with stressful situations and it remains to be seen how researchers could explore this in athletes given that they may possess little conscious awareness of these reactions.

The Coping Function Questionnaire (CFQ; Kowalski and Crocker, 2001) is a sport-specific questionnaire developed to assess problem-focused, emotion-focused and avoidance-focused functions. This questionnaire requires respondents to rate how frequently they have used each coping item in response to a self-reported stressful situation. The CFQ has generally demonstrated good validity and reliability scores in a variety of athletic populations and has recently been used in studies which have examined coping function in relation to type of perfectionism (Crocker et al., 2014) and personality in sport (Allen et al., 2011b). However, the CFQ has a number of limitations that researchers should be aware of. For example, it requires athletes to make inferences about the function of their coping efforts when, ideally, they would be asked to report the strategies they had used to cope. The instrument may also be improved through psychometric evaluation and validation across a wider range of athletic populations (Nicholls and Ntoumanis, 2010). Unfortunately, very few of the preceding studies have actually tested the psychometric properties of these scales (i.e. how valid are the scales with their own data?). To circumvent some of these limitations, Nicholls and Ntoumanis (2010) proposed that future researchers could use ecological momentary assessment (EMA) to assess coping in sport. This method involves providing athletes with electronic "bleepers" and asking them to answer a series of questions when the device bleeps at random or predetermined times. A potential strength of this method is the reduced period of time between the stressful event and the recall of the coping strategies used to manage that stressor. However, a rather obvious limitation of this method is that it is impractical during competitive events (i.e. the performer can't stop play in order to note his/her stressors and coping responses) so it may be best put to use during training or practice or to an exploration of organizational stressors where EMA assessments could be completed outside competition.

Unresolved issues and new directions in research on emotions and coping in sport

The theoretical and research evidence introduced in this chapter would suggest that emotions can have a powerful impact on athletic performance. Indeed, this is becoming a vibrant area of study but an analysis of the research conducted thus far indicates that there are a number of possible directions for future research. First, much of our understanding of emotions and coping in sport has emerged from studies using a university population as their sample. Consequently, there is great scope for researchers to explore the interplay of stress, coping and emotions amongst different populations (e.g. children and young athletes; Thatcher et al., 2011) or even in hostile environments (e.g. polar expeditions). In the former case, a greater understanding of the mechanisms that influence sport enjoyment amongst young participants could inform interventions which seek to increase adherence and commitment to sport. Another area worthy of exploration is how coping develops in young children and athletes and how social support contributes to this process. Second, there remains a paucity of research exploring the psychological stressors that sports officials and coaches are exposed to. As a result, we know very little about how experiencing certain emotions influence their decision making or enjoyment of participation and how they cope with or regulate these emotions. Third, researchers have devoted little attention to the role of conscious and unconscious processing in emotion. Fourth, the mechanisms by which emotional regulation strategies influence self-control resources remain poorly understood. Moreover, few studies have sought to identify the potential costs that might be associated with attempts to regulate an athlete's emotions (e.g. emphasizing the need to reduce anxiety may merely exacerbate this emotion). Finally, researchers may wish to explore how athletes cope with positive emotions. For example, some athletes may experience a feeling of "flatness" in the aftermath of a major competitive success. These emotions may stem from the realization that it may be difficult to recapture the "highs" associated with such achievements or the feeling that one may be aimless due to the absence of intense and goal-directed training programmes that characterized the lead-up to a major event.

Ideas for research projects on emotions and coping in athletes

Here are five suggestions for possible research projects on the topics of emotion and coping in sport psychology.

1. You could build on Martinent and Ferrand's (2015) recent work by exploring whether some appraisal dimensions are more relevant to the competitive sporting environment than others and by extending Lazarus' work to examine whether any additional appraisal dimensions are evident in competitive sporting environments.

2. Few studies have explored how emotional contagion may influence athletic performance. One line of inquiry might be to examine how overt displays of positive or negative emotions by coaches or spectators influence the likelihood that athletes will experience these emotions. For example, if home supporters become increasingly angry at a series of what they consider to be poor decisions by officials, do athletes begin to mimic these emotions? You could conduct experimental studies in which athletes perform tasks in a simulated environment in which crowd mood is manipulated. Alternatively, you could use questionnaires to explore whether there is any convergence between coaches' emotions and those of their athletes.

3. Research investigating the relationship between social support and coping remains relatively scant. Exploring this issue could involve a number of questions. For example, how does the provision of social support influence the coping strategies adopted by athletes? What are the strengths and drawbacks of social support as a coping strategy? Is social support a coping strategy in its own right – much like other problem- and emotion-focused strategies?

4. An individualistic perspective on emotions and regulation has been called "untenable" and authors have started to highlight the importance of social relationships and interdependency in moving forward with emotion research. You could address this issue by exploring the intersubjective or relational perspectives of emotion within teams. One potential line of inquiry would be to investigate how athletes use communal coping in a naturalistic setting. To do so, you could use naturalistic observations and/ or self-confrontation interviews to explore how athletes use "we-talk" within team settings. This approach would allow you to explore how group-referent self-talk influences the team's perceptions of their ability to perform.

5. You could explore the stressors experienced by officials in competition and how they cope with these events. This line of inquiry appears particularly relevant given recent findings which indicate that nearly two thirds of football referees in England experience verbal abuse on a regular basis (Cleland et al., 2015). A phenomenological investigation of officials' experiences being subjected to abuse or being threatened by athletes before, during or after competition may be particularly fruitful. Your study might address a number of important questions: (1) what does it feel like to be on the receiving end of threat and abuse? (2) What strategies do officials use to regulate their emotions during, and in the aftermath of, these verbal attacks? (3) How do these incidents influence referees' desire to continue their involvement or their enjoyment of participation?

Summary

- Emotions have a hugely important bearing on the process and outcome of athletic performance. For example, emotions may influence athletes' motivation to train and their adherence to injury rehabilitation programmes.

- The second section explored the nature of emotions and distinguished between emotions and related constructs such as mood and affect.

- In the third section, we critically evaluated three prominent theories that have sought to explain the emotion–performance relationship in sport.

- The fourth section considered how "positive" and "negative" emotions might influence athletic performance while the fifth section discussed a number of methodological approaches that have been used to measure emotions in athletes.

- In the sixth section, we evaluated a variety of the regulatory processes that athletes use to deal with emotions and stressors. Next, we outlined the various coping strategies that athletes have been found to use in training and competitive contexts.

- Finally, some unresolved issues on emotion in athletes were identified along with five potentially fruitful new directions for future research in this field.

Staying focused in sport
Concentration in sport performers

Introduction

For Dan Carter (a World Cup winner with New Zealand and widely regarded as the greatest out-half in the history of rugby union), "concentration" ("staying in the moment"), or the ability to focus effectively on the task at hand while ignoring distractions, is a vital prerequisite of successful performance in sport. As he put it,

> you have a mindset of just nailing each task, staying in the moment, and it has really helped myself and this team ... It is quite easy to start thinking about the result and what potentially could happen, but you soon lose track.
> (cited in Skysports.com, 2015; see Figure 5.1)

This idea that concentration is crucial for optimal performance applies both to team and individual sports. For example, Alex Ferguson (former manager of Manchester United) proclaimed that in soccer, "without question, at the top level, concentration is a big part of a player's game whether they're a keeper or outfield" (cited in Northcroft, 2009, p. 12). This view is shared by top goalkeeper Petr Cech (the Czech Republic player who holds the Premier league record for the fewest appearances required to reach one hundred "clean sheets") when he revealed that "everything is about concentration" (cited in Szczepanik, 2005, p. 100). Interestingly, Cech's comment was prompted by his observation that opposing teams invariably get at least one chance to score during a game and "it's difficult to be concentrated for the right moment". Not surprisingly, in individual sporting activities, the ability to dwell only on the present moment is also crucially important. Trevor Immelman, the South African golfer, remarked that he had been "so totally in the present" (cited in McRae, 2008, p. 7) during his triumph at the US Masters tournament in 2008. In this regard, perhaps the epitome of a present-centred awareness is that displayed by Michael Johnson, a three times Olympic gold medallist in 400 metres, and nine times a world athletics gold medallist. Remarkably, he claimed that he had learned to cut out all the unnecessary thoughts ... on the track. I simply concentrate. I concentrate on the tangible – on the track, on the race, on the blocks, on the things I have to do. The crowd fades away and the other athletes disappear and now it's just me and this one lane.

(cited in Miller, 1997, p. 64)

Such extraordinary powers of concentration are also evident in Usain Bolt, multiple Olympic gold medallist and the current world record holder in the 100 metre sprint, who advised that you should not "focus on the guy next to you. He might be very quick out of the blocks, which can make you lose concentration. Stay focused on what you're going to do and run your race at all times" (cited in Staph, 2011). By contrast with the preceding examples, an *inability* to focus effectively can mean the difference between success and failure in competitive sport. For example, consider the case of Alicia Sacramore, the US gymnast, whose two falls in the beam and floor routines probably cost the US women's team a gold medal at the Beijing Olympics, who blamed an unusually long delay before the beam routine for making her lose concentration: "I stood there in front of a blank screen. I felt like it was 5 minutes. Nerves got to me" (Ingle, 2008). Similarly, at the 2008 Olympic Games in Beijing, the US rifle-shooter Matthew Emmons missed an opportunity to win a gold medal in the 50 metre three-position target event due to a lapse in concentration. Leading his nearest rival Qiu Jian (China) by 3.3 points as he took his last shot, Emmons lost his focus momentarily and inexplicably misfired, ending up with a 4.4 for his efforts – and fourth place.

Figure 5.1 According to Dan Carter, concentration is vital for success in sport (*source*: courtesy of Inpho photography)

This example dramatically illustrates how concentration can mean the difference between winning and losing an Olympic gold medal (see Figure 5.2). Similarly, Andy Murray blamed a lapse in concentration for his defeat to Novak Djokovic in the 2015 Australian Open tennis final. Specifically, "the third set was frustrating because I got a bit distracted when he fell on the ground after a couple of shots … it appeared he was cramping and then I let it distract me a little bit" (cited in Newman, 2015). Clearly, top athletes not only realize the importance of focusing skills but also have developed informal theories about how their concentration systems work in competitive situations. To illustrate, Garry Sobers proposed:

> concentration's like a shower. You don't turn it on until you want to bathe … You don't walk out of the shower and leave it running. You turn it off, you turn it on … It has to be fresh and ready when you need it.
>
> (cited in White, 2002a, p. 20)

Often, these intuitive theories about how the mind works are accompanied by idiosyncratic concentration techniques – especially in individual sports. For example, Andy Roddick, the former tennis star, revealed that during his 2007 Wimbledon match against his fellow American and friend, Justin Gimmelstob, he avoided making any eye contact with him in case he might lose his concentration as a result (Muscat, 2007). Similarly, the snooker player Mark Williams raised a few eyebrows when he revealed that he had sung a song silently to himself in an effort to block out negative thoughts towards the end of his classic defeat of Ken Doherty in the 2003 world championship final. As he said: "At 16–16, I was singing songs in my head. I was singing Tom Jones' Delilah. I just tried to take my mind off the arena, the crowd, everything" (cited in Everton, 2003, p. 31). Strange as it may seem, however, this curious strategy actually makes psychological sense. To explain, singing to oneself as a deliberate distraction may not only prevent an athlete from thinking too much but also counteract his or her tendency to try to exert conscious control over actions that are better performed automatically (Beilock, 2010a). In attempting to adopt a similar strategy, the snooker star Ronnie O'Sullivan, who won the 2007 UK Championship, counted dots on a spoon to maintain his focus while his semi-final opponent (Mark Selby) was playing. As he said:

> My head was going so I had to find a way to keep it. They won't let me put a towel over my head any more so when Mark was at the table I picked up a spoon. If I lost count of the dots, I just started all over again. My thanks go to the spoon!
>
> (cited in Yates, 2007)

These examples and incidents raise a number of questions. For example, can psychological techniques help athletes to turn on and turn off their concentration systems like a shower? Can athletes learn to suppress interfering information and reorient their focus of attention? What other strategies can they use to achieve and maintain an optimal focus for competition? What is "concentration" anyway and why do athletes lose it so easily in competitive situations?

Figure 5.2   Lapses in concentration can prove costly in sport (*source:* courtesy of Inpho photography)

The purpose of this chapter is to answer these and other relevant questions using the principles and findings of **cognitive sport psychology** – that part of the discipline that is concerned with understanding the role of mental processes (e.g. attention, mental imagery, memory) in athletic performance. In order to achieve this objective, the chapter is organized as follows. Initially, we explore the nature, dimensions and importance of concentration in sport psychology. In the next section, we outline briefly the principal methods used by psychologists to measure attentional processes (including concentration) in athletes. Then, we summarize some key principles of effective concentration that have emerged from research on attention in sport performers. The fourth section addresses the question of why athletes are vulnerable to lapses or loss of concentration. In the fifth section, we review various practical exercises and psychological techniques that are alleged to improve concentration skills in athletes. The sixth section outlines some old problems and new directions for research in this field. Finally, we suggest some ideas for possible research projects on concentration in athletes.

Nature and importance of concentration in sport psychology

In cognitive sport psychology, concentration is regarded as one component of the multidimensional construct of "attention" (Moran, 1996). In cognitive psychology, attentional processes have been invoked to account for selectivity of information processing, intensity of focus, consciousness and/or the allocation of a limited resource capacity to cope with ongoing cognitive demands (Rensink,

2013). In particular, attention involves "focusing on specific features, objects or locations or on certain thoughts or activities" (Goldstein, 2011, p. 391). It is a cognitive system that facilitates the selection of some information for further processing while inhibiting the selection of other information for subsequent analysis (E. Smith and Kosslyn, 2007). Put simply, it is "a concentration of mental activity" (Matlin, 2009, p. 67). Let us now consider the main dimensions and types of attention before examining a topic that we mentioned earlier – namely, the special importance of concentration in sport.

Research on attention is central to cognitive sport psychology because the ability to focus mental effort effectively is associated with optimal athletic performance (see later in this chapter for a discussion of **flow states**). Attentional research is also one of the fastest growing fields in **cognitive neuroscience**. Broadly, it explores the mechanisms by which "voluntary control and subjective experience arise from and regulate our behaviour" (Posner and Rothbart, 2007, p. 1). For psychologists, attention is paradoxical because it is *familiar* but yet *mysterious*. To explain, the term attention is *familiar* because it is used frequently in everyday life – as happens, for example, when a coach asks her students to "pay attention" to something important that she is about to say or demonstrate to her athletes. Indeed, based on such apparent familiarity, William James (1890a) remarked famously:

> Everyone knows what attention is. It is the taking possession by the mind, in clear and vivid form, of one of what may seem several simultaneously possible objects or trains of thought. Focalization, concentration, of consciousness are of its essence. It implies withdrawal from some things in order to deal effectively with others.

> (pp. 403–404)

But attention is also *mysterious* because it refers to many different types and levels of psychological processes ranging from biological arousal or alertness to high level conscious awareness. Not surprisingly, therefore, James' "folk-psychology" approach to attention (i.e. one based on unsystematic but compelling insights drawn from everyday life: Pashler, 1998) has been criticized for its limited scope. Therefore, despite more than a century of research in the field, there is still a great deal of confusion concerning the nature of attention and the mechanisms underlying it. For example, Ashcraft (2006) identified *six* different meanings of this term. Commenting on the multiplicity of approaches and definitions in this field, Pashler (1998, p. 1) subverted James' famous quotation above by observing that perhaps "no one knows what attention is, and ... there may not even be an 'it' to be known about". Of course, modern neuroimaging techniques (e.g. see Gazzaniga et al., 2013) can help to establish the neural mechanisms and brain circuits underlying the "it" of attention. So, undaunted by Pashler's somewhat pessimistic conclusion, we suggest that a great deal of progress has been made in attentional research since the late 1990s. First, most theorists in the field accept that the hallmark of attention is the concentration of mental activity (Matlin, 2009). Second, neuroscientific studies have identified a number of different brain regions activated during attentional processing. For example, Corbetta and

Shulman (2002) concluded that the task of searching for your friend in a crowded room involves activation of frontal and dorsal **parietal lobe regions**. By contrast, redirecting your attention to an unexpected stimulus (e.g. the sound of breaking glass) involves the activation of the ventral frontal cortex (see also E. Smith and Kosslyn, 2007). Third, researchers agree on the *multidimensional* nature of this construct and can distinguish between several different dimensions of attention.

Dimensions of attention

At least three separate dimensions of attention have been identified by cognitive psychologists. The first one is called "concentration" and refers to a person's ability to exert deliberate mental effort on what is most important in any given situation. For example, football players concentrate when they attempt to assimilate coaching instructions delivered before an important match. The second dimension of attention denotes a skill in selective perception – namely, the ability to zoom in on task-relevant information while ignoring potential distractions. This dimension designates the ability to discriminate relevant stimuli (targets) from irrelevant stimuli (distractors) competing for our attention. To illustrate, a tennis player who is preparing to smash a lob from his or her opponent must learn to focus only on the flight of the ball, not on the distracting movement of the player(s) on the other side of the net. As a test of your selective attentional skill, can you focus only on the vocals of a song on the radio, disregarding the instrumental backing? Interestingly, one way of capturing people's attention is through the use of sudden onset stimuli and movement. For example, if you are typing a document on your computer, the blinking on-screen cursor makes it stand out from the static display of text on which you're working. Similarly, internet "pop up" advertising exploits this perceptual principle by trying to "steal" computer users' attention. The third dimension of attention involves a form of mental time-sharing ability whereby athletes learn, as a result of extensive practice, to perform two or more concurrent actions equally well. For example, a skilful basketball player can dribble with the ball while simultaneously looking around for a teammate who is in a good position to receive a pass. To summarize, the construct of attention refers to at least three different cognitive processes: concentration or effortful awareness, selectivity of perception, and/or the ability to coordinate two or more actions at the same time. A possible fourth dimension of attention called "vigilance" has also been postulated (De Weerd, 2002). This dimension designates a person's ability to orient attention and respond to randomly occurring relevant stimuli over an extended period of time.

Unfortunately, the multidimensional nature of attention has occasionally spawned conceptual confusion among sport psychologists. For example, Gauron (1984, p. 43) appeared to suggest that mental time-sharing is a *weakness* rather than a skill when he claimed that athletes could "*suffer* from divided attention" (italics ours). Perhaps this author failed to grasp the fact that repeated practice enables people to spread their attentional resources between concurrent activities – often without any deterioration in performance. Incidentally, research shows that people are capable of doing two or more things at the same time provided that at least one of them is highly practised and the tasks operate in different sensory modalities (Matlin, 2009). If neither task has been practised sufficiently and/or if the concurrent activities in question take place in the same sensory system, errors will probably occur. Box 6.5 in Chapter 6 examines a practical implication of this principle when we explain why it is dangerous to drive a car while listening to a football match on the radio.

Just like other scientists, cognitive psychology researchers have used various metaphors to understand how the mind works. Since the 1950s, a number of metaphors have been coined by cognitive psychologists to describe the selective and divided dimensions of attention (see review by Fernandez-Duque and Johnson, 1999). The earliest metaphors of attention ("filter" approaches) were largely auditory in nature but as a greater range of experimental procedures emerged, visual attention metaphors became more popular. More recently, resource metaphors have dominated cognitive research on attention. One of the most influential accounts of attention is the "spotlight" metaphor (e.g. Posner, 1980; see also Reisberg, 2016). According to this metaphor, **selective attention** resembles a mental beam which illuminates targets that are located either in the external world around us or else in the subjective domain of our own thoughts and feelings. This idea of specifying a target for one's attentional spotlight is important practically as well as theoretically because it is only relatively recently that sport psychologists have begun to explore the question of what exactly athletes should focus on when they are exhorted to "concentrate" by their coaches (see MacPherson et al., 2008; Winter et al., 2014). Unfortunately, the spotlight metaphor of attention is plagued by a number of problems. First, it has not adequately explained the mechanisms by which executive control of one's attentional focus is achieved. Put simply, who or what is directing the spotlight at its target? This question is difficult to answer without postulating a controlling homunculus – a miniature person in one's head, apparently coordinating cognitive operations. Interestingly, this homunculus problem pervades contemporary cognitive neuroscience research. Thus, Yeung (2013) claimed that a central problem for this discipline is how "to account for intelligent, purposive human behaviour without relying on an unspecified intelligent agent – a controlling homunculus" (p. 275). Second, the spotlight model assumes that people's attentional beam sweeps through space en route to its target. However, this assumption is challenged by research evidence that attention is not influenced "by the presence of spatially intervening information" (E. Smith and Kosslyn, 2007, p. 131). Third, the spotlight metaphor neglects the issue of what lies *outside* the beam of our concentration. In other words, it ignores the possibility that unconscious factors can affect people's attentional processes. Interestingly, such factors have attracted increasing scrutiny from cognitive scientists. Nadel and Piattelli-Palmarini (2002, p. xxvi) remarked that although cognitive science began with the assumption that cognition was limited to conscious processes, "much of the domain is now concerned with phenomena that lie behind the vale of consciousness". In this regard, evidence has emerged since the early 2000s that perception without conscious awareness can occur in vision (Merikle, 2007). We shall return to this issue later in the chapter when we consider how unconscious sources of distraction can affect athletes. Fourth, the spotlight model of attention has been concerned mainly with *external* targets – not internal ones. Again, we shall return to this issue later in the chapter when considering how and why *internal* distractions disrupt our concentration. A fifth weakness of the spotlight metaphor is that it neglects emotional influences on attentional processes. For example, anxiety can narrow one's mental spotlight and encourage performers to shine it inwards. Interestingly, as we learned in Chapter 3, attentional control theory (ACT: Eysenck et al., 2007) was developed to account for the effects of anxiety on cognitive performance.

Metaphors have also been coined for **divided attention** or what we call "multitasking" ability in everyday life. The fact that people can sometimes do two or more concurrent tasks equally well suggests that attention is a "resource" or pool of mental energy (Kahneman, 1973). This pool is believed to be available for allocation to competing tasks depending on various strategic principles. For example, motivation, practice and arousal are held to increase spare attentional capacity whereas task difficulty is believed to reduce it (Kahneman, 1973). Unfortunately, like its spotlight counterpart, the resource metaphor of divided attention is somewhat simplistic. Navon and Gopher (1979) have argued that people may have multiple attentional resources rather than a single pool of undifferentiated mental energy. Each of these multiple pools may have its own functions and limits. For example, R. Schmidt and Lee (1999) discovered that the attentional resources required for a motor skill such as selecting a finger movement may be separate from those which regulate a verbal skill such as the pronunciation of a word. Although intuitively appealing, multiple resource theories of attention have been criticized on the grounds of being "inherently untestable" (Palmeri, 2002, p. 298). To explain, virtually any pattern of task interference can be "explained" post hoc by attributing it to the existence of multiple pools of attentional resources.

In general, cognitive models of attention, whether based on spotlight or resource metaphors, have two major limitations. First, they have focused mainly on external (or environmental) determinants of attention and have largely overlooked internal factors (e.g. thoughts and feelings) which can distract athletes. Consider what happened to former athlete Sonia O'Sullivan, the 2000 Olympic silver medallist in the 5,000 metre event in Sydney, who allowed her concentration to slip in the 10,000 metre race at the Games. According to her post-event interview, the thought of the medal she had won prevented her from focusing properly in the next race:

> If I hadn't already got a medal, I might have fought a bit harder. But when you have a medal already, maybe you think about that medal for a moment. It probably was only for a lap … but that is all it takes for a race to get away from you.
>
> (cited in Curtis, 2000)

The second weakness of cognitive models of attention is that they ignore the influence of emotional states. This neglect of the affective dimension of behaviour is lamentable because it is widely known in sport psychology that anxiety impairs attentional processes. The phenomenon of **choking under pressure** (whereby nervousness may cause a sudden deterioration of athletic performance; see also Chapter 3) illustrates how the beam of one's attentional spotlight can be directed *inwards*, or directed towards task-irrelevant thoughts (such as fear of negative evaluation from one's coach), when it should be focused only on the task at hand. We considered the role of emotional factors in sport in Chapter 4.

To summarize, this section of the chapter highlighted two important ideas. First, concentration is just one aspect of the multidimensional construct of attention. In particular, it refers to the ability to pay attention to the task at hand while ignoring distractions from internal as well as external sources. Second, despite their plausibility, cognitive metaphors of attention have certain limitations which hamper theories and research on concentration in athletes. Having sketched the nature of concentration, let us now consider its importance for optimal athletic performance.

Importance of concentration in sport

The importance of concentration in sport is indicated by at least three sources of evidence: anecdotal, descriptive and experimental (see Chapter 1 for a discussion of the main research methods used in sport psychology).

First, as the anecdotal examples and anecdotes at the beginning of this chapter reveal so graphically, many top coaches and athletes attest to the value of focusing skills in sport. Such anecdotal insights are supported by objective evidence in the form of athlete surveys which indicate the importance of concentration to sport performance. For example, Durand-Bush et al. (2001) found that a large sample (n=335) of athletes perceived "focusing" as a vital mental skill in determining successful performance in their sport. Unfortunately, this survey did not explore in-depth what the term "focusing" meant to athletes. Therefore we cannot be sure that athletes and researchers were referring to the same cognitive construct in this study.

The second source is descriptive evidence on the value of concentration in sport which comes from studies of "flow" states or "peak performance" experience of athletes (e.g. see reviews by Harmison, 2007; Swann et al., 2012). These experiences refer to a coveted yet elusive state of mind during which the physical, technical, tactical and psychological components of sporting performance (see Figure 1.2) intertwine perfectly for the athlete in question. Given the importance of such experiences to athletes and musicians, it is not surprising that they have attracted considerable research interest from psychologists (e.g. see S. Jackson and Kimiecik, 2008; Sinnamon et al., 2012; Swann et al., 2012, 2016). A key finding from such research is that flow experiences emanate mainly from a *cognitive* source – namely, a heightened state of concentration. Indeed, S. Jackson et al. (2001, p. 130) defined flow as a "state of concentration so focused that it amounts to absolute absorption in an activity". Likewise, in Swann et al.'s (2016) recent qualitative study of flow experiences in elite golfers within a week of actual peak performances, effortful concentration was perceived as being crucial to "making it happen" on the course.

Overall, studies of peak performance suggest that athletes tend to perform optimally when they are totally absorbed in the task at hand. This state of mind is epitomized in a quote from golfer Jordan Spieth, the winner of the 2015 US Masters and US Open, who remarked that during a recent experience of being in the zone he

> wasn't striking the ball great, but every putt was finding the middle of the hole. You just kind of — everything seems simpler. You don't really see anything else around you. All you see is that line, you see your high point, you see where it's going to roll over en route to going in.
>
> (cited in Rand, 2015)

Unfortunately, research on flow states in sport is plagued by a variety of conceptual and methodological problems that are summarized in Box 5.1.

Box 5.1 Thinking critically about ... flow states in sport

Flow states or peak performance experiences tend to occur when people become absorbed in challenging tasks that demand intense concentration and commitment (see review in S. Jackson and Kimiecik, 2008). In such desirable but fleeting states of mind, performers become so deeply immersed in the activities of the present moment that they lose track of time, feel highly alert and experience a temporary sense of euphoria and joy. Research in this field was pioneered by a Hungarian psychologist named Mihalyi Csikszentmihalyi (pronounced "chick-sent-me-hai") who set out to explore the reasons why some people pursue activities (e.g. painting, mountain-climbing) that appear to offer minimal extrinsic rewards (Csikszentmihalyi, 1975). Briefly, he argued that they do so because of the intrinsic feeling of satisfaction that arises whenever there is a perfect match between the challenge of the task at hand and the skill level of the performer. Since the 1980s, sport psychologists have explored the nature and characteristics of flow states in athletes (e.g. Schuler and Brunner, 2009). According to A. Martin and Jackson (2008), there are nine putative dimensions of flow. These dimensions include

> challenge-skill balance (feeling competent enough to meet the high demands of the situation), action-awareness merging (doing things spontaneously and automatically without having to think), clear goals (having a strong sense of what one wants to do), unambiguous feedback (knowing how well one is doing during the performance itself), concentration on the task at hand (being completely focused on the task at hand), sense of control (having a feeling of total control over what one is doing), loss of self-consciousness (not worrying what others think of oneself), transformation of time (having the sense that time passes in a way that is different from normal), and autotelic experience (feeling the experience to be extremely rewarding).
>
> (A. Martin and Jackson, 2008, p. 146)

continued ...

Box 5.1 continued

Swann et al. (2015a) interviewed ten elite golfers and used "connecting analysis" to understand better how these preceding dimensions influence flow. As with previous research in this area, the authors found that heightened concentration was a key feature of this state. One golfer revealed that during flow his "mind's full with just the task in hand at that particular moment" (p. 64). Given the ephemeral nature of these states of mind, however, it is not surprising that research on flow has encountered a number of conceptual and methodological difficulties. First, consider the proliferation of different terms that have been used to refer to the construct. Although "flow", "peak performance" and "peak experience" are often used synonymously, there are important differences between them. If peak performance is defined as a performance that exceeds a person's previous levels of performance, then, as S. Jackson and Kimiecik (2008, p. 382) pointed out, "a peak performance may not lead to a peak experience and an athlete can probably have a peak experience without having a peak performance". Second, how universal is the flow experience? It would appear that its occurrence requires the confluence of a large number of factors and this might explain why it is such a rare and elusive state. While we should value attempts to better understand this phenomenon it is equally important to explore the attentional processes that underlie athletes attempts to maintain performance proficiency in the face of a variety of challenges that are a ubiquitous feature of their environment. Turning to methodological problems, there is evidence that people are not always reliable judges of their own mental processes. Brewer et al. (1991) discovered that when people were given spurious feedback concerning their performance on certain tasks, they unwittingly distorted their subsequent recall of the way in which they had performed these tasks. In other words, their recollections of task performance were easily contaminated by "leading" information. Is there a danger of similar contamination of athletes' retrospective accounts of flow states? Similarly, some qualitative accounts of the flow experience read like a retrospective rationalization (i.e. drawing on one's theoretical knowledge of a subject) rather than a vivid and rich account of what it felt like to experience this phenomenon at a specific moment in time. Researchers may need to use qualitative approaches that have greater phenomenological sensitivity (e.g. explication interviews; see Petitmengin, 2006) if they are to gain a more nuanced understanding of what it means to experience flow in sport.

Critical thinking questions

Why is it so difficult to predict when flow states are likely to occur? Why, in your view, are these states so rare in sport? Do you think that athletes could experience flow states in practice – or do they happen only in competition? Is it possible to study flow states without disrupting them? Can you think of one advantage and one disadvantage of using questionnaires to assess athletes' peak performance experiences (see S. Jackson et al., 2008)? Apart from psychometric tests, what other methods could you use to study flow states? Do you think that a flow state comes before or after an outstanding athletic performance? Give reasons for your answer. Finally, do you think that athletes can be trained to experience flow states more regularly (see also Box 5.2)?

One of the critical thinking questions in Box 5.1 concerned the apparent rarity of peak experiences in sport. One possible reason why flow states are not more common in sport is that our concentration system is too fragile to maintain the type of absorption that is necessary for them. To explain, psychologists believe that concentration is controlled mainly by the "central executive" component of our working memory system (whose main objective is to keep a small amount of information active in our minds while we make a decision about whether or not to process it further: see D'Esposito and Postle, 2015; Logie, 1999). This component of the memory system regulates what we consciously attend to, such as holding a telephone number in our heads before we write it down. Unfortunately, the working memory system is very limited in its capacity and duration. This limitation helps to explain why people are easily distracted. Put simply, we find it very difficult to focus on our intentions when there is a lot of activity going on around us. Other causes of distractibility are examined briefly later in the chapter. In any case, as soon as we begin to pay attention to task-irrelevant information – something other than the job at hand – our mental energy is diverted and we lose our concentration temporarily. Despite the issues raised in Box 5.1, there is little doubt that athletes who perform at their peak tend to report focusing only on task-relevant information – which is a sign of effective concentration.

The third source of evidence on the importance of concentration in sport comes from experimental research on the consequences of manipulating athletes' attentional focus in competitive situations. For example, a review by Wulf (2013) concluded that an external focus of attention (in which performers direct their attention at the effects that their movements have on the environment) is more effective than an internal one (in which performers focus on their own body movements) in improving the learning and performance of motor skills. Wulf (2013) has argued that an internal focus constrains the automatic control processes that would normally regulate the movement while an external focus allows the motor system to more naturally self-organize. To illustrate, Wulf et al. (2001) discovered that participants who adopted an internal focus produced higher balance errors on a dynamic balance task (stabilometer) when compared to the performance of an external focus of attention group. The results revealed that the external group demonstrated lower probe reaction times (a measure of attentional demands and, hence, the extent to which a movement is automatized) than the internal focus group. Although these findings point to the efficacy of an external focus (especially with relatively simple motor tasks), Wulf (2008) has acknowledged that there might be a "limit to the performance-enhancing effects of external focus instructions for top-level performers" (p. 323). Wulf made this claim having found that an external focus did not enhance movement efficiency (relative to a normal focus condition and to an internal focus condition) when Cirque Du Soleil performers were required to balance on an inflated rubber disk. Despite this admission, Wulf (2016) recently argued that "if movements are not planned in terms of the intended movement effect, but in terms of specific body movements, the outcome will always be less-than-optimal" (p. 338). However, arguments that an internal focus of attention will always prove less-than-optimal seem flawed. Exploring this issue in a series of recent papers, Toner and Moran (2015, 2016) have argued that there are occasions when an internal focus of attention may prove beneficial to performance. For example, when seeking to refine "attenuated" movement patterns in a practice setting, expert performers may need to reinvest conscious attention in order to acquire a more desirable movement pattern (see Carson and Collins, 2016, for a recent discussion of this issue). Furthermore, Rienhoff et al. (2015) showed that an external focus of attention led to a significant decrease in basketball shooting performance relative to internal focusing and no-instruction conditions for players of differing expertise. Rory McIlroy, the world's number 1 ranked golfer, revealed his preference for an internal focus of attention in his quest for improvement. Specifically, he always uses "a couple of little swing thoughts, whatever I'm working on at the time whether it's to do with holding my right elbow or making sure that I turn my shoulder under my chin or whatever it is" (Watson, 2015). Clearly, some elite athletes value the importance of an internal rather than external focus of attention in certain circumstances.

In seeking to resolve the debate over the relative merits of different attentional foci Toner and Moran (2016) suggested that researchers should go beyond restrictive theoretical dichotomies (e.g. "internal" versus "external"; "top-down" versus "bottom-up") because such binary distinctions are "fuzzy" and leave crucial explanatory gaps (since different aspects of attention interact extensively; see Anderson, 2011). Unfortunately, the majority of research exploring attentional processes in skilled performers has relied on the use of standardized laboratory tasks. This approach may only provide a static snapshot of the phenomena of interest and sheds little light on the dynamic nature of attention. For example, using naturalistic investigations (including filming participants and using self-confrontation interviews), Bernier et al. (2011, 2016) found that skilled golfers and figure skaters were able to flexibly adjust their attentional focus (specifically, moving back-and-forth between internal and external foci) across the preparatory, execution and evaluative stages of training and competitive performance. To shed light on the complex and dynamic attentional mechanisms that allow skilled performers to maintain performance proficiency researchers may need to use a variety of methods including both standardized laboratory techniques (e.g. occlusion paradigms, eye-tracking) and phenomenological and naturalistic investigations (e.g. stimulated recall (SR)).

Additional experimental evidence on the efficacy of attentional focus manipulations among athletes comes from research on association/dissociation (see Brick et al., 2014). The use of "associative" attentional techniques (see explanation of term in Morgan and Pollock, 1977) in which athletes are trained to focus on bodily signals such as heart beat, respiratory signals and kinaesthetic sensations has been linked with faster performance in running (K. Masters and Ogles, 1998; Morgan, 2000) and swimming (Couture et al., 1999) in comparison with "dissociative" techniques such as paying attention to thoughts other than those concerned with bodily processes. Overall, K. Masters and Ogles (1998) concluded that whereas associative techniques are typically related to comparatively faster performances by athletes, dissociative techniques are usually linked to a reduction in perceived exertion in endurance events. However, the validity of this conclusion was challenged by Salmon et al. (2010) in a comprehensive review of the research literature in this field. Briefly, these researchers argued that a variety of conceptual and methodological difficulties hamper traditional studies of associative and dissociative attentional techniques. For example, they pointed out that the psychodynamic theory underlying the original use of the term "dissociation" has been largely discredited and supplanted by cognitive constructs. Brick et al. (2014) recently sought to address some of these conceptual issues. They proposed an expansion of the internal/external dimensions of the association and dissociation categories so as to more adequately describe the attentional focus of endurance athletes. They argued that the association category should distinguish between internal sensory monitoring and active self-regulation (e.g. efforts to control thoughts, feelings, actions). They also proposed that the external association category should include outward monitoring (e.g. thoughts relating to other competitors, mile markers etc.). These authors argued that the internal dissociation category should include active distraction (e.g. attentionally demanding tasks) while the external dissociation category should include reference to involuntary distraction (e.g. reflective thoughts, irrelevant daydreams). Recent research by Brick et al. (2015) has found some empirical support for these emergent categories.

Box 5.2 Thinking critically about … research on what long-distance runners think about

Given the apparent complexity of the thought patterns held by long-distance runners, what methods might the researcher use to understand how these athletes deal with issues such as maintaining a desirable pace or coping with feelings of pain or discomfort? A recent study by Samson et al. (2015) used a think-aloud protocol (i.e. a method in which participants state aloud their thoughts as they are performing a task) with ten long-distance runners to shed light on these latter issues. Results revealed that participants' thoughts fell into one or more of three interrelated themes: (a) pace and distance, (b) pace and discomfort, and (c) environment. The most common type of thought related to pace and distance. For example, runners monitored their pace so as to ensure that they were conserving their energy levels and so that they were aware of the distance they had left to cover. The next most common thought, perhaps unsurprisingly, related to thoughts of pain and discomfort. Runners thought about the cause of pain and discomfort such as the steepness of a hill and used motivational self-talk (e.g. "that sucked but it's going to be an awesome run on the way back") in order to cope with pain. The final category of thoughts related to environmental conditions such as the scenery, weather (e.g. "it's hot, it's really humid"), and other runners or cyclists. Overall, the majority of the runners' thoughts (i.e. 72 per cent) were internal in nature while only 28 per cent were external. Interestingly, nearly all of the runners revealed that the beginning of the run was difficult but that it became easier as it progressed.

continued …

Box 5.2 continued

Critical thinking questions

Do you think verbal "think aloud" protocols can provide a comprehensive insight into the thought processes of athletes during online skill execution? Is there, for example, any danger that athletes may censure certain thoughts (e.g. if the athlete considered them frivolous or were worried that revealing them would portray them in a bad light)? What could you, as the experimenter, do to encourage athletes to answer these protocols in a frank and forthright manner? Can you think of any mental skills techniques that could be used to help athletes deal with the pain or discomfort that they experience at the beginning of the run? How might increasing an athlete's bodily awareness (through certain practices such as the Feldenkrais method) improve their pacing strategies?

Methodologically, many studies in this field are flawed because they are based on non-validated measures of association and dissociation. In view of these problems, Salmon et al. (2010) proposed that future research on the relationship between attentional strategies and sustained physical activity could benefit from adopting the theoretical model of mindfulness – a theory and practice derived from Buddhist meditation. We consider this practice in the following section.

Earlier in this chapter, we explained how important it is for athletes to focus on the task at hand while ignoring distractions. But how exactly can athletes develop this rather unnatural type of present-centred awareness? One emerging technique for this purpose is "mindfulness" training – an attentional focusing strategy that originated in the Buddhist meditative tradition (Erisman and Roemer, 2010). According to one of its leading proponents Kabat-Zinn (2005, p. 24), mindfulness involves "an openhearted, moment-to-moment, nonjudgmental awareness" of oneself and of the world. This emphasis on adopting a non-judgemental orientation to distractions is important because it distinguishes mindfulness training from more active cognitive control techniques such as thought suppression. By urging acceptance rather than attempted elimination of intrusive, unwanted thoughts and feelings, mindfulness training purports to help performers to concentrate on the here-and-now. In fact mindfulness would appear to have played an important role in Novak Djokovic's rise to number 1 tennis player in the world. In his book Serve to Win Djokovic reveals that:

> I used to freeze up whenever I made a mistake; I was sure that I wasn't in the same league as the Federers or the Andy Murrays…now, when I blow a serve or shank a backhand, I still get those feelings of self-doubt but I know how to handle them: I acknowledge the negative thoughts and let them slide by, focusing on the moment. That mindfulness helps me process pain and emotions. It lets me focus on what's really important. It helps me turn down the volume in my brain. Imagine how handy that is for me in the middle of a grand slam championship match.

> (cited in Mitchell, 2013)

In terms of empirical support for this approach, Ivarsson et al. (2015) found that a mindfulness intervention (based on the mindfulness, acceptance and committment (MAC) approach) with a group of elite footballers was associated with a clinically relevant reduction in injuries over a six-month period when compared to the injuries sustained by those who took part in a control condition (which involved attending weekly presentations covering topics on group psychology). The authors argued that mindfulness practice might have helped participants to attend to relevant stimuli during competition. They also point to research which has found a relationship between injury and peripheral vision narrowing (Rogers and Landers, 2005).

In a novel experiment, Aherne et al. (2011) investigated the effects of a six week, CD-based mindfulness training programme on elite athletes' flow experiences in training. Results showed that athletes who underwent this training programme experienced greater flow than those in a control group who had received no mindfulness instruction. Although this result is interesting, additional research employing larger samples and controlling for the potential effects of increased attention by the experimenter is needed before firm conclusions can be reached regarding the efficacy of mindfulness training on flow experiences in athletes. What cognitive mechanisms underlie the potentially beneficial effects of mindfulness training? This approach may help performers to improve their selective attention – that is, the ability to disengage quickly from an incorrectly cued spatial location and reorient attention to a correct location (Hodgins and Adair, 2010). Mindful behaviour might also promote a form of cognitive flexibility which helps performers to inhibit automated responses by retaining the flexibility to react to the dynamically unfolding events that characterize many performance environments (Rossano, 2003).

Unfortunately, although mindfulness practice offers considerable promise as a strategy for the enhancement of a host of desirable athletic behaviours (e.g. reorienting one's focus of attention), there are a number of conceptual and methodological issues which hamper research in this area. For example, Davidson and Kaszniak (2015) argued that the construct validity of many mindfulness questionnaires is problematic. The argument here is that these measures require individuals to provide accounts of their own experience which depend on their practice and skill in interrogating their own minds – something that will be likely to change with training. An additional problem concerns the impossibility of blinding participants to which group they are assigned to in mindfulness intervention studies. To explain, participants in the control conditions know they are in the control group and participants in the active meditation/mindfulness practice condition are similarly aware. An ideal solution would be to use a comparison treatment condition that matches the mindfulness intervention in all of the basic non-specific factors. However, this is recognized as a challenging endeavour – one that sport psychology researchers may need to address before they can be confident that mindfulness-based training interventions are having a meaningful impact on athletic performance.

To summarize, the three preceding strands of evidence (anecdotal, descriptive and experimental) converge on the conclusion that concentration is vital for success in sport. This conclusion has been echoed by researchers such as

Abernethy et al. (2007, p. 245), who proclaimed that "it is difficult to conceive of any aspect of psychology that may be more central to the enhancement of skill learning and expert performance than attention". But how can psychologists measure people's attentional skills?

Measurement of attentional processes in athletes

As concentration is a hypothetical construct, and hence unobservable, it cannot be measured directly. Nevertheless, attentional processes can be assessed indirectly using methods drawn from four main paradigms: the psychometric (or individual differences), neuroscientific, experimental and "pupillometry" (the measurement of changes in pupil diameter as a function of cognitive processing) traditions in psychology. Due to space restrictions, we can provide only a brief overview of these paradigms here. For a more detailed review of these methodological approaches, see Summers and Moran (2011).

Psychometric approach

Some sport psychologists have attempted to measure individual differences in attentional processes in athletes through the use of specially designed paper-and-pencil tests. For example, the Test of Attentional and Interpersonal Style (TAIS; Nideffer, 1976) has been used as a screening device in several applied sport psychology settings, such as in the Australian Institute for Sport (Nideffer et al., 2001). It contains 144 items, broken down into seventeen subscales, which purport to measure people's attentional processes in everyday situations (e.g. "When I read, it is easy to block out everything but the book"). Although the original version of this test was not intended for use with athletic populations, several sport-specific versions of the TAIS have emerged. The TAIS is based on Nideffer's model of attention, which can be outlined briefly as follows. According to Nideffer (1976), people's attentional focus varies simultaneously along two independent dimensions – namely, "width" and "direction". With regard to width, attention is believed to range along a continuum from a broad focus (where one is aware of many stimulus features at the same time) to a narrow one (where irrelevant information is excluded effectively). Attentional "direction" refers to the target of one's focus: whether it is external or internal (for a review of external and internal attention, see Chun et al., 2011). These dimensions of width and direction may be combined factorially to yield four hypothetical attentional styles. To illustrate, a narrow external attentional focus in sport is implicated when a golfer looks at the hole before putting. By contrast, a narrow internal focus is required when a gymnast mentally rehearses a skill such as back-flip while waiting to compete. Nideffer (1976) proposed that athletes have to match the attentional demands of a given sport skill or situation with the appropriate attentional focus. Some evidence to support this idea comes from a study by Kress and Statler (2007) on the strategies used by former Olympic cyclists to cope with exertion pain. Depending on what was required at the time, these cyclists reported using a broad external focus (e.g.

concentrating on getting to the finish line), a broad internal focus (concentrating on pedalling and body movements), a narrow external focus (e.g. "staying on the wheel in front of me") or a narrow internal focus (concentrating on a smooth pedalling stroke). Despite its plausibility and popularity, however, the TAIS has several flaws which are discussed in Box 5.3.

Box 5.3 Thinking critically about ... the Test of Attentional and Interpersonal Style

The TAIS (Nideffer, 1976) has been used in sport psychology to investigate the relationship between attentional processes and athletic performance. Unfortunately, its validity and utility have been questioned. So, what are the strengths and weaknesses of this test?

On the positive side, the TAIS has a plausible theoretical rationale and considerable face validity because its assumptions make "intuitive sense to coaches and athletes" (Bond and Sargent, 1995, p. 394). Also, there is some empirical support for its construct validity. Nideffer (1976) reported that unsuccessful swimmers were attentionally "overloaded" when compared to successful counterparts. Similarly, V. Wilson et al. (1985) discovered that volleyball players who had been rated by their coaches as "good concentrators" under competitive stress scored significantly lower on the broad external focus (BET) and broad internal focus (BIT) subscales than did "poor concentrators". Unfortunately, such strengths must be weighed against the following weaknesses of this test. First, it is questionable whether athletes are reliably capable of evaluating their own attentional processes using self-report instruments (Boutcher, 2008). Second, the TAIS assesses perceived, rather than actual, attentional skills. Accordingly, we cannot be sure that athletes who complete it are differentiating between what they actually do and what they would like us to believe that they do in everyday situations requiring attentional processes. Third, the factor structure of the TAIS has not been replicated consistently across different cultural settings (Wada et al., 2003). Fourth, the TAIS fails to differentiate between athletes of different skill levels in sports in which selective attention is known to be important (Summers and Ford, 1990). Fifth, Nideffer's theory is conceptually flawed because it does not distinguish between task-relevant and task-irrelevant information in sport situations. Finally, Boutcher (2008) raised doubts about the predictive validity of the test. Specifically, based on a review of relevant evidence, he concluded that the TAIS has "limited validity and predictive properties for sport performance" (Boutcher, 2008, p. 330). This conclusion echoes that of Cratty (1983, p. 100), who said that the test was only "marginally useful, and the data it produces are not much better than the information a coach might obtain from simply questioning athletes or observing their performance".

Critical thinking questions

From the evidence above, what conclusions would you draw about the validity of the TAIS? If you were redesigning this test, what changes would you make to its content and format? Can a psychological test be useful in applied settings even if its construct validity is questionable? More generally, do you think that paper-and-pencil tests of attention should be augmented by other measurement paradigms? If so, which ones would you suggest and why?

As you can see, the psychometric paradigm, as epitomized by the TAIS, is a popular if somewhat flawed approach to the measurement of attentional processes in athletes. Nevertheless, since the early 2000s, this approach has yielded several promising instruments which claim to measure concentration skills. For example, Hatzigeorgiadis (2002) and Hatzigeorgiadis and Biddle (2000) have developed psychometric tools to measure "cognitive interference" or task-irrelevant, self-preoccupied thinking in sport performers. The Thought Occurrence Questionnaire for Sport (TOQS; Hatzigeorgiadis and Biddle, 2000) is a seventeen-item test comprising three subscales that measures the frequency of participants' performance worries (e.g. "that I am not going to win this competition"), situation-irrelevant thoughts (e.g. "about what I'm going to do when I get home"), and thoughts of escape (e.g. "that I am fed up with it"). Overall, it purports to assess athletes' susceptibility to cognitive interference during sport performance. Participants are typically instructed to complete the questionnaire in relation to their most recent sport encounter. The factorial validity of the TOQS is supported in both adult (Hatzigeorgiadis and Biddle, 2000) and youth sport (Lane et al., 2005) populations.

Neuroscientific approach

The second measurement paradigm in attentional research comes from cognitive neuroscience – a field that is concerned broadly with the identification of the neural substrates of mental processes (Gazzaniga et al., 2013). Since 2000, a variety of neuroscientific techniques such as **electroencephalography** (EEG), functional magnetic resonance imaging (fMRI) and **positron emission tomography** (PET scanning) have been used to reveal which parts of the brain "light up" when a person is paying attention to designated stimuli (Kolb and Whishaw, 2015; see also Mather et al., 2013a). Interestingly, a neuroscientific study using functional imaging technology has revealed that compared to expert golfers, the brains of relative novices have difficulty in filtering out irrelevant information (Milton et al., 2007). Let us now summarize some key findings arising from neuroscientific studies of athletes' attentional processes.

Psychophysiological indices of attention such as heart rate have been monitored in athletes as they perform self-paced skills in target sports like archery, pistol-shooting and rifle-shooting (see reviews by Cooke, 2013; Hatfield and Kerick, 2007; Janelle and Hatfield, 2008). An early finding that emerged from this line of research is that cardiac deceleration (or a slowing of the heart rate) tends to occur among elite rifle-shooters in the seconds before they pull the trigger of their guns. Researchers have used electrocardiograms to assess cardiac activity (typically heart rate acceleration or deceleration) by placing electrodes on the skin to detect electrical activity generated by the heart. This finding is interesting in the light of Garry Sobers' comments in the first section of this chapter because it suggests that expert target sport performers can indeed "switch on" their concentration processes at will. Interestingly, a study by Radlo et al. (2002) reported that dart-throwers' heart rates may vary in accordance with the type of attentional focus that they adopted. For example, when they used an external attentional strategy, their heart rates tended to decline just before they threw the darts. Cooke (2013) proposed that this deceleration in heart rate may facilitate the processing of external information by reducing blood pressure and increasing the flow of environmental information to the brain.

The next methodological innovation in this paradigm occurred with the development of equipment designed to measure continuous patterns of electrical activity in the brain (see Box 5.4). This "brain wave" technology included electroencephalographic methods and those based on **event-related potentials** (ERPs). In a typical EEG experiment, an electrode is attached to a person's scalp in order to detect the electrical activity of neurons in the

---

Box 5.4 In the spotlight Neurofeedback as a technique for enhancing sports performance: promise and limitations

Researchers and practitioners have become increasingly interested in the use of neurofeedback as a potential means of enhancing sports performance. Unfortunately, until recently, EEG studies have been undermined by a variety of methodological limitations (e.g. inconsistency across studies in the location and number of electrodes placed on the scalp; see Park et al., 2015) – and this might explain some of the apparent inconsistencies in the reported location of the effects. An equally important issue is that few studies have used EEG during real-world sporting behaviour. That is, these techniques have been largely used in abstract laboratory tasks lacking ecological validity. Given these apparent limitations, what potential do neurofeedback training approaches hold for the improvement of athletes' concentration skills? Dekker et al. (2014) failed to find any benefit of neurofeedback training with a group of elite table tennis players although Rostami et al. (2012) discovered that elite rifle-shooters demonstrated a significant difference in shot performance when assessed after five weeks of neurofeedback training. In a recent study, Kao et al. (2014) sought to regulate frontal midline theta (Fmθ) amplitude (an EEG signature which is associated with top-down cognitive processing) using neurofeedback training in order to enhance sustained attention in a group of three highly skilled golfers. Results showed partial support for their hypothesis as two of the participants improved their putting performance. However, these researchers failed to observe any change in Fmθ during online skill execution so we cannot be sure that neurofeedback training was responsible for improvements in performance. These results mean that it is still open to question whether patterns characteristic of optimal performance can be trained via the use of EEG-based neurofeedback for individual athletes. Ultimately, it is hoped that the continued development of neurofeedback mechanisms will provide cognitive neuroscientists with a better understanding of the brain–behaviour links underpinning superior performance at the elite level of sport. Perhaps most importantly, developments in mobile EEG technology (addressing some of the issues that plagued its early use such as inability to handle motion artefacts and portability of the equipment) may allow researchers to gain a better understanding of the complexity of the neural mechanisms underpinning performance in dynamic environments.

underlying brain region. Another electrode is then attached to the person's earlobe, where there is no electrical activity to detect. Then the EEG is recorded to indicate the difference in electrical potentials detected by the electrodes (Kolb and Whishaw, 2015). Since the late 1990s, a considerable amount of research has been conducted on EEG activity in athletes (Hatfield and Hillman, 2001). From such research, certain cerebral asymmetry effects have been detected in these performers. For example, in keeping with previous findings from heart rate studies, research suggests that just before expert archers and pistol performers execute their shots, their EEG records tend to display a distinctive shift from left-hemisphere to right-hemisphere activation (Hatfield and Hillman, 2001). This shift is believed to reflect a change in executive control from the verbally based left hemisphere to the visuo-spatially specialized right hemisphere. Put differently, target-shooters display a marked reduction in the extent of their verbal-analytical processes (including self-talk) prior to shot execution. In the light of this finding, perhaps the snooker player Mark Williams' strategy of covert singing (see first section of chapter) was not so daft after all because it may have helped him to avoid thinking too much or from focusing on task-irrelevant thoughts – which can cause paralysis-by-analysis – prior to shot execution (for an explanation of R. Masters' (1992) "conscious processing" or reinvestment hypothesis, see Chapter 3). More generally, EEG research findings suggest that top-class athletes know how to regulate their physiological processes as they prepare for the performance of key skills (for a discussion of expertise in sport, see also Chapter 7). Unfortunately, this theory has not been tested systematically to date as the EEG is a relatively blunt instrument because its data are confounded with the brain's global level of electrical activity. Nevertheless, EEG research in sport has had at least one practical implication. Specifically, it has led to the use of biofeedback techniques designed to help athletes to become more effective at controlling their cortical activity. For example, participants' EEG activity can be measured over a period of time and analysis of their brain activity can be fed back to them. With practice, participants may be able to learn how their internal mental states correspond with a neural signal. It is possible that they could use this information to control the onset or maintenance of particular mental states. In fact, Jason Day, the winner of the 2015 USPGA golf championship, has used a wireless EEG and claims that his "mental game has improved 100% since working with the system…it teaches me how to get in the zone, shows me what it feels like when I'm in the zone and allows me to work on replicating it" (cited in Suarez, 2013).

Staying with brain wave measurement in sport, event-related potentials are brief changes in EEG signals that are synchronized with or "time locked" to some eliciting event or stimulus. Unlike the EEG, which is a measure of continuous electrical activity in the brain, ERPs reflect transient cortical changes that are evoked by certain information-processing events. Typically, ERPs display characteristic peaks of electrical activity that begin a few milliseconds after the onset of a given stimulus (e.g. a loud noise) and continue for up to a second afterwards (for more details, see Kolb and Whishaw, 2015).

Since the 1990s, a methodological innovation in neuroscientific research on attention concerns the use of functional brain imaging techniques. With these procedures (e.g. recall our earlier discussion of positron emission tomography and functional magnetic resonance imaging; see also Chapter 6), researchers can obtain clear and dynamic insights into the specific brain regions that are activated when people perform specific cognitive tasks. Since about 2007, the neural processes underlying athletic expertise have attracted increasing research interest from cognitive neuroscientists (e.g. see Nakata et al., 2010; Wei and Luo, 2010; Yarrow et al., 2009). For example, **transcranial magnetic stimulation** (TMS, a technique in which the functioning of a specific area of the brain is temporarily disrupted through the application of pulsating magnetic fields to the skull using a stimulating coil) has been employed to study attentional processes (e.g. Aglioti et al., 2008; Thomson et al., 2008). Such research has allowed investigators to link several functions of attention to specific anatomical areas in the brain. So far, three separable attention-related neural networks have been identified linked to the functions of achieving and maintaining high sensitivity to incoming stimuli (alerting); selecting information from sensory input (orienting); and monitoring and resolving conflict (executive attention) (for a review, see Posner and Rothbart, 2007).

Although fMRI scans can answer questions concerning the "where" of attention, issues concerning the "how" of attention require methods (such as the EEG) that assess changes in patterns of the brain's neurological activity over time. In this regard, a considerable amount of research has accumulated on the pre-event patterns of EEG activity in certain athletes (Hatfield and Kerick, 2007). For example, there is evidence that superior performance is associated with increased coherence of alpha rhythms prior to execution just as expert golfers and shooters prepare to execute a skill (see Babiloni et al., 2011; Del Percio et al., 2011). Findings from these latter two studies suggest that expertise may be characterized by increased communication between visual–spatial parietal sites and regions responsible for motor control and attentional processing. Such findings lend initial support to the concept of "neural efficiency" in elite athletes. It is possible that such efficiency facilitates the transmission and retrieval of sensorimotor and cognitive information in the brain. In summary, the major advantage of neuroscientific techniques over their psychometric counterparts is that they yield objective data on biological processes which can be recorded while the athlete is performing his or her skills. Unfortunately, the major drawbacks associated with the neuroscientific paradigm are cost and practicality.

Experimental approach

The third approach to the measurement of attentional processes in athletes comes mainly from capacity theory (Kahneman, 1973) in experimental psychology. Briefly, this theory suggests that attention may be defined operationally in terms of the interference between two tasks (a primary task and a secondary task) that are performed simultaneously. Furthermore, it postulates that multiple tasks require more attentional resources than does a single task, and that difficult tasks require more attentional resources than do relatively simple tasks. Because this pool of attentional resources is limited, however, interference will occur any time that a person performs multiple tasks – regardless of the sensory modalities involved. Another postulate of capacity theory is that interference depends primarily on the difficulty level and subsequent demands of the tasks that are being performed (Abernethy, 2001).

Having provided a quick overview of capacity theory, let us now explain the "dual-task paradigm". Briefly, if the two tasks can be performed as well simultaneously as individually, it may be concluded that at least one of them was automatic (i.e. demanding minimal attentional resources). However, if the primary task is performed less well when it is combined with the secondary task, then both tasks are believed to require attentional resources. Adopting this experimental approach, the dual-task method of measuring attention requires participants to perform two tasks over three conditions. In condition one, the person has to perform the primary task on its own. Likewise, in condition two, the person must perform the secondary task on its own. In condition three, however, the person is required to perform both tasks concurrently.

When the dual-task paradigm is used in sport psychology, the primary task usually consists of a self-paced or "closed" skill (i.e. one that can be performed without interference from others such as a golf putt e.g. see Fisher and Etnier, 2014) whereas the secondary task (usually based on reaction time) typically requires the subject to respond as fast as possible to a predetermined probe signal (e.g. an auditory tone). Following comparison of performance between these three conditions, conclusions may be drawn about the attentional demands of the primary and secondary tasks. Using this method, sport psychologists are usually interested in people's performance in condition three – the concurrent task situation. In this condition, participants are required to perform a primary task which is interrupted periodically by the presentation of the probe stimulus. When this probe is presented, the person has to respond to it as rapidly as possible. It is assumed that the speed of responding to the probe is related inversely to the momentary attention devoted to the primary task. Therefore, if a primary task is cognitively demanding, a decrement should be evident in secondary task performance. However, if the performance of the secondary task in the dual-task condition does not differ significantly from that evident in the relevant control condition, then it may be assumed that the primary task is relatively effortless (or automatic).

In summary, the dual-task paradigm is an attempt to measure the spare mental capacity of a person while he or she is engaged in performing some task or mental activity. To illustrate this approach, consider a study by W. Land and G. Tenenbaum (2012), which was designed to investigate the effects of attentional focus on skilled and novice performance. These researchers used a dual-task design to examine the effects of manipulating people's focus of attention (either explicitly on their own golf putting performance or on a distracting secondary task) on performance on a putting task under low-anxiety or high-anxiety experimental conditions. In this study, participants were required to perform the primary task, that is, holing putts while responding as accurately as possible to one of two theoretically derived secondary tasks. The "relevant" secondary task required participants to monitor club head–ball contact and indicate as precisely as possible the moment the club struck the ball by stating the word "hit" out loud at impact. The "irrelevant" secondary task required participants to speak aloud a random letter each time they heard an auditory signal while they were putting. In a third condition, participants were merely asked to focus on holing as many putts as possible. Each condition was completed under evaluative and non-evaluative instructional sets that were designed to manipulate the level of anxiety experienced by the participants. Results showed that putting performance effectiveness (as measured by the mean number of putts made) was maintained under anxiety-provoking conditions, when both of the two secondary task strategies were implemented. The authors found that the relevant secondary task was just as effective at preventing choking under pressure amongst experts as the irrelevant secondary task (which is the most common type of secondary task used by researchers) and that the former may serve as a more practical method of maintaining performance proficiency during on-course performance. Novice performance did not benefit from either secondary task possibly because these strategies prevented them from focusing on component elements of action as they performed the skill. The ingenuity of dual-task paradigms means they have become a popular method of measuring attentional processes in athletes. However, a number of researchers have argued for the need to explore attentional changes in more ecologically valid tasks which involve less forced attentional manipulations (Wilson et al., 2007a). Land and Tenenbaum's use of a "relevant" task provides an example of how researchers can achieve this latter aim. To summarize this section of the chapter, the self-report approach to the measurement of concentration processes is favoured by most sport psychologists for reasons of brevity, convenience and economy. Given the issues raised in Box 5.3, however, the results yielded by psychological tests of concentration must be interpreted cautiously. Also, few, if any, of the available measures of attention deal explicitly with concentration skills. Moreover, no consensus has emerged about the best combination of these methods to use when assessing athletes' attentional processes in applied settings.

Pupillometry

The fourth approach to the measurement of attentional processes involves the use of "pupillometry" or the objective measurement of continuous, task-evoked changes in the diameter of the pupil of the eye as a function of cognitive processing (Laeng et al., 2012; Mathôt and Van der Stigchel, 2015). Pupillometry is particularly suitable for the measurement of "attentional effort" (also known as "mental effort" or "cognitive effort"; Burge et al., 2013; Piquado et al., 2010) – a construct that denotes the motivated allocation of attentional capacity or resources to satisfy cognitively challenging demands (Kahneman, 1973; Sarter et al., 2006). To illustrate the nature of attentional effort, note that trying to multiply 36 by 49 in your head requires more mental exertion than does the effort required to multiply 6 by 9. Technically, the term attentional effort captures the intensive, as distinct from the selective, aspect of cognitive resource allocation.

According to Kahneman (1973), pupil dilation is probably "the best single index" (p. 18) of attentional effort as it reflects "the current rate at which mental energy is used" (Kahneman, 2011, p. 34). Supporting this view, recent evidence (e.g. by Alnaes et al., 2014; Murphy et al., 2014) shows that pupil size predicts brain activity in the locus coeruleus-norepinephrine (LC-NE) system – the one that regulates the allocation of attentional resources to task engagement. Although space limitations preclude a review of research on pupillometry (but see Mathôt and Van der Stigchel, 2015), pupil dilation effects have been demonstrated for cognitive tasks involving multiplication problems (Hess and Polt, 1964), visual search (Porter et al., 2007) and change detection (Unsworth and Robinson, 2015). Furthermore, mounting evidence suggests that the pupil remains dilated throughout the expenditure of cognitive load (Granholm et al., 1996). Unfortunately, apart from Moran et al. (2016), pupillometry has not yet been studied in sport psychology despite its potential importance as a non-invasive, online measure of attentional effort and locus coeruleus activity.

Pupillometry may enable researchers to investigate individual differences in attentional allocation processes among expert athletes as they negotiate dynamic tasks. In a recent study, O'Shea and Moran (2016) used eye-tracking technology to capture pianists' pupil size measurement with a view to exploring whether there were any changes in cognitive effort between executed and imagined piano performance. Results showed that pupil dilation during executed and imagined performance of a musical composition was very similar. Unfortunately, the low sampling rate of the equipment (30Hz; capturing an image of the eye every 33ms) meant that the researchers could only examine the relative size of the pupil and not true pupil dilation. O'Shea and Moran recognized that the use of pupil-size measurements is not a fine-grained method of analysis (i.e. it is unable to detect subtle changes in pupil size). Accordingly, future researchers wishing to use pupillometry as a method of measuring attentional allocation may need to use wavelet analysis (to investigate where pupil measurements are greater or smaller) alongside other eye-tracking metrics (e.g. fixation length and number). Now that we have explained the nature, importance and measurement of concentration in sport, let us consider some psychological principles which govern an optimal focus in athletes.

Principles of effective concentration

Based on general reviews of the relationship between attention and athletic performance (e.g. Moran, 1996), at least five theoretical principles of effective concentration in sport may be identified (Kremer and Moran, 2013; see Figure 5.3). Three of them concern the establishment of an optimal focus and the other two describe how it may be disrupted or lost.

The first principle of effective concentration is that a focused state of mind requires deliberate mental effort and intentionality on the part of the athlete concerned. In short, one must prepare to concentrate rather than hope that it will occur by chance. This principle was endorsed by Ronan O'Gara, the former Ireland and Lions' rugby out-half, who claimed that:

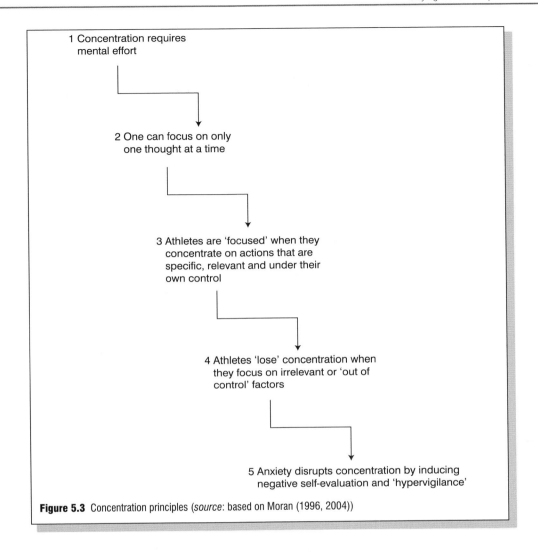

Figure 5.3 Concentration principles (*source*: based on Moran (1996, 2004))

I have to be focused. I have to do my mental preparation. I have to feel that I'm ready. I don't want to be putting myself out there for credit but I have a big impact on how Munster perform. When it's coming up to a big match, rugby is the only thing in my head. Driving around, I visualize certain scenarios, different positions on the pitch, different times when the ball is coming to me.

(cited in English, 2006, p. 70)

Not surprisingly, many athletes use imaginary "switch on" and "switch off" zones in their sports. For example, when top tennis players look for towels behind the baseline during a game to mop up perspiration, they are in their switch off zone. But when they step forward to begin their pre-service routine, they move into their switch on zone. Second, one has to be single-minded. To explain, athletes can focus on only one thought at a time – even though they can divide their attention between two or more concurrent actions (see earlier discussion). Justin Langer, the Australian former cricketer, stated that the key to concentration is "filling your mind with what you need to do to ensure a successful action, for me to bat there must be nothing but the ball in my mind, this occupies my thoughts before every shot" (cited in Barker and Slater, 2015). Indeed, this "one thought" principle may be hardwired into our brains because research shows that the working memory system which regulates conscious awareness (see D'Esposito and Postle, 2015; Logie, 1999) is fragile and limited in duration (unless extensive practice occurs; see also Chapter 7). Third, as we indicated earlier in the chapter, research on the phenomenology of peak performance states indicates that athletes' minds are focused optimally when they are doing what they are thinking. In other words, there is no difference between what athletes are thinking about and what they are doing. By implication, sport performers tend to concentrate most effectively when they direct their mental spotlight (recall our earlier discussion of various metaphors of attention) at actions that are specific, relevant and, above all, under their own control. Fourth, athletes need to refocus regularly in order to keep their minds on track. Research shows that athletes tend to "lose" their concentration when they focus on factors that are outside their control (Moran, 1996). We shall return to this issue in the next section. The fifth principle of effective concentration suggests that athletes should focus outwards when they become anxious. This principle acknowledges the potentially disruptive influence of emotions such as anxiety.

In particular, anxiety impairs concentration systems in several distinctive ways. First, it overloads working memory with worries (or cognitive anxiety; see Chapter 3). Indeed, McCarthy et al. (2013) found that anxiety was associated with an increase in distracting thoughts in a group of youth sport athletes. Second, it tends to restrict the beam of one's mental spotlight and also shifts its focus onto self-referential stimuli. Baumeister (1984) invoked this principle in attempting to explain the psychological mechanisms underlying the phenomenon of choking under pressure (see Chapter 3). Briefly, he postulated that anxiety causes people to monitor their own skills excessively, thereby leading to a sudden deterioration of performance. Third, anxiety precipitates task-irrelevant information processing. Janelle et al. (1999) discovered that anxious drivers who participated in a motor-racing simulation were especially likely to attend to irrelevant cues. Anxiety has also been found to result in the narrowing of driver's visual attention (thereby preventing them from processing relevant information in peripheral locations; see Wilson et al., 2006). Fourth, another way in which anxiety affects sport performance is by its influence on the direction of athletes' attentional focus. In particular, anxiety may encourage them to dwell on real or imagined personal weaknesses (self-focused attention) and on potential threats in the environment, thereby inducing a state of hypervigilance. Interestingly, the conscious processing (or reinvestment) hypothesis postulates that anxiety hampers performance by inducing performers to rely too much either on explicit monitoring (Beilock and Carr, 2001) or on conscious control (R. Masters, 1992) of their skills (see also Chapter 3). It is clear, therefore, that anxiety affects the content, direction and width of athletes' concentration beam (see also Moran et al., 2002). One aspect of this influence of anxiety on attention concerns the phenomenon of **"ego depletion"** (see Box 5.5).

Box 5.5 In the spotlight Exploring the relationship between ego depletion and distractibility

According to Attentional Control Theory (ACT; Eysenck et al., 2007; see Chapter 3), relatively high levels of state anxiety increase the likelihood that individuals will be distracted by irrelevant stimuli (e.g. worries). Fortunately, most people are usually able to counteract such distractions. However, under certain circumstances, especially when one's self-control resources are weakened temporarily (a hypothetical state called "ego depletion"; Baumeister et al., 1998), certain adverse consequences can occur. For example, research suggests that in a state of ego depletion, people may show impaired performance in perceptual-motor tasks (McEwan et al., 2013) and are likely to perform poorly in stressful situations (Englert and Bertrams, 2012).

In a recent study, Englert et al. (2015) found that ego-depleted participants paid more attention to distracting stimuli (statements seeking to induce worry) and performed more poorly in a free-throw basketball task. These authors proposed that one's self-control strength (the process by which one seeks to control and override predominant response tendencies) would determine an athlete's ability to resist/suppress distracting stimuli. To test this idea, Englert et al. manipulated basketball players' self-control strength as they performed a series of free throws. While performing the task, participants listened to a series of worrisome thoughts (which acted as a form of external auditory distraction) presented via headphones. Available self-control strength was manipulated in an ego-depletion task which required participants to transcribe a neutral text by omitting the letters "e" and "n" (the most frequent letters in the German language). This task can be considered a form of self-control as participants had to volitionally override a well-learned writing habit. Results indicated that ego-depleted participants were more distracted by the auditory distraction and that their performance on the free-throw task suffered in comparison to the non-depletion group. The authors argued that participants with intact self-control strength were better equipped to ignore the distracting stimuli. These results suggest that participants may have been able to use selective attention to shift their attention away from irrelevant thoughts. Given these findings it may be useful for future research to consider how athletes can increase their self-control strength. One possible means of doing so might involve the use of relaxation techniques to restore recently depleted self-control strength (see Tyler and Burns, 2008).

In summary, at least five principles govern either the maintenance or loss of an optimal focus for athletes. But why do sport performers lose their concentration in the first place?

Why do athletes lose their concentration?

As we learned from Figure 5.3, when people focus on factors that are either irrelevant to the job at hand or beyond their control, they lose concentration and their performance deteriorates. However, psychologists believe that concentration is never really "lost", but merely redirected at some target that is irrelevant to the task at hand. For example, have you ever had the experience of realizing suddenly that you have been reading the same sentence in a book over and over again without any understanding simply because your mind was "miles away"? If so, then you have distracted yourself by allowing a thought, daydream or feeling to become the target of your attention. By the way, this problem can be overcome by writing down two or three specific study questions before you approach a textbook or notes (see advice in Moran, 2000b). Let us now consider the question of why athletes appear to lose their concentration.

Competitive sport is replete with a variety of distractions that can disrupt athletes' concentration. In general, these distractions fall into two main categories: external and internal (Moran, 1996, 2004). Whereas external distractions are objective stimuli which divert our attentional spotlight away from its intended target, internal distractions include a vast array of thoughts, feelings and/or bodily sensations (e.g. pain, fatigue) which impede athletes' efforts to concentrate on the job at hand. Typical external distractions include such factors as crowd movements, sudden changes in ambient noise levels (e.g. the click of a camera – as happened to the golfer, Ian Poulter, who lost his chance to win the 2009 French Open when a camera click caused him to hit his ball into the water on the fifteenth hole; *The Irish Times*, 2009) and gamesmanship by opponents (e.g. at corner-kicks in football, opposing forwards often stand in front of the goalkeeper to prevent him or her from tracking the incoming ball). Sometimes, these factors merge together. For example, consider what happened to Samantha Stosur in her victory over Serena Williams in the final of the Australian Open tennis championship in 2011 (Fendrich, 2011). Briefly, Williams had lost the first set and was facing a break point in the first game of the second set when she hit a forehand and shouted, "come on!" as Stosur prepared a backhand return. Interestingly, the umpire ruled that Williams' shout had hindered Stosur's ability to complete the point and awarded it to Stosur – thereby putting her ahead 1–0 in that set, which she won to clinch the championship. External distractions also include unpredictable weather conditions (e.g. a golfer may become distracted by windy conditions). As an example of the last of these factors, the Swiss cyclist Fabian Cancellara complained about the distracting effect of the heat he experienced during the 2009 Tour de France: "With the heat like that... there's a lack of concentration among the riders" (cited in Associated Press, 2009). Interestingly, a study by Larrick et al. (2011) analysed data from over 57,000 Major League Baseball games on the relationship between ambient temperature and retaliatory aggression among pitchers. Results showed that, when many relevant variables were controlled for, the probability of a pitcher hitting a batter increased significantly during high temperatures. More generally, distractions lead to impaired performance at the worst possible moment for the performer concerned. For example, the Brazilian marathon runner Vanderlei De Lima was leading the race in the 2004 Olympics in Athens when an unstable spectator suddenly jumped out from the crowd and wrestled him to the ground. Stunned and naturally distracted, De Lima eventually finished third in the event (Goodbody and Nichols, 2004). By contrast, internal distractions are self-generated concerns arising from one's own thoughts and feelings. Typical factors in this category include wondering what might happen in the future, regretting what has happened in the past, worrying about what other people might say or do and/or feeling tired, bored or otherwise emotionally upset (Figure 5.4). A classic example of a costly internal distraction occurred in the case of the golfer Doug Sanders, who missed a putt of less than three feet that would have earned him victory at the 1970 British Open championship in St. Andrews, Scotland. This error not only prevented him from winning his first major tournament, but also deprived him of an estimated £10 million in prize money, tournament invitations and advertising endorsements. Remarkably, Sanders' attentional lapse was precipitated by a cognitive error – thinking too far ahead or in this case, making a victory speech before the putt had been taken. Intriguingly, over 30 years later, he revealed what had gone through his mind at the time: "I made the mistake about thinking which section of the crowd I was going to bow to!" (cited in Gilleece, 1999b). Clearly, Sanders had inadvertently distracted himself by allowing his mental spotlight to shine into the future instead of at the task in hand. As he explained:

> I had the victory speech prepared before the battle was over ... I would give up every victory I had to have won that title. It's amazing how many different things to my normal routine I did on the eighteenth hole. There's something for psychologists there, the way that the final hole of a major championship can alter the way a man thinks.
>
> (cited in G. Moran, 2005, p. 21)

Figure 5.4 Internal distractions can upset athletes' concentration in competitive situations

Unfortunately, despite such vivid accounts of attentional lapses in sport, little research has been conducted on the phenomenology of distractibility – although Gouju et al. (2007) explored athletes' attentional experiences in a hurdle race, especially those arising from the "felt presence" of rival competitors. This general neglect of distractibility is attributable to a combination of theoretical and methodological factors. First, since the 1960s, cognitive researchers have assumed falsely that information flows into the mind in only one direction – from the outside world inwards. In so doing, they ignored the possibility that information (and hence distractions) could travel in the opposite direction – from long-term memory into working memory or current awareness. A second reason why researchers focused on external distractions is simply because they were easier to measure than were their self-generated equivalents. As a result of this combination of factors, the theoretical mechanisms by which internal distractions disrupt concentration are still rather mysterious. Nevertheless, a promising approach to this problem may be found in Wegner's (1994) "ironic processes" model. This model is interesting because it addresses the question of why people often lose their concentration at the most inopportune moment. Briefly, Wegner's (1994) theory proposed that the mind wanders because we try to control it. Put simply, when we are anxious or tired, the decision not to think about something may paradoxically increase the prominence of that phenomenon in our consciousness. In such circumstances, the attempt to block out a certain thought from one's mind may lead to a "rebound" experience whereby the suppressed thought becomes even more prominent in consciousness. In other words, when we are anxious or tired, trying not to think about something may paradoxically increase its prominence in our consciousness. For example, if you try to focus on falling asleep, you will probably achieve only a prolonged state of wakefulness! Similarly, if you attempt to block a certain thought from entering your mind, you may end up becoming more preoccupied with it. This tendency for a suppressed thought to come to mind more readily than a thought that is the focus of intentional concentration is called "hyperaccessibility" and is especially likely to occur under conditions of mental load. Clearly, there are many situations in sport in which such ironic self-regulation failures occur. For example, issuing a negative command to your doubles partner in tennis (such as "whatever you do, don't double-fault") may produce counter-intentional results. What theoretical mechanisms could account for this phenomenon? Briefly, Wegner's (1994) theory proposed that the mind wanders because we try to control it; when people try to suppress a thought, they engage in a controlled (conscious) search for thoughts that are different from the unwanted thought. At the same time, however, our minds conduct an automatic (unconscious) search for any signs of the unwanted thought. In other words, the intention to suppress a thought activates an automatic search for that very thought in an effort to monitor whether or not the act of suppression has been successful. Normally, the conscious intentional system dominates the unconscious monitoring system. But under certain circumstances (e.g. when our working memories are overloaded or when our attentional resources are depleted by fatigue or stress), the ironic system prevails and an ironic intrusion of the unwanted thought occurs. Wegner (1994) attributes this rebound effect to cognitive load. But although this load is believed to disrupt the conscious mechanism of thought control, it does not interfere with the automatic (and ironic) monitoring system. Wegner (1994) proposed that the intention to concentrate creates conditions under which mental load can enhance the monitoring of irrelevant information. To summarize, Wegner's (1994) research helps us to understand why athletes may find it difficult to suppress unwanted or irrelevant thoughts when they are tired or anxious.

Perhaps not surprisingly, Wegner (2002) has investigated ironies of action as well as those of thought. For example, consider what happens when people who are asked not to overshoot the hole in a golf putt are given tasks which impose a heavy mental load on them. In such situations, the unwanted action (overshooting the hole) is exactly what occurs.

Since the 1990s, the applicability of the **ironic theory of mental control** to sport settings has been recognized – originally by Moran (1996, pp. 106ff) but subsequently by scholars such as Janelle (1999) and Binsch et al. (2009). Interestingly, Binsch et al. (2010), found that experienced footballers showed lapses in mental control (i.e. ironic performance) during a penalty kick task when instructed to shoot as accurately as possible whilst remaining careful not to shoot within reach of the goalkeeper. Ironic effects were accompanied by shorter final fixations on the target area (i.e. the open goal space). Research has shown that a longer fixation on the target prior to and during aiming is a characteristic of high levels of skill and accuracy (see Vine et al., 2014, for a review). Binsch et al. proposed two explanations as to why these ironic effects may have occurred. First, for some participants, their initial fixation on the goalkeeper may have lasted too long for them to dedicate a sufficiently lengthy fixation on the open goal space. Second, the remaining participants may have dedicated an insufficiently long final fixation on the open goal space as they subsequently returned their gaze to the keeper. With the former group, the negative instruction not to aim within reach of the keeper may have caused the word "keeper" to remain within conscious awareness meaning that it was difficult for the performers to disengage their visual fixation from this stimuli. In the latter group the word also lingered in their cognitive system and left insufficient time for a proper final fixation on the target. Clearly, this finding raises doubts about the validity of asking anxious athletes not to worry about an important forthcoming athletic event or outcome. Woodman et al. (2015) also showed that ironic processes impair athletic performance. Specifically, they discovered that when instructed not to miss a penalty in a specific direction, anxious hockey players did so a significantly greater number of times when compared to a non-anxiety control condition. Interviews with athletes have also revealed that ironic errors are common in elite sport. To illustrate, in a study by Bertollo et al. (2009) on the mental preparation strategies used by Italy's 2004 Olympic pentathlon squad, one of the athletes explained: "In some circumstances my intention is not to do the best but to avoid making a bad shot. That is when I make a bad shot. *When I think about avoiding the error, I make the error*" (Bertollo et al., 2009, p. 252; italics ours). Interestingly, however, a number of studies (see de la Peña et al., 2008; Toner et al., 2013) have found that avoidant instructions may, on occasion, produce the opposite effect to that proposed by the ironic processes theory. The **"implicit overcompensation hypothesis"** proposes that instructions to avoid a certain action (e.g. leaving a golf putt short of the hole) will trigger an implicit message that it is better to putt the ball firmly (e.g. thereby overshooting the hole) than to leave it short. Toner et al. (2013) found some support for this hypothesis in an experiment where skilled golfers were instructed not to miss a putt to the left or right of the hole. In this study, golfers demonstrated over-compensatory behaviour by missing more putts in the opposite direction to instructions (e.g. missing putts to the left of the hole when instructed not to miss to the right). Further research is required to establish the prevalence of ironic and over-compensatory effects amongst skilled performers.

At this stage, it might be helpful to do some research on distractions. So, if you are interested in exploring the factors that cause athletes to lose their focus, try the exercise in Box 5.6.

Box 5.6 In the spotlight Exploring distractions in sport

The purpose of this exercise is twofold. First, you will find out what the term "concentration" means to athletes. Second, you will try to classify the distractions which they perceive to have affected their performance.

To begin with, find three athletes who compete regularly in different sports (e.g. golf, soccer, swimming). Request their permission to record your interview with them on an electronic voice-recorder. Then, ask them the following questions:

1. What does the term "concentration" mean to you?

2. On a scale of 0 (meaning "not at all important") to 5 (meaning "extremely important"), how important do you think that the skill of concentration is for successful performance in your sport?

3. What sort of distractions tend to upset your concentration before a game/match? Describe the situation and the distraction which results from it.

4. What distractions bother you during the event itself? Describe the situation and the distraction which results from it.

5. Please give me a specific example of how a distraction changed your focus and/or affected your performance. Tell me what the distraction was, how it occurred and how you reacted to it.

6. What techniques do you use, if any, to cope with distractions?

Analysis

Compare and contrast the athletes' answers to your questions. The word "focus" will probably feature in responses to Q 1. Try to establish exactly what athletes mean by this word. You should also find that athletes regard concentration as being very important for successful performance in their sport (Q 2). After you have compiled a list of distractions (Qs 3 and 4), you will probably find that they fall into two main categories: external and internal. Is there any connection between the type of sport which the athletes perform and the distractions that they reported?

Concentration training exercises and techniques

Having explored what concentration is, how to measure it and why we often lose it, we shall now examine the various strategies recommended by sport psychologists for improving focusing skills. Applied sport psychology is replete with strategies which claim to improve concentration skills in athletes (Greenlees and Moran, 2003). Typically, the purpose of these strategies is to help athletes to achieve a focused state of mind in which there is no difference between what they are thinking about and what they are doing. If this happens, the athlete's mind is "cleared of irrelevant thoughts, the body is cleared of irrelevant tensions, and the focus is centred only on what is important at that moment for executing the skill to perfection" (Orlick, 1990, p. 18). But what concentration strategies do sport psychologists recommend to athletes and what do we know about their efficacy?

In general, two types of psychological activities have been alleged to enhance focusing skills in sport performers: concentration training exercises and concentration techniques (Moran, 1996, 2003b). The difference between these activities is that whereas the former ones are intended for use mainly in athletes' training sessions, the latter are designed primarily for competitive situations. Among the plethora of concentration exercises recommended by sport psychologists are such activities as the "concentration grid" (a **visual search task** endorsed by Schmid and Peper (1998), in which the participant is required to scan as many digits as possible within a given time limit), watching the oscillation of a pendulum (which is alleged to show how "mental concentration influences your muscle reactions": Weinberg, 1988, p. 87) and looking at a clock "and saying 'Now' to yourself every alternate 5 and 10 seconds" (L. Hardy and Fazey, 1990, p. 9). Unfortunately, few of these activities are supported by either a coherent theoretical rationale or adequate evidence of empirical validity. For example, take the case of the ubiquitous concentration grid. Surprisingly, no references were cited by Weinberg and Gould (2007) to support their claim that it was used "extensively in Eastern Europe as a pre-competition screening device" or that "this exercise will help you learn to focus your attention and scan the environment for relevant cues" (Weinberg and Gould, 2007, pp. 391 and 392). Despite the absence of such evidence, the grid is recommended unreservedly by Schmid and Peper (1998, p. 324) as a "training exercise for practising focusing ability" and also by Weinberg and Gould (2007) and J. Williams et al. (2010). These endorsements are contradicted by empirical evidence, however. Greenlees et al. (2006) examined the validity of the grid as a concentration exercise over a nine week period with a sample of collegiate soccer players. Results showed no significant effects of the grid on the athletes' concentration skills relative to a control group. Therefore, these authors concluded that the grid "lacks the efficacy that has been ascribed to it in previous literature and anecdotal accounts" (Greenlees et al., 2006, p. 36). Surprisingly, the tool continues to be used by a number of sport psychology researchers (e.g. Laborde et al., 2014).

In summary, there appears to be little empirical justification for the use of generic visual search and/or vigilance tasks in an effort to improve athletes' concentration skills. Indeed, research suggests that general visual skills training programmes are not effective in enhancing athletes' performance in sports such as soccer (Starkes et al., 2001) – a finding which challenges the validity of using visual search tasks like the concentration grid as a training tool. However, a growing body of evidence shows how sports visual training (see box below) may confer certain performance advantages when compared to control and placebo interventions (Smeeton et al., 2013). However, a true test of the efficacy of these training interventions is whether they facilitate the transfer of performance to competition – a finding which has yet to be demonstrated in the research literature.

In contrast to the previous concentration exercises, simulation training (Moran 2003a; Orlick, 1990) appears to have a satisfactory theoretical rationale (for a discussion of the use of simulation training to counteract anxiety, see Chapter 3). This exercise, which is also known as dress rehearsal (Schmid and Peper, 1998), simulated practice (Hodge and McKenzie, 1999) and distraction training (Maynard, 1998), proposes that athletes can learn to concentrate more effectively in real-life pressure situations by simulating them in practice conditions. A number of anecdotal testimonials to the value of this practice have emerged since 2000. Earl Woods, the father and initial coach of Tiger Woods, used such methods on him when he was a boy. Woods Senior claimed:

> all the strategies and tactics of distraction I'd learned I threw at that kid and he would just grit his teeth and play ... and if anyone tries pulling a trick on him these days he just smiles and says "my dad used to do that years ago".
>
> (cited in *Evening Herald*, 2001

Javier Aguirre, the coach of the Mexican national soccer team, instructed his players to practise penalty-taking after every friendly match in the year leading up to the 2002 World Cup in an effort to prepare for the possibility of penalty shootouts in that competition. As he explained: "there will always be noise and that is the best way to practise" (cited in M. Smith, 2002). However, the issue of whether or not it is ever possible to truly simulate a penalty shootout in practice has been debated frequently among football coaches and players. For example, Brian Laudrup (the former Danish international player) claimed that

> it's something you can't really train for because you can be the best in training and then when you have to do it in a final, the goal is getting so small and the goalkeeper so big. I tried it myself so I know how it is.
>
> (cited in Taylor, 2013, p. 6)

Another example of simulation training comes from rugby football. Here, in preparation for an away match against Stade Français where a capacity crowd (80,000 people) were expected to attend, the Harlequins team trained at home under a giant screen playing loud music and YouTube clips. Harlequins won the match (Casey, 2011). As we discovered in Chapter 3, Bob Bowman helped the swimmer Michael Phelps (multiple Olympic champion) to prepare for possible adverse conditions (e.g. having to swim without goggles) in competition by deliberately breaking Phelps' goggles in training races.

Unfortunately, despite its intuitive appeal, simulation training has received little or no empirical scrutiny as a concentration strategy (although see Chapter 3 for a discussion on the "specificity of practice" hypothesis). Nevertheless, some support for its theoretical rationale may be found in cognitive psychology. Research on the "encoding specificity" principle of learning shows that people's recall of information is facilitated by conditions which resemble those in which the original encoding occurred (Matlin, 2009). Based on this principle, the simulation of competitive situations in practice should lead to positive transfer effects to the competition itself. In addition, adversity training may counteract the tendency for novel or unexpected stimuli to distract athletes in competition. The simulation of these factors in training should reduce their attention-capturing qualities subsequently. To summarize, there is some theoretical justification for the belief that simulation training could enhance athletes' concentration skills, but this conclusion is tentative for one important reason. Specifically, even the most ingenious simulations cannot replicate completely the actual arousal experienced by athletes in competitive situations. For example, Ronan O'Gara, the Ireland and Lions' rugby out-half, admitted that although he can practise taking penalty kicks in training, "it's completely different in a match where my heartbeat is probably 115 beats a minute whereas in training it's about 90–100" (cited in Fanning, 2002). Clearly, it is difficult to simulate accurately the emotional aspects of competitive action.

Having reviewed some popular concentration exercises, we should now turn to the second type of attentional skills intervention used in sport psychology – namely, the concentration techniques listed in Figure 5.5.

Specifying performance goals

In Chapter 2, we explained the theory and practice of goal-setting. As you may recall, a "goal" is a future valued outcome (Locke and Latham, 2006). Sport psychologists (e.g. L. Hardy and Jones, 1994) commonly distinguish between result goals (e.g. the outcome of a sporting contest), performance goals (or specific end-products of performance that lie within the athlete's control, e.g. attempting to achieve 90 per cent accuracy in one's serve in tennis) and process goals (or specific behavioural actions that need to be undertaken to achieve a goal – such as tossing the ball up high for greater service accuracy). Using this distinction, some researchers (e.g. G. Winter and Martin, 1991) have proposed that specifying performance goals can improve athletes' concentration skills. According to this theory, athletes such as tennis players could improve their concentration on court by focusing solely on such performance goals as seeking 100 per cent accuracy on their first serves. This suggestion seems plausible theoretically because performance goals encourage athletes to focus on task-relevant information and on controllable actions. Additional support for this idea springs from studies on the correlates of people's best and worst athletic performances. S. Jackson and Roberts (1992) found that collegiate athletes performed worst when they were preoccupied by result goals. Conversely, their best displays coincided with an explicit focus on performance goals. Similarly, Kingston and Hardy (1997)

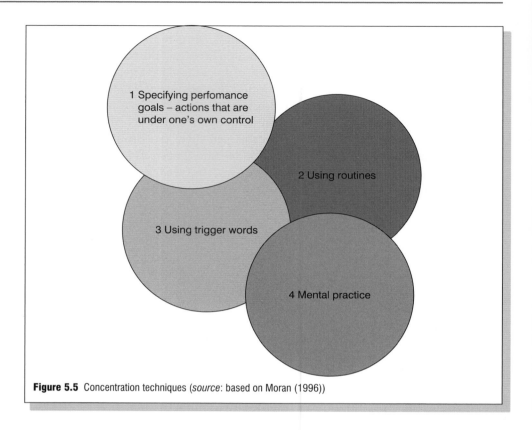

Figure 5.5 Concentration techniques (*source*: based on Moran (1996))

discovered that golfers who focused on specific action goals improved both their performance and their concentration. To summarize, there seems to be some empirical support for the idea that performance goals can facilitate concentration skills in athletes. In this regard, the goal of focusing on the target has led to a fascinating discovery – the "quiet eye" phenomenon (see Box 5.7 below).

Using pre-performance routines

Sport is a highly ritualized activity. Thus, most top-class athletes display characteristic, self-consistent sequences of preparatory actions before they perform key skills. For example, tennis players tend to bounce the ball a preferred number of times before serving and golfers like to go through a systematic series of steps before striking the ball (see Figure 5.6).

These preferred action sequences and/or repetitive behaviours are called "pre-performance routines" (PPRs; for a comprehensive review of research on this topic, see Cotterill, 2010) and are typically conducted prior to the execution of self-paced skills (i.e. actions that are carried out largely at one's own speed and without interference from other people). According to Harle and Vickers (2001), such routines are often used in an effort to improve concentration and performance.

Box 5.7 In the spotlight Exploring the "quiet eye" phenomenon

Since the 1990s, eye-trackers (see Chapter 7) have been used to explore expert–novice differences in attentional processes in sport. Within this field, Vickers (2007) developed an empirical approach called the "vision-in-action" paradigm. This paradigm combines mobile eye-trackers with video-based motion capture systems to investigate athletes' gaze behaviour in situ. Using this method, Vickers (1992, 1996, 2007) discovered a distinctive pattern of gaze behaviour among expert performers prior to skill execution in aiming (target-based) sports such as basketball and golf. Specifically, Vickers reported that prior to free-throw shooting, expert basketball players displayed significantly longer durations of final fixation on targets than did "near-expert" counterparts. This pattern of visual behaviour was named the "quiet eye" period (commonly abbreviated to "quiet eye"; QE; see Panchuk and Vickers, 2013) and is held to designate the time that elapses between the performer's last fixation on a specific target and his/her subsequent initiation of a relevant motor response. More precisely, Vickers (2007) defined QE as "a final fixation or tracking gaze that is located on a specific location or object in the visuomotor workspace within 3° of visual angle (or less) for a minimum of 100 ms" (p. 11) prior to the onset of a critical movement

A wide range of studies have adopted the QE as an objective measure of visuomotor control underpinning the learning, retention and performance of skills under demanding and anxiety-provoking circumstances. It is important to note that the eye is rarely "quiet", however, as small eye movements take place during visual fixation. These movements include what are known as low velocity drifts and high velocity micro saccades. Nevertheless, a number of studies have focused on measuring the QE in a variety of tasks that involve targeting skills (e.g. shooting, golf putting). Generally, these studies have found that skilled performance is characterized by longer QE durations (QEDs; although longer QEDs have not always been found to correlate with better performance; see Horn et al., 2012). For example, Vine and Wilson (2011) found that a 1 hour QE training intervention for low handicap golfers (mean = 2.4) resulted in increases in QE and putting performance in a laboratory putting task compared to a control group. QE trained golfers also revealed an improvement in their putting performance on the course taking 1.92 fewer putts per round while the control group revealed no significant differences in competitive putting performance. Vine et al. (2014) claim that QE is an important mediator of expertise and that it can be trained to improve performance of target skills – even those that are already well practiced (see Chapter 3 for a discussion of the training protocol). For example, researchers can use video modelling and verbal feedback to help participants develop the same QE focus and visual control as expert performers. Interestingly, a number of studies have found that QE durations are shortened under conditions of elevated anxiety (Causer et al., 2011). In one study, biathletes who increased their QE duration were found to be less susceptible to the adverse effects of performance anxiety (Vickers and Williams, 2007).

What cognitive mechanisms might be responsible for the QE effect? Long quiet eye durations are proposed to increase the motor preparation period that involves the fine-tuning of movement parameters responsible for motor programming. Klosterman et al. (2014) suggested that a longer QED may allow performers to inhibit alternative

continued ...

> **Box 5.7 continued**
>
> movement variables and allow for the effective parameterization of a single movement. Other researchers (e.g. Moore et al., 2012) have argued that QE may promote an external focus of attention which is believed to promote automatic behaviour in skilled performers. Although the preceding results point to the promise of the quiet eye as a means of improving an athlete's concentration, a number of methodological issues must be considered when evaluating this body of research. For example, the different sensitivity of the measurements used across studies means that arbitrary definitions of the threshold for determining the QE period have been provided. Additionally there are certain physical characteristics (e.g. position of the eye within the face) of an individual's eye that can make effective calibration of eye tracking systems quite difficult. It is also important to recognize that eye tracking data will not necessarily tell us what an athlete happens to be attending to, or consciously thinking about, during online skill execution (e.g. if the athlete is focused on controlling movement). Using verbal **protocol analysis** whilst capturing visual control may provide a means of addressing this latter problem. Further research is required to determine whether performance and skill differences still hold at varying thresholds (e.g. 1 versus 2 or 2 versus 3 degrees of visual angle), thus examining the importance of the amplitude of eye movement during the QE (Gonzalez et al., 2015). Furthermore, research is necessary to determine whether eye movement differences are mediated by the type of task or level of skill.

At least three types of routines are common in sport. First, pre-event routines are preferred sequences of actions in the run-up to competitive events. Included here are stable preferences for what to do on the night before, and on the morning of, the competition itself. Second, pre-performance routines are characteristic sequences of thoughts and actions which athletes adhere to prior to skill execution – as in the case of tennis players bouncing the ball before serving. Third, post-mistake routines are action sequences which may help performers to leave their errors in the past so that they can refocus on the task at hand. For example, a golfer may "shadow" the correct swing of a shot that had led to an error. A novel study on the efficacy of post-performance routines was conducted recently by Mesagno et al. (2015). Briefly, these researchers found that both pre-performance routines and post-performance routines enhanced the performance of ten-pin bowlers – through improvements in concentration, emotional control, self-confidence, motivation and self-awareness.

Support for the value of PPRs as concentration techniques comes from both theoretical and empirical sources. Theoretically, pre-performance routines may improve concentration for at least three reasons. First, they are intended to encourage athletes to develop an appropriate mental set for skill execution by helping them to focus on task-relevant information. For example, many soccer goalkeepers follow pre-kick routines in an effort to block out any jeering that is directed at them by supporters of opposing teams. Second, such routines may enable athletes to concentrate on the present moment rather than on past events or on possible future outcomes. Third, PPRs may prevent athletes from devoting too much attention to the mechanics of their well-learned skills – a habit which

Figure 5.6 Pre-performance routines help players to concentrate (*source*: courtesy of University College Dublin, Sport)

can unravel automaticity (see Beilock and Carr, 2001; see also Chapter 3). Thus routines may help to suppress the type of inappropriate conscious control that often occurs in pressure situations. A useful five-step pre-performance routine for self-paced skills is described by Singer (2002) and Lidor and Singer (2003).

Augmenting the preceding arguments is empirical evidence derived from case studies which show that routines can improve athletes' concentration skills and performance. For example, Crews and Boutcher (1986) compared the performances of two groups of golfers – those who had been given an eight week training programme of only swing practice and those who had participated in a "practice-plus-routine" programme for the same duration. Results revealed that the more proficient golfers benefited more from using routines than did the less skilled players. An important issue in research on the efficacy of pre-performance routines concerns the degree to which they are actually consistent in competitive situations. Some studies have raised doubts about such consistency. For example, R. Jackson and Baker (2001) analysed the pre-strike routine of the prolific former Welsh international and Lions rugby kicker, Neil Jenkins, who scored 1,049 points in eighty-seven games for his country. As expected, Jenkins reported using a variety of concentration techniques (such as thought-stopping and mental imagery) as part of his pre-kick routine. However, what surprised Jackson and Baker (2001) was that Jenkins varied the timing of his pre-kick behaviour as a function of the difficulty of the kick he faced. This finding shows that routines are not as rigid or stereotyped as was originally believed. Subsequently, R. Jackson (2003) reported that goal-kickers at the 1999 Rugby World Cup varied the duration of their pre-kick routine in accordance with the perceived difficulty of the task. Carson et al. (2014) found that there was little similarity between skilled golfers' practice swings – an important part of a golfer's pre-shot routine – and the "real" swing that they used to execute a shot. Lonsdale and Tam (2008) examined the consistency of the pre-performance routines of a sample of elite National Basketball Association (NBA) players whose "free-throw" behaviour was analysed from television footage. Results showed that, contrary to expectations, the temporal consistency of the basketball players' pre-performance routines was not associated with accurate skill execution. However, there was evidence that behavioural consistency was related to accurate performance. Specifically, Lonsdale and Tam (2008) found that the basketball players were more successful when they adhered to their dominant behavioural sequence prior to their free throws. Having considered research on the relationship between pre-performance behaviour and skilled performance, is there any empirical evidence on the attentional importance of pre-shot routines? Unfortunately, there is a dearth of studies on this issue. However, a case study by D. Shaw (2002) reported that a professional golfer experienced some attentional benefits arising from the use of a pre-shot routine. Although this evidence is anecdotal, the golfer reported that "the new routine had made him more focused for each shot and therefore less distracted by irrelevancies" (D. Shaw, 2002, p. 117). Cotterill et al. (2010) conducted in-depth interviews with a sample of amateur international golfers in an effort to understand the nature and perceived benefits of their PPRs. Results showed that these golfers used routines for attentional purposes such as attempting to "switch on and off" and "staying in the present and not dwelling on the past or engaging in fortune telling" (Cotterill et al., 2010, p. 55).

What theoretical mechanisms could explain the popularity of ritualized behaviour (such as pre-performance routines) in sport? According to R. Jackson and Masters (2006), such behaviour probably serves two purposes simultaneously. First, it consumes working memory resources and hence prevents the performer from "reinvesting" conscious control over skills that are more effectively executed automatically. Second, pre-competitive rituals may provide some temporary relief from excessive anxiety on the part of the performer.

Apart from their apparent variability in different situations, pre-performance routines give rise to other practical issues that need to be addressed here. They may lead to superstitious rituals on the part of the performer. For example, consider the mixture of routines and rituals used by the Australian tennis player Jelena Dokic.

Apparently, she never steps on white lines, she always blows on her right hand while waiting for her opponent to serve and she bounces the ball five times before her own first serve and twice before her second serve (Edworthy, 2002). Furthermore, she insists that "the ball boys and girls always have to pass me the ball with an underarm throw, which is luckier than an overarm throw" (cited in Edworthy, 2002). Clearly, this example highlights the rather fuzzy boundaries between pre-performance routines and superstitious rituals in the minds of some athletes. A study by D. Foster et al. (2006) highlighted the overlap between these two types of ritualized behaviour. Briefly, these authors evaluated the effect of removing superstitious behaviour (e.g. kissing the tape covering a wedding ring on the shooter's hand) and introducing a pre-performance routine (of bouncing the ball, taking a deep breath, visualizing the perfect shot and then using a cue word before executing the skill) for a group of basketballers engaged in free-throw skill execution. Contrary to what was predicted, there was very little difference between performances following either superstitious behaviour or a pre-performance routine perhaps because many of the basketballers had been using superstitious behaviour for years prior to the study whereas the routine was only a recent addition to their mental preparation for skill execution.

At this stage, it may occur to you that routines are merely superstitions in disguise. To explore this issue further, read Box 5.8.

Box 5.8 Thinking critically about ... routines and superstitions in sport: helpful or harmful?

Pre-performance routines (PPRs; Cotterill, 2010) are consistent sequences of thoughts and behaviour displayed by athletes as they prepare to execute key skills. Given some apparently compulsive features of this behaviour, however, it may be argued that routines are not really concentration techniques but merely superstitions. Is this allegation valid?

Superstition may be defined as the belief that, despite scientific evidence to the contrary, certain actions are causally related to certain outcomes. Furthermore, we know that athletes are notoriously superstitious – largely because of the capricious nature of sport (Vyse, 1997). Rafael Nadal must have two water bottles beside the court, perfectly aligned and with the labels facing the baseline. Interestingly, Nadal argued that this wasn't a form of superstitious behaviour as if it was superstition then "why would I keep doing the same thing over and over whether I win or lose? It's a way of placing myself in a match, ordering my surroundings to match the order I seek in my head" (Nadal, 2011). Real Madrid's Cristiano Ronaldo exhibits similarly superstitious behaviours by ensuring that he steps onto the pitch with his right foot first. Dara Howell, the 2014 Olympic champion in slopestyle skiing, used superstitious routines to stay calm during her Olympic-winning performance by always putting on the right ski before the left, grabbing the right pole before the left and doing a fist pound with her coach. The former tennis player Martina Hingis refused to step on the lines on the tennis court for fear of misfortune (Laurence, 1998). In general, sport psychologists distinguish between routines and superstitious behaviour on two criteria: control and purpose. First, consider the issue of control. The essence of superstitious behaviour is the belief that one's fate is governed by factors that lie outside

continued ...

Box 5.8 continued

one's control. But the virtue of a routine is that it allows the player to exert complete control over his or her preparation. Indeed, players often shorten their pre-performance routines in adverse circumstances (e.g. under unfavourable weather conditions). Unfortunately, the converse is true for superstitions. Thus they tend to grow longer over time as performers "chain together" more and more illogical links between behaviour and outcome. A second criterion which may be used to distinguish between routines and rituals concerns the technical role of each behavioural step followed. To explain, whereas each part of a routine should have a rational basis, the components of a superstitious ritual may not be justifiable objectively. Many elements of pre-shot routines in sport are designed to ensure that technique or form is effective and imagery is often used to pre-programme the desired movement pattern. These behaviours appear to be absent from superstitious rituals. Despite these neat conceptual distinctions, the pre-shot routines of many athletes are often invested with magical thinking and superstitious qualities. Schippers and Van Lange (2006) analysed the psychological benefits of superstitious rituals among elite athletes. Based on an examination of the circumstances in which such rituals are displayed before games, these investigators concluded that superstitious behaviour was most likely to occur when games were perceived as especially important. In addition, these researchers reported that players with an external locus of control (i.e. athlete attributes performance outcomes to factors such as luck) tended to display more superstitious rituals than those with an internal locus of control (i.e. attribute outcome to their own behaviour).

As a final point, evidence has emerged to suggest that despite their irrational origins, superstitions may be helpful sometimes to performers. Damisch et al. (2010) conducted a series of intriguing experiments which appear to highlight some benefits of superstitions to motor and cognitive task performance. Specifically, they showed that playing with a ball described as "lucky" seems to improve participants' golf putting accuracy and that the presence of a personal charm enhances participants' performance on memory and anagram tests. Volunteers who kept their fingers crossed finished a dexterity task faster than did participants in a control condition. In an effort to explain these results, Damisch et al. (2010) postulated that "good-luck" superstitions may have increased participants' self-efficacy (or belief in their own ability to succeed on the tasks in question) which, in turn, may have improved their performance. Moreover, superstitions may allow athletes to exert some control over what they feel is a highly uncontrollable situation. In short, although carrying a lucky charm is irrational, it may boost one's confidence and reduce anxiety during high-pressure situations.

Critical thinking questions

Do you think that athletes really understand the difference between routines and rituals? What do you think of the idea that it does not really matter that athletes are superstitious – as long as it makes them feel mentally prepared for competition? What do you think would prove more detrimental to performance – the manipulation of an athlete's pre-performance routine or preventing them from carrying out ritualized behaviours? Can you think of any other explanation – besides one involving a possible boost in self-efficacy or perceived control – for the results reported by Damisch et al. (2010)?

Another problem with routines is that they need to be reviewed and revised regularly in order to avoid the danger of automation. In fact, Lautenbach et al. (2015a) found that tennis players who used a longer pre-performance routine merely maintained performance proficiency under pressure whereas those who had learnt the routine shortly before a high-performance situation actually improved performance. One might argue that if athletes maintain the same pre-performance routines indefinitely, their minds may begin to wander as a consequence of growing accustomed to them or tuning out. Clearly, an important challenge for applied sport psychologists is to help athletes to attain an appropriate level of conscious control over their actions before skill execution. Too much control, however, can cause "reinvestment" – a problem which occurs when relatively automated motor processes are disrupted if they are run using consciously accessed knowledge to control the mechanics of the movements (R. Masters and Maxwell, 2008).

Trigger words as cues to concentrate

Although recent years have witnessed a proliferation of research interest in cognitive sport psychology (see Moran, 2009, 2014), there are many gaps in our understanding of the efficacy of specific cognitive strategies used by athletes in an effort to improve their performance. One of the most popular of these cognitive strategies involves the use of "**trigger words**" or short, vivid and positively phrased verbal reminders designed to help performers to focus on a specific target or to execute a given action. Such verbal prompts are usually regarded as being part of athletes' self-talk – or verbalizations (either covert or overt) addressed to the self that serve both instructional and motivational functions (see reviews by Theodorakis et al., 2012; Van Raalte et al., 2016). For example, the British Olympic athlete Paula Radcliffe, who won the 2007 New York City Marathon, reported using trigger numbers by counting her steps silently to herself in an effort to maintain her concentration in a race. As she explained,

> When I count to 100 three times, it's a mile. It helps me to focus on the moment and not to think about how many miles I have to go. I concentrate on breathing and striding, and I go within myself.
>
> (cited in Kolata, 2007)

More recently, the multiple major golf championship winner Rory McIlroy spoke about the important role that trigger words played in helping him to enter the "zone" during his 2014 Open Championship winning performance at Royal Hoylake. He revealed that "I've got a couple of little trigger words that I'm using this week that I keep telling myself in my head when I'm just about to hit it" (cited in Corrigan, 2014). In a similar vein, consider an incident that occurred during the 2002 Wimbledon Ladies' Singles tennis final between the Williams sisters, Serena and Venus. Briefly, Serena (who defeated Venus 7–6, 6–3) was observed by millions of viewers to be reading something as she sat down during

Figure 5.7 Serena Williams uses trigger words as cues to concentrate (*source*: courtesy of Inpho photography)

the changeovers between games (see Figure 5.7). Afterwards, she explained that she had been reading notes that she had written to herself as trigger words or instructional cues to remind her to "hit in front" or "stay low" (R. Williams, 2002b). She used a similar strategy in 2007 in Wimbledon when she defeated Daniela Hantuchova in the fourth round of the tournament. On this occasion, she used phrases like "get low", "add spin" and "move up" (A. Martin, 2007). A self-report scale designed to measure athletes' use of such self-talk was developed by Zervas et al. (2007).

Many sport performers talk to themselves either silently or out loud when they compete – usually in an effort to motivate themselves. This covert self-talk may involve praise (e.g. "Well done! That's good"), criticism ("You idiot – that's a stupid mistake") and/or instruction ("Swing slowly"). Accordingly, self-talk may be positive, negative or neutral. As a cognitive self-regulatory strategy, self-talk may enhance concentration skills (J. Williams and Leffingwell, 2002). In particular, Landin and Herbert (1999) discovered that tennis players who had been trained to use instructional cues or trigger words (such as "split, turn") attributed their improved performance to enhanced concentration on court. In a meta-analytic review of the effectiveness of self-talk interventions, Hatzigeorgiadis et al. (2011) found that instructional self-talk was more effective for the performance of fine motor tasks than was motivational self-talk. For example, technically demanding tasks which require the precise execution of specific movement patterns (such as a downhill left-to-right putt in golf) may benefit more from instructional self-talk (e.g. make a smooth stroke) than "motivational self-talk" (e.g. "give everything") which seems to be more effective in tasks requiring strength or endurance or when one wants to "psych-up" for competition.

While trigger words may serve an important function as a motivational tool they may also (as evidenced in Rory McIlroy's comments above) help with memory retrieval by activating specific neural networks involved in movement execution. This possibility stems from research by MacPherson et al. (2008) who suggested that performers may adopt what they refer to as "mood words" (which serve a similar function to trigger words). Mood words may reflect various movement capacities and may be drawn from "a list of monosyllabic synonyms for strength, power (force), speed, agility, balance, and endurance" which are generated by the athlete to best fit the movement being carried out (MacPherson et al., 2008, p. 289). Rather than focusing on a specific component of the movement (e.g. part process goal/part swing thought in golf), mood words represent rhythmical properties of the movement and "do not divide the movement into orthogonal units" (MacPherson et al., 2008, p. 289). MacPherson et al. (2008) found that the adoption of a mood word (rhythm) improved the performance and consistency (as measured statistically) of an elite javelin throwers action. By contrast, sub-elite javelin throwers tended to focus on part of the whole throw which may have disrupted the consistency of the whole movement. MacPherson et al. (2008) argue that if carefully selected, mood words may provide a holistic "source of information" (SOI). The use of holistic SOIs may offer the athlete a more comprehensive aide memoire for the skill, rather than a focus on the component parts. MacPherson et al., (2009) further suggested that the employment of holistic SOIs may offer smoother performance than the more limiting use of part-skill cues, which may potentially disjoint subsequent task execution.

Can self-talk improve athletes' concentration? Unfortunately, no published research on this question could be located. However, it is possible that positive and/or instructional self-statements could enhance attentional skills by reminding athletes about what to focus on in a given situation. For example, novice golfers may miss the ball completely on the fairway in the early stages of learning to swing the club properly. In an effort to overcome this problem, golf instructors may advise learners to concentrate on sweeping the grass rather than hitting the ball. This trigger phrase ensures that learners stay "down" on the ball instead of looking up to see where it went. In general, trigger words must be short, vivid and positively phrased to yield maximum benefits. They should also emphasize positive targets (what to aim for) rather than negative ones (what to avoid).

Mental practice

The term mental practice (MP; also known as motor imagery; see detailed discussion in Chapter 6) refers to imaging actions without engaging in the actual physical movements involved. Put simply, it involves "seeing" and "feeling" a skill in one's imagination before physically executing it (Driskell et al., 1994). Although there is considerable empirical evidence that MP facilitates skill-learning and performance (see Chapter 6), its status as a concentration technique remains uncertain. However, from anecdotal evidence, it is clear that mental imagery is used widely by athletes for the purpose of focusing. For example, combining visual and **kinaesthetic imagery** (see Chapter 6) can help to block out distracting thoughts, as Jonny Wilkinson, a Rugby World Cup winner with England, revealed: "I visualise the ball travelling along that path and imagine the sensation of how the ball is going to feel when it hits my foot for the perfect strike" (cited in Bailey, 2014).

In a similar vein, British athlete Jessica Ennis-Hill used imagery to concentrate on her technique during her gold-winning performance in the heptathlon at the 2012 Olympic games: "I use visualisation to think about the perfect technique. If I can get that perfect image in my head, then hopefully it'll affect my physical performance" (cited in Bailey, 2014). Also, Australian golfer Jason Day revealed that he used imagery during the final round of his 2015 USPGA championship to eliminate certain task-irrelevant thoughts and to refocus his concentration: "At one point on Sunday at the PGA, I was thinking about what I'd say at the trophy presentation. And on 18, I'm thinking, 'Don't hook it left.' You just have to stamp those thoughts out and visualize the shot" (cited in Day, 2015). Despite such anecdotal insights, there have been few studies designed to evaluate mental imagery as a concentration technique. Clearly, this topic is ripe for future investigation.

In summary, we have reviewed four psychological techniques that are used regularly in an effort to improve athletes' concentration skills. Unfortunately, there is a dearth of studies that have evaluated the efficacy of these techniques in enhancing concentration skills. Despite the absence of such evidence, these four concentration techniques appear to be both plausible and useful in sport settings. Before we finish the chapter, here are some insights on attentional training from Michael Posner – who has achieved great eminence for his research on the cognitive neuroscience of attention (see Box 5.9).

Box 5.9 In the spotlight A neuroscientist on attentional training

The psychologist Michael Posner has recently argued that people are capable of learning to control their attentional processes through practice. There appears to be two approaches that might help people achieve this latter aim: attention training and attention state training. In a study testing the efficacy of the former type of training, Rosario Rueda et al. (2012) examined how exposure to ten sessions of computerized attentional training would influence childrens' learning and performance of a variety of tasks (including their ability to target their attention). Results indicated that trained children could activate their executive attentional network (which is believed to be involved in the regulation of thoughts and responses) more quickly than untrained children and that this effect was observed two months later without additional training. A second proposed approach involves the use of attention state training and the use of mindfulness meditation in particular. Tang et al. (2007) found that participants exposed to a mere 5 days of a form of mindfulness called integrative body-mind training (IBMT) showed higher executive attention than a control group who were required to perform basic relaxation tasks. In additional studies IBMT produced increases in fractional anisotropy, an index of white matter efficiency (Tang et al., 2012). This result suggests that attentional training can alter the brain networks which play a crucial role in guiding one's attentional processes. While these results are hugely promising, researchers have yet to explore whether such forms of training would have a similar impact on executive functioning in elite performers.

Old problems and new directions in research on concentration in athletes

Despite a considerable amount of research on attentional processes in athletes, some old problems remain. The purpose of this section of the chapter is to identify these unresolved issues and to sketch some potentially fruitful new directions for research in this field.

First, as is evident from the insights of some leading sports performers earlier in this chapter, further research is required on the **meta-attentional** processes of athletes or their intuitive theories about how their own concentration systems work. Such research is important because concentration skills enhancement in applied sport psychology is really an exercise in meta-attentional training whereby athletes learn to understand, and gain some control over, their apparently capricious concentration system. As yet, however, we know very little about the nature, accuracy and/or malleability of athletes' theories of how their own mental processes operate. Second, evidence suggests that performers can flexibly adjust their attentional focus during training and performance and yet we know very little about the cognitive mechanisms that allow them to do so. Similarly, little or nothing is known about the influence of internal distractions – those which arise from athletes' own thoughts and feelings – on performance. However, with the advent of Wegner's (1994, 2002) ironic processes model and the development of novel ways of assessing athletes' susceptibility to cognitive interference (e.g. see the test developed by Hatzigeorgiadis and Biddle, 2000), a greater understanding has emerged of the mechanisms underlying athletes' internal distractions. Third, what is the best way to train concentration skills in athletes? The increasing sophistication of neurofeedback devices has led researchers to explore whether patterns characteristic of optimal performance can be trained via the use of EEG feedback for individual athletes. A related line of inquiry concerns the possibility that certain types of attentional training (e.g. integrative body–mind training) can improve an athlete's executive attention. Fourth, further research is required to explore the relationship between ego depletion and distractibility – this is particularly relevant in light of a recent meta-analysis which revealed that the size of the ego-depletion effect was small (see Hagger and Chatzisarantis, 2016). Does intact self-control mean that athletes are better equipped to ignore distracting stimuli and, if so, what are the precise mechanisms that mediate this effect? Research is also required to explore if athletes can increase their self-control strength and if this has a positive influence on their performance under pressure. Fifth, additional research is needed to establish the precise mechanisms by which emotions (such as anxiety) affect athletes' concentration processes.

One way to address this question is to explore the visual search behaviour of anxious athletes as they tackle laboratory simulations of sport-relevant tasks (see Moran et al., 2002). The use of pupillometry as a measure of "attentional effort" holds some promise in this regard. A sixth fruitful avenue for research on attention in sport comes from cognitive neuroscience. As mentioned earlier, this field is concerned with understanding the biological substrates of cognitive processes through the use of psychophysiological measures (e.g. EEG, ERP, PET scanning, fMRI, and TMS) collected during "real-time" performance of various tasks. Already, such techniques have proved valuable in identifying the main attentional networks in the brain (Posner and Rothbart, 2007). Although these techniques have limitations (e.g. they are likely to be most beneficial when guided by psychological theories; see Cacioppo et al., 2008), they offer intriguing possibilities for the study of attentional processes in athletes.

Ideas for research projects on concentration in athletes

Here are six ideas for possible research projects on attentional processes in athletes.

1. You could fill a gap in the field by exploring the nature and extent of expert–novice differences in athletes' "meta-attentional awareness" (i.e. their understanding of, and control over, how their concentration system works; see Loper and Hallahan, 1982; Reisberg, 1985). Only a handful of studies have been conducted on this topic to date.

2. Using a qualitative approach (e.g. diaries, interviews) you could examine the extent to which performers adapt their attentional focus in order to deal with various challenges (e.g. injury, "performance slumps") that they may encounter over the course of a competitive season. You could also use "stimulated recall" (SR – a method for enhancing reflection by recalling situations through audiotapes or video recordings; see Nyberg, 2015) to help athletes recall their thoughts during training or competition.

3. You could address some of the unresolved questions in research on flow states in athletes. For example, do athletes ever experience such states when practising or training? Or do they occur only in competitive situations? You could use "explication interviews" to better understand the role bodily awareness plays during flow.

4. Empirical studies are required to explore whether mindfulness training (discussed earlier in the chapter) might help performers to maintain performance and movement proficiency by improving their attentional control under pressurized conditions. In this regard, you could replicate and extend Chong et al.'s (2015) work in order to ascertain whether or not mindfulness approaches might improve the acquisition and retention of more complex motor skills such as golf putting. A useful questionnaire to include in such a study is the Mindfulness Inventory for Sport (MIS; Thienot et al., 2014).

5. Further research is required to test Wegner's (1994) theory of ironic control in a sport setting. For example, using the methodology developed by Dugdale and Eklund (2002), can ironic rebound effects be reduced by manipulating athletes' attentional focus? Will the adoption of an external focus of attention reduce the likelihood of experiencing either ironic or over-compensatory effects? Could "quiet eye" training prove helpful in this regard?

6. What methods may be used by athletes to replenish their self-control strength? For example, will relaxation techniques, quiet eye training, or practicing under pressure help them improve self-control strength in real-life competitive settings?

Summary

- The term "concentration" refers to the ability to focus mental effort on what is most important in any situation while ignoring distractions. This ability is a crucial prerequisite of successful performance in sport. Research suggests that the ability to focus effectively is associated with peak performances in athletes. Unfortunately, despite a century of empirical studies on attentional processes, there is still a great deal of confusion about what concentration is and how it can be measured and improved in athletes. Therefore, the purpose of this chapter was to alert you to the progress and prospects of research in this field.

- The second section examined the nature, dimensions and importance of the construct of concentration in sport.

- The third section outlined briefly four approaches to the measurement of attentional processes (including concentration) in athletes.

- The fourth section explained the main principles of effective concentration that have emerged from research on the ideal performance states of athletes.

- The fifth section explored the question of why athletes lose their concentration so easily.

- The sixth section reviewed various practical exercises and psychological techniques that are purported to enhance concentration skills in athletes.

- The seventh section outlined some unresolved issues concerning attentional processes in sport performers.

- Finally, some potentially fruitful new directions for research in this field were suggested.

6

Using imagination in sport
Mental imagery, motor imagery and mental practice in athletes

Introduction

One of our most remarkable cognitive abilities is the capacity to use our imagination to mimic perceptual experiences (e.g. we can "see" a red traffic light in our mind's eye) and motor actions (e.g. we can "kick" a ball virtually). For example, consider how Formula One champion driver Jenson Button practises in his mind: "I'll sit down on a Swiss ball with a steering wheel in my hands and close my eyes. I'll drive around the circuit, practising every gear shift. It's just a little bit of visualization" (cited by Jackson, 2014). This ability to draw on previous experience in order to engage in mental simulation (which is how "imagination" is defined in psychology; see Jung et al., 2016) has been studied under the heading of "mental imagery" and raises many intriguing theoretical and practical questions. For example, at a theoretical level, what are the neurocognitive substrates (i.e. the specific brain circuits and/or underlying psychological processes) of the ability to imagine actions? At a practical level, can imagining an action without executing it (a process known as **motor imagery** or "mental practice", MP; see Di Rienzo et al., 2016; Driskell et al., 1994) really improve its subsequent performance? If so, what is the scientific explanation of this fascinating effect – given that MP provides no actual sensory feedback to the performer?

At the outset, it is clear that motor imagery is widely used by elite athletes. To illustrate, Murphy (1994) reported that 90 per cent of a sample of athletes at the US Olympic Training Centre claimed to use imagery regularly. Likewise, Ungerleider and Golding (1991) discovered that 85 per cent of more than 600 prospective Olympic athletes employed imagery techniques while training for competition. More recently, Clarey (2014) found that Olympic athletes routinely "see" and "feel" themselves performing key actions in their mind's eye as part of their mental training regimes.

Turning to individual athletes, world-class performers like Carli Lloyd (soccer), Wayne Rooney (soccer) and Michael Phelps (swimming) have provided powerful testimonials to the power of imagination in sport. Thus, Lloyd, a two-times Olympic gold-medallist and World Cup winner with the US soccer team, Carli Lloyd (US soccer star and World Cup winner and two-times Olympic gold-medallist for the United States), claimed that "… over the years and definitely over the last four years, I've taken that visualization part to another level … I've basically visualized so many different things on the field, making these big plays, scoring goals" (cited in Jensen, 2015).

Likewise, Rooney, England's leading international goal-scorer, explained that before matches "I lie in bed the night before the game and visualize myself scoring goals or doing well. You're trying to put yourself in that moment and trying to prepare yourself, to have a 'memory' before the game" (Watson, 2012). Note also that Michael Phelps, the most decorated Olympian of all time with a total of twenty-two medals, extolled the importance of kinaesthetic or "feeling oriented" mental imagery (see Figure 6.1) when he said:

> swimmers like to say they can "feel" the water. Even early on, I felt it. I didn't have to fight the water. Instead, I could feel how I moved in it. How to be balanced. What might make me go faster or slower.
>
> (Phelps, 2008a)

Arising from the preceding evidence, the purpose of the present chapter is to explore the psychology of imagination (or more precisely, "mental imagery" and "motor imagery") – in action. But before we begin, some terminological clarification is required.

In cognitive psychology, the term **mental imagery** refers to a "multimodal" (i.e. involving different sensory systems) cognitive simulation process that enables us to represent perceptual information in our minds in the absence

Figure 6.1 Michael Phelps uses kinaesthetic imagery to "feel" the water (*source*: courtesy of Inpho photography)

of actual sensory input (Munzert et al., 2009). Technically, it involves the "voluntary retrieval and representation of sensory information from memory" (Pearson, 2014, p. 178) in the absence of a direct external stimulus. Put simply, imagery enables us to create virtual experiences of sights, sounds and sensations of things that are not present in our environment or actually happening to us. For example, if you close your eyes for a moment you can probably "see" a red traffic light in your mind's eye and "hear" the sound of an ambulance siren in your mind's ear – *even though you are not standing beside a road right now*. Here, the "sight" that you see and the "sound" that you "hear" comes from your *memory* of traffic lights and ambulance sirens, not from actually perceiving them. Similarly, our imagination can simulate perceptual experiences in other senses. For instance, you may be able to "smell" a freshly peeled orange or to "taste" a cup of strong coffee in the absence of these stimuli. Furthermore, with a little more effort, you should be able to imagine *physical* sensations like clenching your fist or stretching both arms high above your head as if you were trying to touch the ceiling. And it is this latter experience that characterizes motor imagery or the mental simulation of a movement without actually executing it (see Hanakawa, 2016). As we mentioned earlier, this cognitive process of "seeing" and "feeling" a movement in one's imagination without actually executing it is also known as "mental practice". Imagery experiences are intriguing not only because they involve different sensory systems but also because they *seem real* to your brain – a crucial point which we shall return to later when we explain how imagery works.

Perhaps not surprisingly, the value of using mental imagery to rehearse and improve actions and movements is recognized in many fields of skilled performance *other* than sport. For example, imagery has been shown to enhance performance among musicians (Bernardi et al., 2013; Wright et al., 2014) and surgeons (Arora et al., 2010, 2011) and also to augment the physical rehabilitation of people who have suffered neurological damage from strokes (e.g. see Harris and Herbert, 2015) or spinal cord injury (see Mateo et al., 2015). So, mental imagery techniques are recommended extensively by sport and performance psychologists (e.g. see Cumming and Ramsey, 2009; Gould et al., 2014; MacIntyre et al., 2013b; Weinberg, 2008) and neuroscientists (e.g. Munzert & Lorey, 2013). Such advocacy is based on an impressive body of experimental evidence. For example, Caliari (2008) found that table tennis players who had been trained to use imagery in order to mentally rehearse a stroke (the forehand drive) improved significantly relative to a control group. Likewise, imagery practice can also improve psychological processes such as the capacity to experience flow states (see Chapter 5). For example, Koehn et al. (2014), using a single-case experimental design (see Chapter 1), found that a six week programme of imagery exercises led to improved performance and increased flow experiences among four elite junior athletes. Arising from such research, imagery has become such a common component of sport psychological interventions that it has been acclaimed as a "central pillar of applied sport psychology" (T. Morris et al., 2004, p. 344). Nevertheless, scepticism remains because some athletes who practise imagery may be regarded as rather eccentric. For example, Jamie George, the England international rugby hooker, encountered some scepticism when he revealed his use of imagery as a concentration technique. Specifically, just before he throws the ball, he uses his imagination to "put myself into my bedroom and let nothing else come into that bubble" (cited in Kitson, 2015, p.8).

To summarize what we have learned so far, athletes (e.g. Jenson Button, Carli Lloyd, Wayne Rooney, Michael Phelps), sport psychologists and neuroscientists endorse the value of imagery as a cognitive tool for giving performers a winning edge in their chosen field. But is this belief in the power of imagery supported by empirical evidence in psychology? Or does it merely reflect some "New Age", pseudo-scientific mysticism?

In attempting to answer these challenging questions, this chapter explores a variety of intriguing issues at three different levels: practical, methodological and theoretical. For example, practically, if mental imagery *does* improve athletic performance, is it possible that athletes could practise their skills in their heads without leaving their armchairs? Turning to methodological issues, how can we measure people's mental images objectively given their intrinsically private and ephemeral nature? At a theoretical level, what happens in our brains when we imagine something and what psychological mechanisms could account for the effects of mental rehearsal on skilled performance? In order to address these questions, we have organized the present chapter as follows.

To begin with, we investigate what mental imagery is, how it can be studied, and its types, modalities (or sensory systems) and dimensions. This section also features a brief analysis of the brain mechanisms underlying motor imagery. The next section of the chapter focuses on mental practice in sport and reviews the main findings, theories and issues in this field. The fourth section examines the measurement of mental imagery skills in sport. The fifth section describes what researchers have learned about the ways in which athletes use mental imagery in various athletic situations. In the sixth section, we sketch some new directions for research on imagery in athletes, with a special emphasis on the growing topic of motor imagery. Finally, we'll provide a few ideas for possible research projects in this field.

What is "mental imagery" and how can we study it?

As we explained earlier, the cognitive (or knowledge-seeking) process of mental imagery enables us to mimic or simulate experiences involving people, places, actions and situations. Formally, the mental representations that give rise to our imagery experiences are generated in working memory in the absence of appropriate sensory input (Pearson et al., 2015).

Remarkably, although imagery is a fleeting and inherently private experience, it *can* be studied objectively (see Box 6.1).

Earlier, we explained that mental imagery is the ability to use information in one's mind to create or simulate perceptual experiences that are normally triggered by sensory input from the world around us. This definition highlights a crucial difference between imagery and the related cognitive process of "perception".

Box 6.1 In the spotlight Studying imagery … from questionnaires to brain imaging

Since the 1880s, psychologists have explored the intriguing but elusive skill of mental imagery. Whereas the earliest studies in this field used *subjective* measures (questionnaires) in which people were asked to describe their imagery experiences, more recent research is based on *objective* tests that measure the speed and accuracy with which people can make decisions or solve problems that are known to require imagery skills. The faster and better that people can do so, the stronger are their imagery skills.

The subjective approach to imagery assessment began when Galton (1883) asked people to visualize familiar experiences such as what they had had for breakfast, the sound of rain against the window, the smell of tobacco, the taste of chocolate and the touch of soap. Building on this idea, Betts (1909) developed a questionnaire in which people were asked to rate, using numbers, the vividness or clarity with which they could imagine items drawn from different sensory modalities such as vision (the sight of the sun sinking below the horizon) and touch (the feeling of running upstairs). Unfortunately, following some doubts about the reliability (i.e. consistency) of these measures, however, the subjective approach gave way to at least three waves of objective measurement techniques.

The first wave of objective imagery measurement began in the 1970s. Here, experimental psychologists like Shepard and his colleagues (e.g. Shepard and Metzler, 1971) devised a "mental rotation" task in which people had to use their imagery skills to make mental comparisons that led to right or wrong answers. Specifically, they had to decide as quickly as possible whether a given pair of objects were identical (i.e. the same object but in a different orientation) or different (mirror images of each other). People reported that they solved such problems by mentally rotating one object until it either matched or did not match the other object. In other words, they used mental imagery to solve a problem involving rotation of objects in space. Interestingly, Madan and Singhal (2013, 2014) developed an objective instrument for the measurement of motor imagery skills. This instrument, called the Test of Ability in Movement Imagery (TAMI), requires participants to make explicit imagined movements from an external imagery perspective (i.e. as if watching oneself or someone else performing movements on a movie screen; see also later in chapter). Having imagined a series of five specific body movements, participants are required to select the appropriate body position from a variety of possible body-positioning images. So, there is a correct answer for each question on the TAMI.

The second wave of objective imagery measurement was prompted in the 1990s by the development of high resolution brain imaging procedures (e.g. functional magnetic resonance imaging, fMRI). fMRI techniques were developed to counteract some of the limitations of existing tools used to explore the brain in action. Specifically, although electroencephalography (EEG) provided a groundbreaking measure of brain activity in the scalp, it suffered from inadequate spatial resolution. Similarly, although positron emission tomography (PET) could measure local brain activity through cerebral blood flow, its accuracy was limited by the decay properties of the radioactive isotope with which participants had to be injected. By contrast, a key advantage of fMRI techniques is that they are non-invasive and offer temporal resolution in the order of seconds and spatial resolution in the order of millimetres (Mather et al., 2013b).

The third wave of objective imagery assessment occurred with the advent of chronometric measures of imagery – which depend on comparing the length of time it takes a person to *imagine* something and to *actually* do it in reality. The rationale here is that if imagined and executed actions recruit similar neural circuits and brain regions (see also Boxes 6.4 and 6.8), then the timing of imagined and actual actions should also be similar. Therefore, there should be a close correspondence between the time required to *mentally* perform a given action and that required to *actually* execute it. Research shows that this is exactly what happens when you compare "real" and "imagined" time for the performance of skilled actions by expert athletes. The time it takes them to imagine performing a given skill such as a tennis serve or a putt in golf is almost identical to that required to actually perform these skills. But significant gaps between real and imagined times for everyday actions can occur for people who may have neurological problems.

Briefly, whereas perception involves making sense of the world from the *outside in* (as information flows into your mind from the world around you), imagery works from the *inside out* because it involves the creative assembly of information that is *already* stored in your mind. Theoretically, therefore, imagery involves perception without sensation. To explain, whereas perception occurs when we interpret sensory input, imagery arises from our interpretation of stored, memory-based information.

A good way of understanding this difference between perception and imagery was proposed by Kosslyn and Rosenberg (2011). Imagine that you're looking at a picture on a television screen linked to a camera and a DVD player. Whereas *perception* is like the screen picture that comes from the camera recording details of the world around us, *mental imagery* is like the picture that comes from the DVD player which plays information stored in its memory.

If imagery resembles perception, then there should be similarities between the neural circuits activated by these two related psychological processes. Put simply, similar parts of the brain should "light up" when we imagine things as when we actually perceive them. For example, visual imagery should be associated with neural activity in the cortical areas (e.g. in the **occipital lobe**) that are specialized for visual perception and motor imagery should be associated with the neural pathways typically triggered by motor actions (e.g. in the cerebellum and basal ganglia; see Box 6.2).

How is imagery information stored in the mind?

Before concluding this section, it is important to mention an important theoretical debate that arose in imagery circles in the 1980s. Briefly, this issue was called the "imagery debate" (see Pearson and Kosslyn, 2015) and revolved around the precise nature of the mental representations that underlie imagery experiences. Note that cognitive psychologists distinguish between the *content* of mental imagery (i.e. the nature of the information being represented) and its *format* (i.e. the nature of the code used to represent it). At the heart of this imagery debate was the following question. Is imagery encoded in the mind in an analogue format (i.e. one that *depicts*

Box 6.2 Thinking critically about ... the neural substrates of motor imagery

What brain areas and cortical networks underlie our ability to imagine movements and actions? As we shall see, motor imagery tends to recruit subcortical motor areas such as the basal ganglia and cerebellum. But before we analyse this finding, some background information is required. Research on the neural substrates of motor imagery was inspired mainly by Jeannerod's (2001, 2004) simulation theory which postulated that motor images are "non-executed actions" (2004, p. 390). In Jeannerod's view, all actions involve a covert stage during which they are prepared or simulated. Based on this tenet, Jeannerod (2001) predicted that "motor imagery ... should involve, in the subject's motor brain, neural mechanisms similar to those operating during the real action" (pp. S103–S104) – the "functional equivalence" hypothesis (explained later in this chapter). In seeking to test this hypothesis, neuroimaging studies have revealed that mentally simulated and actually executed actions share certain mental representations – especially those involved in motor planning – and activate partially overlapping cortical regions called the "core network" (Sauvage et al., 2013). This network includes brain areas such as the premotor cortex, supplementary motor area, the anterior cingulate cortex, inferior and superior parietal regions, and the cerebellum (Hétu et al., 2013). Furthermore, research shows that athletes' level of expertise affects the specific neural networks activated by motor imagery. Specifically, Chang et al. (2011) discovered that elite archers displayed greater activation in premotor and supplementary motor area (SMA) than that found in novice counterparts. By contrast, novice archers displayed higher cerebral activation than expert performers in brain regions such as the basal ganglia and cerebellum. More recently, Jiang et al. (2015) found that motor imagery activated a number of cortical areas in the cerebellum (which plays a crucial role in motor control) as well as some in inferior frontal cortex. They also discovered that participants with strong imagery skills showed activation of the right supplementary motor area (specifically, BA6), which is normally associated with motor planning. Such results are consistent with earlier findings (e.g. Munzert & Zentgraf, 2009) that actual and imagined actions activate similar brain regions in the motor and premotor cortices. They are also compatible with findings that, compared to executed actions, imagined actions have a similar temporal structure and accuracy (Guillot and Collet, 2005) and tend to evoke similar autonomic responses (Mulder et al., 2005).

Critical thinking questions

How well has imagery been measured in studies of the neural substrates of motor imagery? Recently, Seiler et al. (2015) pointed out some methodological weaknesses of studies in this field. For example, investigators typically fail either to screen participants for imagery ability or to include imagery manipulation checks to show that people actually understood and adhered to the imagery instructions that they received in the studies. Such methodological problems hamper the validity of many neuroimaging studies of mental imagery processes.

things) or a propositional format (i.e. one that *describes* things)? Championing the former position, Kosslyn and his colleagues (e.g. see Kosslyn, 1994; Kosslyn et al., 2006) argued that images are visuo-spatial brain representations or depictions ("pictures in the head") and that visual mental images are structurally analogous to visual perceptual representations. In other words, each part of the imagery representation was held to correspond or "map onto" a part of the represented object. So, for example, the distance between the parts of the representation should correspond with the actual distances between the parts. Opposing this depictive view was Pylyshyn (1973, 1981), who argued that visual mental imagery relies on representations that are largely propositional or language-like in nature and that any structural or phenomenal similarities between imagery and perception are illusory. A key point of disagreement between these rival theorists was whether or not mental imagery plays a functional role in cognitive processing. Whereas Kosslyn and his colleagues used neuroscientific evidence to support their argument that visuo-spatial depictions play a crucial role in human cognition, Pylyshyn (1973, 1981) argued that imagery is "epiphenomenal" – an accidental by-product of abstract cognitive processing but not a central part of it – like the pilot light of a CD player. With the advent of functional brain imaging technology in the early 1990s, the imagery debate was quickly resolved because numerous fMRI studies showed that visual mental imagery *is* a depictive representation with strong links to visual perception. Evidence to support this claim comes from studies (see Pearson and Kosslyn, 2015) showing that when one forms a visual image with one's eyes closed, activity occurs in the V1 area (primary visual cortex). One implication of this finding is that it may be possible for future researchers to "decode" the visual imagery that people experience when they dream (Horikawa et al., 2013). Interestingly, Stumbrys et al. (2016) reported that motor imagery can be practised during sleep.

Types, modalities and dimensions of mental imagery

Mental imagery is a complex construct that can be studied with regard to typology, modalities and dimensions. Before summarizing research on these topics, here is a quick overview of key findings.

First, depending on the sensory modality and cognitive systems involved, different types of mental imagery have been identified. Second, recent progress has been made in identifying the neural processes underlying the motor modality of imagery. Third, research suggests that imagery is a multimodal or multisensory experience. In other words, we have the capacity to imagine "seeing", "hearing", "tasting", "smelling" and "feeling" various stimuli and/or sensations. Finally, images differ from each other in dimensions such as controllability and **vividness** (Callow and Hardy, 2005; Moran, 1993). Let us now explore each of these points briefly.

To begin with, whereas sport psychology researchers tend to differentiate between different types of imagery based on their predominant sensory modality (e.g. visual, motor) cognitive neuroscientists tend to use more theoretically based distinctions such as those between visual and spatial imagery processes. To explain, researchers have discovered two distinct cognitive systems that encode and process visual information in different ways (Blajenkova et al., 2006). Whereas object-based imagery represents the shape and colour information of objects, spatial imagery represents location information. More precisely, "visual object imagery" involves mental representations of "the literal appearances of individual objects in terms of their precise form, size, shape, colour and brightness" (Blajenkova et al., 2006, p. 239) and "spatial imagery" involves the mental representations of "the spatial relations amongst objects, parts of objects, locations of objects in space, movements of objects and object parts and other complex spatial transformations" (Blajenkova et al., 2006, pp. 239–240). Historically, visuo-spatial imagery has received far more research attention than has imagery in other modalities (Reisberg, 2013). As one might expect, however, motor imagery is extremely important to athletes. Cognitive researchers have typically defined it as the cognitive rehearsal of a motor action or movement in the absence of overt motor output or "mentally simulating an intended action without actually producing it" (Smith and Kosslyn, 2014, p. 518). This largely proprioceptive or kinaesthetic process is evident whenever people imagine actions without engaging in the actual physical movements involved. We shall return to this topic later in the chapter when we explore "mental practice" or motor imagery training. In the meantime, however, Box 6.2 summarizes what we know about the neural substrates of motor imagery.

Third, as we mentioned earlier, imagery is a multisensory experience. Of the various senses contributing to imagery experiences in daily life, vision has been studied most frequently (Reisberg, 2013). Interestingly, imagery diary studies (Kosslyn et al., 1990) suggest that about two thirds of people's mental images in everyday life are visual in nature. For example, have you ever had the experience of trying to remember where you parked your car as you wandered around a large, congested carpark? If so, then the chances are that you tried to form a mental "picture" of the location of your vehicle. But our imagination is not confined solely to the visual sense. To illustrate, if you pause for a moment and close your eyes, you should also be able to imagine the sensations evoked by feeling the fur of a cat (a tactile image), hearing the sound of your favourite band or song (an auditory image) or experiencing the unpleasant grating sensation of a nail being scraped across a blackboard (a combination of tactile and auditory images).

Visual and auditory sensations are easily imagined in sport (e.g. can you "see" yourself taking a penalty and then "hear" the crowd roar as your shot hits the net?), but the type of feeling-oriented imagery that Michael Phelps referred to earlier in the chapter is more difficult both to conceptualize and to investigate empirically (see Figure 6.2).

Although few studies have been conducted on feeling-oriented imagery in sport, Moran and MacIntyre (1998) and Callow and Hardy (2005) have investigated kinaesthetic imagery processes in elite athletes (see Box 6.3).

To summarize, we have learned that although mental imagery is a multisensory construct, most studies of imagery processes in athletes have been confined to the visual sensory modality.

Figure 6.2 Carli Lloyd uses imagery to improve her performance (*source*: courtesy of Inpho photography)

Box 6.3 In the spotlight Exploring "feel" in athletes: investigating kinaesthetic imagery processes

Historically, research on mental imagery in athletes has focused mainly on visual imagery rather than on motor imagery. This oversight is unfortunate because, as we mentioned earlier in the chapter, elite performers such as Carli Lloyd and Wayne Rooney (soccer), Michael Phelps (swimming) and Jenson Button (racing driver) have reported relying on "touch" and "feel" when rehearsing their skills and movements in their minds before they actually execute them. Such kinaesthetic imagery processes involve feelings of force and motion or the mental simulation of sensations associated with bodily movements. More precisely, kinaesthetic imagery denotes "the sensations of how it feels to perform an action, including the force and effort involved in movement and balance, and spatial location (either of a body part or piece of sports equipment)" (Callow and Waters, 2005, pp. 444–445). In one of the earliest studies of this topic, Moran and MacIntyre (1998) used a combination of qualitative and quantitative methods to investigate the kinaesthetic imagery experiences of a sample (n=12) of elite canoe slalomists participating in World Cup competitions. These athletes were first interviewed about their understanding and use of feeling-oriented imagery in their sport. Then they were assessed using a battery of measures which included specially devised Likert rating scales and the Movement Imagery Questionnaire-Revised (C. Hall and Martin, 1997). Next, in an effort to validate the athletes' subjective reports on their imagery experiences (see later in the chapter for a discussion of this problem), the canoe slalom competitors were timed as they engaged in a "mental travel" procedure during which they had to visualize a recent race in their

continued ...

> **Box 6.3 continued**
>
> imagination and execute it as if they were paddling physically. The time taken to complete these mental races was then compared with actual race times. As expected, there was a significant positive correlation between mental and physical race times ($r=0.78$, $p<0.05$). More recently, Callow and Waters (2005) investigated the efficacy of a kinaesthetic imagery intervention on the confidence of three flat-race jockeys. Using a single-case, multiple-baseline design (for a comprehensive account of single-case research in sport and exercise psychology, see Barker et al., 2011), Callow and Waters (2005) found that the kinaesthetic imagery intervention was associated with a significant increase in confidence for two of the three jockeys involved. Subsequently, Ridderinkhof and Brass (2015) proposed a model of motor imagery which we examine later in the chapter.

Turning to the final points – how images differ from each other – it is clear that images vary in dimensions such as controllability, vividness and **perspective**. "Controllability" refers to the ease with which mental images can be manipulated by the person who creates them. To illustrate, can you imagine a feather falling down from the ceiling of your room, slowly wafting this way and that before gently landing on your desk? Now, see if you can imagine this feather reversing its path floating back up towards the ceiling like a balloon, as if carried higher by a sudden current of air. If you found these mental pictures easy to create, then you probably have reasonably good control over your imagery. As another example of this skill, try to imagine yourself standing in front of where you live. How many windows can you see? Count them. Now, using your imagination as a camera with a zoom lens, try to get a close-up picture of one of the windows. What material are the frames made of? What colour are the frames? Can you see them in a different colour? If you can "see" these details of your windows accurately, then you have good imagery control skills. An interesting measure of imagery controllability was proposed recently by Saimpont et al. (2015). Briefly, in this "finger-thumb opposition task", participants were required to repeatedly execute and imagine – from a first-person/ internal imagery perspective (see brief discussion below) – an auditory paced (1Hz), finger–thumb opposition sequence with their dominant hand. The sequence consisted of touching fingers 2 (the index finger), 4, 3, 5 and was repeated until the auditory pacing stopped. Next, imagery "vividness" refers to people's ability to generate clear or realistic virtual experiences and sensations of imagined objects. It can be measured psychometrically using self-report questionnaires such as the Vividness of Movement Imagery Questionnaire (VMIQ-2; R. Roberts et al., 2008; described later in chapter). A third dimension of mental imagery that has attracted growing research interest is "imagery perspective" or the virtual vantage point used by a person when imagining an action or event. For example, there is a difference between "seeing" something internally (through one's own eyes) and "seeing" it externally (as if watching oneself or someone else on a movie screen). Since the 1970s (e.g. Mahoney and Avener, 1977), imagery researchers have distinguished between a "first-person" visual perspective (whereby people imagine themselves performing a given action) and a "third-person" or "observer" visual perspective (whereby people imagine seeing either themselves or someone else performing the action). Using this distinction, researchers (e.g. Callow et al., 2013) have explored the possibility of differential effects of imagery perspective on motor learning. For example, Hardy and colleagues postulated that external visual imagery (EVI) would be superior to internal visual imagery (IVI) for skills that require positioning the body relative to itself, such as tasks relying heavily on the use of "form". To test this hypothesis, Hardy and Callow (1999) used a series of three tasks relying heavily upon the use of form for successful completion. In all three tasks, (i.e. a karate kata task, a gymnastics floor routine and a technical rock climbing task), the use of EVI was found to have a superior influence on performance compared to the use of IVI. Building on such research, a study by Callow et al. (2013) corroborated the suggestion that EVI is more effective than IVI for "form"-based tasks. In considering possible explanations of this phenomenon, these authors cited Hardy's (1997) cognitive analysis of imagery perspectives. According to this analysis, imagery may enhance the performance in situations when the images that are generated manage to supplement the information that is already available to the performer. So, for tasks that depend on the use of form, EVI seems to be more useful than IVI because the former enables the person to "see" the desired form associated with the appropriate movement. Also, Callow et al. (2013) suggested that IVI would be superior to EVI for tasks that require positioning the body in relation to other external visual features, such as in slalom-based tasks where a performer has to follow a "line" through or around a set course (e.g. downhill slalom skiing). Here, these authors speculated that IVI may allow a performer to see the precise temporal and spatial locations where key movements need to be initiated from the actual viewing angle of the motor action in relation to external visual information.

In summary, mental imagery representations have three important characteristics. First, they are multisensory constructs that enable us to create virtual experiences of absent objects, events and/or experiences. Second, they are believed to be functionally equivalent to percepts in the sense that they share a great deal of the same brain machinery or neural substrates with perception. Third, mental images vary in vividness, controllability and perspective – dimensions which which facilitate their measurement (see later in this chapter). Having explained the nature and types of imagery, let us now consider the topic of mental practice.

Mental practice

As we explained earlier, MP (or motor imagery) refers to a systematic form of covert rehearsal in which people imagine themselves performing an action without engaging in the actual physical movements involved (Driskell et al., 1994). Historically, the term "mental practice" first appeared formally in the title of a psychology paper in a publication by Vandell et al. (1943). However, psychological interest in the phenomenon of mental practice is as old as the discipline of psychology itself. To illustrate, the covert simulation of physical actions had been considered by William James (1890b) in his discussion of "motor images" (p. 708). Indeed, he suggested rather counter-intuitively that by anticipating experiences imaginatively, people actually learn to skate in the *summer* and to swim in the *winter*! Interestingly, the 1890s witnessed various expressions of an idea called the **ideo-motor principle** which suggested that all thoughts have muscular concomitants. For example, in 1899 Henri-Etienne Beaunis (cited in Washburn, 1916, p. 138) proposed that "it is well known that the idea of a movement suffices to produce the movement or make it tend to be produced". Similarly, Carpenter (1894) claimed that low-level neural impulses are similar in imagined movement. Furthermore, he argued that these impulses are similar in nature, but lower in amplitude, to those emitted during actual movement. We shall return to this ideo-motor hypothesis later in the chapter when evaluating theories of mental practice.

During this same era, Anderson (1899) conducted a series of empirical studies demonstrating the effects of mental practice on gymnastic skills. He concluded that gymnastic movements could be learned without actual use of the muscles, solely through mental rehearsal. Subsequently, a surge of research on mental practice occurred under various headings such as "kinaesthetic imagery" (Sullivan, 1921), "symbolic rehearsal" (Sackett, 1934) and "imaginary practice" (Perry, 1939). Since the 1930s, other terms for MP included "visualization" (Gieseking and Leimer, 1932), "implicit practice" (Morrisett, 1956), "covert rehearsal" (Corbin, 1967), "visual motor behaviour rehearsal" (Suinn, 1984), "imagined action" (Decety et al., 1989), "motor imagery" (Decety, 1996a, 1996b), "mental training" (Jeannerod, 1997), "mental simulation" (Allami et al., 2008), "motor imagery practice" (Bovend'eerdt et al., 2012) and, most recently, "motor imagery training" (Mizuguchi et al., 2013).

Unfortunately, as we shall see in the next section, research on mental practice between the 1930s and late 1990s is paradoxical for at least one crucial reason. Specifically, although the *efficacy* of MP was well established by this time, its underlying mechanisms received surprisingly little scrutiny – simply because most MP studies during this era were *atheoretical* in nature. Put differently, they rarely tested conceptually driven hypotheses about the mechanisms underlying MP effects. Therefore, despite at least 70 years of theorizing in this field (as defined by the period between Jacobson's, 1932, **neuromuscular theory of mental practice** and Jeannerod's, 2006, simulation theory account of "mental training", p. 41), little progress was made in understanding how MP works.

Now that we have examined the nature of mental imagery and mental practice, let us explore research methods and findings on MP. Research on athletes' use of mental imagery will be examined in the fifth section of the chapter.

Research on mental practice (MP) in sport

Since the 1890s, hundreds of experimental studies have demonstrated the efficacy of MP in improving skilled performance in sport and other domains. Reviews of this research literature have been conducted, in chronological order, by A. Richardson (1967a, 1967b), Feltz and Landers (1983), Grouios (1992), Murphy and Jowdy (1992), Driskell et al. (1994), Murphy and Martin (2002), van Meer and Theunissen (2009) and Schuster et al. (2011). Before we summarize the general findings of these reviews, here is a brief explanation of the typical research paradigm used in studies of MP.

Typical research design and findings

In general, the experimental paradigm in MP research involves a comparison of the pre- and post-intervention performance of the following groups of participants: those who have been engaged only in physical practice of the skill in question (the physical practice group, PP); those who have mentally practised it (the mental practice group, MP); those who have alternated between physical and mental practice (PP/MP); and, finally, people who have been involved in a control condition. Historically, the target skills investigated in MP research have largely been relatively simple laboratory tasks (e.g. dart-throwing or maze-learning) rather than complex sports skills. After a pre-treatment baseline test has been conducted on the specific skill involved, participants are randomly assigned to one of these conditions (PP, MP, PP/MP or control). Normally, the cognitive rehearsal in the MP treatment condition involves a scripted sequence of relaxing physically, closing one's eyes, and then trying to see and feel oneself repeatedly performing a target skill (e.g. a golf putt) successfully in one's imagination. After this MP intervention has been applied, the participants' performance on this skill is tested again. Then, if the performance of the MP group exceeds that of the control group, a positive effect of mental practice is reported.

Based on this experimental paradigm, a number of general conclusions about mental practice have emerged. First, relative to not practising at all, MP appears to improve skilled performance. However, MP is less effective than is physical practice. More precisely, a meta-analytic review by Driskell et al. (1994) showed that physical practice treatment conditions produced greater statistical effect sizes than was evident in mental rehearsal conditions (recall from Chapter 1 that meta-analysis is a statistical technique which combines the results of a large number of studies in order to determine the overall size of a statistical effect). Statistically, the relative effect sizes of physical practice and mental practice were estimated by these researchers as 0.382 and 0.261 (both Fisher's Z), respectively. These figures can be interpreted with reference to J. Cohen's (1992) suggestion that values of 0.20, 0.50 and 0.80 represent effect sizes that are small, medium and large, respectively. The second general finding from the research literature is that MP, when combined and alternated with physical practice, seems to produce superior skill-learning to that resulting from either mental or physical practice conducted alone. Third, research suggests that mental practice improves the performance of cognitive skills (i.e. those that involve sequential processing activities; e.g. mirror drawing tasks) more than it does for motor skills (e.g. balancing on a stabilometer). Fourth, there seems to be an interaction between the level of expertise of the performer and the type of task which yields the best improvement from mental rehearsal (Driskell et al., 1994). Specifically, expert athletes tend to benefit more from MP than do novices, regardless of the type of skill being practised (either cognitive or physical). Fifth, the positive effects of MP on task performance tend to decline sharply over time. Indeed, according to Driskell et al. (1994), the beneficial effects of visualization are reduced to *half* of their original value after approximately two weeks of time has elapsed. A practical implication of this finding is that in order to gain optimal benefits from mental practice, "refresher" training should be implemented after this critical two week period. Finally, there is evidence that imagery ability mediates the relationship between MP and motor skill performance. More precisely, athletes who display special skills in generating and controlling vivid images tend to benefit more from visualization than do counterparts who lack such abilities. In summary, there is now considerable evidence (much of it experimental) to support the efficacy of mental practice as a technique for improving the performance of a variety of sport skills. These skills include not only "closed" actions (i.e. ones which are self-paced and performed in a relatively static environment) such as golf putting or place-kicking in rugby but also "open" or reactive skills. For example, the rugby tackle (McKenzie and Howe, 1991) and the counter-attacking forehand in table tennis (Lejeune et al., 1994) have shown improvements under mental rehearsal training.

Critical evaluation of research on mental practice

At first glance, the preceding evidence on the efficacy of mental practice conveys the impression of a vibrant and well-established research field in cognitive sport psychology. But closer inspection reveals a less satisfactory picture. Specifically, as we mentioned in the previous section, MP research has encountered many conceptual and methodological criticisms over its century-long history (Murphy and Martin, 2002). Of these criticisms, perhaps the two most persistent concerns have been the "validation" problem and an issue stemming from a lack of field research in the area. The validation problem can be conveyed by a simple question. How do we know that people who claim to be imagining a designated skill are actually using mental imagery? In other words, how can we validate people's subjective reports about their imagery experiences? Let us now sketch these problems in more detail.

The validation problem: how do we know that athletes are actually using imagery?

At the beginning of this chapter, we encountered a quotation from Jenson Button which provided an anecdotal testimonial to the value of mental imagery. As critical psychologists, however, should we accept at face value what athletes and performers tell us about their imagery experiences? After all, cognitive researchers (e.g. Nisbett and Wilson, 1977) and sport psychologists (e.g. Brewer et al., 1991) have warned us that people's retrospective reports on their own mental processes are susceptible to a variety of memory biases and other distortions (e.g. "response sets" whereby people may wish to convey the impression that they have a good or vivid imagination). Unfortunately, few researchers over the past century have attempted either to keep precise records of the imagery scripts used by participants in MP studies or otherwise to validate athletes' reports of their alleged imagery experiences. This neglect is probably attributable to the fact that in order to validate these latter reports, sport psychology researchers require either objective methods (e.g. functional brain imaging techniques to find out if the imagery centres in the brain are activated when the person claims to be visualizing; see Kosslyn et al.,

2001) or experimental procedures (e.g. manipulation checks such as asking people detailed questions about their images; see Murphy and Martin, 2002).

Although the use of brain imaging technology with athletes is prohibited by cost and inconvenience at present, progress has been made in devising theoretically based procedures to check if athletes are really using imagery when they claim to be doing so. For example, Moran and MacIntyre (1998) checked the veracity of canoe slalomists' imagery reports (see Box 6.3) by using a theoretical principle derived from Decety et al. (1989) and MacIntyre (1996). Specifically, this proposition suggests that the greater the congruence between the imagined time and "real" time to complete a mental journey, the more likely it is that imagery is involved. This mental **chronometric paradigm** offers an intriguing way to check whether or not athletes are actually using imagery when claiming to do so. To explore what can be learned from comparing the time it takes to complete actual and imaginary tasks, try the exercise in Box 6.4.

Box 6.4 In the spotlight Mental chronometry in action: exploring the congruence between actual and imagined movements

What is the relationship between imagining an action and actually doing it? Using the mental chronometric paradigm (see Guillot and Collet, 2005, 2010), it is now possible to investigate motor imagery objectively by comparing the duration required to execute real and imagined actions. The logic here is as follows. If imagined and executed actions rely on similar motor representations and activate certain common brain areas (e.g. the parietal and prefrontal cortices, the pre-motor and primary cortices; see Gueugneau et al., 2008), the temporal organization of imagined and actual actions should also be similar. If that is so, there should be a close correspondence between the time required to *mentally* perform a given action and that required for its *actual* execution. Using this logic, Calmels et al. (2006) examined the temporal congruence between actual and imagined movements in gymnastics. They found that the overall times required to perform and imagine a complex gymnastic vault were broadly similar, regardless of the imagery perspective used (i.e. imagining oneself from a first-person perspective or from a third-person perspective). However, the temporal congruence between actual and imagined actions is mediated by a number of factors. Guillot and Collet (2005) concluded that when the skills to be performed are largely automatic (e.g. reaching, grasping) or occur in cyclical movements (e.g. walking, rowing), there is usually a high degree of temporal congruence between actual and imagined performance. But when the skills in question involve complex, attention-demanding movements (e.g. golf putting, tennis serving), people tend to *overestimate* their imagined duration. Although this use of mental chronometry has proved very helpful in motor imagery research, it needs to be augmented by other techniques in order to identify the cognitive mechanisms mediating the relationship between imagined and actual skilled performance. One possible solution to this problem is to use eye-tracking technology (see Chapter 7) as an objective method for investigating online cognitive processing during "eyes open" motor imagery. By comparing the eye movements of people engaged in mental and physical practice, we

continued ...

> **Box 6.4 continued**
>
> may be able to investigate the cognitive processes (especially those concerned with attention) that are activated by imaginary action (see Heremans et al., 2008).
>
> To experience the mental chronometry in action, try this exercise (adapted from Robertson, 2002) at home. Imagine that you are about to write down your name, address and phone number on a sheet of paper. Before you begin this mental task, make sure the second hand of your watch is at the zero position. Then, make a note of how long it took you to write the three pieces of information in your mind's eye. Next, find another piece of paper and repeat the writing exercise. Now, compare the two times that you recorded. If you were to repeat this exercise several times, you would find that the time it takes to write down your name, address and phone number is about the same as it takes to complete this task mentally.

Perhaps not surprisingly, the temporal congruence between actual and imagined movements seems to be affected by intervening variables such as the nature of the skill being performed and the level of expertise of the performers. Reed (2002) compared physical execution times for springboard dives with the time taken to execute this skill mentally. Three groups of divers were used: experts, intermediate performers and novices. Results revealed that, in general, visualization time increased with the complexity of the dives. Also, by contrast with the experts and novices, visualized dive execution time was slower than physical dive execution time. A further complication within this field of mental chronometry emerged from a study by Orliaguet and Coello (1998). Briefly, these researchers found little or no similarity between the timing of actual and imagined putting movements in golfers. Until recently, most research on the congruence between actual and imagined movement execution used skilled tasks (e.g. canoe slalom, diving) in which there were no environmental constraints imposed on the motor system of the performer. However, Papaxanthis et al. (2003) conducted a remarkable study in which cosmonauts were tested on actual and imagined motor skills (e.g. climbing stairs, jumping and walking) before and after a six month space flight. The specific issue of interest to these researchers was the degree to which a long exposure to microgravity conditions could affect the duration of actual and imagined movements. Results showed that, in general, the cosmonauts performed the actual and imagined movements with similar durations before and after the space flight. Papaxanthis et al. (2003) interpreted this finding to indicate that motor imagery and actual movement execution are affected by similar adaptation processes and share common neural pathways. More recently, O'Shea and Moran (2016) used chronometric and **"pupillometry"** (the measurement of changes in pupil dilation as a function of cognitive processing; see Chapter 5) methods to explore the relationship between the executed and imagined movements of expert pianists. Results showed that the pupil-size measurements of pianists during executed and imagined performance were similar, thus supporting functional equivalence theory (see later).

In summary, the fact that the timing of mentally simulated lengthy actions tends to resemble closely the actual movement times involved suggests that motor imagery is functionally equivalent to motor production. Let us now return to the issue of how to assess the veracity of athletes' imagery reports. Another possibility in this regard is to validate such experiences through **functional equivalence theory**. To explain, until the 1980s, the mechanisms underlying mental imagery were largely unknown. However, important theoretical progress on this issue occurred with the discovery that imagery shares some neural pathways and mechanisms with like-modality perception (Farah, 1984; Kosslyn, 1994) and with the preparation and production of motor movements (Jeannerod, 2001). This postulated overlap of neural representations between imagery, perception and motor execution is known as the functional equivalence hypothesis (e.g. Finke, 1979; Jeannerod, 1994). To illustrate, P. Johnson (1982) investigated the effects of imagined movements on the recall of a learned motor task and concluded that "imagery of movements has some functional effects on motor behaviour that are in some way *equivalent* to actual movements" (P. Johnson, 1982, p. 363; italics ours). Other studies (e.g. Roland and Friberg, 1985) suggested a functional equivalence between imagery and perception because "most of the neural processes that underlie like-modality perception are also used in imagery" (Kosslyn et al., 2001, p. 641). According to the functional equivalence hypothesis, mental imagery and perception are functionally equivalent in the sense that they are mediated by similar **neuropsychological** pathways in the brain. Accordingly, interference should occur when athletes are required to activate perceptual and imagery processes concurrently in the same sensory modality. This interference should manifest itself in errors and longer response times when athletes face this dual-task situation. Interestingly, as Figure 6.3 shows, interference can also occur between mental imagery and perception in other situations in everyday life such as driving a car while listening to the radio. Why is it so difficult to use perception and imagination in the same sensory modality? See Box 6.5

Figure 6.3 It is dangerous to listen to a football match while driving a car

Box 6.5 In the spotlight Why you should not listen to football commentaries while driving: interference between imagery and action

It has long been known that people have great difficulty in perceiving and imagining information presented in the same sensory modality. Indeed, research by the British Transport Research Laboratory showed that listening to sport on the radio can affect drivers more than being drunk at the wheel (Massey, 2010). Furthermore, during simulated driving scenarios, there were nearly 50 per cent more incidents involving hard braking while motorists were listening to sport commentaries on the radio than when drivers were driving without the presence of distractions. To experience this difficulty of trying to engage in perception while imagining, try to form a mental image of a friend's face while reading this page. If you are like most people, you should find this task rather difficult because the cognitive activities of forming a visual image and reading text on a page draw upon the same neural pathways. Another example of this "like-modality" interference problem occurs if you try to imagine your favourite song in your "mind's ear" while listening to music on the radio. Just as before, auditory perception and auditory imagery interfere with each other because both tasks compete for the same processing pathways in the brain. An interesting practical implication of this interference phenomenon is that you should not listen to football matches while driving your car because both tasks require visual processing. This time, unfortunately, cognitive interference could result in a nasty accident (see Figure 6.3). Similar interference could occur if you try to visualize an action while driving.

The idea of using cognitive interference to validate imagery reports has certain obvious limitations, however. For example, apart from being modality-specific, it is rather unwieldy if not impractical as it depends on finding a suitable pair of perceptual and imagery tasks. Let us now turn to the second problem afflicting MP research. Why have there been so few imagery studies conducted on elite athletes who have to learn and perform sport skills in field settings?

Lack of field research problem in MP research

Earlier in this chapter, we indicated that most research on mental practice has been carried out in laboratories rather than in real-life settings. Unfortunately, this trend has led to a situation in which few studies on MP have used "subjects who learned actual sport skills, under the same conditions and time periods in which sport activities are typically taught" (Isaac, 1992, p. 192). This neglect of field research is probably attributable to the fact that studies of this type are very time-consuming to conduct – which is a major drawback for elite athletes whose training and travel schedules are usually very busy. In addition, laboratory studies offer a combination of convenience and experimental control which is not easily rivalled in research methodology (see Chapter 1 for a brief summary of research methods in sport and exercise psychology). Since about 2000, there has been an upsurge of interest in "single-case" multiple-baseline research designs (for a comprehensive review of these designs, see Barker et al., 2011). In this paradigm, all participants not only receive the treatment but also act as their own controls because they are required to spend some time earlier in a baseline condition. A major advantage of these research designs is that they cater for individual differences because the intervention in question is administered at different times for each of the different participants in the study. As yet, however, only a handful of imagery studies in sport (e.g. Casby and Moran, 1998) have used single-case research designs.

Despite the conceptual and methodological criticisms discussed above, few researchers deny that MP is effective in improving certain sport skills in certain situations. So, what theoretical mechanisms could account for this MP effect?

Theories of mental practice: overview

Although the efficacy of MP has been demonstrated repeatedly, the precise psychological mechanisms underlying symbolic rehearsal remain unclear. As Foerster et al. (2013) put it, "the neural mechanisms underlying this effect are unknown" (p. 786). The main reason for this equivocal state of affairs is that most MP studies are "one-shot" variations of a standard experimental paradigm (described in the previous section) rather than explicit hypothesis-testing investigations. Nevertheless, we can distinguish between three different waves of theory-building in the attempt to understand the mechanisms underlying MP: early conceptual approaches (e.g. Jacobson, 1931; Sackett, 1934, 1935); applied models in sport psychology (e.g. Holmes and Collins, 2001; Guillot and Collet, 2008); and cognitive neuroscience accounts derived from simulation theory (e.g. Jeannerod, 2001, 2004, 2006).

Evaluation of wave 1: neuromuscular and symbolic learning accounts of MP

The two most prominent early conceptual approaches to MP in the 1930s are the neuromuscular (e.g. Jacobson, 1932) and **cognitive or symbolic theory of mental practice** (Sackett, 1934, 1935) accounts. Although these approaches are often portrayed as "theories" of MP (e.g. see Druckman and Swets, 1988), they were not actually published as such and hence lack many of the essential requirements (e.g. explicit assumptions, falsifiable predictions) of formal scientific models.

The main prediction of the neuromuscular approach to MP is Jacobson's (1932) suggestion that "during imagination or recollection of muscular acts … contraction occurs in some of the muscle-fibers which would engage in the actual performance of the act" (p. 694). Accordingly, MP of an action is deemed to be effective because it is alleged to elicit tiny "innervations" in the peripheral muscles that are actually used in physical performance of the action in question. This neuromuscular account of MP is based on a theory that we mentioned earlier in this chapter – Carpenter's (1891) ideo-motor principle which proposed that all thoughts have muscular concomitants: "ideas, which take full possession of the mind, and from which it cannot free itself, may excite ideo-motor actions" (pp. 124–125). By contrast, the symbolic approach (e.g. Sackett, 1934) suggests that MP works by facilitating central symbolic coding of the sequence of movements in the action to be learned. Unfortunately, Sackett's (1935) main hypothesis about mental practice – that "the influence of such rehearsal is limited to those skills in which there is ideational representation of the movements involved" (p. 113) – seems tautologous. This is so because it is simply a reassertion of the claim it allegedly supports: namely, that imaginatively based symbolic coding "works" best on skills which are amenable to such symbolic coding.

How well are the neuromuscular and symbolic learning accounts of MP supported by relevant evidence? In order to corroborate a neuromuscular explanation of MP, evidence is required to show that there is a strong positive relationship between the muscular activity elicited by imagery of a given skill and that detected during the actual performance of this skill. Unfortunately, a recurrent difficulty for neuromuscular accounts of MP is that there is no *direct* evidence that muscle activation during imagery is associated with improved motor performance. As Guillot et al. (2012a) concluded: "research has not yet demonstrated that the increase in muscle activity fully contributes to performance enhancement" (p. 6). With regard to symbolic learning theory, some evidence is available to support the hypothesis that MP is especially suitable for sensori-motor tasks which involve the sequencing of movements (Driskell et al., 1994). However, it does not easily explain how MP can increase muscle strength (e.g. Reiser et al., 2011; Sidaway and Trzaska, 2005).

Evaluation of wave 2: applied models of motor imagery/mental practice

The second wave of theory-building in MP research occurred with the development of applied models (e.g. Holmes and Collins, 2001; Guillot and Collet, 2008; Murphy et al., 2008) designed to improve the efficacy of MI interventions. Perhaps the most influential of these models is the PETTLEP approach postulated by Holmes and Collins (2001; see also Wakefield et al., 2013, for a critical review of this model).

Explicitly endorsing a "functional equivalence approach" (see our earlier explanation of this term), Holmes and Collins (2001) suggested that "if physical and mental practice are equivalent, then many of the procedures shown to be efficacious in physical practice should also be applied in mental practice" (p. 62). Regrettably, as we shall explain below, this proposition has spawned confusion among researchers who have subsequently tested the PETTLEP model. Before analysing this confusion, however, a brief explanation of the model itself is required.

In an effort to develop a theoretically based checklist for the effective implementation of mental imagery intervention in sport, Holmes and Collins (2001) drew upon Lang's (1977, 1979) **bio-informational theory of imagery** and the functional equivalence hypothesis in **neuroscience** (described earlier) to produce the PETTLEP model. The acronym PETTLEP encapsulated seven practical issues to be considered when designing MP scripts and implementing imagery interventions for optimal efficacy in sport. To explain, "P" refers to the athlete's physical response to the sporting situation, "E" is the environment in which the imagery is performed, "T" is the imagined task, "T" refers to timing (or the pace at which the imagery is performed), "L" is a learning or memory component of imagery, "E" refers to the emotions elicited by the imagery and "P" designates the type of visual imagery perspective used by the practitioner (either first person or third person; see earlier in chapter). Overall, the PETTLEP model proposes that in order to produce optimal "behavioural matching between imagery and action" (Wakefield et al., 2013, p. 117), mental imagery interventions should take into consideration each of the preceding aspects of imagery. Thus, Wakefield et al. (2013) concluded that "a number of studies report that imagery interventions based on PETTLEP principles tend to produce significant improvements in skill and strength performance relative to traditional imagery interventions" (pp. 115–116). Extending these studies, Battaglia et al. (2014) compared the efficacy of a video observation-and-PETTLEP trained group of elite rhythmic gymnasts relative to a group trained in physical practice only, over a six week duration. Results showed that the former group improved their jumping performance significantly more than did the group engaged in physical practice only

Unfortunately, despite its plausibility, the PETTLEP model is afflicted by major conceptual confusion arising from a misunderstanding of the meaning of "functional equivalence" (see Box 6.6 below).

Box 6.6 Thinking critically about … the PETTLEP model of motor imagery: functional equivalence or behavioural matching?

Originally, the term "functional equivalence" designated the concept of partially overlapping *neural* circuitry between imagined and executed action (or the idea that "motor imagery and action preparation and execution share related neural activity"; Wakefield et al., 2013, p. 109). Recently, however, some PETTLEP researchers have used it to refer to imagery/behavioural harmonization (or "the matching of imagery condition behaviours with those of action preparation and execution"; Wakefield et al., 2013, p. 109). This behavioural matching interpretation of functional equivalence is apparent in the suggestion by Winter and Collins (2013) that imagery practitioners should "monitor the equivalence to the physical task to enhance the efficacy of their practice" (p. 301). Additional misunderstanding of functional equivalence is evident in other studies that have tested the predictions of the PETTLEP model. For example, consider the claim by Ramsey et al. (2008) that "the degree of equivalence between the imagery experience and the physical experience is a major determinant of imagery's effectiveness in modulating behaviour" (p. 209). This claim is questionable because it suggests that functional equivalence occurs at the *phenomenological* level – between the *experience* of imagining a skill or movement and that of performing it – rather than at the neural level. By contrast, pioneers of the concept of functional equivalence (e.g. Finke, 1979) postulated that it occurs at the neural and/or representational level – *not* experientially. The difference between these levels is evident from the fact that imagining a marathon does not make one feel as tired or as sore as if one actually competed in the event. Logically, therefore, by confusing phenomenological with representational levels of analysis, Ramsey et al. (2008) appear to have made a "category mistake" (Ryle, 1949) – a conceptual error that occurs when concepts are allocated "to logical types to which they do not belong" (p. 19). Another example of this misunderstanding of functional equivalence is apparent when Cumming and Ramsey

continued …

Box 6.6 continued

(2009) hypothesised that "imagery *more functionally equivalent* to actual performance will have more pronounced effects on subsequent performance compared to less functionally equivalent imagery" (p. 20, italics ours). This phrase "more functionally equivalent" has also been employed by Callow et al. (2013). Unfortunately, it is problematic because it assumes that an objective independent index of degree of functional equivalence is available. But, because no such measure exists at present, we cannot assess the "amount" of putative functional equivalence between two processes. Logically, therefore, any attempt to provide a post hoc "explanation" of a set of experimental results by ascribing them to a factor (i.e. functional equivalence) that cannot be measured independently seems circular. As a consequence, explanations that invoke "functional equivalence" must be treated with caution in the absence of independent validation evidence. Incidentally, for a comprehensive discussion of the problems of circular reasoning (or "double dipping") in psychology and neuroscience, see Hahn (2011) and Kriegeskorte et al. (2009).

Critical thinking questions

Despite its clear theoretical origins, the PETTLEP approach is hampered by certain semantic problems. For example, consider its understanding of functional equivalence. According to Wakefield et al. (2013), "the multiple meanings of functional equivalence have given rise to a decade of confusion in the sports imagery literature" (p. 109). These authors also concluded that this term "may have been more problematic than helpful for the validity of the PETTLEP model" (p. 110). Accordingly, Wakefield et al. (2013) recommended that the term "behavioural matching" should replace "functional equivalence" in research testing the PETTLEP model. Clearly, a precise analysis of the meaning of functional equivalence is required if progress is to be achieved in theoretical understanding of the mechanisms underlying MP.

Evaluation of wave 3: cognitive neuroscientific accounts of MI derived from simulation theory

The most recent wave of theory-building in research on MP was inspired by the simulation theory of action representation (Jeannerod, 1994, 2001, 2004, 2006). As we explained earlier, this theory postulates that "motor imagery ... should involve, in the subject's motor brain, neural mechanisms similar to those operating during the real action" (Jeannerod, 2001, pp. S103–S104) – the functional equivalence hypothesis (explained earlier in this paper).

At first glance, this hypothesis appears to be corroborated by a wealth of empirical evidence derived from neuroimaging, psychophysiological and experimental studies (e.g. see Burianová et al., 2013; Guillot et al., 2012b; Hétu et al., 2013). For example, neuroimaging studies showed that mentally simulated and actually executed actions share similar internal motor representations – especially those involved in motor planning – and activate partially overlapping cortical regions called the "core network" (Sauvage et al., 2013). Second, imagined and executed movements tend to activate psychophysiological systems to similar degrees (for review, see Collet et al., 2013). Third, experimental studies using chronometric measures indicate that there is a close correspondence between duration of imagined skills/movements and that required to actually execute them (for reviews, see Guillot and Collet, 2005; Guillot et al., 2012b). However, when we look more critically at the degree to which the preceding evidence supports the predictions of simulation theory, certain problems become apparent. In particular, these problems concern the clarity and testability of the functional equivalence hypothesis, which is a key tenet of this theory.

Going to the heart of the matter, what exactly does the functional equivalence hypothesis *actually* predict? Unfortunately, the answer to this question is not clear because it appears to depend on the specific psychological processes (e.g. psychophysiological, neural) in question. To illustrate, consider the apparently different versions of this hypothesis provided by Jeannerod (2006) in his chapter on imagined actions. Specifically, in a discussion of dynamic changes in physiological parameters during motor imagery, he asserted that "... imagining a movement relies on the *same mechanisms* as actually performing it, except for the fact that it execution is blocked" (p. 28, italics ours). But in the next sentence, he claimed that "this assumption of a functional equivalence of dynamic imagery and overt action generates a specific prediction, namely, that one should find in motor imagery and related phenomena physiological correlates *similar* to those measured during real action" (pp. 28–29; italics ours). Later in the same chapter, in a discussion of the problem of motor inhibition during the representation of actions, he postulated that "imagined actions ... activate motor areas *almost to the same extent* as executed actions ..." (p. 39, italics ours). Given the complexity of the processes involved, and the subtle distinctions between the words "same", "similar" and "almost to the same extent", it is hardly surprising that applied imagery researchers such as Gould et al. (2014) have mistakenly assumed that the neural substrates of imagined and executed actions are exactly "the same" (p. 62). Unfortunately, such questionable inferences seem inevitable unless the clarity of expression of the functional equivalence hypothesis is improved. This issue of imprecision raises the related problem of the testability of this hypothesis. In this regard, how much overlap is required between the neural substrates of imagined and executed actions in order to corroborate the hypothesis that such processes are "functionally equivalent"? Unfortunately, this question seems intractable at present because there is, as yet, no agreed objective measure of "amount" of functional equivalence. So, what is the best current explanation of mental practice effects?

Explaining mental practice/motor imagery effects

As we indicated earlier in the chapter, Jeannerod's (2001) simulation theory postulated that imagined and executed actions share, to some extent, certain mental representations and underlying mechanisms (see brief review in Moran et al., 2012). This shared motor representation facilitates certain forms of functional equivalence between actual and imagined actions. For example, Debarnot et al. (2014) concluded that the brain changes that occur during *mental* practice of a given motor skill tend to mimic closely those that occur after *physical* practice of the same skill. Building on simulation theory, Ridderinkhof and Brass (2015) developed a model of mental practice/motor imagery called "predictive-processing theory". This theory postulates that motor imagery works through an internal emulation process involving the anticipation of action effects. This emulation mechanism seems to be implemented in brain regions that partially overlap with those regulating overt motor behaviour (e.g. the cerebellum, basal ganglia). According to Ridderinkhof and Brass (2105), the motor representation triggers an internal "emulation" process of the planned motor act that has a high degree of similarity to the actual motor output. The comparison of the anticipated action effect and the internal emulation of the motor act provides an error signal that forms the basis for improving motor performance – even if the actual movement is inhibited. At the neural level, a network of brain regions that is highly overlapping but not identical to the overt motor performance network is involved in kinaesthetic motor imagery (KMI). The kinematic details and precise timing parameters of the motor emulation are probably provided by the cerebellum.

Conclusions about research on mental practice in athletes

In summary, research on MP has shown that the systematic covert rehearsal of motor movements and sport skills has a small but significant positive effect on their actual performance. But this conclusion must be tempered by at least three cautionary notes. First, as Box 6.7 shows, mental practice effects are influenced by a number of intervening variables.

Box 6.7 Thinking critically about ... the effects of mental practice on sport performance

Despite an abundance of research on mental practice since the 1960s, there is a dearth of theoretically driven studies on the nature of, and cognitive mechanisms underlying, motor imagery processes in athletes. Therefore, any conclusions about the effects of MP on sporting performance – especially at the elite level – must be regarded as somewhat tentative because they reflect extrapolations from a body of research literature that was developed using rather different tasks and research designs from those employed in sport psychology. For example, for reasons of convenience and control, the criterion tasks employed by most MP researchers tend to be laboratory tasks (e.g. maze-learning) rather than complex sport skills (e.g. the golf drive). In addition, traditional studies of mental practice have adopted "between groups" experimental designs in laboratory settings rather than either single-case studies or field experiments. Clearly, future studies of mental practice in athletes will benefit from the use of more complex and ecologically valid sport skills than those used to date and also from the adoption of a wider range of experimental research designs than has been evident until now. Nevertheless, there is at least one important lesson to be learned by motor imagery researchers in sport psychology from traditional studies of MP. Specifically, investigators in the latter field have evaluated a range of intervening variables that affect the relationship between MP and skilled performance. These intervening variables offer crucial clues to the design of successful motor imagery interventions. Schuster et al. (2011) conducted a systematic review of the research literature on mental practice in an effort to identify the key elements of successful motor imagery interventions reported in 133 studies in five different disciplines – sport (i.e. research using athlete populations), psychology (i.e. research using healthy participants who were not athletes), education, medicine and music. Schuster et al. (2011) discovered that, in general, successful imagery interventions had a number of key training elements. For example, the imagery training was conducted in individual sessions and added after physical practice of the skill being targeted. In addition, the participants received acoustic and detailed imagery instructions and kept their eyes closed while imagining the execution of the skill. The imagery perspective that seemed to work best was an internal/kinaesthetic one.

Critical thinking questions

All too often, studies on mental practice in sport fail to include either an imagery test or a manipulation check on whether or not participants actually adhered to the imagery instructions provided. Why do you think it is important to evaluate the imagery skills of participants in mental practice research? (As a hint, would it be helpful to find out if people's imagery scores changed over the course of the intervention? If so, why?) Is it possible to evaluate an imagery intervention in the absence of a manipulation check that imagery instructions were followed adequately? Do you think that the duration of a motor imagery intervention affects its efficacy? Give reasons for your answer – and then check your ideas with what Schuster et al. (2011) found in their review.

Second, research on imagery processes in athletes is hampered by inadequate theoretical explanation of the psychological mechanisms underlying MP effects. In this regard, however, the weight of evidence at present tends to favour the functional equivalence model of mental rehearsal. The third cautionary note arises from the possibility that MP research may constrain our understanding of imagery use in athletes. To explain, as Murphy and Martin (2002) observed, research on the symbolic rehearsal of movements and skills may blind us to the many other ways in which athletes use imagery in sport. Put differently, MP research "offers little guidance regarding the many uses of imagery by athletes beyond simple performance rehearsal" (Murphy and Martin, 2002, p. 417). We shall return to this last point in the fifth section of this chapter.

Measuring mental imagery skills in sport

Research on the measurement of mental imagery has a long and somewhat controversial history in psychology. As explained in Box 6.1, it goes back to the earliest days of experimental psychology when Galton (1883) asked people to describe their images and to rate them for vividness. Not surprisingly, this introspective, self-report strategy proved contentious. In particular, as we explained earlier in the chapter, Behaviourists like Watson (1913) attacked it on the grounds that people's imagery experiences could neither be verified independently nor linked directly with observable behaviour. Fortunately, theoretical advances in cognitive psychology (see Kosslyn et al., 2006; Pearson et al., 2015) and the advent of brain imaging techniques in neuroscience (discussed earlier in this chapter) overcame these methodological objections and led to a resurgence of interest in imagery research. Thus imagery is now measured via a combination of techniques that include experimental tasks (e.g. asking people to make decisions and solve problems using imagery processes), timing of behaviour (e.g. comparing imagined with actual time taken to execute an action), neuroscientific procedures (e.g. recording what happens in brain areas activated by imagery tasks) and psychometric tools (e.g. for the assessment of imagery abilities and imagery use in athletes). Arising from these empirical strategies, two questions are especially relevant to this chapter. First, how can psychologists measure people's private experience of mental imagery? Second, what progress has been made in assessing imagery processes in athletes? In order to answer these questions, a brief theoretical introduction is necessary.

Earlier in this chapter, we learned that although mental images are ephemeral constructs, they differ from each other along several psychological dimensions such as vividness and controllability. Over the past century, these two dimensions of imagery have been targeted by psychologists in their attempt to measure this construct. Throughout this period, two different strategies have been used to assess these imagery dimensions. Whereas the subjective approach is based on the idea of asking people about the nature of their images, the objective approach requires people to complete visualization tasks that have right or wrong answers. The logic here is that the better people perform on these tasks, the more imagery skills they are alleged to possess.

These approaches to imagery measurement can be illustrated as follows. The vividness of an image (which refers to its clarity or sharpness) can be assessed using self-report scales in which people are asked to comment on certain experiential aspects of their mental representation. For example, close your eyes and form an image of a friend's face. On a scale of 1 (meaning "no image at all") to 5 (meaning "as clear as in normal vision"), how vivid is your mental image of this face? Similarly, the clarity of an auditory image might be evaluated by asking people such questions as: "If you close your eyes, how well can you hear the imaginary sound of an ambulance siren?" Unfortunately, subjective self-report scales of imagery have certain limitations (Moran, 1993). For example, they are subject to contamination from response sets such as social desirability. Put simply, most people are eager to portray themselves as having a good or vivid imagination regardless of their true skills in that area. For this reason, objective tests of imagery have been developed. Thus the controllability dimension of a visual mental image (which refers to the ease and accuracy with which it can be transformed symbolically) can be measured objectively by requesting people to complete tasks which are known to require visualization abilities. In the Group Mental Rotations Test (GMRT; Vandenberg and Kuse, 1978), people have to make judgements about whether or not the spatial orientation of certain three-dimensional target figures matches (i.e. is congruent with) or does not match (i.e. is incompatible with) various alternative shapes. The higher people's score is on this test, the stronger are their image control skills. For a more comprehensive account of the history of imagery measurement, as well as of the conceptual and methodological issues surrounding it, see J. Richardson (1999).

Let us now turn to the second question guiding this section. What progress has been made in assessing imagery processes in athletes (see also T. Morris et al., 2005)? In general, two types of instruments have been developed in this field: tests of athletes' imagery *skills/abilities* and tests of their imagery *use*. Although an exhaustive review of these measures lies beyond the scope of this chapter, some general trends and issues in imagery measurement may be summarized as follows.

First, among the most popular and psychometrically impressive tests of imagery skills in athletes are the revised version of the Vividness of Movement Imagery Questionnaire (VMIQ-2; R. Roberts et al., 2008) and the revised version of the Movement Imagery Questionnaire (MIQ-3; Williams, et al., 2012). The original VMIQ was a twenty-four-item measure of "visual imagery of movement itself and imagery of kinaesthetic sensations" (Isaac et al., 1986, p. 24). Each of the items presented a different movement or action to be imagined (e.g. riding a bicycle). Respondents are required to rate these items in two ways: "watching somebody else" and "doing it yourself". The ratings were given on a five-point scale where 1 = "perfectly clear and as vivid as normal vision" and 5 = "no image at all". An amended version of this test called the Vividness of Movement Imagery Questionnaire-2 (VMIQ-2) was published by R. Roberts et al. (2008). This test consists of twelve items and assesses the ability to form mental images of a variety of movements visually and kinaesthetically. The visual component is further subdivided into "external" and "internal" visual imagery. Respondents are required to imagine each of the twelve movements and to rate the vividness of each item on a Likert-type scale from 1 ("perfectly clear and vivid") to 5 ("no image at all"). The VMIQ-2 displays impressive psychometric characteristics. For example, Williams et al. (2012) reported internal consistency (Cronbach's alpha) coefficients of 0.94 (for the external visual imagery subscale), 0.93 (for the internal visual imagery subscale) and 0.93 (for the kinaesthetic imagery subscale).

Next, the MIQ-3 (Williams et al., 2012) is a twelve-item questionnaire that assesses the ease or difficulty of generating images of four different movements (i.e. knee lift, jump, arm movement, and waist bend) from three different imagery perspectives – that of kinaesthetic imagery (KI), external visual imagery (EVI) and internal visual imagery (IVI). For each item, participants are required to read a description of the movement, physically perform the movement, and then imagine that movement from the designated perspective. Respondents are then required to rate the resultant image on a seven-point Likert scale ranging from 1 (*very hard to see/feel*) to 7 (*very easy to see/feel*). Subscale scores range from 4 to 28 and higher scores reflect better imagery ability. According to the test developers, the MIQ-3 displays good internal consistency. For example, Williams et al. (2012) reported Cronbach's α values for the subscales as follows: 0.85 (kinaesthetic imagery), 0.83 (external visual imagery) and 0.79 (internal visual imagery).

Next, the Sport Imagery Questionnaire (SIQ; C. Hall et al., 1998, 2005) is a popular, theory-based and reliable tool for measuring the frequency with which athletes use imagery for motivational and cognitive purposes. Based on Paivio's (1985) proposal that imagery affects behaviour through motivational and cognitive mechanisms operating at general and specific levels, the

---

Box 6.8 In the spotlight Comparing self-report and mental chronometry measures of motor imagery ability: an empirical investigation

Earlier in the chapter, we explained that motor imagery (MI) ability can be assessed using a variety of self-report psychometric tests (which typically assess individual differences in imagery dimensions such as vividness and/or controllability) and objective chronometric measures (which are based on a comparison of the difference between the duration of physically executed and imagined actions). Until recently, these different measures of MI were used relatively independently, with little or no analysis of their relationship to each other (but see Saimpont et al., 2015, for an exception to this trend). As a result, it is not clear whether such measures merely duplicate each other or else provide distinctive insights into MI. Against this background, Williams et al. (2015) investigated the relationship between the Movement Imagery Questionnaire (MIQ-3; Williams et al., 2012; described earlier) and a chronometric equivalent of this test. In the latter case, a chronometric measure of MI was obtained by recording the duration of each MIQ-3 movement when physically performed and then imagined. Subsequently, discrepancy scores were calculated. Results showed that for each of the three subscales (kinaesthetic imagery, external visual imagery and internal visual imagery), MI and physical execution times were significantly positively correlated. Thus, people who took longer to physically perform the MIQ-3 movements also took longer to imagine the same movements. Results also indicated that there were no significant correlations between MIQ-3 motor imagery and physical execution times for any of the three different perspectives. S. Williams et al. (2015) interpreted these results as suggesting that the movements used in MIQ-3 are appropriate for use in mental chronometry. They also concluded that the MIQ-3 and its chronometric equivalent appear to assess different aspects of MI. Specifically, they speculated that whereas the MIQ-3 may evaluate people's ability to generate a motor image, the chronometric measure may assess people's ability to maintain and control the image. Clearly, further research is required to test such conjectures empirically.

SIQ is a thirty-item instrument (with five subscales) that asks respondents to rate on a seven-point scale (where 1 = "rarely" and 7 = "often") how often they use five specific categories of imagery: *motivational general-mastery* (e.g. imagining appearing mentally tough, self-confident and in control in front of others), *motivational general-arousal* (e.g. imagining the anxiety, stress and/or excitement associated with competition), *motivational specific* (e.g. imagining achieving an individual goal, such as winning a medal), *cognitive general* (e.g. imagining various strategies, game plans or routines for a competitive event) and *cognitive specific* (e.g. mentally practising specific sport skills). Sample items from these subscales include "I imagine myself appearing self-confident in front of my opponents" (motivational general-mastery), "I imagine the stress and anxiety associated with competing" (motivational general-arousal), "I imagine myself winning a medal" (motivational specific), "I imagine alternative strategies in case my event/game plan fails" (cognitive general) and "I can mentally make corrections to physical skills" (cognitive specific). The six items that comprise each subscale are averaged to yield a score that indicates to what extent respondents use each of the five functions of imagery. Overall, this test appears to have acceptable psychometric characteristics. For example, Mellalieu et al. (2009) reported internal consistency values for the scale that ranged from 0.77 (for the motivational general-arousal subscale) to 0.83 (for the cognitive specific subscale). Another test designed to measure athletes' ability to imagine sport-specific cognitive and motivational content is the Sport Imagery Ability Questionnaire (SIAQ; Williams and Cumming, 2011). This test is a fifteen-item questionnaire which purports to assess the ease with which respondents can imagine five types of imagery functions: skill imagery (images associated with performing various sport skills), strategy imagery (images associated with formulating game plans), goal imagery (images associated with achieving sporting goals and outcomes), affect imagery (images associated with experiencing various sporting feelings and emotions) and mastery imagery (images associated with persisting in the face of adversity). According to Williams and Cumming (2011), the psychometric characteristics of the SIAQ are impressive.

Unfortunately, despite the preceding progress in imagery measurement, a number of conceptual and methodological issues remain in this field (see also T. Morris et al., 2005). First, even though evidence has accumulated from neuroimaging techniques that imagery is a multidimensional construct, most imagery tests in sport and exercise psychology rely on a single imagery scale score. Second, until recently, few imagery tests in sport psychology had either an explicit or an adequate theoretical rationale. This issue prompted Murphy et al. (2008, p. 298) to proclaim that "researchers and theorists need to develop a comprehensive model that will guide imagery investigations". Third, much of the psychometric evidence cited in support of imagery tests in sport psychology comes from the research teams that developed the tests in the first place – which is hardly ideal for independent scientific development. A brief summary of some other issues in the field is contained in Box 6.9.

Box 6.9 Thinking critically about ... imagery tests in sport psychology

Many tests of imagery abilities and imagery use are available in sport psychology (see T. Morris et al., 2005). Which one should you use? Although the answer to this question depends partly on the degree to which the test matches your specific research requirements (e.g. are you studying visual or kinaesthetic imagery or both?), it also depends on psychometric issues. These issues are expressed below in the critical thinking questions.

Critical thinking questions

If the psychometric adequacy of the imagery test is unknown, how would you assess its reliability? What value of a reliability coefficient is conventionally accepted as satisfactory by psychometric researchers? How would you establish the construct validity of an imagery test in sport? Specifically, what other measures of this construct would you use to establish the "convergent validity" of the test? Also, how would you establish the "discriminant validity" of the test (i.e. what measures should your test be unrelated to statistically)? If you were designing an imagery test for athletes from scratch, what precautions would you take to control for response sets (e.g. social desirability) or acquiescence (i.e. the tendency to apply the same rating to all items regardless of the content involved)?

Athletes' use of mental imagery

Having analysed how mental imagery processes have been measured in sport performers, let us now consider how they are *used* by athletes. In general, people use mental imagery for a variety of purposes in everyday life. To illustrate, Kosslyn et al. (1990) asked a sample of university undergraduates to keep a diary or log of their imagery experiences over the course of a week. Results revealed that imagery was used for such functions as problem solving (e.g. trying to work out in advance whether or not a large suitcase would fit into the boot of a car), giving and receiving directions (e.g. using mental maps to navigate through the physical environment), recall (e.g. trying to remember where they had left a lost object), mental practice (e.g. rehearsing what to say in an important interview on the way to work) and motivation (e.g. using images of desirable scenes for mood enhancement purposes). This type of research raises several interesting questions. How widespread is imagery use among athletes (see review by Munroe et al., 2000)? Do elite athletes use it more frequently than less proficient counterparts? For what specific purposes do athletes employ imagery?

Before we explore empirical data on these questions, let us consider briefly some anecdotal reports and textbook accounts of reports on imagery use in sport. In this regard, many testimonials to the value of imagery have emerged from interviews with, and profiles on, athletes in different sports. For example, former world-class performers such as Michael Jordan (basketball), Jack Nicklaus (golf), John McEnroe and Andre Agassi (tennis), George Best and David James (football) all claim to have seen and felt themselves performing key actions successfully in their imagination before or during competition (Begley, 2000). As critical thinkers, however, we should be careful not to be too easily influenced by anecdotal testimonials. A critic once remarked acerbically about another psychologist's work, which was heavily based on colourful examples, that the plural of anecdote is not data! In other words, examples do not constitute empirical evidence. As we explained in Chapter 1, psychologists are wary of attaching too much importance to people's accounts of their own mental processes simply because such insights are often tainted by biases in memory and distortions in reporting. For example, athletes may recall more cases of positive experiences with imagery (i.e. occasions on which their visualization coincided with enhanced performance) than negative experiences with it (where visualization appeared to have no effect).

Turning to the textbooks, many applied sport psychologists have compiled lists of alleged uses of imagery in sport (see Box 6.10).

How can we test the claims made in Box 6.10? To answer this question, two main research strategies have been used by sport psychologists: descriptive and theoretical. Whereas the descriptive approach has tried to establish the *incidence* of general imagery use in athletes, the theoretical approach has examined specific *categories* of imagery use (e.g. imagery as an aid to motivation and cognition) in these performers. These two approaches to imagery use can be summarized as follows.

Box 6.10 Thinking critically about ... athletes' use of mental imagery

Many applied sport psychologists provide lists of alleged applications of mental imagery by athletes. Vealey and Greenleaf (2010) suggested that athletes use imagery to enhance three types of skills: physical (e.g. a golf putt), perceptual (e.g. to develop a strategic game plan) and psychological (e.g. to control arousal levels). Within these three categories, imagery is alleged to be used for the following purposes:

- learning and practising sport skills (e.g. rehearsing a tennis serve mentally before going out to practise it on court)

- learning strategy (e.g. formulating a game plan before a match)

- arousal control (e.g. visualizing oneself behaving calmly in an anticipated stressful situation)

- self-confidence (e.g. "seeing" oneself as confident and successful)

- attentional focusing/refocusing (e.g. focusing on the "feel" of a gymnastics routine)

- error correction (e.g. replaying a golf swing slowly in one's mind in order to rectify any flaws in it)

- interpersonal skills (e.g. imagining the best way to confront the coach about some issue)

- recovery from injury or managing pain (e.g. visualizing healing processes).

Critical thinking questions

Sometimes, speculation goes well beyond the evidence in sport psychology. To explain, there is a big difference between speculating about what athletes *could* use imagery for and verifying what they *actually* use it for in sport situations. For example, few studies have found any evidence that athletes use imagery to enhance either interpersonal skills or recovery from injury. Therefore, despite the unqualified enthusiasm which it commonly receives in applied sport psychology, mental imagery is not a panacea for all ills in sport. Clearly, it is advisable to adopt a sceptical stance when confronted by claims about the alleged use of mental imagery by athletes.

Using the descriptive approach, special survey instruments have been designed to assess imagery use in various athletic populations. This approach has led to some interesting findings. For example, successful athletes appear to use imagery more frequently than do less successful athletes (Durand-Bush et al., 2001). By contrast, Cumming and Hall (2002b) found that recreational sport performers used imagery less than did more proficient counterparts (namely, provincial and international athletes) and also rated it as being less valuable than did the latter group. This trend was apparent even out of season (Cumming and Hall, 2002a). Moreover, as one might expect, visual and kinaesthetic imagery are more popular than other kinds of imagery in athletes (C. Hall, 2001).

Although this type of descriptive research provides valuable baseline data on imagery use among athletes, it does not elucidate the precise tasks or functions for which athletes employ their visualization skills. To fill this gap, a theoretically derived conceptual model of imagery use in athletes was required. C. Hall et al. (1998) postulated a **taxonomy** of imagery use in athletes based on Paivio's (1985) theory that imagery affects both motivational and cognitive processes. As indicated in the previous section, this taxonomy of C. Hall et al. (1998) proposed five categories of imagery use. First, motivational general-mastery involved the imagination of being mentally tough and focused in a forthcoming competitive situation. Second, motivational general-arousal involved imagining the feelings of excitement that accompany an impending competitive performance. Third, motivational specific was implicated in visualizing the achievement of a goal such as winning a race. Fourth, cognitive general imagery occurred when athletes imagined a specific strategy or game plan before or during a match. Fifth, cognitive specific imagery involved mentally rehearsing a skill such as a golf putt or a penalty kick in football.

At first glance, this taxonomy is helpful not only because it distinguishes between imagery *function* and imagery *content* but also because it allows researchers to explore the relationship between these variables and subsequent athletic performance. Short et al. (2002) discovered that both imagery direction (i.e. whether imagery was positive or negative) and imagery function (motivational general-mastery and cognitive specific) can affect people's self-efficacy and performance in golf putting. Despite its heuristic value, however, the classification system by C. Hall et al. (1998) has been criticized for conceptual vagueness. To illustrate, Abma et al. (2002) pointed out that athletes who use cognitive specific imagery regularly (e.g. in rehearsing a particular skill) may be classified as using motivational general-mastery if they believe that mental practice is the best way to boost their confidence. Another limitation of this taxonomy is that it offers no explanation of the cognitive mechanisms underlying imagery processes. Despite such criticisms, the theoretically driven taxonomies developed by C. Hall et al. (1998) and K. Martin et al. (1999) offer greater scope for research on imagery use by athletes than do the rather intuitive classifications promulgated by applied sport psychologists (e.g. Vealey and Greenleaf, 2010).

Let us now summarize some general findings on imagery use in athletes. According to C. Hall (2001), three general trends may be detected in this field. First, athletes tend to use imagery more in pre-competitive than in practice situations – a fact which suggests that they tend to visualize more frequently for the purpose of mental preparation or performance enhancement in competition than for skill acquisition. Second, available evidence suggests that, as predicted by Paivio (1985), imagery is used by athletes for both motivational and cognitive purposes. Although the former category is rather fuzzy and ill-defined, it includes applications like seeing oneself achieving specific goals and feeling oneself being relaxed in competitive situations. It is precisely this latter application that the former British Olympic champion shooter, Richard Faulds, pursued in creating the image of an ice-man prior to winning the 2000 Olympic gold medal for trap-shooting "The image is the ice-man. You walk like an ice-man and think like an ice-man" (quoted in Nichols, 2000, p. 7). With regard to cognitive uses of imagery by athletes, two main applications have been discovered by researchers. First, as is evident from anecdotal and survey evidence, imagery is widely used as a tool for mental rehearsal (a "cognitive specific" application). Second, imagery is often used as a concentration technique. The former England cricket batsman Mike Atherton used to practise in his mind's eye in an effort to counteract anticipated distractions on the big day. This involved visualizing "What's going to come, who's going to bowl, how they are going to bowl, what tactics they will use, what's going to be said to try and get under my skin so that nothing can come as a surprise" (cited in Selvey, 1998). A third general research finding in this field concerns the *content* of athletes' imagery. In this regard, C. Hall (2001, p. 536) claims that athletes tend to use positive imagery (e.g. seeing themselves winning competitive events) and "seldom imagine themselves losing". But is this really true? After all, everyday experience would suggest that many club-level golfers are plagued by negative mental images such as hitting bunkers or striking the ball out of bounds. Nevertheless, C. Hall (2001) concluded that athletes' imagery is generally accurate, vivid and positive in content.

New directions for research on imagery in athletes

Two questions are covered in this section of the chapter. First, what new directions can be identified in research on imagery processes in athletes? Second, does this research shed any light on how the mind works?

At least six new directions may be identified for imagery research on athletes. First, using simulation theory, researchers are beginning to make progress in understanding the neurocognitive mechanisms underlying motor imagery processes in sport (e.g. see Hanakawa, 2016; Ridderinkhof and Brass, 2015). Clearly, empirical studies are required to test the predictions of such simulation theories of motor imagery. Second, very little is known about athletes' **meta-imagery** processes – or their beliefs about the nature and regulation of their own imagery skills (see Moran, 1996). Within this topic, it would be interesting to discover if expert athletes have greater insight into, or control over, their imagery processes than do relative novices (see MacIntyre and Moran, 2007a, 2007b; MacIntyre et al., 2013b). Third, research is required to establish when, and with what effect, athletes use mental imagery in the period immediately prior to competition. Fourth, we need to tackle the old issue of how to validate athletes' reports of their imagery experiences. As we mentioned early in this chapter however, we may be approaching this task with the wrong theory in mind. Put simply, what if imagery were not so much a characteristic that people "have" but something – a cognitive process – that they "do"? If, as Kosslyn et al. (2001) propose, imagery and perception are functionally equivalent, interference should occur when athletes are required to use these processes concurrently in the same modality. As we indicated earlier, this possibility of creating experimental analogues of this type of interference could help to discover whether athletes are really using imagery when they claim to be mentally practising their skills. Psychophysiological indices may also be helpful in "tracking" athletes' imagery experiences. Fifth, more studies are needed to investigate the relationship between **deliberate practice** (defined as a highly structured, focused, purposeful form of practice that involves "trying to exceed one's previous limit, which requires full concentration and effort"; Ericsson & Lehmann, 1999, p. 695; see also Chapter 7) and mental practice (see also Moran, 2016). Sixth, Collet et al. (2011) argued that the multidimensional construct of motor imagery is best measured using a combination of psychometric, behavioural and psychophysiological tools. Furthermore, they proposed a way of combining these different imagery measures into an integrated "motor imagery index". However, this new measure requires additional validation before its widespread usage can be justified. Interestingly, Saimpont et al. (2015) conducted an intriguing study of MI processes recently in which they used a combination of imagery measures of vividness, controllability and timing. Such research provides a robust template for future studies in this field.

Let us now turn to the issue of whether or not imagery research has any implications for the pursuit, in mainstream cognitive psychology, of how the mind works. Moran (2002a) considered several ways in which research on mental imagery in athletes can enrich mainstream cognitive psychology. Up to now, however, cognitive psychology has devoted little attention to the world of athletic performance (although Frederick Bartlett (1932) used tennis and cricket examples when explaining his theory of schemata in the early 1930s). Nevertheless, imagery research in sport may help to enrich cognitive theory in at least two ways. First, it can provide a natural laboratory for the study of neglected topics such as kinaesthetic and meta-imagery processes. For example, relatively little is known about the neural substrates of motor imagery (but see Box 6.2). In addition, it offers a sample of expert participants (see "strength-based approach"; MacIntyre et al., 2013a) and a range of imagery tests (including objective measures like the Test of Ability in Movement Imagery (TAMI); Madan and Singhal, 2013, 2014; described briefly in Box 6.1) which may help researchers to make progress in understanding individual differences in cognitive processes.

Ideas for research projects on imagery in athletes

Here are six suggestions for possible research projects on the topic of mental/motor imagery in sport psychology.

1. First, consider the topic of "embedded" **motor imagery training**. Although there has been a plethora of research on the effects of mental practice/motor imagery training on various sport skills (e.g. Battaglia et al., 2014; also see reviews by Driskell et al., 1994; Wakefield et al., 2013), there has been a dearth of experimental studies on the effects of an "embedded" MI training programme (i.e. one in which athletes are trained to perform imagery between sets of corresponding physical practice trials) on skilled performance (e.g. executing a groundstroke during a rally in tennis). Therefore, it would be interesting to replicate and extend the study by Guillot et al. (2015) on the effects of an embedded MI intervention programme on tennis forehand and backhand groundstroke performance during a rally.

2. Next, it would be interesting to test the validity of the objective Test of Ability in Movement Imagery (TAMI; see Box 6.1) by comparing and contrasting the performance of athletes of different levels of expertise on this test.

3. Next, you may be interested in conducting a research project on **imagery perspective** (i.e. the virtual viewpoint that a person takes when using imagery – either "internal", where a person "looks" at the imagined scene through his or her own eyes, or "external", where the imaginer "looks" at his or her own performance as if watching a video on a movie screen; see discussion earlier in his chapter). Arising from Hardy's (1997) hypothesis that different imagery perspectives have differential effects on skilled performance, it would be interesting to test the suggestion by Callow et al. (2013) that the angle of external visual imagery adopted by the learner could affect sport skill performance. In conducting such a study, however, it is essential to match participants for motor imagery ability as measured by a scale such as the revised version of the Vividness of Movement Imagery Questionnaire (VMIQ-R: R. Roberts et al., 2008) or the Movement Imagery Questionnaire (MIQ-3: Williams et al., 2012).

4. A fourth project idea concerns using the **mental chronometry paradigm** (see Box 6.4; also Guillot and Collet, 2005) to investigate the extent to which the level of *expertise* of the performer affects the congruence between his or her imagined time and the actual time taken to execute a given "closed" skill such as the tennis serve or the golf putting stroke. In general, we would expect that expert athletes should show a closer correspondence between real and imagined time for these skills compared with their novice counterparts.

5. Next, given the relative scarcity of mental practice studies on elite athletes in field settings, it would be interesting to conduct a field study with athletes such as elite rugby or basketball players on the efficacy of mental practice in enhancing skills such as place-kicking or free-throwing, respectively.

6. Finally, consider a possible research project on the construct of "meta-imagery" or people's knowledge of, and control over, their own imagery processes (see Moran, 2002a). By way of background, since the 1980s, cognitive research on mental imagery has been dominated by neuroscientific methods that typically involve comparisons between the imagery performance of participants from clinical populations with those who exhibit apparently normal cognitive functioning. Although this paradigm has been helpful in identifying the basic substrates of imagery processes, it sheds little light on expert–novice differences (explored in detail in Chapter 7). Therefore, to overcome this oversight, MacIntyre et al. (2013a) postulated a "strength-based" approach to the study of mental practice/motor imagery. Briefly, this approach urges researchers to target elite performers (e.g. top athletes) in order to enrich theoretical understanding of the psychological processes that mediate expertise. It would be interesting to compare and contrast the meta-imagery skills of expert and athletes.

Summary

- We began this chapter by introducing mental imagery as a multimodal, cognitive simulation process which enables us to represent in our minds experiences of things which are not physically present or happening right now.

- Both anecdotal and empirical research evidence indicate that this ability is especially useful for the mental rehearsal of future actions. So, the term mental practice (MP) or motor imagery (MI) refers to a form of symbolic rehearsal in which people "see" and "feel" themselves executing a skilled action in their imagination, without overt performance of the physical movements involved.

- Next, having explained what "mental imagery" is, we explored how it can be studied (e.g. using techniques ranging from questionnaires to brain imaging) and discussed the issue of how imagery information is stored in the mind.

- Then, we outlined the nature, types, modalities and dimensions of mental imagery and provided a brief critical evaluation of research on the neural substrates of motor imagery.

- Next, we considered the measurement of mental imagery skills in athletes.

- After that, we sketched some new directions for research on imagery processes in athletes.

- Finally, we outlined some ideas for possible research projects on imagery processes in sport.

7

What lies beneath the surface?
Investigating expertise in sport

Introduction

Whether out of envy or admiration, we have long been fascinated by the exploits of outstanding performers in any field – people who display exceptional talent, knowledge and/or skills in a particular area of human achievement (such as sport). For example, many of us would love to be able to sprint like Usain Bolt, dribble a football like Lionel Messi, drive a golf ball with the power of Rory McIlroy or serve a tennis ball with the skill of Serena Williams. But all we can do is sit and watch as these experts perform apparently impossible athletic feats. In psychology and cognitive neuroscience, research on expertise investigates the mental and neural processes that underlie such exceptional performance – originally, in cognitively rich domains such as chess, but more recently in perceptual-motor activities such as sport. Regardless of the domain under scrutiny, however, certain questions arise when we marvel at the gifts of such expert performers as Bolt, Messi, McIlroy and Williams. For example, are champion athletes born or made? Put differently, what is the relationship between talent, expertise and success in sport? At first glance, the answer to this question seems obvious. If someone has sufficient innate talent and is lucky enough to have received instruction from an excellent coach, then he or she will develop expertise and become successful. But as we shall discover in this chapter, this "talent myth" has largely been discredited by empirical research on the role of practice in the development of expertise (for a review of research in this field, see Hodges and Baker, 2011). Interestingly, Ericsson (2001) observed that "expert performance is similar to an iceberg … only one tenth of the iceberg is visible above the water and the other nine tenths are hidden below it" (p. 2).

For well over a century, scientists have investigated the nature and determinants of expertise. Whereas some early researchers such as Galton (1869) held that genius in any field comes mainly from inherited abilities, others (perhaps most prominently, Anders Ericsson – whose ideas we shall examine in more detail later) have postulated that practice and experience are what really matter. As research findings have accumulated, several flaws have appeared in the "inherited talent" explanation of athletic excellence. First, just like the rest of us, sports stars are often unreliable judges of the factors which influenced their career success. For example, in seeking to explain how they reached the top of the athletic ladder, they may inadvertently *overestimate* the influence of natural ability and *underestimate* the influence of other influences such as environmental factors (see Box 7.9 later in the chapter), physical training regimes and/or the time they spent practising their skills. Second, as coaches and psychologists have discovered, *quality* is better than quantity when it comes to practice. For example, there is a big difference between mindless drills (where athletes repeat basic skills without any specific purpose in mind) and *mindful* practice (also known as "deliberate practice" – where athletes strive purposefully and single-mindedly to achieve specific and challenging goals in a deliberate attempt to improve their skills; discussed later in the chapter). To explain this idea of deliberate practice, consider what Anders Ericsson, the man who coined this term, says about it: "When most people practise, they focus on things they can do effortlessly. Expert practice is different. It entails considerable, specific, and sustained efforts to do something you can't do well – or even at all" (cited in Syed, 2010, pp. 73–74). Third, as is evident from the research cited in this book, success in sport is determined as much by psychological factors (e.g. motivation) and by strategic planning (e.g. anticipating one's opponent's actions, having a "game plan" for a competition) as by innate technical skill. When combined, these three points highlight the importance of experience and practice in determining athletic expertise. This combination of experience and practice lies beneath the surface in Ericsson's (2001) iceberg metaphor of athletic expertise. Thus when we observe a moment of apparently spontaneous genius by Lionel Messi, Tiger Woods or Serena Williams, we should not overlook the fact that this action is a consequence of lots of practice and hard work amounting to at least 10,000 hours or more (see below for an explanation of how this figure was estimated). Similar sentiments were expressed by the former golf champion Gary Player, who quipped paradoxically, "You must work very hard to become a natural golfer!" (cited in MacRury, 1997, p. 95). Although this remark is not intended to dismiss the influence of innate skills in sport, it challenges us to understand the complex interplay that occurs between talent, motivation, practice habits, quality of coaching and family support (see J. Baker and Horton, 2004; Farrow et al., 2007) in shaping athletic expertise. In this regard, as we shall see later in this chapter, some researchers (e.g. Ericsson, 2001, 2002) have gone so far as to proclaim that practice is the *foremost* cause of expert performance in any field. And so, Ericsson and his colleagues have challenged the "talent myth" – the idea that innate ability rather than practice habits is what determines athletic success (Syed, 2010).

Against this background of claims and controversies, this chapter investigates the nature and determinants of athletic expertise. Therefore, it addresses a number of intriguing questions. For example, what makes someone an expert in a given field? Is athletic expertise simply a matter of being endowed with the right genetic "hardware" (e.g. visual acuity skills above the average) or do "software" characteristics such as practice habits and psychological skills play an important role? If sporting excellence lies partly in the mind, how do the knowledge and skills of expert athletes differ from those of less successful counterparts? What stages of learning and development do novice athletes pass through on their journey to expertise? Finally, can research on expertise illuminate any significant principles that might help us to understand how the mind works?

In order to answer these questions, the chapter is organized as follows. In the next section, we explain what "expertise" means and indicate why it has become such an important topic in psychology. The third section addresses the general question of whether athletic success is determined more by hardware or by software characteristics of sport performers. In the fourth section, we outline and evaluate research methods and findings on expert–novice differences in the domain of sport. One of the issues that is raised in this section is the degree to which athletic expertise transfers effectively from one domain to another within a given sport. Specifically, do former top-class football players make expert managers? The fifth section explores the development of expertise in sport performers. Included in this section is an explanation and critique of Ericsson's (1996, 2001) theory that expertise is due mainly to a phenomenon called "deliberate practice". In the sixth section of the chapter, we examine the significance of, and some problems and new directions in, research on expertise in athletes. Finally, some suggestions are provided for possible research projects in this field.

The nature and study of expertise in sport

Expertise, or the growth of specialist knowledge and skills through effortful experience, is currently a "hot topic" both in cognitive psychology (Gobet, 2016; Ullén et al., 2016), cognitive neuroscience (e.g. Ring et al., 2015) and sport psychology (e.g. Swann et al., 2015b; Toner and Moran, 2015). Researchers from these disciplines have generated a considerable volume of studies on the cognitive processes and structures that underlie the skilled performance of experts in various fields ranging from chess to athletic pursuits. To illustrate this trend, expertise has attracted special editions of academic journals such as *Frontiers in Psychology* (Campitelli et al., 2015), *Intelligence* (Detterman, 2014) and *Psychology of Sport and Exercise* (Raab and Harwood, 2015), a comprehensive handbook (Baker and Farrow, 2015), an entire section of the *Handbook of Sport Psychology* (Tenenbaum and Eklund, 2007), and interest from popular science writers (e.g. Colvin, 2010; Gladwell, 2009; Syed, 2010). One index of this trend is evident from the coverage devoted to expertise research in recent handbooks of sport psychology. Specifically, whereas the first edition of the *Handbook of Sport Psychology* (published in 1993) had no chapters on expertise and the second edition (in 2001) had just one chapter, the third edition (2007) has *five* chapters on it. For cognitive psychologists, research on expert–novice differences in sport is important because it provides an empirical window on the topic of knowledge-based perception. Specifically, it can reveal the role of cognitive processes in mediating the relationship between visual perception and skilled action in dynamic yet constrained environments. For psychologists, the study of athletic expertise (see reviews by Hodges and Baker, 2011; Hodges et al., 2006; A. Williams and Ford, 2008) presents at least two intriguing challenges.

Theoretically, it raises the question of how certain people (such as elite athletes) manage to circumvent information-processing limitations when performing complex motor skills (Müller et al., 2009). Methodologically, it poses the challenge of developing objective and valid measures of expert–novice differences. Before we consider the reasons for its popularity among researchers in these disciplines, however, we need to explain precisely what the term expert actually means.

In everyday life, the term "expert" is used in a variety of different ways. For example, at a humorous level, it could refer to someone who is wearing a suit, carrying a laptop computer and who is more than 50km from home! More seriously, this term is often used to refer to the possession of specialist knowledge in a designated field (e.g. medical pathology). For example, an "expert witness" may be summoned to appear in court in order to offer an informed opinion about some legally contentious issue. On other occasions, the term is ascribed to someone who is deemed to be exceptionally skilful in performing a specific task such as tuning a piano or repairing a watch. What these two definitions have in common is the idea that expertise depends on some combination of experience and specialist training in a given field. But how much experience and what duration of training qualifies one as an expert?

In an attempt to answer this question, cognitive psychologists tend to invoke Hayes' (1985) **ten-year rule** when defining expertise. Briefly, Hayes discovered from his study of geniuses in different fields (e.g. musicians, chess players) that nobody had reached expert levels of performance without investing approximately ten years of sustained practice in the field in question. According to Daniel Levitin, a neurologist and musician, "it takes the brain this long to assimilate all that it needs to know to achieve true mastery" (cited in Gladwell, 2009, p. 40). Using this temporal criterion, we can define an expert as someone who has displayed consistent evidence of a high level of proficiency in a specific field as a result of at least *ten years* of sustained training and experience in it (Ericsson and Charness, 1997). By convention, this criterion is deemed equivalent to about 10,000 hours of practice in the field in question. Ericsson et al. (1993) found that expert pianists and violinists had conducted over 10,000 hours of practice between the ages of 8 and 20 years. This figure may be contrasted with about 8,000 hours of practice for the good performers and about 4,000 hours of practice for the average performers. Similar corroboration of this rule has emerged from research in sport with evidence that elite soccer players (Helsen et al., 1998), figure skaters (Starkes et al., 1996) and wrestlers (Hodges and Starkes, 1996) satisfied the stated criterion. However, there is empirical evidence that questions the notion that 10,000 hours of deliberate practice is a prerequisite for the attainment of expertise for all performers across all skill domains. For example, Duffy et al.'s (2004) examination of dart players found an average of 12,839 hours of deliberate practice (with a standard deviation of 7,780 hours) while ice-hockey players have been found to require less than 4,000 hours (see Soberlak and Côté, 2003). Nevertheless, the idea of the ten-year rule is supported by numerous cases within sport. Consider the case of Roger Federer, whose record of achieving seventeen Grand Slam men's tennis titles is unsurpassed.

He won his first Wimbledon singles title in 2003 at the age of 22 years – about ten years after he had begun to specialize in this sport. Also in tennis, Steffi Graf, who won twenty-two Grand Slam titles in her career, began to dominate her rivals consistently in her early to mid-twenties – about ten years after she had played her first professional match as a 13 year old. In golf, Tiger Woods had clocked up about 10,000 hours of dedicated practice by his mid-teen years (Syed, 2010). In fact, by the age of 3 years, he was playing nine holes of golf. At the age of 15, he became the youngest winner of the US junior amateur golf championship (Lehrer, 2010). In summary, it seems that some of the best athletes in these sports have accumulated about 10,000 hours of practice within ten or twelve years of specialization in their chosen sport. Additional support for this rule comes from Ericsson (2002), who claimed that the typical age at which most sport stars reach their peak is between the mid- and late twenties – which is approximately ten years after most young athletes have begun to practise seriously for their sport.

Despite the canonical status of the ten-year rule (or its equivalent, the 10,000 hours of practice rule), many sport psychology researchers have identified problems with it and some exceptions to it. First, research suggests that practice, on its own, is not a sufficient condition for the development of expertise. Gobet and Campitelli (2007) investigated the determinants of expertise among chess players in Argentina. Although results confirmed the importance of practice for the attainment of excellence in this game, considerable variability was also evident (e.g. slower players needed a lot more practice than faster players to attain the status of chess master). Ruthsatz et al. (2014) proposed that the existence of child prodigies in music provide strong support for the argument that nature is the primary driver of exceptional talent. Motivated by such claims, Hambrick et al. (2014) reanalysed findings from research conducted on deliberate practice activities amongst elite chess players and musicians and concluded that "deliberate practice explains a considerable amount of the variance in performance in these domains, but leaves a much larger amount of the variance unexplained" (p. 41). Overall, it would appear that practice is a necessary but not sufficient condition for the development of expertise (see Epstein, 2013, for a detailed discussion). Second, as we mentioned earlier, the *quality* of practice undertaken to become an expert is at least as important as the quantity of practice. In other words, it is probably more important to explore what types of practice work best than simply to count the duration of such practice in hours or years. Third, many people develop expertise in certain complex skills (e.g. learning to cycle) in less than the requisite ten years. Again, this point has not been adequately addressed by proponents of the rule. Fourth, there are obvious exceptions to the ten-year rule in certain domains. For example, in music, Mozart began composing pieces for the violin and piano at the age of 5 years (although it has been estimated that he had accumulated about 3,500 hours of musical practice before he was 6; Syed, 2010). Similarly, Bobby Fischer had attained the status of an international chess master by the age of 16, after playing for only nine years – a remarkable feat (Cloud, 2008). More formally, Hodges et al. (2004) found that length of involvement in sport was not related to subsequent performance by athletes in swimming and triathlon. Regardless of these caveats, however, most researchers agree that the ten-year rule is a robust and useful criterion for distinguishing between expertise and average levels of performance in any given domain of inquiry. In summary, expertise in sport refers to consistently superior performance in athletic activities that takes at least ten years to develop.

Although the ten-year rule has been promulgated in a largely uncritical manner in cognitive neuroscience, it has received considerable scrutiny in sport psychology. Such scrutiny has led to alternative ways of defining athletic expertise. Starkes (2001) suggested that an expert athlete was someone who competed at an international level and whose performance is generally at least two standard deviations above average. However, she acknowledged an obvious limitation of this approach – namely, the fact that this status is easier to achieve in sports where the level of participation (and hence competition) is relatively low. Thus it is easier to be acknowledged as an expert in a little-known sport such as curling as compared with one which is truly global in popularity such as soccer. For this reason, it is unlikely that this alternative approach to defining expertise in sport will supplant the ten-year rule. Unfortunately, there is a great deal of inconsistency among researchers in the definition of expertise. For example, despite the ten-year rule, Werner and Thies (2000, p. 166) defined "experts" in their study as "individuals who had at least three years of extensive experience playing, coaching, or refereeing football". Gulbin and Weissensteiner (2013) introduced the FTEM (Foundations, Talent, Elite, Mastery) framework to guide the development of elite pathways. This framework identifies seven stages of sport excellence including *breakthrough* and *reward* (e.g. representative honours at a national age-group level), *representation* at national senior level, *success* in international competitions, and *sustained success* at the highest level of one's sport. While this framework circumvents some of the problems associated with previous definitions of expertise (i.e. by being more specific) it does not appear to account for between-sport comparisons (i.e. how competitive a sport is in the athlete's country or globally) or the amount of experience an athlete has accrued at a certain level.

In seeking to deal with some of these issues Swann et al. (2015a) put forward a taxonomy of expertise that was more comprehensive, specific and practically useful. When seeking to provide a definition of an athlete's level of expertise within a particular sport, Swann et al. (2015a) recommend that researchers should consider the athlete's highest standard of performance, their success at that level and the amount of experience that they have gained at that level. When comparing athletes across sports, these authors argue that there is a need to consider the competitiveness of the sport within a specific country and within the sport itself. Swann et al. (2015a) presented a classification system which distinguishes between four types of expertise. *Semi-elite* athletes are those who participate just below the top standard possible in their sport (e.g. talent-developmental programmes). *Competitive-elite* regularly compete at the highest level in their sport (e.g. competing in Olympic Games) but have yet to experience success (e.g. medals) at that level. *Successful-elite* athletes compete regularly at the highest level and have experienced some (infrequent) success at this standard. Finally, *world-class* elite athletes have experienced sustained success over a period of time at the very highest level of their sport (e.g. winning gold medals in consecutive Olympics). This classification system is not intended to be definitive but may offer expertise researchers a heuristic device which can be used when selecting their samples (see also Baker et al., 2015, for another taxonomy of expertise).

Having considered the nature of expertise from a theoretical perspective, we should now explore the human face of an expert sport performer – the multiple world champion darts player, Phil "The Power" Taylor (see Figure 7.1). What is so special about this man? For a brief profile of Phil Taylor, see Box 7.1.

Why does the topic of expertise in sport appeal equally to popular science (e.g. see Ross, 2006) as to researchers (e.g. Hodges et al., 2006)? Three main reasons are apparent. First, the existence of athletic expertise gives us a tantalizing glimpse of the benefits which people have attained through dedicated practice and self-development. By implication, our admiration of other people's expertise beguiles us into believing that we too could have untapped potential which could be turned to our advantage.

Figure 7.1 Phil "The Power" Taylor – the greatest darts player of all time? (*source:* courtesy of Inpho photography)

Box 7.1 In the spotlight Profile of an expert sport performer: Phil "The Power" Taylor

Despite its stereotypical association with overweight, tattooed, beer-swilling men in noisy pubs (and they are just the performers!), darts is a popular and skilful game that requires a surprising amount of implicit knowledge of geometry and considerable computational prowess. To explain, the objective of this game, which probably dates back to the Middle Ages, is to throw a set of projectiles (darts) at a board which is placed about eight feet away (approximately 237cm). Put simply, it involves propelling a 27 gram projectile through the air at a target that is about the size of an AAA battery. Different locations on the board yield different points for the dart thrower. It is easy to see that success in darts requires a high degree of concentration, eye–hand coordination and fine motor control skills. To illustrate, players need to be able to stand completely still while controlling the speed, angle and spin of the darts. Apart from these skills, some mathematical proficiency is also required. Indeed, top darts players must be adept at making rapid mental calculations (Smyth, 2009). For example, in most darts tournaments, players start on 501 points and count down to zero. They have to be able to finish with a double that takes them to zero. Thus if they are on 59, they may aim for a single 19 and then a double 20. All of the ingredients of expertise in darts are epitomized in abundance in the career of Phil "The Power" Taylor, sixteen times world champion, who is widely regarded as one of the most successful individual sports performers of all time. To illustrate, apart from his world championship success, he has won the World Matchplay fifteen times, the World Grand Prix eleven times and over a hundred ranking tournaments in his career spanning more than twenty years (O'Sullivan, 2010). So, who is this star performer and what makes him so successful?

Born in Stoke, Phil Taylor was working as a tool machinist when his wife gave him a birthday present of a set of darts in 1986 when he was 26. He began to play once a week and showed enough skill at this sport to represent his county after a mere two years. One day, Eric Bristow (the most famous darts player of his generation) saw him practising and offered to advise him about the game. This advice soon paid off because in 1990, Taylor entered the World Darts Championship – and won it. Ironically, he defeated his mentor, Bristow, in the final! This victory was the first of a series of stunning performances that saw him demolish opponent after opponent with remarkable displays of accurate dart-throwing under intense competitive pressure. Famed for his eye–hand coordination (which he honed as a child by throwing a golf ball against the garden wall), dedication to physical and mental fitness (e.g. he practises for six hours a day: Hughes, 2002), and for his ruthless ability to finish matches when he gets the chance, he deliberately refuses to socialize with his fellow competitors in case he loses his competitive edge. For him, darts is a battle:

> familiarity breeds contempt ... I can see when people play me that they're worried. I can see the fear in their eyes and I know I've got them then ... As soon as he (the opponent) shows weakness, I'm in there, humiliating him. It's like boxing. You need to get your guy on the ropes.
>
> (cited in Kervin, 2001)

Continuing this confrontational theme, he claimed that success in darts is about "reading the body language ... I can see when people's minds are wrong ... In darts you wait for that dip and them you hit them hard" (cited in Ronay, 2008).

In capturing this idea, an adage from the study of attentional skills comes to mind: there is no such thing as a difficult task, only an unpractised task. Second, the study of expert athletic performance is appealing because it enables researchers to examine how skills are acquired and perfected over time in real life rather than artificial contexts. This distinction is an important point because traditional laboratory studies of human skill-learning were confined mainly to short-term activities (e.g. maze-learning) that had little relevance to everyday life. By contrast, contemporary researchers are striving to understand how people become proficient at complex everyday skills such as swimming or playing tennis. Of course, there is also a methodological explanation for the upsurge of research interest in athletic expertise. Specifically, the scientific study of skill-learning in sport is facilitated by the profusion of ranking and rating systems available to researchers – a fact which enables investigators to define and measure "success" in this field with some degree of objectivity. The same point holds true for chess which may explain why it is so popular among problem-solving researchers in cognitive psychology. Third, expert athletes are admired not only for their speed, economy of movement and timing but also because they appear to transcend the limits of what is humanly possible. For example, the Spanish rider Miguel Indurain, who won five successive Tour de France cycling titles between 1991 and 1995, had a resting heart rate of only 28 beats per minute (bpm) (Shontz, 1999). To put this figure in perspective, the average resting heart rate is between 77 and 72bpm whereas that of an experienced endurance athlete is around 40bpm. (The advantage of having a well-trained heart is that it is significantly larger and can pump more blood with each beat than can an untrained heart.) Other sporting champions who have attained extraordinary records in their careers include Tiger Woods (who won four consecutive major golf championships in the 2000–2001 season), Carl Lewis (who won four Olympic long-jump titles in succession between 1984 and 1996), Sir Steve Redgrave (who won an unprecedented five Olympic gold medals at consecutive Games between 1984 and 2000), Michael Phelps (who has won a record twenty-three Olympic gold medals) and Martina Navratilova (who, apart from her brilliant tennis career as a singles player, won an all-time record of thirty-one Grand Slam doubles titles). The existence of such outstanding competitors suggests that the horizons of human physical achievements are expanding. This impression is supported by historical analyses of sporting records. To illustrate, top amateur swimmers and marathon runners at present can routinely beat the records set by Olympic gold medallists in the early 1900s – even though the times recorded by the latter athletes were regarded in that era as being close to the impermeable boundaries of human performance (Ericsson, 2002). Interestingly, the French Institute of Sport in a study of performance improvements in sport over the past century suggested that world records in athletics will probably hit a ceiling around 2060 (Naish, 2009). The Institute analysed over 3,000 world records since the Olympics began in 1896 and concluded that athletes were operating at about 75 per cent of their potential at that time but at about 99 per cent of their potential by 2008. Extrapolating from such estimates, athletes in track and field events should reach their full potential by about 2060.

Analysis of the horizons of human performance in sport can help cognitive scientists to understand how the mind achieves some of its remarkable feats. For example, how do skilled athletes such as Andy Murray (who is widely regarded as the tennis player with one of the best returns of serve in the world today) manage to hit winning returns off tennis balls that travel towards him at over 193 kilometres per hour (kph) or about 120 miles per hour (mph), which is faster than the eye can see? By the way, the current world record for the fastest serve in tennis is held by the Croatian player Ivo Karlovic, who hit a serve of 251kph (or 156mph) in a Davis Cup match against Germany in Zagreb in March 2011. Theoretically, the feat of returning such a serve is impossible because there is about a 200 millisecond time-lag between noticing a stimulus and responding to it. To explain this delay, it takes about 100 milliseconds for a nerve impulse to travel from the eye to the brain and about another 100 milliseconds for a motor message to be sent from the brain back to the muscles. Remarkably, therefore, expert athletes in fast-ball, reactive sports like tennis, hurling (a type of aerial hockey that is played in Ireland and regarded as being one of the fastest games in the world), baseball and cricket manage to overcome the severe time-constraints imposed by this "hardwired" delay in the human information-processing system. In short, they effortlessly achieve the impossible feat of responding to fast-flying balls before they have any conscious knowledge of them! But this feat may not be as paradoxical as it seems. After all, some neuroscientists claim that our conscious awareness of any neural event is delayed by several hundred milliseconds although we do not normally notice this time-lag because we refer this awareness back in time – so that we convince ourselves that we were aware of the stimulus from its onset (Gazzaniga et al., 2002). For an account of the neuroscience of fast-ball sports, see Box 7.2.

Box 7.2 In the spotlight The neuroscience of expertise in fast-ball sports

What neural processes underlie the ability of expert baseball players to hit deliveries that are pitched at them at speeds of over 100 miles an hour? According to Milton et al. (2008), the baseball hitter's brain has to coordinate two main tasks in striking the ball successfully – preparing to swing the bat and interpreting the kinematic movements of the pitcher in an effort to predict the direction of the pitched ball. In order to understand the neural substrates of these skills, Milton et al. (2008) have used brain-imaging technology (e.g. fMRI) to investigate expert–novice differences in baseball players as they imagine swinging their bats to hit the ball. From such research, a number of fascinating insights into the neuroscience of fast-ball sports have emerged. Perhaps the most important one is that expert players typically show less brain activation but greater cortical efficiency than novice counterparts. For example, whereas expert baseball hitters tend to activate mainly the supplementary motor areas of the brain when they imagine hitting, novice players tend to activate the limbic regions (e.g. the amygdala and basal forebrain complex) which generally regulate emotions such as fear and anxiety (see Chapter 3). This activation of the limbic region suggests that novice players have a difficulty in filtering out irrelevant information as they prepare to execute their swings.

The discovery that fast reactions in sport lie mainly in the unconscious mind of the athlete has at least one surprising implication. Specifically, it suggests that contrary to coaching wisdom, top players in fast-ball sports do not actually watch the ball in flight. These findings seem at odds with anecdotal reports from elite performers, however, who claim that they do watch the ball as it is hit. Take for example, Justin Langer's (one of the all-time leading run scorers in test cricket) claim that he sees markings on the ball as it makes contact with the bat (see Mann et al., 2013). Mann et al. reported another leading cricket player who claimed that one of his main aims when batting is to watch the ball come out from underneath his bat. Can these anecdotal claims be corroborated by experimental findings? Until recently, few studies had explored the gaze patterns of truly elite performers. Mann et al. (2013) sought to address this issue by exploring whether the performance of interceptive actions by elite athletes involve fixations using central vision at the moment of bat–ball contact. Many researchers have argued that experts use early signals or "advance cues" from their opponents' body position and/or limb movements to anticipate the type of delivery, trajectory and likely destination of the speeding ball (e.g. see Müller et al., 2009). Perhaps not surprisingly, this capacity to extrapolate accurately from the information yielded by advance cues appears to be a distinctive characteristic of expert athletes. Nevertheless, this should not be taken to mean that skilled performers are incapable of using late ball-flight information to modify their action based on continuous visual feedback from the position of the ball. In fact, Mann et al. (2013) found that two of the world's leading cricket batsman coupled the rotation of their head to the movement of the ball, ensuring the ball remained in a consistent direction relative to their head. These batters were found to use two predictive saccades to anticipate (1) the location of ball-bounce, and (2) the location of bat–ball contact. This approach ensured that they could direct their gaze towards the ball as they hit it.

However, a large volume of evidence indicates that beginners tend to adopt a more constrained visual search process when preparing to execute interceptive actions. For example, Abernethy and Russell (1987) found that top-class squash players based their predictions about ball flight on early signals from opponents' movements (e.g. from both the position of the racquet and the racquet arm) when watching film simulations of squash matches. By contrast, squash beginners looked only at those cues that were yielded by the racquet itself. The significance of this finding is clear. Expert athletes have a knowledge-based rather than an innate speed advantage over less proficient rivals. In general, therefore, speed of reaction in sport depends as much on the mind (because it depends on game-specific knowledge and anticipation skills) as on the body. Put differently, research on anticipatory cue usage suggests that expert athletes have a cognitive rather than a physical advantage over less successful counterparts. This finding raises the contentious question of whether hardware or software explanations of athletic expertise are more plausible scientifically.

What makes an expert in sport? Hardware or software characteristics?

Are sport stars born or made? Unfortunately, it is not really possible to answer this general question scientifically because genetic and environmental factors are inextricably intertwined (see Davids and Baker, 2007). Indeed, as modern neuroscientific research has shown, the activity of acquiring and storing knowledge (a software process) can actually change structural aspects (hardware processes) of the brain. In a remarkable study, Maguire et al. (2000) found that the posterior hippocampi (brain regions that are specialized for the storage of spatial representations of environmental knowledge) of London taxi drivers were significantly larger than those of a matched group of people who did not drive taxis. These authors interpreted this finding as indicating that the thousands of hours spent by taxi drivers in mastering "the knowledge" (i.e. accurate representation of the spatial layout of London's maze of streets) had resulted in structural change to the "map storage" regions of their brains. Building on such research, some progress has been made in identifying the relative contributions of physical (or hardware) and mental (or software) processes to expertise in sport (Yarrow et al., 2009). To start with, let us consider the popular idea that athletic expertise is largely a matter of being born with the right physical hardware such as a muscular physique, fast reactions, acute vision and exceptional sensitivity to peripheral visual information. According to this intuitively appealing theory, success in sport is attributable to the possession of some fixed and prototypical constellation of physiological attributes (which we could call a "superior" nervous system) as well as to exceptional perceptual-motor skills (e.g. rapid reflexes, dynamic visual acuity). Furthermore, it is assumed that by using these advantages, top athletes can run faster, see more clearly and display sharper reactions than average performers. At first glance, this approach is persuasive because it is easily exemplified in sport. To illustrate, Yao Ming, the Chinese basketball player who stands 7 feet 6 inches and weighs 310 pounds (ESPN NBA, 2010), has obvious natural advantages in his sport. Indeed, he has been selected for the National Basketball Association's (NBA) "all star" team on a number of occasions since 2003. Similarly, Venus Williams, who won four Grand Slam events in one season, stands at an impressive height of 6 feet 1 inch (1.85m) and can hit tennis serves that travel at over 120 miles per hour (193kph) (*The Economist*, 1999). In fact, she has been credited with the fastest recorded serve in women's tennis history. Clearly, the hardware possessed by Williams and others is as impressive as their athletic achievements. By contrast, the appearance and actions of most sporting novices seem ungainly, poorly coordinated and badly timed – even to an untutored eye. But this physical theory of athletic expertise is beset by several problems. First, even at an anecdotal level, "bigger" does not always mean "better" in sport (see Box 7.3).

Second, there is little or no empirical evidence that top-class sports performers possess hardware characteristics, such as unusually fast reflexes or extreme visual acuity, that differentiate them significantly from less successful counterparts (A. Williams and Davids, 1998). For example, elite adult athletes do not perform consistently better than novices on tests of visual abilities (A. Williams, 2002b).

Box 7.3 In the spotlight Does size really matter? Is bigger always better in sport?

Does an athlete's physical "hardware" determine his or her success in sport? How important are the three S's of athletic ability – size, strength and speed? Is bigger always better? At first glance, few could argue against the claim that physical factors such as size and strength matter in competitive sport. For example, consider athletics, weightlifting, swimming and rugby. In athletics, Usain Bolt, the Jamaican triple Olympic champion sprinter who broke his own 100m and 200m world records in 2009, has a physique which facilitates his prodigious speed (Gibson, 2009) (see Figure 7.2). Specifically, his height (6 feet 5 inches or 1.96m) enables him to cover the 100m in just forty or forty-one strides – which is between five and seven strides less than that taken by his shorter competitors. Put simply, Bolt's longer leg muscles generate more speed and velocity than that of his rivals. What is even more remarkable about Bolt is that he was born with a condition (scoliosis or curvature of the spine) that could easily have made it impossible for him to play sport at a high level. Indeed, this condition resulted in one of his legs being half an inch shorter than the other (Hattenstone, 2010). More generally, research indicates that elite sprinters have grown by about 6.4 inches over the past century compared with an average population growth of about 2 inches. Perhaps more tellingly, Bolt is a full 11 inches (27.94cm) taller than the world sprint champion of 1929 (Gibson, 2009). Turning to weightlifting, North Korea's recent successes (twelve medals at the 2014 World Weightlifting Championships), have been attributed to their genetic make-up. In seeking to explain this success, British Weightlifting performance director, Tommy Yule, argued that the North Korean weightlifters

> look like what you would want a weightlifter to look like … short arms, long back and short legs – kind of the opposite of the body shape you would want for a sprinter or a discus thrower. The Chinese and the North Korean lifters have the ideal body dimensions to excel.

> (Reynolds, 2015)

In swimming, Michael Phelps, the most successful athlete in Olympic history (because he is a twenty-three-time gold medal winner), not only is very tall (at 6 feet 4 inches or 1.93m) but also has enormous hands and very large feet (he takes size 14 shoes). These physical attributes enable him to "hold onto" the water as he swims. In addition, Phelps has a long torso in relation to his legs (he is almost all "back") which helps him to "plane" on the water like a boat. Also, he has a huge "wingspan" (6 feet 7 inches or 2.01m), long arms (which enables him to take fewer strokes in a single lap), flexible ankles (that act like fins) and a very high endurance capacity in his heart and lungs (Phelps, 2008b). In rugby, the sheer bulk of modern players can be illustrated by comparing the height and weight of some of the backs of the 2013 British and Irish Lions squad with their counterparts from the 1974 squad (Hands, 2009). For example, at centre, Ian McGeechan (1974 squad) was 5 feet 9 inches (1.75m) and weighed 11 stone 3 pounds (71.21kg) whereas Jamie Roberts (2013 squad) is 6 feet 4 inches (1.93m) and weighs 16 stone 9 pounds (107kg). Similarly, at scrum half, Gareth Edwards (1974) was 5 feet 8 inches (1.73m) and weighed 12 stone 9 pounds (80.29kg) whereas Mike Phillips (2013) is 6 feet 3 inches (1.91m) and weighs 16

continued …

Box 7.3 continued

stone 5 pounds (105kg). Clearly, from these four sporting examples, we can conclude that today's athletes are generally taller, stronger and fitter than their predecessors. Perhaps it is this fact that explains why so many of the athletic records set in the early 1900s have been smashed a century later. For example, whereas the men's world record for throwing the hammer in 1900 was 51.10 metres (set by an Irish athlete called John Flanagan), it was 86.74 metres in 2000 (set by a Russian performer named Yuri Sedykh) – a figure which represents an increase of almost 70 per cent in the distance involved! Interestingly, the current female hammer-throwing record is held by Anita Wlodarczyk (Poland), who threw a distance of 82.98 metres in the EAA 7th Kamila Skolimowska Memorial in Warsaw in 2016. But bigger is certainly not always better in sport: big athletes may be clumsier than their smaller counterparts. In sports such as tennis, tall players may have trouble in playing shots aimed at their feet. In addition, tall or strong players may tend to neglect other parts of their game. So, in modern tennis, despite the increasing prevalence of tall (i.e. over 1.8m or 6 feet) stars such as Ivo Karlovic (who, at 6 feet 10 inches or 2.08m, is the tallest player ever on the professional tour), shorter players like Lleyton Hewitt (Australia) and David Ferrer (Spain) (both under 5 feet 11 inches or 1.8m in height) have won as many, if not more, singles titles than their taller counterparts. Of course, there are distinct advantages to being tall and strong in the majority of sports. Big athletes tend to have large lungs and powerful hearts – physical assets which increase their cardiovascular efficiency in pumping oxygenated blood around the body. Larger limbs are advantageous in certain sports: in swimming, long arms can give an athlete leverage for speedy passage through the water. Similarly, long legs are essential for high-jumpers. Of course, there are also sports in which a small stature and a wiry physique are mandatory. Accordingly, marathon runners tend to be slight, if not scrawny, in build and they usually have "slow twitch" muscles. Likewise, successful jockeys are usually small, light, wiry and strong.

Figure 7.2 Usain Bolt has a wonderful physique that facilitates his prodigious speed (*source*: courtesy of Inpho photography)

The same principle seems to apply also to younger athletes. P. Ward and Williams (2003, p. 108) found that elite and sub-elite soccer players were "not meaningfully discriminated on nonspecific tests of visual function throughout late childhood, adolescence or early adulthood". Furthermore, Mann et al. (2007) found that optimal vision is not essential for optimal performance in interceptive tasks (such as batting in cricket) because the human perceptual-motor system can compensate for significant alterations in visual input. More generally, there is little reliable evidence of expert–novice differences in simple reaction time. In fact, as explained earlier, it takes about 200 milliseconds for anyone to react to a given stimulus – regardless of whether that person is an expert athlete or an unfit "couch potato". Remarkably, this finding suggests that there is little or no difference between the average reaction time of a tennis star like Andy Murray and that of a spectator picked randomly from a courtside seat. Indeed, the legendary Australian cricketer Donald Bradman, revealed that tests showed that his reaction time was slower than the average university student (Farrow and Abernethy, 2015). The implication of this point is clear. The rapid reactions exhibited by top athletes in sport situations do not reflect hardwired, innate talents but are probably due instead to acquired skills (such as the ability to read and anticipate what an opponent is likely to do next). In short, expert athletes have a distinct anticipatory advantage over everyone else, which makes it seem as if their reaction times are exceptionally fast (e.g. see Müller et al., 2006, 2009).

The third problem for hardware theories of sporting expertise comes from research findings on the age at which athletes tend to reach their peak level of performance (see Ericsson, 2001). Briefly, if expertise were limited mainly by biological factors, such as the functional capacity of the brain and body, then we would expect that the age at which athletes reach their peak would be around the time that they reach physical maturation – namely, in their late teens. However, research shows that the age at which most athletes attain peak levels of performance occurs many years later – usually, in the mid- to late twenties. This latter finding has challenged the validity of hardware theories of athletic expertise.

In the light of the preceding evidence, expertise in sport appears to be "dependent on perceptual and cognitive skills as well as on physical and motor capabilities" (A. Williams, 2002b, p. 416). Put differently, knowledge-driven factors (software processes) can account significantly for differences between expert and novice athletes in a variety of sports (Starkes and Ericsson, 2003; A. Williams, 2002b; A. Williams et al., 1999). Smith (2016) recently conducted a systematic review of action anticipation studies which have used functional neuroimaging or brain stimulation during sport-specific anticipation tasks and found that experts tended to outperform non-experts and this finding was pronounced when sequences were early occluded or manipulated to show deceptive actions. To illustrate the extent to which exceptional athletic performance is cognitively driven, consider how an expert tennis player and a relative novice might respond to the same situation in a match. Briefly, if a short, mid-court ball is played to an expert performer, she will probably respond to it with an attacking drive either cross-court or down the line followed by an approach to the net in order to volley the anticipated return shot from the opponent. In similar circumstances, however, a novice player is likely to be so preoccupied with the task of returning the ball anywhere back over the net that she will fail to take advantage of this attacking opportunity. In other words, the weaker player is handicapped cognitively (i.e. by an inability to recognize and respond to certain patterns of play) as well as technically. We shall return to this point in the next section of the chapter.

Despite its flaws, the hardware theory of sporting expertise has some merit. There is evidence that people's performance in certain athletic events is facilitated by the type of musculature that they possess (Andersen et al., 2000). Top-class sprinters tend to possess an abundance of "fast twitch" muscles which provide the explosive power which they need for their event. Conversely, "slow" muscle fibres have been shown to be helpful for endurance sports such as long-distance running and cycling. M. Reid and Schneiker (2008) have provided a thorough review of research on the importance of strength and conditioning in top-level professional tennis. In the future, the field of hardware research in sport may serve as a natural laboratory for testing the effects of genetic engineering. For example, in an effort to boost their chances of success, sprinters could be equipped genetically with more "fast twitch" muscles, long-distance runners could be given the genes that create the blood-enhancing hormone erythropoietin, and basketball players may seek artificial height increases! Fortunately for legislators and sports associations, this type of genetic therapy for athletes is not a feasible proposition at present. Worryingly, however, there are a number of commercial genetic tests available – aimed at coaches, parents and sport teams – which claim to provide early information on a child's genetic predisposition for success in speed/power or endurance sports. Webborn et al. (2015) cautioned against the use of these measurements arguing that there remains a lack of universally accepted guidelines and legislation for all forms of genetic testing. The authors recommend that no child or young athlete should be exposed to this form of testing to alter training or for talent identification purposes. Indeed, they note a number of important ethical issues associated with the use of such testing including psychosocial consequences such as impaired self-esteem and social stigma.

In summary, despite its intuitive plausibility, the hardware approach is inadequate for the task of explaining the theoretical mechanisms that underlie athletic expertise. But what about the software approach? Can research on expert–novice differences in cognitive processes help us to understand the nature of athletic expertise?

Expert–novice differences in sport: research methods and findings

After the pioneering research of de Groot (1965) and Chase and Simon (1973) on the cognitive characteristics of chess grand-masters, cognitive psychology researchers have used laboratory simulations of various real-life tasks in order to determine how expert performers differ from novices (see review by P. Ward et al., 2006). Initially, the main fields of expertise investigated were formal knowledge domains such as chess and physics where problem-solving processes and outcomes can be measured objectively. The archetypal research in this regard was a set of studies conducted by de Groot (1965) on chess expertise (for a detailed account of this work, see Gobet and Charness, 2006).

In one of these experiments, de Groot (1965), who was a chess master player, explored how performers of different abilities planned their moves. Briefly, he found that the grand-masters made better moves than less skilled experts – even though they did not appear to consider more moves than the latter players. Some years later, Chase and Simon (1973) discovered that although chess experts were superior to novices in recalling the positions of chess pieces from real or meaningful games, they did not differ from this group in their memory for chess pieces that had been randomly scattered around the board. The evidence for this conclusion came from two key findings. First, whereas chess masters could recall, on average, about sixteen of the twenty-four chess pieces displayed on the board in their correct positions after a single five-second glance, novices could recall only about four such pieces correctly. Second, when the chess pieces were presented in random or meaningless configurations on the board, the experts were no better than the novices at recalling their positions correctly. Indeed, neither group could recall more than two or three chess pieces in their correct location. This classic study shows that expert chess players do not have superior memories to those of novices – but that they use their more extensive knowledge base to **chunk** or code the chess configurations in meaningful ways. Another conclusion from this study is that the cognitive superiority of expert chess players over novices is knowledge based and context specific – not indicative of some general intellectual advantage. In the light of this finding, research on expertise since the 1990s has shifted away from formal knowledge domains (such as chess) towards informal, everyday domains such as sport, music and dance (see coverage of these topics in Ericsson et al., 2006).

Research methods in the study of expertise

Within the domain of sport, a variety of research methods have been used to study expert–novice differences. These methods include both qualitative techniques (such as in-depth interviews, think aloud verbal protocols and thought sampling techniques) and quantitative procedures (e.g. pattern recall and **pattern recognition tasks**, video-based methods such as the **temporal occlusion paradigm** and spatial occlusion paradigm, and eye-tracking technology). Although we shall describe each of these techniques briefly below, additional information on their strengths and weaknesses is available in Hodges et al. (2006, 2007) and Lavallee et al. (2012).

In-depth interviews

Intensive interviews are widely used by researchers in an effort to elicit experts' knowledge and opinions about different aspects of their sports. The advantages and disadvantages of the interview method were mentioned briefly in Box

1.4 in Chapter 1 (see also Côté et al., 2007). Interestingly, Eccles et al. (2002) interviewed the British orienteering squad (n=17) in an attempt to develop a "grounded theory" of how expert performers in this sport manage to divide their attention successfully between three key sources of information: the map, the environment and the travel path. Grounded theory is a qualitative approach in psychology in which researchers build a conceptual model inductively from the data yielded by participants rather than deductively from the researcher's assumptions about the phenomenon in question.

Think aloud verbal protocols and thought sampling techniques

Another approach is the "think aloud" (TA) verbal protocol method whereby people are required to talk about and/or give a running commentary on their thoughts and actions as they tackle real or simulated problems in their specialist domain (for a thorough review of research on protocol analysis, see Ericsson, 2006; M. Fox et al., 2011). This technique was pioneered by de Groot (1965) in an effort to explore the cognitive processes of chess masters as they contemplated their next move in a simulated game. It is a valuable tool as it helps researchers to represent not only what people know (**declarative knowledge**) but also how they perform skilled behaviour (**procedural knowledge**). Of course, there are certain limitations associated with the collection and analysis of verbal protocols. First, protocols are limited to consciously accessible processes on the part of the person studied. Second, a difficulty arises from the fact that recording what people say as they solve a problem may inadvertently distort the quality of the data obtained. Put simply, people may become more self-conscious, guarded and/or spuriously rational if they know that their every utterance is being analysed by a researcher. In spite of these limitations, verbal protocols are useful because they provide researchers with an insight into the cognitive mechanisms that guide real-time skill execution. Whitehead et al. (2015) recently found that "level 2" (i.e. verbal encoding and verbalization of internal representations) and "level 3" (i.e. requires participants to explain their thoughts or motives) think aloud protocols did not impair golf putting performance compared to a no verbalization condition. These authors also found that TA provides richer verbal data than cued retrospective recall (interviews held ten minutes, twenty-four hours and forty-eight hours after performance).

Thought sampling or experience sampling methods (based on Csikszentmihalyi, 1990; Nakamura and Csikszentmihalyi, 2002; see also the method of descriptive experience sampling; Hurlburt and Akhter, 2006) involve equipping athletes with electronic beepers during training or competitive encounters and cueing them randomly to pay attention to their thoughts and experiences at the precise moment in question. Thus athletes are prompted electronically to respond to such questions as "What were you thinking of just now?" Using this technique, researchers can keep track of athletes' thoughts, feelings and focus of attention in real-life situations. In a variation of this procedure, McPherson (2000) asked expert and novice tennis players questions such as "What were you thinking about while playing that point?" and "What are you thinking about now?" during the period between points in competitive tennis matches. Unfortunately, despite its ingenuity, certain flaws in this method are apparent. First, there are obvious practical and ethical constraints surrounding athletes' willingness to be "thought sampled" during competitive situations. Second, little or no data have been gathered to evaluate the reliability of this procedure (for a review, see Hodges et al., 2007). Nevertheless, these techniques could be used by researchers to explore athletes' thought processes during practice and training situations.

Pattern recall and recognition tasks

Pattern recall recognition tasks are based largely on the classic studies of de Groot (1965) and Chase and Simon (1973) on chess experts' memories for briefly presented chess patterns. When these tasks are adapted for use in sport situations, athletes and/or coaches are tested on their ability to remember precise details of rapidly presented, game-relevant information such as the exact positions of players depicted briefly in a filmed sport sequence. In the Chase and Simon (1973) study, expert and novice chess players were asked to study chessboards with pieces on them for five seconds. Next, they had to reconstruct the positions of these pieces on another board. As we indicated previously, results showed that the chess masters were superior to the novices in recalling the pieces – but only if these pieces came from structured game situations. No differences between the groups were evident when the pieces were randomly presented initially. In a typical sport psychological modification of this paradigm, participants may be shown a slide or a video sequence of action from a game-specific situation for a brief duration. Then, they are asked to recall as accurately as possible the relative position of each player in the slide or sequence. Interestingly, the ability to recall and recognize evolving patterns of play seems to be an excellent predictor of athletes' anticipatory skills in team sports (A. Williams, 2002b; for an investigation of the transfer of pattern recall skills between athletes in basketball, netball and hockey, see Abernethy et al., 2005). A limitation of many studies in this field has been their reliance on the use of static images to depict scenes which are typically dynamic and ever-changing when encountered in a real-world situation. To address this issue, Gorman et al. (2012) examined the recall performance of expert and non-expert basketball players who viewed static and moving patterns of play. Participants' accuracy in recalling player positions was compared to their actual positions when presented at the final frame and at successive milliseconds (ms) increments thereafter. Experts were far superior at prospectively encoding elements within the presented pattern – a process which helps them to predict how the scene is likely to unfold quite early in its development.

As a practical illustration of this pattern recall paradigm applied to the sport of rugby, consider the configurations of players displayed in Figure 7.3a and Figure 7.3b. In both cases, the aim of the diagrams is to depict a "three-man defence" tactical strategy. But only one of these patterns is meaningful. Can you identify which of them makes sense and which of them is random or meaningless? Take a moment to examine the diagrams carefully.

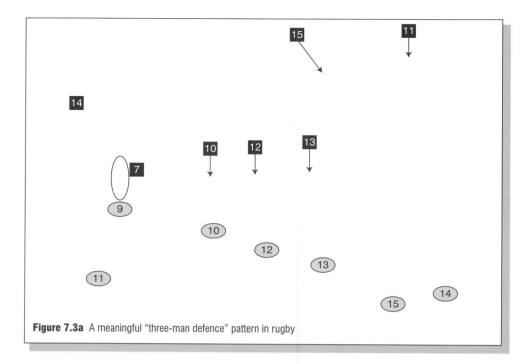

Figure 7.3a A meaningful "three-man defence" pattern in rugby

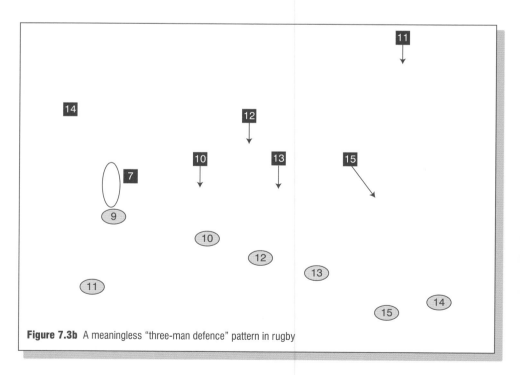

Figure 7.3b A meaningless "three-man defence" pattern in rugby

If you are not knowledgeable about rugby, you should find this task very difficult, if not impossible! But if you were an expert rugby coach, you would quickly realize that Figure 7.3b is the meaningless pattern. To explain, Figure 7.3a portrays an orthodox three-man defence in which the number 10 player covers the opposing number 10, the number 12 takes the opposing number 12, the number 13 covers the opposing number 13 with the winger taking the last person. By contrast, in Figure 7.3b there is no obvious pattern to the defensive alignment. In fact, the only defensive player who is in the correct position is the number 10.

Extrapolating from Chase and Simon's (1973) study, we would expect that expert rugby players or coaches would be able to memorize the pattern of players depicted in the orthodox three-man defence (Figure 7.3a) much better than the meaningless pattern depicted in Figure 7.3b.

Video-based temporal occlusion paradigm

As the term "occlusion" means to hide or to obscure from view, the "occlusion paradigm" involves presenting participants with predictive tasks (e.g. guessing the likely direction of a shot in tennis) based on obscured or incomplete information. By analysing how experts differ from novices in extrapolating from such incomplete information, researchers can establish the relative importance of different cues in making predictive decisions. Typically, two different types of occlusion paradigms are used in sport psychology research – temporal occlusion and spatial occlusion (Hodges et al., 2007).

The temporal occlusion paradigm (e.g. for more details, see Yarrow et al., 2009) is a method which requires participants to guess "what happens next" when asked to view video or film sequences in which key time-based, sport-related information has been occluded deliberately (e.g. by disguising the ball flight-path). Participants are then asked to make anticipatory judgements based on the varying levels of information that they had seen. For example, in an attempt to investigate anticipation skill in soccer goalkeepers, A. Williams and Burwitz (1993) presented participants with video footage that was occluded at four successive points around the point at which the player's foot struck the ball. At the early cut-off points that occurred (prior to foot on ball impact), expert goalkeepers performed significantly better than relative novices in their ability to use what they had seen to make accurate predictions about where the ball would go. Müller et al. (2006) used the temporal occlusion approach to examine anticipation skills in cricket players of different levels of expertise. Results showed that the expert batsmen were significantly better than their less skilled counterparts in picking up advance information about ball flight from early cues such as the position of the arm and hand of the bowlers. Similarly, Rowe et al. (2009) used the temporal occlusion paradigm to explore the effects of deliberately disguising tennis groundstrokes on expert and novice players' anticipation skills. Results demonstrated that, as expected, disguise reduced anticipatory accuracy – but more for the novices than the expert tennis players.

In an ecological variation of the temporal occlusion method, liquid crystal occlusion glasses may be used to replicate film occlusion procedures in actual sport settings. To illustrate, a tennis player may be asked to wear such glasses while receiving a serve on court. Both variations of this paradigm are especially useful for assessing expert–novice differences in advance cue usage (A. Williams, 2002b). For example, a top-class tennis player can guess which side of the court his or her opponent is likely to serve to by making predictions from the direction of the server's ball toss. A right-handed server tossing the ball to his or her right will probably swing the serve to the right of the receiver. The occlusion paradigm has also been used to study how soccer goalkeepers anticipate the direction of penalty kicks against them in the actual pitch environment. Early anticipation of the direction of a penalty kick is vital as goalkeepers have less than half a second to decide which way to dive in an effort to save the shot. Researchers at the Australian Institute of Sport in Canberra have used occlusion goggles with goalkeepers in an effort to vary the amount and type of pre-contact cue information available to them. In this way, the goalkeeper's use of early visual cues from the penalty taker (e.g. his or her posture, foot angle and arm swing) can be analysed (M. Smith, 2003; for a study that investigated anticipation and visual search skills in goalkeepers, see Savelsbergh et al., 2005). From such research, it should be possible to develop anticipatory training programmes for goalkeepers. Unfortunately, few researchers have explored whether instructional programmes can improve athletes' knowledge of situational probabilities in specific sports. In an attempt to address this issue, Romeas et al. (2016) trained skilled soccer players using a three-dimensional multiple object tracking task and found that this improved their decision making accuracy in passing. Further studies are required to corroborate the finding that perceptual-cognitive training exercises can have a transfer effect into competitive performance. Before concluding this brief discussion of the laboratory version of the occlusion paradigm, we need to acknowledge that its fidelity or realism is open to question. For example, to what extent is watching a video sequence of a tennis serve on a large screen equivalent to being on the receiving end of it on court during windy conditions? A detailed discussion of the advantages and disadvantages of this technique may be found in A. Williams et al. (1999).

Video-based spatial occlusion paradigm

Although the temporal occlusion paradigm is helpful in providing insights into the issue of exactly when participants extract certain information from a filmed sequence of movements, the spatial occlusion approach attempts to answer the "where?" question – namely, the issue of exactly which areas of the filmed scene are perceived as most important by viewers. In this spatial occlusion paradigm, specific portions of the visual scene are typically removed or occluded from view and their effects on viewers' accuracy scores are analysed (for more details, see Yarrow et al., 2009). The logic of this method is that if there is a performance decrement when a particular spatial element or area of the stimulus display (e.g. the hips or shoulders of a tennis player model during a simulated serve) is occluded from participants, that area of interest could prove to be especially informative to viewers. Special software packages are now available to enable researchers to be more precise in determining exactly which areas of the stimulus display they wish to occlude. Using these packages, researchers can "clone" the background of any scene and overlay it on the element to be occluded. In this way the element "disappears" or becomes invisible to the participant for as long as is necessary. To illustrate this method, R. Jackson and Morgan (2007) investigated expert–novice differences in tennis players' ability to judge the direction of a serve. Participants of different ability levels were required to look at video clips of tennis serves under various conditions of spatial occlusion and to make appropriate predictions about the likely direction of the ball. Results showed that, as expected, the expert players were more attuned to early advances cues (e.g. from ball toss and serving arm position) than were less proficient counterparts. Loffing and Hagemann (2014) used the spatial occlusion technique to identify the cues used by experienced and novice handball goalkeepers when deciding where an attacker was going to place a ball when taking a penalty. As expected, skilled performers made more accurate predictions and this success appears to have been facilitated by their ability to pick up information using a "global" process rather than a "local" process. In the latter case, novices are reliant on the use of later-occurring, locally presented information (which may contain only one kinematic information source such as the ball or hand) while a "global" strategy allows skilled performers to pick up pattern information earlier in the chain of action by using proximal (i.e. trunk and shoulder) and distal cues (i.e. throwing arm and ball). Similarly, Schorer et al. (2015) compared the anticipation performance of skilled and novice volleyball players and found that the former group also used this global strategy to improve their prediction accuracy.

One recurrent criticism of this spatial occlusion technique, however, concerns the issue of experimenter bias. To explain, the potential areas of interest are rarely specified on theoretical grounds but are usually designated in advance by the researchers themselves. Clearly, this practice raises the question of whether or not experimenters' preconceptions may influence the data collected using this paradigm. Slattery (2010) addressed this problem by basing the areas of interest on empirical data rather than on experimenters' theories.

Cañal-Bruland and Mann (2015) recently called for researchers to broaden the scope of anticipation research by exploring the influence of broader situational or contextual (non-kinematic) sources of information on expert anticipation. These authors argue that contextual information is often processed well before kinematic information becomes available. In addition, performers are likely to adopt different strategies when making decisions and this will influence the type of information processed. Take, for example, a penalty taker in soccer who adopts a keeper-independent strategy which is reliant on contextual information (e.g. the goalkeeper's preference for direction of dive) rather than a keeper-dependent strategy (where the taker prioritizes kinematic cues from the goalkeeper to decide where to place the kick). Little is known about how, or when, contextual and kinematic information interact to inform expert anticipation.

Eye-tracking technology

If, as an old proverb says, the eyes serve as windows to the mind, the study of eye movements can provide insights into the relationship between "looking" (or visual fixation) and "seeing" (or paying attention). Two main types of eye movements have been identified (Kowler, 1999). First, **saccadic eye movements** are conjugate, high-speed jumps of the eyes which shift people's gaze from one location to another (e.g. notice how your gaze is moving from one word to the next while you read this sentence). Second, **smooth pursuit eye movements** help people to fixate on a given target (e.g. a ball) during the intervals between the saccades. These smooth pursuit movements are important because they enable perceivers to compensate for any displacements on the retina that may be caused by variations in either head or object position. Typically, people display about three fixations per second when viewing a scene that is unfamiliar to them (Goldstein, 2011).

A variety of eye trackers (or eye-movement registration systems) have been developed in psychology (for a review, see Duchowski, 2007). Among the most popular of these approaches in sport psychology are the Applied Science Laboratories' (ASL) 5000 SU eye-tracking system and the Tobii system (depicted in Figure 7.4). The Tobii eye-glasses have heralded the arrival of the latest generation of mobile eye trackers. The ASL system is a video-based monocular

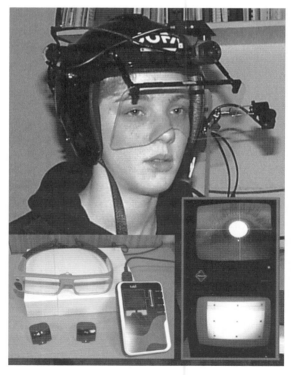

Figure 7.4 Eye-tracking technology allows psychologists to study visual search behaviour in athletes (*source*: courtesy of Andrew Flood, University College Dublin, School of Psychology)

corneal-reflection system that measures the perceiver's point of gaze with respect to video images recorded by an infra-red eye camera and a scene camera (which is usually floor mounted). This system works by detecting two features, namely, the position of the pupil and the corneal reflex, in a video image of the eye. The relative position of these features is used to compute the visual point of gaze. The infra-red eye camera records displacement data from the left or right pupil and cornea.

Using such eye-tracking systems, a considerable amount of research has been conducted on the eye movements of athletes since the late 1990s. Typical stimuli used in these studies include static slides depicting schematic sport situations as well as dynamic video presentations of similar material (see review by A. Williams et al., 1999). Certain inferences are drawn from the location and duration of the perceiver's visual fixations. First, the location of a fixation is usually regarded as an index of the relative importance of a given cue within a stimulus display. Second, the number and duration of fixations recorded (which define "search rate") are believed to reflect the information-processing demands placed on the perceiver. Using such variables, expert–novice differences in visual search strategies have been discovered in such sports as soccer (Helsen and Starkes, 1999; Savelsbergh et al., 2005), tennis (Singer et al., 1996), billiards (Williams et al., 2002), golf (Wilson and Pearcy, 2009), basketball (Vickers, 1996), ice-hockey (Martell and Vickers, 2004) and shotgun shooting (Causer et al., 2010). More recently, changes in pupil diameter have been used to measure attentional effort in eye-tracking studies (e.g. see Moran et al., 2016; O'Shea & Moran, 2016; see also Chapter 5).

A prediction that is frequently tested in this field is that expert athletes will display a more efficient visual search strategy than relatively less skilled counterparts when inspecting sport-specific displays (e.g. see A. Williams et al., 2004). This means that they will show fewer visual fixations of longer length – and focus more on "information rich" areas of the display than will relative novices.

Research findings on expert–novice differences in athletes

Using a combination of the preceding methods, a number of expert–novice differences in sport have been identified. The following research findings summarize what is known about the differences between expert and novice athletes at present. For a more detailed discussion of these research trends, see Beilock (in press), Ericsson and Williams (2007), Hodges et al. (2007) and A. Williams and Ford (2008).

Experts have a more extensive knowledge base of sport-specific information

Expert athletes and coaches know more about their specialist domain than do relative novices but, as we shall see later, this knowledge tends to be "domain specific" or restricted to one specific field. In the case of chess masters, the size of this chess database or "vocabulary" has been estimated at approximately 50,000 "chunks" of information (Simon and Gilmartin, 1973), where a chunk is defined as a meaningful grouping of chess piece positions.

This quantitative advantage associated with expertise means that experienced athletes and coaches possess a larger and better cross-referenced knowledge base about their chosen sport than do relative novices. Typically, this cognitive superiority is evident in three different areas: declarative knowledge (i.e. factual knowledge about the sport in question such as knowing its rules), procedural knowledge (i.e. the ability to perform basic technical skills in this sport accurately and efficiently) and **strategic knowledge** (i.e. the ability to recognize and respond optimally to various patterns of play in the sport). P. Morris et al. (1985) found that people who knew a lot about soccer displayed significantly greater recall of match results than did less knowledgeable participants. Hyllegard (1991) discovered that expert batters were better than novices in predicting the type of pitch they were about to receive in a simulated baseball situation. Abernethy et al. (1994) found that expert snooker players were more adept than novices at planning future shots.

Experts use their knowledge more efficiently to identify, remember and manipulate relevant information

Apart from knowing more about their specialist sport than novices, expert athletes can do more with information deemed relevant. Chase and Simon (1973) discovered that top chess players were better than novices at encoding and recalling meaningful (but not random) patterns from actual game situations. This cognitive advantage of experts over novices has been replicated extensively in sport situations. Thus top athletes and coaches are adept at recognizing and memorizing patterns of play in their sport. Bedon and Howard (1992) found that expert karate practitioners were significantly superior to beginners in memorizing various strategic techniques which had been presented to them. There is also evidence that experts tend to represent problems at a deeper level than novices because they search for principles and rules rather than superficial features of the tasks in question (Woll, 2002).

One explanation of the cognitive superiority of experts over novices comes from skilled memory theory (Chase and Ericsson, 1981). This theory proposes that experts use their long-term memory advantages to enrich the coding of new information. In other words, their rich database of knowledge appears to guide their **chunking** of new information. This proposition is significant for two reasons. First, it highlights a paradox of expertise (E. Smith et al., 1978). Put simply, this paradox concerns the fact that although experts have more knowledge to search through in their database than have novices, they can retrieve information in their specialist domain more quickly. Perhaps the reason for this difference in speed of search and retrieval is that experts' knowledge tends to be extensively cross-referenced whereas that of novices is usually compartmentalized. The second reason that skilled memory theory is significant psychologically is that it challenges a common misconception about the way in which our memory system is designed. Briefly, many people believe that our minds resemble containers which fill up with the knowledge we acquire but which may overflow if we are exposed to too much information. Research on experts, however, shows that our memory system is not passive but expands to accommodate new information. Put simply, the more we know about a given field, the more we can remember in it (Moran, 2000b). Although skilled performers may possess greater generic knowledge (i.e. memory about how a skill is typically performed without reference to a specific performance) they actually possess poorer episodic knowledge (i.e. memory about a specific recent event) than their less-skilled counterparts. This effect is known as "expertise-induced amnesia" (Beilock and Carr, 2001) and may arise for two reasons. First, the procedural knowledge structures that underlie expert level performance are less accessible to conscious recall than the declarative structures underlying novice performance (Gray, 2015). Second, because skilled performers devote less attention to skill execution, they are believed to possess poorer memory for the component processes of movement. Indeed, Beilock et al. (2002) found that expert golfers could recall a significantly greater number of generic steps for a specific putt, but fewer episodic steps, when compared to novice golfers. In summary, the study of expert–novice differences in memory yields several interesting findings about the way in which our minds work.

Experts are faster, more consistent and have better anticipation skills than novices

Classical studies on expertise showed that elite performers are usually faster at solving problems in their specialist field than are novices (Woll, 2002). Experts also tend to be more consistent than novices in performing their skills accurately. For example, top golfers are able to perform basic skills like driving or putting several times more consistently than are average players (Ericsson, 2001). As indicated earlier, a number of laboratory studies of ball sports have shown that expert athletes are superior to novices in using advance cues from opponents to predict accurately shot placement and destination ("What will happen next?") in simulated sport-specific situations. Typically, in these studies, participants are presented with specially prepared video sequences in which key ball-flight information has been occluded selectively. The task is to predict the likely destination or flight-path of the ball in the film. For example, A. Williams and Burwitz (1993) reported that expert soccer players were better able to predict the destination of filmed penalty kicks than novices – but only during conditions of minimal exposure (40 milliseconds after impact). Arising from these findings on expert–novice differences in advance cue utilization, a practical question arises. Do anticipatory abilities in athletes develop over time? This issue is examined in Box 7.4.

Expertise in sport is domain-specific

Research suggests, as mentioned earlier in this section, that the skills of expert athletes tend to be "domain-specific" or confined to one area. In other words, few of the specialist skills acquired by expert athletes transfer to other sporting fields.

Box 7.4 In the spotlight Do anticipatory abilities develop over time?

In sport, the term "anticipation" refers to an athlete's ability to predict task-relevant events accurately. Although it is well known that top performers are adept at this skill (Slattery, 2010; A. Williams and Ward, 2007), little research has been conducted on whether or not this skill can be developed over time. Therefore, in an effort to fill this gap in the literature, Tenenbaum et al. (2000) explored how visual anticipatory abilities developed in young tennis players of different skill levels over time. Using a temporal occlusion paradigm (described earlier in the chapter), high- and low-skilled tennis players from the Israeli Academy of Tennis watched specially prepared video segments and had to predict the final ball location after various tennis strokes (e.g. a backhand down the line, a serve) had been executed by model players. Results showed that, as expected, the more skilful players anticipated ball location more accurately than did less proficient performers. However, contrary to the theory of Ericsson et al. (1993) (see later in the chapter) some differences in visual anticipatory abilities were found to exist between the players of different skill levels from the earliest stages of their development. These latter differences suggest that deliberate practice alone cannot account for differences in anticipation skills in young tennis players. Tenenbaum et al. (2000, p. 126) concluded that "extensive practice is a necessary but not a sufficient condition for developing highly skilled performance". Extending this research on anticipation in handball, Abernethy et al. (2012) investigated the relative efficacy of different perceptual training approaches to the task of improving anticipation skills in novice-level players. More precisely, they compared the effectiveness of explicit instruction, verbal cueing on its own or supplemented with colour cueing, and implicit learning techniques in teaching anticipation skills to these athletes. Results showed that the explicit learning, implicit learning and the verbal cueing conditions provided the greatest sustained improvements in performance (i.e. after a five month retention period) thereby highlighting the benefits of perceptual-cognitive training. The implicit approach was inferior to the explicit and verbal cueing approaches in facilitating pre- to post-training improvements but was superior in promoting the preservation of performance through to a five month retention and under evaluative stress. In a more recent study, Schorer et al. (2015) showed that skilled volleyball players' anticipation performance could be improved using a short-term, full-vision training intervention. In a series of studies, participants were presented with clips that were spatially occluded so that (a) no information from the "setter" was available and (b) the rest of the attackers were occluded and only information from the setter was provided. Participants also viewed "full vision" clips which included information pertaining to both the attackers and the setter. Having being presented with this information participants were asked which player, of four possible options, would receive the ball from the setter. Temporal occlusion involved occluding frames at various points prior to ball–hand contact of the attacking setter. Results indicated that this training was more effective in certain circumstances (i.e. when it involved full vision and when attacking players were occluded) than others (i.e. when the setter was occluded). Together, these findings point to the potential efficacy of training interventions as a means of enhancing anticipation skills but further research is required to determine if these skills lead to improved performance in competitive conditions.

At first glance, this finding is surprising as it challenges the existence of sporting "all-rounders" or athletes who appear to be capable of achieving expert-level performance in several different sports simultaneously. For example, Jim Thorpe won a gold medal as a decathlete and pentathlete in the 1912 Olympic Games before going on to play basketball and baseball professionally. A more recent example of the "all-rounder" is Rebecca Romero, who became an individual world champion in two unrelated Olympic sports – rowing and cycling. More precisely, in 2008, she became the first British woman to win Olympic medals in two different sports when she added a gold medal in cycling (won at the Beijing Games in 2008) to the silver medal that she had won in rowing at the Athens Games in 2004. On closer scrutiny, however, the domain-specificity of athletic skills is not completely surprising. Consider the case of Michael Jordan, who was one of the greatest basketballers of all time. In the late 1990s, he retired from basketball and tried to become a professional baseball player with the Chicago White Sox. Unfortunately, his involvement with this new sport was not a success by his standards and he failed to attain his desired level of expertise in it. Anecdotally, similar experiences are evident in the case of several world-class athletes who tried to become successful golfers on the professional tour (Capostagno, 2002). Among these former athletes are Nigel Mansell (former Formula One world champion) and Ivan Lendl (a former world number 1 tennis player in the 1980s). Of course, as we explained in Chapter 1, we must be cautious about extrapolating from anecdotal examples. Also, we need to be careful to point out that some sports stars do indeed become skilled exponents of another game. John Surtees is the only person to have won world championships on both two and four wheels, in both motorcycle racing and Formula One motor racing (Gallagher, 2008). Despite these last few examples, research suggests that top athletes rarely achieve equivalent levels of expertise in sports outside of their own specialist domain – unless there is a substantial level of overlap between the skills required by the sports in question. An interesting test case of the "transferability" of athletic skills concerns the question of whether or not expert football players also make expert coaches or managers (see Box 7.5).

Experts have more insight into, and control over, their own mental processes

The term **metacognition** refers to people's insight into, and control over, their own mental processes (Matlin, 2009). It has long been assumed that experts are superior to novices in this area. If this principle holds true in sport, then expert athletes and coaches should have greater insight into, and more control over, their minds than do novices. Although few studies have tested this hypothesis, there is some evidence to support it with regard to planning behaviour. McPherson (2000) found that expert collegiate tennis players generated three times as many planning concepts as novices during "between point" periods in tennis matches. Brick et al. (2015) found that elite-level endurance runners used metacognitive strategies such as planning, monitoring, reviewing and evaluating as forms of cognitive control before, during and after races.

Box 7.5 Thinking critically about ... whether or not expert soccer players are likely to become successful managers

Does expertise transfer from one specialist role to another within a given sport? This question comes to mind when we explore whether or not expert footballers become successful managers (Lawrenson, 2008; Marcotti, 2001; Moore, 2000). At the outset, we need a definition of expertise in playing sport. As noted earlier, this might involve a consideration of the athletes' highest standard of performance, their success at that level, and the amount of experience that they have gained at that level. As regards a definition for "success" in management, coaching one's team to win a league championship or cup competition may suffice. Initially, it is easy to think of some excellent football players who subsequently became successful managers. Kenny Dalglish was a star for Liverpool and subsequently managed that club to league championship honours. Similarly, on the international stage, Jack Charlton, who won a World Cup medal with England in 1966, managed the unheralded Republic of Ireland team to a quarter-final place in the World Cup finals in Italy in 1990. Also, legendary stars like Franz Beckenbauer won World Cup medals both as a player and as a manager. From these examples, it is clear that one advantage of possessing playing experience at an elite level is that it adds credibility to one's views on coaching. However, managers who achieved success with teams in the British Premier League such as Arsenal (under Arsène Wenger), Liverpool (under Rafael Benitez) and Manchester United (under Alex Ferguson) were only moderately successful as players. Analysing the archives, Moore (2000) calculated that of the twenty-six managers who had coached winning teams in the Premier League in England between 1945 and 2000, only five had won more than six caps for their countries. Surprisingly, even acknowledged expert managers like Bob Paisley and Bill Shankly (both of Liverpool) and Alex Ferguson (manager of Manchester United, perhaps the most successful club manager in England since the early 1960s) were never capped by their native country, Scotland. In addition, statistics reveal that only one (Jack Charlton) of the eight English World Cup-winning team of 1966 who went into management was subsequently successful in this role. Additional support for the idea that one does not have to be a great player to become a great manager comes from the fact that top managers such as Arsène Wenger (Arsenal), Rafael Benitez (former manager of Inter Milan) and José Mourinho (former manager of Chelsea and Real Madrid) were never capped for their countries at senior international level either. But let us leave the last word on this issue to Arigo Sacchi, who won the Italian league and two European Cups with AC Milan even though he had never even played professional soccer! He said:

> What's the problem here? So I never played. I was never good enough. But so what? If you want to be a good jockey, it's not necessary to have been a horse earlier in your career. In fact, sometimes it's a hindrance.
>
> (cited in Marcotti, 2001)

A key lesson from the preceding discussion is that playing and managing are completely different tasks with different requirements. As Lawrenson (2008) pointed out, an important skill in managing players is the ability to assess talented players with the right mentality. This skill is not part of a player's repertoire – regardless of his or her playing ability. Nevertheless, former elite athletes dominate head coaching roles in professional sports clubs and many of these organizations appear to support a "fast-track" pathway for elite athletes to become high performance coaches. In a recent study seeking to explore the basis for "fast-tracked" pathways, Blackett et al. (in press) found that these appointments (in professional rugby union and football clubs in England) were often based upon the perceived ability of head coaches to gain player "respect". The authors claimed that this "fast-tracking" process was promoted by directors as it ensured the perpetuation of specific playing and coaching philosophies. Playing and managing may very well require different skills and attributes but this appears to be of little concern to those individuals responsible for the appointment of high-performance coaches.

Critical thinking questions

Do you agree with the definitions of success that were used above? How could you analyse scientifically whether or not great players become great managers? Is it enough merely to stack up examples on both sides of the question – or is there another way to proceed? One possibility is to elicit the views of a large sample of expert coaches on this question. An alternative method is to devise a checklist of managerial skills and to survey the views of players and managers on the relative importance of each of these factors. Why do you think that expertise in playing may not transfer to expertise in coaching or management? Remember that coaching largely involves teaching – and it is often quite difficult to teach a skill that one learned intuitively.

Metacognitive experiences and feelings, including internal sensory monitoring (e.g. increased exertional pain) and outward monitoring (e.g. of a competitor), also played an important role in informing and guiding cognitive strategies adopted during performance. These feelings helped athletes to form a representation of the task which, in turn, stimulated the initiation of an appropriate cognitive strategy (e.g. to relax), thereby enabling them to exert cognitive control over performance.

In summary, research shows that expert adult athletes differ consistently from relative novices with regard to a variety of perceptual, cognitive and strategic aspects of behaviour. This conclusion appears to apply equally to young athletes. P. Ward and Williams (2003) discovered that perceptual and cognitive skills discriminated between elite and sub-elite soccer players between the ages of 9 and 17 years. These general findings are consistent with those derived from more formal domains like chess and physics where experts have been shown to display both quantitative and qualitative knowledge advantages over novices. Thus experts' knowledge is better organized and largely domain-specific and is probably represented differently from that of novices. But how do people become athletic experts in the first place? In order to answer this question, we need to consider the role of practice in the acquisition of expertise.

Becoming an expert athlete: Ericsson's theory of "deliberate practice"

Earlier in this chapter, we mentioned the joy of watching expert athletes such as Lionel Messi and Serena Williams. Why do we find it almost impossible to emulate the skills of these players? At one level, the answer to this question is obvious. Most of us lack the hardware and/or sufficient athletic talent to do so. But there is another possibility. Perhaps we simply do not practise hard enough, long enough or well enough to fulfil our potential (see Hodges et al., 2004). This "nurturist" possibility raises an intriguing issue. How important is practice in the development of expertise in any field?

Surprisingly, it is only since the mid-1980s that this question has begun to receive sustained empirical attention in psychology. In this era, several stage theories were developed to account for the development of expertise in young performers in different fields (e.g. see Bloom, 1985; Dreyfus, 1997). Of these approaches, the work of Ericsson has generated the greatest volume of research in recent years.

According to Ericsson et al. (1993, 2006), innate talent is a necessary but not sufficient condition for the development of expertise in a given domain. Instead, top-level performance is believed to be an acquired skill that is attributable largely to the quantity and quality of the performer's practice schedule (where "practice" is understood as any exercise that is designed to fulfil the goal of improving the person's performance). This claim about the primacy of practice is based on two main sources of evidence – first, research which highlights the **plasticity** or amenability of many cognitive characteristics to practice effects, and second, studies on the practice habits of elite musicians. Let us now consider each of these two strands of evidence in more detail.

For a long time, it was assumed that many of our mental limitations (e.g. the fact that our **short-term memory** is very brief and fragile) were caused by flaws in the design of our brain. For example, early cognitive research (see details in Matlin, 2009) showed that the average person's short-term memory span is restricted to between seven and nine units of information – which probably explains why we find it difficult to remember people's mobile phone numbers. However, this structural limitation principle was challenged by Chase and Ericsson (1981) who showed that with between 200 and 400 hours of practice, a person could be trained to remember up to eighty randomly presented digits. Details of this remarkable case study are presented in Box 7.6.

Box 7.6 shows us that practice can circumvent certain information-processing limitations of the mind. Put differently, Chase and Ericsson's (1981) study showed that remarkable changes in performance (albeit in one field only) could be produced in otherwise unexceptional performers simply by practising rigorously over time. Augmenting this line of evidence was other research which showed that practice could induce actual anatomical changes in athletes. For example, evidence indicates that years of intensive practice can increase the size and endurance of athletes' hearts as well as the size of their bone structure (Ericsson, 2002). Thus the playing arm of a professional tennis player is often more heavily muscled and larger boned than his or her non-dominant arm. In summary, a recurring theme of research in modern neuroscience is the malleability or plasticity of anatomical and physiological mechanisms.

The second important influence on Ericsson's work emerged from studies which his research team conducted on the practice habits of eminent musicians

Box 7.6 In the spotlight How practice can improve your memory

One of the oldest tasks in experimental psychology is the memory-span test. This test requires people to recall a number of random digits (e.g. 1, 9, 6, 6, 2, 0, 0, 1) in the precise sequence in which they were presented. Early research (e.g. see details in Matlin, 2009) showed that most people can remember between seven and nine such digits – hence the estimation of the apparent limit on our short-term memory span. But what if one were trained to group or chunk these digits together so that they could be transformed into meaningful units? For example, the previous digit sequence could be segmented into two composite units rather than eight separate digits (e.g. "1966" or the year that England won the World Cup and "2001" or the title of a famous science-fiction film directed by Stanley Kubrick). Using this chunking approach, Chase and Ericsson (1981) trained a volunteer referred to as "SF" (whose original memory span was about the average of seven units) in 230 practice sessions spanning almost two years to achieve a remarkable memory span whereby he could recall accurately eighty-two digits presented randomly! How was this feat accomplished? What chunking strategies were exploited? Interestingly, although SF's memory was no better than average, he was a keen varsity track athlete who used his knowledge of running times to chunk the digits to be remembered into familiar units of 3–4 digits. For example, he might break up seven digits such as 2 2 0 3 4 9 2 into two chunks using the time taken to run a marathon (2 hours and 20 minutes) followed by a near-world record time to run a mile (3 minutes and 49.2 seconds). Remarkably, in keeping with the domain specificity principle explained earlier, SF's extraordinary memory skill was confined to numbers only. Thus he was no better than average in his ability to recall long strings of letters. The clear implication of this study is that people's memory span can be increased if they practise chunking techniques based on specialist knowledge or personal interest. Thus SF managed to increase his short-term memory span for digits tenfold by practising extensively. The lesson is clear. According to Anders Ericsson, "there are apparently no limits to improvements in memory skill with practice" (cited in Syed, 2010, p. 22).

(Gladwell, 2009). Specifically, Ericsson et al. (1993) investigated the nature, type and frequency of violinists' practice at the Berlin Academy of Music. They divided the Academy's violinists into three groups – the elite performers (students who were judged to have the potential to become world-class musicians), good performers (students who were predicted to become regular professional performers) and average performers (who were judged to have the potential to become music teachers). Each of these violinists was asked how many hours they had practised since they had first taken up their instrument. Results showed that almost all these performers had started at about the same age (around 5 years old) and had reportedly practised for about two to three hours per week until they were about 8 years of age. However, significant differences between the groups began to emerge at that time. In particular, the elite performers reported practising for longer durations than their counterparts in the other two groups – six hours a week by the age of 9, eight hours per week by the age of 12, sixteen hours per week by the age of 14 and over thirty hours per week by the age of 20. By this latter age, the elite violinists had clocked up an average of about 10,000 hours of practice (recall the ten-year rule that we explained earlier in this chapter). In contrast, the "good" group of violinists had accumulated about 8,000 hours of practice and the potential music teachers had aggregated about 4,000 hours of practice. Ericsson and his colleagues then compared the practice habits of professional and amateur pianists. Results showed that not only did the expert group practise longer than their less successful counterparts, but also they practised differently – spending more time on perfecting their skills (four to five hours a day on average) than in mindlessly repeating elementary drills. From this evidence, Ericsson et al. (1993, p. 392) concluded that "across many domains of expertise, a remarkably consistent pattern emerges: The best individuals start practice at earlier ages and maintain a higher level of daily practice." Furthermore, these researchers proposed that practice, rather than innate talent, was the main cause of expertise or achievement level – not a correlate of it. More precisely, Ericsson and Charness (1994, p. 738) suggested that expertise is a direct function of the total amount of deliberate practice (or "individualized training on tasks selected by a qualified teacher") that has been undertaken by performers. This proposition is the cornerstone of Ericsson's theory. But what exactly is deliberate practice and how does it change over time?

Deliberate practice

Earlier in the chapter, we highlighted the idea that mindful practice (working deliberately to overcome one's weaknesses rather than engaging in mindless drills) is the key to success in sport. But what exactly does this type of practice involve? According to Ericsson et al. (1993), deliberate practice is a highly structured, focused, purposeful and (typically) not inherently enjoyable form of practice that is particularly relevant to the improvement of performance in any domain. It involves individualized training on tasks that are highly structured by skilled instructors in order to provide "optimal opportunities for learning and skill acquisition" (Ericsson and Charness, 1994, p. 739). The goal of such practice is to challenge the learner to go beyond his or her current level of performance. It may be contrasted with mechanical practice which is characterized solely by mindless repetition of basic drills (see A. Williams et al., 2008). Interestingly, based on the findings of Maguire et al. (2000), some commentators (e.g. Syed, 2010) claim that deliberate practice can build neural connections and increase the size of specific brain areas.

What are the characteristics of deliberate practice? Ericsson et al. (1993, p. 373) suggested that deliberate practice activities are "very high on relevance for performance, high on effort, and comparatively low on inherent enjoyment". More precisely, four criteria of such practice may be specified as follows. First, deliberate practice targets specific skills that can improve performance. Second, it requires hard work and intense concentration on the part of the learner. A practical implication of this feature is that the duration of deliberate practice is determined mainly by the ability of the performer to sustain his or her concentration during the training session. Third, Ericsson believes that deliberate practice activities are not intrinsically rewarding. For example, in sport, a top tennis player may have to spend an hour working repetitively on the ball toss for his or her serve rather than engaging in the more pleasant task of rallying with a partner. A fourth criterion of deliberate practice is that it requires feedback from a specialist coach or instructor. This feedback helps the performer to monitor discrepancies between his or her current level of performance and some designated target standard. In summary, deliberate practice consists of activities that require effort and attention but are not play, not enjoyable intrinsically and not part of one's paid employment. Let us now turn to the issue of how expertise is held to develop from sustained engagement in deliberate practice.

Stages in the development of expertise

People are not born experts in anything: they become that way as a function of practice and instruction. Based on this assumption, several stage theories of expertise have been postulated. Dreyfus (1997) proposed a five-stage model of the transition from novice to expert. These stages are novice (stage 1), advanced beginner (stage 2), competent (stage 3), proficient (stage 4) and expert (stage 5). An alternative approach was proposed by Ericsson and his colleagues (e.g. see Ericsson and Charness, 1994). This model can be explained as follows.

Inspired by the theories of Bloom (1985), Ericsson and his colleagues postulated three stages in the development of expertise. These stages are distinguished from each other largely on the basis of the type of practice engaged in at each phase of development. They may be described in relation to athletic expertise as follows. In stage 1, a child is introduced to a given sport and may display some athletic talent which is recognized by his or her parents. At this stage, practice usually takes the form of "play", which may be defined as an unstructured and intrinsically enjoyable activity. During this era, the child's parents may facilitate skill development by encouraging him or her to take some lessons in the activity in question. Stage 2 can extend over a long period. It is here that a protracted period of preparation occurs during which the young learners are taught to perform their skills better. Therefore, "deliberate practice" begins in earnest in stage 2. As explained previously, this form of practice stems from having a well-defined task with an appropriate level of difficulty for the individual concerned, informative feedback, and opportunities for the correction of errors. During this stage, the young athlete's performance usually improves significantly. Typically, the stage ends with some commitment from the performer to pursue activities in the domain on a full-time basis. Finally, in stage 3, the average amount of daily deliberate practice increases and specialist or advanced coaches are sought by the parents to assist the young performer. Indeed, on occasion, parents of some performers may move home in order to live closer to specialist coaches or advanced training facilities. Stage 3 usually ends either when the performer becomes a full-time competitor in the sport in question or when he or she abandons the sport completely. A fourth stage has been recognized by Ericsson and his colleagues. Here, certain outstanding performers may go beyond the competence (skills and knowledge) of their coaches to achieve exceptional levels of success in their chosen sport. In fact, in order to achieve, and subsequently maintain, their position at an elite level, athletes appear to engage in a process of "continuous improvement" (Toner and Moran, 2014). This phenomenon refers to elite sports performers' ability to continuously improve their skills through deliberate practice, even after they have become experts. See Box 7.7 for a discussion of "continuous improvement" in sport.

Box 7.7 Thinking critically about … "continuous improvement" in elite performers

A key feature of Ericsson's theory of expertise is the proposal that skilled performers will seek to "counteract automaticity", or avoid the excessive proceduralization of skills, in order to continue their skill development. In the past, automaticity, or fluent, effortless and unconscious performance, was regarded as the end point of all skill-learning: it was believed that once this state has been achieved, no further progress is possible. By contrast, Ericsson proposed that an over-reliance on automaticity may reduce the performer's ability to consciously monitor and refine their technical skills during training. Unfortunately, neither Ericsson's work nor that in deliberate practice research more generally has adequately explained the precise cognitive mechanisms that allow performers to improve their performance beyond automaticity. In a series of recent papers, Toner and Moran (2014, 2015) sought to address this latter issue by proposing that "somaesthetic awareness" (see Shusterman, 2008, 2012), or heightened body consciousness, may help us to understand how expert performers avoid "prematurely arrested development" (Ericsson, 2013, p. 893) by alternating between reflective (in the practice context) and unreflective (in the performance context) modes of bodily awareness. These authors pointed to a wide volume of evidence from studies which have used "naturalistic investigations" (e.g. including observations and self-confrontation interviews; see Bernier et al., 2011; Ravn and Christensen, 2014) to explore the attentional foci adopted by elite performers across training and performance contexts. For example, Ravn and Christensen (2014) found that an elite golfer's training regime involved learning to listen to their body and regulating how it should "feel" in order to perform optimally. Anecdotal evidence from elite performers also supports the notion that the alteration of automated procedures plays a crucial role in continuous improvement. For example, in July 2012, Rory McIlroy, the world's number 1 ranked golfer at the time, appeared to be experiencing a performance slump having failed to make the halfway "cut" in a number of recent high profile tournaments (e.g. US Open). To address this issue, McIlroy underwent what his coach, Michael Bannon, described as a "fine tuning process" which hinged on the player learning to consciously discriminate between the inefficient downswing position of his club and the desirable or more efficient one. Four weeks after struggling to make the cut in the British Open, McIlroy achieved a spectacular eight stroke victory in the USPGA Championship. Clearly, McIlroy's quest for technical improvement prompted him to make deliberate conscious refinements to his golf swing in the practice context. Together, this body of evidence suggests that "somaesthetic" training (which involves paying heightened attention to and mastery of our somatic functioning) is crucial for skill-learning and continuous improvement.

Critical thinking questions

What methodological approach (e.g. laboratory-based or naturalistic investigations) do you think would be most effective for an investigation of "continuous improvement" in elite athletes? Can you think how these approaches might be combined to track changes in performers' movement proficiency over time? Toner et al. (2016) recently discussed a number of the "crises" (e.g. injuries, performance slumps, movement disorders) that might confront elite performers. Can you think of any approaches, other than somaesthetic training, that performers might use during practice to identify and subsequently combat these crises?

One interesting implication of Ericsson's stage theory is that it suggests that mere exposure to a given sport will not make someone an expert performer in it. Research shows that the ability to perform to an expert standard in sport does not come from merely watching it but requires instead active interaction with its structure.

A four-stage model of the development of expertise has been postulated by Hodges and Baker (2011). The first stage involves early engagement in sport and typically occurs at about 5 years of age. In this stage, children learn fundamental athletic skills, usually in the context of play. In the second stage or intermediate phase of athlete development, playful involvement in sport changes to more structured and specialized activities. The third stage is expertise or demonstrated world-class performance. The fourth stage involves "masters involvement" in sport for people who continue, or at some later time in their lives, begin or resume competing in events for middle-aged and elderly athletes. Relatively few studies have been conducted on athletes in this age category (Medic, 2010).

Testing the theory of deliberate practice in sport

As we learned above, Ericsson (2001, 2002; Ericsson et al., 1993) postulated that expert performance in sport is largely determined by the amount of domain-specific deliberate practice accumulated by the athletes in question. How well has this proposition been supported in the domain of sport?

Overall, a growing number of studies on this issue lend qualified support to Ericsson's belief in the importance of deliberate practice as a determinant of expertise in sport. For example, consider two reviews of research in this area since 2001. In her review, Starkes (2001) concluded:

> in every sport we have examined to date, we have found that level of skill has a positive linear relationship with amount of accumulated practice throughout one's sports career. The best athletes ... have put in significantly more practice than their lesser skill [sic] counterparts.
>
> (Starkes, 2001, p. 198)

Baker and Young (2014) reached a similar conclusion when they proclaimed that "deliberate practice studies in sport have consistently revealed that experts spend more time overall in training" (p. 142). In a review of seventeen studies that have performed between-group analyses to compare expert and less-skilled performance groups, these authors found only one study that failed to demonstrate significant group differences for global totals of practice. But some caution is necessary when interpreting these conclusions. In particular, certain aspects of Ericsson's theory of deliberate practice appear to be problematic when applied to sport settings. Consider the fact that the theory of deliberate practice emerged originally from research on musicians. There are at least two key differences between the deliberate practice schedules of musicians and those of athletes. First, whereas most musicians tend to practise on their own, athletes tend to train with teammates or practice partners (Summers, 1999). Second, the concept of deliberate practice in sport may differ from that in the domain of music. To illustrate, recall that one of the criteria of such practice stipulated by Ericsson is that the activity in question should be relatively unenjoyable (as well as being purposeful and requiring effort). In sport, however, there is evidence that many athletes (e.g. wrestlers; Hodges and Starkes, 1996) seem to enjoy engaging in mundane deliberate practice activities. Indeed, this even applies in sports such as figure skating which are characterized by the solitary practice of technical skills (Starkes, 2000). This finding was confirmed by Helsen et al. (1998), who analysed the practice habits of soccer and hockey players of various levels of ability. The results of this study revealed two key findings and an anomaly. First, the ten-year rule was confirmed. Specifically, results showed that after this period of time, both the soccer and hockey players realized that a significantly greater investment of training time would be required to enable them to achieve further success. Second, as expected, there was a direct linear relationship between the amount of deliberate practice undertaken by these athletes and the level of proficiency that they attained. But an anomaly also emerged from this study. In particular, these researchers found that contrary to Ericsson's model, those practised activities which were deemed to be most relevant to skill development were also seen by the soccer and hockey players as being most enjoyable. Again, this finding contradicts Ericsson's assertion that deliberate practice of basic skills is not inherently enjoyable. Influenced by such findings, Young and Salmela (2002) assessed middle-distance runners' perceptions of Ericsson's definition of deliberate practice. Briefly, these researchers asked the runners to rate various practice and training activities on the amount of effort and concentration required to perform them and the degree of enjoyment to which they gave rise. Contrary to what Ericsson's theory predicted, Young and Salmela (2002) found that these runners rated the most relevant and most effortful of these training activities as also being the most inherently enjoyable. This finding led these authors to conclude that the construct of deliberate practice in sport should be redefined to refer to activities that are highly relevant for performance improvement, highly demanding of effort and concentration – and highly enjoyable to perform. In summary, there is evidence that top athletes differ from expert musicians by appearing to enjoy the routine practice of basic skills in their domain. Interestingly, a substantial body of evidence has accumulated from researchers such as Côté et al. (2007) to suggest that time spent in "deliberate play" activities (i.e. actions that people engage in purely for the sake of enjoyment such as playing football on the street) is related to athletic success. At the moment, it is unclear whether the benefits children derive from structured environments, such as deliberate practice activities, are superior to the benefits they may gain from engaging in deliberate play activities. A number of researchers have advocated the use of deliberate play as a means of instilling in children a life-long commitment to sport which, in turn, will provide greater opportunities for learning specific skills. However, MacNamara et al. (2015) recently argued that the deliberate play paradigm is often misinterpreted and that allowing children to play without appropriate organization, instruction or feedback is unlikely to result in learning that will ensure prolonged engagement. Instead, these authors propose an approach they term "deliberate preparation" which involves children being supported and guided through a series of developmentally appropriate tasks in an effort to develop the essential movement skills required for proactive and sustained participation.

Another problem encountered in trying to apply or test Ericsson's theory of deliberate practice in sport concerns the phenomenon of early specialization – or prioritizing one activity or sport at a young age. Ericsson et al. (1993) argued that early specialization is crucial for later success in any domain because the sooner one adheres to a systematic regime of deliberate practice, the quicker one will attain expertise. However, in sport, researchers such as J. Baker et al. (2009) have pointed out that early intensive training (e.g. deliberate practice) is potentially hazardous to athletes because it is associated with a pattern of negative developmental outcomes such as increased risk of physical injury, decreased enjoyment of sport, burnout (i.e. a withdrawal from a formerly pursued and enjoyable sport, often accompanied by feelings of exhaustion and depersonalization; Cashmore, 2008) and impaired social skills. In fact, although there is evidence to indicate that intensive training may have a similarly debilitative influence on a significant percentage of elite athletes, few researchers have sought to critically evaluate how adherence to such demanding training regimes influences athlete health and well-being. We consider this issue in greater detail in Box 7.8.

Box 7.8 Thinking critically about … whether or not high-performance sport is a healthy pursuit

Spectators marvel at the explosive brilliance that allows Usain Bolt to cover 100m in nine and a half seconds or Serena Williams to hit a serve over 120mph. Elite athletes possess extraordinary physical capacities that allow them to perform challenging feats with grace, power and precision and also to withstand the rigours of elite performance and training environments. Sport scientists often attribute the development of these physical and mental capacities to the extensive hours committed to deliberate practice. In high performance environments athletes are also supported by a vast array of sport scientists who monitor their training loads to ensure that training has the desired effect on performance. Accordingly, one might assume that such careful attention to physical development would inevitably prove beneficial to an athlete's health and well-being. However, we also know that many elite athletes experience a great number of injuries

continued …

Box 7.8 continued

over their careers (which often necessitate surgery) and are often engaged in physical therapy in order to regain strength or mobility. In fact, engaging in health-compromising behaviours, including playing through pain or injury, appears to be quite commonplace amongst elite performers. For example, a number of studies have found that elite rowers and gymnasts continued to train and compete despite suffering from a number of health problems (Barker-Ruchti and Tinning, 2010; Sinden, 2010). Similarly, Alexias and Dimitropoulou (2011) found that ballet dancers were reluctant to reveal anything about their pain or injury to their choreographer as they believed it would represent a sign of weakness and would only prompt a search for their replacement. What other factors might contribute to athletes and performers reluctance to acknowledge pain or injury? Many athletes have relatively short careers and concerns over impending contract renewals or whether they will remain part of high performance squads may convince them that they have no choice but to perform through pain and injury (Wainwright et al., 2005).

Unfortunately, there are a number of other health-compromising activities that are a ubiquitous feature of elite performance environments. As noted earlier, modern athletes are bigger and faster than their predecessors (see Box 7.3 above) and high-speed collisions involving players of huge size and strength are becoming increasingly prevalent in sports such as rugby union and American football. Incidences of concussion have been increasing to such an extent within these sports that they are no longer taken as a rare, but inevitable, feature of participation, but are instead considered a "public health issue" that requires urgent attention.

There is little doubt that involvement in sport has many health benefits but researchers, participants and the viewing public need to question the taken-for-granted assumption that sport participation is healthy "for all of the people all of the time" (Baker et al., 2015, p. 4). Baker et al. argue that the terms "sport", "physical activity" and "exercise" are used interchangeably in spite of the fact that they refer to different forms of movement. High-performance sport – which is characterized by the necessity to constantly push and extend one's bodily capacities – is likely to have a very different influence on health than involvement in "physical education" or "exercise". Overall, this issue is nicely captured by Waddington (2000) who argued that "to suggest a 30-minute gentle swim three times a week is good for one's health does not mean that running 70 miles a week as a means of preparing for running marathons is good for one's health in an equally simple or unproblematic way" (p. 20).

Critical thinking questions

What might be the long-term health consequences for athletes who experience multiple injuries or surgeries or who continue to expose themselves to punishing training regimes? Should elite performers merely accept that playing through pain and injury is a "necessary evil" and something that they must learn to deal with? Would you be happy with your child or younger sibling striving to reach the top level of a sport in which the latter behaviour is normalized and accepted? Is it "healthy" to play a sport where concussion (i.e. a mild traumatic brain injury) is a commonplace occurrence?

Beilock (2010b) highlighted some benefits of "sampling" a number of sporting activities rather than specializing in one of them at an early age. Specifically, she remarked that sampling not only reduces the chances of burnout but also lowers the likelihood of incurring overuse injuries. Clearly, the vexed issues of "practice" versus "play" and "early specialization" versus "sampling" have both theoretical and practical implications in sport psychology. To summarize, empirical research is generally supportive of Ericsson's claim that deliberate practice is crucial to athletic success. Nevertheless, doubts remain about the validity of extrapolating certain key propositions of Ericsson's theory of deliberate practice to the domain of sport.

Implications of Ericsson's research

At least six interesting implications arise from Ericsson's research on deliberate practice. First, his stage theory of expertise suggests that practice by itself is not sufficient to achieve excellence. Specialist advice and corrective feedback from a skilled instructor are essential for the development of expertise (Ericsson et al., 1993). Second, and as noted above, Ericsson's research raises the intriguing possibility that continuous improvement is possible in skill-learning – even among people who have already achieved the proficiency level of experts.

Third, Ericsson's theories offer suggestions as to why continuous practice is so important to experts. Briefly, if elite performers fail to practise continuously, they will lose the "feel" or kinaesthetic control that guides their skills (see Ericsson, 2001, p. 42). Fourth, Ericsson's research on expertise highlights the role of acquired knowledge rather than innate talent in shaping top-level performance: if someone can master the knowledge and skills required for expertise, expert performance should occur. Ericsson concedes that there may well be individual differences in the degree to which people are motivated to engage in deliberate practice, but a key theme of Ericsson's research is that expertise is inextricably linked to knowledge compilation. Syed (2010) captures this idea neatly by arguing that deliberate practice is transformative. Fifth, research on deliberate practice shows us that concentration is essential for optimal learning (Ericsson, 2001; see also Young and Salmela, 2002). Sixth, the theory of deliberate practice has some interesting implications for talent identification programmes (Summers, 1999). For example, it suggests that instead of attempting to identify precociously talented young performers, sports organizations may be better advised to concentrate instead on searching for youngsters who display the types of psychological qualities (e.g. dedication to practice, determination to improve) which are likely to facilitate and sustain requisite regimes of deliberate practice.

Some criticisms of Ericsson's theories

As one might expect of such an environmentalist approach, Ericsson's theory of expertise has aroused as much controversy as enthusiasm within sport psychology. At a practical level, a recurring theme is that many coaches baulk at the claim that practice is more important than innate talent in determining athletic success.

Against this background of controversy, what are the principal criticisms directed at Ericsson's research on deliberate practice?

At least six criticisms of Ericsson's theories and research may be identified in sport psychology. First, an early objection to the theory of deliberate practice concerned apparently invalid extrapolation from the field of music to that of sport. The argument here is that there are important differences between these fields which Ericsson and his colleagues may have neglected. For example, as we mentioned earlier, deliberate practice is usually undertaken alone by musicians but in pairs or collectively in sport. As a result of this contextual difference, the nature of the practice activities undertaken may differ significantly. For example, the camaraderie generated among teammates who spend a lot of time training together may explain why athletes differ from musicians in their tendency to enjoy performing basic practice drills in their specialist domain (see Young and Salmela, 2002). A second criticism of Ericsson's theory is that it is based on evidence that is correlational rather than experimental in nature. According to this argument, these data may merely indicate that people who are highly motivated in a given field will spend more time practising in it and hence are more likely to become experts. Unfortunately, correlational research designs cannot control adequately for possible intervening variables such as motivation. Therefore, somewhat surprisingly, "it is still unclear how crucial motivation and commitment are as factors necessary to promote practice and engender skill development" (Hodges and Baker, 2011, p. 43). Moreover, correlative studies, based on retrospective-longitudinal designs, are unable to support the conclusion that deliberate practice results in the greatest improvement in performance. To address this issue, Baker and Young (2014) recommend that researchers explore how present performance markers regress upon amounts of deliberate practice while controlling for earlier career performance. Third, like many theories in psychology, Ericsson's stage theory of expertise may be criticized for ignoring important contextual and socioeconomic variables. In particular, this theory lacks a precise analysis of the effects of different resource constraints (e.g. access to suitable training facilities or specialist instructors) on people's progress through the three postulated stages of expertise. In a similar vein, Ericsson has not addressed adequately the impact of socioeconomic variables on the maintenance of deliberate practice schedules. Duffy et al. (2006) have highlighted the importance of environmental factors in determining athletic success (see Box 7.9). A fourth criticism is that Ericsson's claims are difficult to falsify or disprove empirically because it is very difficult to find a performance domain in which people have managed to attain expertise without engaging in extensive practice (Duffy et al., 2006). Fifth, another methodological issue is that Ericsson's theory relies heavily on people's retrospective accounts of their practice schedules. Data obtained retrospectively are potentially contaminated by exaggerations, memory biases and various kinds of response sets. Sixth, Ericsson's research appears to have underplayed the role that innate talent, or certain genetic factors, may play in the attainment of sporting expertise. Despite these criticisms, the theory of deliberate practice has proved to be rich and insightful in helping researchers to understand the nature and development of expertise in sport (see also Davids and Baker, 2007).

It has also stimulated much popular interest in athletic success (e.g. see Colvin, 2010; Gladwell, 2009; Syed, 2010). Before concluding this section, it may be helpful to address another relevant question. What factors are perceived by expert sports performers to have contributed to their success (see Box 7.9)?

What else matters? If deliberate practice can only partially explain why some individuals achieve high levels of expertise then what other factors might play a role? Hambrick et al. (2014) suggested that a number of factors including starting age, intelligence, personality and genes may be important in the development of expertise in all the major domains in which deliberate practice has been studied. First, Gobet and Campitelli (2007) and Howard (2012) found that starting age correlated negatively with chess rating even after statistically controlling for amounts of deliberate practice. These findings indicate that players who start at an early age have an advantage as adult players independent of how much deliberate practice they had accumulated. This evidence would suggest that there may be a "critical period" for the acquisition of certain complex skills. Second, global levels of intelligence (IQ) have been found to correlate with performance in chess and music. For example, Frydman and Lynn (1992) found that young chess players had an average performance IQ of 129 with the best players having a higher IQ (average = 131) than the weakest players (average = 124). Although general intelligence does not always

Box 7.9 In the spotlight How did we get here? What expert athletes tell us about the factors that determined their success

Despite scientific advances that have occurred in understanding the complex determinants of athletic success, two key questions remain largely ignored in this field. First, until the early 2000s, most researchers have tended to focus on "solitary determinants of expertise, often in contrived settings" (Janelle and Hillman, 2003, p. 25), thereby neglecting the impact of real-life environmental influences on athletes such as coaches, family members, the size of the community one grows up in and national sporting governing bodies. This neglect is surprising because it seems plausible that the amount of familial support and coaching advice that an aspiring athlete receives is likely to have a significant bearing on his or her future success. Second, an unresolved issue in expertise research is the relative neglect of athletes' perceptions of, and insights into, the barriers that they have overcome on their journey to elite-level performance. In an attempt to address these two oversights in the literature, Duffy et al. (2006) administered a questionnaire to a large (n=191) sample of international athletes to investigate the factors that were perceived to have either facilitated or inhibited their sporting development and success. Results confirmed that although the athletes acknowledged the importance of natural ability and motivation to their success, family support and dedicated coaches were also regarded as pivotal – especially in the early years of the athletes' careers. At a later stage, specialist coaching, sport science assistance and funding from national governing bodies were perceived as being crucially important. Among the main perceived inhibitors to athletic success were factors such as inadequate sport science support, insufficient funding and poor training facilities. Overall, Duffy et al.'s (2006) research highlighted the relatively neglected influence of environmental factors on the trajectory of athletes' careers.

predict performance (see Lyons et al., 2009 for a study on intelligence in American Football players) there is a clear need for research to explore how certain cognitive abilities (e.g. working memory capacity) influence the development of expertise. Third, certain personality factors including "grit" (i.e. a characteristic representing adherence to the achievement of long-term goals) and "passion" (see Bonneville-Roussy, 2011) positively predicted deliberate practice. Of course, it is important to note that while these personality factors may explain why some people engage in more deliberate practice activities they do not independently explain individual differences in performance. Fourth, in contrast to the meritocratic view that anyone can achieve high levels of success through hard work alone, there is some evidence that individual differences in performance are heritable. Vinkhuyzen et al. (2009) analysed self-report data from 1,685 twin pairs who rated their competence in chess, music, sports, arts and several other domains on a scale from 1 (less competent than most people) to 4 (exceptionally skilled). Results of the genetic analyses revealed that both in aptitude and talent, genetic factors contributed to between 50 per cent and 92 per cent of the observed variation. Further research is required to determine how genetic factors influence objective measures of performance (e.g. proficiency on certain musical tasks) and whether such effects can be accounted for by personality, intelligence or a combination of both.

Researchers in sport have also begun to argue that deliberate practice is a necessary but insufficient condition to explain expertise. In addition to a number of the environmental factors noted above (e.g. familial support), Hopwood et al. (2015) pointed to research which has indicated factors such as genetics, birthdate, birthplace, participation in a variety of sporting experiences, and psychological skills and characteristics as making a telling contribution to the development of sporting expertise. For example, a large number of studies have discovered what has been termed the relative age effect in sporting development. This latter term refers to the finding that those athletes whose birthdate is close to a sport's cut-off date (the date used to group athletes into age bands) are more likely to attain elite levels of performance (Cobley et al., 2009). These athletes are more likely to be chosen for developmental squads because of the physical advantages they hold over peers in their age group who were born further away from the sport's cut-off date. As a result these athletes have greater access to high levels of competition, quality coaching and more opportunities for deliberate practice. While all of the aforementioned factors are likely to play a role in the development of expertise, further research is required to model their relative importance and how they interact to facilitate or hinder skill advancement.

Evaluating research on expertise in sport: significance, problems and new directions

Research on expertise in athletes is important both for theoretical and practical reasons. Theoretically, expertise is one of the few topics that bridge the gap between sport psychology and mainstream cognitive psychology. Indeed, until the advent of research on everyday cognition (see Woll, 2002), research on athletic expertise was seen as falling between two stools in the sense that it was perceived as being too "physical" for cognitive psychology and too "cognitive" for sport psychology (Starkes et al., 2001). However, since about 2001, largely as a result of Ericsson's research programme on the relationship between practice and exceptional performance, athletic skills have begun to attract the interest of researchers from cognitive psychology. Meanwhile, at a practical level, research on athletic expertise is valuable because it has highlighted the need for greater understanding of the practice habits of sport performers of different levels of ability (Starkes, 2001). In addition, it has raised the intriguing practical question of whether or not perceptual training programmes can accelerate the skills of novices so that they can "hasten the journey" to expertise (Schorer et al., 2015). With regard to this issue, research suggests that cognitive interventions designed to develop the knowledge base underlying expertise are probably more effective in facilitating elite performance than are perceptual skills training programmes (see A. Williams, 2002b, 2003).

Despite its theoretical and practical significance, however, research on athletic expertise is hampered by at least three conceptual and methodological problems (see Hodges et al., 2007; Starkes et al., 2001). First, a great deal of confusion has surrounded the use of the term "expert". This term has been applied in a rather cavalier fashion to such heterogeneous groups as inter-varsity level athletes, provincial team members, professional performers and members of national squads – without any obvious recourse to the ten-year rule or 10,000 hours of practice criterion. However, Swann et al.'s (2015a) recent definition may provide researchers with a useful heuristic device for the selection of expert samples. Second, little is known at present about the retention of expertise in sport skills over time. In other words, how long does expertise in a given sport last? The paucity of evidence on this question is a consequence of the fact that most research on athletic expertise uses retrospective recall paradigms rather than longitudinal research designs. Third, the methods used to study expertise in sport (reviewed in the fourth section of this chapter) have been challenged on the grounds that they are often borrowed uncritically and without modification from mainstream psychology. For example, can researchers extrapolate validly from methods in which two-dimensional static slides are used to present dynamic three-dimensional sporting information?

Ideas for research projects on expertise in sport

Here are five suggestions for possible research projects on expertise in sport performers.

1. It is implicitly assumed in sport psychology that the term "expert" applies equally to athletes and coaches. But few studies have examined the similarities and differences between these two types of experts (performers and instructors, respectively) on the recall of sport-specific information presented to them. Therefore, it would be interesting to explore "expert versus expert" differences between athletes and coaches from a particular sport using the pattern recognition paradigm explained earlier in this chapter.
2. Tactical and technical creativity are believed to be key determinants of expertise (see Memmert, 2015, for a detailed discussion) and yet researchers know very little about

how these qualities develop in skilled athletes. Research is required to investigate how "deliberate play", "deliberate preparation" and "deliberate practice" contribute to the development of creativity in children. Another idea would be to explore if skilled performers design practice activities in a way that allows them to test and enhance their creative capacities.

3. In the light of the discovery by Young and Salmela (2002) that Ericsson's criteria of deliberate practice may not always apply to athletes, it would be interesting to investigate systematically the degree to which athletes enjoy the basic practice drills required by their sport. Few studies have been conducted in which the "enjoyability" of practice activities has been compared using an expert–novice paradigm across different sports. A good place to start is by reading McCarthy et al. (2008), who have investigated enjoyment of sport from a developmental perspective.

4. Relatively few studies been conducted on expertise in masters level athletes. As Hodges and Baker (2011, p. 44) concluded: "we know very little about the training and development of elite older athletes". What meta-cognitive strategies do master level athletes use to optimize their training by balancing hard work with rest/recovery? The notion of deliberate recovery could be investigated to explore the mechanisms underpinning offline motor learning during restful states (Baker and Young, 2014; Korman et al., 2007). It would be interesting to address this unresolved issue because it can provide us with valuable information about the relationship between ageing and skill maintenance (see also Medic, 2010).

5. Little is known about the mechanisms underpinning "continuous improvement" in sport (see Box 7.8). For example, you could explore how performers maintain the motivation required to engage in demanding training regimes over a prolonged period. Also, how do these performers learn to deal with a variety of challenges (including the reoccurrence of certain injuries or performance slumps) that are a ubiquitous feature of their performance environments?

Summary

■ We have long been fascinated by the exploits of expert performers in any field – those who display exceptional talent, knowledge and/or outstanding skills in a particular domain such as sport. Until the early 1990s, however, little was known about the psychological differences between expert and novice athletes. The purpose of this chapter was to investigate the nature and significance of research on athletic expertise in sport psychology.

■ The second section explained the meaning of the term "expertise" and indicated some reasons for its current popularity as a research topic.

■ The third section explored the general question of whether athletic success is determined more by hardware (i.e. physical) or by software (i.e. psychological) characteristics of sport performers. As we learned, available evidence largely supports the latter approach.

- The fourth section reviewed a variety of research methods and findings on expert–novice differences in sport.

- The fifth section examined the question of how athletic expertise develops over time. A special feature of this section was an explanation and critique of Ericsson's theory that expertise is largely due to the amount of deliberate practice accumulated by the performer.

- The sixth section evaluated the significance of, as well as some problems and new directions in, research on expertise in athletes.

- Finally, five ideas were provided for research projects in this field.

Team cohesion

Overview

Chapter 1 of the book examined the nature of the discipline and profession of sport psychology. Part 1 investigated the various psychological processes (e.g. motivation, anxiety, concentration, imagery) that affect *individual* athletes in their pursuit of excellence. But athletes rarely compete on their own in sport. Part 2 acknowledges the fact that *group* processes are crucial to success in sport. Oddly, however, group phenomena have been somewhat neglected by investigators in sport psychology. Thus, Carron and Brawley (2008, p. 230) concluded that "the amount of sport and exercise group research is surprisingly limited compared with the amount of research focused on the individual". Fortunately, a recent position statement on the rationale underlying, and optimal strategies for, team-focused approaches in sport psychology was published by Kleinert et al. (2012). Building on the preceding background, Chapter 8 explores the main theories, findings and issues arising from research on team cohesion and associated processes in sport.

8

Exploring team cohesion in sport
A critical perspective

Introduction

Few athletes compete alone in their sports. Instead, most of them interact either *with* or *against* other athletes collectively. Indeed, even in quintessentially individual sports, such as golf or tennis, competitive action is often assessed or aggregated as a team game (e.g. the Ryder Cup in golf or the Davis Cup in tennis) – where "team" is defined as a goal-oriented group of interdependent individuals (Cooke, 2015). Furthermore, many top individual sports performers travel and work with support groups of specialist advisers. For example, golfer Jordan Spieth, a two-time Major winner who has been ranked number 1 in the world, believes that golf is a team game rather than an individual sport – which is why he uses the word "we" when discussing his extraordinary success. Supported by his team of a caddy, coach, manager, trainer and sports chiropractic specialist, he claimed that "I'm the one hitting the shots and hitting the putts and getting the credit … but at the same time … we're competing together all for the same goal" (cited in Gaines, 2015).

Top tennis players rely on similar teams of specialist advisers. Thus, when Novak Djokovic lost to Rafael Nadal in the final of the 2010 US Open tennis championship, he congratulated his opponent *"and his team"* (cited in *Evening Herald*, 2010; italics ours). But what exactly is a "team"? And is "team spirit" essential for the achievement of sporting excellence? In relation to this latter question, many athletes and coaches believe in the importance of a sense of collective unity when competing in team competitions. At first glance, there is plenty of anecdotal evidence to support this latter belief. For example, according to Sven-Göran Eriksson, the former England soccer manager, "the creation of team spirit and the building of 'the good team' is … one of the coach's most important jobs" (Eriksson, 2002, p. 116). And such team-building initiatives by skilful managers can be highly effective. To illustrate, consider the remarkable achievement of manager Otto Rehhagel's team, Greece, in winning the

European Championship in soccer in 2004 despite the absence of individual star players. Similarly, Barcelona, the 2011 and 2015 Champions' League winners, earned universal praise not only for their brilliant passing game but also for their extraordinary team cohesion (see Figure 8.1). For players, this cohesion is often forged in the crucible of competition. To illustrate from a different sport, Jeremy Guscott, the former British and Irish Lions rugby player, claimed:

> tours are about bonding together ... Success depends on whether you come together or you split into factions ... There were times with this Lions squad when we felt invincible – that we could take on the whole world and beat them.
>
> (cited in Guscott, 1997, p. 153)

Similar views were expressed by triple-major winning golfer, Pádraig Harrington, about playing in the Ryder Cup: "I wouldn't want to win five matches out of five and the team lose. I'd happily take no points if we had a European victory" (cited in Gilleece, 2010).

Although these quotations about the importance of teams seem persuasive, they need to be tested using relevant scientific evidence. In this regard, attempts to forge team spirit have led to some rather bizarre practices (e.g. see Boxes 8.6 and 8.7 later in the chapter). So, do team-building exercises in sport really work? Is it true that young people's involvement in school sports builds their "character" and imbues them with a healthy respect for team spirit? Interestingly, it has long been believed that sports participation develops leadership qualities. For example,

Figure 8.1 Barcelona FC, winners of the 2011 Champions' League, displayed remarkable team cohesion (*source*: courtesy of Inpho photography)

the Duke of Wellington is alleged to have remarked that the battle of Waterloo "was won on the playing fields of Eton" (Knowles, 1999, p. 810). But scandals involving cheating in sport are not only ubiquitous today but have a surprisingly long history (e.g. see J. Perry, 2007). For example, consider the infamous "Black Sox scandal" that marred the 1919 World Series in baseball (Asinof, 1988). Eight members of the Chicago White Sox team deliberately lost games, thereby allowing the Cincinnati Reds to win the series. As punishment for such cheating behaviour, these players were banned for life from Major League Baseball. More recently, cheating has been detected in other sports such as rugby. For example, in the infamous "bloodgate" incident involving the English team Harlequins, a club doctor admitted deliberately cutting the lip of a player, Tom Williams, in order to cover up an earlier bogus injury (contrived by having the player bite a fake blood capsule) which enabled a specialist place-kicker to replace him as a substitute at a vital stage of his team's match against Leinster in a Heineken quarter-final in 2009 (Carter, 2010). In order to answer these and other relevant questions, this chapter is organized as follows.

In the next section, we explain how psychologists define key terms such as groups, teams and **group dynamics**. In the third section, we introduce the concept of team spirit, which has been defined operationally by sport psychologists as "cohesion" (also known as "cohesiveness") or the extent to which a group of athletes or players is united by a common purpose and bonds together in pursuit of that objective. This section also examines the measurement of team cohesion and its relationship to athletic performance. Given the assumption that cohesion can be enhanced, the fourth section of the chapter investigates the nature and efficacy of team-building activities in sport psychology. In the fifth section, we briefly evaluate the commonly held belief that team sports foster desirable psychological qualities in participants. The sixth section of the chapter outlines some new directions for research on team cohesion in sport. Finally, specific suggestions are provided for possible research projects in this field.

Unfortunately, due to space restrictions, this chapter is not able to deal with other questions concerning the impact of groups on individual athletic performance. For example, the issue of how the presence of other people such as spectators and/or fellow competitors affects athletes' performance lies beyond the scope of this chapter. This latter topic, which was mentioned briefly in Chapter 1, is called "social facilitation" (or the classic phenomenon by which people tend to perform certain skilled tasks – such as winding a fishing reel – better in the presence of others than they do when performing them in isolation; Gilson, 2014), and was first studied empirically by Triplett (1898 – but see Box 8.1 for an alternative view of this study).

According to social facilitation theory (Zajonc, 1965), the presence of another person tends to increase our arousal levels and this surge in arousal facilitates the likelihood that we will perform the *dominant response* (i.e. a behavioural action that is highly practised and executed without deliberate cognitive control). Furthermore, Zajonc (1965) proposed that when the task to be performed is relatively easy or well learned, the dominant response is likely to be the correct one.

Box 8.1 Thinking critically about ... Triplett's (1898) research on social facilitation: what happens when the data from a seminal study is reanalysed using modern statistics?

It has long been claimed (e.g. by Allport, 1954) that Triplett (1898) conducted the first experimental demonstration in psychology of social facilitation effects. However, this claim is challenged in a provocative paper by Stroebe (2012) which describes a reanalysis of the original data using modern statistical methods.

By way of background, Triplett (1898) was curious to find out if cyclists go faster when racing with others (or when being paced) than they do when riding alone racing against the clock. From his analysis of records of the average speed of cyclists under these different conditions, Triplett (1898) concluded that cyclists do indeed ride faster in competition (or with pacers) than they do when alone. However, he acknowledged that this conclusion should be tempered by awareness that racing cyclists specialize in certain types of races and do not tend to participate in events for which they are not suited. Therefore, the observed differences in speed between cyclists in different race conditions may have been caused by self-selection rather than by social facilitation.

In order to circumvent this methodological constraint, Triplett (1898) conducted an experiment in which forty girls and boys aged between 9 and 15 years performed a simple task (namely, winding a fishing reel) either alone or in competition with another participant. Winding the fishing reel caused a small flag sewn to a cord to traverse a 4m closed circuit. A trial consisted of four circuits of the course, and the duration required for this performance was measured by a stopwatch. After a practice trial, each participant performed six trials, three alone and three with a competitor.

Triplett (1898) categorized his participants into three groups on the basis of their performance during the trials: people who were stimulated positively by competition (n=20), those who were not affected (n=10), and those who were "overstimulated" by competition and performed more slowly (n=10). From a visual inspection of his data (note that quantitative inferential methods such as Student's t-test had not been developed in the 1890s), Triplett concluded "that the bodily presence of another contestant participating simultaneously in the race serves to liberate latent energy not ordinarily available" (p. 533). However, when Strube (2005) reanalysed Triplett's (1898) data using modern statistical methods, he discovered "barely a statistical hint of the social facilitation of performance" (p. 280). Furthermore, Strube (2005) discovered that half of the participants in the original study showed no evidence of social facilitation effects.

Critical thinking questions

Do you think that the validity of the social facilitation effect is threatened by Strube's (2005) and Stroebe's (2012) critical reappraisal of Triplett's (1898) paper? Is it fair to reanalyse scientific data from one era using methods invented in a more modern era? How does the distortion that occurred in summarizing Triplett's (1898) findings compare with that reported for other phenomena in psychology (see Vicente and Brewer, 1993, for an excellent paper on this issue)?

In such circumstances, the increase in arousal caused by the presence of others should create "social facilitation" effects. However, when the task is difficult or not well learned, the dominant response is likely to be the *incorrect* one. In such situations, increased arousal tends to enhance the occurrence of the incorrect dominant response, resulting in a deterioration in performance. Interestingly, a classic meta-analysis by Bond and Titus (1983), which examined the results of over 200 studies using over 20,000 research participants, discovered that the presence of others was significantly associated with enhanced performance on simple tasks but impaired performance on complex tasks.

Reviews of research on social facilitation have been provided by Strauss (2002) and Uziell (2007). Similarly, the converse phenomenon of social loafing in sport, or the tendency for people to exert less effort when working in groups than when working individually (see Karau and Williams, 1993) also lies beyond the scope of this chapter (but see Gilson, 2014, for a brief overview).

Groups, teams and group dynamics in sport

In everyday life, we tend to see any collection of other people as a group. However, social psychologists are much more precise than laypeople in their usage of this term. Thus, Alderfer (1977) defined a "group" as "an intact social system, complete with boundaries, interdependence for some shared purpose, and differentiated member roles" (cited in Hackman and Katz, 2010, p. 1210). It is this sense of mutual interaction or interdependence for a common purpose that distinguishes the members of a group from a mere aggregation of individuals. As Hodge (1995) observed, a collection of people who happen to go for a leisurely swim after work on the same day each week does not, strictly speaking, constitute a "group" because these swimmers do not interact with each other in a structured manner. By contrast, a squad of elite young competitive swimmers who train every morning before going to school *is* a sports group because they not only share a common objective (training for competition) but also interact with each other in formal ways (e.g. by warming up together beforehand). It is this sense of people coming together to achieve a common objective that really defines the term "team" in sport psychology.

Developing this notion, psychologists regard sports *teams* as a special type of group (Carron and Hausenblas, 1998). In particular, teams have four key characteristics – apart from having the defining properties of mutual interaction and task interdependence – that serve to differentiate them from aggregates of strangers (see also Carron et al., 2009). First, they have a collective sense of identity – a "we-ness" rather than a collection of "I-nesses". This collective consciousness emerges when individual team members and non-team members agree that the group is distinguishable from other groups ("us" versus "them"). This "us versus them" mentality is commonly encountered in sports like soccer. Recall from Chapter 2 Alex Ferguson's comment that managers can influence players' motivation by creating issues (e.g. "them and us") to galvanize them into action. Similarly, the leaders of the successful English soccer team Wimbledon FC, of the late 1980s, called themselves the "crazy gang" and their manager Dave Bassett used this self-styled identity as a cohesive force when preparing his team to compete against higher ranked football clubs. Often, this type of social bonding seems to lead to enhanced team performance. The former Liverpool soccer player Alan Hansen was amazed at the intimidatory tactics and "all-for-one" spirit which the Wimbledon players showed in the tunnel before they defeated his team in the 1988 FA Cup Final (Hansen, 1999). Second, sports teams are characterized by a set of distinctive *roles*. As Carron et al. (2009, p. 64) explained, group members "develop a generalized expectation for those individuals who through ability or experience assume specific responsibilities". For example, soccer and rugby teams have acknowledged roles for creative players who generate or exploit scoring opportunities as well as for tough-tackling "enforcers" whose job it is to prevent opponents from playing creatively. The third feature of sports teams is their use of *structured modes of communication* within the group. This type of communication often involves nicknames and shorthand instructions for teammates. Fourth, teams develop *norms* or social rules that prescribe what group members either should or should not do in certain circumstances. Individual performers learn to ignore the idiosyncratic routines of their teammates as they prepare for important competitive events. Having explained the key characteristics of teams, a sports team may be defined as

> a collection of two or more individuals who possess a common identity, have consensus on a shared, purpose, share a common fate, exhibit structured patterns of interaction and communication, hold common perceptions about group structure, are personally and instrumentally interdependent, and consider themselves to be a group.
>
> (Carron and Brawley, 2008, p. 215)

In view of the preceding characteristics, teams are regarded as *dynamic* entities by sport psychologists (for reviews of research in this field, see Beauchamp and Eys, 2008; Bruner et al., 2013; Carron and Eys, 2012; Eys et al., 2010). Interestingly, the term "dynamic" comes from the Greek word *dunamikós,* which means "powerful". Perhaps not surprisingly, certain aspects of team behaviour change over time. For example, Tuckman (1965) has identified four hypothetical stages in the development of any team. In the first stage, *forming*, the team's members come together and engage in an informal assessment of each other's strengths and weaknesses. Second, the *storming* stage is postulated in which interpersonal conflict is common as the players compete for the coach's attention and strive to establish their rank in the pecking order of the team. Third, the *norming* stage occurs when group members begin to see themselves as a team united by a common task and by interpersonal bonds. Finally, the *performing* stage occurs when the members of the team resolve to channel their energies as a cohesive unit into the pursuit of agreed goals. A similar account of the way in which teams change over time has been offered by Whitaker (1999), who identified three stages of evolution: *inclusion* (where new members are preoccupied with how to become a part of the team), *assertion* (where members struggle to establish their position within the hierarchy of the team) and *cooperation* (where members strive to work together to fulfil team goals). Unfortunately, although both of these hypothetical stage models of team development seem plausible intuitively, they have not been validated adequately by empirical evidence.

Having explained that teams are dynamic entities and hence change over time, it is important to clarify what psychologists mean by the term "group dynamics". In general, sport psychologists use this term in at least three different ways (Carron and Hausenblas, 1998; Widmeyer et al., 2002). First, it denotes the scientific study of how athletes behave in groups, especially in face-to-face situations (e.g. when coaches address players in team talks). Second, "group dynamics" refers broadly to a host of factors (e.g. confidence) that are believed to play a role in determining team performance. Third, this term designates the processes that generate *change* in groups (Cashmore, 2008). It is mainly the second and third of these meanings that are explored in this chapter – especially, the question of how team spirit or **cohesion** is related to team performance. Let us now explore this idea of team spirit in more detail.

Team spirit or social cohesion: from popular understanding to psychological analysis

It has long been believed that successful sports teams have a unique spirit or sense of unity that transcends the simple aggregation of their individual components. This idea is captured by an insight from Vince Lombardi (one of the most successful managers in the history of American football): "Build for your team a feeling of oneness, of dependence on one another and of strength to be derived by unity" (cited in Pescosolido and Saavedra, 2012, p. 744). It is also captured by an old Irish proverb which states "ní neart go cur le chéile" (there is no strength without unity). As an example of this unity, consider the extraordinary sense of togetherness displayed by the victorious European team during its 2002 Ryder Cup golf match against the United States. Illustrating this spirit, Darren Clarke, the 2016 Ryder Cup captain but then a member of the European team, revealed that

> we played as a team, we dined as a team, we talked as a team and we won as a team ... The team spirit this week has been the best that I have experienced in this, my third Ryder Cup.

(cited in O'Sullivan, 2002b)

This sense of togetherness among Ryder Cup golfers is epitomized by the quotation from Pádraig Harrington at the beginning of the chapter in which he states that he would prefer to sacrifice individual victories for team success (see Figure 8.2). Before we analyse what team spirit means in sport, however, let us pause for a moment to consider the benefits of teamwork in a rather unusual domain – namely, the animal kingdom. Have you ever wondered why migrating birds fly in a peculiar "V"-like formation (called an "echelon"; Batt, 2007)? According to Mears and Voehl (1994), this pattern is adaptive because as each bird in the "V" flaps its wings, it creates an "uplift" current for the bird behind it. This uplift enables the entire flock of birds to fly significantly farther than any of the individual birds

Figure 8.2 Team spirit helped the European team to victory over the United States in the 2014 Ryder Cup (*source:* courtesy of Inpho photography)

could fly alone. But how can this idea of synergy among flocks of bird apply to sports behaviour? In order to answer this question, we need to analyse what team spirit or cohesion means to athletes, coaches and sport psychologists.

Athletes' and coaches' views on cohesion

Team cohesion has long been valued highly by coaches and sports performers. This high regard is supported by research evidence. For example, team cohesion is associated positively with increased positive affect, increased effort, decreased role ambiguity, decreased cognitive anxiety and decreased social loafing (mentioned earlier) (Statler, 2010). Furthermore, Pescosolido and Saavedra (2012) postulated that **cohesion** is particularly important when teams have to synchronize a response in competitive environments. Specifically, they argued that "understanding players' skill sets, preferences, moods, and habits are important for a synchronous response" (p. 751). Perhaps not surprisingly, many team managers believe that team cohesion can be *enhanced* through appropriate instruction and experience. For example, Sam Torrance, the manager of the European Ryder Cup golf team in 2002, sought advice from two successful soccer managers – Alex Ferguson (then manager of Manchester United) and Sven-Göran Eriksson (then coach of England) (R. Williams, 2002a) – in an effort to enrich the **task cohesion** and **social** cohesion of his players before the match. The key message delivered by these managers was the importance of treating all of the golfers in the team in the same way (R. Williams, 2002c). This principle was appreciated greatly by the players:

in commenting on Torrance's captaincy, Pádraig Harrington said, "everybody got the same treatment, there were no stars in the team ... he kept the spirits up all the way" (cited in A. Reid, 2002). By contrast with this egalitarian approach, Curtis Strange, the captain of the US team, showed evidence of preferential treatment for certain players. For example, he allowed Tiger Woods to engage in his customary early morning practice round on his own before the match whereas he insisted that the other players had to practise together. Some studies on university athletes suggests that perceived inequity, or favouritism on the part of coaches towards certain individuals, decreased team cohesion (Turman, 2003).

In addition to believing that team cohesion can be increased (see L. Martin et al., 2009; see also later in the chapter for some practical techniques in this regard), many athletes and coaches claim that individual performers must learn to subordinate their skills and efforts to the goals of the team. Consider the views of Michael Jordan on this issue. Jordan, who is rated as one of the greatest basketball players of all time, having won six world basketball championships with the Chicago Bulls, remarked that "if you think and achieve as a team, the individual accolades will take care of themselves. Talent wins games but *teamwork and intelligence win championships*" (italics ours; see www.quotesandpoem.com/quotes/listquotes/author/michael-jordan). This view supports the old coaching adage that "there is no I in team" (although – according to the comedian Ricky Gervais's character, David Brent, "there is a 'ME' if you look hard enough" (see www.bioteams.com/2006/02/05/managing_teams_david.html).

Despite this adage, however, there are situations in which the "I" in teams becomes apparent. As an extreme example of this phenomenon, consider what happens when the *captain* of a team challenges the authority of its coach or manager. Two interesting case studies of this problem have occurred in World Cup soccer finals since 2002. The first incident occurred in May 2002 shortly before the World Cup soccer finals in Japan and Korea when Roy Keane, who was then the captain of the Republic of Ireland team, was sent home after a heated argument with his manager, Mick McCarthy. This incident happened in Saipan, the location of the team's training camp for the finals.

By way of background, the relationship between Keane and Mick McCarthy was never cordial. Despite this coolness between the captain and the manager, the team had played very well in qualifying for the World Cup finals. But the relationship between these men changed dramatically in Saipan when Roy Keane gave a controversial interview to a journalist in which he criticized both the training facilities and preparation methods of the Irish squad.

Following this interview, he was summoned to attend a "clear the air" meeting with McCarthy and the rest of the players. At this meeting, Keane not only questioned the adequacy of the Irish team's facilities (citing a lack of training gear and footballs as well as deficient medical support) but also publicly rebuked his manager in a vitriolic speech. Not surprisingly, this speech and its consequences attracted media coverage around the world. More significantly, it raised a debate about an important psychological issue – namely, whether or not one player's striving for perfection can impede the progress of the team. For the manager (and some of the team's senior players), Keane's speech was inexcusable and had to be punished by instant dismissal from the rest of the tournament. This is precisely what happened. Unfortunately, as no physical injury had been involved in prompting Keane's departure, the dismissal left the Ireland squad one player short of the quota permitted by the World Cup organizers. It also left the players emotionally drained by the shock of losing their captain in such highly controversial circumstances.

Although there are two sides to this incident (e.g. why did the manager not try to resolve his differences with his captain privately or through an agreed intermediary before summoning him to a specially convened squad meeting?), McCarthy's decision to dismiss Roy Keane reflects a popular coaching belief that any potential threat to team harmony must be removed instantly. Weinberg and Gould (2007, p. 201) urged players and coaches "to respond to the problem quickly so that negative feelings don't build up". Similarly Sven-Göran Eriksson, former manager of England, warned about the danger of negative thinking within a squad: "A bad atmosphere can spread quickly, particularly if one of the 'leaders of opinion' in the team represents the negative thinking – the captain, for instance" (Eriksson, 2002, p. 116). Curiously, the Irish team performed exceptionally well during this competition in spite of losing its most influential player, and was defeated in the knockout stages by Spain only after a penalty shootout.

The second incident involving a mutiny by a national soccer team's captain occurred in South Africa in June 2010 when Patrice Evra (captain of France) and the other twenty-two players in the national squad refused to participate in a training session organized by the team's manager, Raymond Domenech, after a heated disagreement about tactics. Following a temporary resolution of this problem, the players returned to training but subsequently performed poorly and France was eliminated from the tournament. Several months later, the French Football Federation suspended Evra and the other perceived ringleaders of the team's rebellion (namely, Nicolas Anelka, Franck Ribery and Jeremy Toulalan). Anelka was suspended for *eighteen matches*, thereby effectively ending his international career (L. Davies, 2010). These two incidents show that team captains can sometimes rebel against coaches on the eve of championship finals, but the outcome of such dissent is not always clear-cut. Whereas the Ireland team appeared to "pull together" after its captain's departure, the French squad continued to perform poorly after its mutiny against the national coach.

In this section, we have seen that team spirit or cohesion is important to athletes and coaches. But what progress have psychologists made in understanding and measuring the construct of team cohesion? Also, what does research reveal about the relationship between the cohesion and performance of a team? The remainder of this section addresses these questions.

Cohesion (or cohesiveness) in psychology

Until now, we have used the term "cohesion" to refer to a form of social bonding between individuals in order to achieve a common purpose. Let us now analyse this term in more depth. According to the *New Penguin English Dictionary*, the word "cohesion" comes from the Latin word *cohaerere*, meaning "to stick together" (R. Allen, 2000). In popular expression, cohesion refers to acting or working together as a unit. In physics, however, the term has a slightly different meaning as it designates the molecular attraction by which the particles of a body are united together (R. Allen, 2000). Interestingly, psychologists have combined the common sense and physicists' approach to cohesion when describing it as "the total field of forces which act on members to remain in the group" (Festinger et al., 1950, p. 164). Historically, this definition emerged from psychological research on group integration processes evident in accommodation units for returned US veterans of the Second World War. Apart from Festinger and his colleagues, another seminal figure in research on cohesion was the social psychologist Kurt Lewin, a refugee from German Nazi oppression, who was fascinated by the powerful ways in which groups affect people's behaviour. Adopting a "field of forces" model of human behaviour, Lewin (1935) regarded cohesion as a set of ties (including forces of attraction and repulsion) that bind members of a group together. He proposed that the main objectives of any group were to maintain cohesion and to enhance performance – two recurrent themes throughout the team cohesion literature.

This idea of cohesion as the "glue" that integrates members of a group was echoed subsequently by sport psychologists but with one important modification – namely, the idea that cohesion is a *multidimensional* rather than a unidimensional construct. Adopting this multidimensional perspective, Carron et al. (1998, p. 213) defined cohesion as "a tendency for a group to stick together and remain united in the pursuit of its instrumental objectives and/or for the satisfaction of member affective needs". Based on this proposition, Carron and his colleagues postulated an influential conceptual framework to account for the construct of cohesion (see reviews by Carron and Brawley, 2008; Carron et al., 2007). In this framework, Carron and his colleagues proposed that cohesion emerges from two kinds of perceptions: those arising from group members' perceptions of the group as a totality ("group integration") and those generated by members' perceptions of the personal attractiveness of the group ("individual attractions to group"). Put simply, these dimensions reflect a bifurcation between "task" and "social" components of any group. Carron's analysis of cohesion implies that it is a desirable state. In short, if cohesion reflects people's tendency to stick together in order to pursue common goals, it should be associated with team success.

But is this hypothesis supported by empirical evidence? We shall address this question later in the chapter. Before that, let us quickly sketch some key features of cohesiveness in sport psychology. First, as mentioned above, cohesion is a multidimensional construct. As Carron and his colleagues have suggested, two dimensions of this construct are important – the desire of group members to complete a given task (task cohesion) as well as a need by team members both to form and maintain interpersonal bonds (social cohesion). Based on this proposition, Carron et al. (1998) developed a theoretical model of group cohesion similar to that displayed in Figure 8.3.

Carron et al. (1998) distinguished between two overarching strands of cohesion: "group integration" and "individual attraction to group". Group

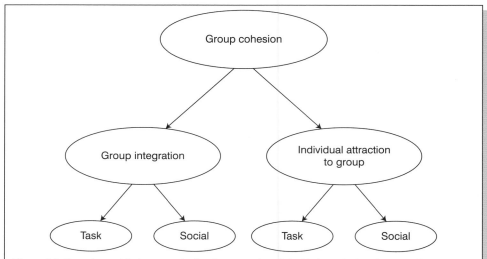

Figure 8.3 Carron's model of group cohesion (*source*: adapted, by kind permission, from A.V. Carron, W. N. Widmeyer, and L. R. Brawley (1985) The development of an instrument to assess cohesion in sport teams: The Group Environment Questionnaire. *Journal of Sport Psychology*, 7, 244–266, p. 248)

integration represents each team member's perception of the closeness, bonding and degree of unity in the group as a whole. Individual attraction to the group refers to each team member's perception of what encourages him or her to remain in the group. Figure 8.3 also shows that both types of perceptions may be divided into "task" and "social" orientations. Combining these various aspects of the construct, four dimensions of cohesion were proposed by Carron et al. (1998). These four dimensions of cohesion are group integration-task (GI-T), group integration-social (GI-S), individual attractions to the group-task (ATG-T) and individual attractions to the group-social (ATG-S). According to S. Burke et al. (2008), these four dimensions are believed to account for the majority of variance in cohesiveness. Applying this model to sport, Hodge (1995) and Hodge and McKenzie (1999) suggested that "task" and "social" cohesion are synonymous with "teamwork" and "team spirit", respectively.

The second characteristic of group cohesion is that it is a *dynamic* process. In other words, cohesion is not a fixed, static property of a group but changes over time as a function of a number of variables such as the degree of success or failure experienced by the team. A soccer team could score highly on cohesion if it has won a considerable number of games in succession, but this cohesion might diminish if the team were to lose one or two important matches. Unfortunately, despite acknowledging the dynamic nature of this construct, few researchers in sport psychology have monitored changes in team cohesion over the course of a competitive season. One exception to this trend is a study by Holt and Sparkes (2001), who followed a university soccer squad throughout a season and found that when the team was eliminated from a mid-season tournament, the players revised their goals for the remainder of the period. This result is not surprising because when a team competes in two tournaments simultaneously, some confusion is likely about which of these tournaments is more important. In this regard, Holt and Sparkes' (2001) research also shows that team cohesion can vary considerably over a competitive season.

The third property of cohesion is that it is characterized by "instrumentality". Put simply, people join or become a team for utilitarian reasons – to achieve a common purpose. Finally, Carron et al. (1998) proposed that the construct of cohesion has an emotional dimension which is derived from social relationships and feelings of togetherness among the players. In summary, cohesion is a multidimensional construct whose practical importance for team performance can be gauged from the variety of contexts in which it has been studied, such as in military settings (Hedlund et al., 2015), in the industrial/organizational sphere (Cannon-Bowers and Bowers, 2011; Mathieu et al., 2010) and, of course, in the world of sport (Rovio et al., 2009; Spink et al., 2015).

Despite the apparent clarity of the preceding theoretical analysis, the construct of cohesion has been criticized on both conceptual and methodological grounds (see reviews by Casey-Campbell and Martens, 2009; Salas et al., 2015). Thus, following a review of cohesion measures, Salas et al. (2015) concluded that studies in this area constitute a "vast, often ambiguous literature that offers little insight about which approaches are most effective" (pp. 366–367). More specifically, at least five problems afflict research on cohesion in sport. First, whereas a minority of investigators define cohesion unidimensionally, the majority study it as a multidimensional construct (Salas et al., 2015). Next, Casey-Campbell and Martens (2009, p. 235) pointed out that the widespread assumption that group cohesion is a dynamic construct "has still to be tested". One way of doing this is to assess cohesion longitudinally – which has rarely occurred to date (Salas et al., 2015). Third, Mudrack (1989a, p. 38) noted a dilemma at the heart of this construct – the fact that although cohesion is alleged to be a property of groups, the group itself "as a distinct entity is beyond the grasp of our understanding and measurement". The problem here is that the "field of forces" approach to cohesion (discussed briefly above) is difficult to operationalize and the "attractions to the group" approach is conceptually inadequate because "it focuses exclusively on individuals at the expense of the group, and therefore may not entirely capture the concept of group cohesiveness" (Mudrack, 1989a, p. 42). Later in the chapter, we shall return to this thorny issue of how to select the most appropriate unit of analysis (group or individual) when studying cohesion in teams. Fourth, another criticism of research on cohesion comes from Mudrack (1989a), who complained that studies in this field have been plagued by "confusion, inconsistency, and almost inexcusable sloppiness". To illustrate this allegation, he listed a variety of meanings spawned by the term cohesion. These include interpersonal attraction, group resistance to break-up, a desire to remain in the group, feelings of group membership, and the value that people place on group membership. As these referents do not share many common features, the meaning of the term "cohesion" is elusive. A similar problem was noted by Widmeyer et al. (2002, p. 298) who concluded that "there is no conceptual or theoretical model that can be used as the basis for defining and measuring cohesion". As an illustration of this difficulty, Mudrack (1989b) reported that of twenty-three investigations conducted between

1975 and 1985, no two studies used the same operational indices of cohesiveness. Unfortunately, there has been little progress in achieving a consensus definition of cohesion. Casey-Campbell and Martens (2009, p. 224) lamented the "lack of consistent definitions and operationalizations" in the field. Finally, Shapcott and Carron (2010) highlighted a recurrent conceptual problem in this field in the form of "reification" – the fallacy of treating an abstraction as a concrete entity. They warned that "reification can arise when individual member responses are summed to reflect a group property without first determining whether some degree of consensus is present" (Shapcott and Carron, 2010, p. 96). For example, they cite the case of two members of a doubles team whose responses are at opposite ends of a continuum of cohesiveness scores. Shapcott and Carron (2010) suggest that it is wrong to reify this property of the team by averaging these extreme scores to indicate that the doubles team has a "moderate" level of cohesiveness. Given such conceptual problems in defining cohesion, what is the best way to measure this construct?

Measuring team cohesion

The profusion of different definitions of cohesion is matched by a plethora of different ways of measuring this construct (see review by Salas et al., 2015). Indeed, so plentiful are such measures (amounting to at least thirty-five tests; Salas et al., 2015) that Casey-Campbell and Martens (2009, p. 224) remarked wryly that "there are approximately as many methods for assessing cohesion as there are researches investigating the construct itself". Although the perceived cohesion of a group can be assessed using methods such as **sociograms** (techniques in which members are asked confidentially to name other group members whom they either like or dislike), specially developed self-report scales are more popular among researchers in this field. One of the earliest of these scales was a measure developed by Martens et al. (1972) called the Sport Cohesiveness Questionnaire (SCQ). This seven-item test requires respondents to rate perceived cohesion in terms of friendship (interpersonal attraction), personal power or influence, enjoyment, closeness, teamwork, sense of belonging and perceived value of membership. Unfortunately, despite its superficial plausibility or face validity, this test has never been validated adequately for use with athletes. Also, it is limited to the extent that it focused more on social cohesion (or the closeness between players) than on task cohesion (or the degree of common purpose between players). To overcome such limitations, two other measures of team cohesion were developed – the Team Cohesion Questionnaire (TCQ; Gruber and Gray, 1982) and the Multidimensional Sport Cohesion Instrument (MSCI; Yukelson et al., 1984). The TCQ contains thirteen items which provide measures of six different factors: satisfaction with team performance, satisfaction with one's own performance, task cohesion, affiliation cohesion, desire for recognition, and value of group membership. Unfortunately, as with its predecessor, little evidence is available on the psychometric adequacy of this test. The MSCI is a twenty-two-item self-report scale which asks people to rate perceived cohesion in terms of such factors as attraction to the group, unity of purpose, quality of teamwork and valued roles (which is alleged to reflect identification with group membership). As with its predecessor, however, the validity of the MSCI is unknown, and it is hampered by the fact that its items relate only to basketball. Apart from their psychometric shortcomings, the TCQ and MSCI suffer from another problem, namely, a flimsy theoretical basis. This problem arose from the fact that many of their items were borrowed from other instruments without adequate theoretical justification (Widmeyer et al., 2002).

By contrast with the preceding measures, the Group Environment Questionnaire (GEQ; Carron et al., 1985) has become the most widely used instrument in research on adult perceptions of team cohesion. The dominance of this test is attributable mainly to two factors: it is based on an explicit conceptual model of cohesion (e.g. see Carron and Brawley, 2008; see also Figure 8.3) and it has impressive psychometric qualities. The GEQ is an eighteen-item self-report questionnaire scale which purports to measure the four key dimensions of team cohesion described in the previous section. The first dimension in this test, which was developed for athletic populations between the ages of 18 and 30 years (Eys et al., 2009), is "group integration-task" (GI-T: five items) which refers to an individual member's perceptions of the similarity, closeness and bonding within the group as a whole with regard to the task it faces. It is measured by items such as "our team is united in trying to reach its goals for performance" or "we all take responsibility for any loss or poor performance by our team". Second, "group integration-social" (GI-S: four items) refers to an individual member's feelings about the similarity and unification of the group as a social unit. A sample item here is that "members of our team would rather go out on their own than get together as a team" (reverse scored) or "our team would like to spend time together in the offseason". Third, "individual attractions to the group-task" (ATG-T: four items) designates a team member's feelings about his or her personal involvement with the group's task. It is typically assessed using items like "I'm not happy with the amount of playing time I get" (reverse scored) or "I do not like this team's style of play" (reverse scored). Fourth, "individual attractions to the group-social" (ATG-S: five items) describes an individual team member's feelings about his or her personal social interactions with the group. A sample item to assess this component of cohesion is "I am not going to miss the members of this team when the season ends" (reverse scored) or "some of my best friends are on this team".

Responses to these items are indicated by choosing the appropriate answer on a nine-point Likert scale ranging from "strongly disagree" (1) to "strongly agree" (9). Negative items are reverse scored to ensure that relatively higher scores on the GEQ reflect stronger perceptions of team cohesiveness among group members. Not surprisingly, it has become very popular in sport psychology and has also been used in exercise settings. For example, Estabrooks and Carron (1999) investigated the relationship between exercise intentions, attitudes and behaviour among a sample of elderly adults in an exercise group. Results showed that, as expected, both social cohesion and task cohesion were associated positively with the participants' attitudes to, and frequency of attendance at, the exercise classes.

In general, the psychometric characteristics of the GEQ are impressive (Dion, 2000; Steca et al., 2013). Specifically, with regard to test reliability, the internal consistency coefficients of the four cohesion subscales range from 0.64 (in the case of "individual attractions to the group-social") to 0.75 (for "individual attractions to the group-task"). Several studies have reported solid factorial validity and satisfactory reliability (with alpha values ranging from 0.63 to 0.81) for the test (Spink et al., 2010). Normative data for this test are also available (see Carron et al., 2002c). Furthermore, Carron et al. (1998) supported the construct validity of the GEQ on the basis of evidence that the four dimensions of cohesion were significantly positively associated with such variables as role clarity in teams and adherence to exercise programmes. They were also significantly negatively correlated with variables like social loafing – defined earlier in this chapter as a tendency for some people within a group to "slacken off" when working towards a common goal. Unfortunately, critical reviewers (e.g. Casey-Campbell and Martens, 2009; Dion, 2000) have noted that the factorial structure of the test remains unclear due to equivocal research findings. Whereas Li and Harmer (1996) replicated Carron's four-factor model in their analysis of cohesion processes in baseball and softball players, Dyce and Cornell's (1996) factor analysis of cohesion data from musicians yielded a three-factor structure. Specifically, these latter investigators concluded "the results support social-task distinctions ... but not the group integration-individual attractions to the group distinctions" (Dyce and Cornell, 1996, p. 264). Carless and De Paola (2000) also reported a three-factor structure for the GEQ – with these factors being task cohesion, social cohesion and attraction to the group. Similar doubts about the factorial validity of the GEQ were raised by Schutz et al. (1994), who discovered that different factor structures emerged depending on the gender of the participants. In an effort to resolve the criticism that the GEQ is not valid for use with young athletes (those aged under 18 years), Eys et al. (2009) and Martin et al. (2011) developed a cohesion perception instruments designed for adolescent (age 13–17 years) athletes. This measures differs from the GEQ, however, because it only assesses task and social cohesion in a general manner (i.e. it does not offer a breakdown of the variables "individual attraction to the group" and "group integration"). More recently, a sport cohesion questionnaire for children has been developed (Martin et al., 2013).

Before concluding this section, we should consider the question of the most appropriate level of analysis to adopt in studying team cohesion (see also Dion, 2000). Put simply, is cohesion investigated best as a property of a *group* (Carless and De Paola, 2000), as a characteristic of its *individual members* (e.g. Hogg, 1992), or perhaps as some *combination* of these different units of analysis (e.g. Widmeyer et al., 1985)? Depending on how this question is answered, different interpretations of the cohesion–performance relationship may emerge. In their meta-analysis of the relationship between cohesion and performance, Gully et al. (1995) discovered that the correlations between these variables was stronger for studies that had used the *group* rather than the individual as the unit of analysis. In an effort to resolve this issue about which unit of analysis to use, Carron et al. (2002a) and Carron and Brawley (2008) provided the following practical suggestions for researchers. First, one should consider the research question being asked. For example, if researchers are interested in exploring the relationship between cohesion and individual adherence behaviour in an exercise group, the individual's perception of group cohesion is crucial. By contrast, if a researcher wishes to explore the relationship between perceived cohesion and team performance in a sport setting, the average level of cohesion in the group is the variable of most interest. Second, cohesion researchers need to consider the type of theory being tested. For example, if such a theory concerns social influences within groups, then the group itself is the most appropriate level of analysis. Third, statistical considerations are important. For example, appropriate statistical procedures need to be used to analyse individual team members' responses because these responses are nested within groups. Having highlighted the complexity of analysing cohesion, let us now turn to a more practical question. What is the relationship between team cohesion and performance?

Team cohesion and performance

For many years, sport psychologists have assumed that team cohesion is positively associated with desirable outcomes such as improved communication between athletes/players, increased expenditure of effort and enhanced team success (Carron and Spink, 1993). But is this assumption supported by empirical evidence? Do cohesive teams really achieve more success than teams in which disharmony reigns? Although there is a well-established positive link between team cohesion and performance (Carron et al., 2002c), this relationship is fraught with difficulty (see Box 8.2 later). For example, there are many anecdotal accounts of sports teams that were highly successful *in spite* of enmity and disharmony between teammates. Thus, the American former basketball star Dennis Rodman was frequently at odds with his fellow players in the Chicago Bulls team of the late 1990s, yet he managed to contribute significantly to this team's extraordinary success in that era (Weinberg and Gould, 2007). Similarly, there are many examples in soccer of teammates actually coming to blows during a competitive match. Thus, in April 2005, two Newcastle Football Club players, Kieron Dyer and Lee Bowyer, traded punches while playing against Aston Villa. In January 2008, two Arsenal players, Emmanuel Adebayor and Nicklas Bendtner, punched each other during their Carling Cup match against Tottenham Hotspur. In speculating on such phenomena, Syer (1986) suggested that the existence of friendship-based cliques in a team may sometimes impede rather than facilitate its success (see also Box 8.2 later in the chapter). This speculation has received little or no empirical scrutiny. However, M. Klein and Christiansen (1969) reported that basketball players who were close friends tended to pass the ball disproportionately frequently to each other – often to the relative neglect of team efficacy. But in general, what conclusions have emerged from studies of the link between team cohesion and performance?

Before reviewing the literature on this issue, it is important to comment briefly on the research paradigms used in cohesion research. In general, studies of the relationship between cohesion and success have adopted either a correlational or an experimental research paradigm (Mullen and Copper, 1994). The correlational approach is more popular among investigators in this field and consists of studies in which perceived levels of team cohesion are elicited from individual members and subsequently correlated with team performance or success. Carron et al. (2002a) investigated the relationship between the perceived cohesiveness of elite basketball and soccer teams and their winning percentages in competitive games. Results revealed quite a strong relationship between team cohesion and success, with correlation values ranging between 0.55 and 0.67. The experimental research paradigm, by contrast, involves evaluation of the effect on team performance of some intervention designed to manipulate the level of cohesion in the group. Few studies in the field have used this paradigm, however. A possible explanation for this neglect is that sport researchers tend to be reluctant to use the artificial and ad hoc groups that are required by the experimental approach. Instead, they prefer to use actual sports teams.

Using the correlational approach, some evidence emerged to indicate that teams could achieve success in spite of enmity between their members. Lenk (1969) suggested that cohesion was not necessary for team success in rowing. Briefly, he investigated the cohesiveness of two teams of German rowers – the 1960 Olympic gold medal winning eight and the 1962 world champions. Although he did not measure team cohesion explicitly, Lenk (1969) assessed group unity by participant observation of social relationships among team members. The results were counter-intuitive because they showed that team success occurred in spite of considerable disharmony among the rowers. Accordingly, this study refuted the traditional view that cohesion is an essential prerequisite of team success; the results challenged "a thesis that seems to have been taken for granted ... [namely that] only small groups, which are low in conflict, or highly integrated can produce especially high performances" (Lenk, 1969, p. 393). Subsequently, he concluded that "sports crews can, therefore, perform top athletic achievements in spite of strong internal conflicts" (Lenk, 1977, p. 38). Of course, as critical consumers of research, we should be cautious about extrapolating too boldly from the results of this study for at least two reasons. First, it is possible that these results are attributable partly to the nature of the sport of rowing. To explain, Syer (1986) noted that it is not too damaging for members of a rowing eight to dislike each other because each one of them has a specific task to perform and is focused on the cox rather than on each other. Thus no matter how much bickering the rowers engaged in with each other, the nature of their sport prevented them from forming cliques that might impede collective performance of the task. Second, Carron et al. (1998) reinterpreted Lenk's results on the grounds that although the rowers in the study had not been socially cohesive, they had been *task* cohesive. So, Lenk's research findings are ambiguous as they have different meanings depending on which aspect of cohesion one examines.

Despite its flaws, Lenk's (1969) study was pivotal in challenging the assumption that cohesion is crucial to team success. Some subsequent studies (e.g. Melnick and Chemers, 1974) found no relationship between cohesiveness and team success whereas others discovered negative relationships between these two variables (e.g. Landers and Luschen, 1974). Research by Carron and Ball (1977) and J. Williams and Hacker (1982) found that team cohesion was associated positively with athletic performance. A review by Widmeyer et al. (1993) claimed that 83 per cent of studies in this field corroborated a positive relationship between team cohesion and performance. Most of these studies found that athletes in successful teams tend to perceive their team as scoring highly in cohesion whereas the converse is true among athletes of unsuccessful teams. But a note of caution regarding this relationship was expressed by Aronson et al. (2002). Briefly, these researchers observed that team cohesion facilitates success *only* if the task facing the team requires close cooperation between members. Furthermore, they warned that team cohesion can impair performance if members of a group are so close emotionally that they allow their social bonds to obscure their critical awareness.

Overall, sport psychologists have shown that the relationship between team cohesion and performance is neither simple nor predictable. Let us consider each of these two points separately. First, as the work of Aronson et al. (2002) indicates, the cohesion–performance relationship is mediated by a host of intervening variables. Consider how the type of sport played may moderate the cohesion–performance relationship. Carron and Chelladurai (1981) speculated that in interactive sports (e.g. basketball, soccer), where team members have to rely on each other, cohesion is likely to be associated with enhanced team success. By contrast, in co-active sports, where athletes play for a team but where individual performance does not depend on teamwork (e.g. golf, rifle-shooting), team cohesiveness should either have no effect or be associated with less team success. This theory was challenged by Matheson et al. (1995) who failed to discover any significant interaction between team cohesion and sport type (a finding supported by Mullen and Copper, 1994). A subsequent review of the literature by Carron and Hausenblas (1998) concluded that in general, team cohesion is positively associated with performance. Similarly, as indicated earlier in the chapter, Carron et al. (2002a) reported that in a large sample of athletes (n=294) from twenty-seven different basketball and soccer teams, cohesion was correlated positively with team success (with *r* values ranging from 0.55 to 0.67). Nevertheless, other variables that are believed to mediate the cohesion–performance relationship include such factors as goal clarity and acceptance (Brawley et al., 1987) and "collective efficacy" or group members' shared beliefs in their conjoint capacity to organize and execute actions to produce a desired goal (Bandura, 1997). According to Feltz and Lirgg (2001), teams with a relatively high degree of team self-efficacy beliefs should perform better, and persist longer when behind, than teams with lower levels of such beliefs. But a team's collective efficacy is thought to be more than the simple aggregate of individual levels of self-efficacy (Spink, 1990). Not surprisingly, therefore, the relationship between team cohesion and performance may be moderated by this intervening variable of collective self-efficacy.

The second counter-intuitive conclusion from the research literature is that team cohesion may be a *consequence* rather than a cause of team success. In other words, the relationship between cohesion and performance may be *circular* rather than linear. This possibility is supported by Mullen and Copper (1994) who concluded that "although cohesiveness may indeed lead the group to perform better, the tendency for the group to experience greater cohesiveness *after* successful performance may be even stronger" (p. 222; italics ours). If this is so, perhaps there is some truth in the old idea that "team spirit" is what a team gains *after* it achieves success! A review by Casey-Campbell and Martens (2009, p. 228) concluded that "existing research appears to provide evidence that the 'performance leads to cohesion' effect seems to be stronger than the 'cohesion leads to performance' effect". A critical perspective on the issue of distinguishing between cause and effect is presented in Box 8.2.

Apart from the preceding conclusions, what other findings have emerged from the research literature on cohesion and performance? One way of answering this question is by augmenting narrative reviews (i.e. those in which researchers draw informal conclusions from reviewing relevant evidence) with meta-analytic reviews of available research. As indicated in Chapter 2, a meta-analysis is literally an analysis of analyses, or a quantitative synthesis of published research on a particular question (e.g. "Does team cohesion affect athletic performance?") in order to determine the effect of one variable on another variable across many different studies and samples.

Box 8.2 Thinking critically about ... the direction of causality in cohesion–performance research

Every psychology student is taught that "correlation does not imply causality". In other words, just because two variables are related to each other does not mean that one *caused* the other. After all, there could be a third, confounding factor which is the real cause of the association in question. Nevertheless, certain correlational research designs allow investigators to draw conclusions about causal relationships between variables in the absence of experimental manipulations or controls. To illustrate, a "cross-lagged panel correlation" research design (Rozelle and Campbell, 1969) can provide useful clues to the question of causality. Briefly, this design is based on the assumption that analysis of the pattern of correlations between variables at different times (note that the term "lagged" means that there is a time-lag between the collection of some of the correlations) allows certain inferences to be drawn about possible causal links between these variables. In particular, if one variable causes another, it seems likely that it should be more strongly related to the second variable *later* in time – because it is assumed that causes take time to produce effects. Using this cross-lagged research design, Bakeman and Helmreich (1975) measured cohesion and performance in water-sports teams on two separate occasions. Results showed that "first-segment" cohesiveness was highly associated with "second-segment" cohesiveness but not with second-segment performance. Accordingly, these authors concluded that team cohesion was not a good predictor of team performance but that successful performance may have contributed to the development of strong cohesiveness.

Critical thinking questions

Why is it important for researchers to indicate the precise time at which team cohesiveness and performance data were collected? Can you think of any flaws in the logic underlying cross-lagged panel research designs? If performance influences cohesion more than cohesion influences performance, what mechanisms could explain this finding? What are the practical implications of this idea that performance affects team cohesion?

The extent of this effect is indicated by the effect size statistic, a number which represents the average strength of the effect in standard score units independent of sample size. Using this statistical technique, Mullen and Copper (1994) examined forty-nine studies of groups derived from a broad cross-section of settings including industrial, military, social and sport psychology. At least five conclusions emerged. First, the authors concluded that the cohesion–performance relationship was small but positive and significant. Interestingly, this relationship was stronger for sports teams than for any other groups (e.g. ad hoc, artificial groups) in the sample. The authors attributed this trend to the fact that sports groups tend to have a unique sense of collective identity, and differ from other groups by virtue of being formally organized according to explicit rules of competition. Second, Mullen and Copper (1994) found that stronger cohesion–performance relationships existed among "real" (i.e. naturally formed) groups than among "artificial" groups. Third, they concluded that performance was more strongly related to cohesion than was cohesion to performance (see also Box 8.2). Fourth, the type of athletic activity (e.g. interactive versus co-active sports) did not seem to mediate the relationship between cohesion and performance in sports teams. Fifth, Mullen and Copper (1994) claimed that commitment to the *task* was the primary component of cohesiveness in the cohesion–performance relationship. This conclusion suggests that team-building techniques aimed at enhancing the other components of cohesion (see Figure 8.3) may not be effective. Mullen and Copper (1994) were sceptical of the merit of fostering interpersonal attraction among members and/or attempting to "pump up" the group in an effort to enhance team performance. Incidentally, the next section examines the nature and efficacy of some popular team-building techniques in sport.

In 2002, Carron et al. (2002b) updated the preceding meta-analytic review by focusing on studies conducted only in the domain of sport. Using a database of forty-six published studies, they discovered that there was a "significant moderate to large" effect size of 0.655 for cohesion on performance – indicating that cohesiveness was significantly associated with team performance in sport. In contrast to the findings of Mullen and Copper (1994), Carron et al. (2002b) found that both task *and* social cohesion were significantly related to athletic performance. Another notable finding emerging from this study was that cohesiveness in female teams was more strongly related to performance than was cohesiveness in male teams. More recently, Eys et al. (2015) investigated the relationship between perceived cohesion and performance using a sample of coaches of male and female sport teams. Interestingly, their results showed a stronger relationship between cohesion and performance for female than for male teams. Such gender differences need to be investigated further in future studies in this field.

So far, we have examined the relationship between cohesion and performance only in relation to the variable of objective team success. But as Kremer and Scully (2002) noted, the focus on only one type of outcome is too narrow as it neglects other ways in which cohesion may affect team dynamics. For example, the cohesion of a group may affect subjective variables such as team satisfaction, team identity and the perceived self-efficacy of a team. These variables could be included fruitfully in future research in this field, although it should be pointed out that "satisfaction" may be either a cause or a consequence of team cohesion. In a longitudinal field study of cohesion, Holt and Sparkes (2001) explored the factors that contributed to the cohesion of a university soccer team over an eight month season. Using a variety of ethnographic methods (such as participant observation and interviews), Holt and Sparkes (2001) identified four main factors that shaped team cohesiveness. These factors were, first, clear and meaningful roles (e.g. in mid-season, some of the teams' midfield players wanted to play a more attacking game to the relative neglect of their defensive duties), second, team goals (in late season, the fact that the team was eliminated from one competition helped to refocus the team for the league campaign), third, personal sacrifices (e.g. the team captain made a three-hour train journey in order to play in the final match of the league) and fourth, communication (especially "on-field" communication among the players).

Before concluding this section, it is worth exploring two intriguing questions. First, can group cohesion ever be *harmful* (see Box 8.3)? Second, would you be surprised to learn that cohesion does not feature in a list of the characteristics of a successful team – at least in the opinion of one successful coach (see Box 8.4)?

Box 8.4 presents former England coach Sven-Göran Eriksson's views on the ingredients of a successful team.

Box 8.3 Thinking critically about ... whether or not team cohesion can ever be harmful

It has long been assumed that high levels of team cohesion are associated with better performance and improved results. In general, empirical research supports this putative connection between cohesion and performance. Carron et al. (2002a) suggested that the relationship between cohesion and performance is reciprocal – with high cohesion leading to improved performance and successful performance in turn increasing cohesion. But Rovio et al. (2009) challenged this conclusion. Briefly, these authors investigated the relationship between the performance of a junior ice-hockey team and various social psychological phenomena (including team cohesion). They used a mixed methodology involving interviews, observational data, a diary and psychometric testing by using the Group Environment Questionnaire (GEQ; Carron et al., 1985). Results showed that despite high social cohesion, the team's performance deteriorated during the season. Based on this finding, Rovio et al. (2009) concluded that cohesion is not always beneficial to team performance.

Critical thinking questions

In the light of the complex relationship between team cohesion and team performance, are you surprised by the findings reported by Rovio et al. (2009)? Can you think of any other explanation of their findings above – besides the one that claims that team cohesion is overvalued? Do you think that the authors' conclusion were justified by the methodology that they used? If you wanted to replicate or extend this study, what methods would *you* choose?

Box 8.4 Thinking critically about ... a coach's view of successful teams

According to the former England soccer manager Sven-Göran Eriksson (2002), who has coached championship winning teams in three countries (Sweden, Portugal and Italy; Every, 2002), there are eight key characteristics of a successful team in sport.

First, the members of the team must have a common vision. Second, they should have a clear understanding of the team's goals. Third, they must have a good understanding of team strategy and tactics. Fourth, they must have "inner discipline" – which involves both knowing and adhering to the rules of the team (e.g. with regard to time-keeping). Fifth, successful teams must have players who complement each other. For example, Eriksson claims that more than one player like Messi in a team could cause problems for it because of the unpredictability of their skills. Sixth, effective teams require a division of roles – but the coach must respect each of them equally. Seventh, players in a successful team must learn to put the common good before their own interests. Finally, the members of a successful team must accept collective responsibility and think of "we" instead of "me".

Critical thinking questions

Notice that Eriksson did not specify "social cohesion" as one of his criteria of successful teams. Do you agree with this decision? If not, why not? Do you think that all of Eriksson's eight team characteristics can be developed psychologically in players? Which ones are the most difficult to develop?

Team-building in sport

Having established the nature, measurement and correlates of team cohesion in sport, let us now consider the main methods by which coaches, managers and psychologists have attempted to enhance it. One popular method in this regard is "team building" (also known as "team development" or "team enhancement") or the use of practical intervention strategies designed to "promote and enhance the functioning of a group" (L. Martin et al., 2009, p. 3). Typically, team-building activities or experiences are intended to enhance aspects of team harmony such as trust, communication and leadership (Statler, 2010). According to Martin et al. (2009, p. 3), the purpose of team-building is "to help a group become more cohesive while working toward its common goals". Increasingly, sports teams try to achieve this latter objective by the use of special training camps – often held away from home either before the competitive season starts or during it. Although such trips are often useful, they may also prove to be counterproductive in generating adverse publicity for the team involved as a result of unruly antics. For example, a team-building trip to Portugal by Liverpool Football Club in February 2007 in preparation for an important Champions' League match turned sour when one of the players (Craig Bellamy) assaulted a teammate (John Arne Riise) with a golf-club during a karaoke session in a local bar (Wallace, 2007). Although anecdotal in nature, this example highlights the danger of assuming that "away days" inevitably foster team cohesion. Howard Wilkinson, a former manager of Leeds United and Sunderland, showed commendable awareness of this problem when he pointed out that there is a big difference between facilitating a temporary form of camaraderie and generating an abiding sense of team cohesion among players. Specifically, he noted that "going out and getting drunk generates a feel-good factor which is different to real team-spirit. I think real team spirit is much more enduring – that (other) feel-good factor cracks under pressure" (cited in Fanning, 2004b). Moving on from anecdotal examples, it is evident that relatively little empirical research has been conducted on the nature and efficacy of team-building techniques in sport psychology (but see Bruner et al., 2013). From the research literature available, however, it is possible to identify some principles and findings as follows.

To begin with, a definition of team-building is required. Several possibilities are available. In one of the earliest definitions in this field, B. Newman (1984, p. 27) proposed that this term denotes an attempt to "promote an increased sense of unity and cohesiveness and enable the team to function together more smoothly and effectively". Subsequently, Bettenhausen (1991, p. 369) described team-building as an attempt "to improve group performance by improving communication, reducing conflict, and generating commitment among work group members". In a similar vein, Brawley and Paskevich (1997, pp. 13–14) defined team-building as "a method of helping the group to (a) increase effectiveness, (b) satisfy the needs of its members, or (c) improve work conditions". More recently, C. Klein et al. (2009, p. 183) defined team-building as "formal and informal team-level interventions that focus on improving social relations and clarifying roles, as well as solving task and interpersonal problems that affect team functioning". In summary, a common theme running through these definitions is the idea that team-building is designed explicitly to enhance team cohesion.

Does team-building actually work? In an attempt to answer this question, C. Klein et al. (2009) reviewed the effects of four team-building strategies – goal-setting, interpersonal relations, problem solving and role clarification – on various indices of team performance, mainly in organizational settings. The results were encouraging as they were "suggestive of the idea that team-building does improve team performance" (C. Klein et al., 2009, p. 212). Similarly, Martin et al. (2009) described the use of four team-building strategies: interpersonal relations, goal-setting, "adventure" and "omnibus". Interpersonal relations strategies focus on developing "an interpersonally competent group" (Spink, 2014, p. 740) in an effort to enhance team cohesion. Goal-setting strategies seek to boost cohesion by developing individual and group (team) goals. Next, "adventure" strategies employ outdoor experiences in an effort to forge or enhance cohesion. Finally, "omnibus" strategies purport to enhance cohesion by encouraging participants to clarify their roles in the team or to make sacrifices for the team. Let us now address the question of how well team-building actually works.

Overall, at least three caveats must be noted when evaluating research and practice in this field (Crace and Hardy, 1997; McLean, 1995). First, team-building should not be regarded as a type of "quick fix, pep talk" which ensures team harmony through the cursory application of some arcane psychological strategies.

Instead, it involves a long-term commitment to the development of task-related and interpersonal dynamics of a team in the interests of enhancing its performance. Emphasizing this point, McLean (1995, p. 424) claimed that team-building "is not a set of exercises that get wheeled out from time to time, but it is a way of thinking which pervades every interpersonal interaction within that group". Second, team-building is not designed to increase similarity or agreement between group members but to enhance mutual respect among teammates. As Yukelson (1997) suggested, sports teams resemble families in the sense that although teammates may not always like or agree with each other, they know that they belong to the same "household". Third, we should acknowledge that most of the principles and strategies of team-building in sport are derived from research on organizational development in business settings (see C. Klein et al., 2009). Although this cross-fertilization of ideas between business and sport has been valuable in certain areas of sport psychology (most notably, perhaps, in goal-setting; see Chapter 2), it has also generated activities (e.g. participation in outdoor adventure weekends) whose appeal is based more on intuition than on empirical evidence. Put simply, the fact that a team-building technique is popular in business does not make it either valid or effective in sport settings. Bearing these caveats in mind, let us now consider the theory and practice of team-building interventions in sport psychology.

Developing team cohesion: from theory to practice

As we learned in the previous section, the main objective of team-building interventions is to increase the effectiveness of a group by enhancing the cohesiveness of its members (Carron et al., 1997). But as cohesion is a multidimensional construct (see earlier in chapter), what aspects of it should team-builders focus on when designing their interventions? More generally, what team-building exercises are most effective in strengthening cohesion? Let us now consider each of these two questions.

According to Mullen and Copper (1994), the three most important dimensions of cohesion are interpersonal attraction, commitment to a common task and pride in the group itself. Most cohesion theorists have explored the first and second of these aspects of cohesion but have tended to neglect the "pride in the group" aspect. Naturally, these different aspects of cohesion have different implications for team-building initiatives. First, if one wishes to strengthen the interpersonal determinants of cohesion, team-building techniques should focus on increasing mutual liking and affiliation among team members. Second, if one wishes to increase group members' commitment to a given task, team-building exercises should be directed at helping them to increase the intrinsic enjoyment of tackling this task. Third, if group pride is seen as the most important dimension of cohesion, activities that "psych up" the group may be appropriate (see also Chapter 3).

In general, two types of team-building interventions may be distinguished in sport psychology – direct and indirect interventions (Eys et al., 2005). In the direct interventions paradigm, the coach, manager or sport psychology consultant works *directly* with the athletes in the team in an effort to increase cohesion among them and to foster a communal vision and sense of identity. In the indirect interventions paradigm, the consultant instructs coaches and managers in the skills of team-building rather than working directly with the athletes or players concerned.

Usually, team-building in sport is conducted through the *indirect* intervention paradigm for three main reasons (Carron and Hausenblas, 1998; Estabrooks and Dennis, 2003). First, most coaches and managers like to be involved in mediating the interventions of consultants to their team members because they tend to know the individual athletes well. Second, many coaches are reluctant to relinquish their control over the team to an outside consultant. Third, some coaches may be wary of the possibility that the consultant in question may use his or her work with the team for personal promotional purposes. Let us now consider some examples of direct and indirect team-building interventions.

Direct team-building interventions

Based on his vast experience as a sport psychology consultant to a variety of university-level athletes in different settings, Yukelson (1997) delineated four stages of direct team-building work with athletes: assessment, education, **brainstorming** and goal-setting. First, he suggested that the consultant must assess the current team situation as accurately as possible. This step requires the consultant to meet relevant coaching staff and listen to and observe the athletes or players in order to determine the goals, expectations and concerns of the entire team. Second, in the education stage, the consultant should provide the team with some elementary information about how groups develop over time. In the third stage, Yukelson (1997) proposed that the consultant should use brainstorming techniques to help the team to generate and prioritize its current needs. In the fourth stage, these needs should be analysed to determine the goals of the team-building intervention. Across these four stages, a number of practical team-building techniques are recommended. These techniques are evaluated in Box 8.5.

Box 8.5 Thinking critically about ... building a great team

Veach and May (2005) proposed the MAPS framework for building a successful team. The acronym MAPS stands for **M**ission, **A**ssessment, **P**lan and **S**ystematic evaluation. Here is a summary of the steps involved in this approach.

■   *Mission*: What does the team stand for? What are its values and how strongly is it committed to achieving excellence? Following discussions with the team and its coaches, develop a concise mission statement that tries to answer these questions as clearly as possible.

■   *Assessment*: Try to assess team strengths and weaknesses by observing how well players work together, communicate with each other and respond to feedback from coaches during practice sessions and competitive matches. Regular appraisal of these qualities is crucial to effective team-building.

- *Plan*: Help the team members and coaches to develop an action plan designed to improve individual and team efforts. This can be done by facilitating team goal-setting meetings and by encouraging open and honest communication about how best to achieve team goals.

- *Systematic evaluation*: You need to review the entire "road map" regularly.

Critical thinking questions

Imagine that you are a sport psychologist hired to engage in direct team-building work with a squad of athletes and coaches. How could you use the MAPS approach to facilitate this task? Do you think that it would be difficult to devise a mission statement for the team if there are lots of conflicting goals among the players? How would you handle a situation in which some of the players rejected the coach's goals for the team? Can you see any contradiction between teaching team members to be self-reliant and yet encouraging them to depend on each other? How would you like to be introduced to the team – as a sport psychologist or as a team-building consultant? Give reasons for your answer.

Apart from the suggestions contained in Box 8.5, a variety of other team-building exercises have been used by coaches and managers in sport. Some of the more unusual ones are described in Box 8.6.

Incidentally, Don Revie was ahead of his time in extolling the psychological value of bingo because research by Julie Winstone (cited in Horwood, 2002) revealed that this activity can yield measurable cognitive benefits. Specifically, she reported that people who played bingo regularly tended to perform faster and more accurately on visual search tasks than those who did not.

Box 8.6 In the spotlight Team-building exercises in soccer: bingo, bathing, drinking and ... injecting monkey testicles!

Soccer coaches and managers have used many unusual strategies in an effort to foster team spirit among their players. Don Revie, who managed the highly successful Leeds United team of the 1960s and 1970s, used to organize games of bingo for his players. In addition, former players claim that he often used to personally soap and massage them in baths after training and matches! Apart from such hands-on techniques, other favourite bonding strategies include playing practical jokes on teammates and engaging in drinking games. The "crazy gang" members of the Wimbledon team of the 1980s used to cut each other's suits, set their clothes on fire and pack talcum powder into teammates' motor-cycle helmets as initiation rites. D. Taylor (2003) reported that when Neil Warnock was manager of Bury, he used to encourage his players to drink cocktails made of raw eggs and sherry after training every Friday. According to Dean Kiely, Bury's goalkeeper at the time, this technique was Warnock's way of saying "we stand and fall together". Perhaps the strangest technique used to enhance team performance was that involving the injection of monkey-testicle serum – allegedly pioneered by Major Frank Buckley (manager of Wolverhampton Wanderers from 1927 to 1944) (Norrish, 2009).

Direct team-building techniques are increasingly evident in sport – even in games which are regarded as quintessentially individual activities such as golf. Consider the various practical strategies used by the captains of the 2002 and 2006 Europe teams in their matches against the United States in the Ryder Cup. Sam Torrance (captain of the 2002 Europe team) used the thirteen month period between the date on which the European team was selected and the match itself (recall that the long delay was caused by the cancellation of the 2001 Ryder Cup match in the wake of the September 11 terrorist attacks) to boost the confidence of his players. He circulated catchy inspirational statements such as "out of the shadows come heroes" and "Curtis has one Tiger – but I've got twelve lions". These motivational phrases were delivered regularly at team meetings and were accompanied by video screenings in which the players were encouraged to view themselves holing putts, hitting wonderful shots and winning tournaments (A. Reid, 2002). He also appealed to his players emotionally: just before the match itself, Torrance addressed the team with the words, "this is going to be the best day of your life. You were born to do this. This is what we practise for. This is what we live for" (cited in A. Reid, 2002). Turning to Europe's team preparation for the 2006 Ryder Cup, a rather different approach was used by the captain, Ian Woosnam, who recruited Jamil Qureshi, a former professional cricketer turned hypnotist and stage entertainer, to help the team of golfers. Qureshi staged a forty-five minute show for the golfers after Woosnam had delivered his opening speech to the team (Donegan, 2006).

Perhaps the most bizarre example of team-building techniques in modern sport is that used by the South African rugby union in preparing its national team for the 2003 World Cup – the infamous Kamp Staaldrad (Kremer and Moran, 2013; Ray, 2003a). Box 8.7 provides some details of this extraordinary boot camp for the South African rugby squad.

Box 8.7 In the spotlight Team-building exercises in rugby: Kamp Staaldraad – a (jack) boot camp that failed

Kamp Staaldraad (from the Afrikaans meaning "Camp Barbed Wire") was a military-type boot camp established under the direction of South Africa's national rugby coach, Rudolf Straeuli, and his assistant Adriaan Heijns (a former Special Services military man from the country's apartheid era). Its goal was to develop team spirit and cohesiveness among the South African rugby squad prior to the 2003 World Cup.

At this camp, the players were forced to undergo a series of torturous and humiliating exercises in an effort to forge team spirit and mental toughness. In particular, the players were allegedly:

- forced to stand naked in a freezing lake and pump up rugby balls underwater (and those who tried to climb out were forced back literally at gunpoint)

- ordered to climb into a foxhole naked and sing the South African national anthem while ice-cold water was poured over their heads (recordings of God Save the Queen (England's national anthem) and the New Zealand All Blacks pre-match haka were played at full volume)

- made to crawl naked across gravel
- coerced into carrying tyres, poles and bags branded with the flag emblems of England and New Zealand
- made to spend a night in the bush, including killing animals and cooking meals.

These unconventional team-building strategies (or alleged human rights violations: see Ray, 2003b) were of little benefit to South Africa as the team lost in the quarter-final of the tournament to New Zealand. Shortly afterwards, Straeuli resigned. The South African public was shocked by revelations surrounding the camp and one of the country's most respected religious figures, Archbishop Ndungane, was reported to have said: "You don't motivate people with jackboot tactics, and the proof is certainly in the World Cup pudding" (cited in Wildman, 2003). Curiously, despite the absence of any scientific evidence to support the strategies used in Kamp Staaldraad, and the worldwide outrage it generated, the team captain, Corne Kriege, claimed that "most of the stuff was really good for team spirit" (cited in *Evening Herald*, 2003, p. 8).

Before concluding this section, we should remember that a great deal of caution is necessary when evaluating the impact of direct team-building interventions. Specifically, when comparing the preparation techniques used by the European and US Ryder Cup teams we must be careful not to fall into the trap of assuming that team success means that team preparation must have been ideal. In other words, we should be wary of post hoc reasoning when attempting to determine the possible causes of a given sporting outcome. This problem is also called the "glow of success" bias and reflects the invalid reasoning procedure by which people think "we won – so we must have been cohesive" (Gill, 2000).

Indirect team-building interventions

As explained previously, indirect team-building involves the sport psychologist working with the coaching staff rather than the team members. Within this paradigm, Carron et al. (1997) developed an influential theoretical model which proposed a four-step intervention process. In the first stage, which typically lasts for less than twenty minutes, the consultant outlines for the team coach or manager both the nature and benefits of team-building. Second, in the "conceptual stage", which takes about the same length of time, the goal of enhanced team cohesion is explained as being the result of three main factors: the team's environment (e.g. the distinctiveness of the team), the team's structure (e.g. norms) and its communication processes. Third, the "practical stage", which takes place in collaboration with the team coach or manager, involves the practical work of generating as many team-building strategies as possible. Fourth, in the "intervention stage", the team-building methods are implemented by the coach or manager with the assistance of trained assistants, if necessary. Box 8.8 presents examples of the various team-building exercises advocated by Carron et al. (1997, 2009).

Box 8.8 In the spotlight Theory and practice of team-building (based on Carron et al., 1997, 2009)

Team-building objective	Possible strategy
Enhancing team distinctiveness	Emphasize unique history or traditions of team and design special team T-shirts or sportswear (e.g. warm-up tracksuits) for players and coaches
Increasing team togetherness	Organize social outings for teammates and design team drills in the lead-up to matches
Clarifying team goals and norms	Set goals in consultation with team members and encourage "goals for the day" exercises
Facilitating team communication	Arrange regular meetings for team members and alternate the role of "social organizer" within team

Evaluating team-building interventions

How effective are the direct and indirect team-building interventions described above? As Pain and Harwood (2009, p. 523) pointed out, despite the importance of team-building to coaches and psychologists, "surprisingly little sport-specific research has been conducted" in this field. Of the handful of published studies on this topic, results are equivocal. To illustrate, Prapavessis et al. (1996) assigned soccer teams to one of three conditions: a team-building intervention condition, an attention-placebo condition or a control condition. The attention-placebo condition consisted of an intervention strategy which involved soccer-specific information (e.g. nutrition) rather than team-building information. The soccer players' perceptions of team cohesion were evaluated before the beginning of the season and also after an eight-week intervention period. Surprisingly, results indicated no significant difference in cohesiveness between the players in the various conditions: the team-building intervention was not effective in this study. By contrast, Pain and Harwood (2009) evaluated a team-building intervention (based on structured team meetings) with a soccer team during a competitive season. Using a single-case research design (see Chapter 1; see also Barker et al., 2011), these researchers reported that their intervention had led to increased team cohesion and improvements in team performance. In the domain of exercise, team-building interventions have also been shown to be moderately effective (Carron and Hausenblas, 1998; L. Martin et al., 2009). For example, Carron et al. (1997) explained how team-building strategies were successful in developing cohesion in, and adherence to, exercise classes for young adults. Also, Estabrooks and Carron (1999, 2000) reported similar results for more elderly exercisers. One possible reason for this apparent discrepancy between team-building effects in sports teams and exercise groups is that a "ceiling effect" may be at work. To explain, the cohesiveness among sport team members is probably greater than that among exercise group members and so interventions designed to enhance cohesion may produce less change in the former than in the latter participants. As Carron and Hausenblas (1998, p. 342) speculated, the "opportunities for increased cohesiveness through team-building are greater in exercise groups". L. Martin et al. (2009) conducted a meta-analysis of research on the efficacy of team-building interventions in sport. Following a review of seventeen relevant studies, the authors concluded that team-building had "a significant moderate effect" on cohesion and performance (L. Martin et al., 2009, p. 11). Furthermore, results showed that the most successful interventions used goal-setting techniques and lasted between two and twenty weeks in duration.

Perhaps a more interesting question for the layperson is: how do athletes themselves react to team-building interventions? Although little or no research data exist on this issue, some relevant insights can be gleaned from athletes' autobiographical accounts of their experiences of team-building. Typically, these accounts reveal considerable scepticism about the merit of team-building activities. Jeremy Guscott, the former England international rugby player who travelled on a seven-week tour of South Africa with the British and Irish Lions in 1997, was very wary of the management consultants who were hired to engage in team-building exercises with the squad prior to its departure. He revealed:

> rugby players are not the most receptive audiences to new-fangled ideas ... I shared the scepticism. I'm a bit old-fashioned about these things and, as far as I'm concerned, a quick drink down the pub would have been enough for me to get to know everyone.
>
> (Guscott, 1997, pp. 19–20)

One of the exercises which was the target of his derision involved the attempt by a subgroup of players to balance a long bamboo cane on the edges of their fingertips before lowering it to the floor. Canoeing and crate-stacking exercises were also used in an effort to develop team spirit among the Lions squad members. As we indicated previously, however, such techniques lack both a coherent theoretical rationale and evidence of empirical validity. Martin Johnson, who captained the England rugby team to victory in the 2003 World Cup, provided some fascinating insights into the motivational ideas and techniques used by the manager, Clive Woodward. Johnson claimed:

> some of the ideas were good, some OK and some just plain crazy – like the computer system (designed to identify true winners) from Mossad ... There was a joystick and you had to line up all these targets and fire things ... At that point, we thought Clive had completely lost it ... we used the program for a couple of months, then we never saw it again.
>
> (cited in Kervin, 2005, p. 72)

Clearly, Johnson was not impressed by fads like the use of computer game playing as a team-bonding exercise. In passing, scepticism about team-building is also prevalent in professional soccer. Recall the story (in Chapter 1) of what happened when a management consultant used an exercise involving plasticine in an attempt to promote team-building among the Sunderland club's soccer players (Dickinson, 2007). Statler (2010) examined some common pitfalls in team-building activities; she noted that some athletes do not feel comfortable in sharing their thoughts with others in a public discussion of team goals. Similarly, sport psychologists engaged in team-building must be sensitive to the possibility that some players will give socially desirable suggestions (i.e. will say what they think the coach wants to hear) rather than honest feedback in group brainstorming sessions. Finally, Statler (2010, p. 333) pointed out that the task of developing a group identity or a team vision is a lengthy process and is "only as great as the commitment to working on it".

Implication of team-building techniques for coaches

At least five practical implications for coaches may be identified from theories of effective team-building (Weinberg and Gould, 2007). First, coaches should try to create a team environment in which open channels of communication exist among teammates and between team members and the coaching or management staff. The assumption here is that clear communication processes foster mutual trust among team members. Practical ways of improving communication in teams include arranging regular team meetings to discuss issues that can be filled into sentences such as "It would be better if ...". Second, although many coaches proclaim that "there is no 'I' in team", it is essential that they recognize the importance of individual roles within groups of athletes. At the very least, all players should be told exactly how they can contribute to the success of the team. Also, if individual players know what skills they have to work on, they are likely to work harder for team objectives. Third, coaches must learn to set challenging group goals for their teams. Fourth, a collective sense of team identity can be strengthened by encouraging teammates to wear similar team clothing. Fifth, successful coaches tend to spend a lot of time in getting to know their players as well as possible (for some practical advice on team-building techniques, see also Estabrooks and Dennis, 2003).

School sports: helpful or harmful?

Participation in school sports is one of the earliest and most powerful ways in which young people are introduced to athletic activities. But what are the psychological benefits and hazards associated with playing competitive sports in school? Does sport build character – or merely *reveal* it? Let us now consider these questions briefly.

At the outset, it is clear that many people have happy memories of youthful days spent on the playing field. For example, Samuel Beckett, a Nobel Prize-winner for literature, wrote fondly of the time he spent playing cricket for Portora Royal School in Enniskillen, Northern Ireland. Sports experience in college/university can be equally enjoyable. To illustrate, consider how the sheer delight of winning the Irish Senior Women's Hockey Cup is captured in the faces of the young women in Figure 8.4.

Figure 8.4 Sheer joy … University College Dublin women's hockey team celebrate winning the Irish Senior Cup in 2014 (*source*: courtesy of University College Dublin, Sport)

Before delving deeper into this topic, however, we must remember that for every winner in competitive sport, there has to be a loser. Not surprisingly, therefore, cheers can quickly turn to tears for young athletes when they equate "winning" with "success" and "losing" with "failure". This problem is exacerbated if excessive emphasis is placed by parents and coaches on winning (S. Murphy, 1999). Psychologically, there are several problems with the assumption that "winning" is the sole, or even primary, goal for sports performers of any age. Apart from being outside one's control, this goal may encourage the view that victory can come only at someone else's expense. But as we learned in Chapter 2, many of the world's top athletes are motivated not by a desire to defeat others but by the goal of improving upon their *own* performance. This idea of seeking to improve one's skills lies at the heart of the developmental models of sport coaching developed by psychologists such as R. Smith and Smoll (2002a) and Smoll and Smith (2005, 2010). These researchers postulate that "success" in sport transcends winning – and instead involves enjoying the challenge of expending maximum effort to develop one's skills. Put simply, according to Ronald Smith:

> the best way to maximize performance is by creating an environment in which athletes are having fun, are highly motivated, they're trying to improve, they're giving maximum effort, and you have a good relationship

with them, so they're more likely to listen to what you tell them. That's the way you get to winning.

(cited in Munsey, 2010, p. 59)

More generally, what do we know about the psychological consequences of participation in youth sports?

The long-term effects of competitive athletic activity in young people have attracted relatively little research attention from psychologists. Therefore, it is difficult to evaluate the widely held assumption that school/youth sports develop "character", team spirit and/or the virtues of sportspersonship (which may be defined broadly as "sport behaviours that carry moral connotations because of their connections to fundamental issues of fairness and respect"; Shields et al., 2007, p. 747). In an early review of the literature in this field, Shields and Bredemeier (2001) proposed that sport does not *automatically* build character – a conclusion echoed by Gould and Carson (2008). Shields and Bredemeier (2001, p. 599) also proposed that "the longer one stays in sport, and the higher the competitive level reached, the more winning becomes the dominant value". This conclusion is endorsed by S. Murphy (1999), who suggested that the longer athletes remain in sport, the less sportingly they behave and the more likely they are to condone cheating and violent behaviour on the field of play! In a similar vein, Miracle and Rees (1994) found no support for the claim that sport builds character in school or anywhere else. Given such research findings, it is not surprising that Shields and Bredemeier (2007) question the evidence underlying the common assumption that participation in sport builds moral attitudes that transfer to other domains in life. Although such a conclusion seems controversial, it has played a valuable role in stimulating popular and scientific debate about the advantages and disadvantages of youth sport involvement. Fortunately, advances have been made in the development of coaching programmes that are designed to enhance enjoyment and to promote moral and ethical development in young athletes (see R. Smith and Smoll, 2002b). Progress is also evident in the measurement of the construct of sportspersonship. Vallerand et al. (1997) reported the development and validation of a psychometric scale to assess a general commitment to fair play in sport as well as a respect for the rules, officials, social conventions and opponents encountered in the specific game in question. Shields et al. (2007), M. Lee et al. (2007) and Kavussanu and Boardley (2009) have developed other potentially valuable questionnaires to measure aspects of sportspersonship/moral behaviour in sport.

Although the link between sport and character development is tenuous, what of the claim that athletic involvement can forge a sense of identity and cohesion among competitors? As before, little or no research exists on this issue, but there is some historical evidence to corroborate the idea that sport fosters cohesion. In Ireland, S. Moran (2001) showed how Gaelic games in the nineteenth century played a significant role in strengthening people's sense of identity in their struggle to establish independent political rule. Unfortunately, problems can arise when this sense of identity becomes rigid or entrenched. In Northern Ireland, allegiance to various sports and teams has a distinctive sectarian dimension (McGinley et al., 1998). A graphic example of the depth of this sectarianism occurred in August 2002 when Neil Lennon, the Northern Ireland player, was forced to retire from international soccer after he had received death threats from "supporters" of his own national team (McIntosh, 2002). These death threats were believed to have been prompted by Lennon's affiliation with the predominantly Catholic team for which he played at the time – Glasgow Celtic.

Finally, can life skills be developed though sport? Although a detailed analysis of this question is beyond the scope of this chapter, research in this field has been reviewed by Gould and Carson (2008). Having defined "life skills" as "those personal assets, characteristics and skills such as goal setting, emotional control, self-esteem, and hard work ethic that can be facilitated or developed in sport and transferred for use in non-sport settings", these authors found that such skills do not automatically result from mere participation in competitive sport: "life skills are taught and not caught" (Gould and Carson, 2008, p. 75).

To summarize, it may be argued that school sports offer potential health, social and psychological benefits to young people. They can help children to discover the benefits of systematic practice (A. Moran, 2001). But to achieve these benefits fully, young sports performers need to be exposed to an enlightened coaching philosophy rather than a "win at all costs" mentality that causes stress to athletes of all ages and levels of ability.

New directions for research on team cohesion

At least seven new directions can be suggested for research on team cohesion in sport. First, in view of formidable definitional and measurement problems in this field (e.g. see Salas et al., 2015), there is an urgent need for conceptual clarification of such key terms as group, team, social cohesion and task cohesion. Second, additional empirical studies are required to test explicit hypotheses about, and/or possible explanations for, group processes in athletes. This type of hypothesis-testing research is preferable to descriptive, atheoretical studies. Third, there is a paucity of knowledge at present about possible *changes* in group dynamics within sports teams over time; additional longitudinal studies (e.g. extending the research of Pain and Harwood, 2009) are required in which such key variables as athletes' social and task cohesion could be measured at various stages over a competitive season. This type of research would rectify the danger of over-reliance on data obtained from "snapshot" studies in this field. Fourth, in examining the relationship between team cohesion and athletic performance, it is important to measure or to control for the moderating influence of such variables as gender. Interestingly, a recent study shows that gender plays a significant role in the relationship between team cohesion and performance (Eys et al., 2015). Fifth, the related emerging topics of "team cognition" (i.e. the study of how teams perform cognitive activities such as making decisions as a unit; Cooke, 2015), "collective intelligence" (Woolley et al., 2015) and "shared mental models" (i.e. the mental representation of knowledge that is shared by team members; Gershgoren et al., 2016) deserves further study. For example, research is required to investigate the role of shared knowledge or interaction across a variety of sport team tasks (e.g. in formulating strategies for upcoming competitive encounters against other teams). Sixth, Eys and Spink (2016) suggested that the concept of "followership" (i.e. the characteristics and behaviour of people who act in accordance with leaders) deserves to be studied in sport psychology (see also below). Finally, the field of sportspersonship or "fair play" (e.g. see Monacis, et al., 2014; Shields et al., 2015) and moral behaviour in sport is ripe for investigation. Indeed, Kavussanu (2008) pointed out that few studies have investigated the consequences of morally relevant behaviour in sport for such variables as team cohesion, team performance and enjoyment.

Ideas for research projects on team cohesion in sport

Here are six ideas for research projects on group processes in athletes.

1. According to Carron and Brawley (2008), studies on group processes in sport are hampered by the use of static, "snapshot" research designs. The problem with this latter approach is that it fails to examine the dynamic nature of groups. Therefore, these authors recommend the use of prospective, longitudinal studies. In order to fill this gap in the field, it would be interesting to investigate possible changes in social and task cohesion in a sports team over the course of a competitive season (for a relevant study in this regard, see Pain and Harwood, 2009).
2. Given the equivocal nature of some of the evidence surrounding the psychometric characteristics of the Group Environment Questionnaire (GEQ; Carron et al., 1985), it would be interesting to conduct a systematic attempt to validate this measure for adult athletes in a sport setting.
3. It would be intriguing to investigate possible gender differences in team cohesion–performance relationships. Specifically, you could extend the study by Eys et al. (2015) by exploring the degree to which clique formation in sports teams affects the relationship between cohesion and performance for male and female teams. As Eys et al. (2015) explained, "the literature of clique formation in sport teams is virtually nonexistent" (p. 105) so research is urgently required on this topic.
4. As research on athlete leadership is scant, you could extend the study of Fransen et al. (2014) by interviewing coaches and players about their perception of the leadership functions played by the team captain.
5. Given the dearth of research on "followership" (see Eys and Spink, 2016), it would be interesting to investigate the degree to which follower behaviour is related to leadership behaviour and/or team cohesion and performance.
6. Additional research is required on the nature, correlates and development of sportspersonship in young athletes (e.g. see Shields et al., 2007, 2015). For example, do athletes' perceptions of team cohesion and coaching climate/values affect their level of sportspersonship?

Summary

- Despite the importance of group processes in athletic performance, less research has been conducted on team-related processes in sport than on the individual characteristics of the performers. To rectify this oversight, the present chapter examined the nature, measurement and correlates of one of the most popular constructs in this field – "team spirit" or "team cohesion" (i.e. the degree of closeness and collaboration that exists between teammates).

- We began by defining key terms such as "groups" (collections of individuals who are bound by a sense of interdependence in pursuit of a common purpose), "teams" (special types of groups which have a collective sense of identity) and "group dynamics" (the study of interactions and changes in groups).

- In the next section, we explored team spirit (also known as "team cohesion") or the extent to which a group of athletes or players is united by a common purpose and bonds together in pursuit of that objective. This section also examined the measurement of team cohesion and its relationship to athletic performance.

- After that, we investigated the nature and efficacy of team-building activities in sport psychology.

- Then, we evaluated the widespread assumption that team sports foster desirable psychological qualities in participants.

- In the next section of the chapter, we sketched some new directions for research on team cohesion in sport.

- Finally, we provided six suggestions for possible research projects in this field.

New directions in sport psychology

Overview

Chapter 1 of the book examined the nature of the discipline and profession of sport psychology. Part 1 investigated the various psychological processes (e.g. motivation, anxiety, concentration, imagery) that affect individual athletes in their pursuit of excellence. Part 2 reviewed team processes in sport. Finally, in Part 3, we explore new directions in the field of sport psychology.

9

New horizons
Embodied cognition and cultural sport psychology

Introduction

In the final chapter, we shall explore some potentially fruitful new directions for research in sport psychology. Although earlier chapters considered unresolved issues and new avenues of inquiry for specific *topics* in this field, the present chapters adopts a different focus and a more abstract approach because it examines new directions for research in sport psychology *itself*. These new directions provide different ways of looking at familiar topics in sport psychology (e.g. perception and cognition) as well as suggestions for studying topics (e.g. cultural aspects of athletes' experience and identity) that have been relatively neglected in most textbooks on sport psychology.

In order to facilitate this task of analysing disciplinary changes, however, we need to remind you of the meaning of a term that we have used regularly throughout this book when discussing theories and methods – namely, "paradigm". According to Kuhn (1962), the term "paradigm" designates a prescribed set of theoretical assumptions and methodological practices that define a particular scientific discipline or sub-discipline. These assumptions and practices concern the type of research questions that are posed by researchers, the nature of the methodological tools that are used to conduct studies, and the issue of how empirical results are typically analysed and interpreted. Put simply, a paradigm is a specific way of looking at, and making sense of, what happens in a given field or discipline. As we shall see, the two new directions in sport psychology that we consider below (i.e. first, cognition and embodied perception in sport and second, **cultural sport psychology**) have arisen mainly from paradigm shifts and clashes in mainstream psychology. To explain, the embodiment movement addresses the neglect by psychologists of how bodily experience shapes our perception of, and interaction with, the world around us. Similarly, the cultural movement emphasizes the importance of seeking a richer, and more contextualized, understanding of people's experience than that which has been offered by empirical psychology in the past.

The chapter is organized in two broad sections as follows. In the first section, we shall evaluate the origin, nature and main assumptions of the paradigm that has dominated psychology for several decades: namely, the **cognitive approach** to mind and behaviour. This approach, which has influenced basic research (e.g. in cognitive neuroscience; Gazzaniga et al., 2014) as well as applied fields such as sport psychology (Moran, 2009), is concerned with the scientific analysis of mental processes (e.g. perception, memory, problem solving) and knowledge structures such as "mental representations" (i.e. concepts and mental images that contain knowledge about the world around us) that underlie human behaviour and experience. You may recall that earlier in the book, we referred to cognitive models of motivation (see Chapter 2) and cognitive components of anxiety (see Chapter 3). In the second section of the chapter, we shall explore two new directions in sport psychology that are prompted by theoretical alternatives to the standard paradigms in psychology. The first of these approaches is the embodiment movement (e.g. Coelho and Fischer, 2016; Körner et al., 2015; M. Wilson, 2002) which challenges the traditional (and rather disembodied) **cognitive paradigm** by arguing that bodily states and bodily dynamics exert a profound, if somewhat neglected, influence on human experience and behaviour. The second theoretical approach which we shall examine is the cultural perspective (e.g. Schinke et al., 2005; Schinke and McGannon, 2015) which argues that cultural aspects of race, ethnicity and gender – all of which have been neglected historically by mainstream psychology – are vital in sculpting people's identity and experience. Interestingly, despite their many differences, the embodied and cultural approaches to the mind are both opposed to the assumption that human cognitive processes are entirely brain-based and universal in nature. Thus, as we shall explain below, embodiment theorists (e.g. Claxton, 2015) propose that the mind cannot be studied on its own as if it were a disembodied computer. Instead, it is best understood by investigating its relationship with a physical body that moves in and interacts with the world. Similarly, a key tenet of the cultural approach is the idea that people's mental processes are shaped by, and grounded in, their social and cultural environments. We shall return to this link between embodiment and culture later in the chapter when we explore some new directions for research in cultural sport psychology.

Origins of the cognitive paradigm in psychology

Given the popularity of the cognitive paradigm, it is not surprising that there has been a recent proliferation of research in "cognitive sport psychology" or the scientific study of mental processes in sports performers. For example, during the past decade alone, publications have appeared on cognitive processes such as anticipation (Aglioti et al., 2008; D. M. Smith, 2016), attention (Milton et al., 2007), expertise (Baker and Farrow, 2015), decision making (Marasso et al., 2014), memory (Buszard et al., 2016) and mental imagery (Moran et al., 2012) in athletes. So, what is the origin of the modern cognitive approach to mind and behaviour?

It is widely agreed that the cognitive paradigm was established in the 1950s as the study of human information processing (for a comprehensive history, see Lachman et al., 1979; Mandler, 2007). Indeed, some scholars believe that its genesis may be traced to a specific date within that period (11 September 1956) on which a group of cognitive pioneers (e.g. H. A. Simon, Allen Newell, Noam Chomsky and George Miller) from different disciplines collaborated in organizing a "Symposium on Information Theory" in the Massachusetts Institute of Technology (MIT). What emerged from this symposium was the proposal that the mind could be studied as an information processing system that functioned in ways that were similar to the operation of a digital computer. Specifically, the internal processes that regulate cognitive activity were likened to the mind's "software" and the brain systems which implement it were regarded as being analogous to the mind's "hardware".

This analogy between mind and computer was enshrined a decade later by Neisser (1967) in *Cognitive Psychology*, the first major textbook in this new field. In this book, Neisser described cognition as "all the processes by which … sensory input is transformed, reduced, elaborated, stored, recovered, and used" (p. 4) and "cognitive psychology" as the study of information processing or the way in which the mind acquires, stores and uses knowledge. Thus, the subject matter of cognitive psychology includes such mental processes as attention, memory, mental imagery, problem solving and decision making.

Interestingly, many early cognitive researchers assumed that cognitive activity or information processing could be studied independently of the "hardware" (brain) on which it was running. Subsequent research challenged this proposition, however. For example, since the 1980s, research has shown that different brain regions are specialized for different cognitive processes (Groome, 2014). For example, the frontal lobes, which include the motor cortex, exert significant control over movement production. Other parts of the frontal lobes appear to control the central executive component of working memory. Similarly, whereas the occipital lobes at the back of the brain typically regulate perception, the temporal lobes tend to control memory. Such discoveries support the claim by cognitive neuroscience (the study of the biological basis of cognition; Reisberg, 2016) that *brain* processes are crucial to the understanding of the mechanisms underlying cognitive activity. As an aside, the term "cognitive neuroscience" was apparently coined in the late 1970s by Michael Gazzaniga and George Miller in the back seat of a taxi as they travelled to a research meeting in New York (Gazzaniga et al., 2014)! According to Gazzaniga et al. (2104), the conjunction of "cognition" (or the process of knowing) and "neuroscience" (the study of how the nervous system is organized) seemed to be an appropriate term to describe the quest to understand how the functions of the brain give rise to the thoughts of an intangible mind. Perhaps not surprisingly, recent years have witnessed a blurring of boundaries between the disciplines of cognitive psychology and cognitive neuroscience. Interestingly, the reciprocal influence of these two disciplines on each other has been analysed recently by Frank and Badre (2015). In particular, these authors used examples from research on memory and decision making to argue that

> it would be a mistake to "skip" the cognitive level and pursue a purely neuroscientific enterprise to studying behaviour … (because) … virtually all

of the major advances in understanding the neural basis of behaviour over the last century have relied fundamentally on principles of cognition for guiding the appropriate measurements, manipulations, tasks, and interpretations.

(p. 14)

Put simply, cognitive psychology augments cognitive neuroscience in the quest to understand how the mind works.

The revolutionary nature of the cognitive paradigm: mind as a representational system

The cognitive paradigm is widely acclaimed as a "revolution" (or perhaps more accurately, as a *counter*-revolution; Miller, 2003) in psychology because it challenged the hegemony of the Behaviourist approach (e.g. Watson, 1930) which had reigned in psychology from about 1920 to the mid-1950s. Briefly, Behaviourists had argued that as mental processes were unobservable and hence impossible to measure objectively, they could not form any part of psychology as the science of behaviour. Strikingly, this claim was refuted by cognitive researchers in the late 1950s who proposed that human behaviour is caused by internal knowledge structures called "mental representations" (mentioned earlier in the chapter) which contain knowledge about the world and ourselves – and which can be studied empirically. This idea of the mind as a representational system emerged from the confluence of at least five significant developments – apart from the MIT symposium mentioned above. First, the emergence of "communication theory" (Shannon and Weaver, 1949) raised the possibility that people may be regarded as "channels" through which information "flows". Second, experimental psychologists like Bruner et al. (1956) developed objective methods for the study of people's thinking strategies and Miller (1956) published his famous paper ("The magical number seven, plus or minus two") which demonstrated some limits on information processing in short-term memory. Third, Chomsky's (1959) devastating critique of Skinner's (1957) book *Verbal Behaviour* showed logically that Behaviourism was inadequate for the task of explaining how people understand and acquire one of our most important cognitive attributes – language. Finally, the advent of digital computers provided psychologists with the metaphor of the mind as a general-purpose, computational system (for a brief overview, see Casey and Moran, 1989). In combination, these developments inspired cognitive researchers in the late 1950s to postulate that the mind is a *representational* system (see also our discussion in Chapter 6 of how imagery information is stored in the mind). In other words, it does not contain knowledge or experiences directly but, instead, stores *symbolic* representations of these phenomena. And so, "thinking", or using one's knowledge and imagination to go beyond the obvious, involves manipulation of our internal (symbolic) representations of the external world. This process takes time. So, for information processing psychologists, all cognitive processes (e.g. memory) may be investigated as a series of hypothetical stages during which unique transformations are performed on incoming sensory information. For example, consider the everyday cognitive task of remembering people's names when we meet them. Technically, in order to remember the name of someone to whom we are introduced at a party, we must "encode" or assimilate the name in working memory (e.g. by repeating it aloud – an acoustic representation), "store" it in some meaningful format in long-term memory (e.g. by labelling a mental image of the person's face tagged with the appropriate name) and finally, be able to "retrieve" it later using a specific recall cue (e.g. the person's face). In this way, the symbolic representation of the person's name has been *transformed* through a sequence of stages from a sound, to an image and, finally, to a verbal response elicited by a social cue (e.g. when someone else joins the conversation, we are expected to introduce our new acquaintance to him/her). This is information processing in action. To summarize, the cognitive revolution culminated in the proposition that mental representations play a crucial role in explaining human behaviour.

In order to test this proposition, cognitive researchers developed theories using sophisticated "box and arrow" flow diagrams that illustrate how knowledge states (mental representations) are transformed into goal states in everyday tasks by various hypothetical processes that occur between sensory input and behavioural output. For example, consider the skill of reading and understanding a long sentence. Here, the cognitive challenge is to hold the first part of the sentence in your memory while making sense of the last few words – and then integrating the material into a meaningful whole while avoiding distractions. The cognitive process that regulates this sentence comprehension activity is called "working memory" (Baddeley, 2012; D'Esposito and Postle, 2015) and can be described as a mental system for storing and manipulating a small amount of currently relevant information for a short period of time. Briefly, this system has three different components – a "central executive" which controls our ability to focus on the task at hand, an "inner voice" that stores and recycles our memory for sounds and an "inner eye" that stores visual and spatial information. You can experience these three processes in action as follows. After you read the next two sentences, close your eyes and imagine standing in front of the house or apartment in which you live. Now, count the number of windows that you can see in your imagination. In this example, the mental image of your house is created by your "inner eye", the task of counting your windows is regulated by your "inner voice" and the entire operation is supervised by your "central executive".

Key assumptions of the cognitive paradigm

Although the tenets of the cognitive paradigm have been explained in detail elsewhere (e.g. Lachman et al., 1979; Mandler, 2007), four of its main assumptions may be highlighted here as follows. To begin with, it assumes that the mind is a general-purpose computational (information processing) system that represents and stores knowledge symbolically – in an abstract or "amodal" format (i.e. independent of any particular sensory modality). Second, mental processes can be studied objectively using a combination of empirical methods such as laboratory experiments (see earlier discussion in Chapter 1), **computer modelling** (the simulation of certain aspects of human cognition using computer programs) and cognitive neuroscientific procedures like eye-tracking systems (see Chapters 5 and 7) and brain-imaging techniques (see Chapter 6). Using these methods, cognitive psychologists typically attempt to explain everyday cognitive activities (e.g. how people remember, pay attention, form mental images or solve problems) by testing theories which involve sequences of hypothetical mental processes ("mechanisms"). Third, the cognitive paradigm assumes that "thinking" is a form of computation in which knowledge is manipulated and transformed symbolically according to formal rules or programs. Thus, for Neisser (1967), the scientific task of exploring cognitive processes is like "trying to understand how a computer has been programmed" (p. 6). Finally, traditional cognitive researchers espoused a "sandwich" (or hamburger) model of the mind in which cognition was "sandwiched" between perception and action (see Hurley, 2001). In this sandwich model, thinking was the "meat" and hence most worthy of study, whereas perception merely served to provide input to the mind and action merely executed its commands (Willems and Francken, 2012). For classical cognitive researchers, people's perceptual and motor systems were "thought to serve merely as peripheral input and output devices" (Wilson, 2002, p. 625). Since the classical cognitive paradigm held that the mind's perceptual and motor systems were largely functionally independent of each other, research on cognitive processes such as thinking "could proceed independently from the study of sensorimotor processes and mechanisms" (Laakso, 2011, p. 410). Based on this latter view, the classical cognitive paradigm advocated a rather disembodied approach to the study of mental processes.

Challenges to the cognitive paradigm in psychology: from emotion to embodiment

In the 1990s, the limitations of the classical cognitive (information processing) paradigm were exposed by a combination of theoretical developments and empirical discoveries (see Laakso, 2011, for a detailed critique of this issue). As we shall see, these discoveries have prompted a debate about whether cognition is computational (i.e. abstract and amodal; as proposed by adherents of the classical cognitive paradigm) or embodied (i.e. rooted in sensorimotor experience; as proposed by **embodiment approaches**). First, some critics of the cognitive paradigm objected to the prevailing view of the mind as a rational computational system that operates relatively independently of emotional experience. For example, Claxton (1980) caricatured the typical participant in a cognitive psychology experiment who "does not feel hungry or tired or inquisitive; it does not think extraneous thoughts or try to understand what is going on. It is, in short, a computer" (p. 13). However, as there is now compelling evidence that emotional factors influence cognitive processing (e.g. see Huntsinger and Schnall, 2013), such factors are becoming more central to the field. Second, the classical information processing paradigm largely neglected the mind's motor output in favour of its sensory input. Identifying this problem some time ago, Adams (1987) observed that cognitive psychology is "preoccupied with disembodied perceptions and higher processes, and indifferently concerned with translating perceptions and higher processes into 'action'" (p. 66). Third, the "**direct perception**" researcher Gibson (1979) challenged the need for mental representational structures. Briefly, he argued that perception evolved in the service of action and "keeping in touch with the environment" (p. 239) by enabling people to extract information directly from it. Specifically, Gibson claimed that

> perception of the environment ... is not mediated by *retinal* pictures, *neural* pictures, or *mental* pictures. *Direct perception* is the activity of getting information from the ambient array of light. I call this a process of *information pickup*, that involves ... looking around, getting around.
>
> (p. 147)

For example, imagine that you are looking for a golf ball that you drove straight up a long fairway. As you walk towards the place where you think that your ball has landed, the image on your retina changes – and the rate of expansion of that image offers important information about how close you are to the ball. In order to account for information extraction from the environment, Gibson (1979) postulated the concept of "**affordance**" to describe the fact that we directly perceive the properties and functions ("action possibilities") of objects. If you look around your environment right now, you will discover which objects (e.g. a cup or a book) invite or "afford" action possibilities like reaching or grasping. So, an affordance is simply an opportunity for action – a latent feature of the environment that provides the possibility of behaviour. For example, a ladder "affords" ascent or descent and a chair "affords" the possibility of sitting (Eysenck and Keane, 2015). By implication, our skills are not stored abstractly as mental representations but as dispositions to respond to environmental triggers. A fourth challenge to the cognitive paradigm came from "embodiment" researchers (e.g. Barsalou, 1999) who argued that cognition is not confined solely to the brain – but is in fact rooted in sensorimotor experience. Specifically, embodiment theorists proposed that cognitive representations are "grounded in, and simulated through, sensorimotor activity" (Slepian et al., 2011, p. 26; see also Laakso, 2011; Shapiro, 2010). For example, when we metaphorically describe something that we do not understand as being "over our heads", we are drawing on our physical inability to see something directly above us (McNerney, 2011). In this case, our cognitive expression has been shaped by our experience in the physical world. More generally, embodiment theorists propose that many of the brain circuits that are responsible for abstract thinking are inextricably linked to those that process sensory experience. Supporting this idea, research on the "functional equivalence" hypothesis (Jeannerod, 1994; see our earlier discussion in Chapter 6) showed that cognitive simulation processes (such as mental imagery) share certain representations, neural structures and theoretical mechanisms with like-modality perception and with motor preparation and execution (Moran et al., 2012). For example, neuroimaging studies show that mentally simulated and executed actions rely on similar neural representations and activate many common brain areas such as the posterior parietal, premotor and supplementary motor cortex (Munzert et al., 2009). Another illustration of simulation comes from the apparent overlap between the neural processes involved in action observation and movement planning. Briefly, research shows that when we watch someone performing an action that is within our motor repertoire, our brains simulate performance of that action (Calvo-Merin et al., 2005). Based on such evidence, it seems clear that the neural substrates of cognition and movement overlap significantly – a point to which we shall return later when we explore possible mechanisms governing embodiment. Before we conclude this section, it is worth noting that "radical embodiment" theorists (e.g. Wilson and Golonka, 2013) claim that there is no need for the concept of internal models/mental representation at all because we are embedded in our environment and can extract information directly from the world around us. Although many embodiment theorists would not go this far in their claims, they are committed to the idea that the body and the environment influence cognitive processes (Schiavio and Altenmüller, 2015).

The embodiment approach in sport psychology: resurrecting the body to study the mind

At the heart of the **embodied cognition** approach are two key ideas. First, cognition and perception are based on action. According to this "action-specific" theory (see review by Philbeck and Witt, 2015), people tend to perceive their environment in terms of their ability to act in it (Witt, 2011) and such perception is influenced by their goals, physiological state and emotions (Proffitt, 2006). Second, cognitive processes are simulations or re-enactments of previously acquired sensory and motor experiences. To experience this idea, consider the various simulation processes elicited by the following sentence: "The sun shone and the crowd cheered as the ball struck the net ... and the scorer punched the air in celebration." According to embodiment theorists, your occipital cortex creates a virtual experience of "seeing" the sun, crowd, ball, net and goal scorer. Likewise, you use your auditory imagery system to "hear" the crowd and perhaps the ball hitting the net. And you may have activated your brain's motor system to simulate what it would feel like to raise your hands in the air.

Intriguingly, evidence has emerged to indicate that bodily information and action abilities can influence our perception in certain situations. For example, Proffitt (2006) reported that the apparent slope of a hill tends to increase when people are tired or laden down by wearing a heavy backpack. He attributed this effect to "energetic considerations" – the idea that wearing a heavy backpack increases the energy required to walk up the hill. The logic here is that if you feel very tired, you probably need to rest. So, perceiving a hill with a real slope of 5 degrees as a 15-degree slope may induce you to rest – which reduces your energy expenditure. Proffitt's "backpack" findings have been challenged (e.g. by Durgin et al., 2012), on the grounds that they may be attributable to "demand characteristics" (i.e. pressure on participants that emanates from the experimental set-up and encourages them to respond in a certain manner; Orne, 1962). For example, if participants are asked to judge the slope of a hill, then wear a backpack, and then judge the slope of the hill again, they may intuitively guess the experimenter's hypothesis that the backpack will influence their judgement and respond accordingly. Since this issue was raised, however, various experimental controls have been introduced to reduce the likelihood that demand characteristics affect perceptual judgements (Witt et al., 2016). Returning to slope perception research, Proffitt (2006) also reported that hills appear to be steeper to people who are in poor physical health compared to healthier counterparts. In a similar vein, Witt et al. (2009) discovered that people who suffered from minor but chronic pain of the lower back tended to misperceive distances. In particular, their estimates of the distance to cones placed at different points in a hallway were greater than those elicited from participants in a comparison group. Also, Witt and her colleagues found that objects that lie beyond one's arm's reach tend to appear closer when perceivers intend to reach out to them with a reach-extending tool by comparison with when they intend to reach *without* such a tool (Witt et al., 2005). Likewise, people who throw a heavy ball to a target tend to perceive that target to be farther away compared with people who throw a light ball (Witt et al., 2004). For recent reviews of action-specific effects on people's estimation of slant, distance, height, weight and speed, see Proffitt and Linkenauger (2013) and Witt and Riley (2014). Interpreting the thrust of the research literature on action-specific effects, Witt (2011) concluded that our perception of the world "reflects the relationship between the environment and the perceiver's ability to act within it" (p. 205). So, how does embodiment provide new directions for research in sport psychology? To answer this question, let us consider recent studies on embodied perception and embodied cognition in sport.

Research on embodied perception in sport: why does the ball or hole look bigger when you're playing well?

In a recent review of research on embodied perception in sport, Gray (2014) begins with an intriguing observation – the fact that peak performance states (see also Chapter 5) in athletic activities are often associated with qualitative *perceptual* changes in the experience of the person involved. For example, John McEnroe, the seven-times Grand Slam tennis champion, revealed that when he played at his best "things slow down, *the ball seems a lot bigger* and you feel like you have more time" (cited in McEnroe and Kaplan, 2002, p. 57; italics ours). The obvious question that arises here is: how can a tennis ball appear bigger on some occasions than others if, as classical perception theory argues, object size perception is based purely on angular size? Well, of course, one possible explanation for this apparent perceptual anomaly is that it could reflect a recall bias (i.e. a distortion in the perceiver's recollection of the events). And such biases are possible given the susceptibility of athletes to memory distortions (Gray et al., 2007). Thus, it is possible that athletes who perform excellently rationalize this experience by reasoning that "I played at my peak level so the ball must have seemed very big to me." Such distortions are unlikely to explain all reports of perceptual distortions, however. So, another possible explanation of such distortions is that they reflects accurate recall of an actual embodied perceptual experience. According to this latter account, McEnroe's perception of the size of the tennis ball was perhaps influenced not only by its retinal image size but also by the accuracy and precision with which McEnroe anticipated the arrival of the ball.

In evaluating the evidence supporting embodied effects on perception in sport, Gray (2014) reviewed a variety of studies on three main types of action-specific variables in sporting contexts: skill level (expert versus less skilled counterparts), task difficulty and task goals. According to the embodiment approach, the predictions for these variables should be as follows. First, if level of expertise affects perception, then balls should be perceived as appearing larger and moving slower as playing level increases because the balls are more "hittable" at higher levels of ability. Evidence to support such "size perception effects" has emerged from studies on goal kicking in American football (Witt and Dorsch, 2009) and archery (Lee et al., 2012). Turning to the second issue, if a sporting task is made more difficult for athletes of a given level of ability, embodiment approaches would predict that there should be changes in perception of the target object. Again, there is evidence to support this hypothesis. Thus, Witt et al. (2008) discovered that golfers perceived the hole as being larger when putting from close range (easy task) as distinct from putting from a longer distance (more difficult task). For example, Witt et al. (2008) conducted a series of studies on relationship between golfing proficiency and perceived hole size. In one of them, they discovered that golfers who had played better than others after a specific round of golf subsequently estimated the hole to be bigger than did counterparts who had not played as well. But was this because the golfers' performance had influenced *perceived* hole size or *remembered* hole size? In order to arbitrate between these possibilities, Witt et al. (2008) conducted two follow-up laboratory studies. In these experiments, participants putted golf balls into a practice hole from a putting mat which was located either close to the hole (0.4m from it) or farther away (2.15m) from it. Then, they had to judge the size of the hole either from memory (Study 2) or while actually viewing the hole (Study 3). Results showed that, in both experiments, estimates of the size of the hole made after easy (close) putts were larger than estimates made after more difficult (farther away) putts. Note that the size estimates should have been similar if the only variables influencing participants' judgement were their visual abilities and the actual size of the hole. Since these estimates were not similar, then it seems that size perception is influenced by the perceiver's current ability to act effectively. But what is *not* clear from these experiments is the direction of causality in this situation. As Witt et al. (2008) queried, do golfers putt better and therefore see the hole as bigger or do they see the hole as bigger first, and then putt better as a result? Clearly, research designed to address this question is urgently required. Finally, embodied approaches predict that objects that are deemed suitable for attainment of a particular goal should be perceived as affording greater opportunity for successful action (e.g. being seen as larger and moving more slowly than usual) as compared with objects that are not deemed as suitable for goal attainment. Some evidence to support this prediction was reported by Gray (2013) using a baseball hitting task. Taken together, Gray (2014) concluded that even when objects in sport are characterized by a constant physical size and speed, they may be perceived differently by athletes – in a way that is consistent with the predictions of embodiment approaches. But what functional benefits do action effects yield for sports performance? At first glance, as Gray (2014) pointed out, they should hamper performance. For example, if a tired tennis player perceives the ball as travelling quicker than it really is, is there not a danger that she will mistime her volley? To answer this question, embodiment theorists might suggest that perception cannot be decoupled from action – and that tired tennis players are likely to display slower racquet head speed than that shown by more rested players as they prepare to volley the ball travelling towards them. So, tired players may need to respond faster than rested players in this case (Gray, 2014). Another perspective on the benefits of action-specific effects was offered by Proffitt and Linkenauger (2013). Consider the case of a basketball player who perceives the hoop to be smaller than it is as a result of missing several consecutive free throws. Here, these authors argued, perceiving the hoop as small may encourage the player either to dribble with the ball or to pass it to a teammate – decisions which might enhance team performance. Interestingly, Gray (2013) used a simulated baseball pitching task to investigate the question of whether a performer is more (or less) likely to act upon an object that is perceived to be bigger (or smaller) than it actually is. He discovered that batters were *more* likely to swing at a pitch when the ball was made artificially *larger* than its regulation size – and *less* likely to swing when it was made artificially smaller than normal. Additional research is required to find out if this effect transfers to real life sporting situations. Before concluding this section, we should mention an interesting training proposal arising from the embodied perception approach. Specifically, Gray (2014) suggested that it may be possible to enhance athletic performance in certain ball sports (e.g. tennis, football, cricket) by using computer simulations to increase the size of target objects. Clearly, experimental research is required to evaluate this possibility.

Research on embodied cognition in sport: do experts simulate experiences differently from novices?

Earlier in the book (see Chapter 7), we explored a number of cognitive differences between expert and novice athletes. One of those differences concerned the fact that expert performers tend to represent problems at a deeper level than do novices because they search for principles and rules rather than superficial features of the tasks in question. Let us now return to this idea but this time from an embodiment perspective. The question here is: do expert athletes simulate sport-related experiences differently from novices and, if so, with what effects? According to Dijkstra and Post (2015), differences in sensorimotor simulation abilities should affect cognitive processing of sport-related information and hence subsequent performance. In an early test of this prediction, Boschker et al. (2002) investigated whether or not expert wall climbers could remember climbing routes better than did relative novices. Results corroborated this hypothesis – leading to the interpretation that the expert climbers may have remembered the routes using the affordances (action possibilities) that the wall had offered (e.g. potential holds for grasping purposes) whereas the novices had probably focused on the structural features of the wall.

Another prediction of the embodiment perspective is that practice – whether mental or physical – should lead to the development of richer, more elaborate mental simulations of relevant movements. Although not a test of this hypothesis directly, a study by Frank et al. (2014) is relevant in this regard. She and her colleagues tested novices as they practised golf putting under one of four conditions: mental practice, physical practice, combined mental and physical practice, and no practice. Both putting performance and mental representation of the putt were assessed prior to and after three days of practice. Results showed that the putting performance of the groups improved along expected lines (with the combined mental and physical practice group performing best and the mental practice only group performing worst). However, participants' mental representations developed differently *between* the groups. Specifically, whereas the physical practice group showed only minor changes in mental representation structures over time, both the mental practice and the combined mental and physical practice group revealed major changes in their representations of the golf putt. To explain, after mental practice and after combined mental and physical practice, participants showed more elaborate representation structures that reflected key functional phases of the movement (i.e. the preparation phase, the swing and the impact phase). From this finding, Frank et al. (2013) concluded that the mental representations of actions develop differently during motor learning – depending on the type of practice undertaken. Additional support for the idea that the learning of a motor action is associated with functional organization of action-related knowledge in long-term memory came from a recent study by Frank et al. (2016) using a golf-putting task. Briefly, these researchers showed that after practice, the mental representation structures of a complex motor action (a golf putt) develop functionally in the sense that they become more similar to the representations of an expert performer.

A final example of a new direction in embodied cognition research in sport comes from recent research (e.g. Toner and Moran, 2015; Toner et al., 2015) on the role of consciousness in facilitating skill development in expert performers. By way of background, traditional information processing theories of skill acquisition (e.g. Fitts and Posner, 1967) claimed that skill learning proceeds inevitably from controlled processing (which is slow, deliberate and effortful in nature) to the development of "automaticity" (an umbrella term that refers to performance that is uncontrolled, unconscious, efficient and fast; Moors, 2013). Challenging this proposition, however, is an emerging body of empirical evidence (e.g. Ravn and Christensen, 2014) and theory (e.g. Montero, 2010; Toner and Moran, 2015, Toner et al., 2015) which suggests that mindful behaviour (including awareness of bodily movement) is a crucial, if neglected, aspect of elite athletes' training regimes. Clearly, such claims concerning the role of "mindedness" in shaping expert performance require empirical testing.

Having considered the embodiment movement as the first of our new directions in sport psychology, let us now turn to the second one – cultural sport psychology.

Cultural sport psychology

Almost three decades ago, Duda and Allison (1990) bemoaned the neglect of topics like race and ethnicity by researchers in sport psychology and concluded that there was a "cultural void" in the field. Supporting this argument, Ram et al. (2004) reported that less than 2 per cent of papers accepted by three North American sport psychology journals contained any significant discussion of either race or ethnicity. This finding was echoed by Peters and Williams (2009) who discovered that less than 5 per cent of papers sampled from three sport psychology journals had examined cultural background as a variable. When combined, these studies led Blodgett et al. (2015) to conclude that sport psychology has "been taken up through mainstream agendas and approaches, with the focus on performance enhancement in ways that are rarely critical and/ or seldom tackle how performances are shaped by the sociocultural" (p. 29). As a result of this neglect, the experiences and identities of culturally diverse people have "continued to be relegated to the margins" (p. 29) despite the increasing globalization of society.

Against this background, the term "cultural sport psychology" (CSP) refers to a growing scholarly movement that challenges "mainstream sport psychology's assumptions in order to facilitate contextualized understandings of marginalized topics and cultural identities" (Blodgett et al., 2015, p. 24). Thus, there has been a recent upsurge of research interest by CSP scholars in topics such as the creation of inclusive sport climates for athletes who are lesbian, gay, bisexual and transgender (LGBT; Krane, 2016); for athletes with either a physical or an intellectual disability (e.g. Burns, 2015; Smith et al., 2016; see Figure 9.1); and for religious and spiritual athletes (Sarkar et al., 2014).

So, what are the main objectives and methods of, and new directions for, this movement in sport psychology? The purpose of this section is to provide a brief review of research in CSP. For a more detailed account of this field, see Blodgett et al. (2015), Schinke and Hanrahan (2009) and Schinke and McGannon (2015).

Objectives and methods of cultural sport psychology

An important goal of research in CSP is to develop a critical understanding of marginalized topics and cultural identities in order to enhance the inclusiveness of sport psychology. For example, consider the issue of elite "athletic acculturation" – the process by which talented young athletes migrate to, and settle in, other countries in order to pursue educational and sporting careers. Until recently,

Figure 9.1 An inclusive society welcomes athletes with disabilities

because of a dearth of research on this process, immigrant athlete acculturation was assumed to be a linear "settling in" process that proceeds from being initially stressful to ultimately satisfying for the sports performer in question. But is this assumption valid? In a recent study, Schinke et al. (2016) interviewed twenty-four elite athletes who had immigrated to Canada during their teenage years. The conversational interviews explored the acculturation challenges that these athletes had faced as they attempted to adjust to a new country and a new sporting environment. In order to elicit their personal stories of acculturation, participants were asked to create drawings that reflected their experiences as immigrant athletes in Canada. These images then served as tools for eliciting narratives ("Can you tell me about what you have drawn in your image?") for the interviews. Following analysis of the verbal transcripts of these interviews, certain themes emerged which were portrayed by Schinke et al. (2016) in a composite vignette of athletes' acculturation experiences. For example, included in the theme "searching for balance" were athletes' sentiments such as "I want to have a good life and a good career that can support me and my family after I'm done [sport]. So, my priorities and my goals shift back and forth" (p. 41). Clearly, such sentiments suggest that the process of acculturation is non-linear and requires constant navigation between competing challenges. More generally, Schinke et al.'s (2016) research indicates that athletes' identities are not fixed or stable but, instead, are fluid in nature and change as a function of cultural context.

Typically, CSP research is characterized by the use of qualitative methods (see also Chapter 1). Recall that qualitative research is concerned with "how people make sense of the world and how they experience events … with the quality and texture of experience, rather than with the identification of cause-effect relationships" (Willig, 2008, p. 8). Two types of qualitative methods are common in CSP – "narrative inquiry" and "**discursive psychology**". Let us now consider each of these approaches briefly in turn.

To begin with, a "narrative" may be regarded as a story containing a plot, characters and a sequence of events that unfolds over time to provide an overarching explanation (Smith and Sparkes, 2009). So, narrative inquiry (see review by Smith, 2010) is an interpretative research method that explores how people communicate their experiences. It hinges on the assumption that people are "storied individuals" or meaning makers who habitually tell stories in order to make sense of themselves and of their world and also to present themselves to others. As Smith (2010) explained, we live *in* and *through* our narratives and we use stories to "guide action … and help frame *who we are* and *who we can be*" (p. 88). Normally, narrative researchers use multiple open-ended interviews with a small number of participants to elicit their stories. To illustrate the importance of narratives to athletes' experiences, some professional golfers seek consultations with sport psychologists not only for practical tips on performance enhancement but also because, as we mentioned in Chapter 1, they felt compelled to tell their story to someone outside their immediate family or social circle (Keefe, 2003). Interestingly, Carless and Douglas (2009) investigated how the stories that female golfers tell affect their career transitions. From this research, a cultural performance narrative was identified in which having a competitive streak was portrayed as being "natural" and failure as an experience that is usually accompanied by feelings of shame. Carless and Douglas (2009) proposed that if such a performance narrative was incompatible with the golfers' personal experience, it could impair their mental well-being. Another example of narrative inquiry in research comes from a study by Toner et al. (2012). This study highlights the "self reflexivity" that characterizes much narrative inquiry approach – the commitment for researchers to acknowledge how their own values and beliefs may have affected their stories. In this vein, the study by Toner et al. (2012) provides a personal narrative by the principal author of this paper concerning the coach–athlete relationship in golf – and how the original story altered through a process of shared critical thinking. On first telling, John (Toner) explained to his co-authors how he considered himself to have been the victim of bad coaching practice following his coach's failure to correctly diagnose an important but subtle fault in his golf swing. The initial rendering of this narrative was a story of blame, betrayal and of a coach who failed to provide the expert advice required. However, having critically reflected upon this version of events with his co-authors, John explores how he came to understand his role in a dysfunctional coaching relationship in a different way. Specifically, rather than being a blameless victim, John began to explore his own contribution to the process of the breakdown in the athlete–coach relationship. For example, his conscious decision not to share his thoughts and feelings about his golf swing with his coach could be construed as an act of stubbornness that led John to "test" his coach in a way that could only lead to failure. Interestingly, Smith (2010) pointed out that until recently, many of the documented narratives of sporting lives have tended to represent the pain and suffering associated with elite sport. Clearly, future research using narrative methods in sport could benefit from exploring the more uplifting side of the athletic experience. In this regard, Day and Wadey (2016) used narrative inquiry methods to illustrate how participation in sport helped two people to recover and grow after they had acquired permanent physical disabilities.

Discursive psychology (e.g. Potter and Wiggins, 2007) is concerned with how people "construct" events in everyday life through their use of language in writing, conversation, media interviews or even through symbolic communication such as text messages. The goal of such analysis is to explore the psychological motives and attitudes that underlie human discourse. According to Locke (2004), discursive psychology has several key tenets. For example, it emphasizes the importance of considering "talk" as a form of contextualized action. So, when analysing an interview with an athlete, discursive analysis would require coding of *both* the questions asked by the interviewer *and* the answers given by the respondent. More generally, as Douglas and Carless (2016) point out, discursive psychology theorists argue that it is a mistake to separate talk and action because talk can achieve things by itself. In addition, discursive analysis, like attribution theory (recall Chapter 2), is interested in the way in which people account for their actions and experiences. For example, Locke (2008) analysed the narratives of performance revealed by two athletes who had been interviewed for a science documentary series on peak performance (being in the "zone"; see also Chapter 1). These athletes were an Olympic champion hurdler and an injury-prone sprinter who had competed at the Olympics. Locke (2008) concluded from her analysis that by referring to concepts like "the zone", these athletes were able to discuss actual (in the case of the hurdler) or potential (in the case of the sprinter) success without appearing to be boasting or making immodest claims. This study is interesting in sport psychology because it provides a different perspective on athletes' accounts of peak performance. Specifically, instead of regarding interviews about peak performance ("zone stories") as anecdotal evidence to support the existence of concepts like "the zone", Locke (2008) suggested that they can be interpreted as narratives constructed to manage or justify athletes' experiences.

This latter interpretation is consistent with discursive psychology's proposal that "meaning" is not some abstract entity located in the mind but is a socially constructed phenomenon which can be analysed through people's use of language.

Some new directions for research in cultural sport psychology

Although space limitations preclude a detailed evaluation of new directions for research in CSP, the following five topics convey a flavour of where the field may be heading. First, just as in cognitive psychology (see earlier in chapter), CSP has shown a growing awareness of the importance of embodiment in exploring the experiences of marginalized groups. For example, Carless and Douglas (in press) used narrative inquiry methods to investigate the embodied experiences of military personnel who had suffered serious injury or emotional trauma while on duty. Second, as there has been a dearth of research on the sporting experiences of people who identify themselves as LGBT (Krane, 2016), relatively little is known about the type of sport climates that are effective in reducing prejudice against LGBT athletes. Furthermore, virtually no research has been conducted as yet on the experiences of LGBT athletes in non-Western cultures. Third, despite the increasing involvement of women in sport, few studies exist on the nature and implications of "athlete mother" identities (McGannon and Busanich, 2016). Thus, for example, research is required on the transition experiences of elite athletes who have given birth and then resumed their sporting careers. Similarly, the question of why women's participation in physical activity seems to decline after motherhood needs to be investigated. Fourth, despite the growth of the Paralympic movement (e.g. the number of Paralympians has increased from about 400 competing at the Games in 1960 to about 4,350 competing at the Rio 2016 Games, see "About the Rio 2016 Paralympics, 2016"), little research has been conducted on the experiences of "parasport" athletes. Clearly, studies are required to address this gap in sport psychology. Finally, as a result of the reintroduction of athletes with intellectual disabilities (ID) into the Paralympics in London in 2012 (note that they had been included in the Sydney Games in 2000), there has been a growth of research interest in the topic of ID in sport (see review by Burns, 2015). As much of this research has explored the value of sport and exercise as a remedial leisure activity to counteract health problems stemming from obesity, relatively little is known at present about the challenges faced by athletes with ID who wish to develop their sporting skills in order to compete against others. Clearly, this topic could provide a fruitful line of inquiry for future investigators.

Summary

- In this chapter, we explored two possible new directions for the discipline of sport psychology – the embodiment approach (which argues that cognitive processes are rooted in sensorimotor experience) and cultural sport psychology (which emphasizes the importance of contextual studies of marginalized topics).

- Before outlining the nature and significance of these approaches, however, we evaluated the origin, nature and main assumptions of the paradigm that has dominated psychology for several decades, namely, the cognitive approach to mind and behaviour.

- This approach is concerned with the scientific analysis of mental processes (e.g. perception, memory, problem solving) and knowledge structures such as "mental representations" (i.e. concepts and mental images that contain knowledge about the world around us) that underlie human behaviour and experience.

- Having explained how embodiment approaches arose as a challenge to traditional cognitive accounts of the mind, we sketched some new directions for research on embodied perception and embodied cognition.

- After that, we examined the nature, objectives and methods of "cultural sport psychology" (CSP), which is broadly concerned with developing a critical understanding of marginalized topics and identities.

- Finally, having explained two key methods used by CSP researchers (narrative inquiry and discursive psychology), we proposed five new directions for research in this field.

Glossary

Achievement goal theory (also known as goal orientation theory)   A theory that postulates two types of motivational orientations in athletes – namely, ego orientation (i.e. focusing mainly on demonstrating one's competence in a given skill by performing better than others) and task orientation (i.e. focusing mainly on acquiring a certain level of competence in a given skill) – depending on how they interpret the meaning of achievement or success. See also **ego orientation** and **task orientation**.

Achievement motivation   The tendency to strive for success or to expend effort and display persistence in attempting to attain a desirable goal.

Action planning   The process by which an individual's intention is translated into specific actions in order to achieve a desired behavioural goal.

Action plans   Specific behavioural acts that serve as stepping stones to goal attainment.

Affordance   A set of actions that a specific object or environmental context "affords" or makes available to the perceiver.

Anecdotal evidence   Subjective evidence derived from examples or personal experience.

Anxiety   An emotional state characterized by worry, feelings of apprehension and/or bodily tension that tends to occur in the absence of real or obvious danger. See also **behavioural anxiety**, **cognitive anxiety** and **somatic anxiety**.

Arousal   A diffuse pattern of alertness and physiological activation that prepares the body for action.

Arousal reappraisal   Interpreting increases in arousal as being beneficial to performance.

Attention   The concentration of mental effort on sensory or mental events. See also **divided attention** and **selective attention**.

Attentional control theory   A theory that postulates that anxiety hampers skilled performance by disrupting attentional control mechanisms in working memory such as attentional inhibition (the process which enables people to ignore irrelevant stimuli) and attentional shifting (the process by which people can switch attention from one task to another depending on changing task requirements).

Attribution   The process of drawing inferences from, or seeking explanations for, events, experiences and behaviour.

Attribution theory   The study of people's explanations for the causes of events or behaviour in their lives.

Attributional retraining   This is a therapeutic strategy that helps people to change the way in which they perceive and think about the meaning of success and failure.

Attributional style   The characteristic manner in which people make sense of, or offer similar explanations for, different events in their lives.

Autonomic nervous system (ANS)   Part of the peripheral nervous system that regulates the body's involuntary muscles (e.g. the heart) and internal organs.

Behavioural anxiety   A component of anxiety that is typically evident in such behaviour as tense facial expressions, changes in communication patterns (e.g. unusually rapid speech delivery) and jerky and inefficient body movements. See also **cognitive anxiety** and **somatic anxiety**.

Biofeedback   A technique that allows people to monitor and gain control over certain bodily functions through the use of specialized equipment.

Bio-informational theory of imagery   A theory that mental images are not "pictures in the head" but consist of stimulus, response and meaning propositions. See also **cognitive or symbolic theory of mental practice** and **neuromuscular theory of mental practice**.

Brainstorming   The generation of ideas or suggestions by members of a group in an effort to solve a problem.

Broaden-and-build theory   This theory proposes that positive emotions can broaden people's momentary thought–action repertoires thereby enhancing their personal resources.

Burnout   A state of withdrawal from a valued activity that is usually caused by chronic stress and accompanied by feelings of physical and mental exhaustion.

Case study   A research method that involves in-depth description or detailed examination of a single person or instance of a situation.

Catastrophe theory   A theory which postulates that high levels of cognitive and somatic anxiety will produce a sudden and dramatic (hence "catastrophic") deterioration in performance.

Choking under pressure   A phenomenon in which athletic performance deteriorates suddenly and significantly as a result of anxiety.

Chronometric paradigm   A method in experimental psychology in which the time-course of information processing activities is used to draw inferences about possible underlying cognitive mechanisms.

Chunk   A well-learned, cognitive unit of information in memory that may contain several smaller components.

Chunking   The process of combining individual items into larger, more meaningful units as an aid to remembering them.

Cognitive anxiety   Worry – or having negative expectations about some current or impending task or situation. See also **behavioural anxiety** and **somatic anxiety**.

Cognitive appraisal   The process of interpreting or making judgements about a given event or situation. See also **primary appraisal** and **secondary appraisal**.

Cognitive approach   A theoretical approach in psychology that investigates the mental processes involved in acquiring, storing and using knowledge. See also **cognitive paradigm**.

Cognitive evaluation theory   A theory of motivation which postulates that rewards which are perceived as controlling tend to impair intrinsic motivation whereas those which are perceived as informative tend to strengthen it.

Cognitive-motivational-relational theory   A theory of emotion which postulates that our emotions are determined by our appraisals of stimuli.

Cognitive neuroscience   An interdisciplinary movement that blends cognitive psychology and neuroscience in the scientific study of how mental activities are executed by the brain.

Cognitive or symbolic theory of mental practice   The theory that mental practice facilitates attention to, and coding and retention of, key elements of the task or skill being learned through imagination. See also **bio-informational theory of imagery** and **neuromuscular theory of mental practice**.

Cognitive paradigm   See **cognitive approach**.

Cognitive processes   Mental activities, such as thinking, by which people acquire, store and use their knowledge.

Cognitive restructuring   A psychological technique that helps people to change the way in which they think so that they can learn to perceive feared situations as controllable challenges.

Cognitive sport psychology   A branch of sport psychology that is concerned with understanding how the mind works in athletic situations.

Cohesion   (also known as team cohesion) The extent to which a group of people is united by a common purpose and bonds together to achieve that objective. See also **social cohesion** and **task cohesion**.

Computer modelling   The attempt to simulate and understand mental processes using computer programs.

Concentration   The ability to focus effectively on the task at hand, or on what is most important in any situation, while ignoring distractions. See also **focus**.

Confidence   A belief in one's ability to perform a certain skill or to achieve a specific goal regardless of prevailing circumstances. See also **self-efficacy**.

Conscious processing hypothesis   A theory which proposes that performance may deteriorate when people try to exert conscious control over skills that had previously been automatic. See also **reinvestment hypothesis**.

Construct   An abstract or theoretical idea in psychology representing something that cannot be observed directly.

Construct validity   The extent to which a psychological test actually measures what it purports to measure.

Controllability   The ease with which mental images can be manipulated by the person who experiences them.

Coping   The use of thoughts and actions to manage demanding situations.

Coping effectiveness   The degree in which a coping strategy or combination of strategies is or are successful in alleviating stress.

Core relational theme   Central or core meaning associated with a certain emotion.

Correlational research A research method that measures the relationship or degree of association between two or more variables. See also **descriptive research** and **experimental research**.

Cultural sport psychology A theoretical movement in sport psychology that seeks to obtain a contextualized understanding of marginalized topics and cultural identities.

Declarative knowledge Knowledge of facts and rules that can be consciously retrieved and declared explicitly.

Deliberate practice A highly structured, purposeful and individualized form of practice in which the learner tries to improve a specific skill under the guidance of a specialist instructor. See also **expertise**.

Descriptive research A group of research methods designed to record and analyse certain aspects of behaviour in natural settings. This category includes such methods as case studies (which are intensive or in-depth analyses of individuals, groups or events), naturalistic observation (where researchers observe behaviour as it occurs in its own natural environment), survey research (where information is collected about the behaviour, experiences or attitudes of many people using a series of questions about the topic of interest) and psychometric testing (where differences between people on some psychological construct are assessed using specially designed, standardized instruments). See also **correlational research** and **experimental research**.

Direct perception A theoretical approach associated with James Gibson which postulates that the mind directly perceives stimuli from the environment without additional cognitive processing.

Direction of anxiety The extent to which a person perceives anxiety to be either facilitative or debilitative of his or her performance.

Discursive psychology The study of how people "construct" events in everyday life through their use of language in writing and conversation and through symbolic communication such as text messages.

Dispositional attributions Explanations of behaviour that invoke personality characteristics as the causes of a given outcome.

Divided attention The ability to perform two or more tasks equally well as a result of extensive practice. See also **selective attention**.

Drive theory A theory of motivation which suggests that behaviour is fuelled from within by drives stemming from basic biological needs.

Dual-task paradigm A research method for studying divided attention in which participants are required to perform two tasks at once.

Effect size Statistical estimation of the effect of one variable on another variable.

Ego depletion Individuals possess a limited supply of willpower which decreases with overuse.

Ego (or "performance") goals Goals that emphasize the importance of demonstrating one's competence by performing better than others. See also **performance goals.**

Ego orientation A type of motivation in which an athlete perceives success as performing better than others on a given task or skill. See also **achievement goal therapy**.

Electroencephalography (EEG)   A neuroscientific technique for recording electrical activity in the brain using special electrodes placed on the scalp.

Electromyographic (EMG) activity   A recording of the electrical activity of the muscles.

Embodied cognition   An interdisciplinary theoretical movement which postulates that many aspects of human cognition are shaped by bodily processes and environmental factors.

Embodiment approach   See **embodied cognition**.

Emotion   Subjective feelings experienced in response to one's environment.

Emotion regulation   The automatic or deliberate use of strategies to initiate, maintain, modify or display emotions.

Epinephrine   A neurotransmitter (also known as adrenaline) that is secreted by the adrenal gland when people are afraid or angry (during the "fight or flight" response) and causes increased heart rate and opening of air passages into the lungs in preparation of the body for strenuous activity. See also **norepinephrine**.

Event-related potential (ERP)   A neuroscientific technique for measuring transient electrical changes in the brain evoked by certain information processing events.

Exercise   Planned, structured and repetitive bodily movements that people engage in to improve or maintain physical fitness and/or health.

Exercise psychology   The scientific study of the psychological antecedents, correlates and consequences of physical activity. It has also been defined as the systematic investigation of the brain and behaviour in physical activity settings.

Experimental research   A research method in which investigators examine the effects of manipulating one or more independent variables, under controlled conditions, on a designated dependent variable. See also **correlational research** and **descriptive research**.

Expertise   Exceptional skills and/or knowledge in a specific area as a result of at least ten years of deliberate practice in it. See also **deliberate practice**.

Extrinsic motivation   The impetus to engage in an activity for external rewards rather than for the satisfaction or enjoyment yielded by the activity itself. See also **intrinsic motivation**.

Eye-tracking technology   The use of special computerized equipment to record and analyse the location, duration and order of people's visual fixations when asked to inspect a given scene.

Fitness   See **physical fitness**.

Flow states   See **peak performance experiences**.

Focus   A figurative term that is commonly used in everyday life to refer to the convergence of one's mental spotlight or concentration system on a given target. In this sense, to focus is to pay specific attention to something. See also **concentration**.

Focus group   A qualitative data collection technique which involves a group discussion led by a trained facilitator and which attempts to understand participants' attitudes, experiences and perceptions of designated ideas or topics. See also **qualitative research**.

Functional equivalence theory   The theory that mental imagery and perception share similar neural mechanisms and pathways in the brain.

Functional magnetic resonance imaging (fMRI)   A neuroscientific imaging technique that detects changes in the activity of the brain by measuring the amount of oxygen brought to a particular location in it.

Goal   See **mastery goals**, **performance goals**, **process goals** and **result goals**.

Goal focus   Refers to whether a designated goal is an outcome (e.g. finishing first in a race), a performance (e.g. the number of putts taken in a round of golf) or a process (e.g. keeping one's head steady as one putts)

Goal orientation theory   See **achievement goal theory**.

Goal-setting   The process by which people establish targets or objectives to attain.

Goal specificity   is the extent to which the target behaviour of a designated goal is precisely defined.

Grounded theory   A qualitative research method that uses a systematic set of procedures to generate a theory from the data collected.

Group   Two or more people who interact with, and exert mutual influence on, each other. See also **team**.

Group dynamics   Psychological processes that generate change in groups.

Hardiness   A set of psychological characteristics that appear to protect people against stress by increasing their commitment to, and perceived control over, pressure situations.

Hemispheric-specific priming   The use of an activity that selectively activates one hemisphere thereby creating an advantage for the performance of an activity that relies on the functions of that hemisphere.

Ideo-motor principle   The theory that all thoughts have muscular concomitants.

Idiographic   An approach in psychology that emphasizes the uniqueness or individuality of behaviour rather than its general principles. See also **nomothetic**.

Imagery   The cognitive ability to simulate in the mind information that is not currently being perceived by the sense organs. See also **mental practice**.

Imagery perspective   The virtual vantage point used by a person when imagining an action or event – for example "seeing" something internally (through one's own eyes) and "seeing" it externally (as if watching oneself or someone else on a movie screen). See also **perspective**.

Implicit overcompensation hypothesis   This theory postulates that avoidant instructions will produce the opposite outcome to that intended by the performer.

Individual zone of optimal functioning (IZOF)   A theory which suggests that optimal performance in sport occurs within a unique and individualized zone of arousal for the athlete concerned.

Internal consistency coefficient   A type of reliability coefficient which assesses the degree to which the items of a test correlate with each other and hence measure the same construct. See also **reliability coefficient**.

Intrinsic motivation   The impetus to engage in an activity for internal rewards such as enjoyment or satisfaction. See also **extrinsic motivation**.

Inverted-U hypothesis   A theory that postulates that the relationship between arousal and performance is curvilinear and takes the form of an inverted-U shape.

Ironic theory of mental control   A theory which proposes that, under certain circumstances, the attempt to consciously suppress a specific thought or action can result in an ironic rebound effect whereby that thought or action becomes even more accessible than before.

Kinaesthetic imagery   Feeling-oriented imagery or the mental simulation of sensations associated with limb positions and bodily movements. See also **motor imagery**.

Likert scale   A numerical rating scale used in tests or questionnaires in which respondents are required to choose a value that represents their attitude or belief concerning a specific topic.

Mastery goals   Goals that are self-referenced (i.e. involve personal improvement rather than comparison with the performance of other people) and that involve the cultivation of a designated level of competence in a given skill. See also **performance goals**.

Mental chronometry paradigm   A method for the investigation of motor imagery which involves the comparison of the actual and imagined duration of executed actions.

Mental imagery   See **imagery**.

Mental practice (also known as **motor imagery**)   The systematic use of mental imagery to rehearse an action in the mind's eye without engaging in the actual physical movements involved. See also **imagery**.

Mental representation   A hypothetical internal structure (e.g. a concept or a mental image) that contains knowledge about some external reality.

Mental toughness   An informal term used loosely to describe athletes' resilience, ability to cope with pressure and determination to persist in the face of adversity.

Meta-analysis   A technique which enables researchers to analyse and combine the results of a number of separate studies on the same topic in order to determine the overall size of a statistical effect.

Meta-attention   People's knowledge about, and control over, their own attentional processes.

Metacognition   People's knowledge about, and control over, their own cognitive processes.

Meta-imagery   People's knowledge about, and control over, their own mental imagery processes.

Mindfulness   An attentional focusing strategy that originated in the Buddhist meditative tradition and that advocates a present-centred, non-judgemental awareness and acceptance (rather than attempted suppression) of external and internal distractions.

Motivation   Factors that initiate, guide and/or sustain behaviour. See also **self-determination theory**.

Motivational climate   The type of learning environment which a coach establishes for an athlete – namely, either ego-oriented or mastery-oriented.

Motor imagery   The cognitive rehearsal of voluntary movement without accompanying bodily movement. It may also be defined as a dynamic mental state during which the representation of a motor action or movement is rehearsed in working memory without any overt motor output. See also **kinaesthetic imagery**.

Motor imagery training   The mental simulation of a movement without actually executing it. See also **mental practice**.

Narrative inquiry   A form of qualitative research that investigates the stories that people create and use over time in order to make sense of themselves and their experience of the world.

Naturalistic observation   A research method in which the investigator observes behaviour in its natural setting and attempts to avoid influencing the participants or behaviour being observed.

Neuromuscular theory of mental practice   The theory that imagination of any physical action elicits a faint pattern of activity in the muscles used to perform that action. See also **bio-informational theory of imagery** and **cognitive or symbolic theory of mental practice**.

Neuropsychological   Pertaining to the study of the psychological effects of brain damage and brain disease. See also **neuropsychology**.

Neuroscience   An interdisciplinary field of research that is concerned mainly with the identification of the neural substrates of mental processes.

Neuroscientific imaging   Brain-scanning techniques that produce pictures of the structure and/or functioning of specific parts of the brain.

Nomothetic   An approach in psychology that seeks to establish general laws of behaviour using data obtained from group comparisons. See also **idiographic**.

Norepinephrine   A type of neurotransmitter in the brain. See also **epinephrine**.

Occipital lobe   A region of the cerebral cortex at the back of the head that is concerned with visual information processing.

Outcome goals   Goals that are based on the outcome of a specific event and usually require some kind of interpersonal comparison. See also **result goals**.

Paradigm   The detailed framework of principles, theories, methods and assumptions that is shared by a group of researchers in a given field.

Paratelic dominance   A state of mind in which the person's behaviour is adventurous, playful and fun-loving. See also **reversal theory** and **telic dominance**.

Parietal lobe   A brain region at the top and rear centre of the head which is believed to be involved in regulating spatial attention and motor control.

Pattern recognition tasks   An experimental technique used by researchers to investigate expert–novice differences in people's ability to remember briefly presented patterns of information in a particular field.

Peak performance experiences (also known as **flow states**)   Coveted but elusive experience in sport where an athlete performs to the best of his or her ability mainly as a result of being totally focused on the task at hand.

Perfectionism   A person's tendency to strive for flawlessness and to set excessively high standards for one's performance.

Performance goals   Behavioural outcomes or targets (such as serving accurately in tennis) that are largely under the control of the performer. See also **mastery goals**. See also **ego goals**.

Perspective   See **imagery perspective**.

Physical activity   Bodily movements that are produced by the skeletal muscles and result in the expenditure of energy.

Physical fitness   The capacity to respond successfully to the physical challenges of life.

Plasticity   A property of the brain that allows it to be moulded by experience and enables it to adapt to and/or compensate for loss of function due to damage.

Positive emotions   Feelings characterized by a lack of negativity.

Positron emission tomography (PET scanning)   A neuroscientific imaging technique that measures the metabolic activity of the brain by tracking radioactive substances injected into the bloodstream.

Pre-performance routines   Preferred sequences of preparatory thoughts and actions that athletes use in an effort to concentrate effectively before the execution of key skills.

Primary appraisal   One's initial perception of a situation as benign, neutral or threatening. See also **cognitive appraisal** and **secondary appraisal**.

Procedural knowledge   Implicit knowledge of how to perform actions and cognitive and/or motor skills.

Process goals   Goals that specify the precise actions or behavioural strategy required in order to execute a particular skill or to attain a specific performance outcome.

Processing efficiency theory   A theory that seeks to explain how anxiety affects skilled performance by distinguishing between performance *effectiveness* (i.e. the quality of task performance) and processing *efficiency* (i.e. the relationship between performance effectiveness and the use of processing resources – in short, performance effectiveness divided by effort) and by postulating that anxiety impairs processing efficiency to a greater extent than it does processing effectiveness.

Protocol analysis   A research method which involves recording what people say as they think aloud while solving a problem. See also **think aloud verbal protocols**.

Psychometric data   Information that is yielded by psychological tests and measures.

Psychometric testing   The use of standardized psychological tests to measure people's abilities, beliefs, attitudes, preferences or activities.

Psychophysiology   A field of psychology that explores the physiological processes underlying behaviour and experience.

Pupillometry   The measurement of changes in pupil diameter as a function of cognitive processing.

Qualitative research   A broad range of data collection techniques used by researchers in an attempt to understand and represent the quality, meaning or richness of people's lived experiences. See also **focus group**.

Quantitative research   A range of research methods which are concerned with measuring and drawing statistical inferences from the data rather than with attempting to understand the subjective meaning or experience of this information.

Quiet eye   The time that elapses between a performer's last visual fixation on a target and the subsequent initiation of a motor response.

Rational emotive behaviour therapy   A form of therapy which attempts to reduce dysfunctional emotions by replacing irrational thoughts with rational ones.

Reinvestment hypothesis   A theory that postulates that skilled performance breaks down when performers "reinvest" in, or attempt to exert conscious control over, actions and movements that are normally performed automatically. See also **conscious processing hypothesis**.

Reliability coefficient   A statistic that is used in psychological measurement to indicate the consistency of a test or the degree to which it can be expected to yield the same results on different occasions. See also **internal consistency coefficient**.

Response set   A tendency to respond to a survey, questionnaire or test in a particular way regardless of the person's actual attitudes or beliefs.

Result goals Behavioural outcomes or targets that can be defined objectively (such as winning a race or defeating an opponent) but which are not directly under one's own control.

Reversal theory A theory of personality which suggests that people alternate or reverse between paired meta-motivational states such as telic and paratelic dominance. See also **paratelic dominance** and **telic dominance**.

Saccadic eye movements A series of high-speed, involuntary jumps of the eye which shift people's gaze from one fixation location to another. See also **smooth pursuit eye movements**.

Secondary appraisal One's perception of the adequacy of one's personal resources in dealing with a source of stress. See also **cognitive appraisal** and **primary appraisal**.

Selective attention The ability to focus on task-relevant information while ignoring distractions. See also **divided attention**.

Self-confrontation interviews A qualitative method which requires subjects to view video recordings of their own actions and to recount any thoughts or emotions they had when performing those actions.

Self-determination theory A general theory of motivation that distinguishes between autonomous motivation (where people experience a sense of volition over, and intrinsic interest in, their actions) and controlled motivation (in which one's behaviour is a function of external contingencies such as rewards). See also **motivation**, **theory of planned behaviour**, **theory of reasoned action** and **transtheoretical model of behaviour change**.

Self-efficacy People's expectations about their ability to perform a given task. See also **confidence**.

Self-serving attributional bias A tendency for people to attribute their successes to internal causes and their failures to external causes.

Self-talk The internal or covert dialogue which people engage in when they "talk" to themselves inside their heads.

Sensation seeking A variable which refers to people's need for, and willingness to take risks in pursuing, various novel, complex or adventurous experiences.

Short-term memory The traditional term for the temporary memory store that can hold a limited amount of information for a brief period of time (usually less than thirty seconds) in the absence of rehearsal. Since the mid-1970s, this term has been largely replaced by "working memory" to reflect an important change in emphasis from a passive store to an active system for the conscious processing and manipulation of temporarily stored information. See also **working memory**.

Simulation training The theory that athletes can learn to concentrate more effectively in real-life pressure situations if they have practised under simulated versions of these conditions.

Single-case research design A group of quasi-experimental research methods that can be used to study the effects, time-course or variability of an independent variable (e.g. an intervention programme) on a designated dependent variable (e.g. behaviour or performance). Although the units in single-case research are typically individual participants, they can also be dyads, small-groups (e.g. teams) or even institutional populations.

Situational attributions   Explanations of behaviour that invoke environmental factors as the causes of a given outcome.

Smooth pursuit eye movements   Eye movements that are activated when a moving target appears within the visual field. These movements serve to centre and stabilize the image of the moving object of interest on the fovea, thereby guaranteeing its high-acuity inspection. See also **saccadic eye movements.**

Snooker   A game played on a billiard table in which people use a cue to hit a white ball to send twenty-one coloured balls in a set order into the pockets around the table.

Social cohesion   The desire by team members to form and maintain interpersonal bonds. See also **cohesion, task cohesion** and **team spirit**.

Social desirability   A bias that occurs when people who are answering questions try to make themselves look good rather than responding truthfully.

Social facilitation   The improvement in people's performance that can occur when they are either part of a group or are being observed by other people.

Social loafing   The tendency of people to work less hard on a task when they are part of a group than as individuals due to diffusion of responsibility.

Sociogram   A technique that is used to measure social cohesion by asking group members confidentially to indicate their like or dislike of other members.

Somatic anxiety   An unpleasant state of bodily tension that is usually accompanied by increased heart rate, rapid breathing and "butterflies" in the stomach. See also **behavioural anxiety** and **cognitive anxiety**.

Spatial occlusion paradigm   A research method commonly used in eye-tracking research in which viewers are required to make judgements about a visual scene from which certain parts have been either occluded from view or removed altogether. See also **temporal occlusion paradigm**.

Sport and exercise psychology   An academic discipline and profession in which the principles, methods and findings of psychology are applied to sport and exercise settings.

Sport psychology   The application of psychological theory and methods to understand the performance, mental processes and well-being of people who are involved in sport.

State anxiety   Transient, situation-specific feelings of fear, worry and physiological arousal.

Strategic knowledge   The ability to recognize and respond to various patterns of play in a given sport.

Survey research   A research method in which questionnaires or interviews are used to obtain information from a sample of people about specific beliefs, attitudes, preferences or activities.

Systematic review   A type of literature review that collects and critically analyses multiple research studies or papers.

Task cohesion   The desire by group members to complete a common task. See also **cohesion** and **social cohesion**.

Task goals   Goals which focus mainly on acquiring competence in a given skill.

Task orientation   A type of motivation in which an athlete perceives success as mastering a given skill or task to a self-defined standard of excellence. See also **achievement goal theory**.

Taxonomy   A scheme of classification used to define a group on the basis of shared characteristics.

Team   A task-related group which is characterized by a collective sense of identity and a set of distinctive roles. See also **group**.

Team building   The attempt to improve team performance by developing communication and cohesion among team members.

Team cohesion   See **cohesion**.

Team goal-setting   The process by which teams plan to achieve certain targets.

Team spirit   A term that is used loosely to indicate the degree of social cohesion that is apparent. See also **social cohesion**.

Telic dominance   A state of mind in which a person's behaviour is serious and goal-directed. See also **paratelic dominance** and **reversal theory**.

Temporal occlusion paradigm   A research method commonly used in eye-tracking research in which people are asked to guess what happens next when viewing information presented in slides, film or video. See also **spatial occlusion paradigm**.

Ten-year rule   The theory that it takes approximately ten years (or approximately 10,000 hours) of sustained deliberate practice to become an expert in any field.

Theory of challenge and threat states   This theory proposes that athletes' emotions will be influenced by the extent to which they respond positively (i.e. view it as a challenge) or negatively (i.e. view it as a threat) to competition.

Theory of planned behaviour   A theory that postulates that human behaviour is guided by four main psychological variables – intentions, attitudes, subjective norms (i.e. perceived social pressures that people feel either to perform or not to perform a given behaviour), and perceived behavioural control.

Theory of reasoned action   A theory that postulates that behavioural intentions rather than attitudes are the main predictors of behaviour. More precisely, attitudes toward the expected result of a given behaviour and subjective norms (or the influences that other people have on a person's attitudes) are held to be the main predictors of behavioural intentions.

Think aloud verbal protocols   A method in which data are collected from what people say as they talk about or give a running commentary on their thoughts and actions as they tackle a cognitive task or problem in their specialist domain. See also **protocol analysis**.

Thought sampling techniques   A research method in which people are equipped with electronic beepers and cued to reveal their thoughts and feelings at specific moments.

Trait anxiety   A consistent and pervasive tendency to perceive certain situations as threatening.

Transcranial magnetic stimulation (TMS)   A neuroscientific technique in which a high-intensity magnetic coil is placed over a person's skull in an effort to stimulate neural activity in the brain.

Transtheoretical model of behaviour change   A dynamic theory that postulates that intentional behavioural change is not an 'all or nothing' phenomenon but reflects a distinctive set of processes that unfold gradually over time.

Trigger words   Instructional cues used by athletes and coaches to help them to concentrate on what is most important when executing a skill.

Valence   The intrinsic attractiveness (positive valence) or aversiveness (negative valence) of an event, object or situation.

Validity   See **construct validity**.

Visual search task   An experimental technique used by researchers to determine people's speed and accuracy in detecting target stimuli presented in complex arrays containing distracters.

Visualization   See **imagery**.

Vividness   The apparent clarity, realism or richness of a mental image.

Working memory   Part of the conscious memory system that stores, retrieves and manipulates transient formation for current use (formerly known as short-term memory). See also **short-term memory**.

References

Abdollahipour, R., Wulf, G., Psotta, R., and Palomo Nieto, M. (2015) Performance of gymnastics skill benefits from an external focus of attention. *Journal of Sports Sciences, 33,* 1807–1813.

Abernethy, A.B. (2001) Attention. In R.N. Singer, H.A. Hausenblas and C.M. Janelle (ed.), *Handbook of Sport Psychology* (2nd edn, pp. 53–58) New York: John Wiley & Sons.

Abernethy, B., and Russell, D. G. (1987) The relationship between expertise and visual search strategy in a racquet sport. *Human Movement Science, 6,* 283–319.

Abernethy, B., Neal, R. J., and Koning, P. (1994) Visual-perceptual and cognitive differences between expert, intermediate, and novice snooker players. *Applied Cognitive Psychology, 8,* 185–211.

Abernethy, B., Baker, J., and Côté, J. (2005) Transfer of pattern recall skills may contribute to the development of sport expertise. *Applied Cognitive Psychology, 19,* 705–718.

Abernethy, B., Maxwell, J. P., Masters, R. S. W., Van der Kamp, J., and Jackson, R. C. (2007) Attentional processes in skill learning and expert performance. In G. Tenenbaum and R. C. Eklund (eds) *Handbook of sport psychology* (3rd edn, pp. 245–263). New York: Wiley.

Abernethy, B., Schorer, J., Jackson, R. C., and Hagemann, N. (2012) Perceptual training methods compared: The relative efficacy of different approaches to enhancing sport-specific anticipation. *Journal of Experimental Psychology: Applied, 18,* 143–153.

Abma, C. L., Fry, M. D., Li, Y., and Relyea, G. (2002) Differences in imagery content and imagery ability between high and low confident track and field athletes. *Journal of Applied Sport Psychology, 14,* 67–75.

About the Rio 2016 Paralympics (2016) Retrieved from https://www.paralympic.org/rio-2016/about-us on 29 August 2016.

Adams, J. A. (1987) Historical review and appraisal of research on the learning, retention and transfer of human motor skills. *Psychological Bulletin, 101,* 41–74.

Aglioti, S. M., Cesari, P., Romani, M., and Urgesi, C. (2008) Action anticipation and motor resonance in elite basketball players. *Nature Neuroscience, 11,* 1109–1116.

Aherne, C., Moran, A., and Lonsdale, C. (2011) The effects of mindfulness training on athletes' flow: An initial investigation. *Sport Psychologist, 25,* 177–189.

Alderfer, C. P. (1977) Group and intergroup relations. In J. R. Hackman and J. L. Suttle (eds) *Improving life at work* (pp. 227–296). Santa Monica, CA: Goodyear.

Alexias, G., and Dimitropoulou, E. (2011) The body as a tool: Professional classical ballet dancers' embodiment. *Research in Dance Education, 12,* 87–104.

Alicke, M. D., Mandel, D. R., Hilton, D. J., Gerstenberg, T., and Lagnado, D. A. (2015) Causal conceptions in social explanation and moral evaluation: A historical tour. *Psychological Science, 10,* 790–812.

Allami, N., Paulignan, Y., Brovelli, A., and Boussaoud, D. (2008) Visuo-motor learning with combinations of different rates of motor imagery and physical practice. *Experimental Brain Research, 184,* 105–113.

Allan, J. L. (2008) The intention-behaviour gap: It's all under control (executive control). *European Health Psychologist, 10,* 62-64.

Allen, M. S., Jones, M. V., and Sheffield, D. (2009) Causal attribution and emotion in the days following competition. *Journal of Sports Sciences, 27,* 461–468.

Allen, M. S., Jones, M. V., and Sheffield, D. (2011a) Are the causes assigned to unsatisfactory performances related to the intensity of emotions experienced after competition? *Sport and Exercise Psychology Review, 7,* 3–9.

Allen, M. S., Greenlees, I., and Jones, M. (2011b) An investigation of the five-factor model of personality and coping behaviour in sport. *Journal of Sports Sciences, 29,* 841–850.

Allen, M. S., Greenlees, I., and Jones, M. (2013) Personality in sport: A comprehensive review. *International Review of Sport and Exercise Psychology, 6,* 184–208.

Allen, R. (2000) *The new Penguin English dictionary.* London: Penguin.

Allport, G. W. (1954). The historical background of social psychology. In G. Lindzey (ed.), *Handbook of social psychology* (Vol. 1, pp. 3–56). Reading, MA: Addison-Wesley.

Alnaes, D., Sneve, M. H., Espeseth, T., Endestad, T., van de Pavert, S. H. P., and Laeng, B. (2014) Pupil size signals mental effort deployed during multiple object tracking and predicts brain activity in the dorsal attention network and the locus coeruleus. *Journal of Vision, 14,* 1–20.

Ames, C. (1992) Achievement goals, motivational climate, and motivational processes. In G. Roberts (ed.) *Motivation in sport and exercise* (pp. 161–176). Champaign, IL: Human Kinetics.

Amorose, A. J., and Anderson-Butcher, D. (2015) Exploring the independent and interactive effects of autonomy-supportive and controlling coaching behaviours on adolescent athletes' motivation for sport. *Sport, Exercise, and Performance Psychology, 4,* 206–221.

Andersen, J. L., Schjerling, P., and Saltin, B. (2000) Muscle, genes and athletic performance. *Scientific American,* September, *283* (3), 48–55.

Anderson, A. (2002) The Assessment of Consultant Effectiveness instrument. *Newsletter Sport and Exercise Psychology Section* (British Psychological Society), *17,* 4–7.

Anderson, B. (2011) There is no such thing as attention. *Frontiers in Psychology, 2,* 246.

Anderson, W. G. (1899) Studies in the effects of physical training. *American Physical Education Review, 4,* 265–278.

Anshel, M. (1995) Anxiety. In T. Morris and J. Summers (eds) *Sport psychology* (pp. 29–62). Brisbane: Wiley.

Anshel, M. (1996) Coping styles among adolescent competitive athletes. *Journal of Social Psychology, 136,* 311–324.

Anshel, M. H., and Kassidis, S. N. (1997) Coping style and situational appraisals, as predictors of coping strategies following stressful events in sport as a function of gender and skill level. *British Journal of Psychology*, *88,* 263–276.

Anthony, D. R., Gucciardi, D. F., and Gordon, S. (in press) A meta-study of qualitative research on mental toughness development. *International Review of Sport and Exercise Psychology.*

Appaneal, R. N., Perna, F. M., and Larkin, K. T. (2007) Psychophysiological response to severe sport injury among competitive male athletes: A preliminary investigation. *Journal of Clinical Sport Psychology, 1,* 68–88.

Arnold, R., and Fletcher, D. (2015) Confirmatory factor analysis of the Sport Emotion Questionnaire in organisational environments. *Journal of Sports Sciences, 33,* 169–179.

Arnold, R., Fletcher, D., and Daniels, K. (2013) Development and validation of the organizational stressor indicator for sport performers (OSI-SP). *Journal of Sport and Exercise Psychology, 35,* 180–196.

Aronson, E., Wilson, T. D., and Akert, R. M. (2002) *Social psychology* (4th edn). Upper Saddle River, NJ: Prentice-Hall.

Arora, S., Aggarwal, R., Sevdalis, N., Moran, A., Sirimanna, P., Kneebone, R., and Darzi, A. (2010) Development and validation of mental practice as a training strategy for laparoscopic surgery. *Surgical Endoscopy, 24,* 179–187.

Arora, S., Aggarwal, R., Sirimanna, P., Moran, A., Grantcharov, T., Kneebone, R., Sevdalis, N., and Darzi, A. (2011) Mental practice enhances surgical technical skills: A randomized controlled study. *Annals of Surgery, 253,* 265–270.

Ashcraft, M. (2006) *Cognition* (4th edn). Upper Saddle River, NJ: Pearson.

Asinof, E. (1988) *Eight men out: The Black Sox and the 1919 world series*. New York: Henry Holt.

Associated Press (2009) Cavendish springs to Stage 2 victory. Associated Press, 5 July 2009. Retrieved from http://sports.espn.go.com/oly/tdf2009/news/story?id=4307025 on 30 September 2010.

Austin, J. (2015) Angry Rory McIlroy aims to control emotions after difficult first day at Wentworth. Retrieved from www.express.co.uk/sport/golf/579035/Angry-Rory-McIlroy-control-emotions-difficult-first-day-Wentworth on 24 October 2016.

Azar, B. (1996) Researchers explore why some athletes "choke". *American Psychological Association Monitor on Psychology, 27,* July, 21.

Babiloni, C., Infarinato, F., Marzano, N., Iacoboni, M., Dassù, F., Soricelli, A., Rossini, P. M., Limatola, C., and Del Percio, C. (2011) Intra-hemispheric functional coupling of alpha rhythms is related to golfer's performance: A coherence EEG study. *International Journal of Psychophysiology, 82,* 260–268.

Baddeley, A. (2012) Working memory: Theories, models, and controversies. *Annual Review of Psychology, 63,* 1–29.

Bailey, M. (2014) Sports visualisation: How to imagine your way to success. Retrieved from www.telegraph.co.uk/men/active/10568898/Sports-visualisation-how-to-imagine-your-way-to-success.html on 24 October 2016.

Bakeman, R., and Helmreich, R. (1975) Cohesiveness and performance: Covariation and causality in an undersea environment. *Journal of Experimental Social Psychology, 11,* 478–489.

Baker, J., and Horton, S. (2004) A review of primary and secondary influences on sport expertise. *High Ability Studies, 15,* 211–228.

Baker, J., and Young, B. (2014) 20 years later: Deliberate practice and the development of expertise in sport. *International Review of Sport and Exercise Psychology, 7,* 135–157.

Baker, J., and Farrow, D. (2015) The Routledge handbook of sport expertise. Abingdon, Oxfordshire: Routledge.

Baker, J., Cobely, S., and Fraser-Thomas, J. (2009) What do we know about early sport specialization? Not much! *High Ability Studies, 20,* 77–89.

Baker, J., Wattie, N., and Schorer, J. (2015) Defining expertise: A taxonomy for researchers in skill acquisition and expertise. In J. Baker and D. Farrow (eds) *The Routledge Handbook of Sport Expertise* (pp. 145–155). Abingdon, Oxfordshire: Routledge.

Bandura, A. (1997) *Self-efficacy: The exercise of control.* New York: Freeman.

Barker, J., and Slater, M. (2015) It's not just cricket. *The Psychologist, 28,* 552–557.

Barker, J., McCarthy, P., Jones, M., and Moran, A. (2011) *Single-case research designs in sport and exercise psychology.* London: Routledge.

Barker-Ruchti, N., and Tinning, R. (2010) Foucault in leotards: Corporeal discipline in women's artistic gymnastics. *Sociology of Sport Journal, 27,* 229–250.

Barlow, M. (2015) "What hope for José and his flops"? *Irish Daily Mail*, 17 December, p. 53.

Barlow, M., Woodman, T., Chapman, C., Milton, M., Stone, D., Dodds, T., and Allen, B. (2015) Who takes risks in high-risk sport? The role of alexithymia. *Journal of Sport and Exercise Psychology, 37,* 83–96.

Barnes, S. (2009) The unfashionable truth about success. *The Times*, 1 June. Retrieved from www.timesonline.co.uk/tol/sport/columnists/simonbarnes/article6401625.ece on 10 March 2011.

Barsade, S. G. (2002) The ripple effect: Emotional contagion and its influence on group behaviour. *Administrative Science Quarterly, 47,* 644–675.

Barsalou L W. (1999) Perceptual symbol systems. *Behavioural and Brain Sciences, 22,* 577–660.

Bartlett, F. C. (1932). *Remembering: A study in experimental and social psychology*. Cambridge: Cambridge University Press.

Batt, B. (2007) Why do migratory birds fly in a V-formation? *Scientific American*, 1 October. Retrieved from www.scientificamerican.com/article/why-do-migratory-birds-fl/ on 13 January 2016.

Battaglia C., D'Artibale E., Fiorilli G., Piazza M., Tsopani D., Giombini A., Calcagno G., and di Cagno, A. (2014) Use of video observation and motor imagery on jumping performance in national rhythmic gymnastics athletes. *Human Movement Science, 38*, 225–234.

Bauman, J. (2008) Sport psychology at the Olympics. *Div47 News: Exercise and Sport Psychology Newsletter, 21*, 2. Retrieved from http://apa47.org/pdfs/summer08newsletter.pdf on 10 March 2011.

Baumeister, R. F. (1984) Choking under pressure: Self-consciousness and the paradoxical effects of incentives on skilled performance. *Journal of Personality and Social Psychology, 46*, 610–620.

Baumeister, R. F., and Showers, C. J. (1986) A review of paradoxical performance effect Choking under pressure in sports and mental tests. *European Journal of Social Psychology, 16*, 361–383.

Baumeister, R. F., Bratslavsky, E., Muraven, M., and Tice, D. M. (1998) Ego depletion: Is the active self a limited resource? *Journal of Personality and Social Psychology, 74*, 1252–1265.

BBC (2003) Snooker: The World Championship. Coverage of the 2003 World Championship, Sheffield. Presented by Hazel Irvine with Steve Dabikd and John Parrott. BBC2, 5 May.

BBC Sport (2008) Little makes Wrexham blunder plea. Retrieved from http://news.bbc.co.uk/sport2/hi/football/teams/w/wrexham/7291542.stm on 21 September 2011.

Beattie, S., Hardy, L., Savage, J., Woodman, T., and Callow, N. (2011) Development and validation of a trait measure of self-confidence. *Psychology of Sport and Exercise, 12*, 184–191.

Beauchamp, M. R., and Eys, M. A. (eds) (2008) *Group dynamics in exercise and sport psychology.* Champaign, IL: Human Kinetics.

Beaumont, C., Maynard, I. W., and Butt, J. (2015) Effective ways to develop and maintain robust sport-confidence: Strategies advocated by sport psychology consultants. *Journal of Applied Sport Psychology, 27*, 301–318.

Bebetsos, E., and Antoniou, P. (2003) Psychological skills of Greek badminton athletes. *Perceptual and Motor Skills, 97*, 1289–1296.

Beckmann, J., Gröpel, P., and Ehrlenspiel, F. (2013) Preventing motor skill failure through hemisphere-specific priming: Cases from choking under pressure. *Journal of Experimental Psychology: General, 142*, 679–691.

Bedon, B. G., and Howard, D. E. (1992) Memory for the frequency of occurrence of karate techniques: A comparison of experts and novices. *Bulletin of the Psychonomic Society, 30*, 117–119.

Begley, S. (2000) Mind games. *Newsweek*, 25 September, pp. 60–61.

Beilock, S. (2010a) *Choke.* New York: Free Press.

Beilock, S. (2010b) How to create a sports superstar. *Psychology Today*, 2 August. Retrieved from www.psychologytoday.com/blog/choke/201008/how-create-sports-superstar?utm_source=twitterfeed&utm_medium=twitter on 8 September 2010.

Beilock, S. (in press) Expert performance: From action to perception to understanding. In J. J. Staszewski (ed.) *Expertise and skill acquisition: The impact of William G. Chase.* New York: Psychology Press.

Beilock, S. L., and Carr, T. H. (2001) On the fragility of skilled performance: What governs choking under pressure? *Journal of Experimental Psychology: General, 130*, 701–725.

Beilock, S. L., Carr, T. H., MacMahon, C., and Starkes, J. L. (2002) When paying attention becomes counterproductive: Impact of divided versus skill-focused attention on novice and experienced performance of sensorimotor skills. *Journal of Experimental Psychology: Applied, 8*, 6–16.

Bennett, P., Lowe, R., and Honey, K. (2003) Brief report. *Cognition and Emotion, 17*, 511–520.

Bensley, D. A. (2010) A brief guide for teaching and assessing critical thinking in psychology. *The Observer* (*Association for Psychological Science*), *23*, 49–53.

Bent, I., McIlroy, R., Mousley, K., and Walsh, K. (2000) *Football confidential.* London: BBC.

Bernardi, N. F., De Buglio, M., Trimarchi, P. D., Chielli, A., and Bricolo, E. (2013) Mental practice promotes motor anticipation: Evidence from skilled music performance. *Frontiers in Human Neuroscience, 7, 451*, 1–14.

Bernier, M., Codron, R., Thienot, E., and Fournier, J. F. (2011) The attentional focus of expert golfers in training and competition: A naturalistic investigation. *Journal of Applied Sport Psychology, 23,* 326–341.

Bernier, M., Trottier, C., Thienot, E., and Fournier, J. (2016) An investigation of attentional foci and their temporal patterns: A naturalistic study in expert figure skaters. *Sport Psychologist, 30,* 256–266.

Bertollo, M., Saltarelli, B., and Robazza, C. (2009) Mental preparation strategies of elite modern pentathletes. *Psychology of Sport and Exercise, 10,* 244–254.

Bettenhausen, K. L. (1991) Five years of group research: What we have learned and what needs to be addressed. *Journal of Management, 17,* 345–381.

Betts, G. H. (1909). *The distribution and functions of mental imagery.* New York: Teachers College, Columbia University

Biddle, S. J. H., and Hanrahan, S. (1998) Attributions and attributional style. In J. L. Duda (ed.) *Advances in sport and exercise psychology measurement* (pp. 3–19). Morgantown, WV: Fitness Information Technology.

Biddle, S. J. H., Hanrahan, S. J., and Sellars, C. N. (2001) Attributions: Past, present and future. In R. N. Singer, H. A. Hausenblas, and C. M. Janelle (eds) *Handbook of sport psychology* (2nd edn, pp. 444–471). New York: Wiley.

Binsch, O., Oudjeans, R. R. D., Bakker, F. C., and Savelsberrgh, G. J. P. (2009) Unwanted effects in aiming actions: The relationship between gaze behaviour and performance in a golf putting task. *Psychology of Sport and Exercise, 10,* 628–635.

Binsch, O., Oudejans, R. R., Bakker, F. C., Hoozemans, M. J., and Savelsbergh, G. J. (2010) Ironic effects in a simulated penalty shooting task: Is the negative wording in the instruction essential? *International Journal of Sport Psychology, 41,* 118–133.

Birrer, D., Wetzel, J., Schmid, J., and Morgan, G. (2012) Analysis of sport psychology consultancy at three Olympic Games: Facts and figures. *Psychology of Sport and Exercise, 13,* 702–710.

Bishop, D. T., Karageorghis, C. L., and Loizou, G. (2007) A grounded theory of young tennis players' use of music to manipulate emotional state. *Journal of Sport and Exercise Psychology, 29,* 584–607.

Blackett, A. D., Evans, A., and Piggott, D. (in press) Why 'the best way of learning to coach the game is playing the game': Conceptualising 'fast-tracked' high-performance coaching pathways. *Sport, Education and Society.*

Blajenkova, O., Kozhevnikov, M., and Motes, M. (2006) Object-spatial imagery: A new self-report imagery questionnaire. *Applied Cognitive Psychology, 20,* 239–265.

Blascovich, J., and Mendes, W. B. (2000) Challenge and threat appraisals: The role of affective cues. In J. Forgas, (ed.) *Feeling and thinking: The role of affect in social cognition* (pp. 59–82). Cambridge: Cambridge University Press.

Blascovich, J., Seery, M. D., Mugridge, C. A., Norris, R. K., and Weisbuch, M. (2004) Predicting athletic performance from cardiovascular indexes of challenge and threat. *Journal of Experimental Social Psychology, 40,* 683–688.

Blau, E. (1998) Nervous issues. *The Guardian* (Review), 2 October, pp. 16–17.

Blodgett, A. T., Schinke, R. J., McGannon, K. R., and Fisher, L. (2015) Cultural sport psychology: Conceptions, evolutions, and forecasts. *International Review of Sport and Exercise Psychology, 8,* 24–43

Bloom, B. S. (1985) Generalizations about talent development. In B. S. Bloom (ed.) *Developing talent in young people* (pp. 507–549). New York: Ballantine.

Bond, C. F., and Titus, L. J. (1983) Social facilitation: A meta-analysis of 241 studies. *Psychological Bulletin, 94,* 265–292.

Bond, J., and Sargent, G. (1995) Concentration skills in sport: An applied perspective. In T. Morris and J. Summers (eds) *Sport psychology: Theory, applications and issues* (pp. 386–419). Chichester, West Sussex: Wiley.

Bonneville-Roussy, A., Lavigne, G. L., and Vallerand, R. J. (2011) When passion leads to excellence: The case of musicians. *Psychology of Music, 39,* 123–138.

Bortoli, L., Bertollo, M., Hanin, Y., and Robazza, C. (2012) Striving for excellence: A multi-action plan intervention model for shooters. *Psychology of Sport and Exercise, 13,* 693–701.

Boschker, M. S. J., Bakker, F. C., and Michaels, C. F. (2002) Memory for the functional characteristics of climbing walls: Perceiving affordances. *Journal of Motor Behaviour, 34,* 25–36.

Boutcher, S. H. (2008) Attentional processes and sport performance. In T. S. Horn (ed.) *Advances in sport psychology* (3rd edn, pp. 325–338). Champaign, IL: Human Kinetics.

Bovend'eerdt, T. J., Dawes, H., Sackley, C., and Wade, D.T. (2012) Practical research-based guidance for motor imagery practice in neurorehabilitation. *Journal of Disability and Rehabilitation, 34,* 2192–2200.

Brady, A., and Maynard, I. (2010) Debate: At an elite level the role of a sport psychologist is entirely about performance enhancement. *Sport & Exercise Psychology Review*, 6, 59–66.

Brawley, L. R., and Paskevich, D. M. (1997) Conducting team building research in the context of sport and exercise. *Journal of Applied Sport Psychology, 9,* 11–40.

Brawley, L. R., Carron, A. V., and Widmeyer, W. N. (1987) Assessing the cohesion of teams: Validity of the Group Environment Questionnaire. *Journal of Sport Psychology, 9,* 275–294.

Breivik, G. (1999) *Empirical studies of risk sport.* Oslo, Norway: Norges Idrettshøgskole, Institutt for Samfunnsfag.

Brewer, B. W., Van Raalte, J. L, Linder, D. E., and Van Raalte, N. S. (1991) Peak performance and the perils of retrospective introspection. *Journal of Sport and Exercise Psychology, 8,* 227–238.

Brick, N., MacIntyre, T., and Campbell, M. (2014) Attentional focus in endurance activity: New paradigms and future directions. *International Review of Sport and Exercise Psychology, 7,* 106–134.

Brick, N., MacIntyre, T., and Campbell, M. (2015) Metacognitive processes in the self-regulation of performance in elite endurance runners. *Psychology of Sport and Exercise, 19,* 1–9.

Bronfenbrenner, U., and Morris, P. A. (2006) The bioecological model of human development. In R. M. Lerner (ed.) *Theoretical models of human development. Volume 1 of Handbook of Child Psychology* (6th edn, pp. 793–828). Hoboken, NJ: Wiley.

Brown, D. J., and Fletcher, D. (2017) Effects of Psychological and Psychosocial Interventions on Sport Performance: A Meta-Analysis. *Sports Medicine, 47,* 77–99.

Brown, O. (2013) Team Justin Rose: The network that helped him to victory at the US Open. Retrieved from www.telegraph.co.uk/sport/golf/usopen/10125392/Team-Justin-Rose-the-network-that-helped-him-to-victory-at-the-US-Open.html on 24 October 2016.

Browne, P. J. (2008) *Reading the green: The inside line on the Irish in the Ryder Cup.* Dublin: Currach Press.

Bruner, J. S., Goodenough, J. J., and Austin, G. A. (1956) *A study of thinking.* New York: John Wiley.

Bruner, M. W., Eys, M. A., Beauchamp, M. R., and Côté, J. (2013) Examining the origins of team building in sport: A citation network and genealogical approach. *Group Dynamics: Theory, Research, and Practice, 17,* 30–42.

Brustad, R. J. (2008) Qualitative research approaches. In T. S. Horn (ed.) *Advances in sport psychology* (3rd edn, pp. 31–43). Champaign, IL: Human Kinetics.

Buckley, W. (2005) Black knight of the fairway. *Sunday Independent* (Sport), 10 July, p. 12.

Buckworth, J., and Dishman, R. K. (2002) *Exercise psychology.* Champaign, IL: Human Kinetics.

Bull, S. J., Albinson, J. G., and Shambrook, C. J. (1996) *The mental game plan.* Eastbourne, East Sussex: Sports Dynamics.

Burge, W. K., Ross, L. A., Amthor, F. R., Mitchell, W. G., Zotov, A., and Visscher, K. M. (2013) Processing speed training increases the efficiency of attentional resource allocation in young adults. *Frontiers in Human Neuroscience, 7,* 684.

Burianová, H., Marstaller, L., Sowman, P., Tesan, G., Rich, A.N., Williams, M., Savage, G., and Johnson, B.W. (2013) Multimodal functional imaging of motor imagery using a novel paradigm. *Neuroimage, 71,* 50–58.

Burke, K. L., Sachs, M. L., Fry, S. J., and Schweighardt, S. L. (2008) *Directory of graduate programs in applied sport psychology* (9th edn). Morgantown, WV: Fitness Information Technology.

Burke, S. M., Carron, A. V., and Shapcott, K. M. (2008) Cohesion in exercise groups: An overview. *International Review of Sport and Exercise Psychology, 1,* 107–123.

Burns, J. (2015) The impact of intellectual disabilities on elite sports performance. *International Review of Sport and Exercise Psychology, 8,* 251–267

Burton, D. (1989) Winning isn't everything: Examining the impact of performance goals on collegiate swimmers' cognitions and performance. *Sport Psychologist, 32,* 105–132.

Burton, D. (1998) Measuring competitive state anxiety. In J. L. Duda (ed.) *Advances in sport and exercise psychology measurement* (pp. 129–148). Morgantown, WV: Fitness Information Technology.

Burton, D., and Naylor, S. (1997) Is anxiety really facilitating? Reaction to the myth that cognitive anxiety always impairs performance. *Journal of Applied Sport Psychology, 9,* 295–302.

Burton, D., and Naylor, S. (2002) The Jekyll/Hyde nature of goals: Revisiting and updating goal-setting in sport. In T. Horn (ed.) *Advances in sport psychology* (2nd edn, pp. 459–499). Champaign, IL: Human Kinetics.

Burton, D., and Weiss, C. (2008) The fundamental goal concept: The path to process and performance success. In T. S. Horn (ed.) *Advances in sport psychology* (3rd edn, pp. 339–375). Champaign, IL: Human Kinetics

Burton, D., Naylor, S., and Holliday, B. (2001) Goal setting in sport. In R. N. Singer, H. A. Hausenblas, and C. M. Janelle (eds) *Handbook of sport psychology* (2nd edn, pp. 497–528). New York: Wiley.

Buszard, T., Farrow, D., Zhu, F. F., Masters, R. S. W. (2016) The relationship between working memory capacity and cortical activity during performance of a novel motor task. *Psychology of Sport and Exercise, 22,* 247–254.

Butler, R. (1996) *Sport psychology in action.* Oxford: Butterworth-Heinemann.

Cacioppo, J. T., Berntson, G. G., and Nusbaum, H. C. (2008) Neuroimaging as a new tool in the toolbox of psychological science. *Current Directions in Psychological Science, 17,* 62–67.

Caliari, P. (2008) Enhancing forehand acquisition in table tennis: The role of mental practice. *Journal of Applied Sport Psychology, 20,* 88–96.

Callow, N., and Hardy, L. (2005) A critical analysis of applied imagery research. In D. Hackfort, J. Duda, and R. Lidor (eds) *The handbook of research in applied sport and exercise psychology: International perspectives* (pp. 21–42). Morgantown, WV: Fitness Information Technology.

Callow, N., and Waters, A. (2005) The effect of kinaesthetic imagery on the sport confidence of flat-race horse jockeys. *Psychology of Sport and Exercise, 6,* 443–459.

Callow, N., Roberts, R., Hardy, L., Jiang, D., and Edwards, M. (2013) Performance improvements from imagery: Evidence that internal visual imagery is superior to external visual imagery for slalom performance. *Frontiers in Human Neuroscience, 7,* 697.

Calmels, C., Holmes, P., Lopez, E., and Naman, V. (2006) Chronometric comparison of actual and imaged complex movement patterns. *Journal of Motor Behaviour, 38,* 339–348.

Calvo-Merino, B., Glaser, D. E., Grèzes, J., Passingham, R. E., and Haggard, P. (2005) Action observation and acquired motor skills: An fMRI study with expert dancers. *Cerebral Cortex, 15,* 1243–1249.

Campbell, A. (2015) Downfall. *The Sunday Times* (News Review), 20 December, pp. 1–3.

Campitelli, G., Connors, M. H., Bilalić, M., and Hambrick, D. Z. (2015) Psychological perspectives on expertise. *Frontiers in Psychology, 6,* 258.

Cañal-Bruland, R., and Mann, D. L. (2015) Time to broaden the scope of research on anticipatory behaviour: A case for the role of probabilistic information. *Frontiers in Psychology, 6,* 1518.

Cannon-Bowers, J. A., and Bowers, C. (2011) Team development and functioning. In S. Zedeck (ed.) *APA handbook of industrial and organisational psychology, Vol 1: Building and developing the organization* (pp. 597–650). Washington, DC: American Psychological Association.

Capostagno, A. (2002) Wegerle pitches up in a whole new ball game. *The Guardian,* 17 January, p. 31.

Carless, D., and Douglas, K. (2009) We haven't got a seat on the bus for you or all the seats are mine: Narratives and career transitions in professional golf. *Qualitative Research in Sport and Exercise, 1,* 51–66.

Carless, D., and Douglas, K. (in press) When two worlds collide: A story about collaboration, witnessing and life story research with soldiers returning from war. *Qualitative Inquiry.*

Carless, S. A., and De Paola, C. (2000) The measurement of cohesion in work teams. *Small Group Research, 13,* 71–88.

Carpenter, W. B. (1891) *Principles of mental physiology* (6th edn). New York: Appleton.

Carpenter, W. B. (1894) *Principles of mental physiology.* New York: Appleton-Century-Crofts.

Carron, A. V., and Ball, J. R. (1977) Cause-effect characteristics of cohesiveness and participation motivation in intercollegiate hockey. *International Review of Sport Sociology, 12,* 49–60.

Carron, A. V., and Chelladurai, P. (1981) Cohesion as a factor in sport performance. *International Review of Sport Sociology, 16,* 2–41.

Carron, A. V., and Spink, K. S. (1993) Team building in an exercise setting. *Sport Psychologist, 7,* 8–18.

Carron, A. V., and Hausenblas, H. (1998) *Group dynamics in sport* (2nd edn). Morgantown, WV: Fitness Information Technology.

Carron, A. V., and Brawley, L. R. (2008) Group dynamics in sport and physical activity. In T. S. Horn (ed.) *Advances in sport psychology* (3rd edn, pp. 213–237). Champaign, IL: Human Kinetics.

Carron, A. V., and Eys, M. A. (2012) *Group dynamics in sport* (4th edn). Morgantown, WV: Fitness Information Technology.

Carron, A. V., Widmeyer, W. N., and Brawley, L. R. (1985) The development of an instrument to assess cohesion in sport teams: The Group Environment Questionnaire. *Journal of Sport Psychology, 7,* 244–266.

Carron, A. V., Spink, K. S., and Prapavessis, H. (1997) Team building and cohesiveness in the sport and exercise setting: Use of indirect interventions. *Journal of Applied Sport Psychology, 9,* 61–72.

Carron, A. V., Brawley, L. R., and Widmeyer, W. N. (1998) The measurement of cohesiveness in sport groups. In J. L. Duda (ed.) *Advances in sport and exercise psychology measurement* (pp. 213–226). Morgantown, WV: Fitness Information Technology.

Carron, A. V., Bray, S. R., and Eys, M. A. (2002a) Team cohesion and team success in sport. *Journal of Sports Sciences, 20,* 119–126.

Carron, A. V., Colman, M. M., Wheeler, J., and Stevens, D. (2002b) Cohesion and performance in sport: A meta analysis. *Journal of Sport and Exercise Psychology, 24,* 168–188.

Carron, A. V., Brawley, L. R., and Widmeyer, W. N. (2002c) *The Group Environment Questionnaire: Test manual.* Morgantown, WV: Fitness Information Technology.

Carron, A. V., Eys, M. A., and Burke, S. M. (2007) Team cohesion: Nature, correlates and development. In S. Jowett and D. Lavallee (eds) *Social psychology in sport* (pp. 91–101). Champaign, IL: Human Kinetics.

Carron, A. V., Burke, S. M., and Shapcott, K. M. (2009) Enhancing team effectiveness. In B. W. Brewer (ed.) *Sport psychology: Handbook of sports medicine* (pp. 64–74). Oxford: Wiley-Blackwell.

Carron, A., Shapcott, K. M., and Martin, L. J. (2014) The relationship between team explanatory style and team success. *International Journal of Sport and Exercise Psychology, 12,* 1–9.

Carson, H. J., and Collins, D. (2016) The fourth dimension: A motoric perspective on the anxiety–performance relationship. *International Review of Sport and Exercise Psychology, 9,* 1–21.

Carson, H. J., Collins, D., and Jones, B. (2014) A case study of technical change and rehabilitation: Intervention design and interdisciplinary team interaction. *International Journal of Sport Psychology, 45,* 57–78.

Carter, H. (2010) Doctor in "bloodgate" rugby scandal cleared to go back to work. *The Guardian,* 1 September, p. 12.

Carver, C. S., Scheier, M. F., and Weintraub, J. K. (1989) Assessing coping strategies: A theoretically based approach. *Journal of Personality and Social Psychology, 56,* 267–283.

Cary, T. (2010) "Team orders" debacle spoils Alonso's victory. *Irish Independent* (Sport), 26 July, p. 21.

Casby, A., and Moran, A. (1998) Exploring mental imagery in swimmers: A single-case study design. *Irish Journal of Psychology, 19,* 525–531.

Casey, B. (2011) Power of the mind key to curing a team with a stutter. *The Irish Times* (Sport), 21 February, p. 5.

Casey, G., and Moran, A. (1989) The computational metaphor and cognitive psychology. *The Irish Journal of Psychology, 10,* 143–161.

Casey-Campbell, M., and Martens, M. L. (2009) Sticking it all together: A critical assessment of the group cohesion-performance literature. *International Journal of Management Reviews, 11,* 223–246.

Cashmore, E. (2008) *Sport and exercise psychology: The key concepts* (2nd edn). London: Routledge.

Causer, J., Bennett, S. J., Holmes, P. S., Janelle, C. M., and Williams, A. M. (2010) Quiet eye duration and gun motion in elite shotgun shooting. *Medicine Science in Sports Exercise, 42,* 1599–1608.

Causer, J., Holmes, P. S., and Williams, A. M. (2011) Quiet eye training in a visuomotor control task. *Medicine and Science in Sports and Exercise, 43,* 1042–1049.

Chang, Y., Lee, J. J., Seo, J. H., Song, H. J., Kim, Y. T., Lee, H. J., Kim, H. J., Lee, J., Kim, W., Woo, M., and Kim, J. G. (2011) Neural correlates of motor imagery for elite archers. *NMR Biomedicine, 24,* 366–372.

Chang, Y. K., Chi, L., and Huang, C. S. (2012) Mental toughness in sport: A review and prospect. *International Journal of Sport and Exercise Psychology, 10,* 79–92.

Chase, W. G., and Simon, H. A. (1973) Perception in chess. *Cognitive Psychology, 4,* 55–81.

Chase, W. G., and Ericsson, K. A. (1981) Skilled memory. In J. R. Anderson (ed.) *Cognitive skills and their acquisition* (pp. 141–189). Hillsdale, NJ: Lawrence Erlbaum Associates.

Chen, J., Xu, T., Jing, J., and Chan, R. C. K. (2011) Alexithymia and emotional regulation: A cluster analytical approach. *BMC Psychiatry, 11,* 33.

Cheng, W. N. K., and Hardy, L. (2016) Three-dimensional model of performance anxiety: Tests of the adaptive potential of the regulatory dimension of anxiety. *Psychology of Sport and Exercise, 22,* 255–263.

Cheng, W. N. K., Hardy, L., and Markland, D. (2009) Toward a three-dimensional conceptualization of performance anxiety: Rationale and initial measurement development. *Psychology of Sport and Exercise, 10,* 271–278.

Cheng, W. N. K., Hardy, L., and Woodman, T. (2011) Predictive validity of a three-dimensional model of performance anxiety in the context of tae-kwon-do. *Journal of Sport and Exercise Psychology, 33,* 40–53.

Chesney, M., Folkman, S., and Chambers, D. (1996) Coping effectiveness training for men living with HIV: Preliminary findings. *International Journal of STD & AIDS, 7*(suppl 2), 75–82.

Chong, Y. W., Kee, Y. H., and Chaturvedi, I. (2015) Effects of brief mindfulness induction on weakening habits: Evidence from a computer mouse control task. *Mindfulness, 6,* 582–588.

Chomsky, N. (1959) A review of B. F. Skinner's (1957) *Verbal behaviour. Language, 35,* 26–58.

Chun, M. M., Golomb, J. D., and Turk-Browne, N. B. (2011) A taxonomy of external and internal attention. *Annual Review of Psychology, 62,* 73–101.

Chunxiao, L., Wang, J., Pyun, D. Y., and Kee, Y. H. (2013) Burnout and its relations with basic psychological needs and motivation among athletes: A systematic review and meta-analysis. *Psychology of Sport and Exercise, 14,* 692–700.

Clarey, C. (2014) Olympians use mental imagery as training, *New York Times.* Retrieved from http://www.nytimes.com/2014/02/23/sports/olympics/olympians-use-imagery-as-mental-training.html?_r=0 on 28 October 2016.

Clark, T. P., Tofler, I. R., and Landon, M. T. (2005) The sport psychiatrist and golf. *Clinics in Sports Medicine, 24,* 959–971.

Clarke, P., Sheffield, D., and Akehurst, S. (2015) The yips in sport: A systematic review. *International Review of Sport and Exercise Psychology, 8,* 156–184.

Claxton, G. (1980) Cognitive psychology: A suitable case for what sort of treatment? In G. Claxton (ed.) *Cognitive psychology: New directions* (pp. 1–25). London: Routledge.

Claxton, G. (2015) *Intelligence in the flesh: Why your mind needs your body much more than it thinks.* London and New Haven, CT: Yale University Press.

Cleland, J., O'Gorman, J., and Bond, M. (2015) The English Football Association's Respect Campaign: The referees' view. *International Journal of Sport Policy and Politics, 7,* 551–563.

Clews, G. J., and Gross, J. B. (1995) Individual and social motivation in Australian sport. In T. Morris and J. Summers (eds) *Sport psychology: Theory, applications and issues* (pp. 90–121). Brisbane: Wiley.

Cloud, J. (2008) The science of experience. *Time.* Retrieved from www.time.com/time/health/article/0,8599,1717927–2,00.html on 19 June 2009.

Clough, P., Earle, K., and Sewell, D. (2002) Mental toughness: The concept and its measurement. In I. Cockerill (ed.) *Solutions in sport psychology* (pp. 32–45). London: Thomson.

Cobley, S., Baker, J., Wattie, N., and McKenna, J. (2009) Annual age-grouping and athlete development. *Sports Medicine, 39,* 235–256.

Coelho, Y., and Fischer, M. (eds) (2016) *Perceptual and emotional embodiment: Foundations of embodied cogntition, Volume 1.* London: Routledge.

Coffee, P. (2014) Attribution theory. In R. C. Eklund and G. Tenenbaum (eds) *Encyclopedia of sport and exercise psychology,* (Vol. 1, pp. 54–57). London: SAGE.

Coffee, P., Greenlees, I., and Allen, M. S. (2015) The TRAMS: The Team-Referent Attributions Measure in Sport. *Psychology of Sport and Exercise, 16,* 150–159.

Cohen, A., Pargman, D., and Tenenbaum, G. (2003) Critical elaboration and empirical investigation of the cusp-catastrophe model: A lesson for practitioners. *Journal of Applied Sport Psychology, 15,* 144–159.

Cohen, A. B., Tenenbaum, G., and English, R. W. (2006) Emotions and golf performance: An IZOF-based applied sport psychology case study. *Behaviour Modification, 30,* 259–280.

Cohen, J. (1992) A power primer. *Psychological Bulletin, 112,* 155–159.

Cohn, M. A., and Fredrickson, B. L. (2006) Beyond the moment, beyond the self: Shared ground between selective investment theory and the broaden-and-build theory of positive emotions. *Psychological Inquiry, 17,* 39–44.

Cohn, P. (2015) *Do you have the mental strength of Novak Djokovic?* Retrieved from http://www.sportspsychologytennis.com/do-you-have-the-mental-strength-of-novak-djokovic/

Collet, C., Guillot, A., Lebon, F., MacIntyre, T., and Moran, A. (2011) Measuring motor imagery using psychometric, behavioural, and psychophysiological tools. *Exercise and Sport Sciences Reviews, 39,* 85–92.

Collet, C., Di Rienzo F., Hoyek N., and Guillot A. (2013) Autonomic nervous system correlates in movement observation and motor imagery. *Frontiers in Human Neuroscience, 7,* 415

Collins, D., Jones, B., Fairweather, M., Doolan, S., and Priestley, N. (2001) Examining anxiety associated changes in movement patterns. *International Journal of Sport Psychology, 31,* 223–242.

Colvin, G. (2010) *Talent is overrated: What really separates world-class performers from everybody else.* London: Penguin.

Connaughton, D., and Hanton, S. (2009) Mental toughness in sport: Conceptual and practical issues. In S. D. Mellalieu and S. Hanton (eds) *Advances in applied sport psychology: A review* (pp. 317–346). Abingdon, Oxfordshire: Routledge.

Connaughton, D., Wadey, R., Hanton, S., and Jones, G. (2008) The development and maintenance of mental toughness: Perceptions of elite performers. *Journal of Sports Sciences, 26,* 83–95.

Connaughton, D., Hanton, S., and Jones, G. (2010) The development and maintenance of mental toughness in the world's best performers. *Sport Psychologist, 24,* 168–193.

Conroy, D. E. (2001) Fear of failure: An exemplar for social development research in sport. *Quest, 53,* 165–183.

Conroy, D. E. (2014) Achievement motive theory. In R. C. Eklund and G. Tenenbaum (eds) *Encyclopedia of sport and exercise psychology* (Vol. 1, pp. 6–9). London: SAGE.

Conroy, D. E., and Hyde, A. L. (2014) Achievement goal theory. In R. C. Eklund and G. Tenenbaum (eds) *Encyclopedia of sport and exercise psychology* (Vol. 1, pp. 1–5). London: SAGE.

Conroy, D. E., Kaye, M. P., and Schantz, L. H. (2008) Quantitative research methodology. In T. S. Horn (ed.) *Advances in sport psychology* (3rd edn, pp. 15–30). Champaign, IL: Human Kinetics.

Cook, C., Crust, L., Littlewood, M., Nesti, M., and Allen-Collinson, J. (2014) "What it takes": Perceptions of mental toughness and its development in an English Premier League Soccer Academy. *Qualitative Research in Sport, Exercise and Health, 6,* 329–347.

Cooke, A. (2013) Readying the head and steadying the heart: A review of cortical and cardiac studies of preparation for action in sport. *International Review of Sport and Exercise Psychology, 6,* 122–138.

Cooke, A., Kavussanu, M., McIntyre, D., and Ring, C. (2010) Psychological, muscular and kinematic factors mediate performance under pressure. *Psychophysiology, 47,* 1109–1118.

Cooke, A., Kavussanu, M., McIntyre, D., Gallichio, G., Willoughby, A., and Ring, C. (2014) Preparation for action: Psychophysiological activity preceding a motor skill as a function of expertise, performance outcome and psychological pressure. *Psychophysiology, 51,* 374–384.

Cooke, N. J. (2015) Team cognition as interaction. *Current Directions in Psychological Science, 24,* 415–419.

Cooper, T. (2003) Join the human race. *The Daily Telegraph* (Weekend), 12 April, p. 15.

Corbetta, M., and Shulman, G. L. (2002) Control of goal-directed and stimulus-driven attention in the brain. *Nature Reviews Neuroscience, 3,* 201–215.

Corbin, C. B. (1967) The effects of covert rehearsal on the development of a complex motor skill. *Journal of General Psychology, 76,* 143–150.

Corrigan, J. (2014) The Open 2014: Rory McIlroy puts in majestic display to race clear and banish memories of recent 'Freaky Fridays'. Retrieved from www.telegraph.co.uk/sport/golf/theopen/10977388/The-Open-2014-Rory-McIlroy-puts-in-majestic-display-to-race-clear-and-banish-memories-of-recent-Freaky-Fridays.html on 24 October 2016.

Corrigan, P. (2007) Countdown to the US PGA: What next for Sergio Garcia? *The Independent,* 4 August. Retrieved from www.independent.co.uk/sport/golf/countdown-to-the-uspga-what-next-for-sergio-garcia-460200.html on 16 December 2008.

Côté, J., Baker, J., and Abernethy, B. (2007) Practice and play in the development of sport expertise. In G. Tenenbaum and R. C. Eklund (eds) *Handbook of sport psychology* (3rd edn, pp. 184–202). New York: Wiley.

Cotterill, S. T. (2010) Pre-performance routines in sport: Current understanding and future directions. *International Review of Sport and Exercise Psychology, 3,* 132–153.

Cotterill, S. T., Sanders, R., and Collins, D. (2010) Developing effective pre-performance routines in golf: Why don't we ask the golfer? *Journal of Applied Sport Psychology, 22,* 51–64.

Couture, R. T., Jerome, W., and Tihanyi, J. (1999) Can associative and dissociative strategies affect the swimming performance of recreational swimmers? *Sport Psychologist, 13,* 334–343.

Cox, R. H., Martens, M. P., and Russell, W. D. (2003) Measuring anxiety in athletes: The revised Competitive State Anxiety Inventory-2. *Journal of Sport and Exercise Psychology, 25,* 519–533.

Crace, R. K., and Hardy, C. J. (1997) Individual values and the team building process. *Journal of Applied Sport Psychology, 9,* 41–60.

Craft, L. C., Magyar, T. M., Becker, B. J., and Feltz, D. L. (2003) The relationship between the Competitive State Anxiety Inventory-2 and sport performance: A meta-analysis. *Journal of Sport and Exercise Psychology, 25,* 44–65.

Cratty, B. J. (1983) *Psychology in contemporary sport.* Englewood Cliffs, NJ: Prentice-Hall.

Cremades, J. G., and Tashman, L. S. (2014) *Becoming a sport, exercise, and performance psychology professional: A global perspective.* London: Routledge.

Crews, D. J., and Boutcher, S. H. (1986) Effects of structured preshot behaviours on beginning golf performance. *Perceptual and Motor Skills, 62,* 291–294.

Crocker, P. R., Gaudreau, P., Mosewich, A. D., and Kljajic, K. (2014) Perfectionism and the stress process in intercollegiate athletes: Examining the 2× 2 model of perfectionism in sport competition (Doctoral dissertation, Edizioni Edra).

Crocker, P. R. E., Tamminen, K. A., and Gaudreau, P. (2015) Coping in sport. In S. D. Mellalieu and S. Hanton (eds) *Contemporary advances in sport psychology: A review* (pp. 28–67). New York: Routledge.

Crust, L. (2008) A review and conceptual re-examination of mental toughness: Implications for future researchers. *Personality and Individual Differences, 45,* 576–583.

Crutchley, P. (2014) One shot: How do athletes perform under the greatest pressure? Retrieved from www.bbc.co.uk/sport/northern-ireland/28982638 on 24 October 2016.

Csikszentmihalyi, M. (1975) *Beyond boredom and anxiety.* San Francisco, CA: Jossey-Bass.

Csikszentmihalyi, M. (1990) *Flow: The psychology of optimal experience.* New York: Harper & Row.

Culver, D. M., Gilbert, W. D., and Trudel, P. (2003) A decade of qualitative research in sport psychology journals: 1990–1999. *Sport Psychologist, 17,* 1–15.

Cumming, J., and Hall, C. (2002a) Athletes' use of imagery in the off-season. *Sport Psychologist, 16,* 160–172.

Cumming, J., and Hall, C. (2002b) Deliberate imagery practice: The development of imagery skills in competitive athletes. *Journal of Sports Sciences, 20,* 137–145.

Cumming, J., and Ramsey, R. (2009) Imagery interventions in sport. In S. D. Mellalieu and S. Hanton (eds) *Advances in applied sport psychology: A review* (pp. 5–36). Abingdon, Oxfordshire: Routledge.

Cunniffe, B., Morgan, K. A., Baker, J. S., Cardinale, M., and Davies, B. (2015) Home versus away competition: Effect on psychophysiological variables in elite rugby union. *International Journal of Sports Physiology & Performance, 10,* 687–694.

Curtis, R. (2000) Sydney 2000. *The Mirror,* 2 October, p. 29.

Cutrona, C. E., and Russell, D. W. (1990) Type of social support and specific stress: Toward a theory of optimal matching. In I. G. Sarason, B. R. Sarason and G. R. Pierce (eds) *Social support: An interactional view* (pp. 319–366). New York: Wiley.

Damisch, L., Stoberock, B., and Musseweiler, T. (2010) Keep your fingers crossed! How superstition improves performance. *Psychological Science, 21,* 1014–1020.

Davids, K., and Baker, J. (2007) Genes, environment and sport performance: Why the nature–nurture dualism is no longer relevant. *Sports Medicine, 37,* 961–980.

Davidson, R. J., and Kaszniak, A. W. (2015) Conceptual and methodological issues in research on mindfulness and meditation. *American Psychologist, 70,* 581–582.

Davies, D. (2001) Relaxed Woods identifies the major pressure points. *The Guardian,* 6 April, p. 26.

Davies, D. (2003) Psychology forms a closer Love. *The Guardian,* 1 April, p. 30.

Davies, L. (2010) Nicolas Anelka suspended for 18 matches by France over World Cup revolt. *The Guardian,* 17 August Retrieved from www.guardian.co.uk/football/2010/aug/17/nicolasanelka-banned-for-18–matches-france on 2 September 2010.

Davis, P. A., Woodman, T., and Callow, N. (2010) Better out than in: The influence of anger regulation on physical performance. *Personality and Individual Differences, 49,* 457–460.

Davis IV, H., Liotti, M., Ngan, E. T., Woodward, T. S., Van Snellenberg, J. X., van Anders, S. M., et al. (2008) fMRI BOLD signal changes in elite swimmers while viewing videos of personal failure. *Brain Imaging and Behaviour, 2,* 84–93.

Day, J. (2015) Jason Day: I can get used to winning majors. Retrieved from http://www.golf.com/tour-and-news/jason-day-winning-majors-battling-vertigo-and-his-team on October 24 2016.

Day, M. C. and Wadey, R. (2016) Narratives of trauma, recovery, and growth: The complex role of sport following permanent acquired disability. *Psychology of Sport and Exercise, 22,* 131–138.

DeAngelis, T. (1996) Seligman: Optimism can be a vaccination. *American Psychological Association Monitor on Psychology, 27,* October, 33.

Debarnot, U., Sperduti, M., DiRienzo, F., and Guillot, A. (2014) Expert bodies, expert minds: How physical and mental training shape the brain. *Frontiers in Human Neuroscience, 8,* 280.

Decety, J. (1996a) Do imagined and executed actions share the same neural substrate? *Cognitive Brain Research, 3,* 87–93.

Decety, J. (1996b) The neurophysiological basis of motor imagery. *Behavioural Brain Research, 77,* 45–52

Decety, J., Jeannerod, M., and Prablanc, C. (1989) The timing of mentally represented actions. *Behavioural and Brain Research, 34,* 35–42.

Deci, E. L. (1971) Effects of externally mediated rewards on intrinsic motivation. *Journal of Personality and Social Psychology, 18,* 105–115.

Deci, E. L., and Ryan, R. M. (1985) *Intrinsic motivation and self-determination in human behaviour.* New York: Plenum.

Deci, E. L., and Ryan, R. M. (1991) A motivational approach to self: Integration in personality. In R. Dienstiber (ed.) *Nebraska symposium on motivation: Perspectives on motivation* (Vol. 38, pp. 37–288). Lincoln, NE: University of Nebraska Press.

Deci, E. L., and Ryan, R. M. (2000) Self-determination theory and the facilitation of intrinsic motivation, social development, and well-being. *American Psychologist, 55,* 68–78.

Deci, E. L., and Ryan, R. M. (2008) Facilitating optimal motivation and psychological well being across life's domains. *Canadian Psychology, 49,* 14–23.

de Groot, A. D. (1965) *Thought and choice in chess.* The Hague, Netherlands: Mouton.

Dekker, M. K., Van den Berg, B. R., Denissen, A. J., Sitskoorn, M. M., and Van Boxtel, G. J. (2014) Feasibility of eyes open alpha power training for mental enhancement in elite gymnasts. *Journal of Sports Sciences, 32,* 1550–1560.

de la Peña, D., Murray, N. P., and Janelle, C. M. (2008) Implicit overcompensation: The influence of negative self-instructions on performance of a self-paced motor task. *Journal of Sports Sciences, 26,* 1323–1331.

Delingpole, J. (2001) Anything to escape the tyranny of comfort. *The Sunday Times* (News Review), 5 August, p. 8.

Del Percio, C., Iacoboni, M., Lizio, R., Marzano, N., Infarinato, F., Vecchio, F., et al. (2011) Functional coupling of parietal alpha rhythms is enhanced in athletes before visuomotor performance: A coherence electroencephalographic study. *Neuroscience, 175,* 198–211.

Derakshan, N., and Eysenck, M. W. (2009) Anxiety, processing efficiency, and cognitive performance: New developments from Attentional Control Theory. *European Psychologist, 14,* 168–176.

D'Esposito, M., and Postle, B. R. (2015) The cognitive neuroscience of working memory. *Annual Review of Psychology, 66,* 115–142.

Detterman, D. K. (2014) Introduction to the intelligence special issue on the development of expertise: Is ability necessary? *Intelligence, 45,* 1–5.

De Weerd, P. (2002) Attention, neural basis of. In L. Nadel (ed.) *Encyclopaedia of cognitive science* (Vol. 1, pp. 238–246). London: Nature Publishing Group.

Dickinson, M. (2007) Hypnotist? Bolton better off with a miracle worker. *Irish Independent,* 21 August, p. 26.

Dijkstra, K., and Post, L. (2015) Mechanisms of embodiment. *Frontiers in Psychology, 6,* 1525.

Dion, K. L. (2000) Group cohesion: From "field of forces" to multidimensional construct. *Group Dynamics, 4,* 7–26.

Di Rienzo, F., Debarnot, U., Daligault, S., Saruco, E., Delpuech, C., Doyon, J., Collet, C., and Guillot, A. (2016) Online and offline performance gains following motor imagery practice: A comprehensive review of behavioural and neuroimaging studies. *Frontiers in Human Neuroscience, 10,* 315.

Dishman, R. K. (1983) Identity crises in North American sport psychology: Academics in professional issues. *Journal of Sport Psychology, 5,* 123–134.

Dixon, L. (2002) Wenger's formula based on science. *The Daily Telegraph* (Sport), 24 December, p. S2.

Dixon, P. (2008) Pádraig Harrington the champion of mind games. *The Times*, 16 July. Retrieved from www.timesonline.co.uk/tol/sport/golf/article4340348.ece on 16 December 2008.

Dixon, P., and Kidd, P. (2006) The golf pro who missed from 3ft and lost £230,000. *The Times*, 21 March, p. 5.

Dobson, R. (1998) In the grip of the yips. *The Guardian* (Sport), 31 March, p. 16.

Doerksen, S. E., and Elavsky, S. (2014) Social cognitive theory. In R. C. Eklund and G. Tenenbaum (eds) *Encyclopedia of sport and exercise psychology* (Vol. 1, pp. 684–688). London: SAGE.

Donegan, L. (2006) How a swing doctor and a mind reader bolster the home defence. *The Guardian* (Supplement: Golf-Ryder Cup countdown), 20 September, p. 7.

Douglas, K., and Carless, D. (2014) *Life story research in sport: Understanding the experiences of elite and professional athletes through narrative*. London: Routledge.

Douglas, K., and Carless, D. (2016) Self-identity: Our most beautify and creative project. In R. J. Schinke, K. R. McGannon and B. Smith (eds) *Routledge international handbook of sport psychology* (pp. 219–227). London: Routledge.

Dowthwaite, P. K., and Armstrong, M. R. (1984) An investigation into the anxiety levels of soccer players. *International Journal of Sport Psychology, 15*, 145–159.

Dreyfus, H. (1997) Intuitive, deliberative, and calculative models of expert performance. In C. E. Zsambok and G. Klein (eds) *Naturalistic decision making* (pp. 17–28). Mahwah, NJ: Lawrence Erlbaum Associates.

Driskell, J. E., Copper, C., and Moran, A. (1994) Does mental practice enhance performance? *Journal of Applied Psychology, 79*, 481–492.

Druckman, D., and Swets, J. A. (1988). *Enhancing human performance: Issues, theories, and techniques*. Washington, DC: National Academy Press.

Duchowski, A. T. (2007) *Eye tracking methodology: Theory and practice* (2nd edn). New York: Springer.

Duda, J., and Nicholls, J. G. (1992) Dimensions of achievement motivation in schoolwork and sport. *Journal of Educational Psychology, 84*, 290–299.

Duda, J., and Whitehead, I. (1998) Measurement of goal perspectives in the physical domain. In J. L. Duda (ed.) *Advances in sport and exercise psychology measurement* (pp. 21–48). Morgantown, WV: Fitness Information Technology.

Duda, J., and Hall, H. (2001) Achievement goal theory in sport. In R. N. Singer, H. A. Hausenblas and C. M. Janelle (eds) *Handbook of sport psychology* (pp. 417–443). New York: Wiley.

Duda, J., and Pensgaard, M. (2002) Enhancing the quantity and quality of motivation: The promotion of task involvement in a junior football team. In I. Cockerill (ed.) *Solutions in sport psychology* (pp. 49–57). London: Thomson.

Duda, J. L., and Allison, M. (1990) Cross-cultural analysis in exercise and sport psychology: A void in the field. *Journal of Sport and Exercise Psychology, 12*, 114–131.

Duffy, L. J., Baluch, B., and Ericsson, K. A. (2004) Dart performance as a function of facets of practice amongst professional and amateur men ana women players. *International Journal of Sport Psychology, 35*, 232–245.

Duffy, P. J., Lyons, D. C., Moran, A. P., Warrington, G. D., and MacManus, C. P. (2006) How we got here: Perceived influences on the development and success of international athletes. *Irish Journal of Psychology, 27*, 150–167.

Dugdale, J. R., and Eklund, R. C. (2002) Do not pay any attention to the umpires: Thought suppression and task-relevant focusing strategies. *Journal of Sport and Exercise Psychology, 24*, 306–319.

Dunn, J. G. H. (1999) A theoretical framework for structuring the content of competitive worry in ice hockey. *Journal of Sport and Exercise Psychology, 21*, 259–279.

Dunn, J. G. H., and Syrotuik, D. G. (2003) An investigation of multidimensional worry dispositions in a high contact sport. *Psychology of Sport and Exercise, 4*, 265–282.

Dunn, J. G. H., Causgrove Dunn, J., Wilson, P., and Syrotuik, D. G. (2000) Re-examining the factorial composition and factor structure of the Sport Anxiety Scale. *Journal of Sport and Exercise Psychology, 22*, 183–193.

Dunn, M. (2015) Caroline Wozniacki hopes she can break fourth-round Wimbledon curse. Retrieved from www.express.co.uk/sport/tennis/587425/Caroline-Wozniacki-Wimbledon-SW19-Tennis-Quarter-Final-Target on 24 October 2016.

Durand-Bush, N., Salmela, J., and Green-Demers, I. (2001) The Ottawa Mental Skills Assessment Tool (OMSAT-3). *Sport Psychologist, 15,* 1–19.

Durgin, F. H., Klein, B., Spiegel, A., Strawser, C. J., and Williams, M. (2012) The social psychology of perception experiments: Hills, backpacks, glucose and the problem of generalizability. *Journal of Experimental Psychology: Human Perception and Performance, 38,* 1582–1595.

Dyce, J. A., and Cornell, J. (1996) Factorial validity of the Group Environment Questionnaire among musicians. *Journal of Social Psychology, 136,* 263–264.

Earle, K., Earle, F., and Clough, P. (2008) Mental toughness and its application for golfers. *Sport and Exercise Psychology Review, 4,* 22–27.

Eccles, D. W., Walsh, S. E., and Ingledew, D. K. (2002) A grounded theory of expert cognition in orienteering. *Journal of Sport and Exercise Psychology, 24,* 68–88.

Edmonds, W. A., Mann, D. T., Tenenbaum, G., and Janelle, C. M. (2006) Analysis of affect-related performance zones: An idiographic method using physiological and introspective data. *Sport Psychologist, 20,* 40–57.

Edwards, T., Kingston, K., Hardy, L., and Gould, D. (2002) A qualitative analysis of catastrophic performances and the associated thoughts, feelings, and emotions. *Sport Psychologist, 16,* 1–19.

Edworthy, S. (2002) Brazil buoyant in World Cup final rehearsal. *The Daily Telegraph* (Sport), 28 June, p. S4.

Elliott, A. J., and Conroy, D. E. (2005) Beyond the dichotomous model of achievement goals in sport and exercise psychology. *Sport and Exercise Psychology Review, 1,* 17–25.

Ellis, A. (1957) Outcome of employing three techniques of psychotherapy. *Journal of Clinical Psychology, 13,* 344–350.

Englert, C., and Bertrams, A. (2012) Anxiety, ego depletion, and sports performance. *Journal of Sport and Exercise Psychology, 34,* 580–599.

Englert, C., and Oudejans, R. R. (2014) Is choking under pressure a consequence of skill-focus or increased distractibility? Results from a tennis serve task. *Psychology, 5,* 1035–1043.

Englert, C., Zwemmer, K., Bertrams, A., and Oudejans, R. R. (2015) Ego depletion and attention regulation under pressure: Is a temporary loss of self-control strength indeed related to impaired attention regulation? *Journal of Sport and Exercise Psychology, 37,* 127–137.

English, A. (2006) *Munster: Our road to glory.* Dublin: Penguin.

Ennis, J. (2012) *Unbelievable - from my childhood dreams to winning Olympic gold.* London: Hodder & Stoughton.

Epstein, D. (2013) *The sports gene: Inside the science of extraordinary athletic performance.* London: Random House.

Ericsson, K. A., Krampe, R. T., and Tesch-Romer, C. (1993) The role of deliberate practice in the acquisition of expert performance. *Psychological Review, 100,* 363–406.

Ericsson, K. A. (ed.) (1996) *The road to excellence: The acquisition of expert performance in the arts and sciences, sports and games.* Mahwah, NJ: Lawrence Erlbaum Associates.

Ericsson, K. A. (2001) The path to expert golf performance: Insights from the masters on how to improve performance by deliberate practice. In P. R. Thomas (ed.) *Optimising performance* (pp. 1–57). Brisbane: Australian Academic Press.

Ericsson, K. A. (2002) Attaining excellence through deliberate practice: Insights from the study of expert performance. In M. Ferrari (ed.) *The pursuit of excellence through education* (pp. 21–55). Hillsdale, NJ: Lawrence Erlbaum Associates.

Ericsson, K. A. (2006) Protocol analysis and expert thought: Concurrent verbalizations of thinking during experts' performance on representative tasks. In K. A. Ericsson, N. Charness, P. J. Feltovich and R. R. Hoffman (eds) *The Cambridge handbook of expertise and expert performance* (pp. 223–241). New York: Cambridge University Press.

Ericsson, K. A. (2013). Experts and their superior performance. In D. Reisberg (ed.) *The Oxford handbook of cognitive psychology* (pp. 886-901). Oxford: Oxford University Press.

Ericsson, K. A., and Charness, N. (1994) Expert performance: Its structure and acquisition. *American Psychologist, 49,* 725–747.

Ericsson, K. A., and Charness, N. (1997) Cognitive and developmental factors in expert performance. In P. J. Feltovich, K. M. Ford and R. R. Hoffman (eds) *Expertise in context* (pp. 3–41). Cambridge, MA: MIT Press.

Ericsson, K. A., and Lehmann, A. C. (1999). Expertise. In M. A. Runco and S.Pritzker (eds.) *Encyclopedia of creativity* (pp. 695–707), New York: Academic Press.

Ericsson, K. A., and Williams, A. M. (2007) Capturing naturally occurring superior performance in the laboratory: Translational research on expert performance. *Journal of Experimental Psychology: Applied, 13*, 115–123.

Ericsson, K. A., Charness, N., Feltovich, P. J., and Hoffman, R. R. (eds) (2006) *The Cambridge handbook of expertise and expert performance.* New York: Cambridge University Press.

Eriksson, S.-G., with Willi Railo (2002) *On management.* London: Carlton.

Erisman, S. M., and Roemer, L. (2010) A preliminary investigation of the effects of experimentally induced mindfulness on emotional responding to film clips. *Emotion, 10,* 72–82.

ESPN NBA (2010) Yao Ming stats. ESPN NBA. Retrieved from http://sports.espn.go.com/nba/players/profile?playerId=1722 on 28 August 2010.

Estabrooks, P., and Carron, A. V. (1999) The influence of the group with elderly exercisers. *Small Group Research, 30,* 438–452.

Estabrooks, P., and Carron, A. V. (2000) The Physical Activity Group Environment Questionnaire: An instrument for the assessment of cohesion in exercise classes. *Group Dynamics, 4,* 230–243.

Estabrooks, P., and Dennis, P. W. (2003) The principles of team building and their application to sport teams. In R. Lidor and K. P. Henschen (eds) *The psychology of team sports* (pp. 99–113). Morgantown, WV: Fitness Information Technology.

Eubank, M., and Collins, D. (2000) Coping with pre-and in-event fluctuations in competitive state anxiety: A longitudinal approach. *Journal of Sports Sciences, 18,* 121–131.

Eubank, M., Niven, A., and Cain, A. (2009) Training routes to registration as a Chartered Sport and Exercise Psychologist. *Sport and Exercise Psychology Review, 5,* 47–50.

Evening Herald (2001) One Tiger that will never crouch. *Evening Herald,* 9 April, p. 61.

Evening Herald (2003) Starved and terrorised – that's rugby. *Evening Herald,* 17 November, p. 8.

Evening Herald (2010) Unbelievable win for Nadal. *Evening Herald,* 14 September, p. 66.

Everton, C. (2003) Williams' bareknuckle victory. *The Guardian,* 7 May, p. 31.

Everton, C. (2009) O'Sullivan snaps cue and claims circuit needs repair. *The Guardian* (Sport), 12 January, p. 12.

Everton, C. (2011) Psychologist helped save O'Sullivan. *The Guardian* (Sport), 20 April, p. 8.

Every, D. (2002) UEFA pro licence mid season master class. *Insight: The FA Coaches Association Journal, 2,* 1–4.

Eys, M., Patterson, M. M., Loughead, T. M., and Carron, A. V. (2005) Team building in sport. In D. Hackfort, J. Duda and R. Lidor (eds) *The handbook of research in applied sport and exercise psychology: International perspectives* (pp. 219–231). Morgantown, WV: Fitness Information Technology.

Eys, M., Loughead, T., Bray, S. R., and Carron, A. V. (2009) Development of a cohesion questionnaire for youth: The Youth Sports Environment Questionnaire. *Journal of Sport and Exercise Psychology, 31,* 390–408.

Eys, M., Burke, S. M. Carron. A. V., and Dennis, P. W. (2010) The sport team as an effective group. In J. M. Williams (ed.) *Applied sport psychology: Personal growth to peak performance* (6th edn, pp. 132–148). New York: McGraw-Hill.

Eys, M. A., and Spink, K. S. (2016) Forecasts to the future. In R. J. Schinke, K. R. McGannon and B. Smith (eds) *Routledge international handbook of sport psychology* (pp. 572–580). London: Routledge

Eys, M. A., Ohlert, J., Evans, B. M., Wolf, S., Martin, L. J., Van Bussel, M., and Steins, C. (2015) Cohesion and performance for female and male sport teams. *The Sport Psychologist, 29,* 97–109.

Eysenck, M. W., and Calvo, M. (1992) Anxiety and performance: The processing efficiency theory. *Cognition and Emotion, 6,* 409–434.

Eysenck, M. W., and Keane, M. T. (2015) *Cognitive psychology: A student's handbook* (7th edn). London: Psychology Press.

Eysenck, M., and Wilson, M. (2016) Sporting performance, pressure and cognition. In D. Groome and M. W. Eysenck (eds) *An introduction to applied cognitive psychology* (2nd edn, pp. 329–350). Abingdon, Oxfordshire: Routledge.

Eysenck, M. W., Derakshan, N., Santos, R., and Calvo, M. G. (2007) Anxiety and cognitive performance: Attentional control theory. *Emotion, 7,* 336–353.

Facione, P. A., Facione, N. C., and Giancarlo, C. A. (1997) The motivation to think in working and learning. In E. A. Jones (ed.) *Preparing competent college graduates: Setting new and higher expectations for student learning—New directions for higher education* (Vol. 96, pp. 67–79). San Francisco, CA: Jossey-Bass.

Fanning, D. (2002) Coping with a stress factor. *Sunday Independent* (Sport), 6 October, p. 6.

Fanning, D. (2004a) Arsène aims to mix war and serenity. *Sunday Independent* (Sport), p. 5.

Fanning, D. (2004b) Wilko a deep thinker trapped by his image. *Sunday Independent* (Sport), 16 November, p. 5.

Farah, M. J. (1984) The neurological basis of mental imagery: A componential analysis. *Cognition, 18,* 245–272.

Farhead, N., and Punt, T. D. (2015) Silencing Sharapova's grunt improves the perception of her serve speed. *Perceptual and Motor Skills, 120,* 722–730.

Farrow, D., and Abernethy, B. (2015) Expert anticipation and pattern recognition. In J. Baker and Farrow, D (eds) *The Routledge handbook of sport expertise* (pp. 9–21). London: Routledge.

Farrow, D., Baker, J., and MacMahon, C. (2007) *Developing sport expertise: Researchers and coaches put theory into practice.* Abingdon, Oxfordshire: Routledge.

Feltz, D. L., and Landers, D. M. (1983) The effects of mental practice on motor skill learning and performance: A meta-analysis. *Journal of Sport Psychology, 5,* 25–57.

Feltz, D. L., and Lirgg, C. D. (2001) Self-efficacy beliefs of athletes, teams, and coaches. In R. N. Singer, H. A. Hausenblas and C. M. Janelle (eds) *Handbook of sport psychology* (2nd edn, pp. 340–361). New York: Wiley.

Fendrich, H. (2011) "Stosur tunes out the distractions". *Milwaukee Wisconsin Journal Sentinel,* 11 September. Retrieved from www.jsonline.com/sports/etc/129631608.html on 24 October 2016.

Fenz, W. D., and Epstein, S. (1967) Gradients of physiological arousal in parachutists as a function of an approaching jump. *Psychosomatic Medicine, 29,* 33–51.

Fernandez-Duque, D., and Johnson, M. L. (1999) Attention metaphors: How metaphors guide the cognitive psychology of attention. *Cognitive Science, 23,* 83–116.

Festinger, L., Schacter, S., and Back, K. (1950) *Social pressures in informal groups.* Stanford, CA: Stanford University Press.

Figgins, S. G., Smith, M. J., Sellars, C. N., Greenlees, I. A., and Knight, C. J. (2016) "You really could be something quite special": A qualitative exploration of athletes' experiences of being inspired in sport. *Psychology of Sport and Exercise, 24,* 82–91.

Finke, R. A. (1979) The functional equivalence of mental images and errors of movement. *Cognitive Psychology, 11,* 235–264.

Fisher, K. M., and Etnier, J. L. (2014) Examining the time course of attention during golf putts of two different lengths in experienced golfers. *Journal of Applied Sport Psychology, 26,* 457–470.

Fitts, P. M., and Posner, M. I. (1967) *Human performance.* Belmont, CA: Brooks/Cole.

Flatman, B. (2009) "Grunt and you're out", Wimbledon players told. *Sunday Times,* 14 June, p. 9.

Flatman, B., and Gadher, D. (2015) *Shrink helps Murray swat away demons.* Retrieved from http://www.thesundaytimes.co.uk/sto/news/uk_news/People/article1574579.ece. on 08 November 2016.

Fletcher, D., Hanton, S., and Mellalieu, S. D. (2006) An organisational stress review: Conceptual and theoretical issues in competitive sport. In S. Hanton and S. D. Mellalieu (eds) *Literature reviews in sport psychology* (pp. 321–374). Hauppauge, NY: Nova Science.

Flett, G. L., and Hewitt, P. L. (2005) The perils of perfectionism in sports and exercise. *Current Directions in Psychological Science, 14,* 14–18.

Floegel T. A., Giacobbi, P. R Jr, Dzierzewski, J. M., Aiken-Morgan, A. T., Roberts, B., McCrae, C. S., Marsiske, M., and Buman, M. P. (2015) Intervention markers of physical activity maintenance in older adults. *American Journal of Health Behaviour, 39,* 487–499.

Foerster, A., Rocha, S., Wiesiolek, C., Chagas, A. P., Machado, G., Silva, E., Fregn, F., and Monte-Silva, K. (2013) Site-specific effects of mental practice combined with transcranial direct current stimulation on motor learning. *European Journal of Neuroscience, 37,* 786–794

Folkman, S. (1991) Coping across the life span: Theoretical issues. In E. M. Cummings, A. L. Greene and K. H. Karraker (eds) *Life-span developmental psychology: Perspectives on stress and coping* (pp. 3–19). Hillsdale, NJ: Lawrence Erlbaum Associates.

Folkman, S. (1992) Making the case for coping. In B. N. Carpenter (ed.) *Personal coping: Theory, research and application* (pp. 31–46). Westport, CT: Praeger.

Forshaw, M. (2012) *Critical thinking for psychology: A student guide.* London: John Wiley & Sons.

Forzoni, R. (2015) *Depression in sport.* Retrieved from http://www.robertoforzoni.com/insights/life-coaching/depression-in-sport/ on 08 November, 2016.

Foster, C., Cowburn, G., Allender, S., and Pearce-Smith, N. (2007) *Physical activity and children review 3: The view of children on the barriers and facilitators to participation in physical activity. A review of qualitative studies.* London: NICE Public Health Collaborating Centre – Physical Activity.

Foster, D. J., Weigand, D. A., and Baines, D. (2006) The effect of removing superstitious behaviour and introducing a pre-performance routine on basketball free-throw performance. *Journal of Applied Sport Psychology, 18,* 167–171.

Fosterling, F. (1988) *Attribution theory in clinical psychology.* Chichester, West Sussex: Wiley.

Fox, M. C., Ericsson, K. A., and Best, R. (2011) Do procedures for verbal reporting of thinking have to be reactive? A meta-analysis and recommendations for best reporting methods. *Psychological Bulletin, 137,* 316–344.

Frank, C., Land, W. M., and Schack, T. (2013) Mental representation and learning: The influence of practice on the development of mental representation structure in complex action. *Psychology of Sport and Exercise, 14,* 353–361.

Frank, C., Land, W. M., Popp, C., and Schack, T. (2014) Mental representation and mental practice: Experimental investigation on the functional links between motor memory and motor imagery. *PLoS ONE, 9,* 1–12.

Frank, C., Land, W. M., and Schack, T. (2016) Perceptual-cognitive changes during motor learning: The influence of mental and physical practice on mental representation, gaze behaviour, and performance of a complex action. *Frontiers in Psychology, 6,* 1981.

Frank, M. J., and Badre, D. (2015) How cognitive theory guides neuroscience. *Cognition, 135,* 14–20.

Fransen, K. I., Vanbeselaere, N., De Cuyper, B., Vande Broek, G., and Boen, F. (2014) The myth of the team captain as principal leader: Extending the athlete leadership classification within sport teams. *Journal of Sports Science, 32,* 1389–1397.

Fraser, A. (2009) For Laura. *Daily Mail,* 23 June, p. 77.

Fredrickson, B. L. (1998) What good are positive emotions? *Review of General Psychology, 2,* 300–319.

Fredrickson, B. L. (2001) The role of positive emotions in positive psychology: The broaden-and-build theory of positive emotions. *American Psychologist, 56,* 218–226.

Freeman, P., and Rees, T. (2009) How does perceived support lead to better performance? An examination of potential mechanisms. *Journal of Applied Sport Psychology, 21,* 429–441.

Freeman, P., Rees, T., and Hardy, L. (2009) An intervention to increase social support and improve performance. *Journal of Applied Sport Psychology, 21,* 186–200.

Frost, R. O., and Henderson, K. J. (1991) Perfectionism and reaction to athletic competition. *Journal of Sport and Exercise Psychology, 13,* 323–335.

Frydman, M., and Lynn, R. (1992) The general intelligence and spatial abilities of gifted young Belgian chess players. *British Journal of Psychology, 83,* 233–235.

Funday Times (2002) Sachin Tendulkar. *The Funday Times* (Supplement to *Sunday Times*), 678, 8 September, p. 12.

Furley, P., Dicks, M., Stendtke, F., and Memmert, D. (2012) "Get it out the way. The wait's killing me." Hastening and hiding during soccer penalty kicks. *Psychology of Sport and Exercise, 13,* 454–465.

Futterman, M. (2014) Why Olympic athletes are learning to hold their breath for more than five minutes. Retrieved from www.wsj.com/articles/olympians-in-search-of-a-breathtaking-experience-1407886417 on 24 October 2016.

Gagné, M., Ryan, R. M., and Bargmann, K. (2003) Autonomy support and need satisfaction in the motivation and well-being of gymnasts. *Journal of Applied Sport Psychology, 15,* 372–389.

Gaines, C. (2015) "Jordan Spieth explains why he believes golf is a team sport, and why he deflects a lot of the credit". *Business Insider,* 14 August. Retrieved from http://uk.businessinsider.com/jordan-spieth-golf-game-2015-8?r=US&IR=T on 13 January 2016.

Gallagher, B. (2008) Six of the best British sporting all-rounders. *The Daily Telegraph,* 29 March. Retrieved from www.telegraph.co.uk/sport/columnists/brendangallagher/2295734/Six-of-the-best-British-sporting-all-rounders.html on 30 August 2010.

Galton, F. (1869) *Hereditary genius.* London: Macmillan.

Galton, F. (1883) *Inquiries into human faculty.* London: Dent.

Gamble, T., and Walker, I. (2016) Wearing a bicycle helmet can increase risk taking and sensation seeking in adults. *Psychological Science, 27,* 289–294.

Gardner, L. A., Vella, S. A., and Magee, C. A. (2015) The relationship between implicit beliefs, anxiety, and attributional style in high-level soccer players. *Journal of Applied Sport Psychology, 27,* 398–411.

Garrod, M. (2011) Rory's major meltdown. *Evening Herald,* 11 April, pp. 64–65.

Garside, K. (2008) Fitter means faster. *The Sunday Times* (Sport), 2 March, p. 15.

Gaudreau, P., Nicholls, A. R., and Levy, A. (2010) The ups and downs of coping and sport achievement: An episodic process analysis of within-person associations. *Journal of Sport and Exercise Psychology, 32,* 298–311.

Gauron, E. (1984) *Mental training for peak performance.* Lansing, NY: Sport Science Associates.

Gazzaniga, M. S., Ivry, R. B., and Mangun, G. R. (2002) *Cognitive neuroscience: The biology of the mind* (4th edn). New York: Norton.

Gazzaniga, M. S., Ivry, R. B., and Mangun, G. R. (2014) *Cognitive neuroscience: The biology of the mind* (4th edn). New York: Norton.

Gee, C. J. (2010) How does sport psychology actually improve athletic performance? A framework to facilitate athletes' and coaches' understanding. *Behaviour Modification, 34,* 386–402.

Geoghegan, T. (2009) What a racket. BBC News Magazine, 22 June. Retrieved from http://news.bbc.co.uk/2/hi/uk_news/magazine/8110998.stm on 22 September 2010.

Gershgoren, L., Basevitch, I., Filho, E., Gershgoren, A., Brill, Y. S., Schinke, R. J., and Tenenbaum, G. (2016) Expertise in soccer teams: A thematic inquiry into the role of shared mental models within team chemistry. *Psychology of Sport and Exercise, 24,* 128–139.

Gibson, J. J. (1979) *The ecological approach to visual perception.* Boston, MA: Houghton Mifflin.

Gibson, O. (2009) From man to superman … how fast will we be by 2030? *The Guardian,* 18 August, p. 3.

Gieseking, W., and Leimer, K. (1932) *Piano technique.* New York: Dover.

Gilbourne, D., and Smith, B. (2009) Editorial. *Qualitative Research in Sport and Exercise, 1,* 1–2.

Gilbourne, D., and Andersen, M. (2011) *Critical essays in applied sport psychology.* Champaign, IL: Human Kinetics.

Gill, Diane L. (2000) *Psychological dynamics of sport and exercise* (2nd edn). Champaign, IL: Human Kinetics.

Gilleece, D. (1996) Breathe deeply and be happy with second. *The Irish Times,* 27 September, p. 11. Retrieved from http://www.irishtimes.com/sport/breathe-deep-and-be-happy-with-second-1.71529 on 08 November 2016.

Gilleece, D. (1999a) Qualifiers do it for themselves. *The Irish Times* (Sport), 19 June, p. 2.

Gilleece, D. (1999b) So near and yet so far. *The Irish Times*, 6 July, p. 23.

Gilleece, D. (2010) "I'd happily take no points if we had a European victory". *Sunday Independent* (Sport), 26 September, p. 7.

Gilovich, T., Keltner, D., and Nisbett, R. E. (2011) *Social psychology* (2nd edn). New York: Norton.

Gilson, T. A. (2014) Social processing effects. In R. C. Eklund and G. Tenenbaum (eds) *Encyclopedia of sport and exercise psychology* (Vol. 2, pp. 702–706). New York: SAGE.

Gladwell, M. (2009) *Outliers: The story of success*. London: Penguin.

Gobet, F. (2016) *Understanding expertise: A multidisciplinary approach*. London: Palgrave.

Gobet, F., and Charness, N. (2006) Expertise in chess. In K. A. Ericsson, N. Charness, P. J. Feltovich, R. R. and Hoffman (eds) *The Cambridge handbook of expertise and expert performance* (pp. 523–538). New York: Cambridge University Press.

Gobet, F., and Campitelli, G. (2007) The role of domain-specific practice, handedness and starting age in chess. *Developmental Psychology, 43,* 159–172.

Gola, H. (2008) Tiger Woods entering a zone where few athletes have ever travelled. *Daily News*. Retrieved from www.nydailynews.com/sports/more_sports/2008/03/16/2008-03-16_tiger_woods_entering_a_zone_where_few_at.html?page=0 on 15 December 2008.

Goldenberg, S. (2003) Footballers who paid the penalty for failure. *The Guardian*, 19 April, p. 6.

Goldstein, E. B. (2011) *Cognitive psychology* (3rd edn). Belmont, CA: Wadsworth/Cengage.

Gonzalez, C. C., Causer, J., Miall, R. C., Grey, M. J., Humphreys, G., and Williams, A. M. (2015) Identifying the causal mechanisms of the quiet eye. *European Journal of Sport Science,* 1–11, Epub ahead of print.

Gonzalez, S. P., Metzler, J. N., and Newton, M. (2011) The influence of a simulated "pep talk" on athlete inspiration, situational motivation, and emotion. *International Journal of Sports Science & Coaching, 6,* 445–459.

Goodbody, J., and Nichols, P. (2004) Marathon marred by invader's attack on race leader. *The Times* (Sport), 30 August, p. 1.

Goodger, K., Lavallee, D., Gorely, T., and Harwood, C. (2010) Burnout in sport: Understanding the process – from early warning signs to individualized intervention. In J. M. Williams (ed.) *Applied sport psychology: Personal growth to peak performance* (6th edn, pp. 492–511). New York: McGraw-Hill.

Gordin, R. D. (2003) Ethical issues in team sports. In R. Lidor and K. P. Henschen (eds) *The psychology of team sports* (pp. 57–68). Morgantown, WV: Fitness Information Technology.

Gordon, S. (2008) Appreciative inquiry coaching. *International Coaching Psychology Review, 3,* 19–31.

Gorman, A. D., Abernethy, B., and Farrow, D. (2012) Classical pattern recall tests and the prospective nature of expert performance. *The Quarterly Journal of Experimental Psychology, 65,* 1151–1160.

Gotwals, J. K., and Dunn, J. G. H. (2009) A multi-method multi-analytic approach to establishing internal construct validity evidence: The Sport Multidimensional Perfectionism Scale 2. *Measurement in Physical Education and Exercise Sciences, 13,* 71–92.

Gotwals, J. K., Dunn, J. G. H., Causgrove-Dunn, J., and Gamache, V. (2010) Establishing validity evidence for the Sport Multidimensional Perfectionism Scale-2 in intercollegiate sport. *Psychology of Sport and Exercise, 11,* 423–432.

Gouju, J.-L., Vermersch, P., and Bouthier, D. (2007) A psycho-phenomenological approach to sport psychology: The presence of the opponents in hurdle races. *Journal of Applied Sport Psychology, 19,* 173–186.

Gould, D. (1998) Goal setting for peak performance. In J. M. Williams (ed.) *Applied sport psychology: Personal growth to peak performance* (3rd edn, pp. 182–196). Mountain View, CA: Mayfield.

Gould, D. (2010) Goal-setting for peak performance. In J. M. Williams (ed.) *Applied sport psychology: Personal growth to peak performance* (6th edn, pp. 201–220). New York McGraw-Hill.

Gould, D., and Carson, S. (2008) Life skills development through sport: Current status and future directions. *International Review of Sport and Exercise Psychology, 1,* 58–78.

Gould, D., Eklund, R. C., and Jackson, S. A. (1993) Coping strategies used by US Olympic wrestlers. *Research Quarterly for Exercise and Sport, 64,* 83–93.

Gould, D., Udry, E., Tuffey, S., and Loehr, J. (1996) Burnout in competitive junior tennis players: I. A quantitative psychological assessment. *Sport Psychologist, 10,* 322–340.

Gould, D., Damarjian, N., and Greenleaf, C. (2002a) Imagery training for peak performance. In J. L. Van Raalte and B. W. Brewer (eds) *Exploring sport and exercise psychology* (2nd edn, pp. 49–74). Washington, DC: American Psychological Association.

Gould, D., Dieffenbach, K., and Moffett, A. (2002b) Psychological characteristics and their development in Olympic champions. *Journal of Applied Sport Psychology, 14,* 172–204.

Gould, D., Voelker, D. F., Damarjian, N., and Greenleaf, C. (2014) Imagery training for peak performance. In J. L. Van Raalte and B. W. Brewer (eds) *Exploring sport and exercise psychology* (3rd edn, pp. 55–82). Washington, DC: American Psychological Association.

Goulding, N. (2011) Allen facing the toughest fight of his life. *Irish Mail on Sunday (The Title),* 27 March, p. 21.

Goyen, M. J., and Anshel, M. H. (1998) Sources of acute competitive stress and use of coping strategies as a function of age and gender. *Journal of Applied Developmental Psychology, 19,* 469–486.

Grange, P., and Kerr, J. H. (2010) Physical aggression in Australian football: A qualitative study of elite athletes. *Psychology of Sport and Exercise, 11,* 36–43.

Granholm, E., Asarnow, R. F., Sarkin, A. J., and Dykes, K. L. (1996) Pupillary responses index cognitive resource limitations. *Psychophysiology, 33,* 457–461.

Gray, R. (2013) Being selective at the plate: Processing dependence between perceptual variables relates to hitting goals and performance. *Journal of Experimental Psychology: Human Perception and Performance, 39,* 1124–1142.

Gray, R. (2014) Embodied perception in sport. *International Review of Sport and Exercise Psychology, 7,* 72–86

Gray, R. (2015) Movement automaticity in sport. In J. Baker and D. Farrow (eds) *Routledge Handbook Of Sport Expertise* (pp. 74–83) Abingdon, Oxfordshire: Routledge.

Gray, R., Beilock, S. L., and Carr, T. H. (2007) "As soon as the bat met the ball, I knew it was gone": Outcome prediction, hindsight bias, and the representation and control of action in novice and expert baseball players. *Psychonomic Bulletin & Review, 14,* 669–675.

Green, C. D. (2003) Psychology strikes out: Coleman R. Griffith and the Chicago Cubs. *History of Psychology, 6,* 267–283.

Green, C. D., and Benjamin, L. T., Jr (2009) *Psychology gets in the game: Sport, mind and behaviour, 1880–1960.* Lincoln, NE: University of Nebraska Press.

Greenlees, I., and Moran, A. (eds) (2003) *Concentration skills training in sport.* Leicester: British Psychological Society (Sport and Exercise Psychology Section).

Greenlees, I., Graydon, J., and Maynard, I. (2000) The impact of individual efficacy beliefs on group goal selection and group goal commitment. *Journal of Sports Sciences, 18,* 451–459.

Greenlees, I., Thelwell, R., and Holder, T. (2006) Examining the efficacy of the concentration grid exercise as a concentration enhancement exercise. *Psychology of Sport and Exercise, 7,* 29–39.

Greenspan, M. J., and Feltz, D. L. (1989) Psychological interventions with athletes in competitive settings: A review. *Sport Psychologist, 3,* 219–236.

Groome, D. (2014) *An introduction to cognitive psychology: Processes and disorders.* London: Routledge.

Gross, J. J. (1998) The emerging field of emotion regulation: An integrative review. *Review of General Psychology, 2,* 271–299.

Grouios, G. (1992) Mental practice: A review. *Journal of Sport Behaviour, 15,* 42–59.

Gruber, J. J., and Gray, G. R. (1982) Responses to forces influencing cohesion as a function of player status and level of male varsity basketball competition. *Research Quarterly for Exercise and Sport, 53,* 27–36.

Gucciardi, D. F., and Dimmock, J. A. (2008) Choking under pressure in sensorimotor skills: Conscious processing or depleted attentional resources? *Psychology of Sport and Exercise, 9,* 45–59.

Gucciardi, D. F., Gordon, S., and Dimmock, J. A. (2009a) Advancing mental toughness research and theory using personal construct psychology. *International Review of Sport and Exercise Psychology, 2,* 54–72.

Gucciardi, D. F., Gordon, S., and Dimmock, J. A. (2009b) Development and preliminary validation of a mental toughness inventory for Australian football. *Psychology of Sport and Exercise, 10,* 201–209.

Gucciardi, D. F., Hanton, S., and Mallett, C. J. (2012) Progressing measurement in mental toughness: A case example of the Mental Toughness Questionnaire 48. *Sport, Exercise, and Performance Psychology, 1,* 194-214.

Gucciardi, D. F., Longbottom, J. L., Jackson, B., and Dimmock, J. A. (2010) Experienced golfers' perspectives on choking under pressure. *Journal of Sport and Exercise Psychology, 32,* 61–83.

Gucciardi, D. F., and Mallett, C. J. (2010) Mental toughness. In S. J. Hanrahan and M. B. Andersen (eds) *Routledge handbook of applied sport psychology* (pp. 547–556). Abingdon, Oxon: Routledge.

Gucciardi, D. F., Gordon, S., and Dimmock, J. A. (2009c) Evaluation of a mental toughness training program for youth-aged Australian footballers: I. A quantitative analysis. *Journal of Applied Sport Psychology, 21,* 307–323.

Gucciardi, D. F., Peeling, P., Ducker, K. J., and Dawson, B. (2016) When the going gets tough: Mental toughness and its relationship with behavioural perseverance. *Journal of Science and Medicine in Sport,* 19, 81–86.

Gueugneau, N., Crognier, L., and Papaxanthis, C. (2008) The influence of eye movements on the temporal features of executed and imagined arm movements. *Brain Research, 1187,* 95–102.

Guillot, A., and Collet, C. (2005) Duration of mentally simulated movement: A review. *Journal of Motor Behaviour, 37,* 10–20.

Guillot, A., and Collet, C. (2008) Construction of the motor imagery integrative model in sport: A review and theoretical investigation of motor imagery use. *International Review of Sport and Exercise Psychology, 1,* 31–44.

Guillot, A., and Collet, C. (eds) (2010) *The neurophysiological foundations of mental and motor imagery.* Oxford: Oxford University Press.

Guillot, A., Di Rienzo, F., MacIntyre, T., Moran, A., and Collet C. (2012a) Imagining is not doing but involves specific motor commands: A review of experimental data related to motor inhibition. *Frontiers in Human Neuroscience, 6,* 247, 1–22.

Guillot, A., Hoyek, N., and Collet, C. (2012b) Understanding the timing of motor imagery: Recent findings and future directions. *International Review of Sport and Exercise Psychology,* 5, 3–22

Guillot A., Di Rienzo F., Pialoux V., Simon G., Skinner S., and Rogowski. I. (2015) Implementation of motor imagery during specific aerobic training session in young tennis players. *PLoS ONE 10, 11,* e0143331.

Gulbin, J., and Weissensteiner, J. (2013) Functional sport expertise systems. In D. Farrow, J. Baker, and C. MacMahon (eds.) *Developing sport expertise: Researchers and coaches put theory into practice* (pp. 45–67). Abingdon, Oxfordshire: Routledge.

Gulliver, A., Griffiths, K. M., Mackinnon, A., Batterham, P. J., and Stanimirovic, R. (2015) The mental health of Australian elite athletes. *Journal of Science and Medicine in Sport, 18,* 255–261.

Gully, S. M., Devine, D. J., and Whitney, D. J. (1995) A meta-analysis of cohesion and performance: Effects of level of analysis and task interdependence. *Small Group Research, 26,* 497–520.

Gunnell, K. E., Crocker, P. R. E., Mack, D. E., Wilson, P. M., and Zumbo, B. D. (2014) Goal contents, motivation, psychological need satisfaction, well-being and physical activity: A test of self-determination theory over 6 months. *Psychology of Sport and Exercise, 15,* 19–29.

Guscott, J., with N. Cain (1997) *The Lions' diary.* London: Michael Joseph.

Gustafsson, H., Kenttä, G., and Hassmén, P. (2011) Athlete burnout: An integrated model and future research directions. *International Review of Sport and Exercise Psychology, 4,* 3–24.

Hackman, J. R., and Katz, N. (2010) Group behaviour and performance. In S. T. Fiske, D. T. Gilbert, and G. Lindzey (eds) *Handbook of social psychology* (5th edn, Vol. 2, pp. 1208–1251). Hoboken, NJ: Wiley.

Hagger, M. S., and Chatzisarantis, N. L. D. (2007) Advances in self-determination theory research in sport and exercise. *Psychology of Sport and Exercise, 8,* 597–599.

Hagger, M. S., and Chatzisarantis, N. L. D. (2008) Self-determination theory and the psychology of exercise. *International Review of Sport and Exercise Psychology, 1,* 79–103.

Hagger, M. S., and Chatzisarantis, N. L. (2016) A multilab preregistered replication of the ego-depletion effect. *Perspectives on Psychological Science, 11,* 546–573.

Hagtvet, K. A., and Hanin, Y. L. (2007) Consistency of performance-related emotions in elite athletes: Generalizability theory applied to the IZOF model. *Psychology of Sport and Exercise, 8,* 47–72.

Hahn, U. (2011) The problem of circularity in evidence, argument, and explanation. *Perspectives on Psychological Science, 6,* 172–182.

Hall, C. R. (2001) Imagery in sport and behaviour. In R. N. Singer, H. A Hausenblas and C. M. Janelle (eds) *Handbook of sport psychology* (2nd edn, pp. 529–549). New York: Wiley.

Hall, C. R., and Martin, K. A. (1997) Measuring movement imagery abilities: A revision of the Movement Imagery Questionnaire. *Journal of Mental Imagery, 21,* 143–154.

Hall, C. R., Mack, D., Paivio, A., and Hausenblas, H. A. (1998) Imagery use by athletes: Development of the Sport Imagery Questionnaire. *International Journal of Sport Psychology, 29,* 73–89.

Hall, C. R., Stevens, D. E., and Paivio, A. (2005) *Sport Imagery Questionnaire: Test manual.* Morgantown, WV: Fitness Information Technology.

Hall, H. K., and Kerr, A. W. (2001) Goal setting in sport and physical activity: Tracing empirical developments and establishing conceptual direction. In G. C. Roberts (ed.) *Advances in motivation in sport and exercise* (pp. 183–233). Champaign, IL: Human Kinetics.

Hambrick, D. Z., Oswald, F. L., Altmann, E. M., Meinz, E. J., Gobet, F., and Campitelli, G. (2014) Deliberate practice: Is that all it takes to become an expert? *Intelligence, 45,* 34–45.

Hammermeister, J., and Burton, D. (2004) Gender differences in coping with endurance sport stress: Are men from Mars and women from Venus? *Journal of Sport Behaviour, 27,* 148–164.

Hanakawa, T. (2016) Organizing motor imageries. *Neurocience Research, 104,* 56–63.

Hands, D. (2009) Ever-growing list of injuries puts emphasis on menace of incredible bulk. *The Times,* 6 July, p. 56.

Hanin, Y. (1997) Emotions and athletic performance: Individual zones of optimal functioning hypothesis. *European Yearbook of Sport Psychology, 1,* 29–72.

Hanin, Y. L. (2000) Individual zones of optimal functioning (IZOF) model: Emotion-performance relationships in sport. In Y. L. Hanin (ed.) *Emotions in sport* (pp. 65–89). Champaign, IL: Human Kinetics.

Hanin, Y. L. (2007) Emotions in sport: Current issues and perspectives. In G. Tenenbaum and R. C. Eklund (eds) *Handbook of sport psychology* (3rd edn, pp. 31–58). Hoboken, NJ: John Wiley.

Hanin, Y., and Syrjä, P. (1995) Performance affect in soccer players: An application of the IZOF model. *International Journal of Sports Medicine, 16,* 260–265.

Hanin, Y. L., and Stambulova, N. B. (2002) Metaphoric description of performance states: An application of the IZOF model. *Sport Psychologist, 16,* 396–415.

Hannigan, M. (2003) Keeping sensible. *The Irish Times,* 20 October, p. 7.

Hanrahan, S. J., and Grove, J. R. (1990) A short form of the Sport Attributional Style Scale. *Australian Journal of Science and Medicine in Sport, 22,* 97–101.

Hanrahan, S. J., and Cerin, E. (2009) Gender, level of participation, and type of sport: Differences in achievement goal orientation and attributional style. *Journal of Science and Medicine in Sport, 12,* 508–512.

Hanrahan, S. J., Grove, J. R., and Hattie, J. A. (1989) Development of a questionnaire measure of sport-related attributional style. *International/Journal of Sport Psychology, 20,* 114–134.

Hansen, A., with J. Thomas (1999) *A matter of opinion*. London: Bantam.

Hanton, S., and Jones, G. (1999) The acquisition and development of cognitive skills and strategies: I. Making the butterflies fly in formation. *Sport Psychologist, 13,* 1–21.

Hanton, S., Thomas, O., and Maynard, I. (2004) Competitive anxiety responses in the week leading up to competition: The role of intensity, direction and frequency dimensions. *Psychology of Sport and Exercise, 15,* 169–181.

Hardy, L. (1990) A catastrophe model of anxiety and performance. In G. Jones and L. Hardy (eds) *Stress and performance in sport* (pp. 81–106). Chichester, West Sussex: Wiley.

Hardy, L. (1996) Testing the predictions of the cusp catastrophe model of anxiety and performance. *Sport Psychologist, 10,* 140–156.

Hardy, L. (1997) The Coleman Roberts Griffith address: Three myths about applied consultancy work. *Journal of Applied Sport Psychology, 9,* 277–294.

Hardy, L., and Nelson, D. (1988) Self-regulation training in sport and work. *Ergonomics, 31,* 1573–1583.

Hardy, L., and Fazey, J. (1990) *Concentration training: A guide for sports performers*. Headingley, Leeds: National Coaching Foundation.

Hardy, L., and Parfitt, C. G. (1991) A catastrophe model of anxiety and performance. *British Journal of Psychology, 82,* 163–178.

Hardy, L., and Jones, J. G. (1994) Current issues and future directions for performance-related research in sport psychology. *Journal of Sports Sciences, 12,* 61–92.

Hardy, L., and Callow, N. (1999) Efficacy of external and internal visual imagery perspectives for the enhancement of performance on tasks in which form is important. *Journal of Sport and Exercise Psychology, 21,* 95–112.

Hardy, L., Jones, G., and Gould, D. (1996) *Understanding psychological preparation for sport: Theory and practice of elite performers*. Chichester, West Sussex: Wiley.

Hardy, L., Beattie, S., and Woodman, T. (2007) Anxiety-induced performance catastrophes: Investigating effort required as an asymmetry factor. *British Journal of Psychology, 98,* 15–31.

Harig, B. (2014) Cup pressure squeezes the best. Retrieved from www.espn.co.uk/golf/rydercup14/story/_/id/11581706/ryder-cup-pressure-squeezes-even-best-game-golf in 24 October 2016.

Harkin, B., Webb, T. L., Chang B. P. I., Prestwich, A., Conner, M., Kellar, I, Benn, Y., and Sheeran, P. (2016) Does monitoring goal progress promote goal attainment? A meta-analysis of the experimental evidence. *Psychological Bulletin, 142,* 198–229.

Harle, S. K., and Vickers, J. N. (2001) Training quiet eye improves accuracy in the basketball free throw. *Sport Psychologist, 15,* 289–305.

Harman, N. (2006) Inner drive is key to Murray's hopes of joining greats. *The Times,* 5 July, p. 67.

Harman, N. (2009) Djokovic winning battle between body and soul. *The Times* (Wimbledon 09 supplement), 22 June, p. 5.

Harmison, R. J. (2007) Peak performance in sport: Identifying ideal performance states and developing athletes' psychological skills. *Professional Psychology: Research and Practice, 37,* 233–243.

Harmon, S. W., and Jones, M. G. (1999) The five levels of web use in education: Factors to consider in planning online courses. *Educational Technology, 39,* 28–32.

Harris, J. E., and Herbert, A. (2015) Utilization of motor imagery in upper limb rehabilitation: A systematic scoping review. *Clinical Rehabilitation, 29,* 1092–1107.

Harwood, C. (2002) Assessing achievement goals in sport: Caveats for consultants and a case for contextualisation. *Journal of Applied Sport Psychology, 14,* 106–119.

Harwood, C., and Biddle, S, (2002) The application of achievement goal theory in youth sport. In I. Cockerill (ed.) *Solutions in sport psychology* (pp. 58–73). London: Thomson.

Harwood, C., Spray, C. M., and Keegan, R. (2008) Achievement goal theories in sport. In T. S. Horn (ed.) *Advances in sport psychology* (3rd edn, pp. 157–185). Champaign, IL: Human Kinetics.

Harwood, C. G., Keegan, R. J., Smith, J. M. J., and Raine, A. S. (2015) A systematic review of the intrapersonal correlates of motivational climate perceptions in sport and physical activity. *Psychology of Sport and Exercise, 18,* 9–25.

Hatfield, B. M., and Hillman, C. H. (2001) The psychophysiology of sport. In R. N. Singer, H. A. Hausenblas and C. M. Janelle (eds) *Handbook of sport psychology* (2nd edn, pp. 362–386). New York: Wiley.

Hatfield, B. M., and Kerick, S. E. (2007) The psychology of superior performance: A cognitive and affective neuroscience perspective. In G. Tenenbaum and R. C. Eklund (eds) *Handbook of sport psychology* (3rd edn, pp. 84–109). New York: Wiley.

Hattenstone, S. (2010) Fast and loose. *The Guardian* (Weekend), 28 August, pp. 30–37.

Hattenstone, S. (2016) Roger Federer: "I need the fire, the excitement, the whole rollercoaster". Retrieved from https://www.theguardian.com/sport/2016/jun/18/roger-federer-interview-tennis-wimbledon-simon-hattenstone on 24 October 2016.

Hatzigeorgiadis, A. (2002) Thoughts of escape during competition: Relationships with goal orientation and self-consciousness. *Psychology of Sport and Exercise, 3,* 195–207.

Hatzigeorgiadis, A., and Biddle, S. J. H. (2000) Assessing cognitive interference in sport: Development of the Thought Occurrence Questionnaire for Sport. *Anxiety, Stress, and Coping, 13,* 65–86.

Hatzigeorgiadis, A., Zourbanos, N., Galanis, E., and Theodorakis, Y. (2011) Self-talk and sport performance: A meta-analysis. *Perspectives on Psychological Science, 6,* 348–356.

Hayes, J. (1985) Three problems in teaching general skills. In J. Segal, S. Chipman and R. Glaser (eds) *Thinking and learning skills, Vol 2: Research and open questions* (pp. 391–406). Hillsdale, NJ: Lawrence Erlbaum Associates.

Hazell, J., Cotterill, S. T., and Hill, D. M. (2014) An exploration of pre-performance routines, self-efficacy, anxiety and performance in semi-professional soccer. *European Journal of Sport Science, 14,* 603–610.

Hedlund, E., Börjesson, M., and Österberg, J. (2015) Team learning in a multinational military staff exercise. *Small Group Research, 46,* 179–203.

Heider, F. (1958) *The psychology of interpersonal relations.* New York: Wiley.

Helsen, W. E., and Starkes, J. L. (1999) A multidimensional approach to skilled perception and performance in sport. *Applied Cognitive Psychology, 13,* 1–27.

Helsen, W. E., Starkes, J., and Hodges, N. J. (1998) Team sports and the theory of deliberate practice. *Journal of Sport and Exercise Psychology, 20,* 12–34.

Hemmings, B., Mantle, H., and Ellwood, J. (2007) *Mental toughness for golf: The minds of winners.* London: Green Umbrella.

Henderlong, J., and Lepper, M. R. (2002) The effects of praise on children's intrinsic motivation: A review and synthesis. *Psychological Bulletin, 128,* 774–795.

Heremans, E., Helsen, W. F., and Feys, P. (2008) The eyes as a mirror of our thoughts: Quantification of motor imagery of goal-directed movements through eye movement registration. *Behavioural and Brain Research, 187,* 351–360.

Hersh, P. (1998) Childhood lost: Olympic gymnast sues parents. *Chicago Tribune.* Retrieved from http://articles.chicagotribune.com/1998-10-22/news/9810220122_1_dominique-moceanu-parents-financial-well-being-jury-trial on 08 November 2016.

Hess, E. H., and Polt, J. M. (1964) Pupil size in relation to mental activity during simple problem-solving. *Science, 143,* 1190–1192.

Hétu, S., Grégoire, M., Saimpont, A., Coll, M-P., Eugène, F., Michon P-E., and Jackson, P. L. (2013) The neural network of motor imagery: An ALE meta-analysis. *Neuroscience & Biobehavioural Reviews, 37,* 930–949.

Hill, D. M., and Hemmings, B. (2015) A phenomenological exploration of coping responses associated with choking in sport. *Qualitative Research in Sport, Exercise and Health, 7,* 521–538.

Hill, D., Hanton, S. M., Matthews, N., and Fleming, S. (2010a) Choking in sport: A review. *International Review of Sport and Exercise Psychology, 3,* 24–39.

Hill, D. M., Hanton, S., Matthews, N., and Fleming, S. (2010b) A qualitative exploration of choking in elite golf. *Journal of Clinical Sport Psychology, 4,* 221–240.

Hill, D. M., Hanton, S., Matthews, N., and Fleming, S. (2011) Alleviation of choking under pressure in elite golf: An action research study. *Sport Psychologist, 25,* 465–488.

Hilmert, C., and Kvasnicka, L. (2010) Blood pressure and emotional responses to stress: Perspectives on cardiovascular reactivity. *Social and Personality Psychology Compass, 4,* 470–483.

Hoberman, J. D. (1992) *Mortal engines: The science of performance and the dehumanization of sport.* New York: Free Press.

Hobfoll, S. E. (2001) The influence of culture, community, and the nested self in the stress process: Advancing conservation of resources theory. *Applied Psychology, 50,* 337–421.

Hodge, K. (1995) Team dynamics. In T. Morris and J. Summers (eds) *Sport psychology: Theory, application and issues* (pp. 190–212). Brisbane: Wiley.

Hodge, K. (2010) Working at the Olympics. In S. J. Hanrahan and M. B. Andersen (eds) *Routledge handbook of applied sport psychology* (pp. 405–413). Abingdon, Oxfordshire: Routledge.

Hodge, K., and McKenzie, A. (1999) *Thinking rugby: Training your mind for peak performance.* Auckland: Reed.

Hodge, K., and Gucciardi, D. F. (2015) Antisocial and prosocial behaviour in sport: The role of motivational climate, basic psychological needs, and moral disengagement. *Journal of Sport and Exercise Psychology, 37,* 257–273.

Hodges, N. J., and Starkes J. L. (1996) Wrestling with the nature of expertise: A sport specific test of Ericsson, Krampe and Tesch-Romer's theory of deliberate practice. *International Journal of Sport Psychology, 27,* 1–25.

Hodges, N. J., and Baker, J. (2011) Expertise: The goal of performance development. In D. Collins, A. Button and H. Richards (eds) *Performance psychology: A practitioner's guide* (pp. 31–46). Edinburgh: Churchill Livingstone/Elsevier.

Hodges, N. J., Kerr, T., Starkes, J. L., Weir, P., and Nananidou, A. (2004) Predicting performance from deliberate practice hours for triathletes and swimmers: What, when and where is practice important? *Journal of Experimental Psychology: Applied, 10,* 219–237.

Hodges, N. J., Starkes, J. L., and MacMahon, C. (2006) Expert performance in sport: A cognitive perspective. In K. A. Ericsson, N. Charness, P. J. Feltovich and R. R. Hoffman (eds) *The Cambridge handbook of expertise and expert performance* (pp. 471–488). Cambridge: Cambridge University Press.

Hodges, N. J., Huys, R., and Starkes, J. L. (2007) A methodological review and evaluation of research of expert performance in sport. In G. Tenenbaum and R. C. Eklund (eds) *Handbook of sport psychology* (pp. 161–183). New York: Wiley.

Hodgins, H. S., and Adair, K. C. (2010) Attentional processes and meditation. *Consciousness and Cognition, 19,* 872–878.

Hodgkinson, M. (2002) The top 10 worst sporting excuses. *The Sunday Times* (Sport), 6 October, p. 24.

Hodgkinson, M (2013) *Andy Murray Wimbledon champion: The full and extraordinary story.* London: Simon & Schuster.

Hogg, M. A. (1992) *The social psychology of group cohesiveness.* Toronto: Harvester Wheatsheaf.

Hoggard, R. (2015) Spieth practices, thrives under pressure. Retrieved from www.golfchannel.com/news/rex-hoggard/spieth-practices-thrives-under-pressure/ on 24 October 2016.

Holmes, P., and Collins, D. (2001) The PETTLEP approach to motor imagery: A functional equivalence model for sport psychologists. *Journal of Applied Sport Psychology, 13,* 60–83.

Holt, N. L., and Sparkes, A. C. (2001) An ethnographic study of cohesiveness in a college soccer team over a season. *Sport Psychologist, 15,* 237–259.

Honigsbaum, M. (2004) Sitting pretty. *Observer Sport Monthly,* August, pp. 15–20.

Hopps, D. (2011) Another player in distress reopens debate on the "black wings" of illness. *The Guardian* (Sport), 25 March, p. 2.

Hopwood, M., Macmahon, C., Farrow, D., and Baker, J. (2015) Is practice the only determinant of sporting expertise? Revisiting Starkes (2000). *International Journal of Sport Psychology, 46,* 631–651.

Horikawa, T., Tamaki, M., Miyawaki, Y., and Kamitani, Y. (2013). Neural decoding of visual imagery during sleep. *Science, 340,* 639–642

Horn, R. R., Okumura, M. S., Alexander, M. G., Gardin, F. A., and Sylvester, C. T. (2012) Quiet eye duration is responsive to variability of practice and to the axis of target changes. *Research Quarterly for Exercise and Sport, 83,* 204–211.

Horwood, J. (2002) Sick of work? Bingo! *The Psychologist, 15,* 544.

Howard, R. W. (2012) Longitudinal effects of different types of practice on the development of chess expertise. *Applied Cognitive Psychology, 26,* 359–369.

Hudson, J., and Walker, N. C. (2002) Metamotivational state reversals during matchplay golf: An idiographic approach. *Sport Psychologist, 16,* 200–217.

Hughes, S. (2002) Darts feels the power of Taylor's tungsten. *The Daily Telegraph* (Sport), 7 January, p. S7.

Hull, C. L. (1943) *Principles of behaviour.* New York: Appleton-Century-Crofts.

Huntsinger, J. R., and Schnall, S. (2013) Emotion-cognition interactions. In D. Riesberg (ed.), *Oxford handbook of cognitive psychology* (pp. 571–584). New York: Oxford University Press.

Hurlburt, R. T., and Akhter, S. A. (2006) The descriptive experience sampling method. *Phenomenology and the Cognitive Sciences, 5,* 271–301.

Hurley, S. (2001) Perception and action: Alternative views. *Synthese, 129,* 3–40.

Hyde, A. L., Doerksen, S. E., Ribeiro, N. F., and Conroy, D. E. (2010) The independence of implicit and explicit attitudes toward physical activity: Introspective access and attitudinal concordance. *Psychology of Sport and Exercise, 11,* 387–393.

Hyllegard, R. (1991) The role of baseball seam pattern in pitch recognition. *Journal of Sport and Exercise Psychology, 13,* 80–84.

Ievleva, L., and Terry, P. C. (2008) Applying sport psychology to business. *International Coaching Psychology Review, 3,* 8–18.

Ingle, S. (2008) Olympics: Tearful Sacramone misses gold but lands on front pages, *The Guardian.* Retrieved from https://www.theguardian.com/sport/2008/aug/13/olympics2008.olympicsgymnastics on 24 October 2016.

Isaac, A. (1992) Mental practice: Does it work in the field? *Sport Psychologist, 6,* 192–198.

Isaac, A., Marks, D., and Russell, E. (1986) An instrument for assessing imagery of movement: The Vividness of Movement Imagery Questionnaire (VMIQ). *Journal of Mental Imagery, 10,* 23–30.

Ivarsson, A., Johnson, U., Andersen, M. B., Fallby, J., and Altemyr, M. (2015) It pays to pay attention: A mindfulness-based program for injury prevention with soccer players. *Journal of Applied Sport Psychology, 27,* 319–334.

Jackson, C. (2014) "Raise your game", BBC Sport. Retrieved from http://www.bbc.co.uk/wales/raiseyourgame/sites/inspiration/heroes/pages/jenson_button2.shtml on 16 November 2015.

Jackson, J. (2010) Wenger wants Arsenal to play without fear. *The Irish Times* (Sport), 8 December, p. 3.

Jackson, R. C. (2003) Pre-performance routine consistency: Temporal analysis of goal kicking in the Rugby Union World Cup. *Journal of Sports Sciences, 21,* 803–814.

Jackson, R. C., and Baker, J. S. (2001) Routines, rituals, and rugby: Case study of a world class goal kicker. *Sport Psychologist, 15,* 48–65.

Jackson, R. C., and Masters, R. S. W. (2006) Ritualized behaviour in sport. *Behavioural and Brain Sciences, 29,* 621–622.

Jackson, R. C., and Mogan, P. (2007) Advance visual information, awareness, and anticipation skill. *Journal of Motor Behaviour, 39,* 341–351.

Jackson, S. A., and Roberts, G. C. (1992) Positive performance states of athletes: Toward a conceptual understanding of peak performance. *Sport Psychologist, 6,* 156–171.

Jackson, S. A., and Kimiecik, J. C. (2008) The flow perspective of optimal experience in sport and physical activity. In T. S. Horn (ed.) *Advances in sport psychology* (3rd edn, pp. 377–399). Champaign, IL: Human Kinetics.

Jackson, S. A., Thomas, P. R., Marsh, H. W., and Smethurst, C. J. (2001) Relationships between flow, self-concept, psychological skills, and performance. *Journal of Applied Sport Psychology, 13,* 129–153.

Jackson, S. A., Martin, A. J., and Eklund, R. C. (2008) Long and short measures of flow: The construct validity of FSS-2, DFS-2, and new brief counterparts. *Journal of Sport and Exercise Psychology, 30,* 561–587.

Jacob, G. (2003) The game. *The Times,* 19 May, p. 5.

Jacobson, E. (1931). Electrical measurements of neuromuscular states during mental activities. *American Journal of Physiology, 96,* 115–121.

Jacobson, E. (1932) Electrophysiology of mental activities. *American Journal of Psychology, 44,* 677–694.

James, W. (1890a) *Principles of psychology (Vol. 1).* Cambridge, MA: Harvard University Press.

James, W. (1890b) *Principles of psychology (Vol. 2).* Cambridge, MA: Harvard University Press.

Janelle, C. M. (1999) Ironic mental processes in sport: Implications for sport psychologists. *Sport Psychologist, 13,* 201–220.

Janelle, C. M., and Hillman, C. H. (2003) Expert performance: Current perspectives. In J. L. Starkes and K. A. Ericsson (eds) *Expert performance in sports: Advances in research on sport expertise* (pp. 19–47). Champaign, IL: Human Kinetics.

Janelle, C. M., and Hatfield, B. D. (2008) Visual attention and brain processes that underlie expert performance: Implications for sport and military psychology. *Military Psychology, 20* (supplement 1), S39–S69.

Janelle, C. M., Singer, R. N., and Williams, A. M. (1999) External distractions and attentional narrowing: Visual search evidence. *Journal of Sport and Exercise Psychology, 21,* 70–91.

Jeannerod, M. (1994) The representing brain: Neural correlates of motor intention and imagery. *Behavioural and Brain Sciences, 17,* 187–245.

Jeannerod, M. (1997) *The cognitive neuroscience of action.* Oxford: Blackwell.

Jeannerod, M. (2001) Neural simulation of action: A unifying mechanism for motor cognition. *NeuroImage, 14,* S103–S109.

Jeannerod, M. (2004) Actions from within. *International Journal of Sport and Exercise Psychology, 2,* 376–402.

Jeannerod, M. (2006) *Motor cognition.* New York: Oxford University Press.

Jensen, M. (2015) Retrieved from http://articles.philly.com/2015-07-03/news/64042592_1_james-galanis-carli-lloyd-germany on 22 June 2016.

Jensen, M. (2nd July, 2015). "Mental toughness key to Carli Lloyd's success". *The Inquirer Daily News,* retrieved from http://www.philly.com/philly/sports/soccer/worldcup/20150702_Carli_Lloyd_tells_The_Inquirer_how_she_stays_focused.html 12 November 2016.

Jiang D., Edwards M. G., Mullins P., and Callow N. (2015). The neural substrates for the different modalities of movement imagery. *Brain and Cognition, 97,* 22–31

John, E. (2010) This much I know: Jessica Ennis. Retrieved from https://www.theguardian.com/lifeandstyle/2010/aug/15/jessica-ennis-this-much-i-know-interview on 24 October 2016.

Johnson, D. W., and Johnson, F. P. (1987) *Joining together: Group therapy and group skills* (3rd edn). Englewood Cliffs, NJ: Prentice-Hall.

Johnson, M. B., Edmonds, W. A., Moraes, L. C., Medeiros Filho, E. S., and Tenenbaum, G. (2007) Linking affect and performance of an international level archer incorporating an idiosyncratic probabilistic method. *Psychology of Sport and Exercise, 8,* 317–335.

Johnson, P. (1982) The functional equivalence of imagery and movement. *Quarterly Journal of Experimental Psychology, Section A, 34,* 349–365.

Jones, G. (1995) More than just a game: Research developments and issues in competitive anxiety in sport. *British Journal of Psychology, 86,* 449–478.

Jones, G., and Swain, A. B. J. (1992) Intensity and direction as dimensions of competitive state anxiety and relationships with competitiveness. *Perceptual and Motor Skills, 74,* 467–472.

Jones, G., and Swain, A. B. J. (1995) Predispositions to experience debilitative and facilitative anxiety in elite and non-elite performers. *Sport Psychologist, 9,* 201–211.

Jones, G., and Hanton, S. (2001) Pre-competitive feeling states and directional anxiety interpretations. *Journal of Sports Sciences, 19,* 385–395.

Jones, G., Hanton, S., and Swain, A. B. J. (1994) Intensity and interpretation of anxiety symptoms in elite and non-elite sports performers. *Personality and Individual Differences, 17*, 657–663.

Jones, G., Hanton, S., and Connaughton, D. (2002) What is this thing called mental toughness? An investigation of elite sport performers. *Journal of Applied Sport Psychology, 14*, 205–218.

Jones, G., Hanton, S., and Connaughton, D. (2007) A framework of mental toughness in the world's best performers. *Sport Psychologist, 21*, 243–264.

Jones, M., Meijen, C., McCarthy, P. J., and Sheffield, D. (2009) A theory of challenge and threat states in athletes. *International Review of Sport and Exercise Psychology, 2*, 161–180.

Jones, M. V. (2012) Emotion regulation and performance. In S. Murphy (ed.) *The Oxford handbook of sport and performance psychology* (pp. 154–172). New York: Oxford University Press.

Jones, M. V., and Uphill, M. (2004) Responses to the Competitive State Anxiety Inventory-2(d) by athletes in anxious and excited scenarios. *Psychology of Sport and Exercise, 5*, 201–212.

Jones, M. V., and Lavallee, D. (2010) A good walk worth watching. *The Psychologist, 23*, 806–809.

Jones, M. V., Lane, A. M., Bray, S. R., Uphill, M., and Catlin, J. (2005) Development and validation of the Sport Emotion Questionnaire. *Journal of Sport and Exercise Psychology, 27*, 407–431.

Jones, S. (1997) Seigne's only song: Je ne regrette rien. *The Sunday Times* (Sport), 5 October, p. 14.

Jordet, G. (2009) When superstars flop: Public status and choking under pressure in international soccer penalty shootouts. *Journal of Applied Sport Psychology, 21*, 125–130.

Jordet, G. (2010) Choking under pressure as self-destructive behaviour. In A. R. Nicholls (ed.) *Coping in sport: Theory, methods, and related constructs* (pp. 239–259). New York: Nova Science Publishers.

Jordet, G., and Hartman, E. (2008) Avoidance motivation and choking under pressure in soccer penalty shootouts. *Journal of Sport and Exercise Psychology, 30*, 452–459.

Jordet, G., Elferink-Gemser, M. T., Lemmink, K. A. P. M., and Visscher, C. (2006) The "Russian roulette" of soccer? Perceived control and anxiety in a major tournament penalty shootout. *International Journal of Sport Psychology, 37*, 281–298.

Jordet, G., Hartman, E., Visscher, C., and Lemmink, K. A. P. M. (2007) Kicks from the penalty mark in soccer: The role of stress, skill, and fatigue for kick outcomes. *Journal of Sports Sciences, 25*, 121–129.

Jung, R. E., Flores, R. A., and Hunter, D. (2016) A new measure of imagination ability: Anatomical brain imaging correlates. *Frontiers in Psychology, 7*, 496.

Kabat-Zinn, J. (2005) *Coming to our senses: Healing ourselves and the world through mindfulness.* New York: Hyperion.

Kahneman, D. (1973) *Attention and effort.* New York: Prentice-Hall.

Kahneman, D. (2011) *Thinking, fast and slow.* London: Macmillan.

Kaiseler, M., Polman, R. C., and Nicholls, A. R. (2012) Effects of the Big Five personality dimensions on appraisal coping, and coping effectiveness in sport. *European Journal of Sport Science, 12*, 62–72.

Kamata, A., Tenenbaum, G., and Hanin, Y. L. (2002) Individual zone of optimal functioning (IZOF): A probabilistic estimation. *Journal of Sport and Exercise Psychology, 24*, 189–208.

Kao, S. C., Huang, C. J., and Hung, T. M. (2014) Neurofeedback training reduces frontal midline theta and improves putting performance in expert golfers. *Journal of Applied Sport Psychology, 26*, 271–286.

Karageorghis, C. I. (2008) The scientific application of music in sport and exercise. In A. M. Lane (ed.) *Sport and exercise psychology: Topics in applied psychology* (pp. 109–137). London: Hodder Education.

Karageorghis, C. I., and Terry, P. C. (2010) *Inside sport psychology.* Champaign, IL: Human Kinetics.

Karageorghis, C. I., Hutchinson, J. C., Jones, L., Farmer, H. L., Ayhan, M. S., Wilson, R. C., Rance, J., Hepworth, C. J., and Bailey, S. G. (2013) Psychological, psychophysical, and ergogenic effects of music in swimming. *Psychology of Sport and Exercise, 14*, 560–568.

Karau, S. J., and Williams, K. D. (1993) Social loafing: A meta-analytic review and theoretical integration. *Journal of Personality and Social Psychology, 65*, 681–706.

Kavussanu, M. (2007) Morality in sport. In S. Jowett and D. E. Lavallee (eds) *Social psychology in sport* (pp. 265–278). Champaign, IL: Human Kinetics.

Kavussanu, M. (2008) Moral behaviour in sport: A critical review of the literature. *International Review of Sport and Exercise Psychology, 1,* 124–138.

Kavussanu, M., and Boardley, I. D. (2009) The Prosocial and Antisocial Behaviour in Sport Scale. *Journal of Sport and Exercise Psychology, 31,* 97–117.

Kay, O. (2016) Inside the mind of Leicester's miracle. Retrieved from www.thetimes.co.uk/article/inside-the-mind-of-leicesters-miracle-dv057mcx6 on 24 October 2016.

Keefe, R. (2003) *On the sweet spot: Stalking the effortless present.* New York: Simon & Schuster.

Keegan, R. (2016) *Being a sport psychologist.* London: Palgrave.

Keh, A. (2010) A few things to think about when lining up that kick. *New York Times,* 30 May. Retrieved from www.nytimes.com/2010/05/31/sports/soccer/31penaltykicks.html on 29 September 2010.

Kelley, H. H. (1967) Attribution theory in social psychology. In D. Levine (ed.) *Nebraska symposium on motivation* (Vol. 15, pp. 192–240). Lincoln, NE: University of Nebraska Press.

Kelly, G. A. (1955) *The psychology of personal constructs*, Vol. 1. New York: Norton.

Kelly, L. (1998) Walton's new mountain. *Irish Independent,* 26 October, p. 9.

Kerr, J. H. (1997). *Motivation and emotion in sport: Reversal theory.* Hove: Psychology Press.

Kersten, P., McCambridge, A., McPherson, K. M., Kayes, N., and Theadom, A. (2015) Bridging the gap between goal intentions and actions: A systematic review in patient populations. *Disability and Rehabilitation, 37,* 563–570.

Kervin, A. (2001) The power and the glory. *The Times* (Sport), 7 August, p. S6.

Kervin, A. (2005) From zero at Twickenham to World Cup heroes in Sydney. *The Times,* 3 October, pp. 72–73.

Kim, K. A., and Duda, J. L. (2003) The coping process: Cognitive appraisals of stress, coping strategies, and coping effectiveness. *Sport Psychologist, 17,* 406–425.

King, D., and Ridley, I. (2006) Arsenal lucky says Nedved as Wegner turns to shrinks to help young stars cope with bullies in Premiership. *Ireland on Sunday,* 2 April, pp. 82–83.

King, L. A. and Burton, C. M. (2003) The hazards of goal pursuit. In E. C. Chang and L. J. Lawrence (eds) *Virtue, vice, and personality: The complexity of behaviour* (pp. 53–69). Washington, DC: American Psychological Association.

Kingston, K. (2014) Goal setting. In R. C. Eklund and G. Tenenbaum (eds) *Encyclopedia of sport and exercise psychology* (Vol. 1, pp. 311–316). London: SAGE.

Kingston, K. M., and Hardy, L. (1997) Effects of different types of goals on processes that support performance. *Sport Psychologist, 11,* 277–293.

Kingston, K. M., and Wilson, K. M. (2009) The application of goal setting in sport. In S. D. Mellalieu and S. Hanton (eds) *Advances in applied sport psychology: A review* (pp. 75–123). Abingdon, Oxfordshire: Routledge.

Kinrade, N. P., Jackson, R. C., Ashford, K. J., and Bishop, D. T. (2010) Development and validation of the decision-specific reinvestment scale. *Journal of Sports Sciences, 28,* 1127–1135.

Kitson, R. (2015) "George's bedroom technique hits the spot", *The Guardian,* 23 Aug, p. 8 (Sport)

Klavora, P. (1978) An attempt to derive inverted-U curves based on the relationship between anxiety and athletic performance. In D. M. Landers and R. W. Christina (eds) *Psychology of motor behaviour and sport* (pp. 369–377). Champaign, IL: Human Kinetics.

Klein, C., DiazGranados, D., Salas, E., Le, H., Burke, C. S., Lyons, R., and Goodwin, G. F. (2009) Does team-building work? *Small Group Research, 40,* 180–222.

Klein, M., and Christiansen, G. (1969) Group composition, group structure and group effectiveness of basketball teams. In J. W. Loy and G. S. Kenyon (eds) *Sport, culture, and society* (pp. 397–408). London: Macmillan.

Kleinert, J., Ohlert, J., Carron, B., Eys, M., Feltz, D., Harwood, C., Linz, L., Seiler, R., and Sulprizio, M. (2012) Group dynamics in sports: An overview and recommendations on diagnostic and intervention. *The Sport Psychologist, 26,* 412–434.

Klostermann, A., Kredel, R., and Hossner, E. J. (2014) On the interaction of attentional focus and gaze: The quiet eye inhibits focus-related performance decrements. *Journal of Sport and Exercise Psychology, 36,* 392–400.

Knowles, E. (ed.) (1999) *The Oxford dictionary of quotations* (5th edn). Oxford: Oxford University Press.

Kobasa, S. C. (1979) Stressful life events, personality, and health: An inquiry into hardiness. *Journal of Personality and Social Psychology, 37,* 1–11.

Koehn, S. (2013) Effects of confidence and anxiety on flow state in competition. *European Journal of Sport Science, 13,* 543–550.

Koehn, S., Morris, T., and Watt, A. P. (2014). Imagery intervention to increase flow state and performance in competition. *The Sport Psychologist, 28,* 48–59.

Kolata, P. (2007) "I'm not really running, I'm not really running ...". *New York Times,* 6 December. Retrieved from www.nytimes.com/2007/12/06/health/nutrition/06Best.html on 8 April 2011.

Kolb, B., and Whishaw, I. Q. (2015) *Fundamentals of human neuropsychology* (7th edn). New York: Worth.

Kontos, A. P., and Feltz, D. L. (2008) The nature of sport psychology. In T. Horn (ed.) *Advances in sport psychology* (3rd edn, pp. 3–14). Champaign, IL: Human Kinetics.

Korman, M., Doyon, J., Doljansky, J., Carrier, J., Dagan, Y., and Karni, A. (2007) Daytime sleep condenses the time course of motor memory consolidation. *Nature Neuroscience, 10,* 1206–1213

Körner, A., Topolinski, S., and Strack, F. (2015) Routes to embodiment. *Frontiers in Psychology, 6,* 940.

Kornspan, A. (2007) The early years of sport psychology: The work and influence of Pierre De Coubertin. *Journal of Sport Behaviour, 30,* 77–93.

Kornspan, A. (2011) A history of sport psychology. In S. M. Murphy (ed.) *Handbook of sport and performance psychology.* Oxford: Oxford University Press.

Kosslyn, S. M. (1994) *Image and brain: The resolution of the imagery debate.* Cambridge, MA: MIT Press.

Kosslyn, S. M., and Rosenberg, R. S. (2011) *Introducing psychology: Brain, person, group* (4th edn). New York: Pearson.

Kosslyn, S. M., Seger, C., Pani, J. R., and Hillger, L. A. (1990) When is imagery used in everyday life? A diary study. *Journal of Mental Imagery, 14,* 131–152.

Kosslyn, S. M., Ganis, G., and Thompson, W. L. (2001) Neural foundations of imagery. *Nature Reviews: Neuroscience, 2,* 635–642.

Kosslyn, S. M., Thompson, W. L., and Ganis, G. (2006) *The case for mental imagery.* Oxford: Oxford University Press.

Kowalski, K. C., and Crocker, P. R. E. (2001) Development and validation of the Coping Function Questionnaire for adolescents in sport. *Journal of Sport and Exercise Psychology, 23,* 136–155.

Kowler, E. (1999) Eye movements and visual attention. In R. A. Wilson and F. C. Keil (eds) *The MIT encyclopedia of the cognitive sciences* (pp. 306–309). Cambridge, MA: MIT Press.

Krane, V. (1994) The Mental Readiness Form as a measure of competitive state anxiety. *Sport Psychologist, 8,* 189–202.

Krane, V. (2016) Inclusion to exclusion. In R. J. Schinke, K. R. McGannon and B. Smith (eds) *Routledge international handbook of sport psychology* (pp. 238–247). London: Routledge.

Kratochwill, T. R., and Levin, J. R. (2010) Enhancing the scientific credibility of single-case intervention research: Randomization to the rescue. *Psychological Methods, 15,* 124–144.

Kremer, J., and Scully, D. (1994) *Psychology in sport.* London: Taylor & Francis.

Kremer, J., and Busby, G. (1998) Modelling participant motivation in sport and exercise: An integrative approach. *Irish Journal of Psychology, 19,* 447–463.

Kremer, J., and Scully, D. (1998) What applied sport psychologists often don't do: On empowerment and independence. In H. Steinberg, I. Cockerill and A. Dewey (eds) *What sport psychologists do* (pp. 21–27). Leicester: British Psychological Society (Sport and Exercise Psychology Section).

Kremer, J., and Scully, D. (2002) The team just hasn't gelled. In I. Cockerill (ed.) *Solutions in sport psychology* (pp. 3–15). London: Thomson.

Kremer, J., and Moran, A. (2008) Swifter, higher, stronger: The history of sport psychology. *The Psychologist, 21,* 740–742.

Kremer, J., and Moran, A. (2013) *Pure sport: Practical sport psychology* (2nd edn). Hove, East Sussex: Routledge.

Kremer, J., Sheehy, N., Reilly, J., Trew, K., and Muldoon, O. (2003) *Applying social psychology.* Basingstoke, Hampshire: Palgrave Macmillan.

Kremer, J., Moran, A., Walker, G., and Craig, C. (2012) *Key concepts in sport psychology.* London: SAGE.

Kress, J. L., and Statler, T. (2007) A naturalistic investigation for former Olympic cyclists' cognitive strategies for coping with exertion pain during performance. *Journal of Sport Behaviour, 30,* 428–452.

Kriegeskorte, N., Simmons, W. K., Bellgowan, P. S. F., and Baker, C. I. (2009) Circular analysis in systems neuroscience: The dangers of double dipping. *Nature Neuroscience, 12,* 535–540.

Kuhn, T. S. (1962). *The structure of scientific revolutions.* Chicago, IL: University of Chicago Press.

Kyllo, L. B., and Landers, D. M. (1995) Goal-setting in sport and exercise: A research synthesis to resolve the controversy. *Journal of Sport and Exercise Psychology, 17,* 117–137.

Laakso, A. (2011) Embodiment and development in cognitive science. *Cognition, Brain, Behaviour: An Interdisciplinary Journal, 4,* 409–425.

Laborde, S., Dosseville, F., and Kinrade, N. P. (2014) Decision-specific reinvestment scale: An exploration of its construct validity, and association with stress and coping appraisals. *Psychology of Sport and Exercise, 15,* 238–246.

Lachman, R., Lachman, J. C. L., and Butterfield, E. C. (1979) *Cognitive psychology and information processing.* Hillsdale, NJ: Lawrence Erlbaum.

Laeng, B., Sirois, S., and Gredebäck, G. (2012) Pupillometry a window to the preconscious? *Perspectives on Psychological Science, 7,* 18–27.

Lalande, D. R., and Vallerand, R. J. (2014) Intrinsic/extrinsic motivation, hierarchical model of. In R. C. Eklund and G. Tenenbaum (eds) *Encyclopedia of sport and exercise psychology* (Vol. 1, pp. 393–395). London: SAGE.

Land, W., and Tenenbaum, G. (2012) An outcome-and process-oriented examination of a golf-specific secondary task strategy to prevent choking under pressure. *Journal of Applied Sport Psychology, 24,* 303–322.

Landers, D. M., and Luschen, G. (1974) Team performance outcome and cohesiveness of competitive coacting groups. *International Review of Sport Sociology, 9,* 57–71.

Landers, D. M., and Arent, S. M. (2010) Arousal-performance relationships. In J.M. Williams (ed.) *Applied sport psychology: Personal growth to peak performance* (6th edn, pp. 221–246). New York: McGraw-Hill.

Landin, D., and Herbert, E. P. (1999) The influence of self-talk on the performance of skilled female tennis players. *Journal of Applied Sport Psychology, 11,* 263–282.

Lane, A. M. (2007) *Mood and human performance: Conceptual, measurement, and applied issues.* Hauppauge, NY: Nova Science.

Lane, A. M. and Devonport, T. J (2009) Can anger and tension really be helpful? Relationships between mood states and emotional intelligence during optimal performance. Paper presented at the Stress Anxiety Research Society Conference, Budapest, Hungary, July 16–18, 2009.

Lane, A. M., Sewell, D. F., Terry, P. C., Bartram, D., and Nesti, M. S. (1999) Confirmatory factor analysis of the Competitive State Anxiety Inventory-2. *Journal of Sports Sciences, 17,* 505–512.

Lane, A. M., Harwood, C., and Nevill, A. M. (2005) Confirmatory factor analysis of the Thought Occurrence Questionnaire for Sport (TOQS) among adolescent athletes. *Anxiety, Stress, and Coping, 18,* 245–254.

Lane, A. M., Beedie, C. J., and Devonport, T. J. (2012a) Measurement issues in emotion and emotion regulation. In D. Lavallee, J. Thatcher and M. Jones (eds) *Coping and emotion in sport* (pp. 79–101). London: Wiley.

Lane, A. M., Beedie, C. J., Jones, M. V., Uphill, M., and Devonport, T. J. (2012b) The BASES expert statement on emotion regulation in sport. *Journal of Sports Sciences, 30,* 1189–1195.

Lane, A. M., Devonport, T. J., Friesen, A. P., Beedie, C. J., Fullerton, C. L., and Stanley, D. M. (2016) How should I regulate my emotions if I want to run faster? *European Journal of Sport Science, 16,* 465–472.

Lang, M. (2010) Surveillance and conformity in competitive youth swimming. *Sport, Education and Society, 15,* 19–37.

Lang, P. J. (1977) Imagery in therapy: An information-processing analysis of fear. *Behaviour Therapy, 8,* 862–886.

Lang, P. J. (1979) A bio-informational theory of emotional imagery. *Psychophysiology, 17,* 495–512.

Larrick, R. P., Timmerman, T. A., Carton, A. M., and Abrevaya, J. (2011) Temper, temperature, and temptation: Heat-related retaliation in baseball. *Psychological Science, 22,* 423–428.

Larsen, R. J., and Fredrickson, B. L. (1999) Measurement issues in emotion research. In D. Kahneman, E. Diener and N. Schwarz (eds) *Well-being: The foundations of hedonic psychology* (pp. 40–60). New York: Russell Sage Foundation.

Lashley, K. (1915) The acquisition of skill in archery. *Carnegie Institutions Publications, 7,* 107–128.

Lau, R. R., and Russell, D. (1980) Attributions in the sports pages: A field test of some current hypotheses about attribution research. *Journal of Personality and Social Psychology, 39,* 29–38.

Laurence, J. (1998) A saunter for champs. *Irish Independent,* 1 July, p. 23.

Lautenbach, F., Laborde, S., Achtzehn, S., and Raab, M. (2014) Preliminary evidence of salivary cortisol predicting performance in a controlled setting. *Psychoneuroendocrinology, 42,* 218–224.

Lautenbach, F., Laborde, S., Mesagno, C., Lobinger, B. H., Achtzehn, S., and Arimond, F. (2015a) Nonautomated pre-performance routine in tennis: An intervention study. *Journal of Applied Sport Psychology, 27,* 123–131.

Lautenbach, F., Laborde, S., Klämpfl, M., and Achtzehn, S. (2015b) A link between cortisol and performance: An exploratory case study of a tennis match. *International Journal of Psychophysiology, 98,* 167–173.

Lavallee, D., Jennings, D., Anderson, A. G., and Martin, S. B. (2005) Irish athletes' attitudes toward seeking a sport psychology consultation. *Irish Journal of Psychology, 26,* 115–121.

Lavallee, D., Kremer, J., Moran, A., and Williams, M. (2012) *Sport psychology: Contemporary themes* (2nd edn). Basingstoke, Hampshire: Palgrave Macmillan.

Lawrence, G. P., Cassell, V. E., Beattie, S., Woodman, T., Khan, M. A., Hardy, L., and Gottwald, V. M. (2014) Practice with anxiety improves performance, but only when anxious: Evidence for the specificity of practice hypothesis. *Psychological Research, 78,* 634–650.

Lawrenson, M. (2008) String of poor signings indicated serious flaw. *The Irish Times,* 5 December, p. 19.

Lazarus, R. S. (1991) Progress on a cognitive-motivational-relational theory of emotion. *American Psychologist, 46,* 819–834.

Lazarus, R. S. (1999) *Stress and emotion: A new synthesis.* New York: Springer.

Lazarus, R.S. (2000) Toward better research on stress and coping. *American Psychologist, 55,* 665–673.

Lazarus, R. S. (2001) Relational meaning and discrete emotions. In K. Scherer, A. Schorr and T. Johnstone (eds) *Appraisal processes in emotion: Theory, methods, research* (pp. 37–67). New York: Oxford University Press.

Lazarus, R. S., and Folkman, S. (1984) *Stress, appraisal, and coping.* New York: Springer.

Lee, M. J., Whitehead, J., and Ntoumanis, N. (2007) Development of the Attitudes to Moral Decision-Making in Youth Sport Questionnaire (AMDYSQ). *Psychology of Sport and Exercise, 8,* 369–392.

Lee, Y., Lee, S., Carello, C., and Turvey, M. T. (2012) An archer's perceived form scales the "hitableness" of archery targets. *Journal of Experimental Psychology. Human Perception and Performance, 38,* 1125–1131.

Leffingwell, T. R., Rider, S. P., and Williams, J. M. (2001) Application of the transtheoretical model to psychological skills training. *Sport Psychologist, 15,* 168–187.

Lehrer, J. (2010) How to raise a superstar. The frontal cortex. Retrieved from www.wired.com/wiredscience/2010/08/how-to-raise-a-superstar/on 8 September 2010.

Lejeune, M., Decker, C., and Sanchez, X. (1994) Mental rehearsal in table tennis performance. *Perceptual and Motor Skills, 79,* 627–641.

Lemyre, P.-N., Roberts, G. C., and Ommundsen, Y. (2002) Achievement goal orientations, perceived ability, and sportspersonship in youth soccer. *Journal of Applied Sport Psychology, 14,* 120–136.

Lemyre, P.-N., Treasure, D. C., and Roberts, G. C. (2006) Influence of variability in motivation and affect on elite athlete burnout susceptibility. *Journal of Sport and Exercise Psychology, 28,* 32–48.

Lenk, H. (1969) Top performance despite internal conflict: An antithesis to a functionalist proposition. In J. W. Loy and G. S. Kenyon (eds) *Sport, culture, and society: A reader on the sociology of sport* (pp. 393–396). Toronto: Collier Macmillan.

Lenk, H. (1977) *Team dynamics.* Champaign, IL: Stipes.

Lepper, M. R., and Greene, D. (1975) Turning play into work: Effects of adult surveillance and extrinsic rewards on children's intrinsic motivation. *Journal of Personality and Social Psychology, 31,* 479–486.

LeUnes, A. (2008) *Sport psychology* (4th edn). New York: Taylor & Francis.

LeUnes, A., and Nation, J. R. (2002) *Sport psychology* (3rd edn). Pacific Grove, CA: Wadsworth.

Lewin, K. (1935) *A dynamic theory of personality.* New York: McGraw-Hill.

Li, F., and Harmer, P. (1996) Confirmatory factor analysis of the Group Environment Questionnaire with an intercollegiate sample. *Journal of Sport and Exercise Psychology, 18,* 49–63.

Lidor, R., and Singer, R. N. (2003) Preperformance routines in self-paced tasks: Developmental and educational considerations. In R. Lidor and K. P. Henschen (eds) *The psychology of team sports* (pp. 69–98). Morgantown, WV: Fitness Information Technology.

Lilienfeld, S. O., Lynn, S. J., Namy, L. L., and Woolf, N. J. (2009) *Psychology: From inquiry to understanding.* Boston, MA: Pearson.

Lim, H. B., Karageorghis, C. I., Romer, L. M., and Bishop, D. T. (2014) Psychophysiological effects of synchronous versus asynchronous music during cycling. *Medicine & Science in Sports & Exercise, 46,* 407–413.

Lippke, S., Schwarzer, R., Ziegelmann, J. P., Scholz, U., and Schüz, B. (2010). Testing stage-specific effects of a stage-matched intervention: A randomized controlled trial targeting physical exercise and its predictors. *Health Education & Behaviour, 37,* 533–546

Locke, A. (2004) Accounting for success and failure: A discursive psychological approach to sport talk. *Quest, 56,* 302–320.

Locke, A. (2008) Managing agency for athletic performance: A discursive approach to the zone. *Qualitative Research in Psychology, 5,* 103–126.

Locke, E. A. (1991) Problems with goal-setting research in sports – and their solution. *Journal of Sport and Exercise Psychology, 8,* 311–316.

Locke, E. A., and Latham, G. P. (1985) The application of goal setting to sports. *Journal of Sport Psychology, 7,* 205–222.

Locke, E. A., and Latham, G. P. (1990) *A theory of goal setting and task performance.* Englewood Cliffs, NJ: Prentice-Hall.

Locke, E. A., and Latham, G. P. (2002) Building a practically useful theory of goal setting and task motivation. *American Psychologist, 57,* 705–717.

Locke, E. A., and Latham, G. P. (2006) New directions in goal-setting theory. *Current Directions in Psychological Science, 15,* 265–278.

Locke, E. A., and Latham, G. S. (2013) Goal setting theory: The current state. In E. A. Locke and G. P. Latham (eds) *New developments in goal setting and task performance* (pp. 623–630). London: Routledge.

Locke, E. A., Shaw, K. N., Saari, L. M., and Latham, G. P. (1981) Goal setting and task performance: 1969–1980. *Psychological Bulletin, 90,* 125–152.

Loehr, J. E. (1982) *Athletic excellence: Mental toughness training for sports.* Denver, CO: Forum.

Loffing, F., and Hagemann, N. (2014) Skill differences in visual anticipation of type of throw in team-handball penalties. *Psychology of Sport and Exercise, 15,* 260–267.

Logie, R. H. (1999) Working memory. *The Psychologist, 12,* 174–178.

Lonsdale, C., and Tam, J. T. M. (2008) On the temporal and behavioural consistency of pre-performance routines: An intra-individual analysis of elite basketball players' free throw shooting accuracy. *Journal of Sports Sciences, 26,* 259–266.

Loper, A. B., and Hallahan, D. P. (1982) Meta-attention: The development of awareness of the attentional process. *Journal of General Psychology, 106,* 27–33.

Lowe, S. (2011) I'm a romantic, says Xavi, heartbeat of Barcelona and Spain. *The Guardian* (Sport), 11 February, pp. 6–7.

Lyons, B. D., Hoffman, B. J., and Michel, J. W. (2009) Not much more than g? An examination of the impact of intelligence on NFL performance. *Human Performance, 22,* 225–245.

McAuley, E. (1985) Success and causality in sport: The influence of perception. *Journal of Sport Psychology, 7,* 13–22.

McAuley, E., and Blissmer, B. (2002) Self-efficacy and attributional processes in physical activity. In T. S. Horn (ed.) *Advances in sport psychology* (2nd edn, pp. 185–205). Champaign, IL: Human Kinetics.

McCann, S. (2008) At the Olympics, everything is a performance issue. *International Journal of Sport and Exercise Psychology, 6,* 267–276.

McCarthy, P. (2011) Positive emotion in sport performance: Current status and future directions. *International Review of Sport and Exercise Psychology, 4,* 50–69.

McCarthy, P. J., Jones, M. V., and Clark-Canter, D. (2008) Understanding enjoyment in youth sport: A developmental perspective. *Psychology of Sport and Exercise, 9,* 142–156.

McCarthy, P. J., Allen, M. S., and Jones, M. V. (2013) Emotions, cognitive interference, and concentration disruption in youth sport. *Journal of Sports Sciences, 31,* 505–515.

McClelland, D. C., Atkinson, J. W., Clark, R. W., and Lowell, E. J. (1953) *The achievement motive.* New York: Appleton-Century-Crofts.

McCormick, A., Meijen, C., and Marcora, S. (2015) Psychological determinants of whole-body endurance performance. *Sports Medicine, 45,* 997–1015.

McEnroe, J., and Kaplan, J. (2002) *You cannot be serious.* New York: G. P. Putnam's Sons.

McEwan, D., Martin Ginis, K. A., and Bray, S. R. (2013) The effects of depleted self-control strength on skill-based task performance. *Journal of Sport and Exercise Psychology, 35,* 239–249.

McGannon, K. R., and Busanich, R. (2016) Athletes and motherhood. In R. J. Schinke, K. R. McGannon, and B. Smith (eds) *The Routledge international handbook of sport psychology* (pp. 286–295). London: Routledge.

McGinty, K. (2006) Kiwi finds his silver lining in clouds of Carton. *Irish Independent,* 18 May, p. 19.

McGinley, M., Kremer, J., Trew, K., and Ogle, S. (1998) Socio-cultural identity and attitudes to sport in Northern Ireland. *Irish Journal of Psychology, 19,* 464–471.

McIlveen, R. (1992) An investigation of attributional bias in a real-world setting. In R. McIlveen, L. Higgins, and A. Wadeley (eds) *BPS manual of psychology practicals* (pp. 78–92). Leicester: British Psychological Society.

McIntosh, M. (2002) Hate drives Lennon out. *The Guardian,* 22 August, p. 34.

MacIntyre, T. (1996) Imagery validation: How do we know that athletes are imaging during mental practice? Unpublished MA thesis, Department of Psychology, University College, Dublin.

MacIntyre, T., and Moran, A. (2007a) A qualitative investigation of imagery use and meta-imagery processes among elite canoe-slalom competitors. *Journal of Imagery Research in Sport and Physical Activity, 2,* 1, Article 3.

MacIntyre, T., and Moran, A. (2007b) A qualitative investigation of meta-imagery processes and imagery direction among elite athletes. *Journal of Imagery Research in Sport and Physical Activity, 2,* 1, Article 4.

MacIntyre, T., Moran, A., Collet, C., and Guillot, A. (2013a) An emerging paradigm: A strength-based approach to exploring mental imagery. *Frontiers in Human Neuroscience, 7,* 104, 1–12.

MacIntyre, T., Moran, A., Collet, C., Guillot, A., Campbell, M., Matthews, J., Mahoney, C., and Lowther, J. (2013b) The BASES expert statement on the use of mental imagery in sport, exercise and rehabilitation contexts. *The Sport and Exercise Scientist, 38,* 10–11.

McKenzie, A. D., and Howe, B. L. (1991) The effect of imagery on tackling performance in rugby. *Journal of Human Movement Studies, 20,* 163–176.

McLean, N. (1995) Building and maintaining an effective team. In T. Morris and J. Summers (eds) *Sport psychology: Theory, applications and issues* (pp. 420–434). Brisbane: Wiley.

McNair, D. M., Lorr, M., and Droppleman, L. F. (1971) *Manual for the Profile of Mood States.* San Diego, CA: Educational and Industrial Testing Services.

McNair, D. M., Lorr, M., and Droppleman, L. F. (1992) *Revised manual for the Profile of Mood States.* San Diego, CA: Educational and Industrial Testing Services.

MacNamara, Á., Collins, D., and Giblin, S. (2015) Just let them play? Deliberate preparation as the most appropriate foundation for lifelong physical activity. *Frontiers in Psychology, 6,* 1548.

McNerney, S. (2011) A brief guide to embodied cognition: Why you are not your brain. *Scientific American,* 4 November. Retrieved from http://blogs.scientificamerican.com/guest-blog/a-brief-guide-to-embodied-cognition-why-you-are-not-your-brain/ on 24 October 2016.

MacPherson, A., Collins, D., and Morriss, C. (2008) Is what you think what you get? Optimizing mental focus for technical performance. *Sport Psychologist, 22,* 288–303.

MacPherson, A. C., Collins, D., and Obhi, S. S. (2009) The importance of temporal structure and rhythm for the optimum performance of motor skills: A new focus for practitioners of sport psychology. *Journal of Applied Sport Psychology, 21,* S48–S61.

McPherson, S. L. (2000) Expert-novice differences in planning strategies during collegiate singles tennis competition. *Journal of Sport and Exercise Psychology, 22,* 39–62.

McRae, D. (2008) Even great players can have tortured minds. *The Guardian* (Sport), 15 July, pp. 6–7.

MacRury, D. (1997) *Golfers on golf.* London: Virgin.

Madan, C. R., and Singhal, A. (2013) Introducing TAMI: An objective test of ability in movement imagery. *Journal of Motor Behaviour, 45,* 153–166.

Madan, C. R., and Singhal, A. (2014) Improving the TAMI for use with athletes. *Journal of Sports Sciences, 32,* 1351–1356.

Maehr, M. L., and Nicholls, J. G. (1980) Culture and achievement motivation: A second look. In N. Warren (ed.) *Studies in cross-cultural psychology* (pp. 221–267). New York: Academic Press.

Maguire, E. A., Gadian, D. G., Johnsrude, I. S., Good, C. D., Ashburner, J., Frackowiak, R. S. J., and Frith, C. D. (2000) Navigation-related structural change in the hippocampi of taxi drivers. *Proceedings of the National Academy of Sciences* (USA), *97,* 4398–4403.

Mahoney, M. J., and Avener, M. (1977) Psychology of the elite athlete: An exploratory study. *Cognitive Therapy and Research, 1,* 135–141.

Mahoney, P. (2007) Swing doctors cash in as Baddeley joins quick-fix gospel's band of disciples. *The Guardian* (Sport), 11 June, p. 5.

Mair, L. (2004) Faldo dismisses fear of failure in a heartbeat. *The Daily Telegraph* (Sport), 15 July, pp. 2–3.

Malhotra, N., Poolton, J. M., Wilson, M. R., Omuro, S., and Masters, R. S. (2015) Dimensions of movement specific reinvestment in practice of a golf putting task. *Psychology of Sport and Exercise, 18,* 1–8.

Mallett, C. J., and Hanrahan, S. J. (2003) Elite athletes: Why does the "fire" burn so brightly? *Psychology of Sport and Exercise, 5,* 183–200.

Mandler, G. (2007) *A history of modern experimental psychology: From James and Wundt to cognitive science.* Cambridge, MA: MIT Press.

Mann, D. L., Spratford, W., and Abernethy, B. (2013) The head tracks and gaze predicts: How the world's best batters hit a ball. *PloS ONE, 8,* e58289.

Mann, D. L., Ho, N. Y., De Souza, N. J., Watson, D. R., and Taylor, S. J. (2007) Is optimal vision required for the successful execution of an interceptive task? *Human Movement Science, 27,* 343–356.

Marasso, D., Laborde, S., Bardaglio, G., and Raab, M. (2014) A developmental perspective on decision making in sports. *International Review of Sport and Exercise Psychology, 7,* 1–23.

Marcotti, G. (2001) Made, not born. *Sunday Tribune* (Sport), 7 October, p. 9.

Martell, S. G., and Vickers, J. N. (2004) Gaze characteristics of elite and near-elite athletes in ice hockey defensive tactics. *Human Movement Science, 22,* 689–712.

Martens, M. P., and Webber S. N. (2002) Psychometric properties of the Sport Motivation Scale: An evaluation with college varsity athletes from the US. *Journal of Sport and Exercise Psychology, 24,* 254–270.

Martens, R. (1977) *Sport competition anxiety test.* Champaign, IL: Human Kinetics.

Martens, R., Landers, R. M., and Loy, J. W. (1972) *Sport cohesiveness questionnaire.* Unpublished manuscript, University of Illinois, Champaign, IL.

Martens, R., Burton, D., Vealey, R. S., Bump, L. A., and Smith, D. E. (1990) Development and validation of the Competitive State Anxiety Inventory-2 (CSAI-2). In R. Martens, R. S. Vealey, and D. Burton (eds) *Competitive anxiety in sport* (pp. 117–190). Champaign, IL: Human Kinetics.

Martin, A. (2007) More than words: Book of Serena the answer to Williams' prayers. *The Guardian* (Sport), 3 July, p. 5.

Martin, A. J., and Jackson, S.A. (2008) Brief approaches to assessing task absorption and enhanced subjective experience: Examining "short" and "core" flow in diverse performance domains. *Motivation and Emotion, 32,* 141–157.

Martin, J. J., and Gill, D. L. (1991) The relationships among competitive orientation, sport-confidence, self-efficacy, anxiety and performance. *Journal of Sport and Exercise Psychology, 13,* 149–159.

Martin, K. A., Moritz, S. E., and Hall, C. (1999) Imagery use in sport: A literature review and applied model. *Sport Psychologist, 13,* 245–268.

Martin, L. C., Carron, A. V., and Burke, S. M. (2009) Team building interventions in sport: A meta-analysis. *Sport and Exercise Psychology Review, 5,* 3–18.

Martin, L. J., Carron, A. V., Eys, M. A., and Loughead, T. M. (2011). Children's perceptions of cohesion. *Sport and Exercise Psychology Review, 7,* 11–25

Martin, L. J., Carron, A. V., Eys, M. A., and Loughead, T. (2013) Validation of the Child Sport Cohesion Questionnaire. *Measurement in Physical Education and Exercise Science, 17,* 105–119.

Martin, S. B., Kellmann, M., Lavallee, D., and Page, S. J. (2002) Development and psychometric evaluation of the Sport Psychology Attitudes – Revised Form: A multiple group investigation. *Sport Psychologist, 16,* 272–290.

Martindale, A., and Collins, D. (2011) Conclusion: Where next? Getting help in your pursuit of excellence. In D. Collins, A. Button, and H. Richards (eds) *Performance psychology: A practitioner's guide* (pp. 393–401). Oxford: Elsevier.

Martinent, G., and Ferrand, C. (2015) A field study of discrete emotions: Athletes' cognitive appraisals during competition. *Research Quarterly for Exercise and Sport, 86,* 51–62.

Martinent, G., Guillet-Descas, E., and Moiret, S. (2015) A reciprocal effects model of the temporal ordering of basic psychological needs and motivation. *Journal of Sport and Exercise Psychology, 37,* 117–126.

Massey, R. (2010) Sport radio "as risky as a drink if you're driving". *Daily Mail,* 2 July, p. 13.

Masters, K. S., and Ogles, B. M. (1998) Associative and dissociative cognitive strategies in exercise and running: 20 years later, what do we know? *Sport Psychologist, 12,* 253–270.

Masters, R. S. W. (1992) Knowledge, "knerves" and know-how: The role of explicit versus implicit knowledge in the breakdown of a complex motor skill under pressure. *British Journal of Psychology, 83,* 343–358.

Masters, R. S. W., and Maxwell, J. P. (2004) Implicit motor learning, reinvestment and movement disruption: What you don't know won't hurt you. In A. M. Williams and N. J. Hodges (eds) *Skill acquisition in sport: Research, theory and practice* (pp. 207–228). London: Routledge.

Masters, R. S. W., and Maxwell, J. P. (2008) The theory of reinvestment. *International Review of Sport and Exercise Psychology, 2,* 160–183.

Masters, R. S. W., Polman, R. C. J., and Hammond, N. V. (1993) "Reinvestment": A dimension of personality implicated in skill breakdown under pressure. *Personality and Individual Differences, 14,* 655–666.

Mateo, S., Di Rienzo, F., Guillot, A., Collet, C., and Rode, G. (2015) Motor imagery reinforces compensation of reach-to-grasp movement after cervical spinal cord injury. *Frontiers in Behavioural Neuroscience, 9,* 234.

Mather, M., Cacioppo, J. T., and Kanwisher, N. C. (2013a) Introduction to the special issue section: 20 years of fMRI – what has it done for understanding cognition? *Perspectives on Psychological Science, 8,* 41–43.

Mather, M., Cacioppo, J., and Kanwisher, N. (2013) How fMRI can inform cognitive theories. *Perspectives on Psychological Science, 8,* 108–113.

Matheson, H., Mathes, S., and Murray, M. (1995) Group cohesion of female intercollegiate coacting and interacting teams across a competitive season. *International Journal of Sport Psychology, 27,* 37–49.

Mathieu, J., Maynard, M. T., Rapp, T., and Gilson, L. (2010) Team effectiveness 1997–2007: A review of recent advancements and a glimpse into the future. In J. A. Wagner and J. R. Hollenbeck (eds) *Readings in organisational behaviour* (pp. 321–380). New York: Routledge.

Mathôt, S., and Van der Stigchel, S. (2015) New light on the mind's eye: The pupillary light response as active vision. *Current Directions in Psychological Science, 24,* 374–378.

Matlin, M. W. (2009) *Cognition* (7th edn). New York: Wiley.

Mauss, I. B., and Robinson, M. D. (2009) Measures of emotion: A review. *Cognition and Emotion, 23,* 209–237.

Maxwell, J. P., and Moores, E. (2007) The development of a short scale measuring aggressiveness and anger in competitive athletes. *Psychology of Sport and Exercise, 8,* 179–193.

Maxwell, J. P., Visek, A. J., and Moores, E. (2009) Anger and perceived legitimacy of aggression in male Hong Kong Chinese athletes: Effects of type of sport and level of competition. *Psychology of Sport and Exercise, 10,* 289–296.

Maynard, I. (1998) *Improving concentration.* Headingley, Leeds: National Coaching Foundation.

Mears, P., and Voehl, F. (1994) *Team building: A structured learning approach.* Delray Beach, FL: St Lucie Press.

Medic, N. (2010) Masters athletes. In S. J. Hanrahan and M. B. Andersen (eds) *Routledge handbook of applied sport psychology* (pp. 387–395). Abingdon, Oxfordshire: Routledge.

Meijen, C., Jones, M. V., Sheffield, D., and McCarthy, P. J. (2014) Challenge and threat states: Cardiovascular, affective, and cognitive responses to a sports-related speech task. *Motivation and Emotion, 38,* 252–262.

Mellalieu, S. D., Hanton, S., and Fletcher, D. (2006a) A competitive anxiety review: Recent directions in sport psychology. In S. Hanton and S. D. Mellalieu (eds) *Literature reviews in sport psychology* (pp. 1–45). Hauppauge, NY: Nova Science.

Mellalieu, S. D., Hanton, S., and O'Brien, M. (2006b) The effects of goal-setting on rugby performance. *Journal of Applied Behaviour Analysis, 39,* 257–261.

Mellalieu, S. D., Hanton, S., and Thomas, O. (2009) The effects of a motivational general-arousal imagery intervention upon preperformance symptoms in male rugby union players. *Psychology of Sport and Exercise, 10,* 175–185.

Melnick, M. J., and Chemers, M. M. (1974) Effects of group structure on the success of basketball teams. *Research Quarterly for Exercise and Sport, 45,* 1–8.

Memmert, D. (2015) *Teaching tactical creativity in sport: Research and practice.* Abingdon, Oxfordshire: Routledge.

Mendes, W. B., Major, B., McCoy, S., and Blascovich, J. (2008) How attributional ambiguity shapes physiological and emotional responses to social rejection and acceptance. *Journal of Personality and Social Psychology, 94,* 278–291.

Merikle, P. (2007) Preconscious processing. In M. Velmans and S. Schneider (eds) *The Blackwell companion to consciousness* (pp. 512–524). Oxford: Blackwell.

Mesagno, C., and Mullane-Grant, T. (2010) A comparison of different pre-performance routines as possible choking interventions. *Journal of Applied Sport Psychology, 22,* 343–360.

Mesagno, C., and Hill, D. M. (2013) Definition of choking in sport: Re-conceptualization and debate. *International Journal of Sport Psychology, 44,* 267–277.

Mesagno, C., Hill, D. M., and Larkin, P. (2015) Examining the accuracy and in-game performance effects between pre-and post-performance routines: A mixed methods study. *Psychology of Sport and Exercise, 19,* 85–94.

Meyers, A. W. (1997) Sport psychology services to the United States Olympic Festival: An experiential account. *Sport Psychologist, 11,* 454–468.

Mezulis, A. H., Abramson, L. Y., Hyde, J. S., and Hankin, B. L. (2004) Is there a universal positivity bias in attributions? A meta-analytic review of individual, developmental, and cultural differences in self-serving attributional bias. *Psychological Bulletin, 130,* 711–747.

Middleton, C. (1996) Losing out as the mind muscles in. *Sunday Telegraph* (Sport), 30 June, p. 15.

Miles, A., and Neil, R. (2013) The use of self-talk during elite cricket batting performance. *Psychology of Sport and Exercise, 14,* 874–881.

Miller, B. (1997) *Gold minds: The psychology of winning in sport.* Marlborough, Wiltshire: Crowood Press.

Miller, G. (1956) The magical number seven, plus or minus two: Some limits on our capacity for processing information. *The Psychological Review, 63,* 81–97.

Miller, G. (2003) The cognitive revolution: A historical perspective. *Trends in Cognitive Sciences, 7,* 141–144.

Milton, J., Solodkin, A., Hlustik, P., and Small, S. L. (2007) The mind of expert performance is cool and focused. *NeuroImage, 35,* 804–813.

Milton, J., Solodkin, A., and Small, S. L. (2008) Why did Casey strike out? The neuroscience of hitting. In D. Gordon (ed.) *Your brain on Cubs: Inside the heads of players and fans* (pp. 43–57). New York: Dana Press.

Miracle, A. W., and Rees, C. R. (1994) *Lessons of the locker-room: The myth of school sports.* Amherst, NJ: Prometheus.

Misirlisoy, E., and Haggard, P. (2014) Asymmetric predictability and cognitive competition in football penalty shootouts. *Current Biology, 24,* 1918–1922.

Mitchell, K. (2010) Hard regime in gym helps Murray find his feet on clay. *The Guardian* (Sport), 29 April, p. 6.

Mitchell, K. (2013) Novak Djokovic mindful of US Open threat posed by Stanislas Wawrinka. Retrieved from https://www.theguardian.com/sport/2013/sep/06/novak-djokovic-us-open-wawrinka on 24 October 2016.

Mizuguchi, N., Nakata, H., Hayashi, T., Sakamoto, M., Muraoka, T., Uchida, Y., and Kanosue, K. (2013) Brain activity during motor imagery of an action with an object: A functional magnetic resonance imaging study. *Neuroscience Research, 76,* 150–155.

Moll, T., Jordet, G., and Pepping, G. J. (2010) Emotional contagion in soccer penalty shootouts: Celebration of individual success is associated with ultimate team success. *Journal of Sports Sciences, 28,* 983–992.

Monacis, L., de Palo, V., and Sinatra, M. (2014) Sportspersonship behaviours: An exploratory investigation of antecedents. *International Journal of Sport Psychology, 45,* 231–245.

Montero, B. (2010) Does bodily awareness interfere with highly skilled movement? *Inquiry: An interdisciplinary Journal of Philosophy, 53,* 105–122.

Moore, G. (2000) Sympathy but little satisfaction for Robson. *The Independent,* 4 December, p. 3.

Moore, L. J., Vine, S. J., Freeman, P., and Wilson, M. R. (2012) Quiet eye training promotes challenge appraisals and aids performance under elevated anxiety. *International Journal of Sport and Exercise Psychology, 11,* 169–183.

Moore, L. J., Wilson, M. R., Vine, S. J., Coussens, A. H., and Freeman, P. (2013) Champ or chump? Challenge and threat states during pressurized competition. *Journal of Sport and Exercise Psychology, 35,* 551–562.

Moore, L. J., Vine, S. J., Wilson, M. R., and Freeman, P. (2015) Reappraising threat: How to optimize performance under pressure. *Journal of Sport and Exercise Psychology, 37,* 339–343.

Moors, A. (2013) Automaticity. In D. Reisbeg (ed.) *The Oxford handbook of cognitive psychology* (pp. 163–175). Oxford: Oxford University Press.

Moran, A. (2014) Cognitive strategies in sport and exercise psychology. In J. L. Van Raalte and B. Brewer (eds) *Exploring sport and exercise psychology* (3rd edn, pp. 83–105). Washington, DC: American Psychological Association.

Moran, A. (2016) Expertise and mental practice. In R. J. Schinke, K. R. McGannon and B. Smith (eds) *The Routledge international handbook of sport psychology* (pp. 421–428). London: Routledge.

Moran, A., Quinn, A., Campbell, M., Rooney, B., Brady, N., and Burke, C. (2016). Using pupillometry to evaluate attentional effort in quiet eye: A preliminary investigation. *Sport, Exercise, and Performance Psychology, 5,* 365–376.

Moran, A. P. (1993) Conceptual and methodological issues in the measurement of mental imagery skills in athletes. *Journal of Sport Behaviour, 16,* 156–170.

Moran, A. P. (1996) *The psychology of concentration in sport performers: A cognitive analysis.* Hove, East Sussex: Psychology Press.

Moran, A. P. (1998) *The pressure putt: Doing your best when it matters most in golf* (audiotape). Aldergrove, Co. Antrim, N. Ireland: Tutorial Services (UK).

Moran, A. P. (2000a) Improving sporting abilities: Training concentration skills. In J. Hartley and A. Branthwaite (eds) *The applied psychologist* (2nd edn, pp. 92–110). Buckingham: Open University Press.

Moran, A. P. (2000b) *Managing your own learning at university: A practical guide* (rev. edn, first published 1997). Dublin: UCD Press.

Moran, A. P. (2001) What makes a winner? The psychology of expertise in sport. *Studies, 90,* 266–275.

Moran, A. P. (2002a) In the mind's eye. *The Psychologist, 15,* 414–415.

Moran, A. P. (2002b) "Shrinking" or expanding? The role of sport psychology in professional football. *Insight – The FA Coaches Journal, 6,* 41–43.

Moran, A. P. (2003a) Improving concentration skills in team-sport performers: Focusing techniques for soccer players. In R. Lidor and K. P. Henschen (eds) *The psychology of team sports* (pp. 161–190). Morgantown, WV: Fitness Information Technology.

Moran, A. P. (2003b) The state of concentration skills training in applied sport psychology. In I. Greenless and A. P. Moran (eds) *Concentration skills training in sport* (pp. 7–19). Leicester: British Psychological Society (Division of Sport and Exercise Psychology).

Moran, A. P. (2004) *Sport and exercise psychology: A critical introduction.* London: Routledge.

Moran, A. P. (2009) Cognitive psychology in sport: Progress and prospects. *Psychology of Sport and Exercise, 10,* 420–426.

Moran, A. P., and MacIntyre, T. (1998) "There's more to an image than meets the eye": A qualitative study of kinaesthetic imagery among elite canoe-slalomists. *Irish Journal of Psychology, 19,* 406–423.

Moran, A. P., Byrne, A., and McGlade, N. (2002) The effects of anxiety and strategic planning on visual search behaviour. *Journal of Sports Sciences, 20,* 225–236.

Moran, A., Egan, A., Bates, U., Coleman, U., Guerin, S., and O'Sullivan, C. (2006) The learning support unit project. The development and evaluation of a learning skills intervention for first year students in UCD Dublin. Final report to Higher Education Authority, Dublin: UCD (pp. vi, 116).

Moran, A. P., Guillot, A., MacIntyre, T., and Collet, C. (2012) Re-imagining motor imagery: Building bridges between cognitive neuroscience and sport psychology. *British Journal of Psychology, 103,* 224–247.

Moran, A. P., Quinn, A., Campbell, M., Rooney, B., Brady, N., and Burke, C. (2016) Using pupillometry to evaluate attentional effort in quiet eye: A preliminary investigation. *Sport, Exercise, and Performance Psychology, 5,* 365–376.

Moran, G. (2005) "Oh dear, so near but yet so far away". *The Irish Times,* 12 July, p. 21.

Moran, S. (2001) The Gaelic Athletic Association and professionalism in Irish sport. *Studies, 90,* 276–282.

Morgan, W. P. (1997) Mind games: The psychology of sport. In D. R. Lamb and R. Murray (eds) *Perspectives in exercise science and sports medicine: Optimizing sport performance* (Vol. 10, pp. 1–62). Carmel, IN: Cooper.

Morgan, W. P. (2000) Psychological factors associated with distance running and the marathon. In D. T. Pedloe (ed.) *Marathon medicine* (pp. 293–310). London: Royal Society of Medicine Press.

Morgan, W. P., and Pollock, M. L. (1977) Psychologic characterization of the elite distance runner. *Annals of the New York Academy of Sciences, 301,* 382–403.

Morris, J. A., and Feldman, D. C. (1996) The dimensions, antecedents, and consequences of emotional labor. *Academy of Management Review, 21,* 986–1010.

Morris, K. (2006) The best players know the value of winning ugly. *Sunday Tribune,* 29 October, p. 24.

Morris, L., Davis, D., and Hutchings, C. (1981) Cognitive and emotional components of anxiety: Literary review and revised worry-emotionality scale. *Journal of Educational Psychology, 73,* 541–555.

Morris, P. E., Tweedy, M., and Gruneberg, M. M. (1985) Interest, knowledge and the memorizing of soccer scores. *British Journal of Psychology, 76,* 415–425.

Morris, T., Spittle, M., and Perry, C. (2004) Mental imagery in sport. In T. Morris and J. Summers (eds) *Sport psychology: Theory, applications and issues* (2nd edn, pp. 344–387). Brisbane: Wiley.

Morris, T., Spittle, M., and Watt, A. P. (2005) *Imagery in sport.* Champaign, IL: Human Kinetics.

Morrisett, L. N. (1956) The role of implicit practice in learning. Unpublished doctoral dissertation, Yale University.

Morrissey, E. (2009) Teenage screams make them so hard to beat. *Sunday Tribune* (Sport), 21 June, p. 16.

Mudrack, P. E. (1989a) Defining group cohesiveness: A legacy of confusion? *Small Group Behaviour, 20,* 37–49.

Mudrack, P. E. (1989b) Group cohesiveness and productivity: A closer look. *Human Relations, 42,* 771–785.

Mulder T., De Vries S., and Zijlstra S. (2005). Observation, imagination and execution of an effortful movement: More evidence for a central explanation of motor imagery. *Experimental Brain Research, 163,* 344–351.

Mullen, B., and Copper, C. (1994) The relation between group cohesiveness and performance: An integration. *Psychological Bulletin, 115,* 210–227.

Müller, S., Abernethy, B., and Farrow, D. (2006) How do world-class cricket batsmen anticipate a bowlers' intention? *Quarterly Journal of Experimental Psychology, 59,* 2162–2186.

Müller, S., Abernethy, B., Reece, J., Rose, M., Eid, M., McBan, R., Hart, T., and Abreu, C. (2009) An in-situ examination of the timing of information pick-up for interception by cricket batsmen of different skill levels. *Psychology of Sport and Exercise, 10,* 644–652.

Munroe, K. J., Giaccobi, P. R., Jr, Hall, C. R., and Weinberg, R. S. (2000) The four W's of imagery use: Where, when, why, and what. *Sport Psychologist, 14,* 119–137.

Munroe-Chandler, K. J., Hall, C. R., and Weinberg, R. S. (2004) A qualitative analysis of the types of goals athletes set in training and competition. *Journal of Sport Behaviour, 27,* 58–74.

Munsey, C. (2010) Coaching the coaches. *APA Monitor on Psychology, 41,* 58–61.

Munzert, J., and Zentgraf, K. (2009) Motor imagery and its implications for understanding the motor system. *Progress in Brain Research, 174,* 219–229.

Munzert, J., and Lorey, B. (2013) Motor and visual imagery in sports. In S. Lacey and R. Lawson (eds), *Multisensory imagery* (pp. 319-341). New York: Springer.

Munzert, J., Lorey, J., and Zentgraf, J. (2009) Cognitive motor processes: The role of motor imagery in the study of motor representations. *Brain Research Reviews, 60,* 306–326.

Murphy, P. R., O'Connell, R. G., O'Sullivan, M., Robertson, I. H., and Balsters, J. H. (2014) Pupil diameter covaries with BOLD activity in human locus coeruleus. *Human Brain Mapping, 35,* 4140–4154.

Murphy, S. M. (1994) Imagery interventions in sport. *Medicine and Science in Sports and Exercise, 26,* 486–494.

Murphy, S. M. (1999) *The cheers and the tears: A healthy alternative to the dark side of youth sports today.* San Francisco, CA: Jossey-Bass.

Murphy, S. M., and Jowdy, D. P. (1992) Imagery and mental practice. In T. S Horn (ed.) *Advances in sport psychology* (pp. 221–250). Champaign, IL: Human Kinetics.

Murphy, S. M., and Martin, K. A. (2002) The use of imagery in sport. In T. Horn (ed.) *Advances in sport psychology* (2nd edn, pp. 405–439). Champaign, IL: Human Kinetics.

Murphy, S. M., Nordin, S., and Cumming, J. (2008) Imagery in sport, exercise, and dance. In T. S. Horn (ed.) *Advances in sport psychology* (3rd edn, pp. 297–324). Champaign, IL: Human Kinetics.

Muscat, J. (2007) Big hitting Roddick has to find his way forward. *The Times,* 26 June, p. 75.

Myers, D., Abell, J., Kolstad, A., and Sani, F. (2010) *Social psychology* (European edn). Maidenhead, Berkshire: McGraw-Hill.

Nadel, L., and Piattelli-Palmarini, M. (2002) What is cognitive science? In L. Nadel (ed.) *Encyclopaedia of cognitive science* (Vol. 1, pp. xiii–xli). London: Nature Publishing Group.

Nadal, R. (2011) Rafael Nadal: my pre-game rituals sharpen my senses before I go into battle. Retrieved from www.telegraph.co.uk/sport/tennis/8703175/Rafael-Nadal-my-pre-game-rituals-sharpen-my-senses-before-I-go-into-battle.html on 24 October 2016.

Naish, J. (2009) Humankind on fast track to a standstill. *Irish Independent,* 18 August, p. 13.

Nakamura, J., and Csikszentmihalyi, M. (2002) The concept of flow. In C. R. Snyder and S. J. Lopez (eds) *Handbook of positive psychology* (pp. 89–105). New York: Oxford University Press.

Nakata, H., Yoshie, M., Miura, A., and Kudo, K. (2010) Characteristics of the athlete's brain: Evidence from neurophysiology and neuroimaging. *Brain Research Reviews, 62,* 197–211.

National Coaching Foundation (1996) *Motivation and mental toughness.* Headingley, Leeds: National Coaching Foundation.

Navon, D., and Gopher, D. (1979) On the economy of the human information-processing system. *Psychological Review, 86,* 214–255.

Navratilova, M. (2009) Martina Navratilova: The grunting has to stop. *Sunday Times,* 7 June. Retrieved from www.timesonline.co.uk/tol/sport/tennis/article6446197.ece on 17 March 2011.

Neil, R., Hanton, S., Mellalieu, S. D., and Fletcher, D. (2011) Competition stress and emotions in sport performers: The role of further appraisals. *Psychology of sport and Exercise, 12,* 460–470.

Neiss, R. (1988) Reconceptualizing arousal: Psychobiological states in motor performance. *Psychological Bulletin, 103,* 345–366.

Neisser, U. (1967) *Cognitive psychology.* New York: Appleton-Century-Crofts.

Nesti, M. (2010) *Psychology in football.* Abingdon, Oxfordshire: Routledge.

Newman, B. (1984) Expediency as benefactor: How team building saves time and gets the job done. *Training and Development Journal, 38,* 26–30.

Newman, P. (2010) The power and the glory. *Irish Independent* (Sport), 6 January, p. 12.

Newman, P. (2015) Australian Open 2015: Andy Murray left frustrated by repeated Novak Djokovic 'distractions' in final defeat. *Independent.* Retrieved from http://www.independent.co.uk/sport/tennis/australian-open-2015-andy-murray-left-frustrated-by-repeated-novak-djokovic-distractions-in-final-10016824.html on 08 November 2016.

Nicholas, M. (2002) Control freak Faldo gives pointer to Hussain's men. *The Daily Telegraph* (Sport), 9 December, p. S6.

Nicholls, A. R., and Polman, R. C. J. (2007) Coping in sport: A systematic review. *Journal of Sports Sciences, 25,* 11–31.

Nicholls, A. R., and Ntoumanis, N. (2010) Traditional and new methods of assessing coping in sport. In A. R. Nicholls (ed) *Coping in Sport: Theory, Methods, and Related Constructs* (pp. 35–51). New York: Nova Science Inc.

Nicholls, A. R., and Levy, A. R. (2016) The road to London 2012: The lived stressor, emotion, and coping experiences of gymnasts preparing for and competing at the World Championships. *International Journal of Sport and Exercise Psychology, 14*, 255–267.

Nicholls, A. R., Holt, N. L., Polman, R. C., and James, D. W. G. (2005) Stress and coping among international adolescent golfers. *Journal of Applied Sport Psychology, 17*, 333–340.

Nicholls, A. R., Polman, R., Levy, A. R., Taylor, J., and Cobley, S. (2007) Stressors, coping, and coping effectiveness: Gender, type of sport, and skill differences. *Journal of Sports Sciences, 25*, 1521–1530.

Nicholls, A. R., Polman, R. C., Levy, A. R., and Hulleman, J. (2012) An explanation for the fallacy of facilitative anxiety: Stress, emotions, coping, and subjective performance in sport. *International Journal of Sport Psychology, 43*, 273–293.

Nicholls, A. R., Perry, J. L., Jones, L., Morley, D., and Carson, F. (2013) Dispositional coping, coping effectiveness, and cognitive social maturity among adolescent athletes. *Journal of Sport and Exercise Psychology, 35*, 229–238.

Nicholls, A. R., Levy, A. R., and Perry, J. L. (2015) Emotional maturity, dispositional coping, and coping effectiveness among adolescent athletes. *Psychology of Sport and Exercise, 17*, 32–39.

Nicholls, J. G. (1984) Achievement motivation: Conceptions of ability, subjective experience, task choice, and performance. *Psychological Review, 91*, 328–346.

Nicholls, J. G. (1989) *The competitive ethos and democratic education.* Cambridge, MA: Harvard University Press.

Nicholls, J. G. (1992) The general and the specific in the development and expression of achievement motivation. In G. Roberts (ed.) *Motivation in sport and exercise* (pp. 31–56). Champaign, IL: Human Kinetics.

Nichols, P. (2000) Ice-man Faulds keeps his cool. *The Guardian* (Sport), 21 September, p. 7.

Nideffer, R. M. (1976) Test of Attentional and Interpersonal Style. *Journal of Personality and Social Psychology, 34*, 394–404.

Nideffer, R. M., Sagal, M.-S., Lowry, M., and Bond, J. (2001) Identifying and developing world-class performers. In G. Tenenbaum (ed.) *The practice of sport psychology* (pp. 129–144). Morgantown, WV: Fitness Information Technology.

Nieuwenhuys, A., and Oudejans, R. R. (2012) Anxiety and perceptual-motor performance: Toward an integrated model of concepts, mechanisms, and processes. *Psychological Research, 76*, 747–759.

Nieuwenhuys, A., Vos, L., Pijpstra, S., and Bakker, F. C. (2011) Meta experiences and coping effectiveness in sport. *Psychology of Sport and Exercise, 12*, 135–143.

Nisbett, R. E., and Wilson, T. D. (1977) Telling more than we can know: Verbal reports on mental processes. *Psychological Review, 84*, 231–259.

Norrish, M. (2009) Andrei Arshavin's feat throws spotlight on ultimate case of monkey business. *The Daily Telegraph*, 11 April. Retrieved from www.telegraph.co.uk/sport/football/teams/arsenal/5202158/Andrei-Arshavins-feat-throws-spotlight-on-ultimate-case-of-monkey-business.html on 10 September 2010.

Northcroft, J. (2009) They shall not pass. *The Sunday Times* (Sport), 8 February, pp. 12–13.

Northcroft, J., and Walsh, D. (2010) England: The team that never was. *The Sunday Times* (Sport), 4 July, pp. 6–7.

Ntoumanis, N., Biddle, S., and Haddock, G. (1999) The mediating role of coping strategies on the relationship between achievement motivation and affect in sport. *Anxiety, Stress and Coping, 12*, 299–327.

Ntoumanis, N., Edmunds, J., and Duda, J. L. (2009) Understanding the coping process from a self-determination theory perspective. *British Journal of Health Psychology, 14*, 249–260.

Nyberg, G. (2015) Developing a "somatic velocimeter" – the practical knowledge of freeskiers. *Qualitative Research in Sport, Exercise and Health, 7*, 109–124.

Oaten, M., and Cheng, K. (2006) Improved self-control: The benefits of a regular program of academic study. *Basic and Applied Social Psychology, 28*, 1–16.

O'Connell, D. G., Hinman, M. R., Hearne, K. F., Michael, Z. S., and Nixon, S. L. (2014) The effects of "grunting" on serve and forehand velocities in collegiate tennis players. *The Journal of Strength and Conditioning Research, 28,* 3469–3475.

Öhman, A., Hamm, A., and Hugdahl, K. (2000) Cognition and the autonomic nervous system: Orienting, anticipation, and conditioning. In J. T. Cacioppo, L. G. Tassinary and G. G. Bernston (eds) *Handbook of psychophysiology* (2nd edn, pp. 533–575). Cambridge: Cambridge University Press.

O'Leary-Kelly, A. M., Martocchio, J. J., and Frink, D. D. (1994) A review of the influence of group goals on group performance. *Academy of Management Journal, 37,* 1285–1301.

Oliver, J. (2010) Ethical practice in sport psychology: Challenges in the real world. In S. J. Hanrahan and M. B. Andersen (eds) *Routledge handbook of applied sport psychology* (pp. 60–68). Abingdon, Oxfordshire: Routledge.

Olusoga, P., Butt, J., Maynard, I., and Hays, K. (2010) Stress and coping: A study of world-class coaches. *Journal of Applied Sport Psychology, 22,* 274–293.

O'Neill, D. F. (2008) Injury contagion in alpine ski racing: The effect of injury on teammates' performance. *Journal of Clinical Sport Psychology, 2,* 278–292.

Onions, C. T. (ed.) (1996) *The Oxford dictionary of English etymology.* Oxford: Clarendon.

Ontennis.com (2016) Djokovic: Nerves are normal. Retrieved from http://ontennis.com/news/djokovic-nerves-are-normal on 28 November 2016.

Orbach, I., Singer, R., and Price, S. (1999) An attribution training programme and achievement in sport. *Sport Psychologist, 13,* 69–82.

Orliaguet, J. P., and Coello, Y. (1998) Differences between actual and imagined putting movements in golf: A chronometric analysis. *International Journal of Sport Psychology, 29,* 157–169.

Orlick, T. (1986) *Psyching for sport: Mental training for athletes.* Champaign, IL: Human Kinetics.

Orlick, T. (1990) *In pursuit of excellence.* Champaign, IL: Leisure Press.

Orne, M. T. (1962) On the social psychology of the psychological experiment: With particular reference to demand characteristics and their implications. *American Psychologist, 17,* 776–783.

O'Rourke, D. J., Smith, R. E., Smoll, F. L., and Cumming, S. P. (2014) Relations of parent- and coach-initiated motivational climates to young athletes' self-esteem, performance anxiety, and autonomous motivation: Who is more influential? *Journal of Applied Sport Psychology, 26,* 395–408.

O'Shea, H., and Moran, A. (2016) Chronometric and pupil-size measurements illuminate the relationship between motor execution and motor imagery in expert pianists. *Psychology of Music, 44,* 1289–1303.

O'Sullivan, J. (2002a) Captain steers a steady ship. *The Irish Times,* 26 September, p. 19.

O'Sullivan, J. (2002b) Clark shows his strength as he leads from the front. *The Irish Times* (Sport), 30 September, p. 4.

O'Sullivan, J. (2010) "The Power" still has that driving force. *The Irish Times* (Sport), 15 September, p. 6.

Otten, M. (2009) Choking vs clutch performance: A study of sport performance under pressure. *Journal of Sport and Exercise Psychology, 31,* 583–601.

Oudejans, R. R. D., and Pijpers, J. R. (2010) Training with mild anxiety may prevent choking under higher levels of anxiety. *Psychology of Sport and Exercise, 11,* 44–50.

Owen, O. (2010) "I'd rather quit than be Ferrari's No. 2 driver" – Massa. *The Guardian* (Sport), 30 July, p. 8.

Oxendine, J. B. (1984) *Psychology of motor learning.* Englewood Cliffs, NJ: Prentice-Hall.

Pain, M., and Harwood, C. (2009) Team building through mutual sharing and open discussion of team functioning. *Sport Psychologist, 23,* 523–542.

Paivio, A. (1985) Cognitive and motivational functions of imagery in human performance. *Canadian Journal of Applied Sport Science, 10,* 22–28.

Palmeri, T. J. (2002) Automaticity. In L. Nadel (ed.) *Encyclopaedia of cognitive science* (Vol. 1, pp. 290–301). London: Nature Publishing Group.

Panchuk, D., and Vickers, J. N. (2013) Expert visual perception: Why having a quiet eye matters in sport. In D. Farrow, J. Baker and C. MacMahon (eds) *Developing expertise in sport: Researchers and coaches put theory into practice* (2nd edn, pp. 195–209). Abingdon, Oxfordshire: Routledge.

Papaxanthis, C., Pozzo, T., Kasprinski, R., and Berthoz, A. (2003) Comparison of actual and imagined execution of whole-body movements after a long exposure to microgravity. *Neuroscience Letters, 339,* 41–44.

Parfitt, G., Hardy, L. and Pates, J. (1995) Somatic anxiety, physiological arousal and performance: Differential effects upon a high anaerobic, low memory demand task. *International Journal of Sport Psychology, 26,* 196–213.

Park, J. L., Fairweather, M. M., and Donaldson, D. I. (2015) Making the case for mobile cognition: EEG and sports performance. *Neuroscience & Biobehavioural Reviews, 52,* 117–130.

Parkes, J. F., and Mallett, C. J. (2011) Developing mental toughness: Attributional style retraining in rugby. *The Sport Psychologist, 25,* 269–287.

Pascarella, E. T. (1999) The development of critical thinking: Does college make a difference? *Journal of College Student Development, 40,* 562–569.

Pashler, H. (ed.) (1998) *Attention.* Hove, East Sussex: Psychology Press.

Passer, M. P., Smith, R., Holt, N., Bremner, A., Sutherland, E., and Vliek, M. L. W. (2009) *Psychology: The science of mind and behaviour* (European edn). London: McGraw-Hill.

Pearson, J. (2014). New directions in mental imagery research: The binocular rivalry technique and decoding fMRI patterns. *Current Directions in Psychological Science, 23,* 178–183.

Pearson, J., and Kosslyn, S. (2015) The heterogeneity of mental representation: Ending the imagery debate. *Proceedings of the National Academy of Sciences, 112,* 10089–10092.

Pearson, J., Naselaris, T., Holmes, E. A., and Kosslyn, S. M. (2015) Mental imagery: Functional mechanisms and clinical application. *Trends in Cognitive Sciences, 29,* 590–602.

Pelé (2006) Pelé, my story. *The Guardian* (Sport), 13 May, p. 8.

Perkins, D., Wilson, G. V., and Kerr, J. H. (2001) The effects of elevated arousal and mood on maximal strength performance in athletes. *Journal of Applied Sport Psychology, 13,* 239–259.

Perry, H. M. (1939) The relative efficiency of actual and imaginary practice in five selected tasks. *Archives of Psychology, 34,* 5–75.

Perry, J. (2007) *Rogues, rotters, rascals and cheats: The greatest sporting scandals.* London: John Blake.

Pescosolido, A. T., and Saavedra, R. (2012) Cohesion and sports teams: A review. *Small Group Research, 43,* 744–758.

Peters, H. J., and Williams, J. M. (2009) Rationale for developing a cultural sport psychology. In R. J. Schinke and S. J. Hanrahan (eds) *Cultural sport psychology* (pp. 13–21). Champaign, IL: Human Kinetics.

Peterson, C., Semmel, A., Von Baeyer, C., Abramson, Y. L., Metalsky, G. I., and Seligman, M. E. P. (1982) The Attributional Style Questionnaire. *Cognitive Therapy and Research, 6,* 287–299.

Peterson, C., Buchanan, G. M., and Seligman, M. E. P. (1995) Explanatory style: History and evolution of the field. In G. M. Buchanan and M. E. P. Seligman (eds) *Explanatory style* (pp. 1–20). Hillsdale, NJ: Lawrence Erlbaum Associates.

Petitmengin, C. (2006) Describing one's subjective experience in the second person: An interview method for the science of consciousness. *Phenomenology and the Cognitive Sciences, 5,* 229–269.

Phelps, M. (2008a) Why pain and disorder led to an iron will to win. *The Guardian* (Sport), 13 December, p. 10.

Phelps, M. (2008b) Perfect physique to rule the pool. *The Guardian* (Sport), 13 December, p. 10.

Philbeck, J. W., and Witt, J. K. (2015) Action-specific influences on perception and post-perceptual processes: Present controversies and future directions. *Psychological Bulletin, 141,* 1120–1144.

Pijpers, J. R., Oudejans, R. R. D., Holsheimer, F., and Bakker, F. C. (2003) Anxiety-performance relationships in climbing: A process-oriented approach. *Psychology of Sport and Exercise, 4,* 283–304.

Pijpers, J. R., Oudejans, R. R., and Bakker, F. C. (2005) Anxiety-induced changes in movement behaviour during the execution of a complex whole-body task. *The Quarterly Journal of Experimental Psychology Section A, 58*, 421–445.

Piquado, T., Isaacowitz, D., and Wingfield, A. (2010) Pupillometry as a measure of cognitive effort in younger and older adults. *Psychophysiology, 47*, 560–569.

Porter, G., Troscianko, T., and Gilchrist, I. D. (2007) Effort during visual search and counting: Insights from pupillometry. *The Quarterly Journal of Experimental Psychology, 60*, 211–229.

Posner, M. I. (1980) Orienting of attention: The VIIth Sir Frederic Bartlett lecture. *Quarterly Journal of Experimental Psychology, 32A*, 3–25.

Posner, M. I., and Rothbart, M. K. (2007) Research on attention networks as a model for the integration of psychological science. *Annual Review of Psychology, 58*, 1–23.

Potter, J., and Wiggins, S. (2007) Discursive psychology. In C. Willig and W. Stainton-Rogers (eds) *Handbook of qualitative research in psychology* (pp. 73–90). London: SAGE.

Prapavessis, H., Carron, A. V., and Spink, K. S. (1996) Team building in sport. *International Journal of Sport Psychology, 27*, 269–285.

Proffitt, D. R. (2006) Embodied perception and the economy of action. *Perspectives on Psychological Science, 1*, 110–122.

Proffitt, D. R., and Linkenauger, S. A. (2013) Perception viewed as a phenotypic expression. In W. Prinz, M. Beisert and A. Herwig (eds) *Action science: Foundations of an emerging discipline* (pp. 171–197). Cambridge, MA: MIT Press.

Pylyshyn, Z. (1973) What the mind's eye tells the mind's brain. *Psychological Bulletin, 80*, 1–24.

Pylyshyn, Z. (1981) The imagery debate: Analogue media versus tacit knowledge. *Psychological Review, 88*, 16–45.

Quested, E., and Duda, J. L. (2010) Exploring the social-environmental determinants of well- and ill-being in dancers: A test of basic needs theory. *Journal of Sport and Exercise Psychology, 32*, 39–60.

Raab, M., and Harwood, C. G. (2015) Special issue: The development of expertise and excellence in sport psychology. *Psychology of Sport and Exercise, 16*, 1–136.

Radlo, S. J., Steinberg, G. M., Singer, R. N., Barba, D. A., and Melnikov, A. (2002) The influence of an attentional focus strategy on alpha brain wave activity, heart rate, and dart-throwing performance. *International Journal of Sport Psychology, 33*, 205–217.

Ram, N., Starek, J., and Johnson, J. (2004) Race, ethnicity, and sexual orientation: Still a void in sport and exercise psychology. *Journal of Sport and Exercise Psychology, 26*, 250–268.

Ramsey, R., Cumming, J., and Edwards, M. G. (2008) Exploring a modified conceptualisation of imagery direction and golf putting performance. *International Journal of Sport and Exercise Psychology, 6*, 207–223.

Rand, B. (2015) Jordan Spieth: On what the zone feels like. Retrieved from www.eyeonthetour.com/?p=18511 on 24 October 2016.

Ravn, S., and Christensen, M. K. (2014) Listening to the body? How phenomenological insights can be used to explore a golfer's experience of the physicality of her body. *Qualitative Research in Sport, Exercise and Health, 6*, 462–477.

Ray, C. (2003a) Steel wire tales land Straeuli in hot water. *The Irish Times* (Sport), 22 November, p. 8.

Ray, C. (2003b) Straeuli given one week to explain away Camp Barbed-Wire. *The Guardian*, 28 November. Retrieved from www.guardian.co.uk/sport/2003/nov/28/rugbyworldcup2003.rugbyunion on 10 September 2010.

Reed, C. L. (2002) Chronometric comparisons of imagery to action: Visualizing versus physically performing springboard dives. *Memory and Cognition, 30*, 1169–1178.

Rees, T., and Freeman, P. (2009) Social support moderates the relationship between stressors and task performance through self-efficacy. *Journal of Social and Clinical Psychology, 28*, 244–263.

Rees, T., and Freeman, P. (2010) Social support and performance in a golf-putting experiment. *Sport Psychologist, 24*, 333–348.

Rees, T., and Freeman, P. (2012) Coping in sport through social support. In D. Lavallee, J. Thatcher and M. Jones (eds) *Coping and emotion in sport* (pp. 102–117). London: Wiley.

Rees, T., Ingledew, D. K., and Hardy, L. (2005) Attribution in sport psychology: Seeking congruence between theory, research and practice. *Psychology of Sport and Exercise, 6,* 189–204.

Reeves, C. W., Nicholls, A. R., and McKenna, J. (2011) The effects of a coping intervention on coping self-efficacy, coping effectiveness, and subjective performance among adolescent soccer players. *International Journal of Sport and Exercise Psychology, 9,* 126–142.

Reid, A. (2002) Subtle captaincy gave Europe edge. *The Sunday Times* (Sport), 6 October, p. 22.

Reid, M., and Schneiker, K. (2008) Strength and conditioning in tennis: Current research and practice. *Journal of Science and Medicine in Sport, 11,* 248–256.

Reisberg, D. (1985) Meta-attention: Do we know when we are being distracted? *Journal of General Psychology, 112,* 291–306.

Reisberg, D. (2013) Mental images. In D. Reisberg (ed.) *The Oxford handbook of cognitive psychology* (pp. 374–387). Oxford: Oxford University Press.

Reisberg, D. (2016) *Cognition* (6th edn). New York: W. W. Norton.

Reiser, M., Busch, D., and Munzert, J. (2011). Strength gains by motor imagery with different ratios of physical to mental practice. *Frontiers in Psychology, 2*:194, 1–8.

Rensink, R. A. (2013) Perception and attention. In D. Reisberg (ed.) *The Oxford handbook of cognitive psychology* (pp. 97–116). Oxford: Oxford University Press.

Rettew, D., and Reivich, K. (1995) Sports and explanatory style. In G. M. Buchanan and M. E. P. Seligman (eds) *Explanatory style* (pp. 73–185). Hillsdale, NJ: Lawrence Erlbaum Associates.

Reynolds, T. (2015) How has North Korea become a weightlifting superpower? Retrieved from www.bbc.co.uk/sport/weightlifting/34768507 on 24 October 2016.

Richards, H. (2012) Coping processes in sport. In D. Lavallee, J. Thatcher and M. Jones (eds) *Coping and emotion in sport* (pp. 1–32). London: Wiley.

Richardson, A. (1967a) Mental practice: A review and discussion, Part I. *Research Quarterly, 38,* 95–107.

Richardson, A. (1967b) Mental practice: A review and discussion, Part II. *Research Quarterly, 38,* 263–273.

Richardson, J. T. E. (1999) *Imagery.* Hove, East Sussex: Psychology Press.

Ridderinkhof, K. R., and Brass, M. (2015) How kinaesthetic motor imagery works: A predictive-processing theory of visualization in sports and motor expertise. *Journal of Physiology – Paris, 109,* 53–63.

Rienhoff, R., Fischer, L., Strauss, B., Baker, J., and Schorer, J. (2015) Focus of attention influences quiet-eye behaviour: An exploratory investigation of different skill levels in female basketball players. *Sport, Exercise, and Performance Psychology, 4,* 62–74.

Ring, C., Cooke, A., Kavussanu, M., McIntyre, D., and Masters, R. (2015) Investigating the efficacy of neurofeedback training for expediting expertise and excellence in sport. *Psychology of Sport and Exercise, 16,* 118–127.

Robazza, C., Bortoli, L., and Hanin, Y. (2004) Precompetition emotions, bodily symptoms, and task-specific qualities as predictors of performance in high-level karate athletes. *Journal of Applied Sport Psychology, 16,* 151–165.

Robazza, C., Pellizzari, M., Bertollo, M., and Hanin, Y. L. (2008) Functional impact of emotions on athletic performance: Comparing the IZOF model and the directional perception approach. *Journal of Sports Sciences, 26,* 1033–1047.

Roberts, G. C. (2001) Understanding the dynamics of motivation in physical activity: The influence of achievement goals on motivational processes. In G. C. Roberts (ed.) *Advances in motivation in sport and exercise* (pp. 1–50). Champaign, IL: Human Kinetics.

Roberts, G. C., and Kristiansen, E. (2010) Motivation and goal-setting. In S. J. Hanrahan and M. B. Andersen (eds) *Routledge handbook of applied sport psychology* (pp. 490–499). Abingdon, Oxfordshire: Routledge.

Roberts, G. C., Treasure, D. C., and Balague, G. (1998) Achievement goals in sport: The development and validation of the Perceptions of Success Questionnaire. *Journal of Sports Sciences, 16,* 337–347.

Roberts, G. C., Treasure, D. C., and Conroy, D. (2007) Understanding the dynamics of motivation in sport: An achievement goal orientation. In G. Tenenbaum and R. C. Eklund (eds) *Handbook of sport psychology* (3rd edn, pp. 3–30). New York: Wiley.

Roberts, R., Callow, N., Hardy, L., Markland, D., and Bringer, J. (2008) Movement imagery ability: Development and assessment of a revised version of the Vividness of Movement Imagery Questionnaire. *Journal of Sport and Exercise Psychology, 30,* 200–221.

Roberts, R., Woodman, T., Lofthouse, S., and Williams, L. (2015) Not all players are equally motivated: The role of narcissism. *European Journal of Sport Science, 15,* 536–542.

Robertson, I. (2002) *The mind's eye: An essential guide to boosting your mental power.* London: Bantam.

Robinson, D. W., and Howe, B. L. (1987) Causal attribution and mood state relationships of soccer players in a sport achievement setting. *Journal of Sport Behaviour, 10,* 137–146.

Rogers, T. M., and Landers, D. M. (2005) Mediating effects of peripheral vision in the life event stress/athletic injury relationship. *Journal of Sport and Exercise Psychology, 27,* 271–288.

Roland, P. E., and Friberg, L. (1985) Localization of cortical areas activated by thinking. *Journal of Neurophysiology, 53,* 1219–1243.

Romeas, T., Guldner, A., and Faubert, J. (2016) 3D-multiple object tracking training task improves passing decision making accuracy in soccer players. *Psychology of Sport and Exercise, 22,* 1–9.

Ronay, B. (2008) Absolute power. *The Guardian,* 25 September. Retrieved from www.guardian.co.uk/sport/2008/sep/25/darts.sportinterviews on 4 September 2011.

Ronay, B. (2010) You only get one chance. *The Guardian* (G2), 6 August, pp. 6–9.

Roseman, I. J. (1991) Appraisal determinants of discrete emotions. *Cognition and Emotion, 5,* 161–200.

Ross, P. E. (2006) The expert mind. *Scientific American, 295,* 64–71.

Rossano, M. J. (2003) Expertise and the evolution of consciousness. *Cognition, 89,* 207–236.

Rostami, R., Sadeghi, H., Karami, K. A., Abadi, M. N., and Salamati, P. (2012) The effects of neurofeedback on the improvement of rifle shooters' performance. *Journal of Neurotherapy, 16,* 264–269.

Rovio, E., Eskola, J., Kozub, S. A., Duda, J. L., and Lintunen, T. (2009) Can high group cohesion be harmful? A case study of a junior ice-hockey team. *Small Group Research, 40,* 421–435.

Rowe, R., Horswill, M. S., Kronvall-Parkinson, M., Poulter, D. R., and McKenna, F. (2009) The effect of disguise on novice and expert tennis players' anticipation ability. *Journal of Applied Sport Psychology, 21,* 178–185.

Rozelle, R. M., and Campbell, D. T. (1969) More plausible rival hypotheses in the cross-lagged panel correlation technique. *Psychological Bulletin, 71,* 74–80.

Rueda, M. R., Checa, P., and Combita, L. M. (2012) Enhanced efficiency of the executive attention network after training in preschool children: Immediate changes and effects after two months. *Developmental Cognitive Neuroscience, 2,* S192–S204.

Ruthsatz, J., Ruthsatz, K. S., and Ruthsatz-Stephens, K. (2014) Putting practice into perspective: Child prodigies as evidence of innate talent. *Intelligence, 45,* 60–65.

Ryan, R. M., and Deci, E. L. (2000) Self-determination theory and the facilitation of intrinsic motivation, social development, and well-being. *American Psychologist, 55,* 68–78.

Ryan, R. M., and Deci, E. L. (2007) Active human nature: Self-determination theory and the promotion and maintenance of sport, exercise, and health. In M. S. Hagger and N. L. D. Chatzisarantis (eds) *Intrinsic motivation and self-determination in exercise and sport* (pp. 1–19). Champaign, IL: Human Kinetics.

Ryle, G. (1949) *The concept of mind.* London: Hutchinson's Universal Library.

Sackett, R. S. (1934) The influence of symbolic rehearsal upon the retention of a maze habit. *Journal of General Psychology, 10,* 376–395.

Sackett, R. S. (1935) The relationship between amount of symbolic rehearsal and retention of a maze habit. *Journal of General Psychology, 13,* 113–128.

Sagar, S., Lavallee, D., and Spray, C. M. (2007) Why young athletes fear failure: Consequences of failure. *Journal of Sports Sciences, 25,* 1171–1184.

Saimpont, A., Malouin, F., Tousignant, B., and Jackson, P. K. (2015) Assessing motor imagery ability in younger and older adults by combining measures of vividness, controllability, and timing of motor imagery. *Brain Research, 1597,* 196–209.

Salas, E., Grossman, R., Hughes, A. M., and Coultas, C. (2015) Measuring team cohesion: Observations from the science. *Human Factors, 57,* 365–374.

Salmon, P., Hanneman, S., and Harwood, B. (2010) Associative/dissociative cognitive strategies in sustained physical activity: Literature review and proposal for a mindfulness-based conceptual model. *Sport Psychologist, 24,* 127–156.

Samson, A., Simpson, D., Kamphoff, C., and Langlier, A. (2015) Think aloud: An examination of distance runners' thought processes. *International Journal of Sport and Exercise Psychology,* Epub ahead of print.

Samulski, D. M. (2008) Editor's note: Counselling Olympic athletes. *International Journal of Sport and Exercise Psychology, 6,* 251–253.

Sarkar, M., Hill, D. M., and Parker, A. (2014) Working with religious and spiritual athletes. Ethical considerations for sport psychologists. *Psychology of Sport and Exercise, 15,* 580–587.

Sarkar, P. (2002) Olympic champion falls to earth and retires. *The Guardian* (Sport), 23 November, p.16.

Sarter, M., Gehring, W. J., and Kozak, R. (2006) More attention must be paid: The neurobiology of attentional effort. *Brain Research Reviews, 51,* 145–160.

Sauvage, C. Jissendi, P., Seignan, S., Manto, M., and Habas, C. (2013) Brain areas involved in the control of speed during a motor sequence of the foot: Real movement versus mental imagery. *Journal of Neuroradiology, 40,* 267–280.

Savelsbergh, G. J. P., van der Kamp, J., Williams, A. M., and Ward, P. (2005) Anticipation and visual search behaviour in expert soccer goalkeepers. *Ergonomics, 48,* 1686–1697.

Scanlan, T. K., and Simons, J. P. (1992) The construct of sport enjoyment. In G. C. Roberts (ed.) *Motivation in sport and exercise* (pp. 199–215). Champaign, IL: Human Kinetics.

Scanlan, T. K., Stein, G. L., and Ravizza, K. (1989) An in-depth study of former elite figure skaters: II. Sources of enjoyment. *Journal of Sport and Exercise Psychology, 11,* 54–64.

Scanlan, T. K., Carpenter, P. J., Lobel, M., and Simons, J. P. (1993) Sources of enjoyment for youth sport athletes. *Pediatric Exercise Science, 5,* 275–285.

Schellenberg, B. J., Gaudreau, P., and Crocker, P. R. (2013) Passion and coping: Relationships with changes in burnout and goal attainment in collegiate volleyball players. *Journal of Sport and Exercise Psychology, 35,* 270–280.

Schiavio, A., and Altenmüller, E. (2015) Exploring music-based rehabilitation for Parkinsonism through embodied cognitive science. *Frontiers in Neurology, 6,* 10.

Schinke, R. J., and Hanrahan, S. J. (eds) (2009) *Cultural sport psychology.* Champaign, IL: Human Kinetics.

Schinke, R. J., and McGannon, K. R. (2015) Cultural sport psychology and intersecting identities: An introduction to the special section. *Psychology of Sport and Exercise, 17,* 45–47.

Schinke, R. J., Michel, G., Danielson, R., and Gauthier, A. (2005) Introduction to cultural sport psychology (special issue). *Athletic Insight, 7.* Retrieved from http://www.athleticinsight.com/Vol7Iss3/IntroductionCulturalSportPsychology.htm on 24 October 2016.

Schinke, R. J., Blodgett, A., McGannon, K. R., and Ge, Y. (2016) Finding one's footing on foreign soil: A composite vignette of elite athlete acculturation. *Psychology of Sport and Exercise, 25,* 36–43.

Schinke, R. J., McGannon, K. R., and Smith, B. (2016) (eds) *Routledge international handbook of sport psychology.* London: Routledge.

Schippers, M. C., and Van Lange, P. A. (2006) The psychological benefits of superstitious rituals in top sport: A study among top sportspersons. *Journal of Applied Social Psychology, 36,* 2532–2553.

Schmid, A., and Peper, E. (1998) Strategies for training concentration. In J. M. Williams (ed.) *Applied sport psychology: Personal growth to peak performance* (3rd edn, pp. 316–328). Mountain View, CA: Mayfield.

Schmidt, R. A., and Lee, T. D. (1999) *Motor control and learning: A behavioural emphasis* (3rd edn). Champaign, IL: Human Kinetics.

Schmidt, U., McGuire, R., Humphrey, S., Williams, G., and Grawer, B. (2005) Team cohesion. In J. Taylor and G. S. Wilson (eds) *Applying sport psychology: Four perspectives* (pp. 171–184). Champaign, IL: Human Kinetics.

Schoenemann, T. J., and Curry, S. (1990) Attributions for successful and unsuccessful health behaviour change. *Basic and Applied Social Psychology, 11,* 421–431.

Schorer, J., Rienhoff, R., Fischer, L., Overbeck, I., Weiß, C., and Baker, J. (2015) Hastening the acquisition of perceptual skill in volleyball players. *International Journal of Sport Psychology, 46,* 608–629.

Schrader, M. P., and Wann, D. L. (1999) High-risk recreation: The relationship between participant characteristics and degree of involvement. *Journal of Sport Behaviour, 22,* 426–441.

Schuler, J., and Brunner, S. (2009) The rewarding effect of flow experience on performance in a marathon race. *Psychology of Sport and Exercise, 10,* 168–174.

Schuster, C., Hilfiker, R., Amft, O., Scheidhauer, A., Andrews, B., Butler, J., Kischka, U., and Etttlin, T. (2011) Best practice for motor imagery: A systematic literature review on motor imagery training elements in five different disciplines. *BMC Medicine, 9,* 75, open access journal. Retrieved from www.biomedcentral.com/1741–7015/9/75 on 28 September 2011.

Schutz, R. W., Eom, H. J., Smoll, F. L., and Smith, R. E. (1994) Examination of the factorial validity of the Group Environment Questionnaire. *Research Quarterly for Exercise and Sport, 65,* 226–236.

Schwartz, D. (2008) Keeping athletes on track: Brains and brawn. *APA Monitor on Psychology, 39,* 7, 54.

Scully, D., and Hume, A. (1995) Sport psychology: Status, knowledge and use among elite level coaches and performers in Ireland. *Irish Journal of Psychology, 16,* 52–66.

Sebbens, J., Hassmén, P., Crisp, D., and Wensley, K. (2016) Mental Health in Sport (MHS): Improving the early intervention knowledge and confidence of elite sport staff. *Frontiers in Psychology, 7,* 911.

Seiler, B. S., Monsma, E., and Newman-Norlund, R. D. (2015) Biological evidence of imagery abilities: Intra-individual differences. *Journal of Sport and Exercise Psychology, 37,* 421–434.

Seligman, M. E. P. (1998) *Learned optimism: How to change your mind and your life* (2nd edn). New York: Pocket Books.

Seligman, M. E. P., Nolen-Hoeksema, S., Thornton, N., and Thornton, K. M. (1990) Explanatory style as a mechanism of disappointing athletic performance. *Psychological Science, 1,* 143–146.

Selvey, M. (1998) Getting up for the Ashes. *The Guardian* (Sport), 20 November, p. 2.

Senko, C., Hulleman, C. S., and Harackiewicz, J. M. (2011) Achievement goal theory at the crossroads: Old controversies, current challenges and new directions. *Educational Psychology, 46,* 26–47.

Seppa, N. (1996) Psychologists making it to the big leagues. *American Psychological Association Monitor on Psychology, 27,* July, p. 28.

Shannon, C., and Weaver, W. (1949) *The mathematical theory of communication.* Urbana, IL: University of Illinois Press.

Shannon, K. (2008) How a champion uses mind control. *Mad About Sport* (*Sunday Tribune Sports Monthly*), March, p. 46.

Shapcott, K. M., and Carron, A. V. (2010) Development and validation of a Team Attributional Style Questionnaire. *Group Dynamics: Theory, Research, and Practice, 14,* 95–113.

Shapiro, L. (2010) *Embodied cognition.* London: Routledge.

Shaw, D. (2002) Confidence and the pre-shot routine in golf: A case-study. In I. Cockerill (ed.) *Solutions in sport psychology* (pp. 108–119). London: Thomson.

Sheard, M. (2010) *Mental toughness: The mindset behind sporting achievement.* London: Routledge.

Sheehy, T., and Hodge, K. (2015) Motivation and morality in Masters athletes: A self-determination theory perspective. *International Journal of Sport and Exercise Psychology, 13*, 273–285.

Sheeran, P. (2002) Intention-behaviour relations: A conceptual and empirical overview. In W. Stroebe and M. Hewstone (eds) *European Review of Social Psychology* (Vol. 12, pp. 1–36). Chichester, West Sussex: Wiley.

Sheeran, P., and Orbell, S. (1999). Implementation intentions and repeated behaviour: Augmenting the predictive validity of the theory of planned behaviour. *European Journal of Social Psychology, 29*, 349–369.

Shepard, R.N., and Metzler, J. (1971). Mental rotation of three-dimensional objects. *Science, 171 (3972)*, 701–703.

Shields, D. L., and Bredemeier, B. L. (2001) Moral development and behaviour in sport. In R. N. Singer, H. A. Hausenblas and C. M. Janelle (eds) *Handbook of sport psychology* (2nd edn, pp. 585–603). New York: Wiley.

Shields, D. L., and Bredemeier, B. L. (2007) Advances in sport morality research. In G. Tenenbaum and R. C. Eklund (eds) *Handbook of sport psychology* (3rd edn, pp. 662–684). New York: Wiley.

Shields, D. L., LaVoi, N. M., Bredemier, B. L., and Power, F. C. (2007) Predictors of poor sportspersonship in youth sports: Personal attitudes and social influences. *Journal of Sport and Exercise Psychology, 29*, 747–762.

Shields, D. L., Funk, C D., and Bredemeier, B L. (2015) Contesting orientations: Measure construction and the prediction of sportspersonship. *Psychology of Sport and Exercise, 20*, 1–10.

Shontz, L. (1999) Area cyclists line up to share a ride with Spain's Indurain. Retrieved from www.post-gazette.com/sports_headlines/19990602cycle6.asp on 29 April 2003.

Short, S. E., Bruggerman, S. G., Engel, S. G., Marback, T. L., Wang, L. J., Willadsen, A., and Short, M. W. (2002) The effect of imagery function and imagery direction on self-efficacy and performance on a golf-putting task. *Sport Psychologist, 16*, 48–67.

Shusterman, R. (2008) *Body consciousness: A philosophy of mindfulness andsomaesthetics*. Cambridge: Cambridge University Press.

Shusterman, R. (2012) *Thinking through the body: Essays in somaesthetics*. Cambridge: Cambridge University Press.

Sidaway, B., and Trzaska, A. (2005) Can mental practice increase ankle dorsiflexor torque? *Physical Therapy, 85*, 1053–1060.

Simon, H. A., and Gilmartin, K. (1973) A simulation of memory for chess positions. *Cognitive Psychology, 5*, 29–46.

Sinden, J. L. (2010) The normalization of emotion and the disregard of health problems in elite amateur sport. *Journal of Clinical Sport Psychology, 4*, 241–256.

Singer, R. N. (2002) Preperformance state, routines, and automaticity: What does it take to realize expertise in self-paced tasks? *Journal of Sport and Exercise Psychology, 24*, 359–375.

Singer, R. N., Cauragh, J. H., Chen, D., Steinberg, G. M., and Frehlich, S. G. (1996) Visual search, anticipation, and reactive comparisons between highly-skilled and beginning tennis players. *Journal of Applied Sport Psychology, 8*, 9–26.

Sinnamon, S., Moran, A., and O'Connell, M. (2012) Flow among musicians: Measuring peak experiences of student performers. *Journal of Research in Music Education, 60*, 6–25.

Sinnett, S., and Kingstone, A. (2010) A preliminary investigation regarding the effect of tennis grunting: Does white noise during a tennis shot have a negative impact on shot perception? *PloS ONE, 5*, e13148 (doi 10.1371/journal.pone.0013148).

Sinnott, K., and Biddle, S. (1998) Changes in attributions, perceptions of success and intrinsic motivation after attributions in children's sport. *International Journal of Adolescence and Youth, 7*, 137–144.

Skinner, B. F. (1957) *Verbal behaviour*. New York: Appleton-Century-Crofts.

Skolnick, A. (2016) *One breath: Freediving, death and the quest to shatter human limits*. London: Corsoir/Little, Brown Book Group.

Slaney, R. B., Rice, K. G., and Ashby, J. S. (2002) A programmatic approach in measuring perfectionism: The Almost Perfect Scales. In G. L. Flett and P. L. Hewitt (eds) *Perfectionism: Theory, research and treatment* (pp. 63–88). Washington, DC: American Psychological Association.

Slattery, P. (2010) An empirical investigation of expertise and anticipation skills in martial arts and combat sports. Unpublished doctoral dissertation, School of Psychology, University College, Dublin.

Slepian, M. L., Weisbuch, M., Rule, N. O., and Ambady, N. (2011) Tough and tender: Embodied categorization of gender. *Psychological Science, 22,* 26–28.

Smeeton, N., Page, J., Causer, J., Wilson, M., Gay, R., and Williams, M. (2013) The BASES expert statement on the effectiveness of vision training programmes. *The Sport and Exercise Scientist, 38,* 12–13.

Smith, A. M., Adler, C. H., Crews, D., Wharen, R. E., Laskowski, E. E., Barnes, K., Bell, C. V., Pelz, D., Brennan, R. D., Smith, J., Sorenson, M. C., and Kaufman, K. R. (2003) The "yips" in golf: A continuum between a focal dystonia and choking. *Sports Medicine, 33,* 13–31.

Smith, B. (2010) Narrative inquiry: Ongoing conversations and questions for sport and exercise psychology research. *International Review of Sport and Exercise Psychology, 3,* 87–107.

Smith, B., and Sparkes, A. C. (2009) Narrative inquiry in sport and exercise psychology: What can it mean and why might we do it? *Psychology of Sport and Exercise, 1,* 1–11.

Smith, B., Perrier, M.-J., and Martin, J. (2016) Disability in sport: A partial overview and some thoughts about the future. In R. J. Schinke, K. R. McGannon and B. Smith (eds) *Routledge international handbook of sport psychology* (pp. 296–303). London: Routledge.

Smith, D. M. (2016) Neurophysiology of action anticipation in athletes: A systematic review. *Neuroscience & Biobehavioural Reviews, 60,* 115–120.

Smith, E. E., and Kosslyn, S. M. (2007) *Cognitive psychology: Mind and brain* (international edn). Upper Saddle River, NJ: Pearson.

Smith, E. E., and Kosslyn, S. M. (2014) *Cognitive psychology: Mind and brain* (2nd edn). Upper Saddle River, NJ: Pearson.

Smith, E. E., Adams, N. E., and Schorr, D. (1978) Fact retrieval and the paradox of intelligence. *Cognitive Psychology, 10,* 438–464.

Smith, M. (2002) Practice makes perfect. *The Daily Telegraph* (Sport), 15 February, p. S3.

Smith, M. (2003) Keepers focus on the spot. *The Daily Telegraph* (Sport), 13 March, p. S3.

Smith, R. E. (2006) Understanding sport behaviour. *Journal of Applied Sport Psychology, 18,* 1–27.

Smith, R. E., and Smoll, F. L. (2002a) *Way to go, coach! A scientifically-proven approach to coaching effectiveness* (2nd edn). Portola Valley, CA: Warde.

Smith, R. E., and Smoll, F. L. (2002b) Youth sport interventions. In J. Van Raalte and B. Brewer (eds) *Exploring sport and exercise psychology* (2nd edn, pp. 341–371). Washington, DC: American Psychological Association.

Smith, R. E., Smoll, F. L., and Schutz, R. W. (1990) Measurement and correlates of sport-specific cognitive and somatic trait anxiety: The Sport Anxiety Scale. *Anxiety Research, 2,* 263–280.

Smith, R. E., Smoll, F. L., and Wiechman, S. A. (1998) Measurement of trait anxiety in sport. In J. L. Duda (ed.) *Advances in sport and exercise psychology measurement* (pp. 105–127). Morgantown, WV: Fitness Information Technology.

Smith, R. E., Smoll, F. L., Cumming, S. P., and Grossbard, J. R. (2006) Measurement of multidimensional sport performance anxiety in children and adults: The Sport Anxiety Scale-2. *Journal of Sport and Exercise Psychology, 28,* 479–501.

Smoll, F. L., and Smith, R. E. (2005) *Sports and your child: Developing champions in sport and life* (2nd edn). Palo Alto, CA: Warde.

Smoll, F. L., and Smith, R. E. (2010) Conducting psychologically oriented coach-training programs: A social-cognitive approach. In J. M. Williams (ed.) *Applied sport psychology: Personal growth to peak performance* (6th edn, pp. 392–416). Boston, MA: McGraw-Hill.

Smyth, C. (2009) How darts players can help children to aim higher in job market. *The Times*, 8 January, p. 15.

Soberlak, P., and Côté, J. (2003) The developmental activities of elite ice hockey players. *Journal of Applied Sport Psychology, 15,* 41–49.

Son, V., Jackson, B., Grove, J. R., and Feltz, D. L. (2011) "I am" versus "we are": Effects of distinctive variants of self-talk on efficacy beliefs and motor performance. *Journal of Sports Sciences, 29,* 1417–1424.

Southgate, G. (2010) We are breeding players that are looking for excuses. *The Sunday Times* (Sport), 4 July p. 7.

Sparkes, A., and Smith, B. (2014) *Qualitative research methods in sport, exercise and health. From process to product.* Abingdon, Oxfordshire: Routledge.

Spielberger, C. S. (1966) Theory and research on anxiety. In C. S. Spielberger (ed.) *Anxiety and behaviour* (pp. 3–20). New York: Academic Press.

Spink, K. S. (1990) Collective efficacy in the sport setting. *International Journal of Sport Psychology, 21,* 380–395.

Spink, K. S. (2014) Team building. In R. C. Eklund and G. Tenenbaum (eds) *Encyclopedia of sport and exercise psychology* (Vol. 2, pp. 740–743). New York: SAGE.

Spink, K. S., Wilson, K. S., and Odnokon, P. (2010) Examining the relationship between cohesion and return to team in elite athletes. *Psychology of Sport and Exercise, 11,* 6–11.

Spink, K. S., Ulvick, J. D., McLaren, C. D., Crozier, A. J., and Fesser, K. (2015) Effects of groupness and cohesion on intention to return in sport. *Sport, Exercise, and Performance Psychology, 4,* 293–302.

Standage, M. (2012) Motivation: Self-determination theory and performance in sport. In S. M. Murphy (ed.) *The Oxford handbook of sport and performance psychology* (pp. 233–249). Oxford: Oxford University Press.

Standage, M., Gillison, F. B., and Emm, L. (2014) Self-determination theory. In R. C. Eklund and G. Tenenbaum (eds) *Encyclopedia of sport and exercise psychology* (Vol. 2, pp. 629–632). London: SAGE.

Stanley, D. M., Lane, A. M., Beedie, C. J., Friesen, A. P., and Devonport, T. J. (2012) Emotion regulation strategies used in the hour before running. *International Journal of Sport and Exercise Psychology, 10,* 159–171.

Staph, J. (2011) Usain Bolt's key to explosive starts. Retrieved from www.stack.com/a/usain-bolts-key-to-explosive-starts on 24 October 2016.

Stapleton, A. B., Hankes, D. M., Hays, K. F., and Parham, W. D. (2010) Ethical dilemmas in sport psychology: A dialogue on the unique aspects impacting practice. *Professional Psychology: Research and Practice, 41,* 143–152.

Starkes, J. (2000) The road to expertise: Is practice the only determinant? *International Journal of Sport Psychology, 31,* 431–451.

Starkes, J. (2001) The road to expertise: Can we shorten the journey and lengthen the stay? In A. Papaionnaou, M. Goudas and Y. Theodorakis (eds) *Proceedings of International Society of Sport Psychology's 10th World Congress of Sport Psychology* (Vol. 3, pp. 198–205). Thessaloniki, Greece: Christodoulidi.

Starkes, J. L., and Ericsson, K. A. (eds) (2003) *Expert performance in sports: Advances in research on sport expertise.* Champaign, IL: Human Kinetics.

Starkes, J. L., Deakin, J. M., Allard, F. M., Hodges, N. J., and Hayes, A. (1996) Deliberate practice in sports: What is it anyway? In K. A. Ericsson (ed.) *The road to excellence: The acquisition of expert performance in the arts and sciences, sports and games* (pp. 81–106). Mahwah, NJ: Lawrence Erlbaum Associates.

Starkes, J. L., Helsen, W., and Jack, R. (2001) Expert performance in sport and dance. In R. N. Singer, H. A. Hausenblas and C. M. Janelle (eds) *Handbook of sport psychology* (2nd edn, pp. 174–201). New York: Wiley.

Statler, T. (2010) Developing a shared identity/vision: Benefits and pitfalls. In S. J. Hanrahan and M. B. Andersen (eds) *Routledge handbook of applied sport psychology* (pp. 325–334). Abingdon, Oxfordshire: Routledge.

Steca, P., Norcini Pala, A., Greco, A., Monzani, D., and d'Addario, M. (2013) A psychometric evaluation of the Group Environment Questionnaire in a sample of professional basketball and soccer players. *Perceptual and Motor Skills, 116,* 262–271.

Stoeber, J., and Stoeber, F. S. (2009) Domains of perfectionism: Prevalence and relationships with perfectionism gender, age, and satisfaction with life. *Personality and Individual Differences, 46,* 530–535.

Strahler, K., Ehrlenspiel, F., Heene, M., and Brand, R. (2010) Competitive anxiety and cortisol awakening response in the week leading up to a competition. *Psychology of Sport and Exercise, 11,* 148–154.

Strauss, B. (2002) Social facilitation in motor tasks: A review of research and theory. *Psychology of Sport and Exercise, 3,* 237–256.

Stroebe, W. (2012) The truth about Triplett (1898), but nobody seems to care. *Perspectives on Psychological Science, 7,* 54–57.

Strube, M. J. (2005) What did Triplett really find? A contemporary analysis of the first experiment in social psychology. *American Journal of Psychology, 118,* 271–286.

Stumbrys, T., Erlacher, D., and Schredl, M. (2016) Effectiveness of motor practice in lucid dreams: A comparison with physical and mental practice. *Journal of Sports Sciences, 34,* 27–34.

Suarez, N. (2013) Jason Day uses brain-training tool to contend in Masters. Retrieved from www.nationalclubgolfer.com/2013/04/15/jason-day-eeg-masters/ on 24 October 2016.

Suinn, R. M. (1984) Imagery and sports. In W. F. Straub and J. M. Williams (eds.) *Cognitive sport psychology* (pp. 253–272). Lansing, NY: Sport Science Associates.

Sullivan, A. H. (1921) An experimental study of kinaesthetic imagery. *American Journal of Psychology, 31,* 54–80.

Summers, J., and Moran, A. (2011) Attention. In T. Morris and P. Terry (eds) *The new sport and exercise psychology companion* (pp. 105–133). Morgantown, WV: Fitness Information Technology.

Summers, J. J. (1999) Skill acquisition: Current perspectives and future directions. In R. Lidor and M. Bar-Eli (eds) *Sport psychology: Linking theory and practice* (pp. 83–107). Morgantown, WV: Fitness Information Technology.

Summers, J. J., and Ford, S. K. (1990) The Test of Attentional and Interpersonal Style: An evaluation. *International Journal of Sport Psychology, 21,* 102–111.

Sutcliffe, P. (1997) Out of tune with the rest of us. *The Sunday Times* (Supplement: Stress Manager, Part 4: Raising Your Game), 8 June, p. 6.

Swain, A. B. J., and Jones, G. (1995) Effects of goal setting interventions on selected basketball skills: A single-subject design. *Research Quarterly for Exercise and Sport, 66,* 51–63.

Swain, A. B. J., and Jones, G. (1996) Explaining performance variance: The relative contributions of intensity and direction dimensions of competitive state anxiety. *Anxiety, Stress and Coping, 9,* 1–18.

Swann, C., Keegan, R. J., Piggott, D., and Crust, L. (2012) A systematic review of the experience, occurrence, and controllability of flow states in elite sport. *Psychology of Sport and Exercise, 13,* 807–819.

Swann, C., Piggott, D., Crust, L., Keegan, R., and Hemmings, B. (2015a) Exploring the interactions underlying flow states: A connecting analysis of flow occurrence in European Tour golfers. *Psychology of Sport and Exercise, 16,* 60–69.

Swann, C., Moran, A., and Piggott, D. (2015b) Defining elite athletes: Issues in the study of expert performance in sport psychology. *Psychology of Sport and Exercise, 16,* 3–14.

Swann, C., Crust, L., Keegan, R., Piggott, D., and Hemmings, B. (2015c) An inductive exploration into the flow experiences of European Tour golfers. *Qualitative Research in Sport, Exercise and Health, 7,* 210–234.

Swann, C., Keegan, R., Crust, L., and Piggott, D. (2016) Psychological states underlying excellent performance in professional golfers: "Letting it happen" vs. "making it happen". *Psychology of Sport and Exercise, 23,* 101–113.

Swift, E. J. (1910) Relearning a skilful act: An experimental study of neuromuscular memory. *Psychological Bulletin, 7,* 17–19.

Syed, M. (2010) *Bounce: How champions are made.* London: Fourth Estate (a division of HarperCollins).

Syer, J. (1986) *Team spirit.* London: Sportspages.

Szczepanik, N. (2005) Focused Cech puts records low on his list of priorities. *The Times,* 30 April, p. 100.

Tamminen, K. A., and Holt, N. L. (2012) Adolescent athletes' learning about coping and the roles of parents and coaches. *Psychology of Sport and Exercise, 13,* 69–79.

Tamminen, K. A., and Crocker, P. R. (2013) "I control my own emotions for the sake of the team": Emotional self-regulation and interpersonal emotion regulation among female high-performance curlers. *Psychology of Sport and Exercise, 14,* 737–747.

Tang, Y.-Y., Ma, Y., Wang, J., Fan, Y., Feng, S., Lu, Q., Yu, Q., Sui, D., Rothbart, M. K., Fan, M., and Posner, M. I. (2007) Short-term meditation training improves attention and self-regulation. Proceeding of the National Academy of Sciences of the United States of America, *104,* 17152–17156.

Tang, Y. Y., Lu, Q., Fan, M., Yang, Y., and Posner, M. I. (2012) Mechanisms of white matter changes induced by meditation. *Proceedings of the National Academy of Sciences, 109,* 10570–10574.

Taylor, D. (2003) Warnock's walks on the wild side keep Blades on edge. *The Guardian* (Sport), 12 April, p. 2.

Taylor, F. W. (1967) *The principles of scientific management.* New York: Norton (originally published in 1911).

Taylor, G. (2002) There is still a reluctance to recognise the part that psychology can play. *The Daily Telegraph* (Sport), 1 June, p. S3.

Taylor, G. J., Bagby, R. M., and Parker, J. D. A. (1999) *Disorders of affect regulation: Alexithymia in medical and psychiatric illness.* Cambridge: Cambridge University Press.

Taylor, L. (2013) Everyday heroes ready for final verse in Bradford odyssey, *The Guardian* (Sport), 23 February, p. 6.

Teigen, K. H. (1994) Yerkes-Dodson: A law for all seasons. *Theory and Psychology, 4,* 525–547.

Tenenbaum, G., and Eklund, R. C. (eds) (2007) *Handbook of sport psychology* (3rd edn). New York: Wiley.

Tenenbaum, G., Spence, R., and Christensen, S. (1999). The effect of goal difficulty and goal orientation on running performance in young female athletes. *Australian Journal of Psychology, 51,* 6-11

Tenenbaum, G., Sar-El, T., and Bar-Eli, M. (2000) Anticipation of ball location in low- and high-skill performers: A developmental perspective. *Psychology of Sport and Exercise, 1,* 117–128.

Terry, P. C., Lane, A. M., and Fogarty, G. (2003) Construct validity of the Profile of Mood States-A for use with adults. *Psychology of Sport and Exercise, 4,* 125–139.

Thatcher, J., Jones, M. V., and Lavallee, D. (eds) (2011) *Coping and emotion in sport* (2nd edn). Abingdon, Oxfordshire: Routledge.

The Economist (1999) Freaks under pressure. *The Economist,* 18 December, pp. 90–92.

The Guardian (2005) How relaxed Chelsea took complete control. *The Guardian* (Sport), 15 October, p. 3.

The Guardian (2012) Gore Vidal quotes: 26 of the best. *The Guardian,* 1st August 2012. Retrieved from www.theguardian.com/books/2012/aug/01/gore-vidal-best-quotes on 2 December 2016.

The Irish Times (2008) Fear pushes me and keeps me practising. *The Irish Times,* 22 July, p. 25.

The Irish Times (2009) Poulter blames photographer. *The Irish Times,* 6 July, p. 5.

Thelwell, R. (2009) Team goal setting in professional football. In B. Hemmings and T. Holder (eds) *Applied sport psychology: A case-based approach* (pp. 161–180). Oxford: Wiley-Blackwell.

Thelwell, R., Weston, N., and Greenlees, I. (2005) Defining and understanding mental toughness within soccer. *Journal of Applied Sport Psychology, 17,* 326–332.

Thelwell, R. C., Lane, A. M., and Weston, N. J. (2007) Mood states, self-set goals, self-efficacy and performance in academic examinations. *Personality and Individual Differences, 42,* 573–583.

The Observer (2004) The 10 lamest sporting excuses. *Observer Magazine,* 3 October. Retrieved from http://observer.guardian.co.uk/osm/story/0,1315413,00.html on 30 December 2008.

Theodorakis, Y., Hatzigeorgiadis, A., and Zourbanos, N. (2012) Cognitions: Self-talk and performance. In S. Murphy (ed.) *Oxford handbook of sport and performance psychology.* Part two: Individual psychological processes in performance (pp. 191–212). New York: Oxford University Press.

The Times (2002) The Premiership today: Bergkamp faces FA probe, Royle lines up raid on Maine Road and Taylor calls in the shrinks. *The Times,* 30 October, p. 43.

The Title (1998) Daly is still fighting off the shakes. *The Title,* 29 November, p. 8.

Thienot, E., Jackson, B., Dimmock, J., Grove, J. R., Bernier, M., and Fournier, J. F. (2014) Development and preliminary validation of the mindfulness inventory for sport. *Psychology of Sport and Exercise, 15,* 72–80.

Thomas, O., Maynard, I., and Hanton, S. (2007) Intervening with athletes in the time leading up to competition: Theory to practice II. *Journal of Applied Sport Psychology, 19,* 398–418.

Thomas, O., Mellalieu, S. D., and Hanton, S. (2009) Stress management in applied sport psychology. In S. D. Mellalieu and S. Hanton (eds) *Advances in applied sport psychology: A review* (pp. 124–161). Abingdon, Oxfordshire: Routledge.

Thomas, P. R., Murphy, S. M., and Hardy, L. (1999) Test of performance strategies: Development and preliminary validation of a comprehensive measure of athletes' psychological skills. *Journal of Sports Sciences, 17,* 697–711.

Thomson, R. H. S., Garry, M. I., and Summers, J. J. (2008) Attentional influences on short-interval intracortica inhibition. *Clinical Neurophysiology, 119,* 52–62.

Thornley, G. (1993) Graf profits as Novotna loses her nerve. *The Irish Times,* 5 July, p. 6.

Thornley, G. (1997) Irish call in two psychologists. *The Irish Times,* 16 October, p. 20.

Thorp, M. (1998) Ferdinand has the faith not to falter at the final hurdle. *The Guardian* (Sport), 22 May, p. 5.

Tolman, E. E. (1932) *Purposive behaviour in animals and men.* New York: Appleton-Century-Crofts.

Toner, J., and Moran, A. (2011) The effects of conscious processing on golf putting proficiency and kinematics. *Journal of Sports Sciences, 29,* 673–683.

Toner, J., and Moran, A. (2014) In praise of conscious awareness: A new framework for the investigation of "continuous improvement" in athletes. *Frontiers in Psychology: Cognition, 5,* 769.

Toner, J., and Moran, A. (2015) Enhancing performance proficiency at the expert level: Considering the role of "somaesthetic awareness". *Psychology of Sport and Exercise, 16,* 110–117.

Toner, J., and Moran, A. (2016) On the importance of critical thinking: A response to Wulf (2015). *Psychology of Sport and Exercise, 22,* 339–340.

Toner, J., Nelson, L., Potrac, P., Gilbourne, D., and Marshall, P. (2012) From "blame" to "shame" in a coach-athlete relationship: A tale of shared critical reflection and the re-storying of narrative experience. *Sports Coaching Review, 1,* 67–78.

Toner, J., Moran, A., and Jackson, R. (2013) The effects of avoidant instructions on golf putting proficiency and kinematics. *Psychology of Sport and Exercise, 14,* 501–507.

Toner, J., Montero, B. G., and Moran, A. (2015) The perils of automaticity. *Review of General Psychology, 19,* 431–442.

Toner, J., Jones, L., and Moran, A. (2016) Bodily crises in skilled performance: Considering the need for artistic habits. *Performance Enhancement & Health, 4,* 50–57.

Torstveit, M. K., Rosenvinge, J. H., and Sundgot-Borgen, J. (2008) Prevalence of eating disorders and the predictive power of risk models in elite athletes: A controlled study. *Scandinavian Journal of Medicine and Science in Sports, 18,* 108–118.

Totterdell, P. (2000) Catching moods and hitting runs: Mood linkage and subjective performance in professional sport teams. *Journal of Applied Psychology, 85,* 848–859.

Travers, L. V., Bohnert, A. M., and Randall, E. T. (2013) Adolescent adjustment in affluent communities: The role of motivational climate and goal orientation. *Journal of Adolescence, 36,* 423–428.

Triplett, N. (1898) The dynamogenic factors in pacemaking and competition. *American Journal of Psychology, 9,* 507–533.

Tuckman, B. W. (1965) Developmental sequence in small groups. *Psychological Bulletin, 63,* 384–399.

Turman, P. D. (2003) Coaches and cohesion: The impact of coaching techniques on team cohesion in the small group sport setting. *Journal of Sport Behaviour, 26,* 86–104.

Turner, M., Jones, M., Sheffield, D., Slater, M., Barker, J., and Bell, J. (2013) Who thrives under pressure? Predicting the performance of elite academy cricketers using the cardiovascular indicators of challenge and threat states. *Journal of Sport and Exercise Psychology, 35,* 387–397.

Turner, M. J., Slater, M. J., and Barker, J. B. (2014) Not the end of the world: The effects of rational-emotive behaviour therapy (REBT) on irrational beliefs in elite soccer academy athletes. *Journal of Applied Sport Psychology, 26,* 144–156.

Tyler, J. M., and Burns, K. C. (2008) After depletion: The replenishment of the self's regulatory resources. *Self and Identity, 7,* 305–321.

Ullén, F., Hambrick, D. Z., and Mosing, M. A. (2016) Rethinking expertise: A multifactorial gene-environment interaction model of expert performance. *Psychological Bulletin, 142,* 427–446.

Ungerleider, R. S., and Golding, J. M. (1991) Mental practice among Olympic athletes. *Perceptual and Motor Skills, 72,* 1007–1017.

Unsworth, N., and Robison, M. K. (2015) Individual differences in the allocation of attention to items in working memory: Evidence from pupillometry. *Psychonomic Bulletin & Review, 22,* 757–765.

Uphill, M. (2008) Anxiety in sport: Should we be worried or excited? In A. Lane (ed.) *Sport and exercise psychology: Topics in Applied Psychology* (pp. 35–51). London: Hodder Education.

Uphill, M., and Jones, M. V. (2004) Coping with emotions in sport: A cognitive motivational relational theory perspective. In D. Lavallee, J. Thatcher and M. V. Jones (eds) *Coping and emotion in sport* (pp. 75–89). New York: Nova Science.

Uphill, M. A., and Jones, M. V. (2007) Antecedents of emotions in elite athletes: A cognitive motivational relational theory perspective. *Research Quarterly for Exercise and Sport, 78,* 79–89.

Uphill, M., and Jones, M. V. (2011) The consequences and control of emotions in elite athletes. In J. Thatcher, M. V. Jones and D. Lavallee (eds) *Coping and emotion in sport* (2nd edn, pp. 213–235). Hove, East Sussex. Routledge.

Uphill, M. A., McCarthy, P. J. and Jones, M. V. (2009) Getting a grip on emotion regulation in sport: Conceptual foundations and practical applications. In S. Mellallieu and S. Hanton (eds) *Advances in applied sport psychology.* Abingdon, Oxfordshire: Routledge.

Uphill, M. A., Lane, A. M., and Jones, M. V. (2012) Emotion Regulation Questionnaire for use with athletes. *Psychology of Sport and Exercise, 13,* 761–770.

Uphill, M., Sly, D., and Swain, J. (2016) From mental health to mental wealth in athletes: Looking back and moving forward. *Frontiers in Psychology, 7,* 935

Uziell, L. (2007) Individual differences in the social facilitation effect: A review and meta-analysis. *Journal of Research in Personality, 41,* 579–601.

Vallerand, R. J. (2007) Intrinsic and extrinsic motivation in sport and physical activity: A review and a look at the future. In G. Tenenbaum and R. C. Eklund (eds) *Handbook of sport psychology* (3rd edn, pp. 59–83). New York: Wiley.

Vallerand, R. J., and Fortier, M. S. (1998) Measures of intrinsic and extrinsic motivation in sport and physical activity: A review and critique. In J. L. Duda (ed.) *Advances in sport and exercise psychology measurement* (pp. 81–101). Morgantown, WV: Fitness Information Technology.

Vallerand, R. J., and Rousseau, F. L. (2001) Intrinsic and extrinsic motivation in sport and exercise. In R. N. Singer, H. A. Hausenblas, and C. M. Janelle (eds) *Handbook of sport psychology* (2nd edn, pp. 389–416). New York: Wiley.

Vallerand, R. J., Brière, N. M., Blanchard, C., and Provencher, P. (1997) Development and validation of the Multidimensional Sportspersonship Orientations Scale. *Journal of Sport and Exercise Psychology, 19,* 197–206.

Vandell, R. A., Davis, R. A., and Clugston, H. A. (1943). The function of mental practice in the acquisition of motor skills. *Journal of General Psychology, 29,* 243–250.

Vandenberg, S., and Kuse, A. R. (1978) Mental rotations: A group test of three-dimensional spatial visualization. *Perceptual and Motor Skills, 47,* 599–604.

Van Meer, J. P., and Theunissen, N. C. M. (2009) Prospective educational applications of mental simulation: A review. *Educational Psychology Review, 21,* 93–112.

Van Raalte, J. L., Vincent, A., and Brewer, B. W. (2016) Self-talk: Review and sport-specific model. *Psychology of Sport and Exercise, 22,* 139–148.

Van Yperen N. W., Blaga, M., and Postmes, T. (2014) A meta-analysis of self-reported achievement goals and nonself-report performance across three achievement domains (work, sports, and education). *PLoS One, 9, 4,* e93594.

Vast, R. L., Young, R. L., and Thomas, P. R. (2010) Emotions in sport: Perceived effects on attention, concentration, and performance. *Australian Psychologist, 45,* 132–140.

Veach, T. L., and May, J. R. (2005) Teamwork: For the good of the whole. In S. Murphy (ed.) *The sport psych handbook* (pp. 171–189). Champaign, IL: Human Kinetics.

Vealey, R. S. (1994) Current status and prominent issues in sport psychology interventions. *Medicine and Science in Sports and Exercise, 26,* 495–502.

Vealey, R. S. (2009) Confidence in sport. In B. W. Brewer (ed.) *Sport psychology: Handbook of sports medicine* (pp. 43–52). Oxford: Wiley-Blackwell.

Vealey, R. S., and Walter, S. M. (1994) On target with mental skills: An interview with Darrell Pace. *The Sport Psychologist, 8,* 428–441.

Vealey, R. S., and Chase, M. A. (2008) Self-confidence in sport. In T. S. Horn (ed.) *Advances in sport psychology* (3rd edn, pp. 65–97). Champaign, IL: Human Kinetics.

Vealey, R. S., and Greenleaf, C. A. (2010) Seeing is believing: Understanding and using imagery in sport. In J. M. Williams (ed.) *Applied sport psychology: Personal growth to peak performance* (6th edn, pp. 267–304). Boston, MA: McGraw-Hill.

Vealey, R. S., and Vernau, D. (2010) Confidence. In S. J. Hanrahan and M. B. Andersen (eds) *Routledge handbook of applied sport psychology* (pp. 518–527). Abingdon, Oxfordshire: Routledge.

Vealey, R. S., Hayashi, S. W., Garner-Holman, M., and Giaccobi, P. (1998) Sources of sport-confidence: Conceptualization and instrument development. *Journal of Sport and Exercise Psychology, 20,* 54–80.

Vicente, K. J., and Brewer, W. F. (1993) Reconstructive remembering of the scientific literature. *Cognition, 46,* 101–128.

Vickers, J. N. (1992) Gaze control in putting. *Perception, 21,* 117–132.

Vickers, J. N. (1996) Control of visual attention during the basketball free throw. *American Journal of Sports Medicine, 24,* S93–S97.

Vickers, J. N. (2007) *Perception, cognition, and decision training: The quiet eye in action.* Champaign, IL: Human Kinetics.

Vickers, J. N., and Williams, A. M. (2007) Performing under pressure: The effects of physiological arousal, cognitive anxiety and gaze control in biathlon. *Journal of Motor Behaviour, 39,* 381–394.

Vidal, J. (2001) Call of the wild. *The Guardian* (G2), 9 June, p. 2.

Vine, S. J., and Wilson, M. R. (2011) The influence of quiet eye training and pressure on attention and visuo-motor control. *Acta Psychologica, 136,* 340–346.

Vine, S. J., Moore, L. J., and Wilson, M. R. (2014) Quiet eye training: The acquisition, refinement and resilient performance of targeting skills. *European Journal of Sport Science, 14,* S235–S242.

Viner, B. (2011) Beyond choke: What became of the sporting imploder? *Evening Herald*, 12 April, pp. 26–27.

Vinkhuyzen, A. A., Van der Sluis, S., Posthuma, D., and Boomsma, D. I. (2009) The heritability of aptitude and exceptional talent across different domains in adolescents and young adults. *Behaviour Genetics, 39*, 380–392.

Vyse, S. (1997) *Believing in magic: The psychology of superstition.* New York: Oxford University Press.

Wada, Y., Iwasaki, S., and Kato, T. (2003) Validity of attentional-style subscales for the Japanese version of the Test of Attentional and Interpersonal Style (TAIS). *Japanese Journal of Psychology, 74,* 263–269.

Waddington, I. (2000) *Sport, health and drugs: A critical sociological perspective.* London: Taylor & Francis.

Wagstaff, C. (2014) Emotion regulation and sport performance. *Journal of Sport and Exercise Psychology, 36,* 401–412.

Wainwright, S. P., Williams, C., and Turner, B. S. (2005) Fractured identities: Injury and the balletic body. *Health, 9,* 49–66.

Wakefield, C. J., Smith, D., Moran, A., and Holmes, P. (2013) Functional equivalence or behavioural matching? A critical reflection on 15 years of research using the PETTLEP model of motor imagery. *International Review of Sport and Exercise Psychology, 6,* 105–121.

Wallace, S. (2007) Benitez vows to act over Bellamy "golf club attack". *The Independent on Sunday,* 19 February. Retrieved from www.independent.co.uk/sport/foofball/premier-league/benitez-vows-to-act-over-bellamy-golf-club-attack-436972.html on 5 September 2010.

Walling, M. D., Duda, J. L., and Chi, L. (1993) The Perceived Motivational Climate in Sport Questionnaire: Construct and predictive validity. *Journal of Sport and Exercise Psychology, 15,* 172–183.

Wang, J., Marchant, D., Morris, T., and Gibbs, P. (2004) Self-consciousness and trait anxiety as predictors of choking in sport. *Journal of Science and Medicine in Sport, 7,* 174–185.

Ward, P., and Williams, A. M. (2003) Perceptual and cognitive skill development in soccer: The multidimensional nature of expert performance. *Journal of Sport and Exercise Psychology, 25,* 93–111.

Ward, P., Williams, A. M., and Hancock, P. A. (2006) Simulation for performance and training. In K. A. Ericsson, N. Charness, P. J. Feltovich, and R. R. Hoffman (eds) *The Cambridge handbook of expertise and expert performance* (pp. 243–262). New York: Cambridge University Press.

Washburn, M. F. (1916) *Movement and mental imagery.* Boston, MA: Houghton Mifflin.

Watson, D., Clark, L. A., and Tellegen, A. (1988) Development and validation of brief measures of positive and negative affect: The PANAS scales. *Journal of Personality and Social Psychology, 54,* 1063–1070.

Watson, J. (17th May 2012). Rooney: I see myself scoring goals the night before a game. *Goals.com.* Retrieved from http://www.goal.com/en-gb/news/2896/premier-league/2012/05/17/3109404/rooney-i-see-myself-scoring-goals-the-night-before-a-game on 12 November 2016.

Watson, J. B. (1913) Psychology as the behaviourist views it. *Psychological Review, 20,* 158–177.

Watson, J. B. (1930) *Behaviourism* (revised edn). Chicago, IL: University of Chicago Press.

Webborn, N., Williams, A., McNamee, M., Bouchard, C., Pitsiladis, Y., Ahmetov, I. et al. (2015) Direct-to-consumer genetic testing for predicting sports performance and talent identification: Consensus statement. *British Journal of Sports Medicine, 49,* 1486–1491.

Webster, R. (1984) *Winning ways.* Sydney: Fontana.

Wegner, D. M. (1994) Ironic processes of mental control. *Psychological Review, 101,* 34–52.

Wegner, D. M. (2002) Thought suppression and mental control. In L. Nadel (ed.) *Encyclopaedia of cognitive science* (Vol. 4, pp. 395–397). London: Nature Publishing Group.

Wei, G., and Luo, J. (2010) Sport expert's motor imagery: Functional imaging of professional motor skills and simple motor skills. *Brain Research, 1341,* 52–62.

Weinberg, R. S. (1988) *The mental ADvantage: Developing your mental skills in tennis.* Champaign, IL: Human Kinetics.

Weinberg, R. S. (2002) Goal setting in sport and exercise: Research to practice. In J. Van Raalte and B. Brewer (eds) *Exploring sport and exercise psychology* (2nd edn, pp. 25–48). Washington, DC: American Psychological Association.

Weinberg, R. S. (2008) Does imagery work? Effects on performance and mental skills. *Journal of Imagery Research in Sport and Physical Activity, 3,* article 1, 1–21.

Weinberg, R. S. (2009) Motivation. In B. W. Brewer (ed.) *Sport psychology: Handbook of sports medicine* (pp. 7–17). Oxford: Wiley-Blackwell.

Weinberg, R. S. (2014) Goal setting in sport and exercise: Research to practice. In J. L. Van Raalte and B. W. Brewer (eds) *Exploring sport and exercise psychology* (pp. 33–54). Washington, DC: American Psychological Association.

Weinberg, R. S., and Comar, W. (1994) The effectiveness of psychological interventions in competitive sports. *Sports Medicine Journal, 18,* 406–418.

Weinberg, R. S., and Weigand, D. A. (1996) Let the discussions continue: A reaction to Locke's comments on Weinberg and Weigand. *Journal of Sport and Exercise Psychology, 18,* 89–93.

Weinberg, R. S., and Gould, D. (2007) *Foundations of sport and exercise psychology* (4th edn). Champaign, IL: Human Kinetics.

Weinberg, R. S., Bruya, L. D., and Jackson, A. (1985) The effects of goal proximity and goal specificity on endurance performance. *Journal of Sport Psychology, 7,* 296–305.

Weinberg, R. S., Bruya, L. D., Garland, H., and Jackson, A. (1990) Effect of goal difficulty and positive reinforcement on endurance performance. *Journal of Sport and Exercise Psychology, 12,* 144–156.

Weinberg, R. S., Stitcher, T., and Richardson, P. (1994) Effects of seasonal goal setting on lacrosse performance. *Sport Psychologist, 8,* 166–175.

Weinberg, R. S., and Gould, D. (2007) *Foundations of sport and exercise psychology* (4th edn). Champaign, IL: Human Kinetics.

Weiner, B. (1985) An attributional theory of achievement motivation and emotion. *Psychological Review, 92,* 548–573.

Weiss, M. R., and Ferrer-Caja, E. (2002) Motivational orientations and sport behaviour. In T. S. Horn (ed.) *Advances in sport psychology* (2nd edn, pp. 101–183). Champaign, IL: Human Kinetics.

Weiss, M. R., and Amorose, A. J. (2008) Motivational orientations and sport behaviour. In T. S. Horn (ed.) *Advances in sport psychology* (3rd edn, pp. 115–155). Champaign, IL: Human Kinetics.

Weiss, M. R., Smith, A. L., and Stuntz, C. P. (2008) Moral development in sport and physical activity. In T. S. Horn (ed.) *Advances in sport psychology* (3rd edn, pp. 187–210). Champaign, IL: Human Kinetics.

Wells, R., Outhred, T., Heathers, J. A., Quintana, D. S., and Kemp, A. H. (2012) Matter over mind: A randomised-controlled trial of single-session biofeedback training on performance anxiety and heart rate variability in musicians. *PloS ONE, 7,* e46597.

Werner, S., and Thies, B. (2000) Is "change blindness" attenuated by domain-specific expertise? An expert-novice comparison of change detection in football images. *Visual Cognition, 7,* 163–173.

Weston, N., Greenlees, I., and Thelwell, R. (2013) A review of Butler and Hardy's (1992) performance profiling procedure. *International Review of Sport and Exercise Psychology, 6,* 1–21.

Weston, N. J. V., Thelwell, R. C., Bond, S., and Hutchings, N. V. (2009) Stress and coping in singlehanded, round-the-world ocean sailing. *Journal of Applied Sport Psychology, 21,* 468–474.

What makes the perfect golf swing? (2015) Retrieved from www.bbc.co.uk/guides/z3yw7ty on 24 October 2016.

Whelan, J. P., Epkins, C., and Meyers, A. W. (1990) Arousal interventions for athletic performance: Influence of mental preparation and competitive experience. *Anxiety Research, 2,* 293–307.

Whitaker, D. (1999) *The spirit of teams.* Marlborough, Wiltshire: Crowood Press.

White, J. (1999) Ferguson assumes full control in title campaign. *The Guardian,* 17 February, p.26.

White, J. (2001) Interview: Stephen Hendry. *The Guardian* (Sport), 15 October, pp. 18–19.

White, J. (2002a) Interview: Garry Sobers. *The Guardian* (Sport), 10 June, pp. 20–21.

White, J. (2002b) Interview: Ian Woosnam. *The Guardian* (Sport), 15 July, pp. 22–23.

White, J. (2002c) A potter's tale: Any colour but the blues. *The Guardian* (Sport), 20 April, pp. 10–11.

White, J. (2003, 14 April) Interview: Peter Ebdon. *The Guardian* (Sport), pp. 20–21.

Whitehead, A. E., Taylor, J. A., and Polman, R. C. (2015) Examination of the suitability of collecting in event cognitive processes using Think Aloud protocol in golf. *Frontiers in Psychology, 6,* 1083.

Whitworth, D. (2008) On the waterfront. *The Times* (Magazine), 13 September, pp. 20–25.

Widmeyer, W. N., Brawley, L. R., and Carron, A. V. (1985) *Measurement of cohesion in sport teams: The Group Environment Questionnaire.* London, Ontario: Sports Dynamics.

Widmeyer, W. N., Carron, A. V., and Brawley, L. R. (1993) Group cohesion in sport and exercise. In R. N. Singer, M. Murphey and L. K. Tennant (eds) *Handbook of research on sport psychology* (pp. 672–694). New York: Macmillan.

Widmeyer, W. N., Brawley, L. R., and Carron, A. V. (2002) Group dynamics in sport. In T. S. Horn (ed.) *Advances in sport psychology* (2nd edn, pp. 285–308). Champaign, IL: Human Kinetics.

Wilde, S. (1998) Freudian slips get new meaning with mind games catching on. *The Times* (Sport), 18 May, p. 33.

Wildman, R. (2003) South Africans probe brutal camp. *The Daily Telegraph*, 26 November. Retrieved from www.telegraph.co.uk/sport/rugbyunion/international/southafrica/2425836/South-Africans-probe-brutal-camp.html on 10 September 2010.

Wilkinson, J. (2006) *My world.* London: Headline.

Willems, R. M., and Francken, J. C. (2012) Embodied cognition: Taking the next step. *Frontiers in Psychology, 3,* 582.

Williams, A. M. (2002a) Visual search behaviour in sport. *Journal of Sports Sciences, 20,* 169–170.

Williams, A. M. (2002b) Perceptual and cognitive expertise in sport. *The Psychologist, 15,* 416–417.

Williams, A. M. (2003) Developing selective attention skill in fast ball sports. In I. Greenlees and A. P. Moran (eds) *Concentration skills training in sport* (pp. 20–32). Leicester: British Psychological Society (Division of Sport and Exercise Psychology).

Williams, A. M., and Burwitz, L. (1993) Advance cue utilization in soccer. In T. Reilly, J. Clarys, and A. Stibbe (eds) *Science and football II* (pp. 239–243). London: E. & F. N. Spon.

Williams, A. M., and Davids, K. (1998) Perceptual expertise in sport: Research, theory and practice. In H. Steinberg, I. Cockerill, and A. Dewey (eds) *What sport psychologists do* (pp. 48–57). Leicester: British Psychological Society.

Williams, A. M., and Ward, P. (2007) Anticipation and decision-making: Exploring new horizons. In G. Tenenbaum and R. C. Eklund (eds) *Handbook of sport psychology* (3rd edn, pp. 203–223). New York: Wiley.

Williams, A. M., and Ford, P. R. (2008) Expertise and expert performance in sport. *International Review of Sport and Exercise Psychology, 1,* 4–18.

Williams, A. M., Davids, K., and Williams, J. G. (1999) *Visual perception and action in sport.* London: E. & F. N. Spon.

Williams, A. M., Singer, R. N., and Frehlich, S. G. (2002) Quiet eye duration, expertise, and task complexity in near and far aiming tasks. *Journal of Motor Behaviour, 34,* 197–207.

Williams, A. M., Janelle, C. M., and Davids, K. (2004) Constraints on the search for visual information in sport. *International/Journal of Sport and Exercise Psychology, 2,* 301–318.

Williams, A. M., Ericsson, K. A., Ward, P., and Eccles, D. W. (2008) Research on expertise in sport: Implications for the military. *Military Psychology, 20,* S123–S145.

Williams, J. M. (2010) Relaxation and energizing techniques for regulation of arousal. In J. Williams (ed.) *Applied sport psychology: Personal growth to peak performance* (6th edn, pp. 247–266). New York: McGraw-Hill.

Williams, J. M., and Hacker, C. M. (1982) Causal relationships among cohesion, satisfaction, and performance in women's intercollegiate field hockey teams. *Journal of Sport and Exercise Psychology, 4,* 324–337.

Williams, J. M., and Leffingwell, T. R. (2002) Cognitive strategies in sport and exercise psychology. In J. Van Raalte and B. W. Brewer (eds) *Exploring sport and exercise psychology* (2nd edn, pp. 75–98). Washington, DC: American Psychological Association.

Williams, J. M., Nideffer, R. M., Wilson. V. E., Sagal, M. S., and Peper, E. (2010) Concentration and strategies for controlling it. In J. M. Williams (ed.) *Applied sport psychology: Personal growth to peak performance* (6th edn, pp. 336–358). Boston, MA: McGraw-Hill.

Williams, K. (2013) Goal setting in sports. In E. A. Locke and G. P. Latham (eds) *New developments in goal setting and task performance* (pp. 375–396). London: Routledge.

Williams, R. (2002a) Captains split on the million dollar question. *The Guardian*, 24 September, p. 28.

Williams, R. (2002b) Sublime Serena celebrates the crucial difference. *The Guardian* (Sport), 8 July, p. 6.

Williams, R. (2002c) Torrance masters the fine art of creating an unbreakable bond. *The Guardian*, 2 October, p. 30.

Williams, S., Guillot, A., Di Rienzo, F., and Cumming, J. (2015) Comparing self-report and mental chronometry measures of motor imagery ability. *European Journal of Sport Sciences, 27*, 1–9

Williams, S. E., and Cumming, J. (2011) Measuring athlete imagery ability: The Sport Imagery Ability Questionnaire. *Journal of Sport and Exercise Psychology, 33*, 416–440.

Williams, S. E., Cumming, J., Ntoumanis, N., Nordin-Bates, S., Ramsey, R., and Hall, C. (2012) Further validation and development of the Movement Imagery Questionnaire. *Journal of Sport and Exercise Psychology, 34*, 621–646.

Willig, C. (2008) *Introducing qualitative reseach in psychology*. New York: McGraw-Hill.

Wilson, A. D., and Golonka, S. (2013) Embodied cognition is not what you think it is. *Frontiers in Psychology, 4*, 58.

Wilson, M. (2002) Six views of embodied cognition. *Psychonomic Bulletin and Review, 9*, 625–636.

Wilson, M. (2008) From processing efficiency to attentional control: A mechanistic account of the anxiety-performance relationship. *International Review of Sport and Exercise Psychology, 1*, 184–201.

Wilson, M., Smith, N. C., Chattington, M., Ford, M., and Marple-Horvat, D. E. (2006) The role of effort in moderating the anxiety–performance relationship: Testing the prediction of processing efficiency theory in simulated rally driving. *Journal of Sports Sciences, 24*, 1223–1233.

Wilson, M., Chattington, M., Marple-Horvat, D. E., and Smith, N. C. (2007a) A comparison of self-focus versus attentional explanations of choking. *Journal of Sport and Exercise Psychology, 29*, 439–456.

Wilson, M., Smith, N. C., and Holmes, P. S. (2007b) The role of effort in influencing the effect of anxiety on performance: Testing the conflicting predictions of processing efficiency theory and the conscious processing hypothesis. *British Journal of Psychology, 98*, 411–428.

Wilson, M., Wood, G., and Vine, S. J. (2009) Anxiety, attentional control and performance impairment in penalty kicks. *Journal of Sport and Exercise Psychology, 31*, 761–775.

Wilson, M. R., and Pearcy, R. C. (2009) Visuomotor control of straight and breaking golf putts. *Perceptual and Motor Skills, 109*, 555–562.

Wilson, M. R., Causer, J., and Vickers, J. N. (2015) Aiming for excellence: The quiet eye as a characteristic of expert visuomotor performance. In J. Baker and D. Farrow (eds) *The Routledge handbook of sport expertise* (pp. 22–37). Abingdon, Oxfordshire: Routledge.

Wilson, P. M., and Rodgers, R. M. (2007) Human nature. In M. S. Hagger and N. L. Chatzisarantis (eds) *Intrinsic motivation and self-determination in exercise and sport* (pp. 101–112). Champaign, IL: Human Kinetics.

Wilson, V., Ainsworth, M., and Bird, E. (1985) Assessment of attentional abilities in male volleyball players. *International Journal of Sport Psychology, 16*, 296–306.

Wimbledon.com (2015) Roger Federer: first round. Retrieved from www.wimbledon.com/en_GB/news/articles/2015-06-30/roger_federer_first_round.html on 24 October 2016.

Winter, G., and Martin, C. (1991) *Sport "psych" for tennis*. Adelaide: South Australian Sports Institute.

Winter, H. (2002) Coaches try to win mind games. *The Daily Telegraph* (Sport), 8 November, p. S3.

Winter, S., and Collins, D. (2013). Does priming really put the gloss on performance? *Journal of Sport & Exercise Psychology, 35,* 299–307.

Winter, S., MacPherson, A. C., and Collins, D. (2014) "To think, or not to think, that is the question". *Sport, Exercise, and Performance Psychology, 3,* 102–115.

Witt, J. K. (2011) Action's effect on perception. *Current Directions in Psychological Science, 20,* 201–206.

Witt, J. K, and Dorsch, T. (2009) Kicking to bigger uprights: Field goal kicking performance influences perceived size. *Perception, 38,* 1328–1340.

Witt, J. K., and Riley, M. (2014) Discovering your inner Gibson: Reconciling action-specific and ecological approaches. *Psychonomic Bulletin & Review, 21,* 1353–1370.

Witt, J. K., Proffitt, D.R., and Epstein, W. (2004) Perceiving distance: A role of effort and intent. *Perception, 33,* 570–590.

Witt, J. K., Proffitt, D.R., and Epstein, W. (2005) Tool use affects perceived distance but only when you intend to use it. *Journal of Experimental Psychology: Human Perception and Performance, 31,* 880–888.

Witt, J. K., Linkenauger, S. A., Bakdash, J. Z., and Proffitt, D. R. (2008) Putting to a bigger hole: Golf performance relates to perceived size. *Psychonomic Bulletin & Review, 15,* 581–585.

Witt, J. K., Linkenauger, S. A., Bakdash, J. Z., Augustyn, J. A., Cook, A. S., and Proffitt, D. R. (2009). The long road of pain: Chronic pain increases perceived distance. *Experimental Brain Research, 192,* 145–148.

Witt, J. K., Linkenauger, S. A., and Wickens, C. (2016) Action-specific effects in perception and their potential applications. *Journal of Applied Research in Memory and Cognition, 5,* 69–76.

Woll, S. (2002) *Everyday thinking: Memory, reasoning and judgment in the real world.* Hillsdale, NJ: Lawrence Erlbaum Associates.

Wollaston, S. (2010) TV review: The men who jump off buildings and Californication. *The Guardian,* 29 July. Retrieved from www.guardian.co.uk/tv-and-radio/2010/jul/29/menwho-jump-off-buildings on 9 August 2010.

Wood, G., and Wilson, M. R. (2010) A moving goalkeeper distracts penalty takers and impairs shooting accuracy. *Journal of Sports Sciences, 28,* 937–946.

Wood, G., and Wilson, M. R. (2012) Quiet-eye training, perceived control and performing under pressure. *Psychology of Sport and Exercise, 13,* 721–728.

Wood, G., Jordet, G., and Wilson, M. R. (2015) On winning the "lottery": Psychological preparation for football penalty shoot-outs. *Journal of Sports Sciences, 33,* 1758–1765.

Woodcock, C., Cumming, J., Duda, J. L., and Sharp, L. A. (2012) Working within an Individual Zone of Optimal Functioning (IZOF) framework: Consultant practice and athlete reflections on refining emotion regulation skills. *Psychology of Sport and Exercise, 13,* 291–302.

Woodman, T., and Hardy, L. (2003) The relative impact of cognitive anxiety and self-confidence upon sport performance: A meta-analysis. *Journal of Sports Sciences, 21,* 443–457.

Woodman, T., Cazenave, N., and Le Scanff, C. (2008). Skydiving as emotion regulation: The rise and fall of anxiety is moderated by alexithymia. *Journal of Sport & Exercise Psychology, 30,* 424–433.

Woodman, T., Davis, P. A., Hardy, L., Callow, N., Glasscock, I., and Yuill-Proctor, J. (2009) Emotions and sport performance: An exploration of happiness, hope, and anger. *Journal of Sport and Exercise Psychology, 31,* 169–188.

Woodman, T., Hardy, L., Barlow, M., and Le Scanff, C. (2010) Motives for participation in prolonged engagement in high-risk sports: An agentic emotion regulation perspective. *Psychology of Sport and Exercise, 11,* 345–352.

Woodman, T., Barlow, M., and Gorgulu, R. (2015) Don't miss, don't miss, d'oh! Performance when anxious suffers specifically where least desired. *The Sport Psychologist, 29,* 213–233.

Woolley, A.W., Aggarwal, I., and Malone, T.W. (2015). Collective intelligence and group performance. *Current Directions in Psychological Science, 24,* 420–24.

Wright, D. J., Wakefield, C. J., and D. Smith D. (2014). Using PETTLEP imagery to improve music performance: A review. *Musicae Scientiae, 18,* 448–463.

Wulf, G. (2008) Attentional focus effects in balance acrobats. *Research Quarterly for Exercise and Sport, 79,* 319–325.

Wulf, G. (2013) Attentional focus and motor learning: A review of 15 years. *International Review of Sport and Exercise Psychology, 6,* 77–104.

Wulf, G. (2016) Why did Tiger Woods shoot 82? A commentary on Toner and Moran (2015). *Psychology of Sport and Exercise, 22,* 337–338.

Wulf, G., McNevin, N., and Shea, C. H. (2001) The automaticity of complex motor skill learning as a function of attentional focus. *The Quarterly Journal of Experimental Psychology: Section A, 54,* 1143–1154.

Yarrow, K., Brown, P., and Krakauer, J. W. (2009) Inside the brain of an elite athlete: The neural processes that support high achievement in sports. *Nature Reviews: Neuroscience, 10,* 585–596.

Yates, P. (2007) Ronnie O'Sullivan finds rhythm on the dot. *The Times.* Retrieved from www.timesonline.co.uk/tol/sport/more_sport/article3060192.ece on 17 December 2007.

Yerkes, R. M., and Dodson, J. D. (1908) The relationship of strength of stimulus to rapidity of habit formation. *Journal of Comparative Neurology and Psychology, 18,* 459–482.

Yeung, N. (2013) Conflict monitoring and cognitive control. In K. N. Osherson and S. Kosslyn (eds) *The Oxford handbook of cognitive neuroscience, Volume 2: The cutting edges* (pp. 275–299). Oxford: Oxford University Press.

Young, B. W., and Salmela, J. H. (2002) Perceptions of training and deliberate practice of middle distance runners. *International Journal of Sport Psychology, 33,* 167–181.

Yukelson, D. (1997) Principles of effective team building interventions in sport: A direct services approach at Penn State University. *Journal of Applied Sport Psychology, 9,* 73–96.

Yukelson, D., Weinberg, R., and Jackson, A. (1984) A multidimensional group cohesion instrument for intercollegiate basketball teams. *Journal of Sport Psychology, 6,* 103–117.

Yusoff, M. S. B., Rahim, A. F. A., Mat Pa, M. N., See, C. M., Ja'afar, R., and Esa, A. R. (2011) The validity and reliability of the USM Emotional Quotient Inventory (USMEQ-i): Its use to measure Emotional Quotient (EQ) of future medical students. *International Medical Journal, 18,* 293–299.

Zajonc, R. B. (1965) Social facilitation. *Science, 149,* 269–274.

Zervas, Y., Stavrou, N. A., and Psychountaki, M. (2007) Development and validation of the Self-Talk Questionnaire (S-TQ) for Sports. *Journal of Applied Sport Psychology, 19,* 142–159.

Zinsser, N., Bunker, L., and Williams, J. M. (2010) Cognitive techniques for building confidence and enhancing performance. In J. M. Williams (ed.) *Applied sport psychology* (pp. 305–335). New York: McGraw-Hill.

Zorpette, G. (1999) Extreme sports, sensation seeking and the brain. *Scientific American* (Work, Home and Play section), *10,* 57–59.

Zuckerman, M. V. (1979) *Sensation seeking: Beyond optimal levels of arousal.* Hillsdale, NJ: Lawrence Erlbaum Associates.

Zuckerman, M. V. (1984) Experience and desire: A new format for sensation seeking scales. *Journal of Behavioural Assessment, 6,* 101–114.

Zuckerman, M. V. (1994) *Behavioural expressions and biosocial bases of sensation seeking.* Cambridge: Cambridge University Press.

Zuckerman, M. V. (2007) *Sensation seeking and risky behaviour.* Washington, DC: American Psychological Association.

Author index

Note: References to multi-author texts are listed as given in the text; however, references with *four* or more authors are listed only under the first name cited along with the year of publication. The method of alphabetisation used is word-by-word. Names commencing with 'Mac' and 'Mc' are listed together.

Subject index

Note: for authors cited, see Author Index.

Taylor & Francis eBooks

Helping you to choose the right eBooks for your Library

Add Routledge titles to your library's digital collection today. Taylor and Francis ebooks contains over 50,000 titles in the Humanities, Social Sciences, Behavioural Sciences, Built Environment and Law.

Choose from a range of subject packages or create your own!

Benefits for you

» Free MARC records
» COUNTER-compliant usage statistics
» Flexible purchase and pricing options
» All titles DRM-free.

Benefits for your user

» Off-site, anytime access via Athens or referring URL
» Print or copy pages or chapters
» Full content search
» Bookmark, highlight and annotate text
» Access to thousands of pages of quality research at the click of a button.

| REQUEST YOUR **FREE** INSTITUTIONAL TRIAL TODAY | **Free Trials Available** We offer free trials to qualifying academic, corporate and government customers. |

eCollections – Choose from over 30 subject eCollections, including:

Archaeology	Language Learning
Architecture	Law
Asian Studies	Literature
Business & Management	Media & Communication
Classical Studies	Middle East Studies
Construction	Music
Creative & Media Arts	Philosophy
Criminology & Criminal Justice	Planning
Economics	Politics
Education	Psychology & Mental Health
Energy	Religion
Engineering	Security
English Language & Linguistics	Social Work
Environment & Sustainability	Sociology
Geography	Sport
Health Studies	Theatre & Performance
History	Tourism, Hospitality & Events

For more information, pricing enquiries or to order a free trial, please contact your local sales team: www.tandfebooks.com/page/sales

 Routledge
Taylor & Francis Group

The home of Routledge books

www.tandfebooks.com